Trusts and Estates Law Handbook

Trusts and Estates Law Handbook

Third Edition

Penelope Reed TEP
Barrister
5 Stone Buildings

Tottel publishing

Tottel Publishing, Maxwelton House, 41–43 Boltro Road, Haywards Heath, West Sussex, RH16 1BJ

A CIP Catalogue record for this book is available from the British Library.

ISBN: 978 1 84592 132 3

Typeset by Phoenix Typesetting, Chatham, Kent
Printed and bound in Great Britain by Athenæum Press Limited, Gateshead, Tyne & Wear

PREFACE

For anyone who thinks that trusts and estates lawyers live in an ivory tower, the new legislation which has had an impact on this latest edition is a barometer of social change. The Civil Partnership Act 2004 has had a huge effect on many of the statutes included in this work. The Gender Recognition Act 2004, which seems to have gone by unnoticed by many commentators, has a surprising impact on the way in which trusts and wills now need to be read in respect of those whose gender has been reassigned.

Yet perhaps the greatest revolution has been the complete overhaul of the concept of mental capacity and the establishment of the new Court of Protection by the Mental Capacity Act 2005, a statute so long in gestation that it was first mooted in 1989. This change has been so momentous that it was felt necessary to include an annotated version of those parts of the Act which relate to the subject matter of this work and to include some of the regulations it has already spawned. I must express my gratitude to David Rees of my Chambers for the invaluable assistance he provided in respect of the Act and the regulations.

Quite apart from new legislation there has been plenty of case law to note, particularly under the Inheritance (Provision for Family and Dependants) Act 1975. May I express a debt of gratitude to the editors of the WTLR for making tracking down new cases in this area so much easier.

I must also thank my unfailingly patient editor Andy Hill and all those who have provided suggestions following the first two editions.

To aid the reader, cross-references appear throughout the commentary and are styled as follows: **[111]**.

Penelope Reed
5 Stone Buildings, Lincoln's Inn
April 2008

CONTENTS

PART I
Annotated Statutes

WILLS ACT 1837

1837 Chapter 26

ARRANGEMENT OF SECTIONS

An Act for the amendment of the Laws with respect to Wills

[3rd July 1837]

General Note
This Act provides the main guidance as to the formalities for the making of wills, the manner of their revocation, and aspects of their construction. It has been considerably amended over the years in particular by the Administration of Justice Act 1982.

1 Meaning of certain words in this Act

... the words and expressions herein-after mentioned, which in their ordinary signification have a more confined or a different meaning, shall in this Act, except where the nature of the provisions or the context of the Act shall exclude such construction, be interpreted as follows; (that is to say,) the word "will" shall extend to a testament, and to a codicil, and to an appointment by will or by writing in the nature of a will in exercise of a power, [and also to an appointment by will of a guardian of a child], [and also to an appointment by will of a representative under section 4 of the Human Tissue Act 2004,] ... and to any other testamentary disposition; and the words "real estate" shall extend to manors, advowsons, messuages, lands, tithes, rents, and hereditaments, ... whether corporeal, incorporeal, or personal, ... and to any estate, right, or interest (other than a chattel interest) therein; and the words "personal estate" shall extend to leasehold estates and other chattels real, and also to monies, shares of government and other funds, securities for money (not being real estates), debts, choses in action, rights, credits, goods, and all other property whatsoever which by law devolves upon the executor or administrator, and to any share or interest therein; and every word importing the singular number only shall extend and be applied to several persons or things as well as one person or thing; and every word importing the masculine gender only shall extend and be applied to a female as well as a male.

Amendment
Repealed in part, in relation to Northern Ireland, by the Statute Law Revision (Northern Ireland) Act 1954, the Statute Law Revision (Northern Ireland) Act 1976, and the Wills and Administration Proceedings (NI) Order 1994, SI 1994/1899, art 38, Sch 3.
First words omitted repealed by the Statute Law Revision Act 1893, s 1, Schedule.
Words from "and also to" to "of a child," in square brackets substituted by the Children Act 1989, s 108(5), (6), Sch 13, para 1, Sch 14, para 1.
Words from "and also to" to "the Human Tissue Act 2004," in square brackets inserted by the Human Tissue Act 2004, s 56, Sch 6, para 1.
Second and third words omitted repealed by the Statute Law (Repeals) Act 1969, s 1, Schedule, Pt III.
Final words omitted repealed by the Trusts of Land and Appointment of Trustees 1996, s 25(2), Sch 4; for savings in relation to entailed interests created before the commencement of that Act, and savings consequential upon the abolition of the doctrine of conversion, see s 25(4), (5) thereof.

Commentary
In essence this is the definition section of the Act. Important points to note are that a "will" under the Act also includes a codicil and a power of appointment exercised by will as well as the appointment of a guardian of a child and a representative who can make decisions as to the use of the deceased's body after death such as organ transplant under the Human Tissue Act 2004. The section also sets out the vitally important distinction between real estate and personal estate, the crucial point being that leaseholds are classified not as land but as personal property.

[1]

2 ...

...

Amendment
Repealed by the Statute Law Revision Act 1874.

[2]

3 All property may be disposed of by will

. . . it shall be lawful for every person to devise, bequeath, or dispose of, by his will executed in manner herein-after required, all real estate and all personal estate which he shall be entitled to, either at law or in equity, at the time of his death, and which, if not so devised, bequeathed, and disposed of, would devolve . . . upon his executor or administrator; and . . . the power hereby given shall extend . . . to all contingent, executory or other future interests in any real or personal estate, whether the testator may or may not be ascertained as the person or one of the persons in whom the same respectively may become vested, and whether he may be entitled thereto under the instrument by which the same respectively were created, or under any disposition thereof by deed or will; and also to all rights of entry for conditions broken, and other rights of entry; and also to such of the same estates, interests, and rights respectively, and other real and personal estate, as the testator may be entitled to at the time of his death, notwithstanding that he may become entitled to the same subsequently to the execution of his will.

Amendment

Repealed, in relation to Northern Ireland, by the Wills and Administration Proceedings (NI) Order 1994, SI 1994/1899, art 38, Sch 3.
First and third words omitted repealed by the Statute Law Revision (No 2) Act 1888; second and fourth words omitted repealed by the Statute Law (Repeals) Act 1969.

Commentary

This section confirms the position that a testator of capacity may dispose of all the property vested in him at the time of his death (provided that his interest survives his death) and importantly may dispose of interests which may vest in him in the future whether or not he has been ascertained at the time as a definite beneficiary (in the sense of having to satisfy a contingency or other condition). On the other hand, a testator cannot leave by his will just a hope of succeeding to someone else's estate: *Izahu v Tamahu Makapuku* (1902) 22 NZLR418.

[3]

4–6

. . .

Amendment

Repealed by the Statute Law (Repeals) Act 1969.

[4]

7 No will of a person under age valid

. . . no will made by any person under the age of [eighteen years] shall be valid.

Amendment

Repealed, in relation to Northern Ireland, by the Wills and Administration Proceedings (NI) Order 1994, SI 1994/1899, art 38, Sch 3.
Words omitted repealed by the Statute Law Revision (No 2) Act 1888; words in square brackets substituted by the Family Law Reform Act 1969, s 3(1)(a).

Commentary

The section in its unamended form referred to wills made by any person under the age of 21 years. In respect of wills made before 1 January 1970, that is still the rule.

[5]

8 . . .

. . .

Amendment
Repealed by the Statute Law (Repeals) Act 1969.

[6]

[9 Signing and attestation of wills

No will shall be valid unless—

(a) it is in writing, and signed by the testator, or by some other person in his presence and by his direction; and

(b) it appears that the testator intended by his signature to give effect to the will; and

(c) the signature is made or acknowledged by the testator in the presence of two or more witnesses present at the same time; and

(d) each witness either—

(i) attests and signs the will; or

(ii) acknowledges his signature,

in the presence of the testator (but not necessarily in the presence of any other witness),

but no form of attestation shall be necessary.]

Amendment
Substituted, in relation to England and Wales, by the Administration of Justice Act 1982, s 17.
Repealed, in relation to Northern Ireland, by the Wills and Administration Proceedings (NI) Order 1994, SI 1994/1899, art 38, Sch 3.

Commentary
This section sets out the formalities required for the making of a will. Whether or not a will has been properly executed has given rise to numerous decisions and for extensive coverage of this subject reference should be made to *Williams on Wills* Eighth Edition. The salient points are as follows.
The will may be written on any material (a wall and an eggshell have sufficed, see: *Re Slavisnky's Estate* (1989) 53 SASR 221; *Re Barnes* (1926) 43 TLR 71 respectively) and can be printed, lithographed or typed as well as holograph (see Interpretation Act 1976, Schedule 1 as to what is meant by writing).
For deaths before 1 January 1983 the unamended provisions of this section applied so that the will had to be signed "at the foot or end thereof". There is a vast body of case law on the meaning of this but in general terms the courts accepted the validity of a signature where it had been made once all the other provisions of the will had been written, and provided it was not a will clearly signed at the top. Now the position is that the will need not be signed at the end or the foot but sub-s (b) provides that it must appear that the testator intended by his signature to give effect to the Will. Therefore a signature that was a signature to an earlier will or different document will not suffice (see *Re White (deceased), Barker v Gribble and another* [1991] Ch 1, [1990] 3 All ER 1) but a testator who writes his name (not his normal signature) before writing out the dispositive parts of the will has been held to be signing the will (see: *Wood v Smith* [1993] Ch 90, [1992] 3 All ER 556). As to the form of the signature, a mark may suffice, as may an unfinished signature, or initials if it appears that that testator intended to sign. Rule 13 of the Non-Contentious Probate Rules 1987 makes provisions for signature by blind and illiterate testators **[Appendix V]**.
This may be one of the attesting witnesses, see *Re Bailey's Goods* (1838) 1 Curt 914. The direction need not be in writing, see: *Parker v Felgate* (1883) 8 PD 171.
This provides for attestation of the signature of the testator which must be made or acknowledged in the presence of the witnesses. Acknowledgement must be in the presence of two witnesses and it is crucial that the witnesses see or have the opportunity to see the signature (*Couser v Couser* [1996] 3 All ER 256). The production of a signed will by the testator or someone on his behalf and a request to the witnesses to attest it may amount to an acknowledgement (see, *Inglesant v Inglesant* (1874) LR 3 P & D 172).
The rules as to attestation are different for deaths before 1 January 1983 but the main change which has been made is that witnesses can now acknowledge their own signatures.
The witnesses must both be present when the testator signs but not necessarily when they sign. However, the testator must be present when they sign or acknowledge their signatures. This has been construed as meaning that he must be able to see them sign if he wishes to (see, for example, *Todd v Earl of Winchelsea* (1826) 2 C & P 488).

While there is no form of attestation clause specified, a standard form should always be used to avoid any difficulties in applying for a grant of probate if it is not clear section 9 has been complied with. For a recent case see : *Borman v Lel* [2002] WTLR 237.
There is a strong presumption that a Will which has been properly executed on the face of it is valid, see: *Sherrington v Sherrington* [2005] WTLR 587 and *Channon v Perkins* [2006] WTLR 425

[7]

10 Appointments by will to be executed like other wills, and to be valid, although other required solemnities are not observed

. . . no appointment made by will, in exercise of any power, shall be valid, unless the same be executed in manner herein-before required; and every will executed in manner herein-before required shall, so far as respects the execution and attestation thereof, be a valid execution of a power of appointment by will, notwithstanding it shall have been expressly required that a will made in exercise of such power should be executed with some additional or other form of execution or solemnity.

Amendment
Repealed, in relation to Northern Ireland, by the Wills and Administration Proceedings (NI) Order 1994, SI 1994/1899, art 38, Sch 3.
Words omitted repealed by the Statute Law Revision (No 2) Act 1888.

Commentary
This section is in two parts. Firstly, a power exercisable by will can only be exercised by a will which complies with section 9 above (see re *Barnett* [1908] 1 Ch 402). The second part of the section provides that powers exercisable by will (but not powers exercisable by other instrument only (see, *Taylor v Meads* (1865) 4 De G J & Sm 597) will be validly exercised if the will complies with section 9, even if the document creating the power requires other formalities.

[8]

11 Saving as to wills of soldiers and mariners

Provided always, . . . that any soldier being in actual military service, or any mariner or seaman being at sea, may dispose of his personal estate as he might have done before the making of this Act.

Amendment
Words omitted repealed by the Statute Law Revision (No 2) Act 1888.

Commentary
Before the Act there was no requirement that the wills of soldiers on active service, mariners or seamen at sea be in writing and this provision means that even if in writing the Will does not have to comply with section 9 above. Initially this exemption applied only to personal property, but the Wills (Soldiers and Sailors) Act 1918 **[77]** extended the exemption to real property and also to the Royal Navy and Marine Forces, not only when at sea but also when on active service. The Act also extended the exemption to cover airmen 'in actual military service' which since the 1939–45 war has meant a solider who is directly concerned with operations of a war which is in progress or is imminent. In recent times a soldier serving in Northern Ireland has been held to fulfil the test (see *Re Jones* [1981] Fam 7**).** Any form of words which expresses what the soldier etc wishes to happen to his goods on death will suffice as in *Re Jones* where the soldier said, "If I don't make it, make sure Annie gets all my stuff."

[9]

12 . . .

. . .

Amendment
Repealed by the Admiralty, &c Acts Repeal Act 1865, s 1.

[10]

13 Publication of will not requisite

. . . every will executed in manner herein-before required shall be valid without any other publication thereof.

Amendment
Repealed, in relation to Northern Ireland, by the Wills and Administration Proceedings (NI) Order 1994, SI 1994/1899, art 38, Sch 3.
Words omitted repealed by the Statute Law Revision (No 2) Act 1888.

Commentary
There is now no requirement that a will be published and the law before this Act can be disregarded. Note, however, that the concept of republication is unhelpfully preserved by the law, although it now means confirmation of an earlier will, eg by reference to it in a codicil. See the reference to republication in section 34 below.

[11]

14 Will not be void on account of incompetency of attesting witness

. . . if any person who shall attest the execution of a will shall at the time of the execution thereof or at any time afterwards be incompetent to be admitted a witness to prove the execution thereof, such will shall not on that account be invalid.

Amendment
Repealed, in relation to Northern Ireland, by the Wills and Administration Proceedings (NI) Order 1994, SI 1994/1899, art 38, Sch 3.
Words omitted repealed by the Statute Law Revision (No 2) Act 1888.

Commentary
As a matter of general law a witness must have the intention of attesting a will when he does so (see: *Sherrington v Sherrington* [2005] WTLR 587), but this section means that if he cannot give evidence as to his attestation the will is nevertheless valid.. It has been held that a will witnessed by someone who is blind, is invalid, see *Re Gibson's Estate* [1949] P 434.

[12]

15 Gifts to an attesting witness, or his or her wife or husband, to be void

. . . if any person shall attest the execution of any will to whom or to whose wife or husband any beneficial devise, legacy, estate, interest, gift, or appointment, of or affecting any real or personal estate (other than and except charges and directions for the payment of any debt or debts), shall be thereby given or made, such devise, legacy, estate, interest, gift, or appointment shall, so far only as concerns such person attesting the execution of such will, or the wife or husband of such person, or any person claiming under such person or wife or husband, be utterly null and void, and such person so attesting shall be admitted as a witness to prove the execution of such will, or to prove the validity or invalidity thereof, notwithstanding such devise, legacy, estate, interest, gift, or appointment mentioned in such will.

Amendment
Repealed, in relation to Northern Ireland, by the Wills and Administration Proceedings (NI) Order 1994, SI 1994/1899, art 38, Sch 3.
Words omitted repealed by the Statute Law Revision (No 2) Act 1888.

Commentary
It is vital that neither a beneficiary under a will nor the husband or wife of such a beneficiary witnesses the testator's signatory. A solicitor who failed to warn a testator of this rule was found liable in negligence in *Ross v Caunters* [1980] Ch 297. The rule does not apply where it was not clear until the death of the testator that the attesting witness would in fact benefit (see *Re Royce's Will Trusts Tildesley v Tildesley and Others* [1959] 3 All ER 278). For the destination of the failed gift, see: *Re Doland* [1970] Ch 267. This provision used to prevent a solicitor who became an executor with the benefit of a charging clause but who had

witnessed the will, from taking advantage of the charging clause, but that rule does not apply to deaths after 1 February 2001 by reason of changes made by the Trustee Act 2000 **[503]**. Note that a beneficiary who attests a will is nevertheless able to give evidence as to due execution. For deaths after 29 May 1968 the gift will be valid if the will would be properly executed without the beneficiary or his spouse attesting (see Wills Act 1968 **[295]**).

[13]

16 Creditor attesting a will charging estate with debts shall be admitted a witness

. . . in case by any will any real or personal estate shall be charged with any debt or debts, and any creditor, or the wife or husband [or civil partner] of any creditor, whose debt is so charged, shall attest the execution of such will, such creditor notwithstanding such charge shall be admitted a witness to prove the execution of such will, or to prove the validity or invalidity thereof.

Amendment

Repealed, in relation to Northern Ireland, by the Wills and Administration Proceedings (NI) Order 1994, SI 1994/1899, art 38, Sch 3.
Words omitted repealed by the Statute Law Revision (No 2) Act 1888.
Words "or civil partner" in square brackets inserted by the Civil Partnership Act 2004, s 71, Sch 4, Pt 1, paras 1, 4, 5.

Commentary

There is therefore no reason why a creditor of the deceased or their spouse should not attest the will.

[14]

17 Executor shall be admitted a witness

. . . no person shall, on account of his being an executor of a will, be incompetent to be admitted a witness to prove the execution of such will, or a witness to prove the validity or invalidity thereof.

Amendment

Repealed, in relation to Northern Ireland, by the Wills and Administration Proceedings (NI) Order 1994, SI 1994/1899, art 38, Sch 3.
Words omitted repealed by the Statute Law Revision (No 2) Act 1888.

Commentary

It is a commonly held misconception that the executor appointed under a will cannot also be a witness. This section makes it clear that is not the case.

[15]

[18 Will to be revoked by marriage

(1) Subject to subsections (2) to (4) below, a will shall be revoked by the testator's marriage.

(2) A disposition in a will in exercise of a power of appointment shall take effect notwithstanding the testator's subsequent marriage unless the property so appointed would in default of appointment pass to his personal representatives.

(3) Where it appears from a will that at the time it was made the testator was expecting to be married to a particular person and that he intended that the will should not be revoked by the marriage, the will shall not be revoked by his marriage to that person.

(4) Where it appears from a will that at the time it was made the testator was expecting to be married to a particular person and that he intended that a disposition in the will should not be revoked by his marriage to that person,—

(a) that disposition shall take effect notwithstanding the marriage; and
(b) any other disposition in the will shall take effect also, unless it appears from the will that the testator intended the disposition to be revoked by the marriage.]

Amendment
Substituted, in relation to England and Wales, by the Administration of Justice Act 1982, s 18(1).
Repealed, in relation to Northern Ireland, by the Wills and Administration Proceedings (NI) Order 1994, SI 1994/1899, art 38, Sch 3.

Commentary
A distinction has to be drawn between wills made before 1 January 1983, and those made afterwards. The original section 18 simply provided that wills would be revoked on the marriage of the testator. A lawful marriage is necessary to revoke the will (see *Pilot v Gainfort* [1931] P 103, 100 LJP 60, 145) but although a void marriage will not revoke the will of the testator, a voidable one (within the meaning of section 12 of the Matrimonial Causes Act 1973) will; see: *Re Roberts* [1978] 3 All ER 225. Section 177 of the Law of Property Act 1925 introduced the concept of wills expressed to be made in contemplation of a particular marriage. Whether or not the will did express that it was made in contemplation of a marriage was a matter of construction of the document concerned (a gift to a fiancé would suffice, see *Re Coleman* [1975] Ch 1).
As far as wills made after 1 January 1983 are concerned, the new section 18 makes a distinction between cases where it appears from the will that the Testator first of all expected to enter into a particular marriage, and secondly intended that marriage not to revoke his will. It is necessary therefore to establish both intention and expectation on the part of the testator and evidence for that must come from the will itself. The second situation is where it appears from one of the gifts made that the testator both expected to enter into a particular marriage and intended that marriage not to revoke the gift. In such a case in the absence of evidence to the contrary the whole will shall stand.
As far as any exercise of a power of appointment is concerned, apart from a change in wording there is little change post-1983. In effect, unless in default of appointment the property would go to the personal representatives of the testator, the exercise will be saved notwithstanding the revocation of the will by a subsequent marriage. This is because a testator entering into a marriage after an appointment might wish his new family to benefit if, in default of appointment, the property went to his next of kin.

[16]

[18A Effect of dissolution or annulment of marriage on wills

(1) Where, after a testator has made a will, *a decree* [an order or decree] of a court [of civil jurisdiction in England and Wales] dissolves or annuls his marriages [or his marriage is dissolved or annulled and the divorce or annulment is entitled to recognition in England and Wales by virtue of Part II of the Family Law Act 1986],—

[(a) provisions of the will appointing executors or trustees or conferring a power of appointment, if they appoint or confer the power on the former spouse, shall take effect as if the former spouse had died on the date on which the marriage is dissolved or annulled, and
(b) any property which, or an interest in which, is devised or bequeathed to the former spouse shall pass as if the former spouse had died on that date,]

except in so far as a contrary intention appears by the will.

(2) Subsection (1)(b) above is without prejudice to any right of the former spouse to apply for financial provision under the Inheritance (Provision for Family and Dependants) Act 1975.

(3) . . .]

Amendment
Inserted, in relation to England and Wales, by the Administration of Justice Act 1982, s 18(2).
Sub-s (1): first words in italics prospectively repealed with savings and subsequent words in square brackets prospectively substituted with savings by the Family Law Act 1996, s 66(1),

Sch 8, para 1, as from a day to be appointed, for savings see s 66(2), Sch 9, para 5 thereof; second words in square brackets inserted, and third words in square brackets substituted, by the Family Law Act 1986, s 53; paras (a), (b) substituted by the Law Reform (Succession) Act 1995, s 3.
Sub-s (3): repealed by the Law Reform (Succession) Act 1995, s 5, Schedule.

Commentary
For deaths which took place before 1 January 1996, the unamended section provided that the appointment of a spouse as executor or a gift in his favour should lapse after divorce or annulment, subject to a contrary intention. The Court of Appeal in *Re Sinclair* [1985] Ch 446 held that this did not have the effect of deeming the spouse to have predeceased the testator thereby accelerating alternative gifts. The amendments to the section clearly spell that out. Note that this section does not affect the ability of an ex-spouse to apply under the Inheritance (Provision for Family and Dependants) Act 1975 **[313]**. It should also be noted that this will only affect wills made before the marriage is dissolved or annulled and therefore republications of the will by execution of the codicil will mean the provision does not apply.

[17]

[18B Will to be revoked by civil partnership

(1) Subject to subsections (2) to (6), a will is revoked by the formation of a civil partnership between the testator and another person.

(2) A disposition in a will in exercise of a power of appointment takes effect despite the formation of a subsequent civil partnership between the testator and another person unless the property so appointed would in default of appointment pass to the testator's personal representatives.

(3) If it appears from a will—

(a) that at the time it was made the testator was expecting to form a civil partnership with a particular person, and

(b) that he intended that the will should not be revoked by the formation of the civil partnership,

the will is not revoked by its formation.

(4) Subsections (5) and (6) apply if it appears from a will—

(a) that at the time it was made the testator was expecting to form a civil partnership with a particular person, and

(b) that he intended that a disposition in the will should not be revoked by the formation of the civil partnership.

(5) The disposition takes effect despite the formation of the civil partnership.

(6) Any other disposition in the will also takes effect, unless it appears from the will that the testator intended the disposition to be revoked by the formation of the civil partnership.]

Amendment
Inserted by the Civil Partnership Act 2004, s 71, Sch 4, Pt 1, paras 1, 2, 5.

Commentary
This section provides similar provisions as to the revocation of a Will by a testator entering into a civil partnership as for a testator entering into a marriage. See the notes to section 18 above. If a testator makes a will in contemplation of the civil partnership this section will not have the effect of revoking it.

[18]

[18C Effect of dissolution or annulment of civil partnership on wills]

[(1) This section applies if, after a testator has made a will—

(a) a court of civil jurisdiction in England and Wales dissolves his civil partnership or makes a nullity order in respect of it, or

(b) his civil partnership is dissolved or annulled and the dissolution or annulment is entitled to recognition in England and Wales by virtue of Chapter 3 of Part 5 of the Civil Partnership Act 2004.

(2) Except in so far as a contrary intention appears by the will—

(a) provisions of the will appointing executors or trustees or conferring a power of appointment, if they appoint or confer the power on the former civil partner, take effect as if the former civil partner had died on the date on which the civil partnership is dissolved or annulled, and

(b) any property which, or an interest in which, is devised or bequeathed to the former civil partner shall pass as if the former civil partner had died on that date.

(3) Subsection (2)(b) does not affect any right of the former civil partner to apply for financial provision under the Inheritance (Provision for Family and Dependants) Act 1975.]

Amendment

Inserted by the Civil Partnership Act 2004, s 71, Sch 4, Pt 1, paras 1, 2, 5.

Commentary

This section makes similar provisions in respect of the dissolution or declaration of nullity in respect of a civil partnership as section 18A in respect of marriages. See the notes to that section. It is clear that gifts will be accelerated as if the former civil partners had died. Former civil partners still have the right to make a claim under the Inheritance (Provision for Family and Dependants) Act 1975 **[313]**.

[19]

19 No will to be revoked by presumption from altered circumstances

. . . no will shall be revoked by any presumption of an intention on the ground of an alteration in circumstances.

Amendment

Repealed, in relation to Northern Ireland, by the Wills and Administration Proceedings (NI) Order 1994, SI 1994/1899, art 38, Sch 3.
Words omitted repealed by the Statute Law Revision (No 2) Act 1888.

Commentary

Nothing other than marriage or entering into a civil partnership will automatically revoke the will including the subsequent birth of children or lifetime dispositions by the testator.

[20]

20 No will to be revoked otherwise than as aforesaid or by another will or codicil, or by destruction thereof

. . . no will or codicil, or any part thereof, shall be revoked otherwise than as aforesaid, or by another will or codicil executed in manner herein-before required, or by some writing declaring an intention to revoke the same and executed in the manner in which a will is herein-before required to be executed, or by the burning, tearing, or otherwise destroying the same by the testator, or by some person in his presence and by his direction, with the intention of revoking the same.

Amendment

Repealed, in relation to Northern Ireland, by the Wills and Administration Proceedings (NI) Order 1994, SI 1994/1899, art 38, Sch 3.
Words omitted repealed by the Statute Law Revision (No 2) Act 1888.

Commentary

The first part of the section deals with revocation by another will. Whether a subsequent testamentary document revokes a will is a matter of construction (see *In the Estate of*

Wayland [1951] 2 All ER 1041). A subsequent inconsistent will has the effect of revoking an earlier will but the fact that it is described as the "last Will" may not be enough (*Re Hawksley's Settlement* [1934] Ch 384 and see also *Broadway v Fernandes* [2007] EWHC 684 (Ch)). The section next deals with revocation by codicil and again it will be a matter of construction whether a codicil effects a revocation of the will and/or supervening codicils. As far as destruction is concerned, there are two elements which must be established: the actual destruction itself, and the testator's intention to revoke the will. Destruction involves not only the obliteration of the materials on which the will is written but also some act which goes to the character of the document as a will, for example, the scoring out in ballpoint pen of the signatures of the testator and witnesses (see *Re Adams* [1990] Ch 501). Intention to revoke may be presumed in certain circumstances (see again *Re Adams* and *Rowe v Clarke* [2005] EWHC 3068). Note that the section contemplates the possibility of partial revocation.

[21]

21 No alteration in a will after execution except in certain cases, shall have any effect unless executed as a will

. . . no obliteration, interlineation, or other alteration made in any will after the execution thereof shall be valid or have any effect, except so far as the words or effect of the will before such alteration shall not be apparent, unless such alteration shall be executed in like manner as herein-before is required for the execution of the will; but the will, with such alteration as part thereof, shall be deemed to be duly executed if the signature of the testator and the subscription of the witnesses be made in the margin or on some other part of the will opposite or near to such alteration, or at the foot or end of or opposite to a memorandum referring to such alteration, and written at the end of some other part of the will.

Amendment

Repealed, in relation to Northern Ireland, by the Wills and Administration Proceedings (NI) Order 1994, SI 1994/1899, art 38, Sch 3.
Words omitted repealed by the Statute Law Revision (No 2) Act 1888.

Commentary

There are only two methods of reviving a revoked will permitted by this section. The first is for the Will to be re-executed. The second is by codicil, but it must appear from the face of the codicil that the testator intended to revive the will (see In the *Goods of Steele* (1868) L R 1 P & D 575). The revocation of a will which revoked an earlier will, does not have the effect of reviving that earlier will. Note section 34 as to when such re-execution will take effect. The final provision simply means that if there has been a partial revocation of the will followed by a complete revocation, the part of the will partially revoked will not be revived when the will is revived unless there is something to show the contrary should be the case.

[22]

22 No revoked will shall be revived otherwise than by re-execution or a codicil, &c

. . . no will or codicil, or any part thereof, which shall be in any manner revoked, shall be revived otherwise than by the re-execution thereof or by a codicil executed in manner herein-before required and showing an intention to revive the same; and when any will or codicil which shall be partly revoked, and afterwards wholly revoked, shall be revived, such revival shall not extend to so much thereof as shall have been revoked before the revocation of the whole thereof, unless an intention to the contrary shall be shown.

Amendment

Repealed, in relation to Northern Ireland, by the Wills and Administration Proceedings (NI) Order 1994, SI 1994/1899, art 38, Sch 3.
Words omitted repealed by the Statute Law Revision (No 2) Act 1888.

Commentary

There are only two methods of reviving a revoked will permitted by this section. The first is for the Will to be re-executed. The second is by codicil, but it must appear from the face of the codicil that the testator intended to revive the will (see In the *Goods of Steele* (1868) L R 1 P & D 575). The revocation of a will which revoked an earlier will, does not have the effect of reviving that earlier will. Note section 34 as to when such re-execution will take effect. The final provision simply means that if there has been a partial revocation of the will followed by a complete revocation, the part of the will partially revoked will not be revived when the will is revived unless there is something to show the contrary should be the case.

[23]

23 Subsequent conveyance or other act not to prevent operation of will

. . . no conveyance or other act made or done subsequently to the execution of a will of or relating to any real or personal estate therein comprised, except an act by which such will shall be revoked as aforesaid, shall prevent the operation of the will with respect to such estate or interest in such real or personal estate as the testator shall have power to dispose of by will at the time of his death.

Amendment

Repealed, in relation to Northern Ireland, by the Wills and Administration Proceedings (NI) Order 1994, SI 1994/1899, art 38, Sch 3.
Words omitted repealed by the Statute Law Revision (No 2) Act 1888.

Commentary

The purpose of this section is to change the old law whereby a change in the interest of the testator in property subsequent to the will could have the effect of revoking the gift. It does no more than leave the court free to construe the will in the ordinary way and see what should be the subject matter of a particular gift.

[24]

24 Wills shall be construed, as to the estate comprised, to speak from the death of the testator

. . . every will shall be construed, with reference to the real estate and personal estate comprised in it, to speak and take effect as if it had been executed immediately before the death of the testator, unless a contrary intention shall appear by the will.

Amendment

Repealed, in relation to Northern Ireland, by the Wills and Administration Proceedings (NI) Order 1994, 1994/1899, art 38, Sch 3.
Words omitted repealed by the Statute Law Revision (No 2) Act 1888.

Commentary

This section is crucial when looking at the subject matter of any gift. If there is no contrary intention shown in the will, then it is the property which the testator owns at the date of his death which will form the subject of a gift.

[25]

25 Residuary devises shall include estates comprised in lapsed and void devises

. . . unless a contrary intention shall appear by the will, such real estate or interest therein as shall be comprised or intended to be comprised in any devise in such will contained, which shall fail or be void by reason of the death of the devisee in the lifetime of the testator, or by reason of such devise being contrary to law or otherwise incapable of taking effect shall be included in the residuary devise (if any) contained in such will.

Amendment

Repealed, in relation to Northern Ireland, by the Wills and Administration Proceedings (NI) Order 1994, SI 1994/1899, art 38, Sch 3.

Words omitted repealed by the Statute Law Revision (No 2) Act 1888.

Commentary

The old law before this Act provided that a devise in the will which failed by lapse or for some other reason did not fall into the residuary devise under the will. This section clearly provides that if such a gift fails, then it will in the normal way fall into residue unless of course there is a contrary intention shown on the face of the will.

[26]

26 A general devise of the testator's lands shall include copyhold and leasehold as well as freehold lands, in the absence of a contrary intention

. . . a devise of the land of the testator, or of the land of the testator in any place or in the occupation of any person mentioned in his will, or otherwise described in a general manner, and any other general devise which would describe a . . . leasehold estate if the testator had no freehold estate which could be described by it, shall be construed to include the . . . leasehold estates of the testator, or his . . . leasehold estates, or any of them, to which such description shall extend, as the case may be, as well as freehold estates, unless a contrary intention shall appear by the will.

Amendment

Repealed, in relation to Northern Ireland, by the Wills and Administration Proceedings (NI) Order 1994, SI 1994/1899, art 38, Sch 3.

First words omitted repealed by the Statute Law Revision (No 2) Act 1888; other words omitted repealed by the Statute Law (Repeals) Act 1969.

Commentary

Before the enactment of this section, a general devise of land did not carry leaseholds with it unless there were no freeholds. This section makes it clear that a general devise will carry leaseholds even where there are also freeholds, unless there is a contrary intention. The section will not apply to a gift of "real estate", see *Re Holt* [1921] 2 Ch 17, and a contrary intention might be shown by a specific gift of leaseholds, see *Re Guyton and Rosenberg's Contracts* [1901] 2 Ch 291.

[27]

27 A general gift of realty or personalty shall include property over which the testator has a general power of appointment

. . . a general devise of the real estate of the testator, or of the real estate of the testator in any place or in the occupation of any person mentioned in his will, or otherwise described in a general manner, shall be construed to include any real estate, or any real estate to which such description shall extend (as the case may be), which he may have power to appoint in any manner he may think proper, and shall operate as an execution of such power, unless a contrary intention shall appear by the will; and in like manner a bequest of the personal estate of the testator, or any bequest of personal property described in a general manner, shall be construed to include any personal estate, or any personal estate to which such description shall extend (as the case may be), which he may have power to appoint in any manner he may think proper, and shall operate as an execution of such power, unless a contrary intention shall appear by the will.

Amendment

Repealed, in relation to Northern Ireland, by the Wills and Administration Proceedings (NI) Order 1994, SI 1994/1899, art 38, Sch 3.

Words omitted repealed by the Statute Law Revision (No 2) Act 1888.

Commentary
The purpose of this section has been said to abolish the distinction between property and a general power over property, see *Re Jacob* [1907] Ch 445. It must first be established that the power which is vested in the testator is a general power. The gift in the will must also be of a general nature to have the effect of exercising the power. Again all of this is subject to a contrary intention in the will.

[28]

28 A devise of real estate without any words of limitation shall pass the fee, &c

. . . where any real estate shall be devised to any person without any words of limitation, such devise shall be construed to pass the fee simple, or other the whole estate or interest which the testator had power to dispose of by will in such real estate, unless a contrary intention shall appear by the will.

Amendment
Repealed, in relation to Northern Ireland, by the Wills and Administration Proceedings (NI) Order 1994, 1994/1899, art 38, Sch 3.
Words omitted repealed by the Statute Law Revision (No 2) Act 1888.

Commentary
Before the enactment of this provision, a gift of real estate without any words of limitation would have given a life estate only. This ensures that a gift of real property without such words and in the absence of a contrary intention will pass either the fee simple (if that is what the testator had) or his interest in the property in question.

[29]

29 The words "die without issue," or "die without leaving issue," &c shall mean a want or failure of issue in the lifetime or at the death of the person, except in certain cases

. . . in any devise or bequest of real or personal estate the words "die without issue" or "die without leaving issue," or "have no issue," or any other words which may import either a want or failure of issue of any person in his lifetime or at the time of his death, or an indefinite failure of his issue, shall be construed to mean a want or failure of issue in the lifetime or at the time of the death of such person, and not an indefinite failure of his issue, unless a contrary intention shall appear by the will, by reason of such person having a prior estate tail, or of a preceding gift, being, without any implication arising from such words, a limitation of an estate tail to such person or issue, or otherwise: Provided, that this Act shall not extend to cases where such words as aforesaid import if no issue described in a preceding gift shall be born, or if there shall be no issue who shall live to attain the age or otherwise answer the description required for obtaining a vested estate by a preceding gift to such issue.

Amendment
Repealed, in relation to Northern Ireland, by the Wills and Administration Proceedings (NI) Order 1994, SI 1994/1899, art 38, Sch 3.
Words omitted repealed by the Statute Law Revision (No 2) Act 1888.

Commentary
The old law before this section was that the words set out there meant an indefinite failure of issue. There has been some doubt as to the circumstances in which this section will apply, but it has not been applied where the words "heirs of the body" were used rather than 'issue' (*Re Leach* [1912] 2 Ch 422). Where the failure of issue before the Act would not have been regarded as an indefinite failure of issue, see *Morris v Morris* (1857) 17 B 198. For a full discussion of the many cases in this area see Chapter 98 of *Williams on Wills* Eighth Edition.

[30]

30 Devise of realty to trustees or executors shall pass the fee, &c, except in certain cases

. . . where any real estate (other than or not being a presentation to a church) shall be devised to any trustee or executor, such devise shall be construed to pass the fee simple or other the whole estate or interest which the testator had power to dispose of by will in such real estate, unless a definite term of years, absolute or determinable, or an estate of freehold, shall thereby be given to him expressly or by implication.

Amendment

Repealed, in relation to Northern Ireland, by the Wills and Administration Proceedings (NI) Order 1994, SI 1994/1899, art 38, Sch 3.
Words omitted repealed by the Statute Law Revision (No 2) Act 1888.

Commentary

This section abrogates the old rule that a gift to a trustee or executor must contain specific words to pass the fee simple.

[31]

31 Trustees under an unlimited devise, where the trust may endure beyond the life of a person beneficially entitled for life, shall take the fee, &c

. . . where any real estate shall be devised to a trustee, without any express limitation of the estate to be taken by such trustee, and the beneficial interest in such real estate, or in the surplus rents and profits thereof, shall not be given to any person for life, or such beneficial interest shall be given to any person for life, but the purposes of the trust may continue beyond the life of such person, such devise shall be construed to vest in such trustee the fee simple, or other the whole legal estate which the testator had power to dispose of by will in such real estate, and not an estate determinable when the purposes of the trust shall be satisfied.

Amendment

Repealed, in relation to Northern Ireland, by the Wills and Administration Proceedings (NI) Order 1994, SI 1994/1899, art 38, Sch 3.
Words omitted repealed by the Statute Law Revision (No 2) Act 1888.

Commentary

This section prevents anything other than a fee simple being given to a trustee in circumstances where, under the old law, nothing other than a determinable fee might pass.

[32]

32 . . .

. . .

Amendment

Repealed, in relation to Northern Ireland, by the Wills and Administration Proceedings (NI) Order 1994, SI 1994/1899, art 38, Sch 3.
Repealed by the Trusts of Land and Appointment of Trustees Act 1996, s 25(2), Sch 4; for savings in relation to entailed interests created before the commencement of that Act, and savings consequential upon the abolition of the doctrine of conversion, see s 25(4), (5) thereof.

[33]

[33 Gifts to children or other issue who leave issue living at the testator's death shall not lapse

(1) Where—

- (a) a will contains a devise or bequest to a child or remoter descendant of the testator; and

(b) the intended beneficiary dies before the testator, leaving issue; and
(c) issue of the intended beneficiary are living at the testator's death,

then, unless a contrary intention appears by the will, the devise or bequest shall take effect as a devise or bequest to the issue living at the testator's death.

(2) Where—
(a) a will contains a devise or bequest to a class of person consisting of children or remoter descendants of the testator; and
(b) a member of the class dies before the testator, leaving issue, and
(c) issue of that member are living at the testator's death,

then, unless a contrary intention appears by the will, the devise or bequest shall take effect as if the class included the issue of its deceased member living at the testator's death.

(3) Issue shall take under this section through all degrees, according to their stock, in equal shares if more than one, any gift or share which their parent would have taken and so that no issue shall take whose parent is living at the testator's death and that no issue shall take whose parent is living at the testator's death and so capable of taking.

(4) For the purposes of this section—
(a) the illegitimacy of any person is to be disregarded; and
(b) a person conceived before the testator's death and born living thereafter is to be taken to have been living at the testator's death.]

Amendment
Substituted, in relation to England and Wales, by the Administration of Justice Act 1982, s 19.
Repealed, in relation to Northern Ireland, by the Wills and Administration Proceedings (NI) Order 1994, SI 1994/1899, art 38, Sch 3.

Commentary
This section has been extensively reviewed in the case of *Ling v Ling* [2002] WTLR 553 where it was held that there was no contrary mention excluding the provisions of sub-s (2).

[34]

34 Act not to extend to wills made before 1838, nor to estates pur autre vie of persons who die before 1838

. . . this Act shall not extend to any will made before the first day of January one thousand eight hundred and thirty-eight; and every will re-executed or republished, or revived by any codicil, shall for the purposes of this Act be deemed to have been made at the time at which the same shall be so re-executed, republished or revived; and this Act shall not extend to any estate pur autre vie of any person who shall die before the first day of January one thousand eight hundred and thirty-eight.

Amendment
Repealed, in relation to Northern Ireland, by the Wills and Administration Proceedings (NI) Order 1994, SI 1994/1899, art 38, Sch 3.
Words omitted repealed by the Statute Law Revision (No 2) Act 1888.

Commentary
This section is important as to the timing of revived, re-executed and republished wills. An estate pur autre vie is an estate which lasts until the death of someone other than the person in possession.

[35]

35 Act not to extend to Scotland

. . . this Act shall not extend to Scotland.

Amendment
Repealed, in relation to Northern Ireland, by the Wills and Administration Proceedings (NI) Order 1994, SI 1994/1899, art 38, Sch 3.
Words omitted repealed by the Statute Law Repeals (No 2) Act 1888.

[36]

36 . . .

. . .

Amendment
Repealed by the Statute Law Revision Act 1874.

[37]

APPORTIONMENT ACT 1870

1870 Chapter 35

ARRANGEMENT OF SECTIONS

An Act for the better Apportionment of Rents and other periodical Payments
[1st August 1870]

General Note
The Apportionment Act is mainly known by draftsmen of trusts and wills because it is excluded as a matter of course, but it was enacted to resolve problems as to the way in which certain income was to be treated.

1 Short title

This Act may be cited for all purposes as "The Apportionment Act 1870."

[38]

2 Rents, etc to be apportionable in respect of time

. . . All rents, annuities, dividends, and other periodical payments in the nature of income (whether reserved or made payable under an instrument in writing or otherwise) shall, like interest on money lent, be considered as accruing from day to day, and shall be apportionable in respect of time accordingly.

Amendment
Words omitted repealed by the Statute Law Revision (No 2) Act 1893.

Commentary
This has the effect that in respect of income which has accrued before the death of a deceased will fall into residue unless of course as is commonly the case that the Act is

excluded. On the other hand any dividends etc which accrue after the date of death will go with any specific gifts of the shares regardless of when the shares are actually transferred to the beneficiary. Any dividend has to be declared in respect of a definite period for the Act to apply (*Re Jowitt* [1922] 2 Ch 442). "Other periodical payments in the nature of income" does not include interest on compensation: *Re Sneyd* [1961] 1 WLR 575. Where a protected life interest comes to en end (as to which see section 33 of the Trustee Act 1925 **[102]** there is no apportionment under this Statute, *Re Gourju's Will Trusts* [1943] Ch 24. For the application of this Act to maintenance of a minor beneficiary under section 31 of the Trustee Act 1925 **[100]** see *Re Joel's Will Trusts* [1967] Ch 14.

[39]

3 Apportioned part of rent, etc to be payable when the next entire portion shall have become due

The apportioned part of any such rent, annuity, dividend, or other payment shall be payable or recoverable in the case of a continuing rent, annuity, or other such payment when the entire portion of which such apportioned part shall form part shall become due and payable, and not before, and in the case of a rent, annuity, or other such payment determined by re-entry, death, or otherwise when the next entire portion of the same would have been payable if the same had not so determined, and not before.

Commentary

This section is really more a matter of general law rather than directly relevant to trusts and estates but its effect is that the day for payment of any sum which is apportioned is not accelerated.

[40]

4 Persons shall have the same remedies for recovering apportioned parts as for entire portions—Proviso as to rents reserved in certain cases

All persons and their respective heirs, executors, administrators, and assigns, and also the executors, administrators, and assigns respectively of persons whose interests determine with their own deaths, shall have such or the same remedies at law and in equity for recovering such apportioned parts as aforesaid when payable (allowing proportionate parts of all just allowances) as they respectively would have had for recovering such entire portions as aforesaid if entitled thereto respectively; provided that persons liable to pay rents reserved out of or charged on lands or other hereditaments of any tenure, and the same lands or other hereditaments, shall not be resorted to for any such apportioned part forming part of an entire or continuing rent as aforesaid specifically, but the entire or continuing rent, including such apportioned part, shall be recovered and received by the heir or other person who, if the rent had not been apportionable under this Act, or otherwise, would have been entitled to such entire or continuing rent, and such apportioned part shall be recoverable from such heir or other person by the executors or other parties entitled under this Act to the same by action at law or suit in equity.

Commentary

This section enables the recovery of the apportioned part of any rents etc. as they would have in respect of the whole rent payable, and see: *Swansea Bank v Thomas* (1879) 40 LT 558.

[41]

5 Interpretation

In the construction of this Act—

The word "rents" includes rent service, rentcharge, and rent seck, and also tithes and all periodical payments or renderings in lieu of or in the nature of rent or tithe.

The word "annuities" includes salaries and pensions.

The word "dividends" includes (besides dividends strictly so called) all payments made by the name of dividend, bonus, or otherwise out of the revenue of trading or other public companies, divisible between all or any of the members of such respective companies, whether such payments shall be usually made or declared, at any fixed times or otherwise; and all such divisible revenue shall, for the purposes of this Act, be deemed to have accrued by equal daily increment during and within the period for or in respect of which the payment of the same revenue shall be declared or expressed to be made, but the said word "dividend" does not include payments in the nature of a return or reimbursement of capital.

Commentary

"Dividends" include the dividends of all companies registered under the Companies Acts (*Re Lysaght* [1898] 1 Ch 115) including private companies (*Re White* [1913]1 Ch 231).

[42]

6 Act not to apply to policies of assurance

Nothing in this Act contained shall render apportionable any annual sums made payable in policies of assurance of any description.

[43]

7 Nor where stipulation made to the contrary

The provisions of this Act shall not extend to any case in which it is or shall be expressly stipulated that no apportionment shall take place.

Commentary

The Act is frequently excluded by draftsmen and see: *Re Lysaght* [1898] 1 Ch 115. A direction that the whole of the proceeds of a business should be paid to the tenant for life pending sale did not exclude the Act, see: *Re Edwards* [1918] 1 Ch 142.

[44]

COLONIAL PROBATES ACT 1892

1892 Chapter 6

ARRANGEMENT OF SECTIONS

An Act to provide for the Recognition in the United Kingdom of Probates and Letters of Administration granted in British Possessions

[20th May 1892]

General Note

The Colonial Probates Act 1892 provides for grants made in colonies and other foreign jurisdictions to be resealed by the Probate Court in England and Wales.

1 Application of Act by Order in Council

Her Majesty the Queen may, on being satisfied that the legislature of any British possession has made adequate provision for the recognition in that possession of probates and letters of administration granted by the courts of the United Kingdom, direct by Order in Council that this Act shall, subject to any exceptions and modifications specified in the Order, apply to that possession, and thereupon, while the Order is in force, this Act shall apply accordingly.

Commentary
The term "British Possession" in this section means any part of Her Majesty's Dominions outside the United Kingdom (see the Interpretation Act 1976, Sch 1). As will be seen, the Colonial Probates Act 1892 (CPA 1892), however, has a far wider ambit than simply British possessions. As to the countries covered by the Act at present see the notes to s 4 below.

[45]

[1A

This Act shall apply in relation to the Hong Kong Special Administrative Region of the People's Republic of China as it applied, immediately before 1st July 1997, to Hong Kong; and the Colonial Probates Act Application Order 1965 shall, in relation to that Region, continue in force accordingly.]

Amendment
Inserted by SI 1997/1572, art 2.

Commentary
This inserted section was of course necessitated by the end of the lease of Hong Kong to Britain. Where other former colonies and protectorates have gained independence, these provisions for the resealing of grants have generally continued to apply by virtue of provisions contained in the statute granting independence. See below for a list of the territories to which the CPA 1892 applies.

[46]

2 Sealing in United Kingdom of colonial probates and letters of administration

(1) Where a court of probate in a British possession to which this Act applies has granted probate or letters of administration in respect of the estate of a deceased person [then (subject to section [109 of the *Supreme Court Act 1981* [Senior Courts Act 1981]], section 42 of the Probate and Legacy Duties Act 1808 and section 99A of the Probates and Letters of Administration Act (Ireland) 1857)] the probate or letters so granted may, on being produced to, and a copy thereof deposited with, a court of probate in the United Kingdom, be sealed with the seal of that court, and, thereupon, shall be of the like force and effect, and have the same operation in the United Kingdom, as if granted by that court.

(2) Provided that the court shall, before sealing a probate or letters of administration under this section, be satisfied—

- (a) . . .
- (b) in the case of letters of administration, that security has been given in a sum sufficient in amount to cover the property (if any) in the United Kingdom to which letters of administration relate;

and may require such evidence, if any, as it thinks fit as to the domicile of the deceased person.

(3) The court may also, if it thinks fit, on the application of any creditor, require, before sealing, that adequate security be given for the payment of debts due from the estate to creditors residing in the United Kingdom.

(4) For the purposes of this section, a duplicate of any probate or letters of administration sealed with the seal of the court granting the same, or a copy thereof certified as correct by or under the authority of the court granting the same, shall have the same effect as the original.

(5) Rules of court may be made for regulating the procedure and practice, including fees and costs, in courts of the United Kingdom, on and incidental to an application for sealing a probate or letters of administration granted in a British possession to which this Act applies . . .

Amendment

Sub-s (1): words from "then (subject to" to "Probates and Letters of Administration Act (Ireland) 1857)" in square brackets inserted by the Finance Act 1975, s 52(1), Sch 12, paras 2, 4.
Sub-s (1): words "109 of the Supreme Court Act 1981" in square brackets substituted by the Supreme Court Act 1981, ss 152(1), 153(4), Sch 5.
Sub-s (1): words "Supreme Court Act 1981" in italics repealed and subsequent words in square brackets substituted by the Constitutional Reform Act 2005, s 59(5), Sch 11, Pt 1, para 1(2).
Sub-ss (2), (5): words omitted repealed by the Finance Act 1975, ss 52(2), 59(5), Sch 13, Part I.

Commentary

For the practice on an application for resealing of the grant, see the Non-Contentious Probate Rules 1987, r 39 **[Appendix V]**. Essentially the court has to be satisfied that any inheritance tax has been paid and an account should be lodged. Note that under sub-s (2) the court may require evidence of domicile although usually the statement in the Inheritance Tax account will be sufficient. No oath is sworn on an application to reseal a grant. The subordinate legislation enacted under sub-s (5), the Non-Contentious Probate (Amendment) Rules 1999, SI 1999/1015 preserved the Rules of the Supreme Court 1965 in respect of non-contentious probate when the Civil Procedure Rules 1998 came into force.

[47]

3 Application of Act to British courts in foreign countries

This Act shall extend to authorise the sealing in the United Kingdom of any probate or letters of administration granted by a British court in a foreign country, in like manner as it authorises the sealing of a probate or letters of administration granted in a British possession to which this Act applies, and the provisions of this Act shall apply accordingly with the necessary modifications.

Commentary

As to the meaning of "British Court in a foreign country" see s 6 below. The procedure for applying for resealing of a grant is the same under this provision as for colonial grants.

[48]

4 Orders in Council

(1) Every Order in Council made under this Act shall be laid before both Houses of Parliament . . .

(2) Her Majesty the Queen in Council may revoke or alter any Order in Council previously made under this Act.

(3) Where it appears to Her Majesty in Council that the legislature of part of a British possession has power to make the provision requisite for bringing this Act into operation in that part it shall be lawful for Her Majesty to direct by Order in Council that this Act shall apply to that part as if it were a separate British possession, and thereupon, while the Order is in force, this Act shall apply accordingly.

Amendment

Sub-s (1): words omitted repealed by the Statute Law (Repeals) Act 1986.

Commentary
There have been a number of Orders in Council made under the CPA 1892 which have now been consolidated into the Colonial Probates Act Application Order 1965, SI 1965/1530 (except for the Order in Council which applied the Act to South Africa and which has been preserved). The CPA 1892 now applies in the following countries: Alberta; Antigua; Australian Capital Territory; Bahamas; Barbados; Belize; Bermuda; Botswana; British Antarctic Territory; British Columbia; British Sovereign Base Areas in Cyprus; Brunei; Cayman Islands; Christmas Island (Australia); Cocos (Keeling) Islands; Cyprus (republic and not therefore Turkish Cyprus); Dominica; Falkland Islands; Falkland Islands Dependencies; Fiji; Gambia; Ghana; Gibraltar; Grenada; Guyana; Hong Kong; Jamaica; Kenya; Kiribati; Lesotho; Malawi; Malaysia; Manitoba; Montserrat; New Brunswick; New Guinea Territory; New South Wales; New Zealand; Newfoundland; Nigeria; Norfolk Island; Northern Territory of Australia; North-West Territories of Canada; Nova Scotia; Ontario; Papua New Guinea; Prince Edward Island; Queensland; St Kitts and Nevis; St Helena; St Lucia; St Vincent; Saskatchewan; Seychelles; Sierra Leone; Singapore; Solomon Islands; South Africa; South Australia; Sri Lanka; Swaziland; Tasmania; Tortola; Trinidad and Tobago; Turks and Caicos Islands; Tuvalu; Uganda; Victoria; Western Australia; Zambia, Zimbabwe

[49]

5 Application of Acts to probates, etc already granted

This Act when applied by an Order in Council to a British possession shall, subject to the provisions of the Order, apply to probates and letters of administration granted in that possession either before or after the passing of this Act.

Commentary
The important question is whether the CPA 1892 applies to a particular country when resealing is sought, not when the grant in that foreign jurisdiction was made.

[50]

6 Definitions

In this Act—

The expression "court of probate" means any court or authority, by whatever name designated, having jurisdiction in matters of probate, and in Scotland means the sheriff court of the county of Edinburgh:

The expression "probate" and "letters of administration" include confirmation in Scotland, and any instrument having in a British possession the same effect which under English law is given to probate and letters of administration respectively:

. . .

The expression "British court in a foreign country" means any British court having jurisdiction out of the Queen's dominions in pursuance of an Order in Council, whether made under any Act or otherwise.

Amendment
Words omitted repealed by the Finance Act 1975, ss 52(2), 59(5), Sch 13, Part I.

[51]

7 Short title

This Act may be cited as the Colonial Probates Act 1892.

[52]

JUDICIAL TRUSTEES ACT 1896

1896 Chapter 35

ARRANGEMENT OF SECTIONS

An Act to provide for the Appointment of Judicial Trustees and otherwise to amend the Law respecting the Administration of Trusts and the Liability of Trustees

[14th August 1896]

General Note

The Judicial Trustees Act 1896 (JTA 1896) introduced a whole new category of trustees, judicial trustees, appointed by and acting under the control of the court.

1 Power of court on application to appoint judicial trustee

(1) Where application is made to the court by or on behalf of the person creating or intending to create a trust, or by or on behalf of a trustee or beneficiary, the court may, in its discretion, appoint a person (in this Act called a judicial trustee) to be a trustee of that trust, either jointly with any other person or as sole trustee, and, if sufficient cause is shown, in place of all or any existing trustees.

(2) The administration of the property of a deceased person, whether a testator or intestate, shall be a trust, and the executor or administrator a trustee, within the meaning of this Act.

(3) Any fit and proper person nominated for the purpose in the application may be appointed a judicial trustee, and, in the absence of such nomination, or if the court is not satisfied of the fitness of a person so nominated, an official of the court may be appointed, and in any case a judicial trustee shall be subject to the control and supervision of the court as an officer thereof.

(4) The court may, either on request or without request, give to a judicial trustee any general or special directions in regard to the trust or the administration thereof.

(5) There may be paid to a judicial trustee out of the trust property such remuneration, not exceeding the prescribed limits, as the court may assign in each case, subject to any rules under this Act respecting the application of such remuneration where the judicial trustee is an official of the court, and the remuneration so assigned to any judicial trustee shall, save as the court may for special reasons otherwise order, cover all his work and personal outlay.

(6) . . . in any case where the court shall so direct, an inquiry into the administration by a judicial trustee of any trust, or into any dealing or transaction of a judicial trustee, shall be made in the prescribed manner.

[(7) Where an application relating to the estate of a deceased person is made to the court under this section, the court may, if it thinks fit, proceed as if the application were, or included, an application under section 50 of the Administration of Justice Act 1985 (power of High Court to appoint substitute for, or to remove, personal representative).]

Amendment
Sub-s (6): words omitted repealed by the Administration of Justice Act 1982, ss 57, 75, Sch 9, Part I.
Sub-s (7): inserted with retrospective effect by the Administration of Justice Act 1985, ss 50(6), 69(5), Sch 9, para 10.

Commentary
Application under sub-s (1) is now made by way of a Part 8 claim under the Civil Procedure Rules 1998, SI 1998/3132. Note that the court has a discretion as to whether or not to appoint a judicial trustee. In general it will not do so unless the administration of the trust has broken down, see *Re Chisholm* (1898) 43 SJ 43; *Re Ratcliff* [1898] 2 Ch 352; *Thomas & Agnes Carvel Foundation v Carvel* [2007] 4 All ER 81. The application can be made by the settlor or intending settlor, trustee or beneficiary. Subsection (2) makes it clear that the section applies to administrators and executors and the JTA 1896 therefore provides an alternative to the procedure for removal of personal representatives under the Administration of Justice Act 1985 (AJA 1985), s 50 **[399]**. Subsection (7) enables the court to treat an application under the JTA 1896 as an application to remove the executor or administrator under the AJA 1985, s 50. Subsection (3) provides for any fit and proper person to be appointed. Solicitors and accountants are regularly appointed but if there is no one appropriate then it is common practice for the court to appoint the Official Solicitor. Although the court can make directions under sub-s (4), the judicial trustee nevertheless has all the usual powers of a trustee which he can exercise, see *Re Ridsel* [1947] Ch 597. The court may provide for the remuneration of the judicial trustee (sub-s (5)) but this may not in any year exceed 15% of the capital value of the trust property (see the Judicial Trustee Rules 1983, SI 1983/370, r 11) **[Appendix IV]**.

[53]

2 Court to exercise jurisdiction

The jurisdiction of the court under this Act may be exercised by the High Court, . . . and (subject to the prescribed definition of the jurisdiction) by any county court judge to whom such jurisdiction may be assigned under this Act.

Amendment
Words omitted repealed by the Courts Act 1971, s 56(4), Sch 11, Part II.

Commentary
Application in fact has to be made to the High Court as no rules have ever been made under the JTA 1896 conferring jurisdiction on the County Court.

[54]

3 . . .

. . .

Amendment
Repealed by the Trustee Act 1925, s 70, Sch 2.

[55]

4 Rules

(1) Rules may be made for carrying into effect this Act, and especially—

- (1) for requiring judicial trustees, who are not officials of the court, to give security for the due application of any trust property under their control:
- (2) respecting the safety of the trust property, and the custody thereof:
- (3) respecting the remuneration of judicial trustees and for fixing and regulating the fees to be taken under this Act so as to cover the expenses of the administration of this Act, and respecting the payment of such remuneration and fees out of the trust property, and, where the judicial trustee is an official of the court, respecting the application of the remuneration and fees payable to him:

(4) for dispensing with formal proof of facts in proper cases:
(5) for facilitating the discharge by the court of administrative duties under this Act without prejudicial proceedings and otherwise regulating procedure under this Act and making it simple and inexpensive:
(6) for assigning jurisdiction under this Act to county court judges and defining such jurisdiction:
(7) respecting the suspension or removal of any judicial trustee, and the succession of another person to the office of any judicial trustee who may cease to hold office, and the vesting in such person of any trust property:
(8) respecting the classes of trusts in which officials of the court are not to be judicial trustees, or are to be so temporarily or conditionally:
(9) respecting the procedure to be followed where the judicial trustee is executor or administrator:
(10) for preventing the employment by judicial trustees of other persons at the expense of the trust, except in cases of strict necessity:
[(11) for the preparation, auditing (by the court or otherwise) and filing of the accounts of any trust of which a judicial trustee has been appointed;
(12) for the making of a report to the court on the accounts of any such trust.]

[(1A) The rules under this Act may make different provision for different classes of trust, trustees, beneficiaries or trust property.]

(2) The rules under this Act may be made by the Lord Chancellor, subject to the consent of the Treasury in matters relating to fees and to salaries and numbers of officers, and to the consent of the authority for making orders under the Solicitors Remuneration Act 1881, in matters relating to the remuneration of solicitors. The rules shall be laid before Parliament and . . . if, within thirty days after such rules have been laid before either House of Parliament during which that House has sat, the House presents to Her Majesty an address against such rules or any of them, such rules or the rule specified in the address shall thenceforward be of no effect.

Amendment

Sub-s (1): amended by the Administration of Justice Act 1982, s 57.
Sub-s (1A): inserted by the Administration of Justice Act 1982, s 57.
Sub-s (2): words omitted repealed by the Statute Law (Repeals) Act 1986.

Commentary

The Judicial Trustee Rules 1983 (SI 1983/370) were made under this section. They can be found in the **[Appendix IV]**. They provide for such matters as the giving of security and guarantees (r 6), and vesting of property and documents (r 7). Rule 8 provides for the trustee to be able to seek the directions of the court on questions of administration or termination of the judicial trusteeship without the need for any formal originating process. Special rules for the filing of accounts by the judicial trustee can be found in rr 9–12.

[56]

5 Definitions

In this Act—

The expression "official of the court" means the holder of such paid office in or connected with the court as may be prescribed.

The expression "prescribed" means prescribed by rules under this Act.

Commentary

As stated above in practice it is the Official Solicitor who is appointed judicial trustee if an officer of the court is needed.

[57]

6 Short title and extent of Act

(1) This Act may be cited as the Judicial Trustees Act, 1896.

(2) This Act shall not extend to any charity . . .

(3) This Act shall not extend to Scotland or Ireland.

(4) . . .

Amendment

Sub-s (2): words omitted repealed by the Charities Act 1960, s 48(2), Sch 7, Part I.
Sub-s (4): repealed by the Statute Law Revision Act 1908.

Commentary

Note in sub-s (2) that the JTA 1896 does not apply to charities.

[58]

PUBLIC TRUSTEE ACT 1906

1906 Chapter 55

ARRANGEMENT OF SECTIONS

An Act to provide for the appointment of a Public Trustee and to amend the Law relating to the administration of Trusts

[21st December 1906]

General Note

The Public Trustee Act 1906 (PTA 1906) established the office of the Public Trustee who has several functions in relation to intestate estates, enduring powers of attorney and under the Mental Health Act 1983 some of which are covered by this work.

ESTABLISHMENT OF PUBLIC TRUSTEE

1 Office of Public Trustee

(1) There shall be established the office of Public Trustee.

(2) The Public Trustee shall be a corporation sole under that name, with a perpetual succession and an official seal, and may sue and be sued under the above name like any other corporation sole, but any instruments sealed by him shall not, by reason of

his using a seal, be rendered liable to a higher stamp duty than if he were an individual.

Commentary

The PTA 1906 came into force on 1 January 1908 and the Office of Public Trustee of England and Wales was established on 29 November 1907.

[59]

POWERS AND DUTIES OF PUBLIC TRUSTEE

2 General powers and duties of public trustee

(1) Subject to and in accordance with the provisions of this Act and rules made thereunder, the public trustee may, if he thinks fit—

(a) act in the administration of estates of small value;
(b) act as custodian trustee;
(c) act as an ordinary trustee;
(d) be appointed to be a judicial trustee;
(e) . . .

(2) Subject to the provisions of this Act, and to the rules made thereunder, the public trustee may act either alone or jointly with any person or body of persons in any capacity to which he may be appointed in pursuance of this Act, and shall have all the same powers, duties, and liabilities, and be entitled to the same rights and immunities and be subject to the control and orders of the court, as a private trustee acting in the same capacity.

(3) The public trustee may decline, either absolutely or except on the prescribed conditions, to accept any trust, but he shall not decline to accept any trust on the ground only of the small value of the trust property.

(4) The public trustee shall not accept any trust which involves the management or carrying on of any business, except in the cases in which he may be authorised to do so by rules made under this Act, nor any trust under a deed of arrangement for the benefit of creditors, nor the administration of any estate known or believed by him to be insolvent.

(5) The public trustee shall not accept any trust exclusively for religious or charitable purposes, and nothing in this Act contained, or in the rules to be made under the powers in this Act contained, shall abridge or affect the powers or duties of the official trustee of charity lands or official trustees of charitable funds.

Amendment

Words omitted repealed by the Criminal Justice Act 1948, s 83, Sch 10, Part I.

Commentary

As to the administration of small estates, see s 3 below. As to the appointment of the Public Trustee as custodian, see s 4. As to appointment as an ordinary trustee, see s 5. As to appointment as a judicial trustee, see the Judicial Trustees Act 1896 **[53]**. Subsection (2) makes it clear that the Public Trustee is in the same position as a private trustee and therefore must seek the directions of the court where a private trustee would have done so, see *Re New Haw Estate Trusts* (1912) 107 LT 191; *Re Leslie Hassop's Estates* [1911] 1 Ch 611. The Public Trustee can only accept trusteeship of an English settlement (*Re Hewitt's Settlement* [1915] 1 Ch 228). The prohibition on the Public Trustee accepting the trusteeship of any trust which involves the management or carrying on of any business is softened by the provisions of the Public Trustee Rules 1912, SI 1912/348, r 7 **[Appendix I]**. If the Public Trustee sees fit she can accept the role as custodian trustee under certain circumstances where she is not involved in the management of the business and does not hold property which might expose her to loss. Save in exceptional circumstances, and where she is secured against such loss, she can act as an ordinary trustee, but with the consent of the Treasury, only for a short period of 18 months with a view to sale or winding up of the business and where the business can be carried on without risk of loss. Subsection (5) prevents the Public Trustee from accepting a trust which involves the selection from amongst a range of charitable objects (see *Re Hampton* (1918) 88 LJ Ch 103) but does not prevent the Public Trustee from becoming the trustee of a will where the whole estate is left to charity.

[60]

(1) IN THE ADMINISTRATION OF SMALL ESTATES

3 Administration of small estates

(1) Any person who in the opinion of the public trustee would be entitled to apply to the court for an order for the administration by the court of an estate, the gross capital value whereof is proved to the satisfaction of the public trustee to be less than one thousand pounds, may apply to the public trustee to administer the estate, and, where any such application is made and it appears to the public trustee that the persons beneficially entitled are persons of small means, the public trustee shall administer the estate, unless he sees good reason for refusing to do so.

(2) On the public trustee undertaking, by declaration in writing signed and sealed by him, to administer the estate the trust property other than stock shall, by virtue of this Act, vest in him, and the right to transfer or call for the transfer of any stock forming part of the estate shall also vest in him, in like manner as if vesting orders had been made for the purpose by the High Court under the Trustee Act, 1893, and that Act shall apply accordingly. As from such vesting any trustee entitled under the trust to administer the estate shall be discharged from all liability attaching to the administration, except in respect of past acts:

Provided that—

- (a) the public trustee shall not exercise the right of himself transferring the stock without the leave of the court; and
- (b) this subsection shall not apply to any copyhold land forming part of the estate, but the public trustee shall, as respects such land, have the like powers as if he had been appointed by the court under section thirty-three of the Trustee Act, 1893, to convey the land, and section thirty-four of that Act shall apply accordingly.

(3) For the purposes of the administration the public trustee may exercise such of the administrative powers and authorities of the High Court as may be conferred on him by rules under this Act, subject to such conditions as may be imposed by the rules.

(4) Rules shall be made under this Act for enabling the public trustee to take the opinion of the High Court on any question arising in the course of any administration without judicial proceedings, and otherwise for making the procedure under this section simple and inexpensive.

(5) Where proceedings have been instituted in any court for the administration of an estate, and by reason of the small value of the estate it appears to the court that the estate can be more economically administered by the public trustee than by the court, or that for any other reason it is expedient that the estate should be administered by the public trustee instead of the court, the court may order that the estate shall be administered by the public trustee, and thereupon (subject to any directions by the court) this section shall apply as if the administration of the estate had been undertaken by the public trustee in pursuance of this section.

Commentary

Subsection (1) is now of little practical importance. The estate must be less than £1000 at the date of the application (see *Re Devereux* [1911] 2 Ch 545). As to vesting under sub-s (2) see also the Trustee Act 1925, s 44 **[113]**. Wide powers are conferred on the Public Trustee to act in the administration of small estates by the Public Trustee Rules 1912, SI 1912/348, rr 12–15 **[Appendix I]**. For the procedure on applications to the court under sub-s (4) see SI 1912/348, r 15. Application can be made both formally and informally. Under sub-s (5) it seems that the criteria in sub-s (1) do not have to be fulfilled (ie estate less than £1,000 and beneficiaries of small means) and it is of wider ambit. The reference to the Trustee Act 1893 should be to the Trustee Act 1925 which replaced it.

[61]

(2) AS CUSTODIAN TRUSTEE

4 Custodian trustee

(1) Subject to rules under this Act the public trustee may, if he consents to act as such, and whether or not the number of trustees has been reduced below the original number, be appointed to be custodian trustee of any trust—

- (a) by order of the court made on the application of any person on whose application the court may order the appointment of a new trustee; or
- (b) by the testator, settlor, or other creator of any trust; or
- (c) by the person having power to appoint new trustees.

(2) Where the public trustee is appointed to be custodian trustee of any trust—

- (a) The trust property shall be transferred to the custodian trustee as if he were sole trustee, and for that purpose vesting orders may, where necessary, be made under the Trustee Act 1893:
- (b) The management of the trust property and the exercise of any power or discretion exercisable by the trustees under the trust shall remain vested in the trustees other than the custodian trustee (which trustees are herein-after referred to as the managing trustees):
- (c) As between the custodian trustee and the managing trustees, and subject and without prejudice to the rights of any other persons, the custodian trustee shall have the custody of all securities and documents of title relating to the trust property, but the managing trustee shall have free access thereto and be entitled to take copies thereof or extracts therefrom:
- (d) The custodian trustee shall concur in and perform all acts necessary to enable the managing trustees to exercise their powers of management or any other power or discretion vested in them (including the power to pay money or securities into court), unless the matter in which he is requested to concur is a breach of trust, or involves a personal liability upon him in respect of calls or otherwise, but, unless he so concurs, the custodian trustee shall not be liable for any act or default on the part of the managing trustees or any of them:
- (e) All sums payable to or out of the income or capital of the trust property shall be paid to or by the custodian trustee: Provided that the custodian trustee may allow the dividends and other income derived from the trust property to be paid to the managing trustees or to such person as they direct, or into such bank to the credit of such person as they may direct, and in such case shall be exonerated from seeing to the application thereof and shall not be answerable for any loss or misapplication thereof:
- (f) The power of appointing new trustees, when exercisable by the trustees, shall be exercisable by the managing trustees alone, but the custodian trustee shall have the same power of applying to the court for the appointment of a new trustee as any other trustee:
- (g) In determining the number of trustees for the purposes of the Trustee Act, 1893, the custodian trustee shall not be reckoned as a trustee:

(h) The custodian trustee, if he acts in good faith, shall not be liable for accepting as correct and acting upon the faith of any written statement by the managing trustees as to any birth, death, marriage, or other matter of pedigree or relationship, or other matter of fact, upon which the title to the trust property or any part thereof may depend, nor for acting upon any legal advice obtained by the managing trustees independently of the custodian trustee:

(i) The court may, on the application of either the custodian trustee, or any of the managing trustees, or of any beneficiary, and on proof to their satisfaction that it is the general wish of the beneficiaries, or that on other grounds it is expedient, to terminate the custodian trusteeship, make an order for that purpose, and the court may thereupon make such vesting orders and give such directions as under the circumstances may seem to the court to be necessary or expedient.

(3) The provisions of this section shall apply in like manner as to the public trustee to any banking or insurance company or other body corporate entitled by rules made under this Act to act as custodian trustee, with power for such company or body corporate to charge and retain or pay out of the trust property fees not exceeding the fees chargeable by the public trustee as custodian trustee.

Commentary
This section is in practice very little used now. The idea is for there to be a custodian trustee whose role is to hold investments and documents while the management of the trust remains in the managing trustees. The persons having power to appoint new trustees can appoint a custodian trustee under this section (*Re Cherrys Trusts* [1914] 1 Ch 83). Subsection (2) sets out the manner in which the custodian and managing trustees, between them, deal with the trust. Subsection (3) reflects the fact that many other bodies have been authorised to act as custodian trustees and not just the Public Trustee. For a full list reference should be made to the Public Trustee Rules 1912, SI 1912/348, r 30 (as amended and substituted **[Appendix I]**); the Public Trustee (Custodian Trustee) Rules 1981, SI 1981/358; the Public Trustee (Custodian Trustee) Rules 1984, SI 1984/109; the Public Trustee (Custodian Trustee) Rules 1985, SI 1985/132; the Public Trustee (Custodian Trustee) Rules 1987, SI 1987/1891; the Public Trustee (Custodian Trustee) Rules 1994, SI 1994/2519. The Public Trustee while acting as custodian trustee cannot also be appointed to act as an ordinary trustee and will need the court to discharge him as custodian trustee (*Re Squire's Settlement* (1946) 62 TLR 133).

[62]

(3) AS AN ORDINARY TRUSTEE

5 Appointment of public trustee to be trustee, executor, etc

(1) The public trustee may by that name, or any other sufficient description, be appointed to be trustee of any will or settlement or other instrument creating a trust or to perform any trust or duty belonging to a class which he is authorised by the rules made under this Act to accept, and may be so appointed whether the will or settlement or instrument creating the trust or duty was made or came into operation before or after the passing of this Act, and either as an original or as a new trustee, or as an additional trustee, in the same cases, and in the same manner, and by the same persons or court, as if he were a private trustee, with this addition, that, though the trustees originally appointed were two or more, the public trustee may be appointed sole trustee.

(2) Where the public trustee has been appointed a trustee of any trust, a co-trustee may retire from the trust under and in accordance with section eleven of the Trustee Act, 1893, notwithstanding that there are not more than two trustees, and without such consents as are required by that section.

(3) The public trustee shall not be so appointed either as a new or additional trustee where the will, settlement, or other instrument creating the trust or duty contains a direction to the contrary, unless the court otherwise order.

(4) Notice of any proposed appointment of the public trustee either as a new or additional trustee shall where practicable be given in the prescribed manner to all persons beneficially interested who are resident in the United Kingdom and whose addresses are known to the persons proposing to make the appointment, or, if such beneficiaries are infants, to their guardians, and if any person to whom such notice has been given within twenty-one days from the receipt of the notice applies to the court, the court may, if having regard to the interests of all the beneficiaries it considers it expedient to do so, make an order prohibiting the appointment being made, provided that a failure to give any such notice shall not invalidate any appointment made under this section.

Commentary

Under sub-s (1) the Public Trustee can be appointed a sole trustee even where the trust instrument expressly states that there should be a minimum number of trustees (see *Re Leslie Harrop's Estates* [1911] Ch 611 and *Re Moxon* [1916] 2 Ch 595) and once appointed can exercise functions as a sole trustee which the trust instrument specifies cannot be exercised without there being a minimum number of trustees, see *Re Duxbury's Settlement Trusts* [1995] 1 WLR 425. For the Trustee Act 1925, s 39 see **[108]**. The prescribed manner for notices referred to in sub-s (4) can be found in the Public Trustee Rules 1912, SI 1912/348, r 40 **[Appendix I]**. The onus is on the person applying to the court objecting to the appointment of the Public Trustee, to show that it would be beneficial to prohibit the appointment, see *Re Firth* [1912] 1 Ch 806.

[63]

6 Power as to granting probate

(1) If in pursuance of any rule under this Act, the public trustee is authorised to accept by that name probates of wills or letters of administration, the court having jurisdiction to grant probate of a will or letters of administration may grant such probate or letters to the public trustee by that name, and for that purpose the court shall consider the public trustee as in law entitled equally with any other person or class of persons to obtain the grant of letters of administration, save that the consent or citation of the public trustee shall not be required for the grant of letters of administration to any other person, and that, as between the public trustee and the widower, widow[, surviving civil partner] or next-of-kin of the deceased, the widower, widow[, surviving civil partner] or next-of-kin shall be preferred, unless for good cause shown to the contrary.

(2) Any executor who has obtained probate or any administrator who has obtained letters of administration, and notwithstanding he has acted in the administration of the deceased's estate, may, with the sanction of the court, and after such notice to the persons beneficially interested as the court may direct, transfer such estate to the public trustee for administration either solely or jointly with the continuing executors or administrators, if any. And the order of the court sanctioning such transfer shall, subject to the provisions of this Act, give to the public trustee all the powers of such executor and administrator, and such executor and administrator shall not be in any way liable in respect of any act or default in reference to such estate subsequent to the date of such order, other than the act or default of himself or of persons other than himself for whose conduct he is in law responsible.

Amendment

Sub-s (1): words ", surviving civil partner" in square brackets in both places they occur inserted by the Civil Partnership Act 2004, s 71, Sch 4, Pt 2, para 6.

Commentary
The Public Trustee Rules 1912, SI 1912/348, r 6(c) **[Appendix I]** provides for the Public Trustee to be able to take a grant. However, note that the Public Trustee does not have to be cited before anyone else can take a grant and, if there are surviving widows and widowers civil partners and next of kin, they will in general be preferred. However, the court has power to make a grant of administration to the Public Trustee passing over the widow and others entitled on intestacy, see *Re Woolley* (1911) 55 SJ 220. Application under s 6(2) is now made by way of a Part 8 claim under the Civil Procedure Rules 1998, SI 1998/3132 **[Appendix VII]**.

[64]

LIABILITY: OFFICERS AND OFFICES: FEES

7 . . .

. . .

Amendment
Repealed by the Public Trustee (Liability and Fees) Act 2002, s 1(1).

Commentary
This section provides protection for beneficiaries where they would have had a cause of action against a private trustee.

[65]

8 Officers and offices

[(1) The Lord Chancellor shall appoint such person as he thinks fit to the office of Public Trustee and the person so appointed shall hold and vacate office in accordance with the terms of his appointment.

(1A) The Public Trustee shall be paid such salary or fees as the Lord Chancellor determines with the consent of the Treasury.

(1B) If one person holds office both as the Public Trustee and as the Accountant General of the *Supreme Court* [Senior Courts] then, if he ceases to be the Accountant General, he shall also cease to be the Public Trustee unless the Lord Chancellor otherwise directs.

(1C) If a vacancy occurs in the office of Public Trustee or the person appointed to hold office is for any reason unable to act for any period such person as the Lord Chancellor appoints as deputy in that office shall, during the vacancy or that period, perform the functions of that office (and any property vested in the Public Trustee may accordingly be dealt with by the deputy in all respects as if it were vested in him instead).]

(2) The Lord Chancellor shall appoint such persons to be officers of the public trustee as, subject to the sanction of the Treasury, he may consider necessary for the purposes of this Act, and those officers shall hold office upon such terms, and be remunerated at such rates and in such manner, as the Treasury may sanction.

(3) Any person appointed to be public trustee or an officer of the public trustee may, and shall, if the Treasury so require, be a person already in the public service.

(4) The public trustee shall, if so directed by the Lord Chancellor with the concurrence of the Treasury, maintain offices in London and elsewhere, and, so far as practicable, buildings already used for public purposes shall be used for such offices.

(5) The salary or remuneration of the public trustee and his officers and such other expenses of executing his office or otherwise carrying this Act into effect as may be sanctioned by the Treasury shall be paid out of moneys provided by Parliament.

Amendment
Sub-ss (1), (1A)-(1C): substituted, for sub-s (1) as originally enacted, by the Public Trustee and Administration of Funds Act 1986, Schedule, para 1.
Sub-s (1B): words "Supreme Court" in italics repealed and subsequent words in square brackets substituted, as from a date to be appointed, by the Constitutional Reform Act 2005, s 59(5), Sch 11, Pt 2, para 4(1), (3).

Commentary
As to sub-s (4), the Public Trustee Rules 1912, SI 1912/348, r 3 **[Appendix I]** provides that the central office of the Public Trustee must be in London but branch offices can be established elsewhere.

[66]

9 Fees charged by public trustee

(1) There shall be charged in respect of the duties of the public trustee such fees, whether by way of percentage or otherwise, [as the Lord Chancellor may fix].

(2) Any expenses which might be retained or paid out of the trust property if the public trustee were a private trustee shall be so retained or paid, and the fees shall be retained or paid in the like manner as and in addition to such expenses.

(3) Such fees shall . . . be applied as an appropriation in aid of moneys provided by Parliament for expenses under this Act, and so far as not so applied shall be paid into the Exchequer.

(4) . . .

(5) The incidence of [any expenses retained or paid] under this section as between capital and income shall be determined by the public trustee.

Amendment
Sub-s (1): words "as the Lord Chancellor may fix" in square brackets substituted by the Public Trustee (Liability and Fees) Act 2002, s 2(1)(a).
Sub-s (3): words omitted repealed by the Public Trustee (Liability and Fees) Act 2002, s 2(1)(b).
Sub-s (4): repealed by the Public Trustee (Liability and Fees) Act 2002, s 2(1)(c).
Sub-s (5): words "any expenses retained or paid" in square brackets substituted by the Public Trustee (Fees) Act 1957, s 1(5).

Commentary
This section should be read together with the Public Trustee (Fees) Act 1957 **[252]**.

[67]

SUPPLEMENTAL PROVISIONS AS TO PUBLIC TRUSTEE

10 Appeal to the court

(1) A person aggrieved by any act or omission or decision of the public trustee in relation to any trust may apply to the court, and the court may make such order in the matter as the court thinks just.

(2) Subject to rules of court, an application under this section to the High Court shall be made to a judge of the Chancery Division of the High Court in Chambers.

Commentary
See s 15 below for the meaning of "Court". Application is made by way of Part 8 claim form and the procedure is set out in the Civil Procedure Rules 1998, SI 1998/3132, Pt 50, r 50.1 and Sch 1 thereto, ie Order 93, rule 2 in Schedule 1 to the CPR. On such an appeal the Public Trustee should not be made a party, see *Re Oddy* [1911] 1 Ch 532 as his function is quasi judicial.

[68]

11 Mode of action of public trustee

(1) The public trustee shall not, nor shall any of his officers, act under this Act for reward, except as provided by this Act.

(2) The public trustee may, subject to the rules made under this Act, employ for the purposes of any trust such solicitors, bankers, accountants, and brokers, or other persons as he may consider necessary, and in determining the persons to be so employed in relation to any trust the public trustee shall have regard to the interests of the trust, but subject to this shall, whenever practicable, take into consideration the wishes of the creator of the trust and of the other trustees (if any), and of the beneficiaries, either expressed or as implied by the practice of the creator of the trust, or in the previous management of the trust.

(3) On behalf of the public trustee such person as may be prescribed may take any oath, make any declaration, verify any account, give personal attendance at any court or place, and do any act or thing whatsoever which the public trustee is required or authorised to take, make, verify, give, or do: Provided that nothing in this Act or in any rule made under this Act shall confer upon any person not otherwise entitled thereto any right to appear, or act, or be heard in or before any court or tribunal, on behalf or instead of the public trustee, or to do any act whatsoever on behalf or on the instructions of the public trustee, which could otherwise only be lawfully done by a barrister or a duly certificated solicitor.

(4) Where any bond or security would be required from a private person . . . upon his appointment to act in any capacity, the public trustee, . . . if he is appointed to act in such capacity as aforesaid, shall not be required to give such bond or security, but shall be subject to the same liabilities and duties as if he had given such bond or security.

(5) The entry of the public trustee by that name in the books of a company shall not constitute notice of a trust, and a company shall not be entitled to object to enter the name of the public trustee on its books by reason only that the public trustee is a corporation, and, in dealings with property, the fact that the person or one of the persons dealt with is the public trustee, shall not of itself constitute notice of a trust.

Amendment

Sub-s (4): words omitted repealed by the Administration of Estates Act 1971, s 12(2), Sch 2, Part II.

Commentary

As to sub-s (1), see s 9 above in respect of the fees which can be charged. As to sub-s (2), there is a wider statutory power given to trustees generally to delegate under the Trustee Act 2000, s 11 **[486]**. Notwithstanding the wide terms of sub-s (3) for the Public Trustee to appoint persons to represent him, it has been stated that an official of the Public Trustee Office should be in court when the public trustee's remuneration is being discussed, see *Re Evans* [1948] Ch 185 at 187.

[69]

12 Application of Act to palatine courts

The provisions of this Act with respect to the High Court shall, in their application to cases within the jurisdiction of a palatine court, include that court, and the public trustee shall provide an address within the county palatine where service upon him of any proceedings under this Act in such palatine court may be effected; the rules of court relating to the exercise of the jurisdiction of a palatine court under this Act shall be made by the authority having power to make general rules and orders of that court.

Commentary
The palatine courts of Lancaster and Durham were merged with the High Court by the Courts Act 1971, s 41.

[70]

INVESTIGATION AND AUDIT OF TRUST ACCOUNTS

13 Investigation and audit of trust accounts

(1) Subject to rules under this Act and unless the court otherwise orders, the condition and accounts of any trust shall, on an application being made and notice thereof given in the prescribed manner by any trustee or beneficiary, be investigated and audited by such solicitor or public accountant as may be agreed on by the applicant and the trustees or, in default of agreement, by the public trustee or some person appointed by him:

Provided that (except with the leave of the court) such an investigation or audit shall not be required within twelve months after any such previous investigation or audit, and that a trustee or beneficiary shall not be appointed under this section to make an investigation or audit.

(2) The person making the investigation or audit (herein-after called the auditor) shall have a right of access to the books, accounts, and vouchers of the trustees, and to any securities and documents of title held by them on account of the trust, and may require from them such information and explanation as may be necessary for the performance of his duties, and upon the completion of the investigation and audit shall forward to the applicant and to every trustee a copy of the accounts, together with a report thereon, and a certificate signed by him to the effect that the accounts exhibit a true view of the state of the affairs of the trust and that he has had the securities of the trust fund investments produced to and verified by him or (as the case may be) that such accounts are deficient in such respects as may be specified in such certificate.

(3) Every beneficiary under the trust shall, subject to rules under this Act, be entitled at all reasonable times to inspect and take copies of the accounts, report, and certificate, and, at his own expense, to be furnished with copies thereof or extracts therefrom.

(4) The auditor may be removed by order of the court, and, if any auditor is removed, or resigns, or dies, or becomes bankrupt or incapable of acting before the investigation and audit is completed, a new auditor may be appointed in his place in like manner as the original auditor.

(5) The remuneration of the auditor and the other expenses of the investigation and audit shall be such as may be prescribed by rules under this Act, and shall, unless the public trustee otherwise directs, be borne by the estate; and, in the event of the public trustee so directing, he may order that such expenses be borne by the applicant or by the trustees personally or partly by them and partly by the applicant.

(6) If any person having the custody of any documents to which the auditor had a right of access under this section fails or refuses to allow him to have access thereto or in anywise obstructs the investigation or audit, the auditor may apply to the court, and thereupon the court shall make such order as it thinks just.

(7) Subject to rules of court, applications under or for the purposes of this section to the High Court shall be made to a judge of the Chancery Division in Chambers.

(8) If any person in any statement of accounts, report, or certificate required for the purposes of this section wilfully makes a statement false in any material particular, he shall be liable on conviction on indictment to imprisonment for a term not exceeding two years, and on summary conviction to imprisonment for a term not

exceeding six months, with or without hard labour, and in either case to a fine in lieu of or in addition to such imprisonment.

Commentary

Reference should be made to the Public Trustee Rules 1912, SI 1912/348, rr 31–37 **[Appendix I]** for the practice and procedure on making an application for the Public Trustee to audit trust accounts. The Public Trustee has power under r 32 to demand a deposit before carrying out the audit.

Rule 37 provides that, before making any order under sub-s (5) the Public Trustee shall, if any of the parties so desire, hear the parties in such manner as he shall think fit. Generally when an application is made the costs of the investigation will come out of the fund, but not if the Public Trustee considers that the investigation was unnecessary, see *Re Utley, Russell v Cubitt* [1912] WN 147.

[71]

RULES: DEFINITIONS: SHORT TITLE AND EXTENT

14 Rules

(1) The Lord Chancellor shall, with the concurrence of the Treasury, make rules for carrying into effect the objects of this Act, and in particular for all or any of the following purposes (that is to say):—

(a) establishing the office of public trustee and prescribing the trusts or duties he is authorised to accept or undertake, and the security, if any, to be given by the public trustee and his officers:
(b) the transfer to and from the public trustee of any property:
(c) the accounts to be kept and an audit thereof:
(d) the establishment and regulations of any branch office:
(e) excluding any trusts from the operation of this Act or any part thereof:
(f) the classes of corporate bodies entitled to act as custodian trustees:
(g) the form and manner in which notices under this Act shall be given.

(2) Every rule under this Act shall be laid before each House of Parliament forthwith, and, if an address is presented to His Majesty by either House of Parliament, within the next subsequent thirty days on which the House has sat next after any such rule is laid before it, praying that the rule may be annulled, His Majesty in Council may annul the rule, and it shall thenceforth be void, but without prejudice to the validity of anything previously done thereunder.

(3) If the rules require a declaration to be made for any purpose, a person who makes such declaration, knowing the same to be untrue in any material particular, shall be guilty of a misdemeanour.

Commentary

Note that the rules which apply are the Public Trustee Rules 1912, SI 1912/348, **[Appendix I]**.

[72]

15 Definitions

In this Act, unless the context otherwise requires,—

the expression "court" means the High Court and, as respects trusts within its jurisdiction, the county court:

the expression "letters of administration" means letters of administration of the estate and effects of a deceased person, whether general or with a will annexed, or limited either in time or otherwise:

the expression "trust" includes an executorship or administratorship; and the expression "trustee" shall be construed accordingly; and the expression "trust property" shall include all property in the possession or under the control wholly or partly of the public trustee by virtue of any trust:

the expression "private trustee" means a trustee other than the public trustee:

the expression "expenses" includes costs and charges:

the expression "prescribed" means prescribed for the time being by rules under this Act:

Other expressions have the same meaning as in the Trustee Act, 1893.

Commentary

Trusts fall within the jurisdiction of the County Court if the fund does not exceed £30,000 in value. Note the application of the PTA 1906 to estates. The reference to the Trustee Act 1893 should now be read as a reference to the Trustee Act 1925.

[73]

16 . . .

. . .

Amendment

Repealed by the Statute Law Revision Act 1927.

[74]

17 Short title and extent

(1) This Act may be cited as the Public Trustee Act 1906.

(2) This Act shall not extend to Ireland or Scotland.

[75]

WILLS (SOLDIERS AND SAILORS) ACT 1918

1918 Chapter 58

ARRANGEMENT OF SECTIONS

An Act to amend the Law with respect to Testamentary Dispositions by Soldiers and Sailors

[6th February 1918]

General Note

The Wills (Soldiers and Sailors) Act 1918 (W(SS)A 1918) should be read together with the Wills Act 1837, s 11 which makes provision for soldiers on active service and sailors at sea to make wills which do not comply with the Wills Act 1837, s 9. The W(SS)A 1918 clarifies certain points of doubt and extends the scope of privileged wills.

1 Explanation of s 11 of Wills Act 1837

In order to remove doubts as to the construction of the Wills Act 1837, it is hereby declared and enacted that section eleven of that Act authorises and always has authorised any soldier being in actual military service, or any mariner or seaman being at sea, to dispose of his personal estate as he might have done before the passing of that Act, though under the age of [eighteen years].

Amendment

Words substituted by the Family Law Reform Act 1969, s 3(1)(b).

Commentary

The W(SS)A 1918 was passed to remove the doubt which had arisen as a result of the decision in *Re Wernher* [1918] 1 Ch 339 as to whether a minor (ie a person under the age of 21 until 31 December 1969, and after that date under 18) could make a will if in a privileged situation under the Wills Act 1837, s 11 **[9]**. The law before the passing of the W(SS)A 1918 was that males of 14 and females of 12 could make wills disposing of their personal estate. As to their ability in relation to real estate see s 3 below.

[76]

2 Extension of s 11 of Wills Act 1837

Section eleven of the Wills Act 1837, shall extend to any member of His Majesty's naval or marine forces not only when he is at sea but also when he is so circumstanced that if he were a soldier he would be in actual military service within the meaning of that section.

Commentary

For the meaning of "actual military service" see the notes to the Wills Act 1837, s 11. Note that this provision does not apply to the merchant service.

[77]

3 Validity of testamentary dispositions of real property made by soldiers and sailors

(1) A testamentary disposition of any real estate in England or Ireland made by a person to whom section eleven of the Wills Act 1837, applies, and who dies after the passing of this Act, shall, notwithstanding that the person making the disposition was at the time of making it under [eighteen years] of age or that the disposition has not been made in such manner or form as was at the passing of this Act required by law, be valid in any case where the person making the disposition was of such age and the disposition has been made in such manner and form that if the disposition had been a disposition of personal estate made by such a person domiciled in England or Ireland it would have been valid.

(2) A testamentary disposition of any heritable property in Scotland made after the passing of this Act by a person to whom section eleven of the Wills Act 1837, applies or to whom it would apply if he were domiciled in England, shall not be invalid by reason only of the fact that such person is under twenty-one years of age, provided always that he is of such age that he could, if domiciled in Scotland, have made a valid testamentary disposition of moveable property.

Amendment

Words substituted by the Family Law Reform Act 1969, s 3(1)(b).

Commentary

The ability for persons in privileged circumstances (including minors, as to which see s 1) to make wills not complying with the Wills Act 1837, s 9 **[7]** is extended by this section to real estate but only in the case of testators dying after 5 February 1918. However, note that a minor entitled to an estate in fee simple who has not married is regarded post-1925 as having an entailed interest in the land (Administration of Estates Act 1925, s 51(3) **[227]**) and can only dispose of an entailed interest by will if of full age (Law of Property Act 1925, s 176 **[177]**).

[78]

4 Power to appoint testamentary guardians

Where any person dies after the passing of this Act having made a will which is, or which, if it had been a disposition of property, would have been rendered valid by section eleven of the Wills Act 1837, any appointment contained in that will of any person as guardian of the infant children of the testator shall be of full force and effect.

Commentary

This section relates to those dying after 5 February 1918.

[79]

5 Short title and interpretation

(1) This Act may be cited as the Wills (Soldiers and Sailors) Act 1918.

(2) For the purposes of section eleven of the Wills Act 1837, and this Act the expression "soldier" includes a member of the Air Force, and references in this Act to the said section eleven include a reference to that section as explained and extended by this Act.

Commentary

Note the extension of the meaning of soldier to a member of the air force. Soldier is a term which does not just include fighting men, see *Re Wingham* [1949] P 187.

[80]

TRUSTEE ACT 1925

1925 Chapter 19

ARRANGEMENT OF SECTIONS

PART I

PART II
GENERAL POWERS OF TRUSTEES AND PERSONAL REPRESENTATIVES

PART III
APPOINTMENT AND DISCHARGE OF TRUSTEES

PART IV
POWERS OF THE COURT

PART V
GENERAL PROVISIONS

An Act to consolidate certain enactments relating to trustees in England and Wales
[9th April 1925]

General Note
Part of the great land law and trusts reforms enacted in 1925, the Trustee Act 1925 (TA 1925) deals with all aspects of trust administration, conferring default powers on trustees which have to a large extent been superseded by the Trustee Act 2000 **[476]**. However, the TA 1925 remains the lynchpin of statutory trusts law notwithstanding.

PART I

1–11

. . .

Amendment
Repealed by the Trustee Act 2000, s 40(1), (3), Sch 2, Pt II, para 18, Sch 4, Pt II.

[81]

PART II
GENERAL POWERS OF TRUSTEES AND PERSONAL REPRESENTATIVES

12 Power of trustees for sale to sell by auction, etc

(1) Where [a trustee has a duty or power to sell property], he may sell or concur with any other person in selling all or any part of the property, either subject to prior charges or not, and either together or in lots, by public auction or by private contract, subject to any such conditions respecting title or evidence of title or other matter as the trustee thinks fit, with power to vary any contract for sale, and to buy in at any auction, or to rescind any contract for sale and to re-sell, without being answerable for any loss.

(2) A [duty] or power to sell or dispose of land includes a *trust* [duty] or power to sell or dispose of part thereof, whether the division is horizontal, vertical, or made in any other way.

(3) This section does not enable an express power to sell settled land to be exercised where the power is not vested in the tenant for life or statutory owner.

Amendment
Sub-ss (1), (2): words in square brackets substituted by the Trusts of Land and Appointment of Trustees Act 1996, s 25(1), Sch 3, para 3(2); for savings in relation to entailed interests created before the commencement of that Act, and savings consequential upon the abolition of the doctrine of conversion, see s 25(4), (5) thereof.

Commentary
This section provides for the methods of sale available to trustees. Subsection (2) was a new section and enabled trustees to sell part of land. Subsection (3) refers to settled land as to which see the Settled Land Act 1925 **[Appendix II]**. For the meaning of "land" in this context see s 68(1)(6) below.

[82]

13 Power to sell subject to depreciatory conditions

(1) No sale made by a trustee shall be impeached by any beneficiary upon the ground that any of the conditions subject to which the sale was made may have been unnecessarily depreciatory, unless it also appears that the consideration for the sale was thereby rendered inadequate.

(2) No sale made by a trustee shall, after the execution of the conveyance, be impeached as against the purchaser upon the ground that any of the conditions

subject to which the sale was made may have been unnecessarily depreciatory, unless it appears that the purchaser was acting in collusion with the trustee at the time when the contract for sale was made.

(3) No purchaser, upon any sale made by a trustee, shall be at liberty to make any objection against the title upon any of the grounds aforesaid.

(4) This section applies to sales made before or after the commencement of this Act.

Commentary
The predecessors to this section were introduced to counteract the effect of *Dunn v Flood* (1885) 25 Ch D 586 where the Court of Appeal refused specific performance of a contract for the sale of land by trustees where conditions were imposed by the trustee which tended to damp the success of the sale. Trustees should however avoid imposing stringent conditions, particularly if it will affect the price at which they can sell, as s 13(1) will not relieve them in such circumstances.

[83]

14 Power of trustees to give receipts

(1) The receipt in writing of a trustee for any money, securities, [investments] or other personal property or effects payable, transferable, or deliverable to him under any trust or power shall be a sufficient discharge to the person paying, transferring, or delivering the same and shall effectually exonerate him from seeing to the application or being answerable for any loss or misapplication thereof.

(2) this section does not, except where the trustee is a trust corporation, enable a sole trustee to give a valid receipt for—

[(a) proceeds of sale or other capital money arising under a trust of land;]

(b) capital money arising under the Settled Land Act 1925.

(3) This section applies notwithstanding anything to the contrary in the instrument, if any, creating the trust.

Amendment
Sub-s (1): word "investments" in square brackets inserted by the Trustee Act 2000, s 40(1), Sch 2, Pt II, para 19.
Sub-s (2): para (a) substituted by the Trusts of Land and Appointment of Trustees Act 1996, s 25(1), Sch 3, para 3(3); for savings in relation to entailed interests created before the commencement of that Act, and savings consequential upon the abolition of the doctrine of conversion, see s 25(4), (5) thereof.

Commentary
The rule before the enactment of this section was that if someone paid money over to trustees with notice of the trust, unless he received a receipt from one of the beneficiaries he would be liable if the money was misapplied. This could only be overcome if the trust instrument conferred an express power on the trustees to give a valid receipt. Subsection (1) enables the trustees to give a valid receipt which will discharge the payer, and note that this is the case whatever is said in the trust instrument (sub-s (3)). The section does not abrogate the general rule that a sole trustee cannot give a receipt for capital monies. For the meaning of "trust corporation" see s 68(1) (18) below.

[84]

15 Power to compound liabilities

A personal representative, or two or more trustees acting together, or, subject to the restrictions imposed in regard to receipts by a sole trustee not being a trust corporation, a sole acting trustee where by the instrument, if any, creating the trust, or by statute, a sole trustee is authorised to execute the trusts and powers reposed in him, may, if and as he or they think fit—

(a) accept any property, real or personal, before the time at which it is made transferable or payable; or

(b) sever and apportion any blended trust funds or property; or
(c) pay or allow any debt or claim on any evidence that he or they think sufficient; or
(d) accept any composition or any security, real or personal, for any debt or for any property, real or personal, claimed; or
(e) allow any time of payment of any debt; or
(f) compromise, compound, abandon, submit to arbitration, or otherwise settle any debt, account, claim, or thing whatever relating to the testator's or intestate's estate or to the trust;

and for any of these purposes may enter into, give, execute, and do such agreements, instruments of composition or arrangement, releases, and other things as to him or them seem expedient, without being responsible for any loss occasioned by any act or thing so done by him or them [if he has or they have discharged the duty of care set out in section 1(1) of the Trustee Act 2000].

Amendment
Words "if he has or they have discharged the duty of care set out in section 1(1) of the Trustee Act 2000" in square brackets substituted by the Trustee Act 2000, s 40(1), Sch 2, Pt II, para 20.

Commentary
The powers conferred by this section are very wide in ambit, but do not enable the trustees to vary the trusts, see *Re Strafford* [1980] Ch 28. The trustees can compromise against the wishes of the beneficiaries but they should ascertain and pay due regard to those wishes, see *Re Ezekial's Settlement Trusts* [1942] Ch 230. Before the coming into force of the Trustee Act 2000, the section required the trustees to act in good faith. The effect of the Trustee Act 2000, s 1 and Sch 1 **[519]** is to impose upon the trustees the statutory duty of care when exercising this power which is clearly a higher standard. The trustees can always apply to the court for directions if they are concerned about exercising their powers under this section.

[85]

16 Power to raise money by sale, mortgage, etc.

(1) Where trustees are authorised by the instrument, if any, creating the trust or by law to pay or apply capital money subject to the trust for any purpose or in any manner, they shall have and shall be deemed always to have had power to raise the money required by sale, conversion, calling in, or mortgage of all or any part of the trust property for the time being in possession.

(2) This section applies notwithstanding anything to the contrary contained in the instrument, if any, creating the trust, but does not apply to trustees of property held for charitable purposes, or to trustees of a settlement for the purposes of the Settled Land Act 1925, not being also the statutory owners.

Commentary
Note that this power applies not just to trusts of land but of any property. Similar power is available under the Trusts of Land and Appointment of Trustees Act 1996, s 6 **[436]**

[86]

17 Protection to purchasers and mortgagees dealing with trustees

No purchaser or mortgagee paying or advancing money on a sale or mortgage purporting to be made under any trust or power vested in trustees, shall be concerned to see that such money is wanted; or that no more than is wanted is raised, or otherwise as to the application thereof.

Commentary
This section provides protection for purchasers and mortgagees dealing with trustees.

[87]

18 Devolution of powers or trusts

(1) Where a power or trust is given to or imposed on two or more trustees jointly, the same may be exercised or performed by the survivors or survivor of them for the time being.

(2) Until the appointment of new trustees, the personal representatives or representative for the time being of a sole trustee, or, where there were two or more trustees of the last surviving or continuing trustee, shall be capable of exercising or performing any power or trust which was given to, or capable of being exercised by, the sole or last surviving or continuing trustee, or other the trustees or trustee for the time being of the trust.

(3) This section takes effect subject to the restrictions imposed in regard to receipts by a sole trustee, not being a trust corporation.

(4) In this section "personal representative" does not include an executor who has renounced or has not proved.

Commentary
Subsection (1) deals with the situation when a trustee dies. Note that the reference to powers in this subsection refers not to fiduciary powers (eg to appoint) but to powers vested in the trustee as trustee, see *Re Harding* [1923] 1 Ch 182. Where the last surviving trustee dies, the personal representative of that trustee can (but note, does not have to) act. Note the definition in sub-s (4) of "personal representatives" for these purposes. When new trustees are appointed the personal representative automatically ceases to have the power to act, see *Re Routledge's Trusts* [1909] 1 Ch 280. Subsection (3) makes it clear that this section will not enable a sole surviving trustee to give a receipt for capital monies. For the meaning of "trust corporation" see s 68(1), (18) below.

[88]

[19 Power to insure]

[(1) A trustee may—

(a) insure any property which is subject to the trust against risks of loss or damage due to any event, and

(b) pay the premiums out of the trust funds.

(2) In the case of property held on a bare trust, the power to insure is subject to any direction given by the beneficiary or each of the beneficiaries—

(a) that any property specified in the direction is not to be insured;

(b) that any property specified in the direction is not to be insured except on such conditions as may be so specified.

(3) Property is held on a bare trust if it is held on trust for—

(a) a beneficiary who is of full age and capacity and absolutely entitled to the property subject to the trust, or

(b) beneficiaries each of whom is of full age and capacity and who (taken together) are absolutely entitled to the property subject to the trust.

(4) If a direction under subsection (2) of this section is given, the power to insure, so far as it is subject to the direction, ceases to be a delegable function for the purposes of section 11 of the Trustee Act 2000 (power to employ agents).

(5) In this section "trust funds" means any income or capital funds of the trust.]

Amendment
Substituted by the Trustee Act 2000, s 34(1).

Commentary
This section was replaced by the Trustee Act 2000 and for the reference in sub-s (4) see **[509]**. The previous section was most unsatisfactory and it is now clear that trustees have power to insure against all risks and can pay the premiums out of both capital and income (sub-s (5)). Note that beneficiaries under a bare trust can direct the trustees not to exercise this power. This section confers the power to insure on trustees but does not impose any duty on them, and it is not clear as a matter of law that such a duty exists, see *Re McEacharn* (1911) 103 LT 900. The trustees will be subject to the statutory duty of care contained in the Trustee Act 2000, s 1 and Sch 1 when exercising this power **[476; 519]**

[89]

20 Application of insurance money where policy kept up under any trust, power or obligation

(1) Money receivable by trustees or any beneficiary under a policy of insurance against the loss or damage of any property subject to a trust or to a settlement within the meaning of the Settled Land Act 1925. . . . shall, where the policy has been kept up under any trust in that behalf or under any power statutory or otherwise, or in performance of any covenant or of any obligation statutory or otherwise, or by a tenant for life impeachable for waste, be capital money for the purposes of the trust or settlement, as the case may be.

(2) If any such money is receivable by any person, other than the trustees of the trust or settlement, that person shall use his best endeavours to recover and receive the money, and shall pay the net residue thereof, after discharging any costs of recovering and receiving it, to the trustees of the trust or settlement, or, if there are no trustees capable of giving a discharge therefor, into court.

(3) Any such money—

(a) if it was receivable in respect of settled land within the meaning of the Settled Land Act 1925, or any building or works thereon, shall be deemed to be capital money arising under that Act from the settled land, and shall be invested or applied by the trustees, or, if in court, under the direction of the court, accordingly;

(b) if it was receivable in respect of personal chattels settled as heirlooms within the meaning of the Settled Land Act, 1925, shall be deemed to be capital money arising under that Act; and shall be applicable by the trustees, or, if in court, under the direction of the court, in like manner as provided by that Act with respect to money arising by sale of chattels as heirlooms as aforesaid;

(c) if it was receivable in respect of [land subject to a trust of land or personal property held on trust for sale], shall be held upon the trusts and subject to the powers and provisions applicable to money arising by a sale under such trust;

(d) in any other case, shall be held upon trusts corresponding as nearly as may be with the trusts affecting the property in respect of which it was payable.

(4) Such money, or any part thereof, may also be applied by the trustees, or, if in court, under the direction of the court, in rebuilding, reinstating, replacing, or replacing the property loss or damaged, but any such application by the trustees shall be subject to the consent of any person whose consent is required by the instrument, if any, creating the trust to the investment of money subject to the trust, and, in the case of money which is deemed to be capital money arising under the Settled Land Act 1925, be subject to the provisions of that Act with respect to the application of capital money by the trustees of the settlement.

(5) Nothing contained in this section prejudices or affects the right of any person to require any such money or any part thereof to be applied in rebuilding reinstating, or

repairing the property lost or damaged, or the rights of any mortgagee, lessor, or lessee, whether under any statute or otherwise.

(6) This section applies to policies effected either before or after the commencement of this Act, but only to money received after such commencement.

Amendment

Sub-s (1): words omitted repealed by the Trustee Act 2000, ss 34(2), 40(3), Sch 4, Pt II.
Sub-s (3): in para (c) words "land subject to a trust of land or personal property held on trust for sale" in square brackets substituted by the Trusts of Land and Appointment of Trustees Act 1996, s 25(1), Sch 3, para 3(5); for savings in relation to entailed interests created before the commencement of that Act, and savings consequential upon the abolition of the doctrine of conversion, see s 25(4), (5) thereof.

Commentary

This section deals with the way in which trustees should deal with insurance monies received. There are extensive references in the section to the Settled Land Act 1925 which is included for reference in Appendix II to this work.

[90]

21 . . .

. . .

Amendment

Repealed by the Trustee Act 2000, s 40(1), (3), Sch 2, Pt II, para 21, Sch 4, Pt II.

22 Reversionary interests, valuations, and audit

(1) Where trust property includes any share or interest in property not vested in the trustees, or the proceeds of the sale of any such property, or any other thing in action, the trustees on the same falling into possession, or becoming payable or transferable may—

(a) agree or ascertain the amount or value thereof or any part thereof in such manner as they may think fit;
(b) accept in or towards satisfaction thereof, at the market or current value, or upon any valuation or estimate of value which they may think fit, any authorised investments;
(c) allow any deductions for duties, costs, charges and expenses which they may think proper or reasonable;
(d) execute any release in respect of the premises so as effectually to discharge all accountable parties from all liability in respect of any matters coming within the scope of such release;

without being responsible in any such case for any loss occasioned by any act or thing so done by them [if they have discharged the duty of care set out in section 1(1) of the Trustee Act 2000].

(2) The trustees shall not be under any obligation and shall not be chargeable with any breach of trust by reason of any omission—

(a) to place any distringas notice or apply for any stop or other like order upon any securities or other property out of or on which such share or interest or other thing in action as aforesaid is derived, payable or charged; or
(b) to take any proceedings on account of any act, default, or neglect on the part of the persons in whom such securities or other property or any of them or any part thereof are for the time being, or had at any time been, vested;

unless and until required in writing so to do by some person, or the guardian of some person, beneficially interested under the trust, and unless also due provision is made to their satisfaction for payment of the costs of any proceedings required to be taken:

Provided that nothing in this subsection shall relieve the trustees of the obligation to get in and obtain payment or transfer of such share or interest or other thing in action on the same falling into possession.

(3) Trustees may, for the purpose of giving effect to the trust, or any of the provisions of the instrument, if any, creating the trust or of any statute, from time to time (by duly qualified agents) ascertain and fix the value of any trust property in such manner as they think proper, and any valuation so made . . . shall be binding upon all persons interested under the trust [if the trustees have discharged the duty of care set out in section 1(1) of the Trustee Act 2000].

(4) Trustees may, in their absolute discretion, from time to time, but not more than once in every three years unless the nature of the trust or any special dealings with the trust property make a more frequent exercise of the right reasonable, cause the accounts of the trust property to be examined or audited by an independent accountant, and shall, for that purpose, produce such vouchers and give such information to him as he may require; and the costs of such examination or audit, including the fee of the auditor, shall be paid out of the capital or income of the trust property, or partly in one way and partly in the other as the trustees, in their absolute discretion, think fit, but, in default of any direction by the trustees to the contrary in any special case, costs attributable to capital shall be borne by capital and those attributable to income by income.

Amendment

Sub-s (1): words "if they have discharged the duty of care set out in section 1(1) of the Trustee Act 2000" in square brackets substituted by the Trustee Act 2000, s 40(1), Sch 2, Pt II, para 22(a).
Sub-s (3): words omitted repealed by the Trustee Act 2000, s 40(1), Sch 2, Pt II, para 22(b).
Sub-s (3): words "if the trustees have discharged the duty of care set out in section 1(1) of the Trustee Act 2000" in square brackets inserted by the Trustee Act 2000, s 40(1), Sch 2, Pt II, para 22(b).

Commentary

Subsection (1) confers on trustees wide powers where there are reversionary or other similar interests comprised in the trust fund when they fall in. Note that the Trustee Act 2000, s 1 and Sch 1 **[476; 519]** require the trustees to comply with the statutory duty of care when exercising the powers contained in sub-s (1). The former less stringent requirement was that the trustees act in good faith. As to the reference in sub-s (2) to a stop order, see the Civil Procedure Rules 1998, SI 1998/3132, Rule 73.11 et seq. Note that sub-s (2) does not detract from the trustees' duty to get in trust property. Subsection (3) empowers the trustees to obtain valuations of the trust property (not just reversionary interests) and these will be binding provided that again they comply with the statutory duty of care imposed on them by the Trustee Act 2000. Subsection (4) empowers the trustees to have their accounts audited by an independent accountant. Note the power to have the Public Trustee audit such accounts (see the Public Trustee Act 1906, s 13 **[71]**).

[91]

23 . . .

. . .

Amendment

Repealed by the Trustee Act 2000, s 40(1), (3), Sch 2, Pt II, para 23, Sch 4, Pt II.

[92]

24 Power to concur with others

Where an undivided share in [any] property, is subject to a trust, or forms part of the estate of a testator or intestate, the trustees or personal representatives may (without prejudice to the [trust] affecting the entirety of the land and the powers of the [trustees] in reference thereto), execute or exercise any [duty or] power vested in them in relation to such share in conjunction with the persons entitled to or having power in that behalf over the other share or shares, and notwithstanding that any one or more of the trustees or personal representatives may be entitled to or interested in any such other share, either in his or their own right or in a fiduciary capacity.

Amendment
Words in square brackets substituted by the Trusts of Land and Appointment of Trustees Act 1996, s 25(1), Sch 3, para 3(6); for savings in relation to entailed interests created before the commencement of that Act, and savings consequential upon the abolition of the doctrine of conversion, see s 25(4), (5) thereof.

Commentary
This section is of less importance since the Trusts of Land and Appointment of Trustees Act 1996, s 6 **[436]** conferred on trustees of land all the powers of an absolute owner but it remains a useful section where the trustee is interested in the other share and therefore would normally be subject to a conflict between his personal interests and his duties as trustee.

[93]

[25 Delegation of trustee's functions by power of attorney]

[(1) Notwithstanding any rule of law or equity to the contrary, a trustee may, by power of attorney, delegate the execution or exercise of all or any of the trusts, powers and discretions vested in him as trustee either alone or jointly with any other person or persons.

(2) A delegation under this section—

(a) commences as provided by the instrument creating the power or, if the instrument makes no provision as to the commencement of the delegation, with the date of the execution of the instrument by the donor; and

(b) continues for a period of twelve months or any shorter period provided by the instrument creating the power.

(3) The persons who may be donees of a power of attorney under this section include a trust corporation.

(4) Before or within seven days after giving a power of attorney under this section the donor shall give written notice of it (specifying the date on which the power comes into operation and its duration, the donee of the power, the reason why the power is given and, where some only are delegated, the trusts, powers and discretions delegated) to—

(a) each person (other than himself), if any, who under any instrument creating the trust has power (whether alone or jointly) to appoint a new trustee; and

(b) each of the other trustees, if any;

but failure to comply with this subsection shall not, in favour of a person dealing with the donee of the power, invalidate any act done or instrument executed by the donee.

(5) A power of attorney given under this section by a single donor—

(a) in the form set out in subsection (6) of this section; or

(b) in a form to the like effect but expressed to be made under this subsection,

shall operate to delegate to the person identified in the form as the single donee of the power the execution and exercise of all the trusts, powers and discretions vested in the donor as trustee (either alone or jointly with any other person or persons) under the single trust so identified.

(6) The form referred to in subsection (5) of this section is as follows—

"THIS GENERAL TRUSTEE POWER OF ATTORNEY is made on [date] by [name of one donor] of [address of donor] as trustee of [name or details of one trust].

I appoint [name of one donee] of [address of donee] to be my attorney [if desired, the date on which the delegation commences or the period for which it continues (or both)] in accordance with section 25(5) of the Trustee Act 1925.

[To be executed as a deed]".

(7) The donor of a power of attorney given under this section shall be liable for the acts or defaults of the donee in the same manner as if they were the acts or defaults of the donor.

(8) For the purpose of executing or exercising the trusts or powers delegated to him, the donee may exercise any of the powers conferred on the donor as trustee by statute or by the instrument creating the trust, including power, for the purpose of the transfer of any inscribed stock, himself to delegate to an attorney power to transfer, but not including the power of delegation conferred by this section.

(9) The fact that it appears from any power of attorney given under this section, or from any evidence required for the purposes of any such power of attorney or otherwise, that in dealing with any stock the donee of the power is acting in the execution of a trust shall not be deemed for any purpose to affect any person in whose books the stock is inscribed or registered with any notice of the trust.

(10) This section applies to a personal representative, tenant for life and statutory owner as it applies to a trustee except that subsection (4) shall apply as if it required the notice there mentioned to be given—

(a) in the case of a personal representative, to each of the other personal representatives, if any, except any executor who has renounced probate;

(b) in the case of a tenant for life, to the trustees of the settlement and to each person, if any, who together with the person giving the notice constitutes the tenant for life; and

(c) in the case of a statutory owner, to each of the persons, if any, who together with the person giving the notice constitute the statutory owner and, in the case of a statutory owner by virtue of section 23(1)(a) of the Settled Land Act 1925, to the trustees of the settlement.]

Amendment

Substituted by the Trustee Delegation Act 1999, s 5(1), (2).

Commentary

The original s 25 enabled delegation only in a case where the trustee was absent abroad for one month. This was amended by the Powers of Attorney Act 1970, s 9 so that delegation for 12 months in any circumstances could take place. When the Enduring Powers of Attorney Act 1985, s 3(3) came into force, there was a certain amount of misuse of the section to provide unlimited delegation. This section now regularises the position and delegation can only take place for 12 months (sub-s (2)). Note there is no provision to remunerate the donee under the power, which should be compared with the position under the Trustee Act 2000, s 32(2) **[507]**. Delegation under this section used to be able to take effect under an enduring power of attorney, as to which see the Trustee Delegation Act 1999, s 6 and the Enduring Powers of Attorney Act 1985.

[94]

INDEMNITIES

26 Protection against liability in respect of rents and covenants

(1) Where a personal representative or trustee liable as such for—

(a) any rent, covenant, or agreement reserved by or contained in any lease; or

(b) any rent, covenant or agreement payable under or contained in any grant made in consideration of a rentcharge; or

(c) any indemnity given in respect of any rent, covenant or agreement referred to in either of the foregoing paragraphs;

satisfies all liabilities under the lease or grant [which may have accrued and been claimed] up to the date of the conveyance hereinafter mentioned, and, where necessary, sets apart a sufficient fund to answer any future claim that may be made in respect of any fixed and ascertained sum which the lessee or grantee agreed to lay out on the property demised or granted, although the period for laying out the same may not have arrived, then and in any such case the personal representative or trustee may convey the property demised or granted to a purchaser, legatee, devisee, or other person entitled to call for a conveyance thereof and thereafter—

(i) he may distribute the residuary real and personal estate of the deceased testator or intestate, or, as the case may be, the trust estate (other than the fund, if any, set apart as aforesaid) to or amongst the persons entitled thereto, without appropriating any part, or any further part, as the case may be, of the estate of the deceased or of the trust estate to meet any future liability under the said lease or grant;

(ii) notwithstanding such distribution, he shall not be personally liable in respect of any subsequent claim under the said lease or grant.

[(1A) Where a personal representative or trustee has as such entered into, or may as such be required to enter into, an authorised guarantee agreement with respect to any lease comprised in the estate of a deceased testator or intestate or a trust estate (and, in a case where he has entered into such an agreement, he has satisfied all liabilities under it which may have accrued and been claimed up to the date of distribution)—

(a) he may distribute the residuary real and personal estate of the deceased testator or intestate, or the trust estate, to or amongst the persons entitled thereto—

  (i) without appropriating any part of the estate of the deceased, or the trust estate, to meet any future liability (or, as the case may be, any liability) under any such agreement, and

  (ii) notwithstanding any potential liability of his to enter into any such agreement; and

(b) notwithstanding such distribution, he shall not be personally liable in respect of any subsequent claim (or, as the case may be, any claim) under any such agreement.

In this subsection "authorised guarantee agreement" has the same meaning as in the Landlord and Tenant (Covenants) Act 1995.]

(2) This section operates without prejudice to the right of the lessor or grantor, or the persons deriving title under the lessor or grantor, to follow the assets of the deceased or the trust property into the hands of the persons amongst whom the same may have been respectively distributed, and applies notwithstanding anything to the contrary in the will or other instrument, if any, creating the trust.

(3) In this section "lease" includes an underlease and an agreement for a lease or underlease and any instrument giving any such indemnity as aforesaid or varying the liabilities under the lease; "grant" applies to a grant whether the rent is created by limitation, grant, reservation, or otherwise, and includes an agreement for a grant and any instrument giving any such indemnity as aforesaid or varying the liabilities under the grant; "lessee" and "grantee" include persons respectively deriving title under them.

Amendment

Sub-s (1): words in square brackets substituted by the Law of Property (Amendment) Act 1926, ss 7, 8(2), Schedule.

Sub-s (1A): inserted by the Landlord and Tenant (Covenants) Act 1995, s 30(1), Sch 1, para 1.

Commentary

This section deals with the situation where a personal representative or trustee is liable in a representative capacity (note in sub-ss (1) and (1A) the words "as such") under a lease or grant (defined in sub-s (3)) but wishes to distribute. In the case of a personal representative he will not be relieved by s 26(1) if he has entered into possession or has entered into a lease in the course of administration, see *Re Owers* [1941] Ch 389. For the meaning of "Authorised Guarantee Agreement" in sub-s (1A) see the Landlord and Tenant (Covenants) Act 1995, ss 16 and 28(1) (outside the scope of this work). Again it seems that the liability of the personal representative on the agreement should be as representative of the deceased and will not apply if it is an agreement entered into by him during the administration. As far as trustees are concerned, they usually enter into a lease not in a representative capacity but fully liable on all the covenants and quaere whether this section protects them in such a case (there would seem to be no authority on the point). Section 26(1) enables the personal representative or trustee to retain a fund to meet future liabilities if required. This section relieves the personal representative or trustee from personal liability. Subsection (2) preserves the right of the lessor or grantor as creditor to follow assets which have been distributed into the hands of overpaid beneficiaries, see *Re Diplock* [1948] Ch 465.

[95]

27 Protection by means of advertisements

(1) With a view to the conveyance to or distribution among the persons entitled to any real or personal property, the trustees of a settlement [, trustees of land, trustees for sale of personal property] or personal representatives, may give notice by advertisement in the Gazette, and [in a newspaper circulating in the district in which the land is situated] and such other like notices, including notices elsewhere than in England and Wales, as would, in any special case, have been directed by a court of competent jurisdiction in an action for administration, of their intention to make such conveyance or distribution as aforesaid, and requiring any person interested to send to the trustees or personal representatives within the time, not being less than two months, fixed in the notice or, where more than one notice is given, in the last of the notices, particulars of his claim in respect of the property or any part thereof to which the notice relates.

(2) At the expiration of the time fixed by the notice the trustees or personal representatives may convey or distribute the property or any part thereof to which the notice relates, to or among the persons entitled thereto, having regard only to the claims, whether formal or not, of which the trustees or personal representatives then had notice and shall not, as respects the property so conveyed or distributed, be liable to any person of whose claim the trustees or personal representatives have not had notice at the time of conveyance or distribution; but nothing in this section—

(a) prejudices the right of any person to follow the property, or any property representing the same, into the hands of any person, other than a purchaser, who may have received it; or

(b) frees the trustees or personal representatives from any obligation to make searches or obtain official certificates of search similar to those which an intending purchaser would be advised to make or obtain.

(3) This section applies notwithstanding anything to the contrary in the will or other instrument, if any, creating the trust.

Amendment

Sub-s (1): first words in square brackets substituted by the Trusts of Land and Appointment of Trustees Act 1996, s 25(1), Sch 3, para 3(7), for savings in relation to entailed interests created before the commencement of that Act, and savings consequential upon the abolition of the doctrine of conversion, see s 25(4), (5) thereof; final words in square brackets substituted by the Law of Property (Amendment) Act 1926, ss 7, 8(2), Schedule.

Commentary

Somewhat oddly the section does not seem to apply to trusts of pure personalty not held on trusts for sale (see the way in which trustees are defined in sub-s (1)). The advertisement required under sub-s (1) should be placed in the London Gazette, and if there is land involved, in a newspaper circulating where the land is situated, which may be satisfied by a London newspaper with a wide geographical circulation, see *R v Westminster Betting Licensing Committee* [1962] 2 QB 750 (the Sporting Life). As to the form of the notice, see *Re Aldhous* [1955] 1 WLR 459. An advertisement under this section should be made promptly, see *Re Kay* [1897] 2 Ch 518. The protection conferred by the section does not relieve the trustees if they have notice of a claim even if the claimant does not answer the advertisement, see *Guardian Trust and Executor Co of New Zealand Ltd v Public Trustee of New Zealand* [1942] AC 115 PC. Subsection (2)(a) preserves the right of a beneficiary or creditor to follow property into the hands of an overpaid beneficiary. The searches referred to in sub-s (2)(b) would seem to be the usual conveyancing searches in relation to land and bankruptcy searches in respect of beneficiaries.

[96]

28 Protection in regard to notice

A trustee or personal representative acting for the purposes of more than one trust or estate shall not, in the absence of fraud, be affected by notice of any instrument, matter, fact or thing in relation to any particular trust or estate if he has obtained notice thereof merely by reason of his acting or having acted for the purposes of another trust or estate.

Commentary

This section would seem to apply to both actual and constructive notice acquired by a trustee when acting in that capacity for another settlement.

[97]

29 . . .

. . .

Amendment

Repealed by the Powers of Attorney Act 1971, s 11(2), (4), Sch 2.

[98]

30 . . .

. . .

Amendment

Repealed by the Trustee Act 2000, s 40(1), (3), Sch 2, Pt II, para 24, Sch 4, Pt II.

[99]

MAINTENANCE ADVANCEMENT AND PROTECTIVE TRUSTS

31 Power to apply income for maintenance and to accumulate surplus income during a minority

(1) Where any property is held by trustees in trust for any person for any interest whatsoever, whether vested or contingent, then, subject to any prior interests or charges affecting that property—

(i) during the infancy of any such person, if his interest so long continues, the trustees may, at their sole discretion, pay to his parent or guardian, if any, or otherwise apply for or towards his maintenance, education, or benefit, the whole or such part, if any, of the income of that property as may, in all the circumstances, be reasonable, whether or not there is—

(a) any other fund applicable to the same purpose; or

(b) any person bound by law to provide for his maintenance or education; and

(ii) if such person on attaining the age of [eighteen years] has not a vested interest in such income, the trustees shall thenceforth pay the income of that property and of any accretion thereto under subsection (2) of this section to him, until he either attains a vested interest therein or dies, or until failure of his interest:

Provided that, in deciding whether the whole or any part of the income of the property is during a minority to be paid or applied for the purposes aforesaid, the trustees shall have regard to the age of the infant and his requirements and generally to the circumstances of the case, and in particular to what other income, if any, is applicable for the same purposes; and where trustees have notice that the income of more than one fund is applicable for those purposes, then, so far as practicable, unless the entire income of the funds is paid or applied as aforesaid or the court otherwise directs, a proportionate part only of the income of each fund shall be so paid or applied.

(2) During the infancy of any such person, if his interest so long continues, the trustees shall accumulate all the residue of that income [by investing it, and any profits from so investing it] from time to time in authorised investments, and shall hold those accumulations as follows:—

(i) If any such person—

(a) attains the age of [eighteen years], or marries under that age [or forms a civil partnership under that age], and his interest in such income during his infancy[, or until his marriage or his formation of a civil partnership,] is a vested interest; or

(b) on attaining the age of [eighteen years] or on marriage[, or formation of a civil partnership,] under that age becomes entitled to the property from which such income arose in fee simple, absolute or determinable, or absolutely, or for an entailed interest;

the trustees shall hold the accumulations in trust for such person absolutely, but without prejudice to any provision with respect thereto contained in any settlement by him made under any statutory powers during his infancy, and so that the receipt of such person after marriage [or formation of a civil partnership], and though still an infant, shall be a good discharge; and

(ii) In any other case the trustees shall, notwithstanding that such person had a vested interest in such income, hold the accumulations as an accretion to the capital of the property from which such accumulations arose, and as one fund with such capital for all purposes, and so that, if such property is settled land, such accumulations shall be held upon the same trusts as if the same were capital money arising therefrom;

but the trustees may, at any time during the infancy of such person if his interest so long continues, apply those accumulations, or any part thereof, as if they were income arising in the then current year.

(3) This section applies in the case of a contingent interest only if the limitation or trust carries the intermediate income of the property, but it applies to a future or contingent legacy by the parent of, or a person standing in loco parentis to, the legatee, if and for such period as, under the general law, the legacy carries interest for the maintenance of the legatee, and in any such case as last aforesaid the rate of interest shall (if the income available is sufficient, and subject to any rules of court to the contrary) be five pounds per centum per annum.

(4) This section applies to a vested annuity in like manner as if the annuity were the income of property held by trustees in trust to pay the income thereof to the annuitant for the same period for which the annuity is payable, save that in any case accumulations made during the infancy of the annuitant shall be held in trust for the annuitant or his personal representatives absolutely.

(5) This section does not apply where the instrument, if any, under which the interest arises came into operation before the commencement of this Act.

Amendment
Sub-s (1): words in square brackets substituted by the Family Law Reform Act 1969, s 1(3), Sch 1, Part I.
Sub-s (2): words "by investing it, and any profits from so investing it" in square brackets substituted by the Trustee Act 2000, s 40(1), Sch 2, Pt II, para 25.
Sub-s (2): in para (i)(a) words "eighteen years" in square brackets substituted by the Family Law Reform Act 1969, s 1(3), Sch 1, Part I.
Sub-s (2): in para (i)(a) words "or forms a civil partnership under that age" in square brackets inserted by the Civil Partnership Act 2004, s 261(1), Sch 27, para 5(1), (2)(a).
Sub-s (2): in para (i)(a) words ", or until his marriage or his formation of a civil partnership," in square brackets substituted by the Civil Partnership Act 2004, s 261(1), Sch 27, para 5(1), (2)(b).
Sub-s (2): in para (i)(b) words "eighteen years" in square brackets substituted by the Family Law Reform Act 1969, s 1(3), Sch 1, Part I.
Sub-s (2): in para (i)(b) words ", or formation of a civil partnership," in square brackets inserted by the Civil Partnership Act 2004, s 261(1), Sch 27, para 5(1), (3).
Sub-s (2): in para (i) words "or formation of a civil partnership" in square brackets inserted by the Civil Partnership Act 2004, s 261(1), Sch 27, para 5(1), (4).

Commentary
In respect of any instrument made before 1 January 1970, references to the age 18 in the section must be read as references to age 21. This statutory power is frequently modified in settlements so that the trustees are given a wider discretion in relation to the maintenance of a minor beneficiary and sometimes by increasing the age at which income becomes payable to a beneficiary (subject of course to the law against excessive accumulations). "Maintenance, education and benefit" in sub-s (1) has the widest of meanings and can cover not only expenditure but also capital investment, see *Re Heyworth's Contingent Reversionary Interest* [1956] Ch 363 and *Re Vestey's Settlement* [1951] Ch 209. The trustees must have regard to the factors set out in the proviso and must consider what will most benefit the minor beneficiary and not shy away from benefiting the child's parent if that is the best course for the child, see *Fuller v Evans* [2000] 1 All ER 636. Provided that the trustees exercise their discretion in good faith the court will not interfere, see *Re Senior* [1936] Ch 27. The section only applies where the gift to the child carries the intermediate income (see sub-s (3)). As far as testamentary gifts are concerned, reference should be made to the Law of Property Act 1925, s 175 **[176]** as to whether a gift carries the intermediate income. Similar rules apply in respect of lifetime settlements, but note that if the settlement itself contains an express direction to accumulate income the power will not be available, see *Re Stapleton* [1946] 1 All ER 323, and reference should always be made to the terms of the trust or will to ensure that the income goes with the capital gift and is not otherwise disposed of. A child in respect of whom income has been allocated under a discretionary trust is not entitled to a contingent interest within the settlement (*Re Vestey's Settlement* [1951] Ch 209). Deferred interests do not in general carry the intermediate income and even if within s 175 the deferral of an interest will, in the absence of special words, amount to a contrary intention, see *Re McGeorge* [1963] Ch 544. On attaining the age of 18 the beneficiary will be entitled to the income and will attain an interest in possession for tax purposes, see *Swales v IRC* [1984] 3 All ER 16 and it can be important to exclude that in certain circumstances (see: *Price v Williams-Wyn* [2006] WTLR 1633). The effect of sub-s (2) is that where a beneficiary dies under the age of 18, or marries under that age, the accumulations of income will not fall into his estate even if he had a vested interest in income. For an analysis of the effect of sub-s (2) see *Re Sharp's Settlement Trusts* [1973] Ch 331.

[100]

32 Power of advancement

(1) Trustees may at any time or times pay or apply any capital money subject to a trust, for the advancement or benefit, in such manner as they may, in their absolute discretion, think fit, of any person entitled to the capital of the trust property or of any share thereof, whether absolutely or contingently on his attaining any specified age or on the occurrence of any other event, or subject to a gift over on his death under any specified age or on the occurrence of any other event, and whether in possession or in remainder or reversion, and such payment or application may be made notwithstanding that the interest of such person is liable to be defeated by the

exercise of a power of appointment or revocation, or to be diminished by the increase of the class to which he belongs:

Provided that—

(a) the money so paid or applied for the advancement or benefit of any person shall not exceed altogether in amount one-half of the presumptive or vested share or interest of that person in the trust property; and

(b) if that person is or becomes absolutely and indefeasibly entitled to a share in the trust property the money so paid or applied shall be brought into account as part of such share; and

(c) no such payment or application shall be made so as to prejudice any person entitled to any prior life or other interest, whether vested or contingent, in the money paid or applied unless such person is in existence and of full age and consents in writing to such payment or application.

[(2) This section does not apply to capital money arising under the Settled Land Act 1925.]

(3) This section does not apply to trusts constituted or created before the commencement of this Act.

Amendment

Sub-s (2): substituted by the Trusts of Land and Appointment of Trustees Act 1996, s 25(1), Sch 3, para 3(8); for savings in relation to entailed interests created before the commencement of that Act, and savings consequential upon the abolition of the doctrine of conversion, see s 25(4), (5) thereof.

Commentary

Note that as with many of the default powers conferred by this Act, it is subject to a contrary intention in the trust instrument, see s 69(2) below. The power will also be excluded if it does not fit with the purpose of the trust, see *IRC v Bernstein* [1961] Ch 399. Advancement in this context means establishing a beneficiary in life or contribution towards the establishment of a beneficiary, see *Pilkington v IRC* [1964] AC 612. However, the power is not just to advance but also to apply capital for the benefit of a beneficiary. This has a wide meaning and the power has been used successfully to pay capital directly to a beneficiary thereby effecting a tax saving (*Re Moxon's Will Trusts* [1958] 1 WLR 165); and to pay capital directly to charity in recognition of a wealthy beneficiary's moral obligations (*Re Clore's Will Trusts* [1966] 1 WLR 955) although for the limits on this jurisdiction see *X v A* [2006] 1 WLR 741. Trustees can use this power to resettle the property (*Re Halsted's Will Trusts* [1937] 2 All ER 570) even in circumstances where the beneficiary will not himself benefit provided that it is for his benefit, see *Pilkington v IRC* [1964] AC 612. This power can also be used in appropriate cases to resettle property on offshore trusts, see *Richard v Mackay* (1997) TLI 23. Although there is some debate on the subject, it is now reasonably well settled that the power of advancement can be used to settle on discretionary trusts. Under sub-s (1)(b), the advance is taken into account at its value at the date of the advance but see *Re Marquess of Abergavenny's Estates Act Trusts* [1981] 1 WLR 843. As to the consents required under sub-s (1)(c), trusts deeds often modify the section to dispense with them, but if the consent of beneficiaries under prior discretionary trusts is not necessary, see *Re Beckett's Settlement* [1940] Ch 279. Under the section the advancement is limited to one half and in practice the trust deed will often modify this to extend to the whole of the fund. Once the trustees have advanced up to one half of the presumptive share of the beneficiary their powers are exhausted and they cannot exercise the power further, see *Re Marquess of Abergavenny's Estates Act Trusts* [1981] 1 WLR 843. The section does not apply to Settled Land Act settlements.

[101]

33 Protective trusts

(1) Where any income, including an annuity or other periodical income payment, is directed to be held on protective trusts for the benefit of any person (in this section called "the principal beneficiary") for the period of his life or for any less period, then, during that period (in this section called the "trust period") the said income shall, without prejudice to any prior interest, be held on the following trusts, namely:—

(i) Upon trust for the principal beneficiary during the trust period or until he, whether before or after the termination of any prior interest, does or attempts to do or suffers any act or thing, or until any event happens, other than an advance under any statutory or express power, whereby, if the said income were payable during the trust period to the principal beneficiary absolutely during that period, he would be deprived of the right to receive the same or any part thereof, in any of which cases, as well as on the termination of the trust period, whichever first happens, this trust of the said income shall fail or determine;

(ii) If the trust aforesaid fails or determines during the subsistence of the trust period, then, during the residue of that period, the said income shall be held upon trust for the application thereof for the maintenance or support, or otherwise for the benefit, of all or any one or more exclusively of the other or others of the following persons (that is to say)—

(a) the principal beneficiary and his or her [spouse or civil partner], if any, and his or her children or more remote issue, if any; or

(b) if there is no [spouse or civil partner] or issue of the principal beneficiary in existence, the principal beneficiary and the persons who would, if he were actually dead, be entitled to the trust property or the income thereof or to the annuity fund, if any, or arrears of the annuity, as the case may be;

as the trustees in their absolute discretion, without being liable to account for the exercise of such discretion, think fit.

(2) This section does not apply to trusts coming into operation before the commencement of this Act, and has effect subject to any variation of the implied trusts aforesaid contained in the instrument creating the trust.

(3) Nothing in this section operates to validate any trust which would, if contained in the instrument creating the trust, be liable to be set aside.

[(4) In relation to the dispositions mentioned in section 19(1) of the Family Law Reform Act 1987, this section shall have effect as if any reference (however expressed) to any relationship between two persons were construed in accordance with section 1 of that Act.]

Amendment

Sub-s (1): in para (ii)(a), (b) words “spouse or civil partner” in square brackets substituted by the Civil Partnership Act 2004, s 261(1), Sch 27, para 6.

Sub-s (4): inserted by the Family Law Reform Act 1987, s 33(1), Sch 2, para 2, Sch 3, para 1.

Commentary

This section was introduced because of the popularity of protected life interests and provided a short-hand method of including them in trusts and wills. Note that sub-s (3) preserves the general position at law which is that a settlor cannot take for himself a protective life interest as a man cannot settle property so as to defeat his creditors on bankruptcy, see *Re Burroughs-Fowler* [1916] 2 Ch 251. The circumstances in which forfeiture will take place under this section are very widely drafted, see *Re Pozot's Settlement* [1952] Ch 427. For a thorough analysis of all the cases where it has been held that a protected life interest has been forfeited, see Underhill and Hayton *Law of Trusts and Trustees* (17th edn), but the following are some examples: *Edmunds v Edmunds* [1965] 1 WLR 58 (order of divorce court requiring immediate charge of interest); *Re Baring's Settlement Trusts* [1940] Ch 737 (sequestration order) an order under the Trustee Act 1925, s 57 **[126]** (as to which see below) reducing the right of the protected life tenant to income, see *Re Mair* [2935] Ch 562; the exercise of the power of advancement (as to which see s 32 above) and the giving of consent by the protected life tenant does not operate as a forfeiture (see *Re Rees* [1954] Ch 202) and there was no forfeiture where a divorce court varied trusts on a divorce (*General Accident Fire and Life Assurance Corporation v IRC* [1963] 1 WLR 1207). As for the lifting of protected life interests under the Variation of Trusts Act 1958 see **[256]**.

[102]

PART III
APPOINTMENT AND DISCHARGE OF TRUSTEES

34 Limitation of the number of trustees

(1) Where, at the commencement of this Act, there are more than four trustees of a settlement of land, or more than four trustees holding land on trust for sale, no new trustees shall (except where as a result of the appointment the number is reduced to four or less) be capable of being appointed until the number is reduced to less than four, and thereafter the number shall not be increased beyond four.

(2) In the case of settlements and dispositions [creating trusts of land] made or coming into operation after the commencement of this Act—

- (a) the number of trustees thereof shall not in any case exceed four, and where more than four persons are named as such trustees, the four first named (who are able and willing to act) shall alone be the trustees, and the other persons named shall not be trustees unless appointed on the occurrence of a vacancy;
- (b) the number of the trustees shall not be increased beyond four.

(3) This section only applies to settlements and dispositions of land, and the restrictions imposed on the number of trustees do not apply—

- (a) in the case of land vested in trustees for charitable, ecclesiastical, or public purposes; or
- (b) where the net proceeds of the sale of the land are held for like purposes; or
- (c) to the trustees of a term of years absolute limited by a settlement on trusts for raising money, or of a like term created under the statutory remedies relating to annual sums charged on land.

Amendment

Sub-s (2): words in square brackets substituted by the Trusts of Land and Appointment of Trustees Act 1996, s 25(1), Sch 3, para 3(9); for savings in relation to entailed interests created before the commencement of that Act, and savings consequential upon the abolition of the doctrine of conversion, see s 25(4), (5) thereof.

Commentary

This section applies only to trusts and dispositions of land, which is defined by section 68(1)(6) below. There is no restriction on the number of trustees of other settlements. It is not entirely clear how the restriction in section 34(2) applies where more than four trustees of a personalty settlement purchase land. The reference in subsection (3)(c) is to one of the methods whereby a person entitled to an annual sum charged on land can enforce his right under section 121(4) of the Law of Property Act 1925.

[103]

35 Appointments of trustees of settlements and [and trustees of land]

[(1) Appointments of new trustees of land and of new trustees of any trust of the proceeds of sale of the land shall, subject to any order of the court, be effected by separate instruments, but in such manner as to secure that the same persons become trustees of land and trustees of the trust of the proceeds of sale.]

(2) Where new trustees of a settlement are appointed, a memorandum of the names and addresses of the persons who are for the time being the trustees thereof for the purposes of the Settled Land Act 1925, shall be endorsed on or annexed to the last or only principal vesting instrument by or on behalf of the trustees of the settlement, and such vesting instrument shall, for that purpose, be produced by the person having the possession thereof of the trustees of the settlement when so required.

[(3) Where new trustees of land are appointed, a memorandum of the persons who are for the time being the trustees of the land shall be endorsed on or annexed to the conveyance by which the land was vested in trustees of land; and that conveyance shall be produced to the persons who are for the time being the trustees of the land by the person in possession of it in order for that to be done when the trustees require its production.]

(4) This section applies only to settlements and dispositions of land.

Amendment

Section heading: words in square brackets substituted by the Trusts of Land and Appointment of Trustees Act 1996, s 25(1), Sch 3, para 3(10)(c); for savings in relation to entailed interests created before the commencement of that Act, and savings consequential upon the abolition of the doctrine of conversion, see s 25(4), (5) thereof.
Sub-ss (1), (3): substituted by the Trusts of Land and Appointment of Trustees Act 1996, s 25(1), Sch 3, para 3(10)(a), (b); for savings in relation to entailed interests created before the commencement of that Act, and savings consequential upon the abolition of the doctrine of conversion, see s 25(4), (5) thereof.

Commentary

For the meaning of settlements, see section 68(15) below. "New trustees" referred to in the section include additional trustees, see section 68(7) below. This section reflects the practice where a trust for sale is created by the use of two documents—one to convey the land to trustees for sale and the other to declare the trusts. It should be read in conjunction with section 24 of the Law of Property Act 1925 **[149]** which in essence provides that persons with the power to appoint new trustees of land are bound to appoint the same person as trustees of the land and the proceeds of sale, but the purchaser is not concerned to see that they have been properly appointed. Subsection (2) applies to strict settlements (as to which see the Settled Land Act 1925 **[Appendix II]**). In cases where the trust of land is created by a single document, or there is no trust for sale, the section will not apply.

[104]

36 Power of appointing new or additional trustees

(1) Where a trustee, either original or substituted, and whether appointed by a court or otherwise, is dead, or remains out of the United Kingdom for more than twelve months, or desires to be discharged from all or any of the trusts or powers reposed in or conferred on him, or refuses or is unfit to act therein, or is incapable of acting therein, or is an infant, then, subject to the restrictions imposed by this Act on the number of trustees,—

(a) the person or persons nominated for the purpose of appointing new trustees by the instrument, if any, creating the trust; or

(b) if there is no such person, or no such person able and willing to act, then the surviving or continuing trustees or trustee for the time being, or the personal representatives of the last surviving or continuing trustee;

may, by writing, appoint one or more other persons (whether or not being the persons exercising the power) to be a trustee or trustees in the place of the trustee so deceased remaining out of the United Kingdom, desiring to be discharged, refusing, or being unfit or being incapable, or being an infant, as aforesaid.

(2) Where a trustee has been removed under a power contained in the instrument creating the trust, a new trustee or new trustees may be appointed in the place of the trustee who is removed, as if he were dead, or, in the case of a corporation, as if the corporation desired to be discharged from the trust, and the provisions of this section shall apply accordingly, but subject to the restrictions imposed by this Act on the number of trustees.

(3) Where a corporation being a trustee is or has been dissolved, either before or after the commencement of this Act, then, for the purposes of this section and of any enactment replaced thereby, the corporation shall be deemed to be and to have been from the date of the dissolution incapable of acting in the trusts or powers reposed in or conferred on the corporation.

(4) The power of appointment given by subsection (1) of this section or any similar previous enactment to the personal representatives of a last surviving or continuing trustee shall be and shall be deemed always to have been exercisable by the executors for the time being (whether original or by representation) of such surviving or continuing trustee who have proved the will of their testator or by the administrators for the time being of such trustee without the concurrence of any executor who has renounced or has not proved.

(5) But a sole or last surviving executor intending to renounce, or all the executors where they all intend to renounce, shall have and shall be deemed always to have had power, at any time before renouncing probate, to exercise the power of appointment given by this section, or by any similar previous enactment, if willing to act for that purpose and without thereby accepting the office of executor.

[(6) Where, in the case of any trust, there are not more than three trustees—]

- (a) the person or persons nominated for the purpose of appointing new trustees by the instrument, if any, creating the trust; or
- (b) if there is no such person, or no such person able and willing to act, then the trustee or trustees for the time being;

may, by writing appoint another person or other persons to be an additional trustee or additional trustees, but it shall not be obligatory to appoint any additional trustee, unless the instrument, if any, creating the trust, or any statutory enactment provides to the contrary, nor shall the number of trustees be increased beyond four by virtue of any such appointment.

[(6A) A person who is either—

- (a) both a trustee and attorney for the other trustee (if one other), or for both of the other trustees (if two others), under a registered power; or
- (b) attorney under a registered power for the trustee (if one) or for both or each of the trustees (if two or three),

may, if subsection (6B) of this section is satisfied in relation to him, make an appointment under subsection (6)(b) of this section on behalf of the trustee or trustees.

(6B) This subsection is satisfied in relation to an attorney under a registered power for one or more trustees if (as attorney under the power)—

- (a) he intends to exercise any function of the trustee or trustees by virtue of section 1(1) of the Trustee Delegation Act 1999; or
- (b) he intends to exercise any function of the trustee or trustees in relation to any land, capital proceeds of a conveyance of land or income from land by virtue of its delegation to him under section 25 of this Act or the instrument (if any) creating the trust.

(6C) In subsections (6A) and (6B) of this section "registered power" means [an enduring power of attorney or lasting power of attorney registered under the Mental Capacity Act 2005].

(6D) Subsection (6A) of this section—

- (a) applies only if and so far as a contrary intention is not expressed in the instrument creating the power of attorney (or, where more than one, any of them) or the instrument (if any) creating the trust; and
- (b) has effect subject to the terms of those instruments.]

(7) Every new trustee appointed under this section as well before as after all the trust property becomes by law, or by assurance, or otherwise, vested in him, shall have the same powers, authorities, and discretions, and may in all respects act as if he had been originally appointed a trustee by the instrument, if any, creating the trust.

(8) The provisions of this section relating to a trustee who is dead include the case of a person nominated trustee in a will but dying before the testator, and those relative

to a continuing trustee include a refusing or retiring trustee, if willing to act in the execution of the provisions of this section.

[(9) Where a trustee [lacks capacity to exercise] his functions as trustee and is also entitled in possession to some beneficial interest in the trust property, no appointment of a new trustee in his place shall be made by virtue of paragraph (b) of subsection (1) of this section unless leave to make the appointment has been given by [the Court of Protection].]

Amendment

Sub-s (6): words in square brackets substituted by the Trusts of Land and Appointment of Trustees Act 1996, s 25(1), Sch 3, para 3(11); for savings in relation to entailed interests created before the commencement of that Act, and savings consequential upon the abolition of the doctrine of conversion, see s 25(4), (5) thereof.
Sub-ss (6A)-(6D): inserted by the Trustee Delegation Act 1999, s 8.
Sub-s (6C): words substituted by the Mental Capacity Act 2005, s 67(1), Sch 6, para 3(1), (2)(a).
Sub-s (9): substituted by the Mental Health Act 1959, s 149(1), Sch 7, Pt I.
Sub-s (9): words substituted by the Mental Capacity Act 2005, s 67(1), Sch 6, para 3(1), (2)(b)(i), (ii).

Commentary

The meaning of "trustee" in subsection (1) is important (see s 68(17)) and where the context admits includes personal representatives. However, as the Court is precluded from appointing personal representatives under section 41(4) (as to which see below) it seems unlikely that this power enables personal representatives to appoint new ones. As to the circumstances in which the power can be exercised, a trustee who is dead includes one who has predeceased the testator (see subsection (8)). Where a trustee is out of the UK for more than twelve months he can be replaced under this section whether he agrees or not (see: *Re Stoneham's Settlement Trusts* [1953] Ch 59) This provision is often excluded by modern trust deeds which contemplate the appointment of offshore trustees. The section covers cases where the trustee disclaims office (see: *Re Birchall* (1889) 40 Ch D 436). As to unfitness to act, a bankrupt trustee is unfit (see, for example, *Re Adam's Trust* (1879) 12 Ch D 634). A person is incapable of acting if he is lacks mental capacity to exercise his functions as trustee as explained in the Mental Capacity Act 2005 **[562]**. The test is issue specific. If a trustee is being removed on this basis and is also a beneficiary in possession, an application will need to be made to the Court of Protection before the appointment is made. A trustee may be incapable by reason of old age and infirmity, see: *Re Cutler* (1895) 39 SJ 484. The appointment of the new trustee should be in writing (a will is not writing, see: *Re Parker's Trusts* [1894] 1 Ch 707) and in practice is almost always by deed so that section 40 (see below) automatically vests the trust property in the new trustees. The power given by subsection (1) is permissive only and the trustees are not obliged to exercise it, see: *Re Knight's Will* (1884) 26 Ch 82. As to subsection (2), that will only apply where there is express power under the trust instrument to remove a trustee and that has been exercised. The primary persons entitled to appoint under this section are those nominated in the trust instrument but not if they have a more limited power under the trust instrument (see: *Re Sichel's Settlement* [1916] 1 Ch 358). The object of subsection (5) is to enable an executor intending to renounce to appoint new trustees without jeopardising his chance to renounce. Subsections 6(A) to 6(D) were inserted by the Trustee Delegation Act 1999 and apply only in relation to enduring powers of attorney created on or after 1st March 2000. Their object is to enable a trustee who is also the attorney under a registered enduring power to appoint additional trustees under section 36(6) but only if he satisfies subsection (6B). This is to circumvent the problem that two trustees are required to give a receipt for capital money which might not be achieved if one of the trustees is incapable. The power is in addition to the ability of the trustee to remove the incapable trustee under subsection (1). As far as subsection (7) is concerned, see also section 18 above (evolution of interests of trustees).

[105]

37 Supplemental provisions as to appointment of trustees

(1) On the appointment of a trustee for the whole or any part of trust property—

(a) the number of trustees may, subject to the restrictions imposed by this Act on the number of trustees, be increased; and

(b) a separate set of trustees, not exceeding four, may be appointed for any part of the trust property held on trusts distinct from those relating to any other part or parts of the trust property, notwithstanding that no new trustees or trustee are or is to be appointed for other parts of the trust property, and any existing trustee may be appointed or remain one of such separate set of trustees, or, if only one trustee was originally appointed, then, save as hereinafter provided, one separate trustee may be so appointed; and

(c) it shall not be obligatory, save as hereinafter provided, to appoint more than one new trustee where only one trustee was originally appointed, or to fill up the original number of trustees where more than two trustees were originally appointed, but, except where only one trustee was originally appointed, and a sole trustee when appointed will be able to give valid receipts for all capital money, a trustee shall not be discharged from his trust unless there will be either a trust corporation or at least two [persons] to act as trustees to perform the trust; and

(d) any assurance or thing requisite for vesting the trust property, or any part thereof, in a sole trustee, or jointly in the persons who are the trustees, shall be executed or done.

(2) Nothing in this Act shall authorise the appointment of a sole trustee, not being a trust corporation, where the trustee, when appointed, would not be able to give valid receipts for all capital money arising under the trust.

Amendment

Sub-s (1): in para (c) word in square brackets substituted by the Trusts of Land and Appointment of Trustees Act 1996, s 25(1), Sch 3, para 3(12); for savings in relation to entailed interests created before the commencement of that Act, and savings consequential upon the abolition of the doctrine of conversion, see s 25(4), (5) thereof.

Commentary

These provisions supplement section 36 above. Subsection (1)(b) enables trustees of distinct parts of the fund to be appointed, and the parts of the fund do not need to be permanently distinct, see: *Re Hetherington's Trusts* (1887) 34 Ch D 211. Subsections (1)(a) and (c) and (2) provide for the number of trustees once the appointment has been effected. Essentially the trustees of land must not exceed 4 (see section 34 above) but neither must the trust be left with a sole trustee who cannot give a receipt for capital monies and an outgoing trustee will not be discharged if the effect of his retirement and the appointment of the new trustee would be to that effect. The Public Trustee can of course be appointed as a sole trustee. The term "individuals" in s 37(1)(c) means natural persons and did not include a body corporate, *Jasmine Trustees Ltd. v Wells & Hind* [2007] 1 All ER 1142.

[106]

38 Evidence as to a vacancy in a trust

(1) A statement, contained in any instrument coming into operation after the commencement of this Act by which a new trustee is appointed for any purpose connected with land, to the effect that a trustee has remained out of the United Kingdom for more than twelve months or refuses or is unfit to act, or is incapable of acting, or that he is not entitled to a beneficial interest in the trust property in possession, shall, in favour of a purchaser of a legal estate, be conclusive evidence of the matter stated.

(2) In favour of such purchaser any appointment of a new trustee depending on that statement, and any vesting declaration, express or implied, consequent on the appointment, shall be valid.

Commentary
Note that this section only applies in relation to trusts involving land. As to the reference to the trustee not having a beneficial interest in possession see the notes to section 36 in particular subsection (9).

[107]

39 Retirement of trustee without a new appointment

(1) Where a trustee is desirous of being discharged from the trust, and after his discharge there will be either a trust corporation or at least two [persons] to act as trustees to perform the trust, then, if such trustee as aforesaid by deed declares that he is desirous of being discharged from the trust, and if his co-trustees and such other person, if any, as is empowered to appoint trustees, by deed consent to the discharge of the trustee, and to the vesting in the co-trustees alone of the trust property, the trustee desirous of being discharged shall be deemed to have retired from the trust, and shall, by the deed, be discharged therefrom under this Act, without any new trustee being appointed in his place.

(2) Any assurance or thing requisite for vesting the trust property in the continuing trustees alone shall be executed or done.

Amendment
Sub-s (1): word in square brackets substituted by the Trusts of Land and Appointment of Trustees Act 1996, s 25(1), Sch 3, para 3(13); for savings in relation to entailed interests created before the commencement of that Act, and savings consequential upon the abolition of the doctrine of conversion, see s 25(4), (5) thereof.

Commentary
For the meaning of "trust corporation" see section 68(1)(18) below. Before the amendment made by the 1996 Act there had to be left either two individuals or a trust corporation. Now an individual and a corporate trustee (not a trust corporation) can be left. This section probably does not enable retirement from part of the trusts only. The section can be used in conjunction with section 36(1) to appoint a new trustee in place of the trustee who desires to be discharged.

[108]

40 Vesting of trust property in new or continuing trustees

(1) Where by a deed a new trustee is appointed to perform any trust, then—

(a) if the deed contains a declaration by the appointor to the effect that any estate or interest in any land subject to the trust, or in any chattel so subject, or right to recover or receive any debt or other thing in action so subject, shall vest in the persons who by virtue of the deed become or are the trustees for performing the trust, the deed shall operate, without any conveyance or assignment, to vest in those persons as joint tenants and for the purposes of the trust the estate interest or right to which the declaration relates; and

(b) if the deed is made after the commencement of this Act and does not contain such a declaration, the deed shall, subject to any express provision to the contrary therein contained, operate as if it had contained such a declaration by the appointor extending to all the estates interests and rights with respect to which a declaration could have been made.

(2) Where by a deed a retiring trustee is discharged under [section 39 of this Act or section 19 of the Trusts of Land and Appointment of Trustees Act 1996] without a new trustee being appointed, then—

(a) if the deed contains such a declaration as aforesaid by the retiring and continuing trustees, and by the other person, if any, empowered to appoint trustees, the deed shall, without any conveyance or assignment, operate to vest in the continuing trustees alone, as joint tenants, and for the purposes of the trust, the estate, interest, or right to which the declaration relates; and

(b) if the deed is made after the commencement of this Act and does not contain such a declaration, the deed shall, subject to any express provision to the contrary therein contained, operate as if it had contained such a declaration by such persons as aforesaid extending to all the estates, interests and rights with respect to which a declaration could have been made.

(3) An express vesting declaration, whether made before or after the commencement of this Act, shall, notwithstanding that the estate, interest or right to be vested is not expressly referred to, and provided that the other statutory requirements were or are complied with, operate and be deemed always to have operated (but without prejudice to any express provision to the contrary contained in the deed of appointment or discharge) to vest in the persons respectively referred to in subsections (1) and (2) of this section, as the case may require, such estates, interests and rights as are capable of being and ought to be vested in those persons.

(4) This section does not extend—

(a) to land conveyed by way of mortgage for securing money subject to the trust, except land conveyed on trust for securing debentures or debenture stock;

(b) to land held under a lease which contains any covenant, condition or agreement against assignment or disposing of the land without licence or consent, unless, prior to the execution of the deed containing expressly or impliedly the vesting declaration, the requisite licence or consent has been obtained, or unless, by virtue of any statute or rule of law, the vesting declaration, express or implied, would not operate as a breach of covenant or give rise to a forfeiture;

(c) to any share, stock, annuity or property which is only transferable in books kept by a company or other body, or in manner directed by or under an Act of Parliament.

In this subsection "lease" includes an underlease and an agreement for a lease or underlease.

(5) For purposes of registration of the deed in any registry, the person or persons making the declaration expressly or impliedly, shall be deemed the conveying party or parties, and the conveyance shall be deemed to be made by him or them under a power conferred by this Act.

(6) This section applies to deeds of appointment or discharge executed on or after the first day of January, eighteen hundred and eighty-two.

Amendment

Sub-s (2): words in square brackets substituted by the Trusts of Land and Appointment of Trustees Act 1996, s 25(1), Sch 3, para 3(14); for savings in relation to entailed interests created before the commencement of that Act, and savings consequential upon the abolition of the doctrine of conversion, see s 25(4), (5) thereof.

Commentary

Subsection (1) is not confined to cases where an appointment is made under section 36 (as to which see above) but applies to any appointment, including one made under an express power, and it applies as well to a bare trust, see: *London & County Banking Company v Goddard* [1897] 1 Ch 642. Subsection (2) on the other hand is confined to cases where the trustee is being discharged under section 39 (as to which see above) or under section 19 of the Trusts of Land and Appointment of Trustees Act 1996 **[450]**. The section when it applies obviates the need for an express vesting declaration. Note however that certain types of property are excluded from its operation by subsection (4)-mortgages because of the need to keep the trusts off the face of the transfer of the mortgage, leases where there is a need to obtain licence to assign so that automatic vesting would constitute a breach of trust and stocks and shares where a particular form of transfer is required.

PART IV
POWERS OF THE COURT

APPOINTMENT OF NEW TRUSTEES

41 Power of court to appoint new trustees

(1) The court may, whenever it is expedient to appoint a new trustee or new trustees, and it is found inexpedient difficult or impracticable so to do without the assistance of the court, make an order appointing a new trustee or new trustees either in substitution for or in addition to any existing trustee or trustees, or although there is no existing trustee.

In particular and without prejudice to the generality of the foregoing provision, the court may make an order appointing a new trustee in substitution for a trustee who . . . [[lacks capacity to exercise] his functions as trustee], or is a bankrupt, or is a corporation which is in liquidation or has been dissolved.

(2) The power conferred by this section may, in the case of a deed of arrangement within the meaning of the Deeds of Arrangement Act 1914, be exercised either by the High Court or by the court having jurisdiction in bankruptcy in the district in which the debtor resided or carried on business at the date of the execution of the deed.

(3) An order under this section, and any consequential vesting order or conveyance, shall not operate further or otherwise as a discharge to any former or continuing trustee than an appointment of new trustees under any power for that purpose contained in any instrument would have operated.

(4) Nothing in this section gives power to appoint an executor or administrator.

Amendment

Sub-s (1): words omitted repealed by the Criminal Law Act 1967, s 10, Sch 3, Pt III.
Sub-s (1): words “lacks capacity to exercise” substituted by the Mental Capacity Act 2005, s 67(1), Sch 6, para 3(1), (3).
Sub-s (1): words to “as trustee” in square brackets substituted by the Mental Health Act 1959, s 149(1), Sch 7, Pt I.

Commentary

For the meaning of “court” in subsection (1) see section 67(1) below. Application under this section is made by way of Part 8 claim form in accordance with part 8 of the Civil Procedure Rules 1998 and should be made by a beneficiary or a trustee. This section enables the court to replace a trustee against his will, but the jurisdiction will not be exercised where there is someone who is willing to make an appointment out of court see: *Re Higginbottom* [1982] 3 Ch 132 unless the circumstances are exceptional (*Re May’s Will Trusts* [1941] Ch 104). Note that the Court may appoint the Public Trustee or a judicial trustee. It is clear that the section is of general application and does not just apply to the circumstances set out in subsection (1), see: *Re Henderson, Henderson v Henderson* [1940] Ch 764 . Note also that a corporate trustee in liquidation may be removed which is wider that section 36(3) (as to which see above). As to guidance on who will be appointed as a new trustee, see: *Re Tempest* (1866) 1 Ch App 485. The Court used to be reluctant to appoint an offshore trustee (*Re Guibert* (1852) 16 Jur 852) but quaere whether that practice would be followed today. Traditionally also a beneficiary and his solicitor would not be appointed but that practice is frequently departed from. Although there is nothing in the rules of court now requiring it, evidence of fitness of the new trustee and consent to act are still in practice required. Subsection (4) makes it clear that this section does not enable the court to replace a personal representative or appoint additional personal representatives, but note the powers of the court under section 50 of the Administration of Justice Act 1985 **[399]** and section 1 of the Judicial Trustee Act 1896 **[53].** Apart from this section the court has an inherent jurisdiction to remove and appoint trustees.

[110]

42 Power to authorise remuneration

Where the court appoints a corporation, other than the Public Trustee, to be a trustee either solely or jointly with another person, the court may authorise the corporation to charge such remuneration for its services as trustee as the court may think fit.

Commentary

This section is far less important since the coming into force of the Trustee Act 2000 which by section 29 enables trust corporations to charge reasonable remuneration **[504]**.

[111]

43 Powers of new trustee appointed by the Court

Every trustee appointed by a court of competent jurisdiction shall, as well before as after the trust property becomes by law, or by assurance, or otherwise, vested in him, have the same powers, authorities, and discretions, and may in all respects act as if he had been originally appointed a trustee by the instrument, if any, creating the trust.

Commentary

This provision corresponds with section 36(7) above on the appointment of trustees out of Court.

[112]

VESTING ORDERS

44 Vesting orders of land

In any of the following cases, namely:

- (i) Where the court appoints or has appointed a trustee, or where a trustee has been appointed out of court under any statutory or express power;
- (ii) Where a trustee entitled to or possessed of any land or interest therein, whether by way of mortgage or otherwise, or entitled to a contingent right therein, either solely or jointly with any other person—
  - (a) is under disability; or
  - (b) is out of the jurisdiction of the High Court; or
  - (c) cannot be found, or, being a corporation, has been dissolved;
- (iii) Where it is uncertain who was the survivor of two or more trustees jointly entitled to or possessed of any interest in land;
- (iv) Where it is uncertain whether the last trustee known to have been entitled to or possessed of any interest in land is living or dead;
- (v) Where there is no personal representative of a deceased trustee who was entitled to or possessed of any interest in land, or where it is uncertain who is the personal representative of a deceased trustee who was entitled to or possessed of any interest in land;
- (vi) Where a trustee jointly or solely entitled to or possessed of any interest in land, or entitled to a contingent right therein, has been required, by or on behalf of a person entitled to require a conveyance of the land or interest or a release of the right, to convey the land or interest or to release the right, and has wilfully refused or neglected to convey the land or interest or release the right for twenty-eight days after the date of the requirement;
- (vii) Where land or any interest therein is vested in a trustee whether by way of mortgage or otherwise, and it appears to the court to be expedient;

the court may make an order (in this Act called a vesting order) vesting the land or interest therein in any such person in any such manner and for any such estate or interest as the court may direct, or releasing or disposing of the contingent right to such person as the court may direct:

Provided that—

(a) Where the order is consequential on the appointment of a trustee the land or interest therein shall be vested for such estate as the court may direct in the persons who on the appointment are the trustees; and

(b) Where the order relates to a trustee entitled or formerly entitled jointly with another person, and such trustee is under disability or out of the jurisdiction of the High Court or cannot be found, or being a corporation has been dissolved, the land interest or right shall be vested in such other person who remains entitled, either alone or with any other person the court may appoint.

Commentary

For the meaning of "court" see section 67(1) below. An application for an order under this section is made by way of Part 8 claim form in accordance with Part 8 of the Civil Procedure Rules 1998. The most common use of this section is where new trustees are appointed under section 41, and the Court vests the trust property in them under subsection (1). Although the section applies to appointments out of court, section 40 (as to which see above) will normally vest the property in the new trustees. Under subsection (2) the court may vest the trust assets in the remaining trustees without removing the trustee under a disability, see: *Re Harrison's Settled Trusts* [1965] 1 WLR 1492. The section has been used to vest trust property in a beneficiary absolutely entitled, see: *Re Godfrey* (1883) 23 Ch D 483.

[113]

45 Orders as to contingent rights of unborn persons

Where any interest in land is subject to a contingent right in an unborn person or class of unborn persons who, on coming into existence would, in respect, thereof, become entitled to or possessed of that interest on any trust, the court may make an order releasing the land or interest therein from the contingent right, or may make an order vesting in any person the estate or interest to or of which the unborn person or class of unborn persons would, on coming into existence, be entitled or possessed in the land.

Commentary

For the meaning of "court" see section 67(1) below and for the meaning of "land" see section 68(1)(6). For "contingent right" see section 68(1)(2). Orders under this section are rare but application should be made by way of Part 8 claim form in accordance with Part 8 of the Civil Procedure Rules 1998.

[114]

46 Vesting order in place of conveyance by infant mortgagee

Where any person entitled to or possessed of any interest in land, or entitled to a contingent right in land, by way of security for money, is an infant, the court may make an order vesting or releasing or disposing of the interest in the land or the right in like manner as in the case of a trustee under disability.

Commentary

This section confers powers on the court to deal with interest in land which an infant may hold by way of mortgage. For the meaning of "court" see section 67(1) below. For the meaning of "contingent right" see section 68(1)(2). Applications (which are rare) should be made by way of Part 8 claim form in accordance with Part 8 of the Civil Procedure Rules 1998.

[115]

47 Vesting order consequential on order for sale or mortgage of land

Where any court gives a judgment or makes an order directing the sale or mortgage of any land, every person who is entitled to or possessed of any interest in the land, or entitled to a contingent right therein, and is a party to the action or proceeding in which the judgment or order is given or made or is otherwise bound by the judgment or order, shall be deemed to be so entitled or possessed, as the case may be, as a trustee for the purpose of this Act, and the court may, if it thinks expedient, make an order vesting the land or any part thereof for such estate or interest as that court thinks fit in the purchaser or mortgagee or in any other person:

Provided that, in the case of a legal mortgage, the estate to be vested in the mortgagee shall be a term of years absolute.

Commentary

This section enables the court (defined in section 67(1)) to vest land in a purchaser or mortgagee when it orders sale or mortgage. The proviso ensures that mortgages take effect only as provided for by the Law of Property Act 1925 section 85–87. For examples of orders where this provision might be used, see: section 14 of the Trusts of Land and Appointment of Trustees Act 1996 **[445]** sections 90 and 91 of the Law of Property Act 1925 (sale of mortgaged land) Sections 32 and 38 of the Administration of Estates Act 1925 **[207; 213].**

[116]

48 Vesting order consequential on judgement for specific performance, etc

Where a judgment is given for the specific performance of a contract concerning any interest in land, or for sale or exchange of any interest in land, or generally where any judgment is given for the conveyance of any interest in land either in cases arising out of the doctrine of election or otherwise, the court may declare—

(a) that any of the parties to the action are trustees of any interest in the land or any part thereof within the meaning of this Act; or

(b) that the interests of unborn persons who might claim under any party to the action, or under the will or voluntary settlement of any deceased person who was during his lifetime a party to the contract or transaction concerning which the judgment is given, are the interests of persons who, on coming into existence, would be trustees within the meaning of this Act;

and thereupon the court may make a vesting order relating to the rights of those persons, born and unborn, as if they had been trustees.

Commentary

For the meaning of "court" see section 67(1) below. For the meaning of "conveyance" see section 68(1)(3) below. Usually when an order for specific performance is made the Court will enforce it by use of its powers under section 39 of the Supreme Court Act 1981.

[117]

49 Effect of vesting order

A vesting order under any of the foregoing provisions shall in the case of a vesting order consequential on the appointment of a trustee, have the same effect—

(a) as if the persons who before the appointment were the trustees, if any, had duly executed all proper conveyances of the land for such estate or interest as the court directs; or

(b) if there is no such person, or no such person of full capacity, as if such person had existed and been of full capacity and had duly executed all proper conveyances of the land for such estate or interest as the court directs;

and shall in every other case have the same effect as if the trustee or other person or description or class of persons to whose rights or supposed rights the said provisions respectively relate had been an ascertained and existing person of full capacity, and had executed a conveyance or release to the effect intended by the order.

Commentary
For the meaning of "court" see section 67(1) below. For the meaning of conveyance see section 68(1) (3) below. Usually when an order for specific performance is made the Court will enforce it by use of its powers under section 39 of the Supreme Court Act 1981.

[118]

50 Power to appoint person to convey

In all cases where a vesting order can be made under any of the foregoing provisions, the court may, if it is more convenient, appoint a person to convey the land or any interest therein or release the contingent right, and a conveyance or release by that person in conformity with the order shall have the same effect as an order under the appropriate provision.

Commentary
For the meaning of "court" see section 67(1) below. For an example of an order made under this section see: *Hipkin v Hipkin* [1962] 1 WLR 49. An application for such order which can be a useful adjunct to an order for sale made by the Court should be made not by the purchaser but by the person having the conduct of the sale, see: *Moorhead v Kirkwood* [1919] 1 Ir. R 225.

[119]

51 Vesting orders as to stock and things in action

(1) In any of the following cases, namely:—

(i) Where the court appoints or has appointed a trustee, or where a trustee has been appointed out of court under any statutory or express power;

(ii) Where a trustee entitled, whether by way of mortgage or otherwise, alone or jointly with another person to stock or to a thing in action—

(a) is under disability; or

(b) is out of the jurisdiction of the High Court; or

(c) cannot be found, or, being a corporation, has been dissolved; or

(d) neglects or refuses to transfer stock or receive the dividends or income thereof, or to sue for or recover a thing in action, according to the direction of the person absolutely entitled thereto for twenty-eight days next after a request in writing has been made to him by the person so entitled; or

(e) neglects or refuses to transfer stock or receive the dividends or income thereof, or to sue for or recover a thing in action for twenty-eight days next after an order of the court for that purpose has been served on him;

(iii) Where it is uncertain whether a trustee entitled alone or jointly with another person to stock or to a thing in action is alive or dead;

(iv) Where stock is standing in the name of a deceased person whose personal representative is under disability;

(v) Where stock or a thing in action is vested in a trustee whether by way of mortgage or otherwise and it appears to the court to be expedient;

the court may make an order vesting the right to transfer or call for a transfer of stock, or to receive the dividends or income thereof, or to sue for or recover the thing in action, in any such person as the court may appoint:

Provided that—

(a) Where the order is consequential on the appointment of a trustee, the right shall be vested in the persons who, on the appointment, are the trustees; and

(b) Where the person whose right is dealt with by the order was entitled jointly with another person, the right shall be vested in that last- mentioned person either alone or jointly with any other person whom the court may appoint.

(2) In all cases where a vesting order can be made under this section, the court may, if it is more convenient, appoint some proper person to make or join in making the transfer:

Provided that the person appointed to make or join in making a transfer of stock shall be some proper officer of the bank, or the company or society whose stock is to be transferred.

(3) The person in whom the right to transfer or call for the transfer of any stock is vested by an order of the court under this Act, may transfer the stock to himself or any other person, according to the order, and the [Registrar of Government Stock and any company] shall obey every order under this section according to its tenor.

(4) After notice in writing of an order under this section it shall not be lawful for the [Registrar of Government Stock or any company] to transfer any stock to which the order relates or to pay any dividends thereon except in accordance with the order.

(5) The court may make declarations and give directions concerning the manner in which the right to transfer any stock or thing in action vested under the provisions of this Act is to be exercised.

(6) The provisions of this Act as to vesting orders shall apply to shares in ships registered under the [Merchant Shipping Act 1995] as if they were stock.

Amendment

Sub-s (3): words "Registrar of Government Stock and any company" in square brackets substituted by SI 2004/1662, art 2, Sch, Pt 2, para 10(1), (2)(a).

Sub-s (4): words "Registrar of Government Stock or any company" in square brackets substituted by SI 2004/1662, art 2, Sch, Pt 2, para 10(1), (2)(b).

Sub-s (6): words in square brackets substituted by the Merchant Shipping Act 1995, s 314(2), Sch 13, para 13.

Commentary

For the meaning of "court" see section 67(1) below. For the meaning of "stock" see section 68(1)(14). Stock under this section includes an application for letters patent, see: *Re Defense Supplies Corporations' Application* (1948) 65 RPC 172. The section also applies to stock held by infants, see: *Re Dehaynin* [1910] 1 Ch 223. This section will be of particular use where there has been an appointment of trustees out of Court because stock will not vest automatically under section 40, although things in action will. Application for an Order under this section should be made by way of Part 8 claim form in accordance with Part 8 of the Civil Procedure Rules 1998. The proper form of order under this section is that the right to call for a transfer of and to transfer the stock or shares and to receive the dividends on them should vest in the new trustees and they should transfer the stock or shares into their own names, see: *Re Gregson* [1893] 3 Ch 233.

[120]

52 Vesting orders of charity property

The powers conferred by this Act as to vesting orders may be exercised for vesting any interest in land, stock, or thing in action in any trustee of a charity or society over which the court would have jurisdiction upon action duly instituted, whether the appointment of the trustee was made by instrument under a power or by the court under its general or statutory jurisdiction.

Commentary

For the meaning of "land" see section 68(1)(6) below. See also section 16 of the Charities Act 1960 for the vesting of charity property in the Official custodian for Charities.

[121]

53 Vesting orders in relation to infants' beneficial interests

Where an infant is beneficially entitled to any property the court may, with a view to the application of the capital or income thereof for the maintenance, education, or benefit of the infant, make an order—

(a) appointing a person to convey such property; or
(b) in the case of stock, or a thing in action, vesting in any person the right to transfer or call for a transfer of such stock, or to receive the dividends or income thereof, or to sue for and recover such thing in action, upon such terms as the court may think fit.

Commentary
For the meaning of "court" see section 67(1) below. For the meaning of "maintenance education and benefit" see the notes to section 31(1) above. This section only applies where an order is sought with a view to application of the capital or income "for the maintenance education or benefit" of the minor, see: *Re Heyworth's Contingent Reversionary Interest* [1956] Ch 364 but that requirement might be fulfilled if what is proposed is the transfer property to a settlement for the benefit of the minor, see: *Re Meux* [1958] Ch 154 and see now the power of the Court to approve arrangements on behalf of minor beneficiaries under the Variation of Trusts Act 1958 **[256]**. This section has been used to bar the entailed interests of minors allowing variation of the trusts without having to provide a benefit for those with subsequent interests upon the basis that this was for the benefit of the minor, see: *Re Bristol's Settled Estates* [1965] 1 WLR 469; *Re Lansdowne's Will Trusts* [1967] Ch 603.

[122]

[54 Jurisdiction in regard to mental patients]

[(1) Subject to subsection (2), the Court of Protection may not make an order, or give a direction or authority, in relation to a person who lacks capacity to exercise his functions as trustee, if the High Court may make an order to that effect under this Act.]

(2) [Where a person lacks capacity to exercise his functions as a trustee and a deputy is appointed for him by the Court of Protection or an application for the appointment of a deputy] has been made but not determined, then, except as respects a trust which is subject to an order for administration made by the High Court, [the Court of Protection] shall have concurrent jurisdiction with the High Court in relation to—
(a) mortgaged property of which [the person concerned] has become a trustee merely by reason of the mortgage having been paid off;
(b) matters consequent on the making of provision by [the Court of Protection] for the exercise of a power of appointing trustees or retiring from a trust;
(c) matters consequent on the making of provision by [the Court of Protection] for the carrying out of any contract entered into by [the person concerned];
(d) property to some interest in which [the person concerned] is beneficially entitled but which, or some interest in which, is held by [the person concerned] under an express, implied or constructive trust.

[(2A) Rules may be made in accordance with Part 1 of Schedule 1 to the Constitutional Reform Act 2005 with respect to the exercise of the jurisdiction referred to in subsection (2).]

(3) . . .

Amendment
Substituted by the Mental Health Act 1959, s 149(1), Sch 7, Part I.
Sub-s (1): substituted by the Mental Capacity Act 2005, s 67(1), Sch 6, para 3(1), (4)(a).
Sub-s (2): words from "Where a person" to "of a deputy" substituted by the Mental Capacity Act 2005, s 67(1), Sch 6, para 3(1), (4)(b)(i).
Sub-s (2): words "the Court of Protection" in each place they occur substituted by the Mental Capacity Act 2005, s 67(1), Sch 6, para 3(1), (4)(b)(ii).
Sub-s (2): words "the person concerned" in each place they occur substituted by the Mental Capacity Act 2005, s 67(1), Sch 6, para 3(1), (4)(b)(iii).
Sub-s (2A): substituted by the Constitutional Reform Act 2005, s 12(2), Sch 1, Pt 2, para 6.
Sub-s (3): repealed by the Mental Capacity Act 2005, s 67(1), (2), Sch 6, para 3(1), (4)(c), Sch 7.

Commentary

Reference should be made to the Mental Capacity Act 2005 **[562]**. The test of whether someone does not have capacity to exercise their functions as trustee is an issue specific one. A deputy replaces the office of a receiver for someone who lacks capacity to deal with some or all of their affairs. This section confers on the Court of Protection jurisdiction to deal with matters which would otherwise have to be referred to the High court where a trustee is incapable of carrying out his functions as such and a deputy has been appointed or is in the process of being appointed.

[123]

55 Orders made upon certain allegations to be conclusive evidence

Where a vesting order is made as to any land under this Act or under [sections 15 to 20 of the Mental Capacity Act 2005 or any corresponding provisions having effect in Northern Ireland], founded on an allegation of any of the following matters namely—

[(a) that a trustee or mortgagee lacks capacity in relation to the matter in question;] or

(b) that a trustee or mortgagee or the personal representative of or other person deriving title under a trustee or mortgagee is out of the jurisdiction of the High Court or cannot be found, or being a corporation has been dissolved; or

(c) that it is uncertain which of two or more trustees, or which of two or more persons interested in a mortgage, was the survivor; or

(d) that it is uncertain whether the last trustee or the personal representative of or other person deriving title under a trustee or mortgagee, or the last surviving person interested in a mortgage is living or dead: or

(e) that any trustee or mortgagee has died intestate without leaving a person beneficially interested under the intestacy or has died and it is not known who is his personal representative or the person interested;

the fact that the order has been so made shall be conclusive evidence of the matter so alleged in any court upon any question as to the validity of the order; but this section does not prevent the court from directing a reconveyance or surrender or the payment of costs occasioned by any such order if improperly obtained.

Amendment

Words from "sections 15 to 20" to "in Northern Ireland" substituted by the Mental Capacity Act 2005, s 67(1), Sch 6, para 3(1), (5)(a).
Para (a) substituted by the Mental Capacity Act 2005, s 67(1), Sch 6, para 3(1), (5)(b).

Commentary

Note that this section does not cover all the circumstances in which the court can make a vesting order, including those in section 44(v).

[124]

56 Application of vesting order to property out of England

The powers of the court to make vesting orders under this Act shall extend to all property in any part of His Majesty's dominions except Scotland.

Commentary

As to where intangible movable property is situate for these purposes, see: *Re Helbert Wagg and Co. Ltd's Claim* [1956] 1 Ch.

[125]

JURISDICTION TO MAKE OTHER ORDERS

57 Power of court to authorise dealings with trust property

(1) Where in the management or administration of any property vested in trustees, any sale, lease, mortgage, surrender, release, or other disposition, or any purchase,

investment, acquisition, expenditure, or other transaction, is in the opinion of the court expedient, but the same cannot be effected by reason of the absence of any power for that purpose vested in the trustees by the trust instrument, if any, or by law, the court may by order confer upon the trustees, either generally or in any particular instance, the necessary power for the purpose, on such terms, and subject to such provisions and conditions, if any, as the court may think fit and may direct in what manner any money authorised to be expended, and the costs of any transaction, are to be paid or borne as between capital and income.

(2) The court may, from time to time, rescind or vary any order made under this section, or may make any new or further order.

(3) An application to the court under this section may be made by the trustees, or by any of them, or by any person beneficially interested under the trust.

(4) This section does not apply to trustees of a settlement for the purposes of the Settled Land Act 1925.

Commentary

For the meaning of "court" see section 67(1) below. Application is made by way of Part 8 claim form in accordance with Part 8 of the Civil Procedure Rules 1998. For the section to apply the Court must be satisfied that what is proposed is expedient for the trust as a whole (see: *Re Craven's Estate (no. 2)* [1937] Ch 431). The Court only has jurisdiction where the trustees do not have power, see: *Re Thomas* [1930] 1 Ch 194. Neither can the Court use this section to vary trusts, see: *Chapman v Chapman* [1954] AC 429 but see now the jurisdiction of the Court under the Variation of Trusts Act 1958 **[256]**. The section applies to charitable trusts, see: *Re Harvey, Westminster Bank Ltd. V Askwith* [1941] 3 All ER 284. The section has often been used to extend the trustees' powers of investment and delegation, see: *Anker-Petersen v Anker-Petersen* (1998) 12 TLI 166. This aspect of the jurisdiction has become far less important now that the Trustee Act 2000 **[476]** is in force. For some other examples of the way in which the Court has used this section see, for example: partition of land: *Re Thomas* [1930] 1 Ch 194; sale of chattels *Re Hope's Will Trusts, Hope v Thorp* [1929] 2 Ch 36; sale where requisite consent refused to trustees: *Re Beale's Settlement Trusts, Huggins v Beale* [1932] 2 Ch 15; raising of capital to pay debts of beneficiary *Re Salting, Baillie-Hamilton v Morgan* [1932] 2 Ch 57; purchasing a home for a beneficiary, *Re Power's Will Trusts* [1947] Ch 472; (now section 8 of the Trustee Act 2000 would govern) **[483]**. As to subsection (3) the trustees are normally the applicants for an order under this section. Subsection (4) disapplies this section to strict settlements but section 64 of the Settled Land Act 1925 **[Appendix II]** provides an even wider power. See also Settled Land and Trustee Acts (Court's General Powers) Act 1943 **[239]** which extends the section to trusts of land.

[126]

58 Persons entitled to apply for orders

(1) An order under this Act for the appointment of a new trustee or concerning any interest in land, stock, or thing in action subject to a trust, may be made on the application of any person beneficially interested in the land, stock, or thing in action, whether under disability or not, or on the application of any person duly appointed trustee thereof.

(2) An order under this Act concerning any interest in land, stock, or thing in action subject to a mortgage may be made on the application of any person beneficially interested in the equity of redemption, whether under disability or not, or of any person interested in the money secured by the mortgage.

Commentary

A contingent interest will be enough to satisfy the requirements of this section, see: *Re Sheppard's Trusts* (1862) 4 D.F.& J. 423.

[127]

59 Power to give judgment in absence of a trustee

Where in any action the court is satisfied that diligent search has been made for any person who, in the character of trustee, is made a defendant in any action, to serve him with a process of the court, and that he cannot be found, the court may hear and determine the action and give judgment therein against that person in his character of a trustee as if he had been duly served, or had entered an appearance in the action, and had also appeared by his counsel and solicitor at the hearing, but without prejudice to any interest he may have in the matters in question in the action in any other character.

Commentary

An action also will include a Part 8 claim. Note that Defendant trustees no longer enter an appearance but acknowledge service under Part 10 of the Civil Procedure Rules 1998.

[128]

60 Power to charge costs on trust estate

The court may order the costs and expenses of and incident to any application for an order appointing a new trustee, or for a vesting order, or of and incident to any such order, or any conveyance or transfer in pursuance thereof, to be raised and paid out of the property in respect whereof the same is made, or out of the income thereof, or to be borne and paid in such manner and by such persons as to the court may seem just.

Commentary

Where the application is for the benefit of the estate or fund as a whole, the usual order will be for costs to come out of the estate, but this will not be the practice where trustees have been removed under section 41 or where there has been the need to seek a vesting order under one of the preceding section (e.g. sections 44 or 51) because a trustee has failed to transfer trust assets, see: *Re Knox's Trusts* [1895] 2 Ch 483. In those cases the defaulting trustee should expect to pay the costs.

[129]

61 Power to relieve trustee from personal liability

If it appears to the court that a trustee, whether appointed by the court or otherwise, is or may be personally liable for any breach of trust, whether the transaction alleged to be a breach of trust occurred before or after the commencement of this Act, but has acted honestly and reasonably, and ought fairly to be excused for the breach of trust and for omitting to obtain the directions of the court in the matter in which he committed such breach, then the court may relieve him either wholly or partly from personal liability for the same.

Commentary

This section confers on the Court a discretion to relieve a trustee and how that discretion is exercised will vary from case to case, see: *Re Pauling's Settlement Trusts* [1964] Ch 303. For the section to apply there has first of all to be a breach of trust and not just an imprudent act on the part of the trustees, see: *Re Rosenthal* [1972] 1 WLR 1273. The trustee has the burden of establishing that he has acted honestly and reasonably and ought fairly to be excused, which requirements are cumulative and not alternative, see: *Re Stuart* [1897] 2 Ch 583 and *National Trustees Company of Australasia Ltd. V General Finance Company of Australasia Ltd.* [1905] AC 373. The jurisdiction is not narrow and is designed to relieve an honest trustee, see: *Re Allsop Whittaker v Bamford* [1914] Ch 1. In looking at the question of whether the trustee has been reasonable the question is whether a reasonable man would have dealt with property in the way in which the trustee dealt with the trust property, see: *Re Turner* [1897] 1 Ch 536. The fact that the trustee has acted on legal advice will not necessarily excuse him, see: *Marsden v Regan* [1954] 1 WLR 423; The Court will be slower to relieve a remunerated trustee (see: *Bartlett v Barclays Bank Trust Co. Ltd.* [1980] Ch 515) than a lay trustee (see: *Wohleton v Canada Permanent Trust Co* (1976) 70 DLR (3d.) 257). Although the old practice was that the section need not be pleaded, this is almost certainly not the case under the new Civil Procedure Rules 1998 (see Part 16 as to statements of case).

[130]

62 Power to make beneficiary indemnify for breach of trust

(1) Where a trustee commits a breach of trust at the instigation or request or with the consent in writing of a beneficiary, the court may, if it thinks fit, . . . make such order as to the court seems just, for impounding all or any part of the interest of the beneficiary in the trust estate by way of indemnity to the trustee or persons claiming through him.

(2) This section applies to breaches of trust committed as well before as after the commencement of this Act.

Amendment
Sub-s (1): words omitted repealed by the Married Women (Restraint upon Anticipation) Act 1949, s 1(4), Sch 2.

Commentary
For the meaning of "court" see section 67(1) below. The section will not bite if the beneficiary simply had notice of the breach—there must be more active involvement on the part of the beneficiary, although it is not necessary for the beneficiary to know that what has happened is a breach of trust, simply the facts that give rise to it, see: *Re Somerset* [1894] 1 Ch 265. This section can operate in favour of a former trustee, see: *Re Pauling's Settlement Trusts* [1964] Ch 303. The interest of a beneficiary notwithstanding that it has been assigned for value can nevertheless be impounded under this section, as was the case under the former law, see: *Bolton v Curre* [1895] 1 Ch 544.

[131]

PAYMENT INTO COURT

63 Payment into court by trustees

(1) Trustees, or the majority of trustees, having in their hands or under their control money or securities belonging to a trust, may pay the same into court; . . .

(2) The receipt or certificate of the proper officer shall be a sufficient discharge to trustees for the money or securities so paid into court.

(3) Where money or securities are vested in any persons as trustees, and the majority are desirous of paying the same into court, but the concurrence of the other or others cannot be obtained, the court may order the payment into court to be made by the majority without the concurrence of the other or others.

(4) Where any such money or securities are deposited with any banker, broker, or other depository, the court may order payment or delivery of the money or securities to the majority of the trustees for the purpose of payment into court.

(5) Every transfer payment and delivery made in pursuance of any such order shall be valid and take effect as if the same had been made on the authority or by the act of all the persons entitled to the money and securities so transferred, paid, or delivered.

Amendment
Sub-s (1): words omitted repealed by the Administration of Justice Act 1965, s 36(4), Sch 3.

Commentary
Trustees should use their power to pay in under this section as a last resort, and if they do so without justification, they may be found liable to pay the costs, see: *Re Beddoe* [1893] 1 Ch 547; *Re Salaman* [1908] 1 Ch 4. The effect of payment in is draconian and will result in the retirement of the trustees who cannot then exercise any discretionary powers, see: *Re Nettlefold* (1888) 59 LT 315. The trustees remain liable for breach of trust notwithstanding the

payment into court, see: *A-G v Allford* (1855) 2 Sm. & G. 488. Now that trustees have protection under section 27 (see above) and can apply to the Court for directions under Part 64 of the Civil Procedure Rules 1998, there is little need for this section. The only use might be where a beneficiary cannot be found and an order under *Re Benjamin* is not appropriate.

[132]

[63A Jurisdiction of County Court]

[(1) The county court has jurisdiction under the following provisions where the amount or value of the trust estate or fund to be dealt with in the court does not exceed the county court limit—

section 41;
section 42;
section 51;
section 57;
section 60;
section 61;
section 62.

(2) The county court has jurisdiction under the following provisions where the land or the interest or contingent right in land which is to be dealt with in the court forms part of a trust estate which does not exceed in amount or value the county court limit—

section 44;
section 45;
section 46.

(3) The county court has jurisdiction—

(a) under sections 47 and 48 of this Act, where the judgment is given or order is made by the court;
(b) under sections 50 and 56, where a vesting order can be made by the court;
(c) under section 53, where the amount or value of the property to be dealt with in the court does not exceed the county court limit; and
(d) under section 63 (including power to receive payment of money or securities into court) where the money or securities to be paid into court do not exceed in amount or value the county court limit.

(4) Any reference to the court in section 59 of this Act includes a reference to the county court.

(5) In this section, in its application to any enactment, 'the county court limit' means the amount for the time being specified by an Order in Council under section 145 of the County Courts Act 1984 as the county court limit for the purposes of that enactment (or, where no such Order in Council has been made, the corresponding limit specified by Order in Council under section 192 of the County Courts Act 1959).]

Amendment

Inserted by the County Courts Act 1984, s 148(1), Sch 2, para 1.

Commentary

The county court limit referred to in subsection (5) currently stands at £30,000.

[133]

PART V
GENERAL PROVISIONS

64 Application of Act to Settled Land Act Trustees

(1) All the powers and provisions contained in this Act with reference to the appointment of new trustees, and the discharge and retirement of trustees, apply to

and include trustees for the purposes of the Settled Land Act 1925, and trustees for the purpose of the management of land during a minority, whether such trustees are appointed by the court or by the settlement, or under provisions contained in any instrument.

(2) Where, either before or after the commencement of this Act, trustees of a settlement have been appointed by the court for the purposes of the Settled Land Acts 1882 to 1890, or of the Settled Land Act 1925, then, after the commencement of this Act—

(a) the person or persons nominated for the purpose of appointing new trustees by the instrument, if any, creating the settlement, though no trustees for the purposes of the said Acts were thereby appointed; or

(b) if there is no such person, or no such person able and willing to act, the surviving or continuing trustees or trustee for the time being for the purposes of the said Acts or the personal representatives of the last surviving or continuing trustee for those purposes,

shall have the powers conferred by this Act to appoint new or additional trustees of the settlement for the purposes of the said Acts.

(3) Appointments of new trustees for the purposes of the said Acts made or expressed to be made before the commencement of this Act by the trustees or trustee or personal representatives referred to in paragraph (b) of the last preceding subsection or by the persons referred to in paragraph (a) of that subsection are, without prejudice to any order of the court made before such commencement, hereby confirmed.

[134]

Commentary

This section applies the powers and provisions in relation to the discharge and appointment of trustees to Settled Land Act trustees.

65 . . .

. . .

Amendment

Repealed by the Criminal Law Act 1967, s 10, Sch 3, Pt I.

[135]

66 Indemnity to banks, etc

This Act, and every order purporting to be made under this Act, shall be a complete indemnity to the Bank of England[, the Registrar of Government Stock, any previous Registrar of Government Stock], and to all persons for any acts done pursuant thereto, and it shall not be necessary for the Bank[, the Registrar of Government Stock, any previous Registrar of Government Stock] or for any person to inquire concerning the propriety of the order, or whether the court by which the order was made had jurisdiction to make it.

Amendment

Words ", the Registrar of Government Stock, any previous Registrar of Government Stock" in square brackets in both places they occur inserted by SI 2004/1662, art 2, Sch, Pt 2, para 10(1), (3).

Commentary

As to the indemnity given to the Bank under this section see: *Re Spurling* [1909] 1 Ch 199.

[136]

67 Jurisdiction of the "court"

(1) In this Act "the court" means the High Court . . . or the county court, where those courts respectively have jurisdiction.

(2) The procedure under this Act in . . . county courts shall be in accordance with the Acts and rules regulating the procedure of those courts.

Amendment

Words omitted repealed by the Courts Act 1971, s 56, Sch 11, Part II.

Commentary

See section 63A above in relation to the jurisdiction of the County Court.

[137]

68 Definitions

[(1)] In this Act, unless the context otherwise requires, the following expressions have the meanings hereby assigned to them respectively, that is to say:—

(1) "Authorised investments" mean investments authorised by the instrument, if any, creating the trust for the investment of money subject to the trust, or by law;

(2) "Contingent right" as applied to land includes a contingent or executory interest, a possibility coupled with an interest, whether the object of the gift or limitation of the interest, or possibility is or is not ascertained, also a right of entry, whether immediate or future, and whether vested or contingent;

(3) "Convey" and "conveyance" as applied to any person include the execution by that person of every necessary or suitable assurance (including an assent) for conveying, assigning, appointing, surrendering, or otherwise transferring or disposing of land whereof he is seised or possessed, or wherein he is entitled to a contingent right, either for his whole estate or for any less estate, together with the performance of all formalities required by law for the validity of the conveyance; "sale" includes an exchange;

(4) "Gazette" means the London Gazette;

(5) "Instrument" includes Act of Parliament;

(6) "Land" includes land of any tenure, and mines and minerals, whether or not severed from the surface, buildings or parts of buildings, whether the division is horizontal, vertical or made in any other way, and other corporeal hereditaments; also a manor, an advowson, and a rent and other incorporeal hereditaments, and an easement, right, privilege, or benefit in, over, or derived from . . . ; and in this definition "mines and minerals" include any strata or seam of minerals or substances in or under any land, and powers of working and getting the same . . . ; and "hereditaments" mean real property which under an intestacy occurring before the commencement of this Act might have devolved on an heir;

(7) "Mortgage" and "mortgagee" include a charge or chargee by way of legal mortgage, and relate to every estate and interest regarded in equity as merely a security for money, and every person deriving title under the original mortgagee;

(8) . . .

(9) "Personal representative" means the executor, original or by representation, or administrator for the time being of a deceased person;

(10) "Possession" includes receipt of rents and profits or the right to receive the same, if any; "income" includes rents and profits; and "possessed" applies

to receipt of income of and to any vested estate less than a life interest in possession or in expectancy in any land;

(11) "Property" includes real and personal property, and any estate share and interest in any property, real or personal, and any debt, and any thing in action, and any other right or interest, whether in possession or not;

(12) "Rights" include estates and interests;

(13) "Securities" include stocks, funds, and shares; . . . and "securities payable to bearer" include securities transferable by delivery or by delivery and endorsement;

(14) "Stock" includes fully paid up shares, and so far as relates to vesting orders made by the court under this Act, includes any fund, annuity, or security transferable in books kept by any company or society, or by instrument of transfer either alone or accompanied by other formalities, and any share or interest therein;

(15) "Tenant for life," "statutory owner," "settled land," "settlement," "trust instrument," "trustees of the settlement" . . . "term of years absolute" and "vesting instrument" have the same meanings as in the Settled Land Act 1925, and "entailed interest" has the same meaning as in the Law of Property Act 1925;

(16) "Transfer" in relation to stock or securities, includes the performance and execution of every deed, power of attorney, act, and thing on the part of the transferor to effect and complete the title in the transferee;

(17) "Trust" does not include the duties incident to an estate conveyed by way of mortgage, but with this exception the expressions "trust" and "trustee" extend to implied and constructive trusts, and to cases where the trustee has a beneficial interest in the trust property, and to the duties incident to the office of a personal representative, and "trustee" where the context admits, includes a personal representative, and "new trustee" includes an additional trustee;

(18) "Trust corporation" means the Public Trustee or a corporation either appointed by the court in any particular case to be a trustee, or entitled by rules made under subsection (3) of section four of the Public Trustee Act 1906, to act as custodian trustee;

(19) "Trust for sale" in relation to land means an immediate . . . trust for sale, whether or not exercisable at the request or with the consent of any person . . . ;

(20) "United Kingdom" means Great Britain and Northern Ireland.

[(2) Any reference in this Act to paying money or securities into court shall be construed as referring to paying the money or transferring or depositing the securities into or in the *Supreme Court* [Senior Courts] or into or in any other court that has jurisdiction, and any reference in this Act to payment of money or securities into court shall be construed—

(a) with reference to an order of the High Court, as referring to payment of the money or transfer or deposit of the securities into or in the *Supreme Court* [Senior Courts]; and

(b) with reference to an order of any other court, as referring to payment of the money or transfer or deposit of the securities into or in that court.]

[(3) Any reference in this Act to a person who lacks capacity in relation to a matter is to a person—

(a) who lacks capacity within the meaning of the Mental Capacity Act 2005 in relation to that matter, or

(b) in respect of whom the powers conferred by section 48 of that Act are exercisable and have been exercised in relation to that matter.]

Amendment

Sub-s (1): words omitted from paras (6), (19) repealed by the Trusts of Land and Appointment of Trustees Act 1996, s 25(2), Sch 4, for savings in relation to entailed interests created before the commencement of that Act, and savings consequential upon the abolition of the doctrine of conversion, see s 25(4), (5) thereof; para (8) repealed, and words omitted from para (13) repealed, by the Administration of Justice Act 1965, s 17(1), Sch 1; words omitted from para (15) repealed by the Mental Health Act 1959 s 149(2), Sch 8, Part I.
Sub-s (2): inserted by the Administration of Justice Act 1965, s 17(1), Sch 1.
Sub-s (2): words "Supreme Court" in italics in both places they occur repealed and subsequent words in square brackets substituted, from a date to be appointed, by the Constitutional Reform Act 2005, s 59(5), Sch 11, Pt 2, para 4(1), (3).
Sub-s (3): inserted, from a date to be appointed, by the Mental Capacity Act 2005, s 67(1), Sch 6, para 3(1), (6).

Commentary

These definitions are referred to throughout the notes to the various sections in which the expressions appear. Note under subsection (1) "authorised investments" will now be those permitted by the Trustee Act 2000 **[476]**.

[138]

69 Application of Act

(1) This Act, except where otherwise expressly provided, applies to trusts including, so far as this Act applies thereto, executorships and administratorships constituted or created either before or after the commencement of this Act.

(2) The powers conferred by this Act on trustees are in addition to the powers conferred by the instrument, if any, creating the trust, but those powers, unless otherwise stated, apply if and so far only as a contrary intention is not expressed in the instrument, if any, creating the trust, and have effect subject to the terms of that instrument.

(3) . . .

Amendment

Sub-s (3): repealed by the Statute Law (Repeals) Act 1978, s 1, Sch 1, Part XVII.

Commentary

Subsection (2) is crucial, making it clear that the default powers conferred by the Act are subject to a contrary intention in the trust instrument and indeed it is common practice to exclude and modify the powers under this Act in modern settlements. The presence of a provision in a settlement or will which is inconsistent with a statutory power will be enough to exclude it and express exclusion is not required, see: *Re Erskine's Settlement, Hollis v Piggott* [1971] 1 All ER 572.

[139]

70 Enactments repealed

. . . without prejudice to the provisions of section thirty-eight of the Interpretation Act 1889:

- (a) Nothing in this repeal shall affect any vesting order or appointment made or other thing done under any enactment so repealed, and any order or appointment so made may be revoked or varied in like manner as if it has been made under this Act;
- (b) References in any document to any enactment repealed by this Act shall be construed as references to this Act or to the corresponding enactment in this Act.

Amendment
Words omitted repealed by the Statute Law Revision Act 1950.

[140]

71 Short title, commencement, extent

(1) This Act may be cited as the Trustee Act, 1925.

(2) . . .

(3) This Act, except where otherwise expressly provided, extends to England and Wales only.

(4) The provisions of this Act bind the Crown.

Amendment
Sub-s (2): repealed by the Statute Law Revision Act 1950.

[141]

SCHEDULE 1

. . .

Amendment
Repealed by the Statute Law (Repeals) Act 1978.

[142]

SCHEDULE 2

. . .

Amendment
Repealed by the Statute Law Revision Act 1950.

[143]

LAW OF PROPERTY ACT 1925

1925 Chapter 20

ARRANGEMENT OF SECTIONS

PART I
GENERAL PRINCIPLES AS TO LEGAL ESTATES, EQUITABLE INTERESTS AND POWERS

PART II
CONTRACTS, CONVEYANCES AND OTHER INSTRUMENTS

PART IV
EQUITABLE INTERESTS AND THINGS IN ACTION

PART VI
POWERS

PART VII
PERPETUITIES AND ACCUMULATIONS

PART X
WILLS

PART XI
MISCELLANEOUS

PART XII
CONSTRUCTION, JURISDICTION, AND GENERAL PROVISIONS

An Act to consolidate the enactments relating to Conveyancing and the Law of Property in England and Wales

[9th April 1925]

General Note
In many ways this Act underpins all the other legislation of 1925 and indeed beyond. Only those sections which have a direct bearing on trusts and estates have been reproduced and annotated here.

PART I
GENERAL PRINCIPLES AS TO LEGAL ESTATES, EQUITABLE INTERESTS AND POWERS

2 Conveyances overreaching certain equitable interests and powers

(1) A conveyance to a purchaser of a legal estate in land shall overreach any equitable interest or power affecting that estate, whether or not he has notice thereof, if—

(i) the conveyance is made under the powers conferred by the Settled Land Act 1925 or any additional powers conferred by a settlement, and the equitable interest or power is capable of being overreached thereby, and the statutory requirements respecting the payment of capital money arising under the settlement are complied with;

(ii) the conveyance is made by [trustees of land] and the equitable interest or power is at the date of the conveyance capable of being overreached by such trustees under the provisions of subsection (2) of this section or independently of that subsection, and [the requirements of section 27 of this Act respecting the payment of capital money arising on such a conveyance] are complied with;

(iii) the conveyance is made by a mortgagee or personal representative in the exercise of his paramount powers, and the equitable interest or power is capable of being overreached by such conveyance, and any capital money arising from the transaction is paid to the mortgagee or personal representative;

(iv) the conveyance is made under an order of the court and the equitable interest or power is bound by such order, and any capital money arising from the transaction is paid into, or in accordance with the order of, the court.

[(1A) An equitable interest in land subject to a trust of land which remains in, or is to revert to, the settler shall (subject to any contrary intention) be overreached by the conveyance if it would be so overreached were it an interest under the trust.]

(2) [Where the legal estate affected is subject to [a trust of land], then if at the date of a conveyance made after the commencement of this Act [by the trustees], the trustees (whether original or substituted) are either—]

(a) two or more individuals approved or appointed by the court or the successors in office of the individuals so approved or appointed; or

(b) a trust corporation,

[any equitable interest or power having priority [to the trust]] shall, notwithstanding any stipulation to the contrary, be overreached by the conveyance, and shall, according to its priority, take effect as if created or arising by means of a primary trust affecting the proceeds of sale and the income of the land until sale.

(3) The following equitable interests and powers are excepted from the operation of subsection (2) of this section, namely—

(i) Any equitable interest protected by a deposit of documents relating to the legal estate affected;

(ii) The benefit of any covenant or agreement restrictive of the user of land;

(iii) Any easement, liberty, or privilege over or affecting land and being merely an equitable interest (in this Act referred to as an "equitable easement");

(iv) The benefit of any contract (in this Act referred to as an "estate contract") to convey or create a legal estate, including a contract conferring either expressly or by statutory implication a valid option to purchase, a right of pre-emption, or any other like right;

(v) Any equitable interest protected by registration under the Land Charges Act 1925 other than—

(a) an annuity within the meaning of Part II of that Act;

(b) a limited owner's charge or a general equitable charge within the meaning of that Act.

(4) Subject to the protection afforded by this section to the purchaser of a legal estate, nothing contained in this section shall deprive a person entitled to an equitable charge of any of his rights or remedies for enforcing the same.

(5) So far as regards the following interests, created before the commencement of this Act (which accordingly are not within the provisions of the Land Charges Act 1925), namely—

(a) the benefit of any covenant or agreement restrictive of the user of the land;

(b) any equitable easement;

(c) the interest under a puisne mortgage within the meaning of the Land Charges Act 1925 unless and until acquired under a transfer made after the commencement of this Act;

(d) the benefit of an estate contract, unless and until the same is acquired under a conveyance made after the commencement of this Act;

a purchaser of a legal estate shall only take subject thereto if he has notice thereof, and the same are not overreached under the provisions contained or in the manner referred to in this section.

Amendment

Sub-s (1): words in square brackets substituted by the Trusts of Land and Appointment of Trustees Act 1996, s 25(1), Sch 3, para 4(2)(a); for savings in relation to entailed interests created before the commencement of that Act, and savings consequential upon the abolition of the doctrine of conversion, see s 25(4), (5) thereof.

Sub-s (1A): inserted by the Trusts of Land and Appointment of Trustees Act 1996, s 25(1), Sch 3, para 4(2)(b); for savings in relation to entailed interests created before the commencement of that Act, and savings consequential upon the abolition of the doctrine of conversion, see s 25(4), (5) thereof.

Sub-s (2): first and fourth words in square brackets substituted by the Law of Property (Amendment) Act 1926, s 7, Schedule; other words in square brackets substituted by the Trusts of Land and Appointment of Trustees Act 1996, s 25(1), Sch 3, para 4(2)(c), for savings in relation to entailed interests created before the commencement of that Act, and savings consequential upon the abolition of the doctrine of conversion, see s 25(4), (5) thereof.

Commentary

Overreaching occurs where the transfer of the legal estate does not defeat equitable interests but the purchaser is not concerned to see the concurrence of those having such interests. For the meaning of "conveyance in subsection (1) see section 205(1)(iii) below and purchaser section 205(1)(xxi). As to subsection (1)(ii) for the overreaching powers in the Settled Land Act 1925 see section 72 thereof **[Appendix II]**. For the meaning of trustees of land (subsection (1)(ii) see the Trusts of Land and Appointment of Trustees Act 1996 **[431]**. Subsection (2) stresses the importance of trusts of land having at least two trustees or a trust corporation so that equitable interests are overreached.

[144]

9 Vesting orders and dispositions of legal estates operating as conveyances by an estate owner

(1) Every such order, declaration, or conveyance as is hereinafter mentioned, namely—

(a) every vesting order made by any court or other competent authority;

(b) every vesting declaration (express or implied) under any statutory power;

(c) every vesting instrument made by the trustees of a settlement or other persons under the provisions of the Settled Land Act 1925;
(d) every conveyance by a person appointed for the purpose under an order of the court or authorised under any statutory power to convey in the name or on behalf of an estate owner;
(e) every conveyance made under any power reserved or conferred by this Act,

which is made or executed for the purpose of vesting, conveying, or creating a legal estate, shall operate to convey or create the legal estate disposed of in like manner as if the same had been a conveyance executed by the estate owner of the legal estate to which the order, declaration, vesting instrument, or conveyance relates.

(2) Where the order, declaration, or conveyance is made in favour of a purchaser, the provisions of this Act relating to a conveyance of a legal estate to a purchaser shall apply thereto.

(3) The provisions of the Trustee Act 1925 relating to vesting orders and orders appointing a person to convey shall apply to all vesting orders authorised to be made by this Part of this Act.

Commentary
For vesting orders see Trustee Act 1925 sections 44–49 **[113–118]** and the Settled Land Act 1925 sections 12 and 16 **[Appendix II]** and sections 38(2), and 43(2) of the Administration of Estates Act 1925 **[213, 218]**

[145]

20 Infants not to be appointed trustees

The appointment of an infant to be a trustee in relation to any settlement or trust shall be void, but without prejudice to the power to appoint a new trustee to fill the vacancy.

Commentary
Where a minor does become a trustee see section 36(1) of the Trustee Act 1925 **[105]** for the powers to replace the minor.

[146]

21 Receipts by married infants

A married infant shall have power to give valid receipts for all income (including statutory accumulations of income made during the minority) to which the infant may be entitled in like manner as if the infant were of full age.

Commentary
Note that married male and female infants are here treated equally. For statutory accumulations of income see section 31 of the Trustee Act 1925 **[100].**

[147]

[22 Conveyances on behalf of persons suffering from mental disorder and as to land held by them [in trust]

(1) Where a legal estate in land (whether settled or not) is vested [either solely or jointly with any other person or persons, in a person lacking capacity (within the meaning of the Mental Capacity Act 2005) to convey or create a legal estate, a deputy appointed for him by the Court of Protection or (if no deputy is appointed] for him) any person authorised in that behalf shall, under an order of [the Court of Protection], or of the court, or under any statutory power, make or concur in making all requisite dispositions for conveying or creating a legal estate in his name and on his behalf.

(2) If land [subject to a trust of land] is vested, either solely or jointly with any other

person or persons, in a person who [lacks capacity (within the meaning of that Act) to exercise] his functions as trustee, a new trustee shall be appointed in the place of that person, or he shall be otherwise discharged from the trust, before the legal estate is dealt with [by the trustees].

[(3) Subsection (2) of this section does not prevent a legal estate being dealt with without the appointment of a new trustee, or the discharge of the incapable trustee, at a time when the donee of [an enduring power of attorney or lasting power of attorney (within the meaning of the 2005 Act) is entitled to act for the trustee who lacks capacity in relation to the dealing].]

Amendment

Substituted by the Mental Health Act 1959, s 149(1), Sch 7, Part I.
Section heading: words in square brackets substituted by the Trusts of Land and Appointment of Trustees Act 1996, s 25(1), Sch 3, para 4(6); for savings in relation to entailed interests created before the commencement of that Act, and savings consequential upon the abolition of the doctrine of conversion, see s 25(4), (5) thereof.
Sub-s (1): words from ", either solely" to "is appointed" substituted by the Mental Capacity Act 2005, s 67(1), Sch 6, para 4(1), (2)(a)(i).
Sub-s (1): words "the Court of Protection" substituted by the Mental Capacity Act 2005, s 67(1), Sch 6, para 4(1), (2)(a)(ii).
Sub-s (2): words "lacks capacity (within the meaning of that Act) to exercise" substituted by the Mental Capacity Act 2005, s 67(1), Sch 6, para 4(1), (2)(b).
Sub-s (2): words "subject to a trust of land" and "by the trustees" in square brackets substituted by the Trusts of Land and Appointment of Trustees Act 1996, s 25(1), Sch 3, para 4(6); for savings in relation to entailed interests created before the commencement of that Act, and savings consequential upon the abolition of the doctrine of conversion, see s 25(4), (5) thereof.
Sub-s (3): inserted by the Trustee Delegation Act 1999, s 9.
Sub-s (3): words from "an enduring power" to the end substituted by the Mental Capacity Act 2005, s 67(1), Sch 6, para 4(1), (2)(c).

Commentary

This section has been substantially amended by the Mental Capacity Act 2005 **[562]** to take into account the issue specific approach to capacity. It is capacity to carry out his functions as a trustee which is important. Note that a deputy is now appointed under the Mental Capacity Act 2005 to carry out the functions of a trustee who is not capable of doing so himself, rather than a receiver as under the old law. Subsection (3) inserted by the Trustee Delegation Act 1999 **[471]** has the effect of softening the impact of subsection (2) so that where there is a trustee of land who is incapable of carrying out his functions but who has granted an enduring power of attorney or (as they can no longer be granted) a lasting power of attorney under the Mental Capacity Act 2005, the donee can carry out the duties as trustees. See also sections 36(6A) and (6D) of the Trustee act 1925 **[105]**.

[148]

[24 Appointment of trustees of land

(1) The persons having power to appoint new trustees of land shall be bound to appoint the same persons (if any) who are for the time being trustees of any trust of the proceeds of sale of the land.

(2) A purchaser shall not be concerned to see that subsection (1) of this section has been complied with.

(3) This section applies whether the trust of land and the trust of proceeds of sale are created, or arise, before or after the commencement of this Act.]

Amendment

Substituted by the Trusts of Land and Appointment of Trustees Act 1996, s 25(1), Sch 3, para 4(7); for savings in relation to entailed interests created before the commencement of that Act, and savings consequential upon the abolition of the doctrine of conversion, see s 25(4), (5) thereof.

Commentary
This section should be read together with section 35 of the Trustee Act 1925 **[104]**.

[149]

27 Purchaser not to be concerned with the trusts of the proceeds of sale which are to be paid to two or more trustees or to a trust corporation

[(1) A purchaser of a legal estate from trustees of land shall not be concerned with the trusts affecting the land, the net income of the land or the proceeds of sale of the land whether or not those trusts are declared by the same instrument as that by which the trust of land is created.]

[(2) Notwithstanding anything to the contrary in the instrument (if any) creating a [trust] of land or in [any trust affecting the net proceeds of sale of the land if it is sold], the proceeds of sale or other capital money shall not be paid to or applied by the direction of fewer than two persons as [trustees], except where the trustee is a trust corporation, but this subsection does not affect the right of a sole personal representative as such to give valid receipts for, or direct the application of, proceeds of sale or other capital money, nor, except where capital money arises on the transaction, render it necessary to have more than one trustee.]

Amendment
Sub-s (1): substituted by the Trusts of Land and Appointment of Trustees Act 1996, s 25(1), Sch 3, para 4(8)(a); for savings in relation to entailed interests created before the commencement of that Act, and savings consequential upon the abolition of the doctrine of conversion, see s 25(4), (5) thereof.
Sub-s (2): substituted by the Law of Property (Amendment) Act 1926, s 7, Schedule; words in square brackets substituted by the Trusts of Land and Appointment of Trustees Act 1996, s 25(1), Sch 3, para 4(8)(b), for savings in relation to entailed interests created before the commencement of that Act, and savings consequential upon the abolition of the doctrine of conversion, see s 25(4), (5) thereof.

Commentary
A sole trustee cannot give a valid receipt for capital monies. A sole personal representative can of course act alone (section 39 of the Administration of Estates Act 1925) **[214]**. For the meaning of trust corporation see section 205 (1)(xxviii) below.

[150]

31 [Trust] of mortgaged property where right of redemption is barred

(1) Where any property, vested in trustees by way of security, becomes, by virtue of the statutes of limitation, or of an order for foreclosure or otherwise, discharged from the right of redemption, it shall be held by them [in trust—

(a) to apply the income from the property in the same manner as interest paid on the mortgage debt would have been applicable; and

(b) if the property is sold, to apply the net proceeds of sale, after payment of costs and expenses, in the same manner as repayment of the mortgage debt would have been applicable.]

[(2) Subsection (1) of this section] operates without prejudice to any rule of law relating to the apportionment of capital and income between tenant for life and remainderman.

(3) . . .

[(4) Where—

(a) the mortgage money is capital money for the purposes of the Settled Land Act 1925;

(b) land other than any forming the whole or part of the property mentioned in subsection (1) of this section is, or is deemed to be, subject to the settlement; and

(c) the tenant for life or statutory owner requires the trustees to execute with respect to land forming the whole or part of that property a vesting deed such as would have been required in relation to the land if it had been acquired on a purchase with capital money,

the trustees shall execute such a vesting deed.]

(5) This section applies whether the right of redemption was discharged before or after the first day of January, nineteen hundred and twelve, but has effect without prejudice to any dealings or arrangements made before that date.

Amendment

Section heading: words in square brackets substituted by the Trusts of Land and Appointment of Trustees Act 1996, s 5, Sch 2, para 1(6); for savings in relation to entailed interests created before the commencement of that Act, and savings consequential upon the abolition of the doctrine of conversion, see s 25(4), (5) thereof.

Sub-ss (1), (2): words in square brackets substituted by the Trusts of Land and Appointment of Trustees Act 1996, s 5, Sch 2, para 1(2), (3); for savings in relation to entailed interests created before the commencement of that Act, and savings consequential upon the abolition of the doctrine of conversion, see s 25(4), (5) thereof.

Sub-s (3): repealed by the Trusts of Land and Appointment of Trustees Act 1996, ss 5, 25(2), Sch 2, para 1(4); for savings in relation to entailed interests created before the commencement of that Act, and savings consequential upon the abolition of the doctrine of conversion, see s 25(4), (5) thereof.

Sub-s (4): substituted by the Trusts of Land and Appointment of Trustees Act 1996, s 5, Sch 2, para 1(5); for savings in relation to entailed interests created before the commencement of that Act, and savings consequential upon the abolition of the doctrine of conversion, see s 25(4), (5) thereof.

Commentary

This section is designed to deal with the situation when a mortgage in which the trustees have invested is subject to foreclosure. As to subsection (2), there does not appear to be a rule of law which applies to the apportionment of income after foreclosure, but as to the manner in which the loss should be borne between the life tenant and the remaindermen, see the Australian case: *Trust company of Australia v Braid* [1998] 4 VR 97 and as to the distribution of the funds when the property is ultimately sold, see: *Re Horn* [1924] 2 Ch, 222.

[151]

33 Application of Part I to personal representatives

The provisions of this Part of this Act relating to [trustees of land] apply to personal representatives holding [land in trust], but without prejudice to their rights and powers for purposes of administration

Commentary

See section 33 of the Administration of Estates Act 1925 **[208]**.

[152]

34 Effect of future dispositions to tenants in common

(1) An undivided share in land shall not be capable of being created except as provided by the Settled Land Act 1925 or as hereinafter mentioned.

(2) Where, after the commencement of this Act, land is expressed to be conveyed to any persons in undivided shares and those persons are of full age, the conveyance shall (notwithstanding anything to the contrary in this Act) operate as if the land had been expressed to be conveyed to the grantees, or, if there are more than four grantees, to the four first named in the conveyance, as joint tenants [in trust for the persons interested in the land]:

Provided that, where the conveyance is made by way of mortgage the land shall vest in the grantees or such four of them as aforesaid for a term of years absolute (as provided by this Act) as joint tenants subject to cesser on redemption in like manner as if the mortgage money had belonged to them on a joint account, but without prejudice to the beneficial interests in the mortgage money and interest.

(3) A devise bequest or testamentary appointment, coming into operation after the commencement of this Act, of land to two or more persons in undivided shares shall operate as a devise bequest or appointment of the land to the personal representatives of the testator, and (but without prejudice to the rights and powers of the personal representatives for purposes of administration) [in trust for the persons interested in the land].

[(3A) In subsections (2) and (3) of this section references to the persons interested in the land include persons interested as trustees or personal representatives (as well as persons beneficially interested).]

(4) . . .

Amendment

Sub-s (2): words in square brackets substituted by the Trusts of Land and Appointment of Trustees Act 1996, s 5, Sch 2, para 3(2); for savings in relation to entailed interests created before the commencement of that Act, and savings consequential upon the abolition of the doctrine of conversion, see s 25(4), (5) thereof.
Sub-s (3): words omitted repealed and words in square brackets substituted by the Trusts of Land and Appointment of Trustees Act 1996, ss 5, 25(2), Sch 2, para 3(3), Sch 4; for savings in relation to entailed interests created before the commencement of that Act, and savings consequential upon the abolition of the doctrine of conversion, see s 25(4), (5) thereof.
Sub-s (3A): inserted by the Trusts of Land and Appointment of Trustees Act 1996, s 5, Sch 2, para 3(4); for savings in relation to entailed interests created before the commencement of that Act, and savings consequential upon the abolition of the doctrine of conversion, see s 25(4), (5) thereof.
Sub-s (4): repealed by the Trusts of Land and Appointment of Trustees Act 1996, ss 5, 25(2), Sch 2, para 3(5), Sch 4; for savings in relation to entailed interests created before the commencement of that Act, and savings consequential upon the abolition of the doctrine of conversion, see s 25(4), (5) thereof.

Commentary

After the 1925 property legislation, undivided shares in land could not be created except behind trusts. For the Settled Land Act 1925, see **[Appendix II]**. The Trusts of Land and Appointment of Trustees Act 1996 **[435]** had the effect of removing the trust for sale imposed by section 34 and replacing it with a trust of land.

[153]

36 Joint tenancies

(1) Where a legal estate (not being settled land) is beneficially limited to or held in trust for any persons as joint tenants, the same shall be held [in trust], in like manner as if the persons beneficially entitled were tenants in common, but not so as to sever their joint tenancy in equity.

(2) No severance of a joint tenancy of a legal estate, so as to create a tenancy in common in land, shall be permissible, whether by operation of law or otherwise, but this subsection does not affect the right of a joint tenant to release his interest to the other joint tenants, or the right to sever a joint tenancy in an equitable interest whether or not the legal estate is vested in the joint tenants:

Provided that, where a legal estate (not being settled land) is vested in joint tenants beneficially, and any tenant desires to sever the joint tenancy in equity, he shall give to the other joint tenants a notice in writing of such desire or do such other acts or things as would, in the case of personal estate, have been effectual to sever the tenancy in equity, and thereupon [the land shall be held in trust on terms] which would have been requisite for giving effect to the beneficial interests if there had been an actual severance.

[Nothing in this Act affects the right of a survivor of joint tenants, who is solely and beneficially interested, to deal with his legal estate as if it were not held [in trust].]

(3) Without prejudice to the right of a joint tenant to release his interest to the other joint tenants no severance of a mortgage term or trust estate, so as to create a tenancy in common, shall be permissible.

Amendment

Sub-s (1): words in square brackets substituted by the Trusts of Land and Appointment of Trustees Act 1996, s 5, Sch 2, para 4(2); for savings in relation to entailed interests created before the commencement of that Act, and savings consequential upon the abolition of the doctrine of conversion, see s 25(4), (5) thereof.
Sub-s (2): first words in square brackets substituted by the Trusts of Land and Appointment of Trustees Act 1996, s 5, Sch 2, para 4(3), for savings in relation to entailed interests created before the commencement of that Act, and savings consequential upon the abolition of the doctrine of conversion, see s 25(4), (5) thereof; second words in square brackets inserted by the Law of Property (Amendment) Act 1926, s 7, Schedule, words in square brackets therein substituted by the Trusts of Land and Appointment of Trustees Act 1996, s 5, Sch 2, para 4(3), for savings in relation to entailed interests created before the commencement of that Act, and savings consequential upon the abolition of the doctrine of conversion, see s 25(4), (5) thereof.

Commentary

Subsection (1) brings into effect section 34 above, as amended by the Trusts of Land and Appointment of Trustees Act 1996. As to severance of the joint tenancy within subsection (2), see: *Burgess v Rawnsley* [1975] Ch 429. Subsection (2) does not prevent severance of a joint tenancy in equity any of the ways which were available before 1926. So, the alienation or agreement to alienate a share by one joint tenant will effect a severance, see: *Burgess v Rawnsley* (supra) and *Hunter v Babbage* (1995) 69 P 7 CR 548 and so it seems a unilateral decision by one joint tenant communicated to the other: *Hawksley v May* [1956] 1 QB 304; *Re Draper's conveyance* [1969] 1 Ch 486. The making of mutual wills will also effect a severance: *Re Wilfred's Estate* (1869) 11 Ch D 267.

[154]

PART II
CONTRACTS, CONVEYANCES AND OTHER INSTRUMENTS

52 Conveyances to be by deed

(1) All conveyances of land or of any interest therein are void for the purpose of conveying or creating a legal estate unless made by deed.

(2) This section does not apply to—

(a) assents by a personal representative;
(b) disclaimers made in accordance with [sections 178 to 180 or sections 315 to 319 of the Insolvency Act 1986] or not required to be evidenced in writing;
(c) surrenders by operation of law, including surrenders which may, by law, be effected without writing;
(d) leases or tenancies or other assurances not required by law to be made in writing;
(e) receipts [other than those falling within section 115 below];
(f) vesting orders of the court or other competent authority;
(g) conveyances taking effect by operation of law.

Amendment

Sub-s (2): words in square brackets in para (b) substituted by the Insolvency Act 1986, s 439(2), Sch 14; words in square brackets in para (e) substituted by the Law of Property (Miscellaneous Provisions) Act 1989, s 1, Sch 1, para 2.

Commentary
If a deed is not used in accordance with subsection (1) the instrument may still take effect in equity under the doctrine in *Walsh v Lonsdale* (1882) 21 Ch D 9. As to assents under subsection (2)(a), these must comply with section 36(4) of the Administration of Estates Act 1925 **[211]** and be in writing. As far as subsection (2)(g) is concerned this would include probates and letters of administration as to which see Administration of Estates Act 1925, Part I **[181]**.

[155]

53 Instruments required to be in writing

(1) Subject to the provisions hereinafter contained with respect to the creation of interests in land by parol—

(a) no interest in land can be created or disposed of except by writing signed by the person creating or conveying the same, or by his agent thereunto lawfully authorised in writing, or by will, or by operation of law;

(b) a declaration of trust respecting any land or any interest therein must be manifested and proved by some writing signed by some person who is able to declare such trust or by his will;

(c) a disposition of an equitable interest or trust subsisting at the time of the disposition, must be in writing signed by the person disposing of the same, or by his agent thereunto lawfully authorised in writing or by will.

(2) This section does not affect the creation or operation of resulting, implied or constructive trusts.

Commentary
As to subsection (b) the trust need not be created by writing but must be evidenced in writing in existence at the date when an action is brought to enforce the trust: *Forster v Hale* (1798) 3 Ves 696 and *Rochefoucauld v Boustead* [1897] 1 Ch 196. It is the owner of the beneficial interest in the trust and not the trustee who must sign the declaration: *Tierney v Wood* (1854) 19 Beav 330 and *Grey v IRC* [1960] AC 1. The declaration must be a present and irrevocable declaration of trust (*Re Cozens* [1913] 2 Ch 478). Subsection (b) applies only to land, but subsection (c) applies to all property. What is more, the disposition itself has to be in writing and not just evidenced in writing. The subsection applies to a declaration of trust of an existing equitable interest, see: *Grey v IRC* [1960] AC 1. It does not however apply where the transferor has the legal title, see: *Vandervell v IRC* [1967] 2AC 291. It does not apply where there is a nomination under a pension fund which can be revoked, see: *Re Danish Bacon Co. Ltd. Staff Pension Fund Trusts* [1971] 1 WLR 248. An option given to trustees in respect of property held on resulting trust for the settlor, was held not to be within the section: *Re Vandervell's Trusts (No. 2)* [1974] Ch 269. As to the operation of subsection (2) see: *Oughtred v IRC* [1960] AC 202.

[156]

55 Savings in regard to last two sections

Nothing in the last two foregoing sections shall—

(a) invalidate dispositions by will; or

(b) affect any interest validly created before the commencement of this Act; or

(c) affect the right to acquire an interest in land by virtue of taking possession; or

(d) affect the operation of the law relating to part performance.

Commentary
This section applies also to section 54 which is not covered in this work. The doctrine of part performance (subsection (d) is no longer of great importance since the abolition of section 40 of this Act by the Law of Property (Miscellaneous Provisions) Act 1989.

[157]

PART IV
EQUITABLE INTERESTS AND THINGS IN ACTION

130 ... entailed interests in real and personal property

(1)–(3) ...

(4) In default of and subject to the execution of a disentailing assurance or the exercise of the testamentary power conferred by this Act, an entailed interest (to the extent of the property affected) shall devolve as an equitable interest, from time to time, upon the persons who would have been successively entitled thereto as the heirs of the body (either generally or of a particular class) of the tenant in tail or other person, or as tenant by the curtesy, if the entailed interest had, before the commencement of this Act, been limited in respect of freehold land governed by the general law in force immediately before such commencement, and such law had remained unaffected.

(5) Where personal chattels are settled without reference to settled land on trusts creating entailed interests therein, the trustees, with the consent of the usufructuary for the time being if of full age, may sell the chattels or any of them, and the net proceeds of any such sale shall be held in trust for and shall go to the same persons successively, in the same manner and for the same interests, as the chattels sold would have been held and gone if they had not been sold, and the income of investments representing such proceeds of sale shall be applied accordingly.

(6) ...

(7) In this Act where the context so admits "entailed interest" includes an estate tail (now made to take effect as an equitable interest) created before the commencement of this Act.

Amendment

Section heading: words omitted repealed by the Trusts of Land and Appointment of Trustees Act 1996, s 25(2), Sch 4; for savings in relation to entailed interests created before the commencement of that Act, and savings consequential upon the abolition of the doctrine of conversion, see s 25(4), (5) thereof.

Sub-ss (1)–(3), (6): repealed by the Trusts of Land and Appointment of Trustees Act 1996, s 25(2), Sch 4; for savings in relation to entailed interests created before the commencement of that Act, and savings consequential upon the abolition of the doctrine of conversion, see s 25(4), (5) thereof.

Commentary

Much of the importance of this section has gone with the abolition of entailed interests under the Trusts of Land and Appointment of Trustees Act 1996 **[431]**. For "testamentary power" in subsection (4) see section 176 below. Essentially entailed interests after 1926 took effect as equitable rather than legal interests but the tenant in tail will be a tenant for life under the Settled Land Act 1925 **[Appendix II]**. Subsection (5) supplements section 67 of the Settled Land Act 1925 **[Appendix II]** and will not apply where the chattels are heirlooms.

[158]

131 Abolition of the rule in Shelley's case

Where by any instrument coming into operation after the commencement of this Act an interest in any property is expressed to be given to the heir or heirs or issue or any particular heir or any class of the heirs or issue of any person in words which, but for this section [(and paragraph 5 of Schedule 1 to the Trusts of Land and Appointment of Trustees Act 1996)] would, under the rule of law known as the Rule in Shelley's case, have operated to give to that person an interest in fee simple or an entailed interest, such words shall operate in equity as words of purchase and not of limitation, and shall be construed and have effect accordingly, and in the case of an interest in any property expressed to be given to an heir or heirs or any particular heir or class of heirs, the same person or persons shall take as would in the case of freehold land have answered that description under the general law in force before the commencement of this Act.

Amendment

Words in square brackets inserted by the Trusts of Land and Appointment of Trustees Act 1996, s 25(1), Sch 3, para 4(14); for savings in relation to entailed interests created before the commencement of that Act, and savings consequential upon the abolition of the doctrine of conversion, see s 25(4), (5) thereof.

Commentary

This section abolished a rule which Sir Robert Megarry in his Law of Real Property described as "notorious". Essentially a gift to X for life remainder to his heirs was construed as a gift of the fee simple to X with nothing going to the heirs.

[159]

132 As to heirs taking by purchase

(1) A limitation of real or personal property in favour of the heir, either general or special, of a deceased person which, if limited in respect of freehold land before the commencement of this Act, would have conferred on the heir an estate in the land by purchase, shall operate to confer a corresponding equitable interest in the property on the person who would, if the general law in force immediately before such commencement had remained unaffected, have answered the description of the heir, either general or special, of the deceased in respect of his freehold land, either at the death of the deceased or at the time named in the limitation, as the case may require.

(2) This section applies whether the deceased person dies before or after the commencement of this Act, but only applies to limitations or trusts created by an instrument coming into operation after such commencement.

Commentary

See also section 51(1) of the Administration of Estates Act 1925 **[227]**. Heir in this section has been construed strictly (*Re Bourke's WT* [1980] 1 WLR 539) but for a more relaxed interpretation, see: *Re Kilvert* [1957] Ch 388 and *Lightfoot v Maybury* [1914] AC 782.

[160]

134 Restriction on executory limitations

(1) Where there is a person entitled to—

(a) an equitable interest in land for an estate in fee simple or for any less interest not being an entailed interest, or

(b) any interest in other property, not being an entailed interest,

with an executory limitation over on default or failure of all or any of his issue, whether within or at any specified period or time or not, that executory limitation shall be or become void and incapable of taking effect, if and as soon as there is living any issue who has attained the age of [eighteen years] of the class on default or failure whereof the limitation over was to take effect.

(2) This section applies where the executory limitation is contained in an instrument coming into operation after the thirty-first day of December, eighteen hundred and eighty-two, save that, as regards instruments coming into operation before the commencement of this Act, it only applies to limitations of land for an estate in fee, or for a term of years absolute or determinable on life, or for a term of life.

Amendment
Sub-s (1): words in square brackets substituted by the Family Law Reform Act 1969, ss 1(3), 28(3), Sch 1.

Commentary
See also section 29 of the Wills Act 1837 **[30]**. Before 1882 in the case of a gift to X but if he died without issue to Y, X would not know until his death whether or not the gift would go over to Y. This section provides that the moment that any issue of X attain 18, the gift over to Y becomes void and the gift to X becomes absolute. See also *Re Booth* [1900] 1 Ch 768.

[161]

137 Dealings with life interests, reversions and other equitable interests

(1) The law applicable to dealings with equitable things in action which regulates the priority of competing interests therein, shall, as respects dealings with equitable interests in land, capital money, and securities representing capital money effected after the commencement of this Act, apply to and regulate the priority of competing interests therein.

This subsection applies whether or not the money or securities are in court.

(2)

(i) In the case of a dealing with an equitable interest in settled land, capital money or securities representing capital money, the persons to be served with notice of the dealing shall be the trustees of the settlement; and where the equitable interest is created by a derivative or subsidiary settlement, the persons to be served with notice shall be the trustees of that settlement.

(ii) In the case of a dealing with an equitable interest in [land subject to a trust of land, or the proceeds of the sale of such land, the persons to be served with notice shall be the trustees.]

(iii) In any other case the person to be served with notice of a dealing with an equitable interest in land shall be the estate owner of the land affected.

The persons on whom notice is served pursuant to this subsection shall be affected thereby in the same manner as if they had been trustees of personal property out of which the equitable interest was created or arose.

This subsection does not apply where the money or securities are in court.

(3) A notice, otherwise than in writing, given to, or received by, a trustee after the commencement of this Act as respects any dealing with an equitable interest in real or personal property, shall not affect the priority of competing claims of purchasers in that equitable interest.

(4) Where, as respects any dealing with an equitable interest in real or personal property—

(a) the trustees are not persons to whom a valid notice of the dealing can be given; or

(b) there are no trustees to whom a notice can be given; or

(c) for any other reason a valid notice cannot be served, or cannot be served without unreasonable cost or delay;

a purchaser may at his own cost require that—

(i) a memorandum of the dealing be endorsed, written on or permanently annexed to the instrument creating the trust;

(ii) the instrument be produced to him by the person having the possession or custody thereof to prove that a sufficient memorandum has been placed thereon or annexed thereto.

Such memorandum shall, as respects priorities, operate in like manner as if notice in writing of the dealing had been given to trustees duly qualified to receive the notice at the time when the memorandum is placed on or annexed to the instrument creating the trust.

(5) Where the property affected is settled land, the memorandum shall be placed on or annexed to the trust instrument and not the vesting instrument.

Where the property affected is land [subject to a trust of land], the memorandum shall be placed on or annexed to the instrument whereby the equitable interest is created.

(6) Where the trust is created by statute or by operation of law, or in any other case where there is no instrument whereby the trusts are declared, the instrument under which the equitable interest is acquired or which is evidence of the devolution thereof shall, for the purposes of this section, be deemed the instrument creating the trust.

In particular, where the trust arises by reason of an intestacy, the letters of administration or probate in force when the dealing was effected shall be deemed such instrument.

(7) Nothing in this section affects any priority acquired before the commencement of this Act.

(8) Where a notice in writing of a dealing with an equitable interest in real or personal property has been served on a trustee under this section, the trustees from time to time of the property affected shall be entitled to the custody of the notice, and the notice shall be delivered to them by any person who for the time being may have the custody thereof; and subject to the payment of costs, any person interested in the equitable interest may require production of the notice.

(9) The liability of the estate owner of the legal estate affected to produce documents and furnish information to persons entitled to equitable interests therein shall correspond to the liability of a trustee for sale to produce documents and furnish information to persons entitled to equitable interests in the proceeds of sale of the land.

(10) This section does not apply until a trust has been created, and in this section "dealing" includes a disposition by operation of law.

Amendment

Sub-ss (2), (5): words in square brackets substituted by the Trusts of Land and Appointment of Trustees Act 1996, s 25(1), Sch 3, para 4(15); for savings in relation to entailed interests created before the commencement of that Act, and savings consequential upon the abolition of the doctrine of conversion, see s 25(4), (5) thereof.

Commentary

This section extends the rule in *Dearle v Hall* (1828) 3 Russ 1 to equitable interests in unregistered land. The section does not apply to the creation of a new equitable interest (*Hill v Peters* [1918] 2 Ch 273, *Compaq Computer v Abercorn Group* [1993] BCLC 602). For the meaning of "capital money" in subsection (1) see section 205(1)(xxvi) below.

[162]

138 Power to nominate a trust corporation to receive notices

(1) By any settlement or other instrument creating a trust, a trust corporation may be nominated to whom notices of dealings affecting real or personal property may be given, whether or not under the foregoing section, and in default of such nomination the trustees (if any) of the instrument, or the court on the application of any person interested, may make the nomination.

(2) The person having the possession or custody of any instrument on which notices under that section may be endorsed shall cause the name of the trust corporation to whom notices may be given to be endorsed upon that instrument.

(3) Notice given to any trust corporation whose name is so endorsed shall operate in the same way as a notice or endorsement under the foregoing section.

(4) Where a trust corporation is acting for the purposes of this section a notice given to a trustee of the trust instrument of a dealing relating to the trust property shall forthwith be delivered or sent by post by the trustee to the trust corporation, and until received by the corporation shall not affect any priority.

(5) A trust corporation shall not be nominated for the purposes of this section—

- (a) unless that corporation consents to act; or
- (b) where that corporation has any beneficial interest in or charge upon the trust property; or
- (c) where a trust corporation is acting as the trustee or one of the trustees of the instrument creating the trust.

(6) Where a trust corporation acting for the purposes of this section becomes entitled to any beneficial interest in or charge upon the trust property, another trust corporation shall be nominated in its place and all documents relating to notices affecting the trust shall be delivered to the corporation so nominated.

(7) A trust corporation acting for the purposes of this section shall be bound to keep a separate register of notices of dealings in respect of each equitable interest and shall enter therein—

- (a) the date of the notice;
- (b) the name of the person giving the notice;
- (c) short particulars of the equitable interest intended to be affected; and
- (d) short particulars of the effect of the dealing if mentioned in the notice.

(8) The trust corporation may, before making any entry in the register, require the applicant to pay a fee not exceeding the prescribed fee.

(9) Subject to the payment of a fee not exceeding the prescribed fee, the trust corporation shall permit any person who would, if the corporation had been the trustee of the trust investment, have been entitled to inspect notices served on the trustee, to inspect and take copies of the register and any notices held by the corporation.

(10) Subject to the payment by the applicant of a fee not exceeding the prescribed fee, the trust corporation shall reply to all inquiries respecting notices received by the corporation in like manner and in the same circumstances as if the corporation had been the trustee of the trust instrument.

(11) In this section "prescribed fee" means the fee prescribed [by the Lord Chancellor] in cases where the Public Trustee acts as a trust corporation for the purposes of this section.

Amendment

Sub-s (11): words "by the Lord Chancellor" in square brackets substituted by the Public Trustee (Liability and Fees) Act 2002, s 2(2).

Commentary

This section should be read together with section 137. It provides an easy method for trustees of appointing in effect a Registrar by nominating a trust corporation to receive notices. For the Public Trustee, see the Public Trustee Act 1906 **[59]** For the meaning of "trust corporation" see section 205(1)(xxviii) below.

[163]

PART VI
POWERS

155 Release of powers simply collateral

A person to whom any power, whether coupled with an interest or not, is given may by deed release, or contract not to exercise, the power.

Commentary

The distinction between powers collateral (i.e. powers where the donee has no interest in the property) and other powers is no longer of great importance particularly as this section provides that such collateral powers can be released or the donee can contract not to exercise them. The section does not apply in the case of a power coupled with a duty or in the nature of a trust as to which see: *Re Wills Trust Deed* [1964] Ch 219 and *Muir v IRC* [1966] 1WLR 1269 and see also *Re Evered* [1910] 2 Ch 147.

[164]

156 Disclaimer of power

(1) A person to whom any power, whether coupled with an interest or not, is given may by deed disclaim the power, and, after disclaimer, shall not be capable of exercising or joining in the exercise of the power.

(2) On such disclaimer, the power may be exercised by the other person or persons or the survivor or survivors of the other persons, to whom the power is given, unless the contrary is expressed in the instrument creating the power.

Commentary

See section 155 above for an alternative method of extinguishing a power. Where there is more than one donee and only one disclaims that does not prevent the other donees exercising the power.

[165]

157 Protection of purchasers claiming under certain void appointments

(1) An instrument purporting to exercise a power of appointment over property, which, in default of and subject to any appointment, is held in trust for a class or number of persons of whom the appointee is one, shall not (save as hereinafter provided) be void on the ground of fraud on the power as against a purchaser in good faith:

Provided that, if the interest appointed exceeds, in amount or value, the interest in such property to which immediately before the execution of the instrument the appointee was presumptively entitled under the trust in default of appointment, having regard to any advances made in his favour and to any hotchpot provision, the protection afforded by this section to a purchaser shall not extend to such excess.

(2) In this section "a purchaser in good faith" means a person dealing with an appointee of the age of not less than twenty-five years for valuable consideration in money or money's worth, and without notice of the fraud, or of any circumstances from which, if reasonable inquiries had been made, the fraud might have been discovered.

(3) Persons deriving title under any purchaser entitled to the benefit of this section shall be entitled to like benefit.

(4) This section applies only to dealings effected after the commencement of this Act.

Commentary

As to the law on a fraud on a power, see *Thomas on Powers*. The section provides very limited protection. If X makes a bad appointment of the whole fund in which Y has a one third interest in default and Y being 25 years of age then sells the fund to Z, Z is protected up to the one third interest of Y.

[166]

158 Validation of appointments where objects are excluded or take illusory shares

(1) No appointment made in exercise of any power to appoint any property among two or more objects shall be invalid on the ground that—

(a) an unsubstantial, illusory, or nominal share only is appointed to or left unappointed to devolve upon any one or more of the objects of the power; or

(b) any object of the power is thereby altogether excluded;

but every such appointment shall be valid notwithstanding that any one or more of the objects is not thereby, or in default of appointment, to take any share in the property.

(2) This section does not affect any provision in the instrument creating the power which declares the amount of any share from which any object of the power is not to be excluded.

(3) This section applies to appointments made before or after the commencement of this Act.

Commentary

Before this Act unless there was some contrary intention shown in the power itself the appointor could not exclude one of the objects of a power, and indeed appointing a nominal amount might also be set aside (*Wilson v Piggott* (1794) 2 Ves Jun 351). Subject to any contrary intention in the instrument creating the power the appointor can now exclude one of the objects of the power.

[167]

159 Execution of powers not testamentary

(1) A deed executed in the presence of and attested by two or more witnesses (in the manner in which deeds are ordinarily executed and attested) is so far as respects the execution and attestation thereof, a valid execution of a power of appointment by deed or by any instrument in writing, not testamentary, notwithstanding that it is expressly required that a deed or instrument in writing, made in exercise of the power, is to be executed or attested with some additional or other form of execution or attestation or solemnity.

(2) This section does not operate to defeat any direction in the instrument creating the power that—

(a) the consent of any particular person is to be necessary to a valid execution;

(b) in order to give validity to any appointment, any act is to be performed having no relation to the mode of executing and attesting the instrument.

(3) This section does not prevent the donee of a power from executing it in accordance with the power by writing, or otherwise than by an instrument executed and attested as a deed; and where a power is so executed this section does not apply.

(4) This section applies to appointments by deed made after the thirteenth day of August, eighteen hundred and fifty-nine.

Commentary

As to the execution of powers by Will, see section 10 of the Wills Act 1837 **[8]** and for the wills of soldiers and sailors see the Wills (Soldiers and Sailors) Act 1918 **[76]**.

[168]

160 Application of Part VI to existing powers

This Part of this Act applies to powers created or arising either before or after the commencement of this Act.

[169]

PART VII
PERPETUITIES AND ACCUMULATIONS

PERPETUITIES

161 Abolition of the double possibility rule

(1) The rule of law prohibiting the limitation, after a life interest to an unborn person, of an interest in land to the unborn child or other issue of an unborn person is hereby abolished, but without prejudice to any other rule relating to perpetuities.

(2) This section only applies to limitations or trusts created by an instrument coming into operation after the commencement of this Act.

Commentary

This section was enacted to abolish the rule in *Whitby v Mitchell* (1890) 44 Ch D 85 which essentially provided that if land was left to a person unborn at the date of the gift, any remainder to his or her issue was void. The modern law of perpetuities will still apply to those gifts as to which see the Perpetuities and Accumulations Act 1964 **[266]**.

[170]

162 Restrictions on the perpetuity rule

(1) For removing doubts, it is hereby declared that the rule of law relating to perpetuities does not apply and shall be deemed never to have applied—

(a) To any power to distrain on or to take possession of land or the income thereof given by way of indemnity against a rent, whether charged upon or payable in respect of any part of that land or not; or

(b) To any rentcharge created only as an indemnity against another rentcharge, although the indemnity rentcharge may only arise or become payable on breach of a condition or stipulation; or

(c) To any power, whether exercisable on breach of a condition or stipulation or not, to retain or withhold payment of any instalment of a rentcharge as an indemnity against another rentcharge; or

(d) To any grant, exception, or reservation of any right of entry on, or user of, the surface of land or of any easements, rights, or privileges over or under land for the purpose of—

(i) winning, working, inspecting, measuring, converting, manufacturing, carrying away, and disposing of mines and minerals;

(ii) inspecting, grubbing up, felling and carrying away timber and other trees, and the tops and lops thereof;

(iii) executing repairs, alterations, or additions to any adjoining land, or the buildings and erections thereon;

(iv) constructing, laying down, altering, repairing, renewing, cleansing, and maintaining sewers, watercourses, cesspools, gutters, drains, water-pipes, gas-pipes, electric wires or cables or other like works.

(2) This section applies to instruments coming into operation before or after the commencement of this Act.

Commentary

The effect of this section is to exempt from the perpetuity rule (as to which see the Perpetuities and Accumulations Act 1964 **[266]**) certain interests which are in the main ancillary to other interests. See also *Dunn v Blackdown Properties Ltd.* [1961] Ch 433 (right to use sewer and drains not within subsection (1)(d)(iv)).

[171]

163 . . .

. . .

Amendment

Repealed by the Perpetuities and Accumulations Act 1964, ss 4(6), 15(5).

[172]

ACCUMULATIONS

164 General restrictions on accumulation of income

(1) No person may by any instrument or otherwise settle or dispose of any property in such manner that the income thereof shall, save as hereinafter mentioned, be wholly or partially accumulated for any longer period than one of the following, namely:—

(a) the life of the grantor or settlor; or

(b) a term of twenty-one years from the death of the grantor, settlor or testator; or

(c) the duration of the minority or respective minorities of any person or persons living or en ventre sa mere at the death of the grantor, settlor or testator; or

(d) the duration of the minority or respective minorities only of any person or persons who under the limitations of the instrument directing the accumulations would, for the time being, if of full age, be entitled to the income directed to be accumulated.

In every case where any accumulation is directed otherwise than as aforesaid, the direction shall (save as hereinafter mentioned) be void; and the income of the property directed to be accumulated shall, so long as the same is directed to be accumulated contrary to this section, go to and be received by the person or persons who would have been entitled thereto if such accumulation had not been directed.

(2) This section does not extend to any provision—

(i) for payment of the debts of any grantor, settlor, testator or other person;

(ii) for raising portions for—

(a) any child, children or remoter issue of any grantor, settlor or testator; or

(b) any child, children or remoter issue of a person taking any interest under any settlement or other disposition directing the accumulations or to whom any interest is thereby limited;

(iii) respecting the accumulation of the produce of timber or wood;

and accordingly such provisions may be made as if no statutory restrictions on accumulation of income had been imposed.

(3) The restrictions imposed by this section apply to instruments made on or after the twenty-eighth day of July, eighteen hundred, but in the case of wills only where the testator was living and of testamentary capacity after the end of one year from that date.

Commentary

Only one of the periods in subsection(1) (as supplemented by the additional periods contained in section 13 of the Perpetuities and Accumulations Act 1964 **[278]**) can be chosen *Re Errington* (1897) 76 LT 616. If no express period is chosen by the instrument, it might be implied, see: *Re Rochford's ST* [1965] Ch 111. What period has been chosen is a matter of construction: *Jagger v Jagger* (1883) 25 Ch D. 729; *Re Ransome* [1957] Ch 348 If the period chosen for accumulation exceeds the perpetuity period, it is wholly void, see; *Marshall v Holloway* (1820) 2 Swans 432. If on the other hand the period cannot exceed the perpetuity period but exceeds the relevant accumulation period, only the excess accumulation over the permitted period will be void, *Eyre v Marsden* (1838) 2 Keen 564. For gifts which carry the intermediate income (in order to see where any excessive accumulation should go) see section 175 below. This section does not apply where the grantor or settlor is a body corporate as they are not a "person" for the purposes of this section and that can be important in respect of employee benefit trusts, see: *Re Dodwell & Co. Ltd.'s Trust* [1979] Ch 301.

[173]

165 Qualification of restrictions on accumulation

Where accumulations of surplus income are made during a minority under any statutory power or under the general law, the period for which such accumulations are made is not (whether the trust was created or the accumulations were made before or after the commencement of this Act) to be taken into account in determining the periods for which accumulations are permitted to be made by the last preceding section, and accordingly an express trust for accumulation for any other permitted period shall not be deemed to have been invalidated or become invalid, by reason of accumulations also having been made as aforesaid during such minority.

Commentary

This is an important exception to the general rule. Under section 31 of the Trustee Act 1925 **[100]** trustees are given a power to maintain an infant and subject thereto they must accumulate the income. Indeed they are obliged to do so as a matter of general law as the child cannot give them a valid receipt for it.

[174]

166 Restriction on accumulation for the purchase of land

(1) No person may settle or dispose of any property in such manner that the income thereof shall be wholly or partially accumulated for the purchase of land only, for any longer period than the duration of the minority or respective minorities of any person or persons who, under the limitations of the instrument directing the accumulation, would for the time being, if of full age, be entitled to the income so directed to be accumulated.

(2) This section does not, nor do the enactments which it replaces, apply to accumulations to be held as capital money for the purposes of the Settled Land Act 1925 or the enactments replaced by that Act, whether or not the accumulations are primarily liable to be laid out in the purchase of land.

(3) This section applies to settlements and dispositions made after the twenty-seventh day of June eighteen hundred and ninety-two.

Commentary

Essentially where income is accumulated for the sole purpose of purchasing land (as to which see *Re Knapp* [1929] 1 Ch 341) then only the fourth period specified under section 164 above (that is minority of a beneficiary) can be chosen. This does not apply to accumulations under the Settled Land Act 1925 **[Appendix II]**.

[175]

PART X
WILLS

175 Contingent and future testamentary gifts to carry the intermediate income

(1) A contingent or future specific devise or bequest of property, whether real or personal, and a contingent residuary devise of freehold land, and a specific or residuary devise of freehold land to trustees upon trust for persons whose interests are contingent or executory shall, subject to the statutory provisions relating to

accumulations, carry the intermediate income of that property from the death of the testator, except so far as such income, or any part thereof, may be otherwise expressly disposed of.

(2) This section applies only to wills coming into operation after the commencement of this Act.

Commentary

For the statutory provisions relating to accumulations see sections 164 to 166 above and section 13 of the Perpetuities and Accumulations Act 1964 **[278]**. Income under this section is completely disposed of if a gift of it is made elsewhere regardless of whether that gift is disclaimed: *Re Hatfield's WT* [1956] Ch 469. Deferred or contingent pecuniary legacies are not covered by the section and will not normally carry interest until the future event or contingency occurs: *Re George* (1877) 5 Ch D 837 although it is different if the legacy is directed to be set aside (e.g. *Re Medlock* (1886) 55 LJ Ch 738) or where it is a legacy for a minor child (*Re Bowlby* [1904] 2 Ch 685). The section is silent on the question of deferred residuary gifts but in general residuary gifts of personalty will not carry the intermediate income (*Re Geering* [1964] Ch 136 and *Re Gillett's Will Trusts* [1950] 2 Ch 102). The section appears to contain an anomaly in respect of future residuary devises as they seem to carry the income if contingent but not vested (*Re McGeorge* [1963] Ch 544).

[176]

176 Power for tenant in tail in possession to dispose of property by specific devise or bequest

(1) A tenant in tail of full age shall have power to dispose by will, by means of a devise or bequest referring specifically either to the property or to the instrument under which it was acquired or to entailed property generally—

(a) of all property of which he is tenant in tail in possession at his death; and

(b) of money (including the proceeds of property directed to be sold) subject to be invested in the purchase of property, of which if it had been so invested he would have been tenant in tail in possession at his death;

in like manner as if, after barring the entail, he had been tenant in fee simple or absolute owner thereof for an equitable interest at his death, but, subject to and in default of any such disposition by will, such property shall devolve in the same manner as if this section had not been passed.

(2) This section applies to entailed interests authorised to be created by this Act as well as to estates tail created before the commencement of this Act, but does not extend to a tenant in tail who is by statute restrained from barring or defeating his estate tail, whether the land or property in respect whereof he is so restrained was purchased with money provided by Parliament in consideration of public services or not, or to a tenant in tail after possibility of issue extinct, and does not render any interest which is not disposed of by the will of the tenant in tail liable for his debts or other liabilities.

(3) In this section "tenant in tail" includes an owner of a base fee in possession who has power to enlarge the base fee into a fee-simple without the concurrence of any other person.

(4) This section only applies to wills executed after the commencement of this Act, or confirmed or republished by codicil executed after such commencement.

Commentary

This section is of less importance since entailed interests were abolished by the Trusts of Land and Appointment of Trustees Act 1996 **[431]**. This section enables the tenant in tail in possession to bar the entail by Will, but does not apply to a tenant in tail in remainder nor to entails which could not otherwise be barred under the Fines and Recoveries Act 1833. The Will must refer to the property which is entailed or the instrument under which it is entailed specifically, see: *Acheson v Russell* [1951] Ch 67.

[177]

179 Prescribed forms for reference in wills

The Lord Chancellor may from time to time prescribe and publish forms to which a testator may refer in his will, and give directions as to the manner in which they may be referred to, but, unless so referred to, such forms shall not be deemed to be incorporated in a will.

[178]

PART XI
MISCELLANEOUS

184 Presumption of survivorship in regard to claims to property

In all cases where, after the commencement of this Act, two or more persons have died in circumstances rendering it uncertain which of them survived the other or others, such deaths shall (subject to any order of the court), for all purposes affecting the title of property, be presumed to have occurred in order of seniority, and accordingly the younger shall be deemed to have survived the elder.

Commentary

The Court may declare that the section does not apply but the presumption is a matter of substantive law and not evidence, see *Re Cohn* [1945] Ch 5. See also *Re Bate* [1947] 2 All ER 418; *Re Lindop* [1942] Ch 377 and *Hickman v Peacey* [1945] AC 304 as to the operation of the section. Note that for inheritance tax purposes, section 4(2) of the Inheritance Tax Act 1984 provides that for the purposes of assessing the size of the estate of persons who have died in circumstances where it is not possible to say who survived whom, it is deemed that they died in the same instant. For the modification of this rule in respect of spouses see section 46(3) of the Administration of Estates Act 1925 **[221].**

[179]

PART XII
CONSTRUCTION, JURISDICTION, AND GENERAL PROVISIONS

205 General definitions

(1) In this Act unless the context otherwise requires, the following expressions have the meanings hereby assigned to them respectively, that is to say:—

(i) "Bankruptcy" includes liquidation by arrangement; also in relation to a corporation means the winding up thereof;

(ii) "Conveyance" includes a mortgage, charge, lease, assent, vesting declaration, vesting instrument, disclaimer, release and every other assurance of property or of an interest therein by any instrument, except a will; "convey" has a corresponding meaning; and "disposition" includes a conveyance and also a devise, bequest, or an appointment of property contained in a will; and "dispose of" has a corresponding meaning;

(iii) "Building purposes" include the erecting and improving of, and the adding to, and the repairing of buildings; and a "building lease" is a lease for building purposes or purposes connected therewith;

[(iiiA) . . .]

(iv) "Death duty" means estate duty, . . . and every other duty leviable or payable on a death;

(v) "Estate owner" means the owner of a legal estate, but an infant is not capable of being an estate owner;

(vi) "Gazette" means the London Gazette;

(vii) "Incumbrance" includes a legal or equitable mortgage and a trust for securing money, and a lien, and a charge of a portion, annuity, or other capital or annual sum; and "incumbrancer" has a meaning corresponding with that of incumbrance, and includes every person entitled to the benefit of an incumbrance, or to require payment or discharge thereof;

(viii) "Instrument" does not include a statute, unless the statute creates a settlement;

(ix) "Land" includes land of any tenure, and mines and minerals, whether or not held apart from the surface, buildings or parts of buildings (whether the division is horizontal, vertical or made in any other way) and other corporeal hereditaments; also a manor, an advowson, and a rent and other incorporeal hereditaments, and an easement, right, privilege, or benefit in, over, or derived from land; . . . ; and "mines and minerals" include any strata or seam of minerals or substances in or under any land, and powers of working and getting the same . . . ; and "manor" includes a lordship, and reputed manor or lordship; and "hereditament" means any real property which on an intestacy occurring before the commencement of this Act might have devolved upon an heir;

(x) "Legal estates" mean the estates, interests and charges, in or over land (subsisting or created at law) which are by this Act authorised to subsist or to be created as legal estates; "equitable interests" mean all the other interests and charges in or over land . . . ; an equitable interest "capable of subsisting as a legal estate" means such as could validly subsist or be created as a legal estate under this Act;

(xi) "Legal powers" include the powers vested in a chargee by way of legal mortgage or in an estate owner under which a legal estate can be transferred or created; and "equitable powers" mean all the powers in or over land under which equitable interests or powers only can be transferred or created;

(xii) "Limitation Acts" means the Real Property Limitation Acts 1833, 1837 and 1874, and "limitation" includes a trust;

[(xiii) . . .]

(xiv) a "mining lease" means a lease for mining purposes, that is, the searching for, winning, working, getting, making merchantable, carrying away, or disposing of mines and minerals, or purposes connected therewith, and includes a grant or licence for mining purposes;

(xv) "Minister" means [the Minister of Agriculture, Fisheries and Food];

(xvi) "Mortgage" includes any charge or lien on any property for securing money or money's worth; "legal mortgage" means a mortgage by demise or subdemise or a charge by way of legal mortgage and "legal mortgagee" has a corresponding meaning; "mortgage money" means money or money's worth secured by a mortgage; "mortgagor" includes any person from time to time deriving title under the original mortgagor or entitled to redeem a mortgage according to his estate interest or right in the mortgaged property; "mortgagee" includes a chargee by way of legal mortgage and any person from time to time deriving title under the original mortgagee; and "mortgagee in possession" is, for the purposes of this Act, a mortgagee who, in right of the mortgage, has entered into and is in possession of the mortgaged property; and "right of redemption" includes an option to repurchase only if the option in effect creates a right of redemption;

(xvii) "Notice" includes constructive notice;

(xviii) "Personal representative" means the executor, original or by representation, or administrator for the time being of a deceased person, and as regards any liability for the payment of death duties includes any person who takes possession of or intermeddles with the property of a deceased person without the authority of the personal representatives or the court;

(xix) "Possession" includes receipt of rents and profits or the right to receive the same, if any; and "income" includes rents and profits;

(xx) "Property" includes any thing in action, and any interest in real or personal property;

(xxi) "Purchaser" means a purchaser in good faith for valuable consideration and includes a lessee, mortgagee or other person who for valuable consideration acquires an interest in property except that in Part I of this Act and elsewhere where so expressly provided "purchaser" only means a person who acquires an interest in or charge on property for money or money's worth; and in reference to a legal estate includes a chargee by way of legal mortgage; and where the context so requires "purchaser" includes an intending purchaser; "purchase" has a meaning corresponding with that of "purchaser"; and "valuable consideration" includes marriage[, and formation of a civil partnership,] but does not include a nominal consideration in money;

(xxii) "Registered land" has the same meaning as in the [Land Registration Act 2002;] . . .

(xxiii) "Rent" includes a rent service or a rentcharge, or other rent, toll, duty, royalty, or annual or periodical payment in money or money's worth, reserved or issuing out of or charged upon land, but does not include mortgage interest; "rentcharge" includes a fee farm rent; "fine" includes a premium or foregift and any payment, consideration, or benefit in the nature of a fine, premium or foregift; "lessor" includes an underlessor and a person deriving title under a lessor or underlessor; and "lessee" includes an underlessee and a person deriving title under a lessee or underlessee, and "lease" includes an underlease or other tenancy;

(xxiv) "Sale" includes an extinguishment of manorial incidents, but in other respects means a sale properly so called;

(xxv) "Securities" include stocks, funds and shares;

(xxvi) "Tenant for life", "statutory owner", "settled land", "settlement", "vesting deed", "subsidiary vesting deed", "vesting order", "vesting instrument", "trust instrument", "capital money" and "trustees of the settlement" have the same meanings as in the Settled Land Act 1925;

(xxvii) "Term of years absolute" means a term of years (taking effect either in possession or in reversion whether or not at a rent) with or without impeachment for waste, subject or not to another legal estate, and either certain or liable to determination by notice, re-entry, operation of law, or by a provision for cesser on redemption, or in any other event (other than the dropping of a life, or the determination of a determinable life interest); but does not include any term of years determinable with life or lives or with the cesser of a determinable life interest, nor, if created after the commencement of this Act, a term of years which is not expressed to take effect in possession within twenty-one years after the creation thereof where required by this Act to take effect within that period; and in this definition the expression "term of years" includes a term for less than a year, or for a year or years and a fraction of a year or from year to year;

(xxviii) "Trust Corporation" means the Public Trustee or a corporation either appointed by the court in any particular case to be a trustee or entitled by rules made under subsection (3) of section four of the Public Trustee Act 1906 to act as custodian trustee;

(xxix) "Trust for sale", in relation to land, means an immediate . . . trust for sale, whether or not exercisable at the request or with the consent of any person . . . ; "trustees for sale" mean the persons (including a personal representative) holding land on trust for sale; . . . ;

(xxx) "United Kingdom" means Great Britain and Northern Ireland;

(xxxi) "Will" includes codicil.

[(1A) Any reference in this Act to money being paid into court shall be construed as referring to the money being paid into the *Supreme Court* [Senior Courts] or any other court that has jurisdiction, and any reference in this Act to the court, in a context referring to the investment or application of money paid into court, shall be construed, in the case of money paid into the *Supreme Court* [Senior Courts], as referring to the High Court, and in the case of money paid into another court, as referring to that other court.]

(2) Where an equitable interest in or power over property arises by statute or operation of law, references to the creation of an interest or power include references to any interest or power so arising.

(3) References to registration under the Land Charges Act 1925 apply to any registration made under any other statute which is by the Land Charges Act 1925 to have effect as if the registration had been made under that Act.

Amendment

Sub-s (1): para (iiiA) inserted by the County Courts Act 1984, s 148(1), Sch 2, para 15.
Sub-s (1): para (iiiA) repealed by SI 1991/724, art 2(8), Schedule, Part I.
Sub-s (1): in para (iv) words omitted repealed by the Finance Act 1949, s 52(9), (10), Sch 11, Part IV.
Sub-s (1): in para (ix) words omitted repealed by the Trusts of Land and Appointment of Trustees Act 1996, s 25(2), Sch 4; for savings in relation to entailed interests created before the commencement of that Act, and savings consequential upon the abolition of the doctrine of conversion, see s 25(4), (5) thereof.
Sub-s (1): in para (x) words omitted repealed by the Trusts of Land and Appointment of Trustees Act 1996, s 25(2), Sch 4; for savings in relation to entailed interests created before the commencement of that Act, and savings consequential upon the abolition of the doctrine of conversion, see s 25(4), (5) thereof.
Sub-s (1): para (xiii) substituted by the Mental Health Act 1959, s 149(1), Sch 7, Part I.
Sub-s (1): para (xiii) repealed by the Mental Capacity Act 2005, s 67(1), (2), Sch 6, para 4(1), (3), Sch 7.
Sub-s (1): in para (xv) words "the Minister of Agriculture, Fisheries and Food" in square brackets substituted by SI 1955/554.
Sub-s (1): in para (xxi) words ", and formation of a civil partnership," in square brackets inserted by the Civil Partnership Act 2004, s 261(1), Sch 27, para 7.
Sub-s (1): in para (xxii) words "Land Registration Act 2002;" in square brackets substituted by the Land Registration Act 2002, s 133, Sch 11, para 2(1), (13)(a).
Sub-s (1): in para (xxii) words omitted repealed by the Land Registration Act 2002, ss 133, 135, Sch 11, para 2(1), (13)(b), Sch 13.
Sub-s (1): in para (xxix) words omitted repealed by the Trusts of Land and Appointment of Trustees Act 1996, s 25(2), Sch 4; for savings in relation to entailed interests created before the commencement of that Act, and savings consequential upon the abolition of the doctrine of conversion, see s 25(4), (5) thereof.
Sub-s (1A): inserted by the Administration of Justice Act 1965, ss 17, 18, Sch 1.
Sub-s (1A): words "Supreme Court" in italics in both places they occur repealed and subsequent words in square brackets substituted, from a date to be appointed, by the Constitutional Reform Act 2005, s 59(5), Sch 11, Pt 2, para 4(1), (3).

Commentary

The definitions contained in this section are used not just in this statute but throughout the 1925 legislation and indeed more recent legislation. Reference is therefore made to this section throughout this work.

[180]

ADMINISTRATION OF ESTATES ACT 1925

1925 Chapter 23

ARRANGEMENT OF SECTIONS

PART I
DEVOLUTION OF REAL ESTATE

PART II
EXECUTORS AND ADMINISTRATORS

PART III
ADMINISTRATION OF ASSETS

PART IV
DISTRIBUTION OF RESIDUARY ESTATE

PART V
SUPPLEMENTAL

An Act to consolidate Enactments relating to the Administration of the Estates of Deceased Persons

[9th April 1925]

General Note

Part of the great property law reforms of 1925, the Administration of Estates Act 1925 (AEA 1925) governs the manner in which estates are administered. It has been extensively repealed and amended over the years and reference should also be made to the Intestate Estates Act 1952, the Administration of Estates (Small Payments) Act 1965, the Family Provision Act 1966, the Law of Property (Miscellaneous Provisions) Act 1994 and the Law Reform (Succession) Act 1995 (all of which are reproduced in this work).

PART I
DEVOLUTION OF REAL ESTATE

1 Devolution of real estate on personal representative

(1) Real estate to which a deceased person was entitled for an interest not ceasing on his death shall on his death, and notwithstanding any testamentary disposition thereof, devolve from time to time on the personal representative of the deceased, in like manner as before the commencement of this Act chattels real devolved on the personal representative from time to time of a deceased person.

(2) The personal representatives for the time being of a deceased person are deemed in law his heirs and assigns within the meaning of all trusts and powers.

(3) The personal representatives shall be the representative of the deceased in regard to his real estate to which he was entitled for an interest not ceasing on his death as well as in regard to his personal estate.

Commentary

This section had the effect of assimilating the law in relation to the devolution on personal representatives of personal property on the one hand, (which always vested in them) and real estate, which before the Land Transfer Act 1897 did not. For the meaning of "real estate" see s 3(1) below. Terms of years absolute are defined in the Law of Property Act 1925, s 205(1)(xxvii) **[180]**. For an explanation as to an "interest not ceasing on his death" see ss 3(3)–(5) below. The use of the words "from time to time" in sub-s (1) has the effect that the property will devolve on personal representatives by succession. Subsection (2) has the effect of making the personal representative of the last surviving trustee, trustee for the time being of any property of which the deceased was trustee and see the Trustee Act 1925, s 18 **[88]**.

[181]

2 Application to real estate of law affecting chattels real

(1) Subject to the provisions of this Act, all enactments and rules of law, and all jurisdiction of any court with respect to the appointment of administrators or to probate or letters of administration, or to dealings before probate in the case of chattels real, and with respect to costs and other matters in the administration of personal estate, in force before the commencement of this Act, and all powers, duties, rights, equities, obligations, and liabilities of a personal representative in force at the commencement of this Act with respect to chattels real, shall apply and attach to the personal representative and shall have effect with respect to real estate vested in him, and in particular all such powers of disposition and dealing as were before the commencement of this Act exercisable as respects chattels real by the survivor or survivors of two or more personal representatives, as well as by a single personal representative, or by all the personal representatives together, shall be exercisable by the personal representatives or representative of the deceased with respect to his real estate.

(2) Where as respects real estate there are two or more personal representatives, a conveyance of real estate devolving under this Part of this Act [or a contract for such a conveyance] shall not . . . be made without the concurrence therein of all such representatives or an order of the court, but where probate is granted to one or some of two or more persons named as executors, whether or not power is reserved to the other or others to prove, any conveyance of the real estate [or contract for such a conveyance] may be made by the proving executor or executors for the time being, without an order of the court, and shall be as effectual as if all the persons named as executors had concurred therein.

(3) Without prejudice to the rights and powers of a personal representative, the appointment of a personal representative in regard to real estate shall not, save as hereinafter provided, affect—

- (a) any rule as to marshalling or as to administration of assets;
- (b) the beneficial interest in real estate under any testamentary disposition;
- (c) any mode of dealing with any beneficial interest in real estate, or the proceeds of sale thereof;
- (d) the right of any person claiming to be interested in the real estate to take proceedings for the protection or recovery thereof against any person other than the personal representative.

Amendment

Sub-s (2): words in square brackets inserted, and words omitted repealed, by the Law of Property (Miscellaneous Provisions) Act 1994, ss 16(1), 21(2), Sch 2.

Commentary

Subsection (1) confers on personal representatives all the powers they had prior to the AEA 1925 in relation to chattels real, to the real property held by them. Therefore before 1925, an executor who derived title from the will could bring proceedings in respect of chattels real—now he can do so in respect of real property. An administrator, however, who derives authority from the grant, could not. Subsection (2) requires all administrators and all proving executors join a conveyance. Subsection (3) which was declaratory of the previous law makes it clear that the personal representative takes in a representative capacity only.

[182]

3 Interpretation of Part I

(1) In this Part of this Act "real estate" includes—

(i) Chattels real, and land in possession, remainder, or reversion, and every interest in or over land to which a deceased person was entitled at the time of his death; and

(ii) Real estate held on trust (including settled land) or by way of mortgage or security, but not . . . money secured or charged on land.

(2) A testator shall be deemed to have been entitled at his death to any interest in real estate passing under any gift contained in his will which operates as an appointment under a general power to appoint by will, or operates under the testamentary power conferred by statute to dispose of an entailed interest.

(3) An entailed interest of a deceased person shall (unless disposed of under the testamentary power conferred by statute) be deemed an interest ceasing on his death, but any further or other interest of the deceased in the same property in remainder or reversion which is capable of being disposed of by his will shall not be deemed to be an interest so ceasing.

(4) The interest of a deceased person under a joint tenancy where another tenant survives the deceased is an interest ceasing on his death.

(5) On the death of a corporator sole his interest in the corporation's real and personal estate shall be deemed to be an interest ceasing on his death and shall devolve to his successor.

This subsection applies on the demise of the Crown as respects all property, real and personal, vested in the Crown as a corporation sole.

Amendment

Sub-s (1): words omitted from para (ii) repealed by the Trusts of Land and Appointment of Trustees Act 1996, s 25(2), Sch 4; for savings in relation to entailed interests created before the commencement of that Act, and savings consequential upon the abolition of the doctrine of conversion, see s 25(4), (5) thereof.

Commentary

The power to dispose of an entailed interest by will referred to in sub-s (2) is contained in the Law of Property Act 1925 **[177]**, s 176 and see *Acheson v Russell* [1975] Ch 67. If not so disposed of, it will cease on death in accordance with sub-s (3). Subsection (4) applies to beneficial joint tenancies and an interest held in common will pass to the personal representatives.

[183]

PART II
EXECUTORS AND ADMINISTRATORS

GENERAL PROVISIONS

4 . . .

. . .

Amendment

Repealed by the Supreme Court of Judicature (Consolidation) Act 1925, s 226, Sch 6.

[184]

5 Cesser of right of executor to prove

Where a person appointed executor by a will—

(i) survives the testator but dies without having taken out probate of the will; or

(ii) is cited to take out probate of the will and does not appear to the citation; or

(iii) renounces probate of the will;

his rights in respect of the executorship shall wholly cease, and the representation to the testator and the administration of his real and personal estate shall devolve and be committed in like manner as if that person had not been appointed executor.

Commentary

Once a grant has been made then the personal representatives of the deceased representative can take over (as to which see s 7 below) but not before. As to citation to take a grant see the Supreme Court Act 1981, s 112 and the notes thereto **[351]**. An executor can renounce probate in writing but only before he has intermeddled in the estate, see *Re Bigg's Estate* [1966] P 118.

[185]

6 Withdrawal of renunciation

(1) Where an executor who has renounced probate has been permitted, whether before or after the commencement of this Act, to withdraw the renunciation and prove the will, the probate shall take effect and be deemed always to have taken effect without prejudice to the previous acts and dealings of and notices to any other personal representative who has previously proved the will or taken out letters of administration, and a memorandum of the subsequent probate shall be endorsed on the original probate or letters of administration.

(2) This section applies whether the testator died before or after the commencement of this Act.

Commentary

An executor cannot withdraw a renunciation as of right but the Probate Registrar has power to give leave to an executor to retract the renunciation, see the Non-Contentious Probate Rules 1987, SI 1987/2024, r 37(3) **[Appendix V]**. Application is made ex parte to a Registrar with an affidavit in support. As to an example of the refusal to allow an executor to retract, see *Re Toscani* [1912] P 1.

[186]

7 Executor of executor represents original testator

(1) An executor of a sole or last surviving executor of a testator is the executor of that testator.

This provision shall not apply to an executor who does not prove the will of his testator, and, in the case of an executor who on his death leaves surviving him some other executor of his testator who afterwards proves the will of that testator, it shall cease to apply on such probate being granted.

(2) So long as the chain of such representation is unbroken, the last executor in the chain is the executor of every preceding testator.

(3) The chain of such representation is broken by—

- (a) an intestacy; or
- (b) the failure of a testator to appoint an executor; or
- (c) the failure to obtain probate of a will;

but is not broken by a temporary grant of administration if probate is subsequently granted.

(4) Every person in the chain of representation to a testator—

- (a) has the same rights in respect of the real and personal estate of that testator as the original executor would have had if living; and
- (b) is, to the extent to which the estate whether real or personal of that testator has come to his hands, answerable as if he were an original executor.

Commentary
This section provides for there to be chains of executors so that if probate is granted to A and B, and A dies, the executorship vests in B. However, when B dies, provided that he appoints an executor, C, who proves his will, C will become executor of the original deceased as well. The proviso to sub-s (1) applies where A has proved and B has not. When A dies appointing D his executor who proves, D will take over but only for so long as B does not prove. Where the chain is broken as in sub-s (3), then an administrator de bonis non has to be appointed in the usual order for priority in taking a grant (see the Non-Contentious Probate Rules 1987, SI 1987/2024, r 20 **[Appendix V]**). Note that the grant of a temporary grant will not break the chain provided that a grant of probate then issues (see sub-s (3)).

[187]

8 Right of proving executors to exercise powers

(1) Where probate is granted to one or some of two or more persons named as executors, whether or not power is reserved to the others or other to prove, all the powers which are by law conferred on the personal representative may be exercised by the proving executor or executors for the time being and shall be as effectual as if all the persons named as executors had concurred therein.

(2) This section applies whether the testator died before or after the commencement of this Act.

Commentary
The old rule was that probate granted for the benefit of one executor benefited all those named. This section, which should be read together with s 5, sets out the circumstances where the rights of a named executor will cease and makes it clear that the powers are exercisable by the proving executors only.

[188]

[9 Vesting of estate in Public Trustee where intestacy or lack of executors

(1) Where a person dies intestate, his real and personal estate shall vest in the Public Trustee until the grant of administration.

(2) Where a testator dies and—

- (a) at the time of his death there is no executor with power to obtain probate of the will, or
- (b) at any time before probate of the will is granted there ceases to be any executor with power to obtain probate,

the real and personal estate of which he disposes by the will shall vest in the Public Trustee until the grant of representation.

(3) The vesting of real or personal estate in the Public Trustee by virtue of this section does not confer on him any beneficial interest in, or impose on him any duty, obligation or liability in respect of, the property.]

Amendment
Substituted by the Law of Property (Miscellaneous Provisions) Act 1994, s 14(1).

Commentary
See also in this regard the Law of Property (Miscellaneous Provisions) Act 1994, s 14 **[418]**. The old s 9 provided for the estate of a deceased dying intestate or in the circumstances set out here to vest in the probate judge, that is, the President of the Family Division. Henceforth, that function will be assumed by the Public Trustee whose office is established by the Public Trustee Act 1906 **[59]**. The Public Trustee has no duties to discharge in this role, nor is he a trustee within the meaning of the Trustee Act 1925 **[138]** (see *Re Deans* [1954] 1 WLR 332 and *Earnshaw v Hartley* [2000] Ch 155). However, notices to quit to terminate the deceased's tenancy can be served on him and land charges registered against him (*Smith v Mather* [1948] 2 KB 212; *Wirral v Smith* (1982) 43 P & CR 312).

[189]

10–14 . . .

. . .

Amendment
Repealed by the Supreme Court of Judicature (Consolidation) Act 1925, s 226, Sch 6.

[190]

15 Executor not to act while administration is in force

Where administration has been granted in respect of any real or personal estate of a deceased person, no person shall have power to bring any action or otherwise act as executor of the deceased person in respect of the estate comprised in or affected by the grant until the grant has been recalled or revoked.

Commentary
An executor can of course bring an action before a grant is obtained because his authority derives from the will. However, while there is a grant of administration in force the executor cannot act, see *Re West, Barclays Bank Ltd v Handley* [1947] WN 2.

[191]

16 . . .

. . .

Amendment
Repealed by the Supreme Court of Judicature (Consolidation) Act 1925, s 226, Sch 6.

[192]

17 Continuance of legal proceedings after revocation of temporary administration

[(1)] If, while any legal proceeding is pending in any court by or against an administrator to whom a temporary administration has been granted, that administration is revoked, that court may order that the proceeding be continued by or against the new personal representative in like manner as if the same had been originally commenced by or against him, but subject to such conditions and variations, if any, as that court directs.

[(2) The county court has jurisdiction under this section where the proceedings are pending in that court.]

Amendment
Sub-s (1): numbered as such by the County Courts Act 1984, s 148(1), Sch 2, Part III, para 11.
Sub-s (2): inserted by the County Courts Act 1984, s 148(1), Sch 2, Part III, para 11.

Commentary
For the procedure on substituting the new personal representative for the old, see the Civil Procedure Rules 1998, SI 1998/3132, r 19.2(4)(a) and para 5 of the Practice Direction to that rule. Any application to substitute should be supported by evidence that one grant has been revoked, that a new grant has been issued, and the stage of the proceedings which has been reached.

[193]

18–20 . . .

. . .

Amendment
Repealed by the Supreme Court of Judicature (Consolidation) Act 1925, s 226, Sch 6.

[194]

21 Rights and liabilities of administrator

Every person to whom administration of the real and personal estate of a deceased person is granted, shall, subject to the limitations contained in the grant, have the same rights and liabilities and be accountable in like manner as if he were the executor of the deceased.

Commentary

This section makes it clear that the office of administrator is the same as the office of executor but note that there is no chain of representation as far as administrators are concerned (s 7 above).

[195]

[21A Debtor who becomes creditor's executor by representation or administrator to account for debt to estate

(1) Subject to subsection (2) of this section, where a debtor becomes his deceased creditor's executor by representation or administrator—

(a) his debt shall thereupon be extinguished; but

(b) he shall be accountable for the amount of the debt as part of the creditor's estate in any case where he would be so accountable if he had been appointed as an executor by the creditor's will.

(2) Subsection (1) of this section does not apply where the debtor's authority to act as executor or administrator is limited to part only of the creditor's estate which does not include the debt; and a debtor whose debt is extinguished by virtue of paragraph (a) shall not be accountable for its amount by virtue of paragraph (b) of that subsection in any case where the debt was barred by the Limitation Act 1939 before he became the creditor's executor or administrator.

(3) In this section "debt" includes any liability, and "debtor" and "creditor" shall be construed accordingly.]

Amendment

Inserted by the Limitation Amendment Act 1980, s 10.

Commentary

A limitation defence can be pleaded either by or against a personal representative. It was at one time considered that the defence would not be available in a case where the debtor became the personal representative (see *Seagram v Knight* (1867) LR Ch App 628). However, that decision was held to be wrong in *Bowring-Hanbury Trustee v Bowring-Hanbury* [1943] Ch 194. This section puts the matter beyond doubt, extinguishing the debt but making the debtor/executor accountable to the estate for it, except in cases where the grant is limited to a part of the estate not comprising the debt or where it is statute barred. The reference to the Limitation Act 1939 includes a reference to the Limitation Act 1980 (Sch 3 to that Act).

[196]

SPECIAL PROVISIONS AS TO SETTLED LAND

22 Special executors as respects settled land

(1) A testator may appoint, and in default of such express appointment shall be deemed to have appointed, as his special executors in regard to settled land, the persons, if any, who are at his death the trustees of the settlement thereof, and probate may be granted to such trustees specially limited to the settled land.

In this subsection "settled land" means land vested in the testator which was settled previously to his death and not by his will.

(2) A testator may appoint other persons either with or without such trustees as aforesaid or any of them to be his general executors in regard to his other property and assets.

Commentary

This section will become of less and less importance in the future in the light of the abolition of strict settlements by the Trusts of Land and Appointment of Trustees Act 1996 **[431]**. For the meaning of "settlement" and "settled land" see the Settled Land Act 1925, s 1 **[Appendix II]** and s 55(1)(xxiv) below. Essentially, in a case where the deceased died the tenant for life of settled land, the legal estate will be vested in him but it does not pass to his general personal representatives but to special personal representatives, either appointed by his will, or in default deemed to be the trustees of the settlement. See also the Non-Contentious Probate Rules 1987, SI 1987/2024, r 29(2) **[Appendix V]** which provide that the special representatives are first entitled to a grant, followed by the special personal representatives. In the absence of any special representatives the general personal representatives will be trustees (Settled Land Act 1925, s 30(3) **[Appendix II]**).

[197]

23 Provisions where, as respects settled land, representation is not granted to the trustees of the settlement

(1) Where settled land becomes vested in a personal representative, not being a trustee of the settlement, upon trust to convey the land to or assent to the vesting thereof in the tenant for life or statutory owner in order to give effect to a settlement created before the death of the deceased and not by his will, or would on the grant of representation to him, have become so vested, such representative may—

(a) before representation has been granted, renounce his office in regard only to such settled land without renouncing it in regard to other property;

(b) after representation has been granted, apply to the court for revocation of the grant in regard to the settled land without applying in regard to other property.

(2) Whether such renunciation or revocation is made or not, the trustees of the settlement, or any person beneficially interested thereunder, may apply to the High Court for an order appointing a special or additional personal representative in respect of the settled land, and a special or additional personal representative, if and when appointed under the order, shall be in the same position as if representation had originally been granted to him alone in place of the original personal representative, if any, or to him jointly with the original personal representative, as the case may be, limited to the settled land, but without prejudice to the previous acts and dealings, if any, of the personal representative originally constituted or the effect of notices given to such personal representative.

(3) The court may make such order as aforesaid subject to such security, if any, being given by or on behalf of the special or additional personal representative, as the court may direct, and shall, unless the court considers that special considerations apply, appoint such persons as may be necessary to secure that the persons to act as representatives in respect of the settled land shall, if willing to act, be the same persons as are the trustees of the settlement, and an office copy of the order when made shall be furnished to the [principal registry of the Family Division of the High Court] for entry, and a memorandum of the order shall be endorsed on the probate or administration.

(4) The person applying for the appointment of a special or additional personal representative shall give notice of the application to the [principal registry of the Family Division of the High Court] in the manner prescribed.

(5) Rules of court may be made for prescribing for all matters required for giving effect to the provisions of this section, and in particular—

(a) for notice of any application being given to the proper officer;

(b) for production of orders, probates, and administration to the registry;

(c) for the endorsement on a probate or administration of a memorandum of an order, subject or not to any exceptions;

(d) for the manner in which the costs are to be borne;

(e) for protecting purchasers and trustees and other persons in a fiduciary position, dealing in good faith with or giving notices to a personal representative before notice of any order has been endorsed on the probate or administration or a pending action has been registered in respect of the proceedings.

Amendment

Sub-ss (3), (4): words in square brackets substituted by the Administration of Justice Act 1970, s 1(6), Sch 2, para 3.

Commentary

See also the notes to s 22 in respect of special personal representatives. Subsection (1) provides an exception to the general rule that there cannot be a partial renunciation of office (see s 5 above). Circumstances where settled land might become vested in someone other than the trustee of the settlement include where there are no trustees, or they refuse to act, or where there has been a general grant but no grant limited to settled land (*Re Bridgett and Hayes Contract* [1928] Ch 163). For the procedure under sub-s (2) for appointing an additional personal representative, see *Re Clifton* [1931] P 222. As to the prescribed manner of the notice under sub-s (4) see the Non-Contentious Probate Rules 1987, SI 1987/2024, r 67 **[Appendix V]**. Application should first be made to the Chancery Division (by way of a Part 8 claim form) for a direction to make the application, see *Practice Direction* [1928] WN 225. For the rules of court referred to in sub-s (5) see the Non-Contentious Probate Rules 1987, SI 1987/2024.

[198]

24 Power for special personal representatives to dispose of settled land

(1) The special personal representatives may dispose of the settled land without the concurrence of the general personal representatives, who may likewise dispose of the other property and assets of the deceased without the concurrence of the special personal representatives.

(2) In this section the expression "special personal representatives" means the representatives appointed to act for the purposes of settled land and includes any original personal representative who is to act with an additional personal representative for those purposes.

Commentary

This section provides an exception to the general rule in s 2(2) that personal representatives should act together.

[199]

DUTIES, RIGHTS AND OBLIGATIONS

[25 Duty of personal representatives

The personal representative of a deceased person shall be under a duty to—

(a) collect and get in the real and personal estate of the deceased and administer it according to law;

(b) when required to do so by the court, exhibit on oath in the court a full inventory of the estate and when so required render an account of the administration of the estate to the court;

(c) when required to do so by the High Court, deliver up the grant of probate or administration to that court.]

Amendment

Substituted by the Administration of Estates Act 1971, s 9.

Commentary

Before the amendment of this section by the Administration of Estates Act 1971 **[305]** an inventory and account of the estate was automatically required. An application for an inventory and account is non-contentious business and should be made to the Probate Registry, see: *CI v NS* [2004] EWHC 659.

[200]

26 Rights of action by and against personal representative

(1), (2) . . .

(3) A personal representative may distrain for arrears of a rentcharge due or accruing to the deceased in his lifetime on the land affected or charged therewith, so long as the land remains in the possession of the person liable to pay the rentcharge or of the persons deriving title under him, and in like manner as the deceased might have done had he been living.

(4) A personal representative may distrain upon land for arrears of rent due or accruing to the deceased in like manner as the deceased might have done had he been living.

Such arrears may be distrained for after the termination of the lease or tenancy as if the term or interest had not determined, if the distress is made—

(a) within six months after the termination of the lease or tenancy;

(b) during the continuance of the possession of the lessee or tenant from whom the arrears were due.

The statutory enactments relating to distress for rent apply to any distress made pursuant to this subsection,

(5), (6) . . .

Amendment

Sub-ss (1), (2), (5), (6): repealed by the Law Reform (Miscellaneous Provisions) Act 1934, s 1(7).

Commentary

At common law before 32 Hen 8 c 37 was passed, personal representatives could not sue for arrears of rent or rentcharge which had accrued during the lifetime of the deceased. This is the successor section to the statutes which remedied that.

[201]

27 Protection of persons on probate or administration

(1) Every person making or permitting to be made any payment or disposition in good faith under a representation shall be indemnified and protected in so doing, notwithstanding any defect or circumstance whatsoever affecting the validity of the representation.

(2) Where a representation is revoked, all payments and dispositions made in good faith to a personal representative under the representation before the revocation thereof are a valid discharge to the person making the same; and the personal representative who acted under the revoked representation may retain and reimburse himself in respect of any payments or dispositions made by him which the person to whom representation is afterwards granted might have properly made.

Commentary

This section protects personal representatives in the event of the revocation of the grant, even in circumstances where the "deceased" proves to be alive! See *Re Bloch* (1959) Times, 2 July.

[202]

28 Liability of person fraudulently obtaining or retaining estate of deceased

If any person, to the defrauding of creditors or without full valuable consideration, obtains, receives or holds any real or personal estate of a deceased person or effects the release of any debt or liability due to the estate of the deceased, he shall be charged as executor in his own wrong to the extent of the real and personal estate received or coming to his hands, or the debt or liability released, after deducting—

(a) any debt for valuable consideration and without fraud due to him from the deceased person at the time of his death; and

(b) any payment made by him which might properly be made by a personal representative.

Commentary

This section sets out the statutory basis for the liability of a executor de son tort—a person who intermeddles in the estate of a deceased (as to which see: *James v Williams* [2000] Ch 1). Note that the section will not apply to a case where the real personal representatives sue, as they will do so, on the basis of the executor de son tort's trespass to goods or land belonging to them. At common law, an executor de son tort had no right to deduct debts owed to him whereas sub-s (2) recognises his right to do so. This section was considered in *Jackson v Pollard* (1993) 67 P & CR 327 (where the acts of interference were held not to be in the nature of acts of an executor).

[203]

29 Liability of estate of personal representative

Where a person as personal representative of a deceased person (including an executor in his own wrong) wastes or converts to his own use any part of the real or personal estate of the deceased, and dies, his personal representative shall to the extent of the available assets of the defaulter be liable and chargeable in respect of such waste or conversion in the same manner as the defaulter would have been if living.

Commentary

The common law rule (not changed by this section) is that a personal representative is liable only to the extent that assets come into his hands. That therefore defines the liability of the personal representative of the defaulter under this section, who in turn cannot be liable for anything more than the assets in his hands.

[204]

30 Provisions applicable where administration granted to nominee of the Crown

(1) Where the administration of the real and personal estate of any deceased person is granted to a nominee of the Crown (whether the Treasury Solicitor, or a person nominated by the Treasury Solicitor, or any other person), any legal proceeding by or against that nominee for the recovery of the real or personal estate, or any part or share thereof, shall be of the same character, and be instituted and carried on in the same manner, and be subject to the same rules of law and equity (including, except as otherwise provided by this Act, the rules of limitation under the statutes of limitation or otherwise), in all respects as if the administration had been granted to such nominee as one of the persons interested under this Act in the estate of the deceased.

(2) An information or other proceeding on the part of His Majesty shall not be filed or instituted, and a petition of right shall not be presented, in respect of the real or personal estate of any deceased person or any part or share thereof, or any claim thereon, except . . . subject to the same rules of law and equity within and subject to which a proceeding for the like purposes might be instituted by or against a subject.

(3) The Treasury Solicitor shall not be required, when applying for or obtaining administration of the estate of a deceased person for the use or benefit of His Majesty, to deliver, nor shall . . . the High Court or the Commissioners of Inland Revenue be entitled to receive in connexion with any such application or grant of administration, any affidavit, statutory declaration, account, certificate, or other statement verified on oath; but the Treasury Solicitor shall deliver and the said Division and Commissioners respectively shall accept, in lieu thereof, an account or particulars of the estate of the deceased signed by or on behalf of the Treasury Solicitor.

(4) References in sections two, four . . . and seven of the Treasury Solicitor Act 1876, and in subsection (3) of section three of the Duchy of Lancaster Act, 1920, to "personal estate" shall include real estate.

Amendment

Sub-s (2): words omitted repealed by the Limitation Act 1939, s 34(4), Schedule.
Sub-s (3): words omitted repealed by the Administration of Justice Act 1970, s 54(3), Sch 11.
Sub-s (4): words omitted repealed by the Statute Law (Repeals) Act 1981.

Commentary

Subsections (1) and (2) make it clear that the Crown is in no different a position to any other administrator when proceedings are brought by or against it and this has particular ramifications in relation to limitation periods under the Limitation Act 1980. So for example the Crown normally has a 30-year limitation period for the recovery of land, but as administrator will be subject to the usual 12 year rule (Limitation Act 1980, Sch 1, para 10). Subsection (3) relieves the Crown from the administrator's oath.

[205]

31 Power to make rules

Provision may be made by rules of court for giving effect to the provisions of this Part of this Act so far as relates to real estate and in particular for adapting the procedure and practice on the grant of letters of administration to the case of real estate.

Commentary

The current rules of court are the Non-Contentious Probate Rules 1987, SI 1987/2024 **[Appendix V]**.

[206]

PART III
ADMINISTRATION OF ASSETS

32 Real and personal estate of deceased are assets for payment of debts

(1) The real and personal estate, whether legal or equitable, of a deceased person, to the extent of his beneficial interest therein, and the real and personal estate of which a deceased person in pursuance of any general power (including the statutory power to dispose of entailed interests) disposes by his will, are assets for payment of his debts (whether by specialty or simple contract) and liabilities, and any disposition by will inconsistent with this enactment is void as against the creditors, and the court shall if necessary, administer the property for the purpose of the payment of the debts and liabilities.

This subsection takes effect without prejudice to the rights of incumbrancers.

(2) If any person to whom any such beneficial interest devolves, or is given, or in whom any such interest vests, disposes thereof in good faith before an action is brought or process is sued out against him, he shall be personally liable for the value

of the interest so disposed of by him, but that interest shall not be liable to be taken in execution in the action or under the process.

Commentary

Previously the primary liability for the payment of debts fell on personal property but sub-s (1) puts real and personal property on a par, and see *Re Harland-Peck, Hercy v Mayglothing* [1941] Ch 182. See ss 34 and 35 below as to the payment of debts. Subsection (2) prevents the following or tracing of assets disposed of before proceedings are issued, and has the effect that the testator's debts become those of the beneficiary disposing of the asset (see *Re Hedgely, Small v Hedgely* (1886) 34 Ch D 379). It is the creditors who can pursue the beneficiary, who remains personally liable, see *Worthington & Co Ltd v Abbott* [1910] 1 Ch 588.

[207]

33 Trust for sale

[(1) On the death of a person intestate as to any real or personal estate, that estate shall be held in trust by his personal representatives with the power to sell it.]

(2) [The personal representatives shall pay out of—

- (a) the ready money of the deceased (so far as not disposed of by his will, if any); and
- (b) any net money arising from disposing of any other part of his estate (after payment of costs),

all] such funeral, testamentary and administration expenses, debts and other liabilities as are properly payable thereout having regard to the rules of administration contained in this Part of this Act, and out of the residue of the said money the personal representative shall set aside a fund sufficient to provide for any pecuniary legacies bequeathed by the will (if any) of the deceased.

(3) During the minority of any beneficiary or the subsistence of any life interest and pending the distribution of the whole or any part of the estate of the deceased, the personal representatives may invest the residue of the said money, or so much thereof as may not have been distributed, [under the Trustee Act 2000].

(4) The residue of the said money and any investments for the time being representing the same, [and any part of the estate of the deceased which remains] unsold and is not required for the administration purposes aforesaid, is in this Act referred to as "the residuary estate of the intestate."

(5) The income (including net rents and profits of real estate and chattels real after payment of rates, taxes, rent, costs of insurance, repairs and other outgoings properly attributable to income) of so much of the real and personal estate of the deceased as may not be disposed of by his will, if any, or may not be required for the administration purposes aforesaid, may, however such estate is invested, as from the death of the deceased, be treated and applied as income, and for that purpose any necessary apportionment may be made between tenant for life and remainderman.

(6) Nothing in this section affects the rights of any creditor of the deceased or the rights of the Crown in respect of death duties.

(7) Where the deceased leaves a will, this section has effect subject to the provisions contained in the will.

Amendment

Sub-s (1): substituted by the Trusts of Land and Appointment of Trustees Act 1996, s 5, Sch 2, para 5(1), (2); for savings in relation to entailed interests created before the commencement of that Act, and savings consequential upon the abolition of the doctrine of conversion, see s 25(4), (5) thereof.

Sub-s (2): words from "The personal representatives" to "of costs), all" in square brackets substituted by the Trusts of Land and Appointment of Trustees Act 1996, s 5, Sch 2, para 5(1), (3); for savings in relation to entailed interests created before the commencement of that Act,

and savings consequential upon the abolition of the doctrine of conversion, see s 25(4), (5) thereof.
Sub-s (3): words "under the Trustee Act 2000" in square brackets substituted by the Trustee Act 2000, s 40(1), Sch 2, Pt II, para 27.
Sub-s (4): words "and any part of the estate of the deceased which remains" in square brackets substituted by the Trusts of Land and Appointment of Trustees Act 1996, s 5, Sch 2, para 5(1), (4); for savings in relation to entailed interests created before the commencement of that Act, and savings consequential upon the abolition of the doctrine of conversion, see s 25(4), (5) thereof.

Commentary
Subsection (1) in its unamended form imposed a trust for sale, but the Trusts of Land and Appointment of Trustees Act 1996 has replaced statutory trusts for sale with trusts with a power to sell (see Trusts of Land and Appointment of Trustees Act 1996, s 5 **[435]**). Subsection (2) has the effect that property of the deceased which is undisposed of, is available before any other assets for the payment of debts. There is no definition of "testamentary and administration charges" in this Act but see *Re Eleanor Taylor's Estate and Will Trusts* [1969] 2 Ch 245. The rules governing the payment of debts are set out in s 34(3) and Sch 1, Pt II below. As to the power of investment conferred by the Trustee Act 2000 referred to in sub-s (3), see the Trustee Act 2000, s 3 **[478]**. "Residuary estate" as defined in sub-s (4) does not include property which is subject to an express trust for sale where there is a partial intestacy, see *Re Eleanor Taylor's Estate and Will Trusts* [1969] 2 Ch 245. Subsection (7) applies the section only insofar as the estate is not disposed of by will, see *Re Trollope's Will Trusts, Public Trustee v Trollope* [1927] 1 Ch 596.

[208]

34 Administration of assets

(1), (2) . . .

(3) Where the estate of a deceased person is solvent his real and personal estate shall, subject to rules of court and the provisions hereinafter contained as to charges on property of the deceased, and to the provisions, if any, contained in his will, be applicable towards the discharge of the funeral, testamentary and administration expenses, debts and liabilities payable thereout in the order mentioned in Part II of the First Schedule to this Act.

Amendment
Sub-s (1): repealed by the Insolvency Act 1985, s 235, Sch 10.
Sub-s (2): repealed by the Administration of Estates Act 1971, s 12(2), (4), (6), Sch 2, Part II.

Commentary
See Sch 1, Pt II below and the commentary thereon for the manner in which debts should be paid out of the estate. Insolvent estates can be administered by the personal representatives out of court, by the court under an administration order, or by the court in bankruptcy. For a full discussion see *Butterworths Wills, Probate and Administration Service*, para E [251] ff. The order is subject to a contrary intention and most wills direct the debts to be paid out of the residuary estate, and see *Re Kempthorne, Charles v Kempthorne* [1930] 1 Ch 268 and *Re James, Lloyd's Bank Ltd v Atkins* [1947] Ch 256.

[209]

35 Charges on property of deceased to be paid primarily out of the property charged

(1) Where a person dies possessed of, or entitled to, or, under a general power of appointment (including the statutory power to dispose of entailed interests) by his will disposes of, an interest in property, which at the time of his death is charged with the payment of money, whether by way of legal mortgage, equitable charge or otherwise (including a lien for unpaid purchase money), and the deceased has not by will deed or other document signified a contrary or other intention, the interest so charged, shall as between the different persons claiming through the deceased, be

primarily liable for the payment of the charge; and every part of the said interest, according to its value, shall bear a proportionate part of the charge on the whole thereof.

(2) Such contrary or other intention shall not be deemed to be signified—

(a) by a general direction for the payment of debts or of all the debts of the testator out of his personal estate, or his residuary real and personal estate, or his residuary real estate; or

(b) by a charge of debts upon any such estate;

unless such intention is further signified by words expressly or by necessary implication referring to all or some part of the charge.

(3) Nothing in this section affects the right of a person entitled to the charge to obtain payment or satisfaction thereof either out of the other assets of the deceased or otherwise.

Commentary

This section applies not only in the obvious case where land is subject to a mortgage, but also where there is a lien for unpaid purchase monies, see *Re Birmingham, Savage v Stannard* [1959] Ch 523, or a charge on a share created by the Articles of Association of the company, see *Re Turner, Tennant v Turner* [1938] Ch 593. Someone given an option to purchase property comprised in the estate is not a beneficiary within sub-s (1) and the debt is therefore not paid out of the property (*Re Fison's Will Trusts* [1950] Ch 394). The provision of a special fund (other than by way of a direction covered by sub-s (2)) will signify a contrary intention (*Re Fegan, Fegan v Fegan* [1928] 1 Ch 45). But not a direction made in the lifetime of the deceased not directed to his death, see *Re Nicholson, Nicholson v Boulton* [1923] WN 251. Where the fund set aside to pay the debts is insufficient to cover the secured debt, it is thrown back on the property on which it is charged, see *Re Birch, Hunt v Thorn* [1909] 1 Ch 787. The taking out of an endowment policy at the same time as a mortgage and charging it to a Building Society was regarded as sufficient evidence of contrary intention for a flat to pass free of mortgage notwithstanding there were no words to that effect in the Will, see *Ross v Perrin-Hughes* (2004) The Times November 24.

[210]

36 Effect of assent or conveyance by personal representative

(1) A personal representative may assent to the vesting, in any person who (whether by devise, bequest, devolution, appropriation or otherwise) may be entitled thereto, either beneficially or as a trustee or personal representative, of any estate or interest in real estate to which the testator or intestate was entitled or over which he exercised a general power of appointment by his will, including the statutory power to dispose of entailed interests, and which devolved upon the personal representative.

(2) The assent shall operate to vest in that person the estate or interest to which the assent relates, and, unless a contrary intention appears, the assent shall relate back to the death of the deceased.

(3) . . .

(4) An assent to the vesting of a legal estate shall be in writing, signed by the personal representative, and shall name the person in whose favour it is given and shall operate to vest in that person the legal estate to which it relates; and an assent not in writing or not in favour of a named person shall not be effectual to pass a legal estate.

(5) Any person in whose favour an assent or conveyance of a legal estate is made by a personal representative may require that notice of the assent or conveyance be written or endorsed on or permanently annexed to the probate or letters of administration, at the cost of the estate of the deceased, and that the probate or letters of administration be produced, at the like cost, to prove that the notice has been placed thereon or annexed thereto.

(6) A statement in writing by a personal representative that he has not given or made an assent or conveyance in respect of a legal estate, shall, in favour of a purchaser, but without prejudice to any previous disposition made in favour of another purchaser deriving title mediately or immediately under the personal representative, be sufficient evidence that an assent or conveyance has not been given or made in respect of the legal estate to which the statement relates, unless notice of a previous assent or conveyance affecting that estate has been placed on or annexed to the probate or administration.

A conveyance by a personal representative of a legal estate to a purchaser accepted on the faith of such a statement shall (without prejudice as aforesaid and unless notice of a previous assent or conveyance affecting that estate has been placed on or annexed to the probate or administration) operate to transfer or create the legal estate expressed to be conveyed in like manner as if no previous assent or conveyance had been made by the personal representative.

A personal representative making a false statement, in regard to any such matter, shall be liable in like manner as if the statement had been contained in a statutory declaration.

(7) An assent or conveyance by a personal representative in respect of a legal estate shall, in favour of a purchaser, unless notice of a previous assent or conveyance affecting that legal estate has been placed on or annexed to the probate or administration, be taken as sufficient evidence that the person in whose favour the assent or conveyance is given or made is the person entitled to have the legal estate conveyed to him, and upon the proper trusts, if any, but shall not otherwise prejudicially affect the claim of any person rightfully entitled to the estate vested or conveyed or any charge thereon.

(8) A conveyance of a legal estate by a personal representative to a purchaser shall not be invalidated by reason only that the purchaser may have notice that all the debts, liabilities, funeral, and testamentary or administration expenses, duties, and legacies of the deceased have been discharged or provided for.

(9) An assent or conveyance given or made by a personal representative shall not, except in favour of a purchaser of a legal estate, prejudice the right of the personal representative or any other person to recover the estate or interest to which the assent or conveyance relates, or to be indemnified out of such estate or interest against any duties, debts, or liability to which such estate or interest would have been subject if there had not been any assent or conveyance.

(10) A personal representative may, as a condition of giving an assent or making a conveyance, require security for the discharge of any such duties, debt, or liability, but shall not be entitled to postpone the giving of an assent merely by reason of the subsistence of any such duties, debt or liability if reasonable arrangements have been made for discharging the same; and an assent may be given subject to any legal estate or charge by way of legal mortgage.

(11) This section shall not operate to impose any stamp duty in respect of an assent, and in this section "purchaser" means a purchaser for money or money's worth.

(12) This section applies to assents and conveyances made after the commencement of this Act, whether the testator or intestate died before of after such commencement.

Amendment

Sub-s (3): repealed by the Law of Property (Miscellaneous Provisions) Act 1994, s 21(2), Sch 2.

Commentary

Note that this section deals with assents of real property and not of personalty for which there are at common law no formalities. An assent of equitable interests in land can take place informally (*Re Edwards' Will Trusts* [1982] Ch 30). For the meaning of "real estate" see s 3(1) above. A deed is not necessary unless there are covenants included. See the Settled Land Act 1925, s 8 **[Appendix II]** for vesting assents in respect of settlements created by will before the coming into effect of the Trusts of Land and Appointment of Trustees Act 1996 on 1 January 1997. A personal representative must still assent to the vesting of property in himself whether as a beneficiary or trustee (see *Re King's Will Trusts* [1964] Ch 542). An assent will only work if the legal estate has devolved on the personal representatives in accordance with s 1 above, and if it has not, a conveyance will be needed, see *Re Stirrup's Contract* [1986] 1 WLR 449. Advantage cannot be taken of sub-s (7) where the assent contains a recital casting doubt on the assentee's rights, see *Re Duce and Boots Chemists (Southern) Ltd's Contract* [1937] Ch 642.

[211]

37 Validity of conveyance not affected by revocation of representation

(1) All conveyances of any interest in real or personal estate made to a purchaser either before or after the commencement of this Act by a person to whom probate or letters of administration have been granted are valid, notwithstanding any subsequent revocation or variation, either before or after the commencement of this Act, of the probate or administration.

(2) This section takes effect without prejudice to any order of the court made before the commencement of this Act, and applies whether the testator or intestate died before or after such commencement.

Commentary

For the meaning of purchaser see s 55(1)(xviii). This section applies to purchasers of settled land, see *Re Bridgett & Hayes* [1928] Ch 163.

[212]

38 Right to follow property and powers of the court in relation thereto

(1) An assent or conveyance by a personal representative to a person other than a purchaser does not prejudice the rights of any person to follow the property to which the assent or conveyance relates, or any property representing the same, into the hands of the person in whom it is vested by the assent or conveyance, or of any other person (not being a purchaser) who may have received the same or in whom it may be vested.

(2) Notwithstanding any such assent or conveyance the court may, on the application of any creditor or other person interested,—

(a) order a sale, exchange, mortgage, charge, lease, payment, transfer or other transaction to be carried out which the court considers requisite for the purpose of giving effect to the rights of the persons interested;

(b) declare that the person, not being a purchaser, in whom the property is vested is a trustee for those purposes;

(c) give directions respecting the preparation and execution of any conveyance or other instrument or as to any other matter required for giving effect to the order;

(d) make any vesting order, or appoint a person to convey in accordance with the provisions of the Trustee Act 1925.

(3) This section does not prejudice the rights of a purchaser or a person deriving title under him, but applies whether the testator or intestate died before or after the commencement of this Act.

[(4) The county court has jurisdiction under this section where the estate in respect of which the application is made does not exceed in amount or value the county court limit.]

Amendment

Sub-s (4): inserted by the County Courts Act 1984, s 148(1), Sch 2, Part III, para 12.

Commentary

This section expressly reserves the right to follow assets into the hands of beneficiaries and sub-s (2) sets out the orders which the court can make to facilitate this. As to vesting orders and appointing persons to convey within sub-s (2)(d), see the Trustee Act 1925, ss 4–51 **[113–120]** and section 9 of the Law of Property Act 1925 **[145]**. Assets cannot be followed into the hands of a purchaser, for the meaning of which, see s 55(1)(xviii). The county court has jurisdiction in respect of estates which do not exceed £30,000 (the County Courts Act 1984, s 23 and the County Court Jurisdiction Order 1981, SI 1981/1123).

[213]

39 Powers of management

(1) In dealing with the real and personal estate of the deceased his personal representatives shall, for purposes of administration, or during a minority of any beneficiary or the subsistence of any life interest, or until the period of distribution arrives, have—

(i) [as respects the personal estate,] the same powers and discretions, including power to raise money by mortgage or charge (whether or not by deposit of documents), as a personal representative had before the commencement of this Act, with respect to personal estate vested in him . . . ; and

[(ii) as respects the real estate, all the functions conferred on them by Part I of the Trusts of Land and Appointment of Trustees Act 1996;]

(iii) all the powers [necessary] so that every contract entered into by a personal representative shall be binding on and be enforceable against and by the personal representative for the time being of the deceased, and may be carried into effect, or be varied or rescinded by him, and, in the case of a contract entered into by a predecessor, as if it had been entered into by himself.

[(1A) Subsection (1) of this section is without prejudice to the powers conferred on personal representatives by the Trustee Act 2000.]

(2) Nothing in this section shall affect the right of any person to require an assent or conveyance to be made.

(3) This section applies whether the testator or intestate died before or after the commencement of this Act.

Amendment

Sub-s (1): in para (i) words in square brackets inserted and words omitted repealed, para (ii) substituted and word in square brackets in para (iii) substituted by the Trusts of Land and Appointment of Trustees Act 1996, s 25(1), (2), Sch 3, para 6(1), (2), Sch 4; for savings in relation to entailed interests created before the commencement of that Act, and savings consequential upon the abolition of the doctrine of conversion, see s 25(4), (5) thereof.
Sub-s (1A): inserted by the Trustee Act 2000, s 40(1), Sch 2, Pt II, para 28.

Commentary

Once the personal representatives have assented, the period of distribution referred to in sub-s (1) comes to an end, see *Re Trollope's Will Trusts, Public Trustee v Trollope* [1927] 1 Ch 596. For the powers conferred by the Trusts of Land and Appointment of Trustees Act 1996, Pt I see **[431]**. For the powers conferred by the Trustee Act 2000 referred to in sub-s (1A) (investment, acquisition of land, delegation and insurance) see **[476]**.

[214]

40 Powers of personal representative for raising money, etc

(1) For giving effect to beneficial interests the personal representative may limit or demise land for a term of years absolute, with or without impeachment for waste, to

trustees on usual trusts for raising or securing any principal sum and the interest thereon for which the land, or any part thereof, is liable, and may limit or grant a rentcharge for giving effect to any annual or periodical sum for which the land or the income thereof or any part thereof is liable.

(2) This section applies whether the testator or intestate died before or after the commencement of this Act.

Commentary

This section provides a method whereby money can be raised by the personal representative to satisfy a beneficial interest (for example the statutory legacy referred to in section 46 below). It is in practice very rarely used.

[215]

41 Powers of personal representative as to appropriation

(1) The personal representative may appropriate any part of the real or personal estate, including things in action, of the deceased in the actual condition or state of investment thereof at the time of appropriation in or towards satisfaction of any legacy bequeathed by the deceased, or of any other interest or share in his property, whether settled or not, as to the personal representative may seem just and reasonable, according to the respective rights of the persons interested in the property of the deceased:

Provided that—

(i) an appropriation shall not be made under this section so as to affect prejudicially any specific devise or bequest;

(ii) an appropriation of property, whether or not being an investment authorised by law or by the will, if any, of the deceased for the investment of money subject to the trust, shall not (save as hereinafter mentioned) be made under this section except with the following consents:—

(a) when made for the benefit of a person absolutely and beneficially entitled in possession, the consent of that person;

(b) when made in respect of any settled legacy share or interest, the consent of either the trustee thereof, if any (not being also the personal representative), or the person who may for the time being be entitled to the income:

If the person whose consent is so required as aforesaid is an infant or [lacks capacity (within the meaning of the Mental Capacity Act 2005) to give the consent, it] shall be given on his behalf by his parents or parent, testamentary or other guardian . . . [or a person appointed as deputy for him by the Court of Protection], or if, in the case of an infant, there is no such parent or guardian, by the court on the application of his next friend;

(iii) no consent (save of such trustee as aforesaid) shall be required on behalf of a person who may come into existence after the time of appropriation, or who cannot be found or ascertained at that time;

(iv) if [no deputy is appointed for a person who lacks capacity to consent] then, if the appropriation is of an investment authorised by law or by the will, if any, of the deceased for the investment of money subject to the trust, no consent shall be required on behalf of the [said person];

(v) if, independently of the personal representative, there is no trustee of a settled legacy share or interest, and no person of full age and capacity entitled to the income thereof, no consent shall be required to an appropriation in respect of such legacy share or interest, provided that the appropriation is of an investment authorised as aforesaid.

[(1A) The county court has jurisdiction under proviso (ii) to subsection (1) of this section where the estate in respect of which the application is made does not exceed in amount or value the county court limit.]

(2) Any property duly appropriated under the powers conferred by this section shall thereafter be treated as an authorised investment, and may be retained or dealt with accordingly.

(3) For the purposes of such appropriation, the personal representative may ascertain and fix the value of the respective parts of the real and personal estate and the liabilities of the deceased as he may think fit, and shall for that purpose employ a duly qualified valuer in any case where such employment may be necessary; and may make any conveyance (including an assent) which may be requisite for giving effect to the appropriation.

(4) An appropriation made pursuant to this section shall bind all persons interested in the property of the deceased whose consent is not hereby made requisite.

(5) The personal representative shall, in making the appropriation, have regard to the rights of any person who may thereafter come into existence, or who cannot be found or ascertained at the time of appropriation, and of any other person whose consent is not required by this section.

(6) This section does not prejudice any other power of appropriation conferred by law or by the will (if any) of the deceased, and takes effect with any extended powers conferred by the will (if any) of the deceased, and where an appropriation is made under this section, in respect of a settled legacy, share or interest, the property appropriated shall remain subject to all [trusts] and powers of leasing, disposition, and management or varying investments which would have been applicable thereto or to the legacy, share or interest in respect of which the appropriation is made, if no such appropriation had been made.

(7) If after any real estate has been appropriated in purported exercise of the powers conferred by this section, the person to whom it was conveyed disposes of it or any interest therein, then, in favour of a purchaser, the appropriation shall be deemed to have been made in accordance with the requirements of this section and after all requisite consents, if any, had been given.

(8) In this section, a settled legacy, share or interest includes any legacy, share or interest to which a person is not absolutely entitled in possession at the date of the appropriation, also an annuity, and "purchaser" means a purchaser for money or money's worth.

(9) This section applies whether the deceased died intestate or not, and whether before or after the commencement of this Act, and extends to property over which a testator exercises a general power of appointment, including the statutory power to dispose of entailed interests, and authorises the setting apart of a fund to answer an annuity by means of the income of that fund or otherwise.

Amendment

Sub-s (1): in para (ii) words from "lacks capacity" to "give the consent, it" substituted by the Mental Capacity Act 2005, s 67(1), Sch 6, para 5(1), (2)(a)(i).

Sub-s (1): in para (ii) words from "or a person" to "the Court of Protection" substituted by the Mental Capacity Act 2005, s 67(1), Sch 6, para 5(1), (2)(a)(ii).

Sub-s (1): in para (ii) words omitted repealed by the the Mental Health Act 1959, s 149(1), Sch 7, Pt I.

Sub-s (1): in para (iv) words "no deputy is appointed for a person who lacks capacity to consent" substituted by the Mental Capacity Act 2005, s 67(1), Sch 6, para 5(1), (2)(b).

Sub-s (1): in para (iv) words "said person" in square brackets substituted by the Mental Health Act 1959, s 149(1), Sch 7, Pt I.

Sub-s (1A): inserted by the County Courts Act 1984, s 148(1), Sch 2, Part III, para 13.

Sub-s (6): word "trusts" in square brackets substituted by the Trusts of Land and Appointment of Trustees Act 1996, s 25(1), Sch 3, para 6(1), (3); for savings in relation to entailed interests created before the commencement of that Act, and savings consequential upon the abolition of the doctrine of conversion, see s 25(4), (5) thereof.

Commentary

The need for the consents in sub-s (1) is often dispensed with by the will. Appropriation takes place at the value of the asset at the time of appropriation and not date of death, see *Robinson v Collins* [1975] 1 WLR 309. An appropriation cannot take place if the value of the asset exceeds the entitlement of the beneficiary (although the beneficiary could purchase the asset from the personal representatives). Beneficiaries cannot in general insist on assets being appropriated to them, although at common law a residuary beneficiary may insist on assets being appropriated to him, see *Re Marshall* [1914] 1 Ch 192, but subject to the overriding duty of the personal representatives to hold the balance fairly between beneficiaries, as to which see *Lloyd's Bank plc v Duker* [1987] 1 WLR 1324. See also the surviving spouse's right to require appropriation of the matrimonial home or any interest in it to her under the Intestate Estates Act 1952, s 5 **[246]**. This power does not enable the personal representative to appropriate assets in his own favour, see *Kane v Radley-Kane* [1999] Ch 974. As to the reference to the county court in sub-s (1A), the county court has jurisdiction in respect of estates which do not exceed £30,000 (the County Courts Act 1984, s 23 and the County Court Jurisdiction Order 1981, SI 1981/1123).

[216]

42 Power to appoint trustees of infants' property

(1) Where an infant is absolutely entitled under the will or on the intestacy of a person dying before or after the commencement of this Act (in this subsection called "the deceased") to a devise or legacy, or to the residue of the estate of the deceased, or any share therein, and such devise, legacy, residue or share is not under the will, if any, of the deceased, devised or bequeathed to trustees for the infant, the personal representatives of the deceased may appoint a trust corporation or two or more individuals not exceeding four (whether or not including the personal representatives or one or more of the personal representatives), to be the trustee or trustees of such devise, legacy, residue or share for the infant, and to be trustees of any land devised or any land being or forming part of such residue or share for the purposes of the Settled Land Act 1925, and of the statutory provisions relating to the management of land during a minority, and may execute or do any assurance or thing requisite for vesting such devise, legacy, residue or share in the trustee or trustees so appointed.

On such appointment the personal representatives, as such, shall be discharged from all further liability in respect of such devise, legacy, residue, or share, and the same may be retained in its existing condition or state of investment, or may be converted into money, and such money may be invested in any authorised investment.

(2) Where a personal representative has before the commencement of this Act retained or sold any such devise, legacy, residue or share, and invested the same or the proceeds thereof in any investments in which he was authorised to invest money subject to the trust, then, subject to any order of the court made before such commencement, he shall not be deemed to have incurred any liability on that account, or by reason of not having paid or transferred the money or property into court.

Commentary

Although at first sight this section appears to apply to a minor entitled under an intestacy, it only applies where there are absolute interests and not where children are contingently entitled, see *Re Yerburgh, Yerburgh v Yerburgh* [1928] WN 208. Under s 47 below, which provides for the interests arising on an intestacy, children are normally contingently entitled. However, the section could apply where the child had married before attaining majority, see *Re Wilks, Keefer v Wilks* [1935] Ch 645.

[217]

43 Obligations of personal representative as to giving possession of land and powers of the court

(1) A personal representative, before giving an assent or making a conveyance in favour of any person entitled, may permit that person to take possession of the land, and such possession shall not prejudicially affect the right of the personal representative to take or resume possession nor his power to convey the land as if he were in possession thereof, but subject to the interest of any lessee, tenant or occupier in possession or in actual occupation of the land.

(2) Any person who as against the personal representative claims possession of real estate, or the appointment of a receiver thereof, or a conveyance thereof, or an assent to the vesting thereof, or to be registered as proprietor thereof under the [Land Registration Act 2002], may apply to the court for directions with reference thereto, and the court may make such vesting or other order as may be deemed proper, and the provisions of the Trustee Act 1925, relating to vesting orders and to the appointment of a person to convey, shall apply.

(3) This section applies whether the testator or intestate died before or after the commencement of this Act.

[(4) The county court has jurisdiction under this section where the estate in respect of which the application is made does not exceed in amount or value the county court limit.]

Amendment

Sub-s (2): words "Land Registration Act 2002" in square brackets substituted by the Land Registration Act 2002, s 133, Sch 11, para 3.
Sub-s (4): inserted by the County Courts Act 1984, s 148(1), Sch 2, Part III, para 14.

Commentary

This section enables the personal representatives to delay assenting to the vesting of the assets of the estate (as to which see s 36 above) until the liabilities are ascertained but to enable the beneficiary to go into possession. For vesting orders under the Trustee Act 1925 referred to in sub-s (2), see the Trustee Act 1925, ss 44–50 **[113–119]**. As to the reference to the county court in sub-s (4), the county court has jurisdiction in respect of estates which do not exceed £30,000 (the County Courts Act 1984, s 23 and the County Court Jurisdiction Order 1981, SI 1981/1123).

[218]

44 Power to postpone distribution

Subject to the foregoing provisions of this Act, a personal representative is not bound to distribute the estate of the deceased before the expiration of one year from the death.

Commentary

This gives statutory effect to the idea of the administrator's or executor's year. However, see s 36(10) above which means that if administration is in fact complete the personal representatives cannot delay an assent.

[219]

PART IV
DISTRIBUTION OF RESIDUARY ESTATE

45 Abolition of descent to heir, curtesy, dower and escheat

(1) With regard to the real estate and personal inheritance of every person dying after the commencement of this Act, there shall be abolished—

(a) All existing modes rules and canons of descent, and of devolution by special occupancy or otherwise, of real estate, or of a personal inheritance, whether operating by the general law or by the custom of gavelkind or borough english or by any other custom of any county, locality, or manor, or otherwise howsoever; and

(b) Tenancy by the curtesy and every other estate and interest of a husband in real estate as to which his wife dies intestate, whether arising under the general law or by custom or otherwise; and

(c) Dower and freebench and every other estate and interest of a wife in real estate as to which her husband dies intestate, whether arising under the general law or by custom or otherwise: Provided that where a right (if any) to freebench or other like right has attached before the commencement of this Act which cannot be barred by a testamentary or other disposition made by the husband, such right shall, unless released, remain in force as an equitable interest; and

(d) Escheat to the Crown or the Duchy of Lancaster or the Duke of Cornwall or to a mesne lord for want of heirs.

(2) Nothing in this section affects the descent or devolution of an entailed interest.

Commentary

This section abolishes the old rules relating to the devolution of real property on an intestacy. Note that the rules remain of relevance in relation to the manner in which entailed interests pass by virtue of sub-s (2) which since 1925 can only take effect in equity under the Settled Land Act 1925 **[Appendix II]** and have been abolished altogether for interests created after 1 January 1997 by the Trusts of Land and Appointment of Trustees Act 1996 **[431]**.

[220]

46 Succession to real and personal estate on intestacy

(1) The residuary estate of an intestate shall be distributed in the manner or be held on the trusts mentioned in this section, namely:—

[(i) If the intestate leaves a [spouse or civil partner], then in accordance with the following Table:

TABLE

If the intestate—	
(1) leaves— (a) no issue, and (b) no parent, or brother or sister of the whole blood, or issue of a brother or sister of the whole blood	the residuary estate shall be held in trust for the surviving [spouse or civil partner] absolutely
(2) leaves issue (whether or not persons mentioned in sub-paragraph (b) above also survive)	the surviving [spouse or civil partner] shall take the personal chattels absolutely and, in addition, the residuary estate of the intestate (other than the personal chattels) shall stand charged with the payment of a [fixed net sum], free of death duties and costs, to the surviving [spouse or civil partner] with interest thereon from the date of the death . . . [at such rate as the Lord Chancellor may specify by order] until paid or appropriated, and, subject to providing for that sum and the interest thereon, the residuary estate (other than the personal chattels) shall be held— (a) as to one half upon trust for the surviving [spouse or civil partner] during his or her life, and, subject to such life interest, on the statutory trusts for the issue of the intestate, and (b) as to the other half, on the statutory trusts for the issue of the intestate.

(3) leaves one or more of the following, that is to say, a parent, a brother or sister of the whole blood, or issue of a brother or sister of the whole blood, but leaves no issue	the surviving [spouse or civil partner] shall take the personal chattels absolutely and, in addition, the residuary estate of the intestate (other than the personal chattels) shall stand charged with the payment of a [fixed net sum], free of death duties and costs, to the surviving [spouse or civil partner] with interest thereon from the date of the death . . . [at such rate as the Lord Chancellor may specify by order] until paid or appropriated, and, subject to providing for that sum and the interest thereon, the residuary estate (other than the personal chattels) shall be held— (a) as to one half in trust for the surviving [spouse or civil partner] absolutely, and (b) as to the other half— (i) where the intestate leaves one parent or both parents (whether or not brothers or sisters of the intestate or their issue also survive) in trust for the parent absolutely or, as the case may be, for the two parents in equal shares absolutely (ii) where the intestate leaves no parent, on the statutory trusts for the brothers and sisters of the whole blood of the intestate.]

[The fixed net sums referred to in paragraphs (2) and (3) of this Table shall be of the amounts provided by or under section 1 of the Family Provision Act 1966]

(ii) If the intestate leaves issue but no [spouse or civil partner], the residuary estate of the intestate shall be held on the statutory trusts for the issue of the intestate;

(iii) If the intestate leaves [no [spouse or civil partner] and] no issue but both parents, then . . . the residuary estate of the intestate shall be held in trust for the father and mother in equal shares absolutely;

(iv) If the intestate leaves [no [spouse or civil partner] and] no issue but one parent, then . . . the residuary estate of the intestate shall be held in trust for the surviving father or mother absolutely;

(v) If the intestate leaves no [[spouse or civil partner] and no issue and no] parent, then . . . the residuary estate of the intestate shall be held in trust for the following persons living at the death of the intestate, and in the following order and manner, namely:—

First, on the statutory trusts for the brothers and sisters of the whole blood of the intestate; but if no person takes an absolutely vested interest under such trusts; then

Secondly, on the statutory trusts for the brothers and sisters of the half blood of the intestate; but if no person takes an absolutely vested interest under such trusts; then

Thirdly, for the grandparents of the intestate and, if more than one survive the intestate, in equal shares; but if there is no member of this class; then

Fourthly, on the statutory trusts for the uncles and aunts of the intestate (being brothers or sisters of the whole blood of a parent of the intestate); but if no person takes an absolutely vested interest under such trusts; then

Fifthly, on the statutory trusts for the uncles and aunts of the intestate (being brothers or sisters of the half blood of a parent of the intestate) . . .

(vi) In default of any person taking an absolute interest under the foregoing provisions, the residuary estate of the intestate shall belong to the Crown or to the Duchy of Lancaster or to the Duke of Cornwall for the time being, as the case may be, as bona vacantia, and in lieu of any right to escheat.

The Crown or the said Duchy or the said Duke may (without prejudice to the powers reserved by section nine of the Civil List Act 1910, or any other powers), out of the whole or any part of the property devolving on them respectively, provide, in accordance with the existing practice, for dependents, whether kindred or not, of the intestate, and other persons for whom the intestate might reasonably have been expected to make provision.

[(1A) The power to make orders under subsection (1) above shall be exercisable by statutory instrument subject to annulment in pursuance of a resolution of either House of Parliament; and any such order may be varied or revoked by a subsequent order made under the power.]

(2) A husband and wife shall for all purposes of distribution or division under the foregoing provisions of this section be treated as two persons.

[(2A) Where the intestate's [spouse or civil partner] survived the intestate but died before the end of the period of 28 days beginning with the day on which the intestate died, this section shall have effect as respects the intestate as if the [spouse or civil partner] had not survived the intestate.]

[(3) Where the intestate and the intestate's [spouse or civil partner] have died in circumstances rendering it uncertain which of them survived the other and the intestate's [spouse or civil partner] is by virtue of section one hundred and eighty-four of the Law of Property Act 1925, deemed to have survived the intestate, this section shall, nevertheless, have effect as respects the intestate as if the [spouse or civil partner] had not survived the intestate.

(4) The interest payable on [the fixed net sum] payable to a surviving [spouse or civil partner] shall be primarily payable out of income.]

Amendment

Sub-s (1): para (i) substituted by the Intestates' Estates Act 1952, s 1.
Sub-s (1): words "spouse or civil partner" in square brackets in each place they occur substituted by the Civil Partnership Act 2004, s 71, Sch 4, Pt 2, para 7.
Sub-s (1): in para (i) in the Table, in paras (2), (3) in column 2 words "fixed net sum" in square brackets substituted by the Family Provision Act 1966, s 1.
Sub-s (1): in para (i) in the Table, in paras (2), (3) in column 2 words omitted repealed by the Statute Law (Repeals) Act 1981.
Sub-s (1): in para (i) in the Table, in paras (2), (3) in column 2 words "at such rate as the Lord Chancellor may specify by order" in square brackets substituted by the Administration of Justice Act 1977, s 28(1)(a).
Sub-s (1): in para (i) words from "The fixed net" to "Family Provision Act 1966" in square brackets inserted by the Family Provision Act 1966, s 1.
Sub-s (1): in para (iii) words from "no" to "and" in square brackets substituted by the Intestates' Estates Act 1952, s 1.
Sub-s (1): in para (iii) words omitted repealed by the Intestates' Estates Act 1952, s 1.
Sub-s (1): in para (iv) words from "no" to "and" in square brackets substituted by the Intestates' Estates Act 1952, s 1.
Sub-s (1): in para (iv) words omitted repealed by the Intestates' Estates Act 1952, s 1.
Sub-s (1): in para (v) words in square brackets ending with the words "issue and no" substituted by the Intestates' Estates Act 1952, s 1.
Sub-s (1): in para (v) words omitted repealed by the Intestates' Estates Act 1952, s 1.
Sub-s (1A): inserted by the Administration of Justice Act 1977, s 28(1).
Sub-s (2A): inserted by the Law Reform (Succession) Act 1995, s 1(1), (3).
Sub-s (2A): words "spouse or civil partner" in square brackets in both places they occur substituted by the Civil Partnership Act 2004, s 71, Sch 4, Pt 2, para 7.
Sub-s (3): inserted by the Intestates' Estates Act 1952, s 1(4).
Sub-s (3): words "spouse or civil partner" in square brackets in each place they occur substituted by the Civil Partnership Act 2004, s 71, Sch 4, Pt 2, para 7.

Sub-s (4): inserted by the Intestates' Estates Act 1952, s 1(4).
Sub-s (4): words "the fixed net sum" in square brackets substituted by the Family Provision Act 1966, s 1.
Sub-s (4): words "spouse or civil partner" in square brackets substituted by the Civil Partnership Act 2004, s 71, Sch 4, Pt 2, para 7.

Commentary
This is a vitally important section which governs the distribution of an estate on intestacy. The order of distribution was changed substantially by the Intestates' Estates Act 1952 **[242]** which applies to deaths after 1 January 1953. Personal chattels to which the surviving spouse or civil partner is entitled are defined by s 55 (1)(x). The statutory trusts referred to are those set out in s 33(1) above as that section has been amended by the Trusts of Land and Appointment of Trustees Act 1996, and see s 47 below. The fixed net sum referred to is set from time to time by statutory instrument, made under the Family Provision Act 1966 **[292]**. It currently stands at £200,000 where the deceased died leaving a surviving spouse or civil partner but no issue and at £125,000 where there were issue. Subsections (2A) and (3) have the following effect. As far as deaths between 1925 and 1 January 1953 are concerned, the Law of Property Act 1925 **[144]**, s 184 **[179]** will apply so that in circumstances where it is not possible to say the order in which husband and wife died, the elder will be presumed to have died first. After 1 January 1953, sub-s (2) disapplies that general rule so that neither is presumed to have died before the other (sub-s (3)). After 1 January 1996 a spouse or civil partner has to survive the other for 28 days to benefit (see Law Reform (Succession) Act 1995). Since 2004 these rules have applied equally to civil partners.

[221]

47 Statutory trusts in favour of issue and other classes of relatives of intestate

(1) Where under this Part of this Act the residuary estate of an intestate, or any part thereof, is directed to be held on the statutory trusts for the issue of the intestate, the same shall be held upon the following trusts, namely:—

(i) In trust, in equal shares if more than one, for all or any the children or child of the intestate, living at the death of the intestate, who attain the age of [eighteen] years or marry under that age [or form a civil partnership under that age], and for all or any of the issue living at the death of the intestate who attain the age of [eighteen] years or marry[, or form a civil partnership,] under that age of any child of the intestate who predeceases the intestate, such issue to take through all degrees, according to their stocks, in equal shares if more than one, the share which their parent would have taken if living at the death of the intestate, and so that no issue shall take whose parent is living at the death of the intestate and so capable of taking;

(ii) The statutory power of advancement, and the statutory provisions which relate to maintenance and accumulation of surplus income, shall apply, but when an infant marries [or forms a civil partnership,] such infant shall be entitled to give valid receipts for the income of the infant's share or interest;

(iii) . . .

(iv) The personal representatives may permit any infant contingently interested to have the use and enjoyment of any personal chattels in such manner and subject to such conditions (if any) as the personal representatives may consider reasonable, and without being liable to account for any consequential loss.

(2) If the trusts in favour of the issue of the intestate fail by reason of no child or other issue attaining an absolutely vested interest—

(a) the residuary estate of the intestate and the income thereof and all statutory accumulations, if any, of the income thereof, or so much thereof as may not have been paid or applied under any power affecting the same, shall go, devolve and be held under the provisions of this Part of this Act as if the intestate had died without leaving issue living at the death of the intestate;

(b) references in this Part of this Act to the intestate "leaving no issue" shall be construed as "leaving no issue who attain an absolutely vested interest";

(c) references in this Part of this Act to the intestate "leaving issue" or "leaving a child or other issue" shall be construed as "leaving issue who attain an absolutely vested interest."

(3) Where under this Part of this Act the residuary estate of an intestate or any part thereof is directed to be held on the statutory trusts for any class of relatives of the intestate, other than issue of the intestate, the same shall be held on trusts corresponding to the statutory trusts for the issue of the intestate (other than the provision for bringing any money or property into account) as if such trusts (other than as aforesaid) were repeated with the substitution of references to the members or member of that class for references to the children or child of the intestate.

[(4) References in paragraph (i) of subsection (1) of the last foregoing section to the intestate leaving, or not leaving, a member of the class consisting of brothers or sisters of the whole blood of the intestate and issue of brothers or sisters of the whole blood of the intestate shall be construed as references to the intestate leaving, or not leaving, a member of that class who attains an absolutely vested interest.]

[(5) . . .]

Amendment

Sub-s (1): in para (i) word "eighteen" in square brackets in both places it occurs substituted by the Family Law Reform Act 1969, s 3(2).
Sub-s (1): in para (i) words "or form a civil partnership under that age" in square brackets inserted by the Civil Partnership Act 2004, s 71, Sch 4, Pt 2, para 8(1), (2).
Sub-s (1): in para (i) words ", or form a civil partnership," in square brackets inserted by the Civil Partnership Act 2004, s 71, Sch 4, Pt 2, para 8(1), (3).
Sub-s (1): in para (ii) words ", or forms a civil partnership," in square brackets inserted by the Civil Partnership Act 2004, s 71, Sch 4, Pt 2, para 8(1), (4).
Sub-s (1): para (iii) repealed by the Law Reform (Succession) Act 1995, ss 1(2)(a), (3), 5, Schedule.
Sub-s (4): inserted by the Intestates' Estates Act 1952, s 1(3)(c).
Sub-s (5): inserted by the Intestates' Estates Act 1952, s 1(3)(c); repealed by the Family Provision Act 1966, ss 9, 10, Sch 2.

Commentary

For the meaning of the statutory trusts see section 33 above. This section defines the terms of the trust in two separate categories of case: where there are issue who succeed on intestacy (sub-ss (1) and (2)); and where there are other classes of relatives (sub-s (3)). Brothers and sisters of the whole blood mean those siblings with a common parent.

[222]

[47A Right of surviving spouse to have his own life interest redeemed

(1) Where a surviving [spouse or civil partner] is entitled to the interest in part of the residuary estate, and so elects, the personal representative shall purchase or redeem the life interest by paying the capital value thereof to the tenant for life, or the persons deriving title under the tenant for life, and the costs of the transaction; and thereupon the residuary estate of the intestate may be dealt with and distributed free from the life interest.

(2) . . .

(3) An election under this section shall only be exercisable if at the time of the election the whole of the said part of the residuary estate consists of property in possession, but, for the purposes of this section, a life interest in property partly in possession and partly not in possession shall be treated as consisting of two separate life interests in those respective parts of the property.

[(3A) The capital value shall be reckoned in such manner as the Lord Chancellor may by order direct, and an order under this subsection may include transitional provisions.

(3B) The power to make orders under subsection (3A) above shall be exercisable by statutory instrument subject to annulment in pursuance of a resolution of either House of Parliament; and any such order may be varied or revoked by a subsequent order made under the power.]

(4) . . .

(5) An election under this section shall be exercisable only within the period of twelve months from the date on which representation with respect to the estate of the intestate is first taken out:

Provided that if the surviving [spouse or civil partner] satisfies the court that the limitation to the said period of twelve months will operate unfairly—

- (a) in consequence of the representation first taken out being probate of a will subsequently revoked on the ground that the will was invalid, or
- (b) in consequence of a question whether a person had an interest in the estate, or as to the nature of an interest in the estate, not having been determined at the time when representation was first taken out, or
- (c) in consequence of some other circumstances affecting the administration or distribution of the estate,

the court may extend the said period.

(6) An election under this section shall be exercisable, except where the tenant for life is the sole personal representative, by notifying the personal representative (or, where there are two or more personal representatives of whom one is the tenant for life, all of them except the tenant for life) in writing; and a notification in writing under this subsection shall not be revocable except with the consent of the personal representative.

(7) Where the tenant for life is the sole personal representative an election under this section shall not be effective unless written notice thereof is given to the [[Senior Registrar] of the Family Division of the High Court] within the period within which it must be made; and provision may be made by probate rules for keeping a record of such notices and making that record available to the public.

In this subsection the expression "probate rules" means rules [of court made under section 127 of the *Supreme Court Act 1981* [Senior Courts Act 1981]].

(8) An election under this section by a tenant for life who is an infant shall be as valid and binding as it would be if the tenant for life were of age; but the personal representative shall, instead of paying the capital value of the life interest to the tenant for life, deal with it in the same manner as with any other part of the residuary estate to which the tenant for life is absolutely entitled.

(9) In considering for the purposes of the foregoing provisions of this section the question when representation was first taken out, a grant limited to settled land or to trust property shall be left out of account and a grant limited to real estate or to personal estate shall be left out of account unless a grant limited to the remainder of the estate has previously been made or is made at the same time.]

Amendment

Inserted by the Intestates' Estates Act 1952, s 2.

Sub-s (1): words "spouse or civil partner" in square brackets substituted by the Civil Partnership Act 2004, s 71, Sch 4, Pt 2, para 9.

Sub-ss (2), (4): repealed by the Administration of Justice Act 1977, ss 28(2), 32(4), Sch 5, Pt VI.

Sub-ss (3A), (3B): inserted by the Administration of Justice Act 1977, s 28(3).

Sub-s (5): in the proviso words "spouse or civil partner" in square brackets substituted by the Civil Partnership Act 2004, s 71, Sch 4, Pt 2, para 9.
Sub-s (7): words in square brackets ending with the words "the High Court" substituted by the Administration of Justice Act 1970, s 1(6), Sch 2, para 4.
Sub-s (7): words "Senior Registrar" in square brackets substituted by the Supreme Court Act 1981, s 152(1), Sch 5.
Sub-s (7): words "of court made under section 127 of the Supreme Court Act 1981" in square brackets substituted by the Supreme Court Act 1981, s 152(1), Sch 5.
Sub-s (7): words "Supreme Court Act 1981" in italics repealed and subsequent words in square brackets substituted, from a date to be appointed, by the Constitutional Reform Act 2005, s 59(5), Sch 11, Pt 1, para 1(2).

Commentary

The rules referred to in sub-ss (3A) and (3B) are the Intestate Succession (Interest and Capitalisation) Order 1977, SI 1977/ 1491 which governs the way in which the spouse or civil partner's life interest is valued for deaths post 16 September 1977. The "probate rules" referred to in sub-s (7) are the Non-Contentious Probate Rules 1987, SI 1987/2024 **[Appendix V]**. Rule 56 provides for Form 6 to be filed in the Principal Registry of the Family Division to fulfil the requirements of sub-s (7). See section 48 below for the powers of the personal representatives to raise the capital sum required to redeem by securing it on the residuary estate. For the ability of the spouse or civil partner to require appropriation of the matrimonial home see Sch 2 to the Intestates' Estates Act 1952 **[251]**.

[223]

48 Powers of personal representative in respect of interests of surviving spouse

(1) . . .

(2) The personal representatives may raise—

(a) [the fixed net sum] or any part thereof and the interest thereon payable to the surviving [spouse or civil partner] of the intestate on the security of the whole or any part of the residuary estate of the intestate (other than the personal chattels), so far as that estate may be sufficient for the purpose of the said sum and interest may not have been satisfied by an appropriation under the statutory power available in that behalf; and

(b) in like manner the capital sum, if any, required for the purchase or redemption of the life interest of the surviving [spouse or civil partner] of the intestate, or any part thereof not satisfied by the application for that purpose of any part of the residuary estate of the intestate;

and in either case the amount, if any, properly required for the payment of the costs of the transaction.

Amendment

Sub-s (1): repealed by the Intestates' Estates Act 1952, s 2.
Sub-s (2): in para (a) words "the fixed net sum" in square brackets substituted by the Family Provision Act 1966, s 1.
Sub-s (2): in paras (a), (b) words "spouse or civil partner" in square brackets substituted by the Civil Partnership Act 2004, s 71, Sch 4, Pt 2, para 10.

Commentary

For the fixed net sum see section 46 above. For the right of the spouse or civil partner to redeem his life interest see section 47A above.

[224]

49 Application to cases of partial intestacy

[(1)] Where any person dies leaving a will effectively disposing of part of his property, this Part of this Act shall have effect as respects the part of his property not so disposed of subject to the provisions contained in the will and subject to the following modifications:—

[(aa)], (a) . . .

(b) The personal representative shall, subject to his rights and powers for the purposes of administration, be a trustee for the persons entitled under this Part of this Act in respect of the part of the estate not expressly disposed of unless it appears by the will that the personal representative is intended to take such part beneficially.

[(2), (3) . . .

(4) The references in subsection (3) of section forty-seven A of this Act to property are references to property comprised in the residuary estate and, accordingly, where a will of the deceased creates a life interest in property in possession, and the remaining interest in that property forms part of the residuary estate, the said references are references to that remaining interest (which, until the life interest determines, is property not in possession).]

Amendment

Sub-s (1): para (aa) inserted by the Intestates' Estates Act 1952, s 3, repealed, together with para (a), by the Law Reform (Succession) Act 1995, ss 1(2)(b), 5, Schedule.
Sub-ss (2), (3): inserted by the Intestates' Estates Act 1952, s 3; repealed by the Law Reform (Succession) Act 1995, ss 1(2)(b), (3), 5, Schedule.
Sub-s (4): inserted by the Intestates' Estates Act 1952, s 3.

Commentary

In cases of partial intestacy it is the will which must be looked at first before the intestacy rules apply and these will yield to any contrary intention in the will, see *Re McKee* [1931] 2 Ch 145; *Re Plowman* [1943] Ch 269; *Re Taylor* [1969] 2 WLR 1371. Note that for deaths before 1 January 1996, there were rules whereby the surviving spouse and children had to bring into account benefits received by them under the will. For a full discussion see *Butterworths Wills, Probate and Administration Service* para 269 et seq and see *Re Young, Young v Young* [1951] Ch 185; *Re Morton, Morton v Warham* [1956] Ch 644; *Re Grover's Will Trusts* [1971] Ch 168.

[225]

50 Construction of documents

(1) References to any Statutes of Distribution in an instrument inter vivos made or in a will coming into operation after the commencement of this Act, shall be construed as references to this Part of this Act; and references in such an instrument or will to statutory next of kin shall be construed, unless the context otherwise requires, as referring to the persons who would take beneficially on an intestacy under the foregoing provisions of this Part of this Act.

(2) Trusts declared in an instrument inter vivos made, or in a will coming into operation, before the commencement of this Act by reference to the Statutes of Distribution, shall, unless the contrary thereby appears, be construed as referring to the enactments (other than the Intestates' Estates Act 1890) relating to the distribution of effects of intestates which were in force immediately before the commencement of this Act.

[(3) In subsection (1) of this section the reference to this Part of this Act, or the foregoing provisions of this Part of this Act, shall in relation to an instrument inter vivos made, or a will or codicil coming into operation, after the coming into force of section 18 of the Family Law Reform Act 1987 (but not in relation to instruments inter vivos made or wills or codicils coming into operation earlier) be construed as including references to that section.]

Amendment

Sub-s (3): inserted by the Family Law Reform Act 1987, s 33(1), Sch 2, para 3.

Commentary

This section deals with post 1926 wills and inter vivos settlements and will still refer to the statutes of distribution which Part IV of the AEA 1925 superseded. For cases under sub-s (1)

(ii) "Administrator" means a person to whom administration is granted:

(iii) "Conveyance" includes a mortgage, charge by way of legal mortgage, lease, assent, vesting, declaration, vesting instrument, disclaimer, release and every other assurance of property or of an interest therein by any instrument, except a will, and "convey" has a corresponding meaning, and "disposition" includes a "conveyance" also a devise bequest and an appointment of property contained in a will, and "dispose of" has a corresponding meaning:

[(iiiA) "the County Court limit", in relation to any enactment contained in this Act, means the amount for the time being specified by an Order in Council under section 145 of the County Courts Act 1984 as the county court limit for the purposes of that enactment (or, where no such Order in Council has been made, the corresponding limit specified by Order in Council under section 192 of the County Courts Act 1959);]

(iv) "the Court" means the High Court and also the county court, where that court has jurisdiction . . .

(v) "Income" includes rents and profits:

(vi) "Intestate" includes a person who leaves a will but dies intestate as to some beneficial interest in his real or personal estate:

[(via) "Land" has the same meaning as in the Law of Property Act 1925;]

(vii) "Legal estates" mean the estates charges and interests in or over land (subsisting or created at law) which are by statute authorised to subsist or to be created at law; and "equitable interests" mean all other interests and charges in or over land . . . :

(viii) . . .

(ix) "Pecuniary legacy" includes an annuity, a general legacy, a demonstrative legacy so far as it is not discharged out of the designated property, and any other general direction by a testator for the payment of money, including all death duties free from which any devise, bequest, or payment is made to take effect:

(x) "Personal chattels" mean carriages, horses, stable furniture and effects (not used for business purposes), motor cars and accessories (not used for business purposes), garden effects, domestic animals, plate, plated articles, linen, china, glass, books, pictures, prints, furniture, jewellery, articles of household or personal use or ornament, musical and scientific instruments and apparatus, wines, liquors and consumable stores, but do not include any chattels used at the death of the intestate for business purposes nor money or securities for money:

(xi) "Personal representative" means the executor, original or by representation, or administrator for the time being of a deceased person, and as regards any liability for the payment of death duties includes any person who takes possession of or intermeddles with the property of a deceased person without the authority of the personal representatives or the court, and "executor" includes a person deemed to be appointed executor as respects settled land:

(xii) "Possession" includes the receipt of rents and profits or the right to receive the same, if any:

(xiii) "Prescribed" means prescribed by rules of court . . . :

(xiv) "Probate" means the probate of a will:

(xv), (xvi) . . . :

(xvii) "Property" includes a thing in action and any interest in real or personal property:

(xviii) "Purchaser" means a lessee, mortgagee, or other person who in good faith acquires an interest in property for valuable consideration, also an intending purchaser and "valuable consideration" includes marriage, [and formation of a civil partnership,] but does not include a nominal consideration in money:

(xix) "Real estate" save as provided in Part IV of this Act means real estate, including chattels real, which by virtue of Part I of this Act devolves on the personal representative of a deceased person:

(xx) "Representation" means the probate of a will and administration, and the expression "taking out representation" refers to the obtaining of the probate of a will or of the grant of administration:

(xxi) "Rent" includes a rent service or a rentcharge, or other rent, toll, duty, or annual or periodical payment in money or money's worth, issuing out of or charged upon land, but does not include mortgage interest; and "rentcharge" includes a fee farm rent:

(xxii) . . .

(xxiii) "Securities" include stocks, funds, or shares:

(xxiv) "Tenant for life," "statutory owner," . . . "settled land," "settlement," "trustees of the settlement," "term of years absolute," "death duties," and "legal mortgage," have the same meanings as in the Settled Land Act 1925, and "entailed interest" and "charge by way of legal mortgage" have the same meanings as in the Law of Property Act 1925:

(xxv) "Treasury solicitor" means the solicitor for the affairs of His Majesty's Treasury, and includes the solicitor for the affairs of the Duchy of Lancaster:

(xxvi) "Trust corporation" means the public trustee or a corporation either appointed by the court in any particular case to be a trustee or entitled by rules made under subsection (3) of section four of the Public Trustee Act 1906, to act as custodian trustee:

(xxvii) . . .

(xxviii) "Will" includes codicil.

(2) References to a child or issue living at the death of any person include child or issue en ventre sa mere at the death.

(3) References to the estate of a deceased person include property over which the deceased exercises a general power of appointment (including the statutory power to dispose of entailed interests) by his will.

Amendment

Sub-s (1): para (iiiA) inserted by the County Courts Act 1984, s 148(1), Sch 2, Part III, para 15.
Sub-s (1): words omitted from para (iv) repealed by the Courts Act 1971, s 56(4), Sch 11, Part II.
Sub-s (1): para (via) inserted by the Trusts of Land and Appointment of Trustees Act 1996, s 25(1), Sch 3, para 6(1), (5); for savings in relation to entailed interests created before the commencement of that Act, and savings consequential upon the abolition of the doctrine of conversion, see s 25(4), (5) thereof.
Sub-s (1): in para (vii) words omitted repealed by the Trusts of Land and Appointment of Trustees Act 1996, s 25(2), Sch 4; for savings in relation to entailed interests created before the commencement of that Act, and savings consequential upon the abolition of the doctrine of conversion, see s 25(4), (5) thereof.
Sub-s (1): para (viii) repealed by the Mental Capacity Act 2005, s 67(1), Sch 6, para 5(1), (3), Sch 7.
Sub-s (1): words omitted from para (xiii) repealed by the Supreme Court Act 1981, s 152(4), Sch 7.
Sub-s (1): para (xv) repealed by the Law of Property (Miscellaneous Provisions) Act 1994, s 21(2), Sch 2.
Sub-s (1): paras (xvi), (xxii) repealed by the Supreme Court Act 1980, s 152(4), Sch 7.
Sub-s (1): in para (xviii) words "and formation of a civil partnership," in square brackets inserted by the Civil Partnership Act 2004, s 71, Sch 4, Pt 2, para 12.

Sub-s (1): in para (xxiv) word omitted repealed by the Trusts of Land and Appointment of Trustees Act 1996, s 25(2), Sch 4; for savings in relation to entailed interests created before the commencement of that Act, and savings consequential upon the abolition of the doctrine of conversion, see s 25(4), (5) thereof.
Sub-s (1): para (xxvii) repealed by the Trusts of Land and Appointment of Trustees Act 1996, s 25(2), Sch 4; for savings in relation to entailed interests created before the commencement of that Act, and savings consequential upon the abolition of the doctrine of conversion, see s 25(4), (5) thereof.

Commentary

See throughout these notes references to this definition section. As to the jurisdiction of the County Court (sub-s (1)(iiiA)) that currently applies to estates worth less than £30,000. The most used definition is that of personal chattels contained in (1)(x). The definition has been held to include racehorses (*Re Hutchinson* [1955] Ch 255); manuscripts (*Re Tomline* [1931] Ch 521); a collection of clocks (*Re Crispin* [1975] Ch 245); and a yacht (*Re Chaplin* [1950] Ch 517) but does not include medical records (*R v Mid-Glamorgan FHS* [1995] 1 WLR 110).

[231]

56 Repeal

The Acts mentioned in the Second Schedule to this Act are hereby repealed to the extent specified in the third column of that Schedule, but as respects the Acts mentioned in Part I of that Schedule only so far as they apply to deaths occurring after the commencement of this Act.

[232]

57 Application to Crown

(1) The provisions of this Act bind the Crown and the Duchy of Lancaster, and the Duke of Cornwall for the time being as respects the estates of persons dying after the commencement of this Act, but not so as to affect the time within which proceedings for the recovery of real or personal estate vesting in or devolving on His Majesty in right of His Crown, or His Duchy of Lancaster, or on the Duke of Cornwall, may be instituted.

(2) Nothing in this Act in any manner affects or alters the descent or devolution of any property for the time being vested in His Majesty either in right of the Crown or of the Duchy of Lancaster or of any property for the time being belonging to the Duchy of Cornwall.

Commentary

As to the Crown taking on intestacy an estate as bona vacantia see section 46(1)(vi) above. Prior to this section land escheating to the Crown did not vest in the personal representatives (*Re Hartley* [1899] P 40).

[233]

58 Short title, commencement and extent

(1) This Act may be cited as the Administration of Estates Act 1925.

(2) . . .

(3) This Act extends to England and Wales only.

Amendment

Sub-s (2): repealed by the Statute Law Revision Act 1950.

[234]

SCHEDULE 1

Section 34

PART I

. . .

Amendment
Repealed by the Insolvency Act 1985, s 235(3), Sch 10, Pt III.

PART II
ORDER OF APPLICATION OF ASSETS WHERE THE ESTATE IS SOLVENT

1 Property of the deceased undisposed of by will, subject to the retention thereout of a fund sufficient to meet any pecuniary legacies.

2 Property of the deceased not specifically devised or bequeathed but included (either by a specific or general description) in a residuary gift, subject to the retention out of such property of a fund sufficient to meet any pecuniary legacies, so far as not provided for as aforesaid.

3 Property of the deceased specifically appropriated or devised or bequeathed (either by a specific or general description) for the payment of debts.

4 Property of the deceased charged with, or devised or bequeathed (either by a specific or general description) subject to a charge for the payment of debts.

5 The fund, if any, retained to meet pecuniary legacies.

6 Property specifically devised or bequeathed, rateably according to value,

7 Property appointed by will under a general power, including the statutory power to dispose of entailed interests, rateably according to value.

8 The following provisions shall also apply—
(a) The order of application may be varied by the will of the deceased.
(b) . . .

Amendment
Para 8: words omitted repealed by the Finance (No 2) Act 1983, s 16(4), Sch 2, Part II, in relation to deaths on or after 26 July 1983.

Commentary
See s 34(3) above and the notes thereto, in particular in relation to a contrary intention in the will (para 8). Paragraph 1 includes a lapsed share of income, see *Re Tong, Hilton v Bradbury* [1931] 1 Ch 202. As to the way in which debts payable out of property in para 6 are concerned, see *Re John* [1933] Ch 370. Paragraph 7 includes entailed property barred under the deceased's will (the Law of Property Act 1925 **[177]**, s 176). Paragraph 7 does not include property where there has been no express exercise of the general power of appointment but it has passed into residue, see *Re Hartley* [1900] 1 Ch 152. After these statutory categories have been exhausted, and only then, can recourse be had to property which is subject to an option to purchase in the will, see *Re Eve* [1956] Ch 479.

[235]

SCHEDULE 2

. . .

Amendment
Repealed by the Statute Law Revision Act 1950.

[236]

COLONIAL PROBATES (PROTECTED STATES AND MANDATED TERRITORIES) ACT 1927

1927 Chapter 43

ARRANGEMENT OF SECTIONS

An Act to enable the Colonial Probates Act 1892, to be applied to certain Protected States and Mandated Territories

[22nd December 1927]

General Note

This Act extends the Colonial Probates Act 1892 and reference should be made to that Act and the notes thereto.

1 Extension of Colonial Probates Act 1892 to certain protected states and mandated territories

The power of His Majesty to apply the Colonial Probates Act 1892 to British possessions shall include a power to apply the said Act to any territories, being either territories under His Majesty's protection or territories in respect of which a mandate on behalf of the League of Nations has been accepted by His Majesty, to which it cannot be applied by virtue of the provisions of the Foreign Jurisdiction Acts 1890 and 1913, and the said Act shall accordingly have effect as if references therein to British possessions included references to such territories as aforesaid.

Commentary

The League of Nations did of course terminate but the Act continued to apply to territories administered under the trusteeship system of the United Kingdom.

[237]

2 Short title

This Act may be cited as the Colonial Probates (Protected States and Mandated Territories) Act 1927, and the Colonial Probates Act 1892, and this Act may be cited together as the Colonial Probates Act 1892 and 1927.

[238]

SETTLED LAND AND TRUSTEE ACTS (COURT'S GENERAL POWERS) ACT 1943

1943 Chapter 25

ARRANGEMENT OF SECTIONS

An Act to extend temporarily the powers of the court under section sixty-four of the Settled Land Act 1925, and section fifty-seven of the Trustee Act 1925; and to amend the first-mentioned section as respects improvements

[6th July 1943]

General Note

The Settled Land and Trustee Acts (Court's General Powers) Act 1943 (SLTA(CGP)A 1943) should be read together with the Trustee Act 1925, s 57 **[126]** which it extends. It also extends the Settled Land Act 1925, s 64. That Act is not annotated in this work in light of the fact that strict settlements were abolished by the Trusts of Land and Appointment of Trustees Act 1996 and while there will be many settlements around for a while, their demise is inevitable. However the Act can be found in **Appendix II** to this work. The SLTA(CGP)A 1943 was originally passed as a temporary measure but was made permanent by the Emergency Laws (Miscellaneous Provisions Act) 1953.

1 Extension of powers under 15 Geo 5 c 18, s 64 and c 19, s 57

(1) The jurisdiction of the court under section sixty-four of the Settled Land Act 1925 (which confers power on a tenant for life to effect under an order of the court any transaction, including an application of capital money), and, so far as regards [trustees of land], the jurisdiction of the court under section fifty-seven of the Trustee Act 1925 (under which the court may make an order conferring on trustees power to effect any transaction, including an expenditure of money, and may direct in what manner money to be expended is to be paid as between capital and income) shall include power, in the circumstances specified in subsection (2) of this section, to make an order authorising any expense of action taken or proposed in or for the management of settled land or of [land subject to a trust of land], as the case may be, to be treated as a capital outgoing, notwithstanding that in other circumstances that expense could not properly have been so treated.

(2) The said circumstances are that the court is satisfied—

(a) that the action taken or proposed was or would be for the benefit of the persons entitled under the settlement, or under the [trust of land], as the case may be, generally; and either

(b) that the available income from all sources of a person who, as being beneficially entitled to possession or receipt of rents and profits of the land or to reside in a house comprised therein, might otherwise have been expected to bear the expense of the action taken or proposed has been so reduced . . . as to render him unable to bear the expense thereof, or unable to bear it without undue hardship; or

(c) in a case in which there is no such person as aforesaid, that the income available for meeting that expense has become insufficient . . .

(3) In determining whether to make such an order as aforesaid the court shall have regard to all the circumstances of the case, including the extent of the obligations, whether legally enforceable or not and whether or not relating to the land, of the person referred to in paragraph (b) of the last preceding subsection, the extent to which other persons entitled under the settlement or [trust of land] are likely to benefit from the action taken or proposed or from the relief which would accrue to that person from the making of the order, and the extent to which the making of the order would be likely to involve a loss to any other person so entitled without his receiving any corresponding benefit.

(4) Such an order as aforesaid may be made notwithstanding that the action in question was taken, or the expense thereof discharged, before the passing of this Act or before the application for the order, and the court may direct such adjustments of accounts and such repayments to be made as may appear to the court to be requisite for giving full effect to the purposes of any such order.

(5) In this section—

the expression "management" includes all the acts referred to in subsection (2) of section one hundred and two of the Settled Land Act 1925, and references in this section to expense of management include references to the expense of the employment of a solicitor, accountant, surveyor, or other person in an advisory or supervisory capacity; and

. . .

(6) . . .

Amendment
Sub-ss (1), (3): words in square brackets substituted by the Trusts of Land and Appointment of Trustees Act 1996, s 25(1), Sch 3, para 8(a), (b); for savings in relation to entailed interests created before the commencement of that Act, and savings consequential upon the abolition of the doctrine of conversion, see s 25(4), (5) thereof.
Sub-s (2): words in square brackets substituted by the Trusts of Land and Appointment of Trustees Act 1996, s 25(1), Sch 3, para 8(b), for savings in relation to entailed interests created before the commencement of that Act, and savings consequential upon the abolition of the doctrine of conversion, see s 25(4), (5) thereof; words omitted repealed by the Emergency Laws (Miscellaneous Provisions) Act 1953, ss 9, 14, Sch 3.
Sub-ss (5), (6): words omitted repealed by the Emergency Laws (Miscellaneous Provisions) Act 1953, ss 9, 14, Sch 3.

Commentary
The notes to the Trustee Act 1925, s 57 **[126]** should be consulted when looking at the powers of the court under this section. The original s 57 applied to trusts of land but the SLTA(CGP)A 1943 extends the powers of the court so that it can approve proposals whereby the expenses of managing land are taken from capital rather than income which would have been beyond the scope of the original s 57. Note the retrospective nature of the jurisdiction under this section in sub-s (4).

[239]

2 . . .

. . .

Amendment
Repealed by the Statute Law Revision Act 1950.

[240]

3 Short title

This Act may be cited as the Settled Land and Trustee Acts (Court's General Powers) Act 1943.

[241]

INTESTATES' ESTATES ACT 1952

1952 Chapter 64

ARRANGEMENT OF SECTIONS

PART I
AMENDMENTS OF LAW OF INTESTATE SUCCESSION

PART III
GENERAL

An Act to amend the law of England and Wales, about the property of persons dying intestate; to amend the Inheritance (Family Provision) Act 1938; and for purposes connected therewith

[30th October 1952]

General Note
The Intestates' Estates Act 1952 (IEA 1952) extensively amended the Administration of Estates Act 1925 in relation to intestacy in respect of deaths which occurred after 1 January 1953. The important right of a surviving spouse or civil partner to acquire the matrimonial home is set out in s 5 and Sch 2 below. Reference should be made to the AEA 1925 and the commentary thereon for the main impact of this Act.

PART I
AMENDMENTS OF LAW OF INTESTATE SUCCESSION

1 Succession to estate of intestate leaving a surviving spouse

. . .

Amendment
This section amends the Administration of Estates Act 1925, ss 46–48.
Repealed in part by the Family Provision Act 1966, s 10(2), Sch 2.

[242]

2 Right of surviving spouse to have life interest redeemed

. . .

Amendment
This section inserts the Administration of Estates Act 1925, s 47A, and repeals s 48(1) of that Act.

[243]

3 Partial Intestacies

. . .

Amendment
This section amends s 49 of the Administration of Estates Act 1925, in relation to a person dying intestate after 1 January 1953.
Sub-s (2): repealed by the Law Reform (Succession) Act 1995, s 5, Schedule, in relation to an intestate dying on or after 1 January 1996.

[244]

4 Reproduction of enactments in Administration of Estates Act 1925, as amended

In accordance with the provisions of the foregoing sections, sections forty-six to forty-nine of the principal Act shall have effect as respects a person dying intestate after the commencement of this Act as set out in the First Schedule to this Act.

[245]

5 Rights of surviving spouse [or civil partner] as respects the matrimonial [or civil partnership] home

The Second Schedule to this Act shall have effect for enabling the surviving [spouse or civil partner] of a person dying intestate after the commencement of this Act to acquire the matrimonial [or civil partnership] home.

Amendment

Section heading: words "or civil partner" and "or civil partnership" in square brackets inserted by the Civil Partnership Act 2004, s 71, Sch 4, Pt 2, para 13(1), (4).
Words "spouse or civil partner" in square brackets substituted by the Civil Partnership Act 2004, s 71, Sch 4, Pt 2, para 13(1), (2).
Words "or civil partnership" in square brackets inserted by the Civil Partnership Act 2004, s 71, Sch 4, Pt 2, para 13(1), (3).

Commentary

Reference should be made to Sch 2 and the notes thereto. It is established that the surviving spouse or now a civil partner can appropriate under this section even when the value of the house exceeds the value of his or her absolute interest, see *Re Phelps, Wells v Phelps* [1980] Ch 275. The rights are now available to civil partners.

[246]

6 Interpretation and construction

(1) In this Part of this Act the expression "intestate" has the meaning assigned to it by section fifty-five of the principal Act.

(2) The references in subsection (1) of section fifty of the principal Act (which relates to the construction of documents) to Part IV of that Act, or to the foregoing provisions of that Part, shall in relation to an instrument inter vivos made or a will coming into operation, after the commencement of this Act, but not in relation to instruments inter vivos made or wills coming into operation earlier, be construed as including references to this Part of this Act and the Schedules to be read therewith.

[247]

7, 8 . . .

. . .

Amendment

Section 7 repealed by the Inheritance (Provision for Family and Dependants) Act 1975, s 26(2), Schedule.
Section 8 repealed by the Family Provision Act 1966, s 10(2), Sch 2.

[248]

PART III
GENERAL

9 Short title and commencement

(1) This Act may be cited as the Intestates' Estates Act 1952.

(2) This Act shall come into operation on the first day of January, nineteen hundred and fifty-three.

[249]

SCHEDULE 1
SECTIONS 46 TO 49 OF ADMINISTRATION OF ESTATES ACT 1925, AS AMENDED BY PART I OF THIS ACT AS RESPECTS PERSONS DYING AFTER THE COMMENCEMENT OF THIS ACT

Section 4

. . .

Commentary

This Schedule sets out the Administration of Estates Act 1925, ss 46–49, as amended by Pt I of this Act in relation to persons dying on or after 1 January 1953.

[250]

SCHEDULE 2
RIGHTS OF SURVIVING SPOUSE [OR CIVIL PARTNER] AS RESPECTS THE MATRIMONIAL [OR CIVIL PARTNERSHIP] HOME

Section 5

1 (1) Subject to the provisions of this Schedule, where the residuary estate of the intestate comprises of interest in a dwelling-house in which the surviving [spouse or civil partner] was resident at the time of the intestate's death, the surviving [spouse or civil partner] may require the personal representative in exercise of the power conferred by section forty-one of the principal Act (and with due regard to the requirements of that section as to valuation) to appropriate the said interest in the dwelling-house in or towards satisfaction of any absolute interest of the surviving [spouse or civil partner] in the real and personal estate of the intestate.

(2) The right conferred by this paragraph shall not be exercisable where the interest is—

- (a) a tenancy which at the date of the death of the intestate was a tenancy which would determine within the period of two years from that date; or
- (b) a tenancy which the landlord by notice given for that date could determine within the remainder of that period.

(3) Nothing in subsection (5) of section forty-one of the principal Act (which requires the personal representative, in making an appropriation to any person under that section, to have regard to the rights of others) shall prevent the personal representative from giving effect to the right conferred by this paragraph.

(4) The reference in this paragraph to an absolute interest in the real and personal estate of the intestate includes a reference to the capital value of a life interest which the surviving [spouse or civil partner] has under this Act elected to have redeemed.

(5) Where part of a building was, at the date of the death of the intestate, occupied as a separate dwelling, that dwelling shall for the purposes of this Schedule be treated as a dwelling-house.

Commentary

Personal representatives have power to appropriate under the Administration of Estates Act 1925, s 41 **[216]** but it is their power to exercise and beneficiaries cannot normally require them to exercise the power. These provisions enable the surviving spouse or civil partner to insist that a dwelling house or interest in one in which he or she resides is appropriated to him or her. Sub-paragraph (5) extends the meaning of dwelling house, but note that unprotected tenancies are excluded (sub-para (2)). For the right of the surviving spouse or civil partner to redeem his or her life interest referred to in sub-para (4) see the Administration of Estates Act 1925, s 47A(1) **[223]**.

2 Where—

(a) the dwelling-house forms part of a building and an interest in the whole of the building is comprised in the residuary estate; or
(b) the dwelling-house is held with agricultural land and an interest in the agricultural land is comprised in the residuary estate; or
(c) the whole or part of the dwelling-house was at the time of the intestate's death used as a hotel or lodging house; or
(d) a part of the dwelling-house was at the time of the intestate's death used for purposes other than domestic purposes,

the right conferred by paragraph 1 of this Schedule shall not be exercisable unless the court, on being satisfied that the exercise of that right is not likely to diminish the value of assets in the residuary estate (other than the said interest in the dwelling-house) or make them more difficult to dispose of, so orders.

Commentary
Application under this paragraph can be made by the personal representatives as well as the spouse or civil partner (see para 4(2) below). Application is made in accordance with the Civil Procedure Rules 1998, SI 1998/3132, Pt 8.

3 (1) The right conferred by paragraph 1 of this Schedule.
(a) shall not be exercisable after the expiration of twelve months from the first taking out of representation with respect to the intestate's estate;
(b) shall not be exercisable after the death of the surviving [spouse or civil partner];
(c) shall be exercisable, except where the surviving [spouse or civil partner] is the sole personal representative, by notifying the personal representative (or, where there are two or more personal representatives of whom one is the surviving [spouse or civil partner], all of them except the surviving [spouse or civil partner]) in writing.

(2) A notification in writing under paragraph (c) of the foregoing sub-paragraph shall not be revocable except with the consent of the personal representative; but the surviving [spouse or civil partner] may require the personal representative to have the said interest in the dwelling-house valued in accordance with section forty-one of the principal Act and to inform him or her of the result of that valuation before he or she decides whether to exercise the right.

(3) Subsection (9) of the section forty-seven A added to the principal Act by section two of this Act shall apply for the purposes of the construction of the reference in this paragraph to the first taking out of representation, and the promise to subsection (5) of that section shall apply for the purpose of enabling the surviving [spouse or civil partner] to apply for an extension of the period of twelve months mentioned in this paragraph.

Commentary
The time limit of 12 months is measured from the date of the grant and for this purposes grants limited to settled land or trust property or limited to real or personal estate are left out of account, see the Administration of Estates Act 1925, s 47A(9) **[223]** applied by sub-para (3). The time limit can be extended as can the time limit for redeeming the spouse or civil partner's life interest contained in s 47A (under s 47A(5)). The valuation which can be required under sub-para (2) should be the market value of the interest at the date of appropriation, not death, see the Administration of Estates Act 1925, s 41 **[216]** and *Robinson v Collins* [1975] 1 WLR 309.

4 (1) During the period of twelve months mentioned in paragraph 3 of this Schedule the personal representative shall not without the written consent of the surviving [spouse or civil partner] sell or otherwise dispose of the said interest in the dwelling-house except in the course of administration owing to want of other assets.

(2) An application to the court under paragraph 2 of this Schedule may be made by the personal representative as well as by the surviving [spouse or civil partner], and if, on an application under that paragraph, the court does not order that the right conferred by paragraph 1 of this Schedule shall be exercisable by the surviving [spouse or civil partner], the court may authorise the personal representative to dispose of the said interest in the dwelling-house within the said period of twelve months.

(3) Where the court under sub-paragraph (3) of paragraph 3 of this Schedule extends the said period of twelve months, the court may direct that this paragraph shall apply in relation to the extended period as it applied in relation to the original period of twelve months.

(4) This paragraph shall not apply where the surviving [spouse or civil partner] is the sole personal representative or one of two or more personal representatives.

(5) Nothing in this paragraph shall confer any right on the surviving [spouse or civil partner] as against a purchaser from the personal representative.

Commentary

The protection afforded by sub-para (1) is unnecessary if the spouse or civil partner is the sole personal representative or one of them (sub-para (4)). As to sub-para (2) see the commentary to para 2 above.

5 (1) Where the surviving [spouse or civil partner] is one of two or more personal representatives, the rule that a trustee may not be a purchaser of trust property shall not prevent the surviving [spouse or civil partner] from purchasing out of the estate of the intestate an interest in a dwelling-house in which the surviving [spouse or civil partner] was resident at the time of the intestate's death.

(2) The power of appropriation under section forty-one of the principal Act shall include power to appropriate an interest in a dwelling-house in which the surviving [spouse or civil partner] was resident at the time of the intestate's death partly in satisfaction of an interest of the surviving [spouse or civil partner] in the real and personal estate of the intestate and partly in return for a payment of money by the surviving [spouse or civil partner] to the personal representative.

Commentary

Sub-paragraph (1) was necessary in the case where the spouse or civil partner was the personal representative to abrogate the self-dealing rule. As to sub-para (2), the normal rule is that an asset cannot be appropriated under the Administration of Estates Act 1925, s 41 **[216]** where its value exceeded the value of the beneficiary's interest. This sub-paragraph enables equality money to be paid by the spouse or civil partner, and see *Re Phelps, Wells v Phelps* [1980] Ch 275.

6 [(1) Where the surviving spouse or civil partner lacks capacity (within the meaning of the Mental Capacity Act 2005) to make a requirement or give a consent under this Schedule, the requirement or consent may be made or given by a deputy appointed by the Court of Protection with power in that respect or, if no deputy has that power, by that court.]

(2) A requirement or consent made or given under this Schedule by a surviving [spouse or civil partner] who is an infant shall be as valid and binding as it would be if he or she were of age, and, as respects an appropriation in pursuance of paragraph 1 of this Schedule, the provisions of section forty-one of the principal Act as to obtaining the consent of the infant's parent or guardian, or of the court on behalf of the infant, shall not apply.

Commentary
Sub-paragraph (1) makes it clear that a deputy appointed under the Mental Capacity Act 2005 or the Court of Protection can exercise these functions. An infant spouse or civil partner can notwithstanding their usual lack of legal capacity exercise their rights under this section.

7 (1) Except where the context otherwise requires, references in this Schedule to a dwelling-house include references to any garden or portion of ground attached to and usually occupied with the dwelling-house or otherwise required for the amenity or convenience of the dwelling-house.

(2) This Schedule shall be construed as one with Part IV of the principal Act.

Amendment
Schedule heading: words "or Civil Partner" and "or Civil Partnership" in square brackets inserted by the Civil Partnership Act 2004, s 71, Sch 4, Pt 2, para 13(1), (4).
Para 1: in sub-paras (1), (4) words "spouse or civil partner" in square brackets in each place they occur substituted by the Civil Partnership Act 2004, s 71, Sch 4, Pt 2, para 13(1), (2).
Para 3: words "spouse or civil partner" in square brackets in each place they occur substituted by the Civil Partnership Act 2004, s 71, Sch 4, Pt 2, para 13(1), (2).
Para 4: in sub-paras (1), (2), (4), (5) words "spouse or civil partner" in square brackets in each place they occur substituted by the Civil Partnership Act 2004, s 71, Sch 4, Pt 2, para 13(1), (2).
Para 5: words "spouse or civil partner" in square brackets in each place they occur substituted by the Civil Partnership Act 2004, s 71, Sch 4, Pt 2, para 13(1), (2).
Para 6: sub-para (1) substituted by the Mental Capacity Act 2005, s 67(1), Sch 6, para 8.

Commentary
For Part IV of the principal Act, see **[220]**.

[251]

PUBLIC TRUSTEE (FEES) ACT 1957

1957 Chapter 12

ARRANGEMENT OF SECTIONS

An Act to make further provision as to the fees chargeable by the Public Trustee, and for purposes connected therewith

[21st March 1957]

General Note
The Public Trustee (Fees) Act 1957 (PT(F)A 1957) refers back to section 9 of the Public Trustee Act 1906 and should be read together with that section

1 Orders fixing fees

(1) The power of the [Lord Chancellor] under subsection (1) of section nine of the Public Trustee Act 1906 (in this Act referred to as "the principal Act") . . . to fix the fees chargeable in respect of the duties of the public trustee shall be exercisable by

order made by statutory instrument (in this Act referred to as a "fees order"); and, subject to the provisions of this Act, any fees order made after the passing of this Act may contain such incidental and supplementary provisions as may appear to the [Lord Chancellor] to be necessary or expedient for the purposes of the order.

(2) Every fees order made after the passing of this Act shall indicate, with respect to every fee fixed by the order, whether it is to be payable out of capital or out of income.

(3) Where a fees order made after the passing of this Act provides that a fee is to be payable out of capital, and it appears to the public trustee, in the case of a particular trust fund in respect of which the fee is payable, that there are special reasons which render it expedient that the fee should be paid out of income, the public trustee may direct that the fee shall in that case be payable out of income:

Provided that, if a person of full age is for the time being beneficially entitled in possession to the income of the trust fund (being so entitled directly under the trust in relation to which the fee is payable, and not by virtue of a derivative settlement), the public trustee shall not give a direction under this subsection in respect of that trust fund except with the consent in writing of that person.

(4) The power conferred by the last preceding subsection shall apply to any trust, whether accepted by the public trustee after or before the passing of this Act.

(5) As from the date on which the first fees order made after the passing of this Act comes into operation (in this Act referred to as "the commencement date"), subsection (5) of section nine of the principal Act (which relates to the incidence of the fees and expenses of the public trustee as between capital and income) shall cease to apply to fees; and accordingly in that subsection, in relation to any time on or after the commencement date, for the words "the fees and expenses" there shall be substituted the words "any expenses retained or paid".

Amendment

Sub-s (1): words "Lord Chancellor" in square brackets in both places they occur substituted by the Public Trustee (Liability and Fees) Act 2002, s 2(3)(a).
Sub-s (1): words omitted repealed by the Public Trustee (Liability and Fees) Act 2002, s 2(3)(b).

Commentary

The Public Trustee (Fees) Order 1999, SI 1999/855 currently applies. These legislative provisions exclude the possibility of remuneration becoming payable under the Trustee Act 2000, s 29 **[504]**.

[252]

2 Transitional and supplementary provisions

(1) Nothing in the preceding section shall be construed as affecting the validity of any order or other instrument made for the purposes of subsection (1) of section nine of the principal Act before the passing of this Act.

(2) Where, in the case of a trust fund,—

(a) a judgment or order of the court has been given or made before the commencement date, whether before or after the passing of this Act, whereby provision is made as to the incidence, as between the capital and income of the fund, of any fee chargeable by the public trustee, or

(b) any fee chargeable by the public trustee in respect of the fund or the income thereof has been commuted before the commencement date, whether before or after the passing of this Act, or

(c) by reason of any other special circumstances existing before the commencement date it appears to the public trustee to be expedient to exclude or suspend the operation of any new fees order in relation to that fund or the income thereof, the public trustee shall direct that, notwithstanding the coming into operation of any fees order made after the passing of this Act, the fees in force under subsection (1) of section nine of the principal Act immediately before the commencement date shall continue after that date to apply to that trust fund and the income thereof, and that the provisions of any such fees order shall not apply in relation thereto.

(3) A direction under the last preceding subsection may be given either before or after the commencement date; and, where such a direction is given after the commencement date, it may be made so as to have effect as from that date.

(4) Any direction given by the public trustee under this Act may be given so as to be in force either for a period specified in the direction or indefinitely until the direction is revoked by him.

Commentary

This section preserves the position in respect of cases where it has been fixed by order that the fees are to be paid out of income or capital before the PT(F)A 1957 comes into force, and where there has been a court order made either before or after the Act specifying whether fees should come out of income or capital.

[253]

3 Interpretation

(1) In this Act "trust fund" includes any part of a trust fund, and also includes an estate administered by the public trustee and any part of such an estate; and "trust" includes an executorship or administratorship, and also includes the administration of an estate in pursuance of section three of the principal Act (which relates to the administration of small estates by the public trustee), and any reference to the acceptance of a trust shall be construed accordingly.

(2) Subject to the preceding subsection, expressions used in this Act and in the principal Act have the same meaning in this Act as in that Act.

Commentary

For definitions in the Public Trustee Act 1906, see s 15 of that Act **[73]**.

[254]

4 Short title, citation and extent

(1) This Act may be cited as the Public Trustee (Fees) Act 1957; and the Public Trustee Act 1906, and this Act may be cited together as the Public Trustee Acts 1906 and 1957.

(2) This Act shall not extend to Scotland or to Northern Ireland.

[255]

VARIATION OF TRUSTS ACT 1958

1958 Chapter 53

ARRANGEMENT OF SECTIONS

An Act to extend the jurisdiction of courts of law to vary trusts in the interests of beneficiaries and sanction dealings with trust property

[23rd July 1958]

General Note
The Variation of Trusts Act 1958 (VTA 1958) was passed as a response to the House of Lords decision in *Chapman v Chapman* [1954] AC 429 which held that the court had no jurisdiction to approve the variation of trusts on behalf of an infant or unborns.

1 Jurisdiction of courts to vary trusts

(1) Where property, whether real or personal, is held on trusts arising, whether before or after the passing of this Act, under any will, settlement or other disposition, the court may if it thinks fit by order approve on behalf of—

(a) any person having, directly or indirectly, an interest, whether vested or contingent, under the trusts who by reason of infancy or other incapacity is incapable of assenting, or

(b) any person (whether ascertained or not) who may become entitled, directly or indirectly, to an interest under the trusts as being at a future date or on the happening of a future event a person of any specified description or a member of any specified class of persons, so however that this paragraph shall not include any person who would be of that description, or a member of that class, as the case may be, if the said date had fallen or the said event had happened at the date of the application to the court, or

(c) any person unborn, or

(d) any person in respect of any discretionary interest of his under protective trusts where the interest of the principal beneficiary has not failed or determined,

any arrangement (by whomsoever proposed, and whether or not there is any other person beneficially interested who is capable of assenting thereto) varying or revoking all or any of the trusts, or enlarging the powers of the trustees of managing or administering any of the property subject to the trusts:

Provided that except by virtue of paragraph (d) of this subsection the court shall not approve an arrangement on behalf of any person unless the carrying out thereof would be for the benefit of that person.

(2) In the foregoing subsection "protective trusts" means the trusts specified in paragraphs (i) and (ii) of subsection (1) of section thirty-three of the Trustee Act 1925, or any like trusts, "the principal beneficiary" has the same meaning as in the said subsection (1) and "discretionary interest" means an interest arising under the trust specified in paragraph (ii) of the said subsection (1) or any like trust.

(3) . . . The jurisdiction conferred by subsection (1) of this section shall be exercisable by the High Court, except that the question whether the carrying out of any arrangement would be for the benefit of a person falling within paragraph (a) of the said subsection (1) *shall be determined by order of [the authority having jurisdiction under [Part VII of the Mental Health Act 1983], if that person is a patient within the meaning of [the said Part VII]]* [who lacks capacity (within the meaning of the Mental Capacity Act 2005) to give his assent is to be determined by the Court of Protection].

(4) . . .

(5) Nothing in the foregoing provisions of this section shall apply to trusts affecting property settled by Act of Parliament.

(6) Nothing in this section shall be taken to limit *the powers conferred by section sixty-four of the Settled Land Act 1925, section fifty-seven of the Trustee Act 1925, or [the powers of the authority having jurisdiction under [Part VII of the Mental Health Act 1983]]* [the powers of the Court of Protection].

Amendments
Sub-s (3): words omitted repealed by the County Courts Act 1959, s 204, Sch 3.

Sub-s (3): words from "shall be determined" to the end in italics repealed and subsequent words in square brackets substituted, from a date to be appointed, by the Mental Capacity Act 2005, s 67(1), Sch 6, para 9(a).
Sub-s (3): words in square brackets beginning with the words "the authority having" substituted by the Mental Health Act 1959, s 149(1), Sch 7, Pt I.
Sub-s (3): words "Part VII of the Mental Health Act 1983" in square brackets substituted by the Mental Health Act 1983, s 148, Sch 4, para 14(a).
Sub-s (3): words "the said Part VII" in square brackets substituted by the Mental Health Act 1983, s 148, Sch 4, para 14(a).
Sub-s (4): repealed by the County Courts Act 1959, s 204, Sch 3.
Sub-s (6): words from "the powers conferred" to the end in italics repealed and subsequent words in square brackets substituted, from a date to be appointed, by the Mental Capacity Act 2005, s 67(1), Sch 6, para 9(b).
Sub-s (6): words "Part VII of the Mental Health Act 1983" in square brackets substituted by the Mental Health Act 1983, s 148, Sch 4, para 14(b).
Sub-s (6): words in square brackets beginning with the words "the powers of the authority" substituted by the Mental Health Act 1959, s 149(1), Sch 7, Pt I.

Commentary
The court under the VTA 1958 can approve an arrangement (which means any proposal to revoke or vary any of the trusts, see *Re Steed's Will Trusts* [1960] Ch 407) on behalf of various categories of persons. As far as s 1(1)(a) is concerned the court has assumed that a minor beneficiary under a discretionary trust has an "interest", see *Re Bristols's Settled Estates* [1965] 1 WLR 469, as does a minor, who may become a beneficiary, see *Re Suffert's Settlement* [1961] Ch 1. As far as others suffering from lack of capacity within the Mental Capacity Act 2005 are concerned within sub-s (1)(a), if the arrangement needs to be approved on their behalf alone then an application can be made and dealt with by the Court of Protection. If there are others on whose behalf the arrangement needs to be approved, the application should be submitted to the Court of Protection first for it to decide if the arrangement is for the benefit of the person lacking capacity (see sub-s (3)).
Subsection (1)(b) covers those who may fall within a particular class, or satisfy a particular description on a future date, but do not at present fall within that description, see *Knocker v Youle* [1986] 1 WLR 934. Protective trusts referred to in sub-s (1)(d) are those mentioned in the Trustee Act 1925, s 33 **[102]** and like trusts (see sub-s (2)). Note that the proviso to sub-s (1) does not apply to this category and therefore benefit to the beneficiary on whose behalf the court is approving does not have to be shown.
The court has no power to approve the arrangement on behalf of anyone other than the beneficiaries mentioned in sub-s (1)(a)–(d), see: *Goulding v James* (1997) 2 All ER 239. The VTA 1958 does not permit the court to approve a complete resettlement, see *Re Towler's Settlement Trusts* [1964] Ch 158 although the courts will approve a compete revocation and new declaration if it is in fact a variation, see *Re Holt's Settlement, Wilson v Holt* [1969] Ch 100. Insurance policies held on bare trusts for minors have been held to fall within this section, see: *Re CD* [2004] 3 All ER 780.
The court may approve a settlement notwithstanding a tax mitigation motive and that it involves foreign trustees, see for a recent example, *Re the Colin Richard Douglas 1990 Settlement* (2000) 2 ITELR 682. In the case of approval on behalf of a person within sub-s (1)(a)–(c) the court must be satisfied the arrangement is for their benefit. The benefit need not be financial or material, see *Re Holt's Settlement, Wilson v Holt* [1969] Ch 100, and see *Re Towler's Settlement Trusts* [1964] Ch 158 and *Re Weston's Settlement, Weston v Weston* [1969] 1 Ch 223. Benefit has to be shown on a balance of probabilities, see *Re Druce's Settlement Trusts Pothecary v Druce* [1962] 1 WLR 363 and the court can take a risk on behalf of an infant if it is a risk that an adult would take, see *Re Cohen's Settlement Trusts* [1959] 1 WLR 865. The postponement of a minor beneficiary's interests for sound tax planning reasons my be for their benefit, see: *Ridgewell v Ridgewell* [2007] EWHC 2666.
As far as protective trusts are concerned, benefit does not have to be shown but the court will look at the arrangement and the intention of the settlor in creating the trust, see *Re Steed's Will Trusts* [1960] Ch 407 and evidence of the financial position of the protected life tenant is usually required (*Re Baker's Settlement* [1964] 1 WLR 336). As to sub-s (3), the county court does have limited jurisdiction (the County Courts Act 1984, s 23) but it is rarely used.
Application is by a Part 8 claim form in accordance with the procedure under the Civil Procedure Rules 1998, SI 1998/3132, Part 8 and is governed by Part 64 and the Practice Direction thereto. Trustees ought not to apply unless there is no one else who can make the application, see *Re Druce's Settlement Trusts Pothecary v Druce* [1962] 1 WLR 363.

2 Extent and provisions as to Northern Ireland

(1) This Act shall not extend to Scotland.

(2) The foregoing section shall not extend to Northern Ireland .

Amendment
Sub-s (2): words omitted repealed by the Northern Ireland Constitution Act 1973, s 41(1), Sch 6, Part I.

Commentary
This provision does not prevent trusts governed by the law of Scotland and Northern Ireland being varied or indeed trusts of other jurisdictions, see *Re Paget's Settlement, Baillie v De Brossard* [1965] 1 WLR 1046 and see the Recognition of Trusts Act 1987 **[400]**.

[257]

3 Short title

This Act may be cited as the Variation of Trusts Act 1958.

[258]

WILLS ACT 1963

1963 Chapter 44

ARRANGEMENT OF SECTIONS

An Act to repeal the Wills Act 1861 and make new provision in lieu thereof; and to provide that certain testamentary instruments shall be probative for the purpose of the conveyance of heritable property in Scotland

[31st July 1963]

General Note
The Wills Act 1963 (WA 1963) revolutionised the rules providing for the formal validity of wills where there was a foreign element providing that if the will was executed in accordance with one of seven systems of law, it would be formally valid. Note that although one section of the Act deals with construction, the WA 1963 is otherwise concerned with formal validity and not capacity which is, in general terms, governed by the domicile of the testator.

1 General rule as to formal validity

A will shall be treated as properly executed if its execution conformed to the internal law in force in the territory where it was executed, or in the territory where, at the time of its execution or of the testator's death, he was domiciled or had his habitual residence, or in a state of which, at either of those times, he was a national.

Commentary
These provisions govern the formal validity of wills rather than the question of the testator's capacity which is governed by the law of his domicile. The rules only apply to testators dying on or after 1 January 1964. This section however gives formal validity to a will in circumstances far wider than where it is executed in accordance with the internal law of the

testator's domicile. For cases where there is more than one internal law applicable to the territory or state, see s 6 below. And see s 6(1) for the meaning of "will". There is no statutory definition of "habitual residence" but it would seem to be a far wider concept than domicile, see *Cruse v Chittum* [1974] 2 All ER 940; *Kapur v Kapur* [1984] FLR 920.

[259]

2 Additional rules

(1) Without prejudice to the preceding section, the following shall be treated as properly executed—

(a) a will executed on board a vessel or aircraft of any description, if the execution of the will conformed to the internal law in force in the territory with which, having regard to its registration (if any) and other relevant circumstances, the vessel or aircraft may be taken to have been most closely connected;

(b) a will so far as it disposes of immovable property, if its execution conformed to the internal law in force in the territory where the property was situated;

(c) a will so far as it revokes a will which under this Act would be treated as properly executed or revokes a provision which under this Act would be treated as comprised in a properly executed will, if the execution of the later will conformed to any law by reference to which the revoked will or provision would be so treated;

(d) a will so far as it exercises a power of appointment, if the execution of the will conformed to the law governing the essential validity of the power.

(2) A will so far as it exercises a power of appointment shall not be treated as improperly executed by reason only that its execution was not in accordance with any formal requirements contained in the instrument creating the power.

Commentary

Subsections (1)(a) and (b) provide yet more systems of law which can apply to render a will formally valid—sub-s (1)(a) relating to wills executed on board a vessel and sub-s (1)(b) to the law of the territory where immovable property is situated. Subsection (1)(c) renders valid a will which revokes a previous will which is regarded as formally valid under the WA 1963, provided that it complies with one of the systems of law which would have applied to the original will. Therefore, a will executed in England by a testator then domiciled and habitually resident in Spain and with real property in England, will be formally valid if executed in accordance with the laws of England and/or Spain. If by the time a later revoking will is executed in accordance with Spanish law but the testator is domiciled and habitually resident in England with no real property other than in England, that later will is formally valid insofar as it revokes the earlier will, but not otherwise formally valid to dispose of property. Subsections (1)(d) and (2) relate to powers of appointment exercised by a will which will be validly exercised if the will conforms with one of the systems of law provided for under s 1 or the law governing the essential validity of the power. Other than that, formal requirements of the instrument creating the power do not have to be complied with.

[260]

3 Certain requirements to be treated as formal

Where (whether in pursuance of this Act or not) a law in force outside the United Kingdom falls to be applied in relation to a will, any requirement of that law whereby special formalities are to be observed by testators answering a particular description, or witnesses to the execution of a will are to possess certain qualifications, shall be treated, notwithstanding any rule of that law to the contrary, as a formal requirement only.

Commentary

This section has the effect that specific requirements relating to the way in which a will is to be executed in certain circumstances, must be regarded as a matter of formality only, and can be ignored if the testator in question executes a will which is formally valid in accordance with one of the systems of law which applies to him.

[261]

4 Construction of wills

The construction of a will shall not be altered by reason of any change in the testator's domicile after the execution of the will.

Commentary

Wills are in general construed in accordance with the law of the domicile of the testator unless there is a contrary intention shown in the will. This provision (not relating this time to formal validity but to matters of construction) provides that it is the domicile of the testator at the time when the will was executed which is relevant to the question of construction.

[262]

5 . . .

. . .

Amendment

Repealed by the Succession (Scotland) Act 1964, s 34(2), Sch 3.

[263]

6 Interpretation

(1) In this Act—

"internal law" in relation to any territory or state means the law which would apply in a case where no question of the law in force in any other territory or state arose;

"state" means a territory or group of territories having its own law of nationality;

"will" includes any testamentary instrument or act, and "testator" shall be construed accordingly.

(2) Where under this Act the internal law in force in any territory or state is to be applied in the case of a will, but there are in force in that territory or state two or more systems of internal law relating to the formal validity of wills, the system to be applied shall be ascertained as follows—

(a) if there is in force throughout the territory or state a rule indicating which of those systems can properly be applied in the case in question, that rule shall be followed; or

(b) if there is no such rule, the system shall be that with which the testator was most closely connected at the relevant time, and for this purpose the relevant time is the time of the testator's death where the matter is to be determined by reference to circumstances prevailing at his death, and the time of execution of the will in any other case.

(3) In determining for the purposes of this Act whether or not the execution of a will conformed to a particular law, regard shall be had to the formal requirements of that law at the time of execution, but this shall not prevent account being taken of an alteration of law affecting wills executed at that time if the alteration enables the will to be treated as properly executed.

Commentary

Subsection (1) provides some important definitions, and in particular the way in which "internal law" is defined has the effect of excluding the doctrine of renvoi. Section 6(2)(a) and (b) deal with the problem where the law to be applied under the WA 1963 is of a territory where more than one system of law applies. Subsection (3) deals with the time at which one looks in determining whether a will was executed in accordance with the law of a particular territory. In general terms that will be the date of execution but if there is a retroactive change in the law which validates the will, then that can be taken into account, apparently without any limitation in time. If, however, that retrospective alteration invalidates the will, it seems it is not to be taken into account.

[264]

7 Short title, commencement, repeal and extent

(1) This Act may be cited as the Wills Act 1963.

(2) This Act shall come into operation on 1st January 1964.

(3) . . .

(4) This Act shall not apply to a will of a testator who died before the time of the commencement of this Act and shall apply to a will of a testator who dies after that time whether the will was executed before or after that time, but so that the repeal of the Wills Act 1861 shall not invalidate a will executed before that time.

(5) It is hereby declared that this Act extends to Northern Ireland . . . .

Amendment

Sub-s (3): repeals the Wills Act 1861.

Sub-s (5): words omitted repealed by the Northern Ireland Constitution Act 1973, Sch 6, Part I.

Commentary

The rules before the WA 1963 came into force were quite different and this section makes it clear that the WA 1963 only applies to wills executed post 1 January 1964. Reference should be made to *Williams on Wills* (7th edn) for the old rules.

[265]

PERPETUITIES AND ACCUMULATIONS ACT 1964

1964 Chapter 55

ARRANGEMENT OF SECTIONS

An Act to modify the law of England and Wales relating to the avoidance of future interests in property on grounds of remoteness and governing accumulations of income from property

[16th July 1964]

General Note
The Perpetuities and Accumulations Act 1964 (PAA 1964) substantially amended the common law rule requiring equitable interests to vest within the perpetuity period and the rule limiting the time for which income can be accumulated. The Law Commission is currently considering legislation to amend the law further.

PERPETUITIES

1 Power to specify perpetuity period

(1) Subject to section 9 (2) of this Act and subsection (2) below, where the instrument by which any disposition is made so provides, the perpetuity period applicable to the disposition under the rule against perpetuities, instead of being of any other duration, shall be of a duration equal to such number of years not exceeding eighty as is specified in that behalf in the instrument.

(2) Subsection (1) above shall not have effect where the disposition is made in exercise of a special power of appointment, but where a period is specified under that subsection in the instrument creating such a power the period shall apply in relation to any disposition under the power as it applies in relation to the power itself.

Commentary
Before the PAA 1964 came into force on 15 July 1964, the perpetuity period applicable to trusts was any lives in being at the date of the creation of the trust (including the lives of children conceived but not born) plus 21 years. Draftsmen often chose royal lives to extend the perpetuity period. Subsection (1) enables an 80 year period to be chosen in respect of post-15 July 1964 trusts. Subsection (2) preserves the common law position that the perpetuity period applicable to the exercise of a special power of appointment (that is an appointment amongst a specified class) is that of the instrument creating the power. As to the meaning of period being "specified" see: *Re Green's Will Trusts* [1985] 3 All ER 455.

[266]

2 Presumptions and evidence as to future parenthood

(1) Where in any proceedings there arises on the rule against perpetuities a question which turns on the ability of a person to have a child at some future time, then—

- (a) subject to paragraph (b) below, it shall be presumed that a male can have a child at the age of fourteen years or over, but not under that age, and that a female can have a child at the age of twelve years or over, but not under that age or over the age of fifty-five years; but
- (b) in the case of a living person evidence may be given to show that he or she will or will not be able to have a child at the time in question.

(2) Where any such question is decided by treating a person as unable to have a child at a particular time, and he or she does so, the High Court may make such order as it thinks fit for placing the persons interested in the property comprised in the disposition, so far as may be just, in the position they would have held if the question had not been so decided.

(3) Subject to subsection (2) above, where any such question is decided in relation to a disposition by treating a person as able or unable to have a child at a particular time, then he or she shall be so treated for the purpose of any question which may arise on the rule against perpetuities in relation to the same disposition in any subsequent proceedings.

(4) In the foregoing provisions of this section references to having a child are references to begetting or giving birth to a child, but those provisions (except subsection (1)(b)) shall apply in relation to the possibility that a person will at any time have a child by adoption, legitimation or other means as they apply to his or her ability at that time to beget or give birth to a child.

Commentary

At common law men or women of any age were deemed to be able to have children (see as an example, *Ward v Van der Loeffe* [1924] AC 653). It is important to note the definition of "having a child" in sub-s (4) which means that the presumption will work to exclude the possibility of a woman over 55 adopting a child. The advent of fertilisation techniques means that evidence under sub-s (1)(b) might be brought to show that a woman could have a child over the age of 55, but usually the subsection is used to adduce evidence that a younger woman is not able to have children. Subsections (2) and (3) contain provisions as to what should happen if the presumption should prove to be wrong. There is no guidance from reported cases as to the way in which the jurisdiction would be exercised.

[267]

3 Uncertainty as to remoteness

(1) Where, apart from the provisions of this section and sections 4 and 5 of this Act, a disposition would be void on the ground that the interest disposed of might not become vested until too remote a time, the disposition shall be treated, until such time (if any) as it becomes established that the vesting must occur, if at all, after the end of the perpetuity period, as if the disposition were not subject to the rule against perpetuities; and its becoming so established shall not affect the validity of anything previously done in relation to the interest disposed of by way of advancement, application of intermediate income or otherwise.

(2) Where, apart from the said provisions, a disposition consisting of the conferring of a general power of appointment would be void on the ground that the power might not become exercisable until too remote a time, the disposition shall be treated, until such time (if any) as it becomes established that the power will not be exercisable within the perpetuity period, as if the disposition were not subject to the rule against perpetuities.

(3) Where, apart from the said provisions, a disposition consisting of the conferring of any power, option or other right would be void on the ground that the right might be exercised at too remote a time, the disposition shall be treated as regards any exercise of the right within the perpetuity period as if it were not subject to the rule against perpetuities and, subject to the said provisions, shall be treated as void for remoteness only if, and so far as, the right is not fully exercised within that period.

(4) Where this section applies to a disposition and the duration of the perpetuity period is not determined by virtue of section 1 or 9 (2) of this Act, it shall be determined as follows:—

- (a) where any persons falling within subsection (5) below are individuals in being and ascertainable at the commencement of the perpetuity period the duration of the period shall be determined by reference to their lives and no others, but so that the lives of any description of persons falling within paragraph (b) or (c) of that subsection shall be disregarded if the number of persons of that description is such as to render it impracticable to ascertain the date of death of the survivor;
- (b) where there are no lives under paragraph (a) above the period shall be twenty-one years.

(5) The said persons are as follows:—

- (a) the person by whom the disposition was made;
- (b) a person to whom or in whose favour the disposition was made, that is to say—
  - (i) in the case of a disposition to a class of persons, any member or potential member of the class;
  - (ii) in the case of an individual disposition to a person taking only on certain conditions being satisfied, any person as to whom some of the conditions are satisfied and the remainder may in time be satisfied;

(iii) in the case of a special power of appointment exercisable in favour of members of a class, any member or potential member of the class;
(iv) in the case of a special power of appointment exercisable in favour of one person only, that person or, where the object of the power is ascertainable only on certain conditions being satisfied, any person as to whom some of the conditions are satisfied and the remainder may in time be satisfied;
(v) in the case of any power, option or other right, the person on whom the right is conferred;

(c) a person having a child or grandchild within sub-paragraphs (i) to (iv) of paragraph (b) above, or any of whose children or grandchildren, if subsequently born, would by virtue of his or her descent fall within those sub-paragraphs;
(d) any person on the failure or determination of whose prior interest the disposition is limited to take effect.

Commentary

The provisions contained in this section are commonly known as the "wait and see" provisions. They soften the common law rule against perpetuities which provided that if any interest under the trust would vest outside the perpetuity period, applying that rule at the outset, then that interest was void. These provisions enable those interested to wait and see whether or not the gift will vest outside the perpetuity period and only when it is clear that it will not, is it treated as void. Subsections (2) and (3) apply similar rules to general powers of appointment which might be exercisable outside the perpetuity period and rights options and powers. Subsections (4) and (5) were introduced because it was feared that too many lives in being at common law might need to be taken into account in applying the wait and see provisions. At common law the draftsman could specify as many lives as he wished as lives in being and, as noted above, royal lives clauses were common. Subsections (4) and (5) specify the lives in being which can be taken into account and it is clear that royal lives (unless they actually fall within the various categories set out) will not be taken into account. The restriction on who can be a life in being applies only for the purposes of these provisions, and indeed recourse should not be had to these provisions unless it is clear that at common law the gift is void and is not validated by any of the other provisions of the PAA 1964 (eg ss 4 and 5). It is not entirely clear how sub-s (4)(a) will work to exclude lives in being where it is impracticable to ascertain the death of the survivor. A member of a pension scheme has been held to be a life in being within sub-s (5)(d) (see *Re Thomas Meadows & Co Ltd* [1971] Ch 278).

[268]

4 Reduction of age and exclusion of class members to avoid remoteness

(1) Where a disposition is limited by reference to the attainment by any person or persons of a specified age exceeding twenty-one years, and it is apparent at the time the disposition is made or becomes apparent at a subsequent time—

(a) that the disposition would, apart from this section, be void for remoteness, but
(b) that it would not be so void if the specified age had been twenty-one years,

the disposition shall be treated for all purposes as if, instead of being limited by reference to the age in fact specified, it had been limited by reference to the age nearest to that age which would, if specified instead, have prevented the disposition from being so void.

(2) Where in the case of any disposition different ages exceeding twenty-one years are specified in relation to different persons—

(a) the reference in paragraph (b) of subsection (1) above to the specified age shall be construed as a reference to all the specified ages, and
(b) that subsection shall operate to reduce each such age so far as is necessary to save the disposition from being void for remoteness.

(3) Where the inclusion of any persons, being potential members of a class or unborn persons who at birth would become members or potential members of the

class, prevents the foregoing provisions of this section from operating to save a disposition from being void for remoteness, those persons shall thenceforth be deemed for all the purposes of the disposition to be excluded from the class, and the said provisions shall thereupon have effect accordingly.

(4) Where, in the case of a disposition to which subsection (3) above does not apply, it is apparent at the time the disposition is made or becomes apparent at a subsequent time that, apart from this subsection, the inclusion of any persons, being potential members of a class or unborn persons who at birth would become members or potential members of the class, would cause the disposition to be treated as void for remoteness, those persons shall, unless their exclusion would exhaust the class, thenceforth be deemed for all the purposes of the disposition to be excluded from the class.

(5) Where this section has effect in relation to a disposition to which section 3 above applies, the operation of this section shall not affect the validity of anything previously done in relation to the interest disposed of by way of advancement, application of intermediate income or otherwise.

(6) . . .

[(7) For the avoidance of doubt it is hereby declared that a question arising under section 3 of this Act or subsection (1)(a) above of whether a disposition would be void apart from this section is to be determined as if subsection (6) above had been a separate section of this Act.]

Amendment

Sub-s (6): repeals the Law of Property Act 1925, s 163.
Sub-s (7): inserted by the Children Act 1975, s 108(1)(a), Sch 3, para 43.

Commentary

At common law a gift to a class will be void if that class might be increased or decreased outside the perpetuity period. At common law the rule of convenience (known as the rule in *Andrews v Partington* (1791) 3 Bro CC 401) will apply in some cases to close the class (a full discussion of this rule is outside the scope of this work and reference to its operation should be made to *Underhill & Hayton's Law of Trusts and Trustees*). If that rule des not apply, this section reduces the age whereby the member of the class is to attain a vested interest to 21. It applies only to trusts created after 15 July 1964, although there was a similar although more restrictive provision for dispositions made since 1925 in the Law of Property Act 1925 **[172]**, s 163. Note that the wait and see provisions of s 3 should be applied before this section. If the reduction of ages in sub-ss (1) and (2) does not save the gift, then sub-ss (3) and (4) exclude latecoming beneficiaries from the class. For the meaning of "member of a class" see s 15(3) below.

[269]

5 Condition relating to death of surviving spouse

Where a disposition is limited by reference to the time of death of the survivor of a person in being at the commencement of the perpetuity period and any spouse of that person, and that time has not arrived at the end of the perpetuity period, the disposition shall be treated for all purposes, where to do so would save it from being void for remoteness, as if it had instead been limited by reference to the time immediately before the end of that period.

Commentary

At common law a gift to the widow of a life in being was treated as void as the life in being might marry someone born after the date of the gift. This section provides that the rule against perpetuities shall not apply in such circumstances.

[270]

6 Saving and acceleration of expectant interests

A disposition shall not be treated as void for remoteness by reason only that the interest disposed of is ulterior to and dependent upon an interest under a disposition which is so void, and the vesting of an interest shall not be prevented from being accelerated on the failure of a prior interest by reason only that the failure arises because of remoteness.

Commentary

The rule at common law was that if an interest was intended to take effect on the exhaustion and determination of an earlier interest which was void for perpetuity, it too was void (for an explanation see *Re Hubbard's Will Trusts* [1963] Ch 275). This section abolishes that rule for dispositions after 15 July 1964.

[271]

7 Powers of appointment

For the purposes of the rule against perpetuities, a power of appointment shall be treated as a special power unless—

(a) in the instrument creating the power it is expressed to be exercisable by one person only, and

(b) it could, at all times during its currency when that person is of full age and capacity, be exercised by him so as immediately to transfer to himself the whole of the interest governed by the power without the consent of any other person or compliance with any other condition, not being a formal condition relating only to the mode of exercise of the power:

Provided that for the purpose of determining whether a disposition made under a power of appointment exercisable by will only is void for remoteness, the power shall be treated as a general power where it would have fallen to be so treated if exercisable by deed.

Commentary

An important distinction needs to be drawn between general powers of appointment and special powers for the purposes of the rule against perpetuities. This section makes it clear beyond doubt in respect of post-15 July 1964 dispositions the basis upon which powers are to be treated as general or special, which was a cause of some doubt at common law. At common law a general power of appointment by will only was void if it could be exercised outside the perpetuity period (*Wollaston v King* (1868) LR 8 Eq 165) but see now s 3(3) above and the proviso to sub-s (b). As far as special powers are concerned, provided they were exercisable within the perpetuity period, then the fact they might not be exercised was not important (*Bray v Hammersley* (183) 3 Sims 513). The PAA 1964 only applies to instruments creating the special power coming into effect after the Act but the definition of special powers applies to pre-PAA 1964 dispositions (see s 15(5) below).

[272]

8 Administrative powers of trustees

(1) The rule against perpetuities shall not operate to invalidate a power conferred on trustees or other persons to sell, lease, exchange or otherwise dispose of any property for full consideration, or to do any other act in the administration (as opposed to the distribution) of any property, and shall not prevent the payment to trustees or other persons of reasonable remuneration for their services.

(2) Subsection (1) above shall apply for the purpose of enabling a power to be exercised at any time after the commencement of this Act notwithstanding that the power is conferred by an instrument which took effect before that commencement.

Commentary
This section reinforces the common law rule that the rule against perpetuities does not affect the exercise by trustees of administrative rather than dispositive powers. The section applies to pre-15 July 1964 trusts and will trusts.

[273]

9 Options relating to land

(1) The rule against perpetuities shall not apply to a disposition consisting of the conferring of an option to acquire for valuable consideration an interest reversionary (whether directly or indirectly) on the term of a lease if—

(a) the option is exercisable only by the lessee or his successors in title, and
(b) it ceases to be exercisable at or before the expiration of one year following the determination of the lease.

This subsection shall apply in relation to an agreement for a lease as it applies in relation to a lease, and "lessee" shall be construed accordingly.

(2) In the case of a disposition consisting of the conferring of an option to acquire for valuable consideration any interest in land, the perpetuity period under the rule against perpetuities shall be twenty-one years, and section 1 of this Act shall not apply:

Provided that this subsection shall not apply to a right of pre-emption conferred on a public or local authority in respect of land used or to be used for religious purposes where the right becomes exercisable only if the land ceases to be used for such purposes.

Commentary
Before sub-s (1) came into force the rule was that an option to purchase the reversion of a lease (although not to renew the lease) was void as against the successors in title of the original grantor, unless its exercise was limited to the perpetuity period (see *Woodall v Clifton* [1905] 2 Ch 257). This subsection renders enforceable options contained in leases provided that the conditions set out in the subsection are fulfilled. Subsection (2) is of more general application and has been held to render void a right to re-purchase in a contract unlimited in time, see: *Wilson v Truelove* (2003) 23 EG 136. Note that the wait and see provisions of s 3 above apply.

[274]

10 Avoidance of contractual and other rights in cases of remoteness

Where a disposition inter vivos would fall to be treated as void for remoteness if the rights and duties thereunder were capable of transmission to persons other than the original parties and had been so transmitted, it shall be treated as void as between the person by whom it was made and the person to whom or in whose favour it was made or any successor of his, and no remedy shall lie in contract or otherwise for giving effect to it or making restitution for its lack of effect.

Commentary
At common law the law against perpetuities had no place as between the original contracting parties, see *Hutton v Watling* [1948] Ch 26. This section overrules that general principle so that if the contract would offend the perpetuities rule with regard to third parties, it will also do so with regard to successors in title.

[275]

11 Rights for enforcement of rentcharges

(1) The rule against perpetuities shall not apply to any powers or remedies for recovering or compelling the payment of an annual sum to which section 121 or 122

of the Law of Property Act 1925 applies, or otherwise becoming exercisable or enforceable on the breach of any condition or other requirement relating to that sum.

(2) . . .

Amendment

Sub-s (2): amends the Law of Property Act 1925, s 121(6).

Commentary

The Law of Property Act 1925, s 121(6) in its unamended form relieved certain rights of re-entry to secure payment in respect of rentcharges from the perpetuity rule. This section provides that for rentcharges created after 15 July 1964, the rule against perpetuities shall not apply to any remedy for enforcing a rentcharge. Section 121(6) now reads: "The rule of law relating to perpetuities does not apply to any powers or remedies conferred by this section.".

[276]

12 Possibilities of reverter, conditions subsequent, exceptions and reservations

(1) In the case of—

(a) a possibility of reverter on the determination of a determinable fee simple, or

(b) a possibility of a resulting trust on the determination of any other determinable interest in property,

the rule against perpetuities shall apply in relation to the provision causing the interest to be determinable as it would apply if that provision were expressed in the form of a condition subsequent giving rise, on breach thereof, to a right of re-entry or an equivalent right in the case of property other than land, and where the provision falls to be treated as void for remoteness the determinable interest shall become an absolute interest.

Where a disposition is subject to any such provision, or to any such condition subsequent, or to any exception or reservation, the disposition shall be treated for the purposes of this Act as including a separate disposition of any rights arising by virtue of the provision, condition subsequent, exception or reservation.

Commentary

At common law there was the anomalous situation that the possibility of an interest reverting to the grantor or a resulting trust in his favour arising on the determination of an interest was not subject to the perpetuity rule (see *Re Cooper's Conveyance Trusts* [1956] 1 WLR 1096). This section dispenses with that anomaly and treats determinable interests as if they were conditional. Note that the wait and see provision in s 3 above will apply and if after 21 years (assuming no lives in being) the gift has not reverted, it will belong to the donee absolutely.

[277]

ACCUMULATIONS

13 Amendment of s 164 of Law of Property Act 1925

(1) The periods for which accumulations of income under a settlement or other disposition are permitted by section 164 of the Law of Property Act 1925 shall include—

(a) a term of twenty-one years from the date of the making of the disposition, and

(b) the duration of the minority or respective minorities of any person or persons in being at that date.

(2) It is hereby declared that the restrictions imposed by the said section 164 apply in relation to a power to accumulate income whether or not there is a duty to exercise that power, and that they apply whether or not the power to accumulate extends to income produced by the investment of income previously accumulated.

Commentary
For section 164 of the Law of Property Act 1925 as amended by this section see **[173]**. Note that the Law of Property Act 1925, s 165 **[174]** disregards accumulations made during minorities (for example under the Trustee Act 1925, s 31(2) **[100]**). This section makes it clear by sub-s (2) that it applies to a power as well as a duty to accumulate.

[278]

14 Right to stop accumulations

Section 2 above shall apply to any question as to the right of beneficiaries to put an end to accumulations of income under any disposition as it applies to questions arising on the rule against perpetuities.

Commentary
Where beneficiaries are not only entitled to the accumulations but also to the underlying capital, they can put an end to the accumulations and for these purposes the presumptions as to a person being beyond child bearing etc contained in s 2 above apply.

[279]

SUPPLEMENTAL

15 Short title, interpretation and extent

(1) This Act may be cited as the Perpetuities and Accumulations Act 1964.

(2) In this Act—

"disposition" includes the conferring of a power of appointment and any other disposition of an interest in or right over property, and references to the interest disposed of shall be construed accordingly;

"in being" means living or en ventre sa mere;

"power of appointment" includes any discretionary power to transfer a beneficial interest in property without the furnishing of valuable consideration;

"will" includes a codicil;

and for the purposes of this Act a disposition contained in a will shall be deemed to be made at the death of the testator.

(3) For the purposes of this Act a person shall be treated as a member of a class if in his case all the conditions identifying a member of the class are satisfied, and shall be treated as a potential member if in his case some only of those conditions are satisfied but there is a possibility that the remainder will in time be satisfied.

(4) Nothing in this Act shall affect the operation of the rule of law rendering void for remoteness certain dispositions under which property is limited to be applied for purposes other than the benefit of any person or class of persons in cases where the property may be so applied after the end of the perpetuity period.

(5) The foregoing sections of this Act shall apply (except as provided in section 8 (2) above) only in relation to instruments taking effect after the commencement of this Act, and in the case of an instrument made in the exercise of a special power of appointment shall apply only where the instrument creating the power takes effect after that commencement;

Provided that section 7 above shall apply in all cases for construing the foregoing reference to a special power of appointment.

(6) This Act shall apply in relation to a disposition made otherwise than by an instrument as if the disposition had been contained in an instrument taking effect when the disposition was made.

(7) This Act binds the Crown.

(8) Except in so far as the contrary intention appears, any enactment of the Parliament of Northern Ireland passed for purposes similar to the purposes of this Act shall bind the Crown.

(9) This Act shall not extend to Scotland or (apart from subsection (8) above) to Northern Ireland.

Commentary

Note that under the definitions in sub-s (1) a life in being includes a child conceived but not born. Subsection (6) makes it clear that the PAA 1964 applies to dispositions other than those in writing.

[280]

ADMINISTRATION OF ESTATES (SMALL PAYMENTS) ACT 1965

1965 Chapter 32

ARRANGEMENT OF SECTIONS

An Act to provide for increasing the limits in enactments and instruments which allow property to be disposed of on death without probate or other proof of title, or in pursuance of a nomination made by the deceased; to extend certain of the said enactments relating to an intestate's property to cases where the deceased leaves a will; and for connected purposes

[5th August 1965]

General Note

The Administration of Estates (Small Payments) Act 1965 (AE(SP)A 1965) enabled certain small payments (which have from time to time been increased) to be paid to the person entitled without any need for there to be a grant of representation.

1 Increase in amounts disposable on death without representation

(1) In the enactments and instruments listed in Schedule 1 to this Act, of which—

(a) those listed in Part I are enactments authorising the disposal of property on death, without the necessity for probate or other proof of title, to persons appearing to be beneficially entitled thereto, to relatives or dependants of the deceased or to other persons described in the enactments, but subject to a limit which is in most cases £100 and which does not in any case exceed £100;

(b) those listed in Part II are enactments giving power to make rules or regulations containing corresponding provisions subject to a limit of £100; and

(c) those listed in Part III are such rules and regulations as aforesaid and instruments containing corresponding provisions made under other enactments and containing a limit which does not in any case exceed £200;

the said limit shall, subject to the provisions of that Schedule, in each case be [£5,000] instead of the limit specified in the enactment or instrument; and for references to the said limits in those enactments and instruments there shall accordingly be substituted references to [£5,000].

(2) . . .

Amendments

Sub-s (1): sum "£5,000" substituted, so far as relates to any enactment and in relation to deaths occurring after 11 May 1984, by SI 1984/539.

Sub-s (2): repealed by the National Debt Act 1972, s 17(1), Schedule.

Commentary

Originally the AE(SP)A 1965 raised the limit for payments under the various statutes set out in the Schedule to £500 from 5 September 1965, which was then increased to £1,500 for deaths between 10 August 1975 and 11 May 1984 and thereafter to £5,000.

[281]

2 Increase in amounts disposable on death by nomination

(1) In the enactments and instrument listed in Schedule 2 to this Act (which enable a person by nomination to dispose of property on his death up to a limit of £100 or, in some cases, £200) the said limit shall, subject to the provisions of that Schedule, in each case be [£5,000] instead of the limit specified in the enactments or instrument; and for references to the said limits in the said enactments and instrument there shall accordingly be substituted references to [£5,000].

(2) This section shall apply in relation to any nomination delivered at or sent to the appropriate office, or made in the appropriate book, after the expiration of a period of one month beginning with the date on which this Act is passed.

Amendments

Sub-s (1): sum "£5,000" substituted, so far as relates to any enactment, and in relation to deaths occurring after 11 May 1984, by SI 1984/539.

Commentary

See the notes to s 1 above for various amounts which have applied from time to time.

[282]

3 Extension of certain enactments relating to intestacies to cases where deceased leaves a will

(1) The enactments mentioned in Schedule 3 to this Act (all of which are listed in Part I of Schedule 1 to this Act) shall have effect subject to the amendments in that Schedule, which are amendments extending the operation of those enactments to cases where the deceased leaves a will.

(2) This section shall not extend to Northern Ireland.

Commentary

The amendments made to the various Acts in question extending them to where the deceased left a will are set out in Schedule 3 to the Act which is not reproduced here as it is outside the scope of this work.

[283]

4 Estate duty

. . .

Commentary

This section repeals the Local Government Superannuation Act 1953, s 25(2), the Industrial and Provident Societies Act 1965, s 24(4), and so much of the London Midland and Scottish Railway Act 1924, s 61(11), the Southern Railway Act 1924, s 99(12), and the London and North Eastern Railway Act 1944, s 3(12), as contain corresponding provisions.

[284]

5 Power to amend or repeal corresponding or superseded enactments

(1) If it appears to the Treasury that any provision in an Act (including a local Act) passed before this Act corresponds to any provision amended by section 1 or section 2 of this Act [or to section 66(1) and (2), 67 or 68 of the Friendly Societies Act 1974] [or to section 6(1) of the National Debt Act 1972] . . . and contains a limit of less than £500, the Treasury may by order substitute a limit of £500 for the limit contained in that provision, but subject to such exceptions, if any, including exceptions as regards the operation of the order in Northern Ireland, the Isle of Man, the Channel Islands or any other place outside Great Britain as may be specified in the order; and an order under this subsection may make such consequential amendments in the Act to which it relates as appear to the Treasury to be expedient.

(2) If it appears to the Treasury that any provision in a local Act passed before the Local Government Superannuation Act 1953 is wholly or mainly superseded by section 25(1) of the said Act of 1953 as amended by section 1 of this Act, the Treasury may by order repeal that provision.

(3) Any order under subsection (1) of this section amending a local Act may repeal any provision of that Act corresponding to any provision repealed by section 4 of this Act.

(4) No order shall be made under this section in respect of any provision in a local Act the Bill for which was promoted by a local authority except on the application of that authority or their successors.

(5) Any order under this section shall be made by statutory instrument subject to annulment in pursuance of a resolution of either House of Parliament.

Amendments

Sub-s (1): first words in square brackets inserted by the Friendly Societies Act 1974, s 116(1), Sch 9, para 19.
Sub-s (1): second words in square brackets inserted by the National Debt Act 1972, s 6(3)
Sub-s (1): words omitted repealed by the Trustee Savings Banks Act 1985, ss 4(3), 7(3), Sch 4.

Commentary

This enables future legislation to be amended by statutory instrument if it does not fit in with s 1.

[285]

6 Power to provide for further increases

(1) The Treasury may from time to time by order direct that—

(a) sections 1 and 2 of this Act, so far as they relate to any enactment; and

(b) . . . [. . .] [and section 68 of the Friendly Societies Act 1974] (which contain provisions similar to the enactments to which section 1 of this Act relates but subject to a limit of £500); [and

(c) . . .

(d) section 6(1) of the National Debt Act 1972;] [and

(e) sections 66 and 67 of the said Act of 1974 (which contain provisions similar to the enactments to which section 2 of this Act relates but subject to a limit of £500);]

shall have effect as if for references to £500 there were substituted references to such higher amount as may be specified in the order.

(2) Any order under this section shall apply in relation to deaths occurring after the expiration of a period of one month beginning with the date on which the order comes into force, except that, so far as section 2 of this Act has effect by virtue of any such order, subsection (2) of that section shall apply as if for the reference to the date on which this Act is passed there were substituted a reference to the date on which the order comes into force [and that any such order made by virtue of subsection (1)(e) of this section shall apply in relation to any nomination delivered at or sent to the appropriate office, or made in the appropriate book, after the expiration of a period of one month beginning with the date on which the order comes into force.]

(3) Where an order under this section ... specifying any amount is in force, references in section 5(1) of this Act to £500 shall be construed as references to the amount specified in the order.

(4) Any order under this section may be revoked by a subsequent order and shall be made by statutory instrument; and no such order shall be made unless a draft of the order has been laid before Parliament and approved by a resolution of each House of Parliament.

Amendments

Sub-s (1): in para (b) first words omitted repealed by the Judicial Pensions Act 1981, s 36(2), Sch 4, the Statute Law (Repeals) Act 1986, the Parliamentary and other Pensions Act 1972, s 24(4), and the Parliamentary and other Pensions Act 1987, ss 2, 6(2), Schs 2, 4.
Sub-s (1): in para (b) second words omitted inserted by the Parliamentary and other Pensions Act 1972, s 24(4), the Friendly Societies Act 1974, s 116(1), Sch 9, para 2, and the Parliamentary and other Pensions Act 1987, s 6(2), Sch 4.
Sub-s (1): in para (b) words in square brackets inserted by the Friendly Societies Act 1974, s 116(1), Sch 9, para 20;
Sub-s (1): para (c), as inserted by the Merchant Shipping Act 1970, s 100(1), Sch 3, para 11, repealed by the Merchant Shipping Act 1995, s 314(1), Sch 12.
Sub-s (1): para (d) inserted by the National Debt Act 1972, s 6(3).
Sub-s (1): para (e) inserted by the Friendly Societies Act 1974, s 116(1), Sch 9, para 20.
Sub-s (2): words in square brackets inserted by the Friendly Societies Act 1974, s 116(1), Sch 9, para 20.
Sub-s (3): words omitted repealed by the Trustee Savings Banks Act 1985, ss 4(3), 7(3), Sch 4.

Commentary

See the notes to s 1 for instances where this power has been used in the past and the limits applying.

[286]

7 Short title, interpretation, extent, commencement and repeals

(1) This Act may be cited as the Administration of Estates (Small Payments) Act 1965.

(2) Any reference in this Act to an enactment or instrument shall be construed as including a reference to that enactment or instrument as amended, extended or applied by any other enactment or instrument.

(3) The amendment of any instrument by this Act shall be without prejudice to any power of amending or revoking that instrument.

(4) Save as otherwise expressly provided, so far as this Act amends or gives power to amend, or repeals, any provision which extends to any place outside Great Britain it shall have the same extent.

(5) Subject to sections 2 (2) and 6 (2) of this Act, this Act shall apply in relation to deaths occurring after the expiration of a period of one month beginning with the date on which it is passed.

(6) The enactments mentioned in Schedule 4 to this Act are hereby repealed to the extent specified in the third column of that Schedule, but this subsection shall not affect the operation of those enactments in relation to deaths occurring before the expiration of the said period.

[287]

SCHEDULE 1
STATUTORY PROVISIONS AUTHORISING DISPOSAL OF PROPERTY ON DEATH WITHOUT REPRESENTATION

Section 1

PART I
ENACTMENTS

. . .

Amendments
Repealed in part by the Statute Law (Repeals) Act 2004.

Commentary
This Schedule amends the Friendly Societies Act 1829; the Army Pensions Act 1830; the Loan Societies Act 1940; the Navy and Marines (Property of Deceased) Act 1865; the Provident Nominations and Small Intestacies Act 1883; the Great Western Railway Act 1885; the Regimental Debts Act 1893; the Merchant Shipping Act 1894; the Taff Vale Railways Act 1895; the Friendly Societies Act 1896; the Superannuation (Ecclesiastical Commissioners and Queen Anne's Bounty) Act 1914; the School Teachers (Superannuation) Act 1922; the Constabulary (Ireland) Act 1922; the London Midland and Scottish Railway Act 1924; the Southern Railway Act 1924; the Teachers (Superannuation) Act 1925; the Government Annuities Act 1929; the Superannuation (Various Services) Act 1938; the Greenwich Hospital Act 1942; the London and North Eastern Railway Act 1944; the Local Government Superannuation Act 1953; the Building Societies Act 1962 and the Industrial and Provident Societies Act 1965.

PART II
ENABLING ENACTMENTS

. . .

Commentary
This Schedule amends the Pensions and Yeomanry Pay Act 1884; the Elementary School Teachers (Superannuation) Act 1898; the Post Office Savings Bank Act 1954 and the Trustee Savings Banks Act 1954.

PART III
INSTRUMENTS

. . .

Commentary
This Schedule amends the Rules of the Supreme Court; the amended regulations dated 11th July 1907 and made by the Secretary of State for War under section 4 of the Pensions and Yeomanry Pay Act 1884; SR & O 1913/1332; regulation dated 27th November 1920 and made by the Secretary of State for Air under section 4 of the Pensions and Yeomanry Pay Act 1884 as applied to the Royal Air Force by the Air Force (Application of Enactments) (No 2) Order 1918; SR & O 1922/945; SR & O 1927/1184; SR & O 1929/1048; SR & O 1933/1149; SR & O 1936/70; SR & O 1936/626; SR & O 1938/303; SR & O 1938/304; SR & O 1938/556; SR & O 1945/1164; SI 1956/1217; SI 1956/1657; SI 1957/356; SI 1959/735; SI 1960/1146; SI 1962/2756 and SI 1964/1148.

[288]

SCHEDULE 2
STATUTORY PROVISIONS AUTHORISING DISPOSAL OF PROPERTY ON DEATH BY NOMINATION

Section 2

. . .

Commentary

This Schedule amends the Trade Union Act Amendment Act 1876; the Great Western Railway Act 1885; the Taff Vale Railway Act 1895; the Friendly Societies Act 1896; the London Midland and Scottish Railway Act 1924; the Southern Railway Act 1924; the Trustee Savings Banks Regulations 1929 and the Industrial and Provident Societies Act 1965.

[289]

SCHEDULE 3
EXTENSION OF ENACTMENTS RELATING TO INTESTACIES

Section 3

. . .

Amendments

Repealed in part by the Industrial Relations Act 1971, s 169, Sch 9, the Friendly Societies Act 1974, s 116(4), Sch 11, the Statute Law (Repeals) Act 1974, the Building Societies Act 1986, s 120(2), Sch 19, Pt I, and the Statute Law (Repeals) Act 1998.

Commentary

This Schedule contains amendments to the Great Western Railway Act 1885, s 45(8), the Taff Vale Railway Act 1895, s 18(10), the London Midland and Scottish Railway Act 1924, s 61(11), the Southern Railway Act 1924, s 99(12) and the Industrial and Provident Societies Act 1965, s 25(1).

The various Acts amended by this Schedule are printed in the original Queen's Printer's copy, but are in general terms outside the scope of this work.

[290]

SCHEDULE 4

. . .

Amendments

Repealed by the Statute Law (Repeals) Act 1974.

[291]

FAMILY PROVISION ACT 1966

1966 Chapter 35

ARRANGEMENT OF SECTIONS

An Act to amend the law of England and Wales in relation to the rights after a person's death of that person's spouse or former spouse and children, and to repeal section 47(5) of the Administration of Estates Act 1925, as amended

[17th November 1966]

General Note

The Family Provision Act 1966 (FPA 1966) should be read together with the provisions of the Administration of Estates Act 1925, Pt IV dealing with the distribution of the estate of the deceased on intestacy.

1 Increase of net sum payable to surviving husband or wife on intestacy

(1) In the case of a person dying after the coming into force of this section, section 46(1) of the Administration of Estates Act 1925, as amended by section 1 of the Intestates' Estates Act 1952 and set out in Schedule 1 to that Act, shall apply as if the net sums charged by paragraph (i) on the residuary estate in favour of a surviving [spouse or civil partner] were as follows, that is to say,—

(a) under paragraph (2) of the Table (which charges a net sum of £5,000 where the intestate leaves issue) a sum of £8,750 or of such larger amount as may from time to time be fixed by order of the Lord Chancellor; and

(b) under paragraph (3) of the Table (which charges a net sum of £20,000 where the intestate leaves certain close relatives but no issue) a sum of £30,000 or of such larger amount as may from time to time be so fixed.

(2) Accordingly in relation to the estate of a person dying after the coming into force of this section sections 46, 48 and 49 (as so amended and set out) of the Administration of Estates Act 1925 shall be further amended as follows—

(a) in the Table in section 46(1)(i) for the words "net sum of £5,000" in paragraph (2), and for the words "net sum of £20,000" in paragraph (3), there shall in each case be substituted the words "fixed net sum", and at the end of the Table there shall be added—

"The fixed net sums referred to in paragraphs (2) and (3) of this Table shall be of the amounts provided by or under section 1 of the Family Provision Act 1966";

(b) in sections 46(4) and 48(2)(a) for the words "the net sum of £5,000 or, as the case may be, £20,000", and in section 49(1)(aa) for the words "the net sum of £5,000 or £20,000", there shall in each case be substituted the words "the fixed net sum";

and any reference in any other enactment to the said net sum of £5,000 or the said net sum of £20,000 shall have effect as a reference to the corresponding net sum of the amount fixed by or under this section.

(3) Any order of the Lord Chancellor under this section fixing the amount of either of the said net sums shall have effect (and, so far as relates to that sum, shall supersede any previous order) in relation to the estate of any person dying after the coming into force of the order.

(4) Any order of the Lord Chancellor under this section shall be made by statutory instrument, and a draft of the statutory instrument shall be laid before Parliament.

Amendment

Sub-s (1): words "spouse or civil partner" in square brackets substituted by the Civil Partnership Act 2004, s 71, Sch 4, Pt 2, para 14.

Commentary

The FPA 1966 enabled the lump sum payable to a surviving spouse on intestacy to be increased from time to time by order made by the Lord Chancellor. The power has been exercised by the Family Provision (Intestate Succession) Orders 1972 (SI 1972/916), 1977 (SI 1977/415), 1981 (SI 1981/255), 1987 (SI 1987/799) and 1993 (SI 1993/2906). The effect of these provisions is as follows:

Date of death on or after	*Death without issue*	*Death with issue*
1 July 1972 but before 15 March 1977	£40,000	£15,000
15 March 1977 but before 1 March 1981	£55,000	£25,000
1 March 1981 but before 1 June 1987	£85,000	£40,000
1 June 1987 but before 1 December 1993	£125,000	£75,000
1 December 1993	£200,000	£125,000

[292]

2–10

. . .

Amendment
Repealed by the Inheritance (Provision for Family and Dependants) Act 1975, s 26(2), Schedule.

[293]

10 Short title, repeal, etc

(1) This Act may be cited as the Family Provision Act 1966.

(2) . . .

(3) Nothing in this Act extends to Scotland or to Northern Ireland.

(4) . . .

Amendment
Sub-ss (2), (4): repealed by the Inheritance (Provision for Family and Dependants) Act 1975, s 26(2), Schedule.

[294]

WILLS ACT 1968

1968 Chapter 28

ARRANGEMENT OF SECTIONS

An Act to restrict the operation of section 15 of the Wills Act 1837

[30th May 1968]

General Note
The Wills Act 1968 was passed to relax the effect of the Wills Act 1837, s 15 and should be read with that section.

1 Restriction of operation of Wills Act 1837, s 15

(1) For the purposes of section 15 of the Wills Act 1837 (avoidance of gifts to attesting witnesses and their spouses) the attestation of a will by a person to whom or to whose spouse there is given or made any such disposition as is described in that section shall be disregarded if the will is duly executed without his attestation and without that of any other such person.

(2) This section applies to the will of any person dying after the passing of this Act, whether executed before or after the passing of this Act.

Commentary

The Wills Act 1968 only applies to deaths after 29 May 1968. Its effect is that, provided there are at least two witnesses who attest who are not beneficiaries under the will or spouses of beneficiaries, any witnesses who do in fact benefit or who are spouses of beneficiaries can be disregarded and can therefore take under the will. Before the passing of the Wills Act 1968 such a witness, even if there were two other non-benefiting witnesses, could not take under the will, see *In the Estate of Bravda* [1968] 1 WLR 479.

[295]

2 Short title and extent

(1) This Act may be cited as the Wills Act 1968.

(2) This Act does not extend to Scotland or Northern Ireland.

[296]

ADMINISTRATION OF ESTATES ACT 1971

1971 Chapter 25

ARRANGEMENT OF SECTIONS

An Act to provide for the recognition, without resealing, of certain grants of administration and confirmations throughout the United Kingdom; to allow for the inclusion of real estate in any part of the United Kingdom in the inventory of the estate of a person dying domiciled in Scotland; to amend the law with respect to the grant of administration by the High Court and resealing by that Court of administration granted outside the United Kingdom and to exempt from stamp duty guarantees given under the law so amended; to make provision with respect to the duties and rights of personal representatives; and for connected purposes

[12th May 1971]

General Note

The Administration of Estates Act 1971 (AEA 1971) treats the equivalent of grants of probate in Scotland and Northern Ireland as grants of representation for English law without the need for resealing. Resealing of grants from other jurisdictions is dealt with elsewhere in this work. It also amends the law in relation to the administration of estates.

RECIPROCAL RECOGNITION OF GRANTS

1 Recognition in England and Wales of Scottish confirmations and Northern Irish grants of representation

(1) Where a person dies domiciled in Scotland—

(a) a confirmation granted in respect of all or part of his estate and noting his Scottish domicile, and

(b) a certificate of confirmation noting his Scottish domicile and relating to one or more items of his estate,

shall, without being resealed, be treated for the purposes of the law of England and Wales as a grant of representation (in accordance with subsection (2) below) to the executors named in the confirmation or certificate in respect of the property of the deceased of which according to the terms of the confirmation they are executors or, as the case may be, in respect of the item or items of property specified in the certificate of confirmation.

(2) Where by virtue of subsection (1) above a confirmation or certificate of confirmation is treated for the purposes of the law of England and Wales as a grant of representation to the executors named therein then, subject to subsections (3) and (5) below, the grant shall be treated—

(a) as a grant of probate where it appears from the confirmation or certificate that the executors so named are executors nominate; and

(b) in any other case, as a grant of letters of administration.

(3) Section 7 of the Administration of Estates Act 1925 (executor of executor represents original testator) shall not, by virtue of subsection (2)(a) above, apply on the death of an executor named in a confirmation or certificate of confirmation.

(4) Subject to subsection (5) below, where a person dies domiciled in Northern Ireland a grant of probate of his will or letters of administration in respect of his estate (or any part of it) made by the High Court in Northern Ireland and noting his domicile there shall, without being resealed, be treated for the purposes of the law of England and Wales as if it had been originally made by the High Court in England and Wales.

(5) Notwithstanding anything in the preceding provisions of this section, a person who is a personal representative according to the law of England and Wales by virtue only of those provisions may not be required, under section 25 of the Administration of Estates Act 1925, to deliver up his grant to the High Court.

(6) This section applies in relation to confirmations, probates and letters of administration granted before as well as after the commencement of this Act, and in relation to a confirmation, probate or letters of administration granted before the commencement of this Act, this section shall have effect as if it had come into force immediately before the grant was made.

(7) In this section "confirmation" includes an additional confirmation, and the term "executors", where used in relation to a confirmation or certificate of confirmation, shall be construed according to the law of Scotland.

Commentary

Subsections (1)–(3) deal with a person who dies domiciled in Scotland. The "confirmation" referred to is the Scottish equivalent of a grant but which contains an inventory of the deceased's assets, unlike an English grant. A certificate of confirmation is issued by the Probate Court, if asked for, to show that certain assets were comprised in the estate of the deceased. For the Administration of Estates Act 1925, s 7 (referred to in sub-s (3) and which establishes a chain of representation once there has been a grant) see **[187]**. The terminology contained in sub-ss (1)–(3) must be construed in accordance with the Law of Scotland (sub-s (7)). Subsection (4) deals with Northern Ireland grants and note that the Administration of Estates Act 1925, s 7 applies to them. The AEA 1971 applies to confirmations and grants made before its commencement (sub-s (6)).

[297]

2 Recognition in Northern Ireland of English grants of representation and Scottish confirmations

(1) Where a person dies domiciled in England and Wales a grant of probate of his will or letters of administration in respect of his estate (or any part of it) made by the High Court in England and Wales and noting his domicile there shall, without being resealed, be treated for the purposes of the law of Northern Ireland as if it had been originally made by the High Court in Northern Ireland.

(2) Where a person dies domiciled in Scotland—

(a) a confirmation granted in respect of all or part of his estate and noting his Scottish domicile, and

(b) a certificate of confirmation noting his Scottish domicile and relating to one or more items of his estate,

shall, without being resealed, be treated for the purposes of the law of Northern Ireland as a grant of representation (in accordance with subsection (3) below) to the executors named in the confirmation or certificate in respect of the property of the deceased of which according to the terms of the confirmation they are executors or, as the case may be, in respect of the item or items of property specified in the certificate of confirmation.

(3) Where by virtue of subsection (2) above a confirmation or certificate of confirmation is treated for the purposes of the law of Northern Ireland as a grant of representation to the executors named therein then, subject to subsection (4) below, the grant shall be treated—

(a) as a grant of probate where it appears from the confirmation or certificate that the executors so named are executors nominate; and

(b) in any other case, a grant of letters of administration.

(4) Notwithstanding anything in any enactment or rule of law, subsection (3)(a) above shall not operate to entitle an executor of a sole or last surviving executor of a testator, whose will has been proved in Scotland only, to act as the executor of that testator.

(5) This section applies in relation to probates, letters of administration and confirmations granted before as well as after the commencement of this Act, and—

(a) in relation to a probate, letters of administration or confirmation granted, and resealed in Northern Ireland, before the commencement of this Act, this section shall have effect as if it had come into force immediately before the grant was so resealed; and

(b) a probate, letters of administration or confirmation granted but not resealed in Northern Ireland before the commencement of this Act shall, for the purposes of this section, be treated as having been granted at the commencement of this Act.

(6) In this section "confirmation" includes an additional confirmation, and the term "executors", where used in relation to a confirmation or certificate of confirmation shall be construed according to the law of Scotland.

Commentary

This section contains similar provisions in relation to the recognition of grants in respect of persons domiciled in England and Wales and Scotland by Northern Ireland. Note that sub-s (4) precludes a chain of executorship arising in relation to a Scottish executor. Note that every oath in England and Wales requires a statement of domicile (Non-Contentious Probate Rules 1987, SI 1987/2024, r 8(2) **[Appendix V]**).

[298]

3 Recognition in Scotland of English and Northern Irish grants of representation

(1) Where a person dies domiciled in England and Wales or in Northern Ireland a grant of probate or letters of administration

(a) from the High Court in England and Wales and noting his domicile there, or

(b) from the High Court in Northern Ireland and noting his domicile there

shall, without being resealed, be of the like force and effect and have the same operation in relation to property in Scotland as a confirmation given under the seal of office of the Commissariot of Edinburgh to the executor or administrator named in the probate or letters of administration.

(2) This section applies in relation to probates and letters of administration granted before as well as after the commencement of this Act, and in relation to a probate or letters of administration granted before the commencement of this Act, this section shall have effect as if it had come into force immediately before the grant was made.

Commentary

This section contains similar provisions in relation to the recognition of English and Northern Irish grants in Scotland. Note that every oath in England and Wales requires a statement of domicile (Non-Contentious Probate Rules 1987, SI 1987/2024, r 8(2) **[Appendix V]**).

[299]

4 Evidence of grants

(1) In England and Wales and in Northern Ireland—

(a) a document purporting to be a confirmation, additional confirmation or certificate of confirmation given under the seal of office of any commissariat in Scotland shall, except where the contrary is proved, be taken to be such a confirmation, additional confirmation or certificate of confirmation without further proof; and

(b) a document purporting to be a duplicate of such a confirmation or additional confirmation and to be given under such a seal shall be receivable in evidence in like manner and for the like purposes as the confirmation or additional confirmation of which it purports to be a duplicate.

(2) In England and Wales and in Scotland—

(a) a document purporting to be a grant of probate or of letters of administration issued under the seal of the High Court in Northern Ireland or of the principal or district probate registry there shall, except where the contrary is proved, be taken to be such a grant without further proof; and

(b) a document purporting to be a copy of such a grant and to be sealed with such a seal shall be receivable in evidence in like manner and for the like purposes as the grant of which it purports to be a copy.

(3) In Scotland and in Northern Ireland—

(a) a document purporting to be a grant of probate or of letters of administration issued under the seal of the High Court in England and Wales or of the principal or a district probate registry there shall, except where the contrary is proved, be taken to be such a grant without further proof; and

(b) a document purporting to be a copy of such a grant and to be sealed with such a seal shall be receivable in evidence in like manner and for the like purposes as the grant of which it purports to be a copy.

Commentary
This section deals with what documents will be regarded as grants in each jurisdiction.

[300]

5 Property outside Scotland of which deceased was trustee

(1) A confirmation or additional confirmation granted in respect of property situated in Scotland of a person who died domiciled there, which notes that domicile, may contain or have appended thereto and signed by the sheriff clerk a note or statement of property in England and Wales or in Northern Ireland held by the deceased in trust, being a note or statement which has been set forth in any inventory recorded in the books of the court of which the sheriff clerk is clerk.

(2) Section 1 or, as the case may be, section 2 of this Act shall apply in relation to property specified in such a note or statement as is mentioned in subsection (1) above as it applies in relation to property specified in the confirmation or additional confirmation concerned.

Commentary
This section is required as a confirmation will set out an inventory of the assets of the estate and this will include trust property in England and Wales or Northern Ireland.

[301]

6 Inventory of Scottish estate may include real estate in any part of the United Kingdom

(1) It shall be competent to include in the inventory of the estate of any person who dies domiciled in Scotland any real estate of the deceased situated in England and Wales or Northern Ireland, and accordingly in section 9 of the Confirmation of Executors (Scotland) Act 1858 the word "personal" wherever it occurs is hereby repealed.

(2) Section 14(2) of the Succession (Scotland) Act 1964 (act of sederunt to provide for description of heritable property) shall apply in relation to such real estate as aforesaid as it applies in relation to heritable property in Scotland.

Commentary
This section affects Scottish practice and is outside the scope of this work.

[302]

7 Consequential amendments

Schedule 1 to this Act, which contains amendments consequential on the preceding provisions of this Act, shall have effect.

RIGHTS AND DUTIES OF PERSONAL REPRESENTATIVES IN ENGLAND AND WALES

[303]

8 . . .

. . .

Amendment
Repealed by the Supreme Court Act 1981, ss 152(4), 153(4), (5), Sch 7.

[304]

9 Duties of personal representatives

. . .

Commentary
This section substitutes the Administration of Estates Act 1925, s 25.
Please see s 9 of AEA 1925 **[189]**.

[305]

10 Retainer, preference and the payment of debts by personal representatives

(1) The right of retainer of a personal representative and his right to prefer creditors are hereby abolished.

(2) Nevertheless a personal representative—

(a) other than one mentioned in paragraph (b) below, who, in good faith and at a time when he has no reason to believe that the deceased's estate is insolvent, pays the debt of any person (including himself) who is a creditor of the estate; or

(b) to whom letters of administration had been granted solely by reason of his being a creditor and who, in good faith and at such a time pays the debt of another person who is a creditor of the estate;

shall not, if it subsequently appears that the estate is insolvent, be liable to account to a creditor of the same degree as the paid creditor for the sum so paid.

Commentary
Prior to the commencement of the AEA 1971 a personal representative had power to retain out of the assets in his hands a debt owed to himself, and pay debts of one creditor of the deceased in priority to another. The old law of retainer and preference will apply to estates where the testator died prior to 1 January 1972 but is of little practical importance now. However, note the protection in sub-s (2) to personal representatives who pay off debts not realising that the deceased's estate is insolvent and required to be administered as an insolvent estate, as to which see AEA 1925 **[181]**. Creditor administrators are not protected under sub-s (2) if they pay their own debts, even if they are acting in good faith. For the payment of debts in the administration of estates, see generally the Administration of Estates Act 1925, s 34 **[209]**.

[306]

MISCELLANEOUS AND SUPPLEMENTAL

11 Sealing of Commonwealth and Colonial grants

(1) The following provisions of section 2 of the Colonial Probates Act 1892, that is to say—

(a) subsection (2)(b) (which makes it a condition precedent to sealing in the United Kingdom letters of administration granted in certain overseas countries and territories that a sufficient security has been given to cover property in the United Kingdom); and

(b) subsection (3) (power of the court in the United Kingdom to require that adequate security is given for the payment of debts due to creditors residing in the United Kingdom);

shall not apply to the sealing of letters of administration by the High Court in England and Wales under that section, and the following provisions of this section shall apply instead.

(2) A person to whom letters of administration have been granted in a country or territory to which the said Act of 1892 applies shall on their being sealed by the High Court in England and Wales under the said section 2 have the like duties with respect to the estate of the deceased which is situated in England and Wales and the debts of

the deceased which fall to be paid there as are imposed by section 25(a) and (b) of the Administration of Estates Act 1925 on a person to whom a grant of administration has been made by that court.

(3) As a condition of sealing letters of administration granted in any such country or territory, the High Court in England and Wales may, in cases to which [section 120 of the *Supreme Court Act 1981* [Senior Courts Act 1981]] (power to require administrators to produce sureties) applies and subject to the following provisions of this section and subject to and in accordance with probate rules . . . require one or more sureties, in such amount as the court thinks fit, to guarantee that they will make good, within any limit imposed by the court on the total liability of the surety or sureties, any loss which any person interested in the administration of the estate of the deceased in England and Wales may suffer in consequence of a breach by the administrator of his duties in administering it there.

(4) A guarantee given in pursuance of any such requirement shall enure for the benefit of every person interested in the administration of the estate in England and Wales as if contained in a contract under seal made by the surety or sureties with every such person and, where there are two or more sureties, as if they had bound themselves jointly or severally.

(5) No action shall be brought on any such guarantee without the leave of the High Court.

(6) Stamp duty shall not be chargeable on any such guarantee.

(7) Subsections (2) to (6) above apply to the sealing by the High Court in England and Wales of letters of administration granted by a British court in a foreign country as they apply to the sealing of letters of administration granted in a country or territory to which the Colonial Probates Act 1892 applies.

(8) In this section—

"letters of administration" and "British court in a foreign country" have the same meaning as in the Colonial Probates Act 1892; and

["probate rules" means rules of court made under section 127 of the *Supreme Court Act 1981* [Senior Courts Act 1981]].

Amendment

Sub-s (3): words "section 120 of the Supreme Court Act 1981" in square brackets substituted by the Supreme Court Act 1981, s 152(1), Sch 5.
Sub-s (3): words "Supreme Court Act 1981" in italics repealed and subsequent words in square brackets substituted, from a date to be appointed, by the Constitutional Reform Act 2005, s 59(5), Sch 11, Pt 1, para 1(2).
Sub-s (3): words omitted repealed by the Supreme Court Act 1981, s 152(4), Sch 7.
Sub-s (8): definition "probate rules" substituted by the Supreme Court Act 1981, s 152(1), Sch 5.
Sub-s (8): in definition "probate rules" words "Supreme Court Act 1981" in italics repealed and subsequent words in square brackets substituted, from a date to be appointed, by the Constitutional Reform Act 2005, s 59(5), Sch 11, Pt 1, para 1(2).

Commentary

This section should be read together with the Colonial Probate Acts 1892 and 1927 **[45, 237]**. Subsections (3)–(6) provide that the court can ask for a guarantee if the Supreme Court 1981, s 120 applies, **[359]**, although in fact the Non-Contentious Probate Rules, SI 1987/2024 **[Appendix V]** currently in force do make general provision for a guarantee to be required.

[307]

12 Repeals and savings

(1) The enactments specified in Part I of Schedule 2 to this Act (which include an enactment of the Parliament of Northern Ireland) are hereby repealed to the extent

specified in the third column of that Schedule and the Government of Ireland (Re-sealing of Probates etc) Order 1923 is hereby revoked.

(2) So far as they relate to England and Wales only, the enactments specified in Part II of Schedule 2 to this Act are hereby repealed to the extent specified in the third column of that Schedule.

(3) Nothing in this Act shall affect the liability of any person for, or alter the incidence of, estate duty, including estate duty payable under the law for the time being in force in Northern Ireland.

(4) The following provisions of this Act, that is to say—

(a) . . .

(b) section 11 (other than subsection (2)); and

(c) the repeals specified in Part II of Schedule 2 to this Act, other than the repeal of section 34(2) of the Administration of Estates Act 1925;

shall not apply in relation to grants of administration made by the High Court before the commencement of this Act or to sealing by that court before the commencement of this Act of administration granted in any country or territory outside the United Kingdom.

(5) Any administration bond given before the commencement of this Act . . . under the Colonial Probates Act 1892 may be enforced and assigned as if this Act had not been passed.

(6) Section 10 of this Act and the repeal by this section of section 34(2) of the Administration of Estates Act 1925 shall not apply in relation to the estates of persons dying before the commencement of this Act.

Amendment

Sub-ss (4), (5): words omitted repealed by the Supreme Court Act 1981, s 152(4), Sch 7.

[308]

13 . . .

. . .

Amendment

Repealed by the Northern Ireland Constitution Act 1973, s 41(1), Sch 6, Pt I.

[309]

14 Short title, commencement and extent

(1) This Act may be cited as the Administration of Estates Act 1971.

(2) Section 13 of this Act and this section shall come into force on the passing of this Act and the remaining provisions of this Act shall come into force on 1st January 1972; and, notwithstanding anything in section 36 of the Interpretation Act 1889, any reference in this Act, or in any Act passed after the passing of this Act, to the commencement of this Act shall be construed as a reference to 1st January 1972.

(3) Sections 1 and [9] to 11 of this Act and subsections (2) and (4) to (6) of section 12 of this Act extend to England and Wales only.

(4) Sections 3 and 6 of this Act extend to Scotland only.

(5) Section 2 of this Act extends to Northern Ireland only.

Amendment

Sub-s (3): figure in square brackets substituted by the Supreme Court Act 1981, s 152(1), Sch 5.

[310]

SCHEDULE 1
AMENDMENTS CONSEQUENTIAL ON SS 1

Section 7

. . .

Commentary

This Schedule contains amendments to the Confirmation and Probate Amendment Act 1859, s 1, the Executors (Scotland) Act 1900, s 6, the Conveyancing (Scotland) Act 1924, s 5(2)(b), the Law Reform (Miscellaneous Provisions) (Scotland) Act 1940, s 6(1), and the Succession (Scotland) Act 1964, s 32(2)(b).

[311]

SCHEDULE 2
ENACTMENTS REPEALED

Section 12

PART I
ENACTMENTS RELATING TO ABOLITION OF RESEALING

Chapter	*Short Title*	*Extent of Repeal*
20 & 21 Vict c 79	The Probate and Letters of Administration Act (Ireland) 1857	In section 27 the words "probates, letters of administration".
		Sections 94 and 95.
21 & 22 Vict c 56	The Confirmation and Probate Act 1858	In section 9 the word "personal" in each place where it occurs.
		Sections 13 and 14.
		Schedule (F).
22 & 23 Vict 31	The Court of Probate Act (Ireland) 1859	Section 25.
23 & 24 Vict c 5	The Indian Securities Act 1860	In section 1 the words from "and probate or" to the end of the section.
38 & 39 Vict c 41	The Intestates Widows and Children (Scotland) Act 1875	In section 3, the words from "and where such" to the end of the section.
39 & 40 Vict c 24	The Small Testate Estates (Scotland) Act 1876	In section 3, the words from "and where such" to the end of the section.
39 & 40 Vict c 70	The Sheriff Courts (Scotland) Act 1876	Sections 42 and 43.
44 & 45 Vict c 12	The Customs and Inland Revenue Act 1881	In section 34 the words from "and the fees" to the end of the section.
57 & 58 Vict c 30	The Finance Act 1894	Section 16(4).
		Section 23(7).
10 & 11 Geo 5 c 67	The Government of Ireland Act 1920	Section 28(5).
15 & 16 Geo 5 c 49	The Supreme Court of Judicature (Consolidation) Act 1925	Section 168. Section 169.
		In section 174(2) the words "probates, letters of administration".
18 & 19 Geo 5 c 26	The Administration of Justice Act 1928	Section 10.
22 & 23 Geo 5 c 11	The Northern Ireland (Miscellaneous Provisions) Act 1932	Section 2.
1955 c 24 (NI)	The Administration of Estates Act (Northern Ireland) 1955	Section 27.
4 & 5 Eliz 2 c 46	The Administration of Justice Act 1956	Section 17(3).
1970 c 31	The Administration of Justice Act 1970	In section 54(6) the words from "and the amendment" to the end of the section.
		In Schedule 2, paragraph 1.

PART II
ENACTMENTS RELATING TO ADMINISTRATION IN ENGLAND AND WALES

Chapter	*Short Title*	*Extent of Repeal*
20 & 21 Vict c 77	The Court of Probate Act 1857	In section 73, the words "upon his giving such security (if any) as the court shall direct".
		Section 82.
39 & 40 Vict c 18	The Treasury Solicitor Act 1876	In section 2, the last paragraph, both as originally enacted and as applied by section 3 of the Duchy of Lancaster Act 1920.
54 & 55 Vict c 39	The Stamp Act 1891	In Schedule 1, in the heading beginning "Bond on obtaining letters of administration" the words "England or".
6 Edw 7 c 55	The Public Trustee Act 1906	In section 11(4), the words "upon the grant to him of administration, or" and the words "if administration is granted to him or".
15 & 16 Geo 5 c 23	The Administration of Estates Act 1925	Section 34(2).
12, 13 & 14 Geo 6 c 29	The Consular Conventions Act 1949	In section 1(3) the words "(including liabilities under the administration bond)".
		Section 1(5).
12, 13 & 14 Geo 6 c 47	The Finance Act 1949	In Schedule 8, in paragraph 8, the words "and Bond on obtaining letters of administration".

[312]

INHERITANCE (PROVISION FOR FAMILY AND DEPENDANTS) ACT 1975

1975 Chapter 63

ARRANGEMENT OF SECTIONS

An Act to make fresh provisions for empowering the court to make orders for the making out of the estate of a deceased person of provision for the spouse, former spouse, child, child of the family or dependant of that person; and for matters connected therewith

[12th November 1975]

General Note

This Act, which followed on from the 1938 Act, provides for the court to make provision in certain specified circumstances. There are equivalents of this Act in many other common law jurisdictions.

1 Application for financial provision from deceased's estate

(1) Where after the commencement of this Act a person dies domiciled in England and Wales and is survived by any of the following persons—

[(a) the spouse or civil partner of the deceased;

(b) a former spouse or former civil partner of the deceased, but not one who has formed a subsequent marriage or civil partnership;]

[(ba) any person (not being a person included in paragraph (a) or (b) above) to whom subsection (1A) [or (1B)] below applies;]

(c) a child of the deceased;

(d) any person (not being a child of the deceased) who, in the case of any marriage [or civil partnership] to which the deceased was at any time a party, was treated by the deceased as a child of the family in relation to that marriage [or civil partnership];

(e) any person (not being a person included in the foregoing paragraphs of this subsection) who immediately before the death of the deceased was being maintained, either wholly or partly, by the deceased;

that person may apply to the court for an order under section 2 of this Act on the ground that the disposition of the deceased's estate effected by his will or the law relating to intestacy, or the combination of his will and that law, is not such as to make reasonable financial provision for the applicant.

[(1A) This subsection applies to a person if the deceased died on or after 1st January 1996 and, during the whole of the period of two years ending immediately before the date when the deceased died, the person was living—

(a) in the same household as the deceased, and
(b) as the husband or wife of the deceased.]

[(1B) This subsection applies to a person if for the whole of the period of two years ending immediately before the date when the deceased died the person was living—

(a) in the same household as the deceased, and
(b) as the civil partner of the deceased.]

(2) In this Act "reasonable financial provision"—

(a) in the case of an application made by virtue of subsection (1)(a) above by the husband or wife of the deceased (except where *the marriage with the deceased was the subject of a decree of judicial separation and at the date of death the decree was in force*[, at the date of death, a separation order under the Family Law Act 1996 was in force in relation to the marriage] and the separation was continuing), means such financial provision as it would be reasonable in all the circumstances of the case for a husband or wife to receive, whether or not that provision is required for his or her maintenance;

[(aa) in the case of an application made by virtue of subsection (1)(a) above by the civil partner of the deceased (except where, at the date of death, a separation order under Chapter 2 of Part 2 of the Civil Partnership Act 2004 was in force in relation to the civil partnership and the separation was continuing), means such financial provision as it would be reasonable in all the circumstances of the case for a civil partner to receive, whether or not that provision is required for his or her maintenance;]

(b) in the case of any other application made by virtue of subsection (1) above, means such financial provision as it would be reasonable in all the circumstances of the case for the applicant to receive for his maintenance.

(3) For the purposes of subsection (1)(e) above, a person shall be treated as being maintained by the deceased, either wholly or partly, as the case may be, if the deceased, otherwise than for full valuable consideration, was making a substantial contribution in money or money's worth towards the reasonable needs of that person.

Amendment

Sub-s (1): paras (a), (b) substituted by the Civil Partnership Act 2004, s 71, Sch 4, Pt 2, para 15(1), (2).
Sub-s (1): para (ba) inserted by the Law Reform (Succession) Act 1995, s 2(2).
Sub-s (1): in para (ba) words "or (1B)" in square brackets inserted by the Civil Partnership Act 2004, s 71, Sch 4, Pt 2, para 15(1), (3).
Sub-s (1): in para (d) words "or civil partnership" in square brackets in both places they occur inserted by the Civil Partnership Act 2004, s 71, Sch 4, Pt 2, para 15(1), (4).
Sub-s (1A): inserted by the Law Reform (Succession) Act 1995, s 2(3).
Sub-s (1B): inserted by the Civil Partnership Act 2004, s 71, Sch 4, Pt 2, para 15(1), (5).
Sub-s (2): in para (a) words from "the marriage with" to "was in force" in italics repealed and subsequent words in square brackets substituted by the Family Law Act 1996, s 66(1), Sch 8, para 27(2), as from a day to be appointed; for savings see s 66(2), Sch 9, para 5 thereof.
Sub-s (2): para (aa) inserted by the Civil Partnership Act 2004, s 71, Sch 4, Pt 2, para 15(1), (6).

Commentary

Subsection (1) sets out the various categories of person who are entitled to apply for reasonable financial provision under the Inheritance (Provision for Family and Dependants) Act 1975 (I(PFD)A 1975). The deceased needs to have been domiciled in England and Wales, as to which see: *Agulian v Cyganik* [2006] EWCA Civ 129. The amendments to include civil partners take effect where the deceased died on or after 5 December 2005.

Subsection (1)(a) (husband or wife or civil partner of the deceased) includes a separated spouse (see sub-s (2)(a)) and a person who in good faith has entered into a void marriage (see s 25(4) and the notes thereto) and a party to a polygamous marriage (see Matrimonial Proceedings (Polygamous Marriages) Act 1972.
Subsection (1)(b) (former spouse or civil partner of the deceased). For the meaning of this see s 25(1) below.
Subsection (1)(ba) and 1(A) (cohabitant). This new category was introduced in respect of deaths after 1 January 1996. "Lived as husband and wife" was discussed in *Re Watson* [1999] 1 FLR 878 and held to cover a couple who did not have sexual relations. However, a couple who maintained separate households would not fall within this subsection although the claim succeeded under subsection 1(e): *Churchill v Roach* [2003] WTLR 779 and a claim succeeded where the claimant was not lawfully in the country, see: *Witkowska v Kaminski* [2006] EWHC 1940. The Court's approach to the two year period should be broad and a temporary separation should not be taken into account, see: *Gully v Dix* [2004] 1 FLR 918. Subsection 1B covers claims by persons living together as civil partners although as there is no requirement for any sexual relationship it remains to be seen how the law will interpret that. It is not clear whether a cohabitee will be outside the ambit of subsection 1(1B) because the deceased died before, or within two years of, the date when it first became possible to become a civil partner under the 2004 Act. However, cohabitees of the same sex qualified under the Act before the amendment, see: *Saunders v Garrett* [2005] WTLR 749
Subsection (1)(c) (child). For the meaning of "child" in this context, see s 25(1) below. Note that adult children can apply.
Subsection (1)(d) (any person treated as a child of the family). See s 3(3) below for the factors the court must take into account in deciding whether someone has been treated as a child of the family. The phrase is not itself defined in the I(PFD)A 1975 but see a full discussion of this section by the Court of Appeal in *Re Leach, Leach v Linderman* [1986] Ch 226 and *Re Callaghan* [1985] Fam 1 which made it clear it could apply to adults.
Subsection (1)(e) (any person being wholly or partly maintained by the deceased immediately before his death). Note the definition of "maintained" in sub-s (3). This subsection has been considered in a number of cases including: *Re Beaumont, Martin v Midland Bank Trust Co Ltd* [1980] Ch 444; *Jelley v Iliffe* [1981] Fam 128; *Re B* [2000] Ch 662; *Boutte v Rose* (a mother dependent on payments made in respect of her disabled minor daughter); *Ross v Newbery and Institute of Cancer Research* [1998] 1 FLR 1041; *Graham v Murphy* [1997] 1 FLR 860; *Malone v Harrison* [1979] 1 WLR 1353; *Harrington v Gill* (1983) 4 FLR 265; *Bishop v Plumley* [1991] 1 WLR 582. The maintenance must be immediately before the death of the deceased (see *Layton v Martin* [1986] 2 FLR 227).
The standard of provision for a spouse or civil partner is more generous than that for any other category of applicant (see sub-s (2)(a)). Section 3(2) below requires the court to have regard to what would have been awarded on a divorce, as to which see *White v White* [2001] AC 596 and *Miller v Miller* [2006] 2 AC 618, and how those principles apply in this jurisdiction in *Re Cunliffe* [2006] Ch 36. Provision is more than is required simply to maintain the applicant. In all other cases the standard of provision is maintenance (sub-s (2)(b)) as to which see *Re Coventry, Coventry v Coventry* [1980] Ch 462 at 484.

[313]

2 Powers of court to make orders

(1) Subject to the provisions of this Act, where an application is made for an order under this section, the court may, if it is satisfied that the disposition of the deceased's estate effected by his will or the law relating to intestacy, or the combination of his will and that law, is not such as to make reasonable financial provision for the applicant, make any one or more of the following orders—

(a) an order for the making to the applicant out of the net estate of the deceased of such periodical payments and for such term as may be specified in the order;

(b) an order for the payment to the applicant out of that estate of a lump sum of such amount as may be so specified;

(c) an order for the transfer to the applicant of such property comprised in that estate as may be so specified;

(d) an order for the settlement for the benefit of the applicant of such property comprised in that estate as may be so specified;

(e) an order for the acquisition out of property comprised in that estate of such property as may be so specified and for the transfer of the property so acquired to the applicant or for the settlement thereof for his benefit;

(f) an order varying any ante-nuptial or post-nuptial settlement (including such a settlement made by will) made on the parties to a marriage to which the deceased was one of the parties, the variation being for the benefit of the surviving party to that marriage, or any child of that marriage, or any person who was treated by the deceased as a child of the family in relation to that marriage;

[(g) an order varying any settlement made—

(i) during the subsistence of a civil partnership formed by the deceased, or

(ii) in anticipation of the formation of a civil partnership by the deceased,

on the civil partners (including such a settlement made by will), the variation being for the benefit of the surviving civil partner, or any child of both the civil partners, or any person who was treated by the deceased as a child of the family in relation to that civil partnership].

(2) An order under subsection (1)(a) above providing for the making out of the net estate of the deceased of periodical payments may provide for—

(a) payments of such amount as may be specified in the order,

(b) payments equal to the whole of the income of the net estate or of such portion thereof as may be so specified,

(c) payments equal to the whole of the income of such part of the net estate as the court may direct to be set aside or appropriated for the making out of the income thereof of payments under this section,

or may provide for the amount of the payments or any of them to be determined in any other way the court thinks fit.

(3) Where an order under subsection (1)(a) above provides for the making of payments of an amount specified in the order, the order may direct that such part of the net estate as may be so specified shall be set aside or appropriated for the making out of the income thereof of those payments; but no larger part of the net estate shall be so set aside or appropriated than is sufficient, at the date of the order, to produce by the income thereof the amount required for the making of those payments.

(4) An order under this section may contain such consequential and supplemental provisions as the court thinks necessary or expedient for the purpose of giving effect to the order or for the purpose of securing that the order operates fairly as between one beneficiary of the estate of the deceased and another and may, in particular, but without prejudice to the generality of this subsection—

(a) order any person who holds any property which forms part of the net estate of the deceased to make such payment or transfer such property as may be specified in the order;

(b) varying the disposition of the deceased's estate effected by the will or the law relating to intestacy, or by both the will and the law relating to intestacy, in such manner as the court thinks fair and reasonable having regard to the provisions of the order and all the circumstances of the case;

(c) confer on the trustees of any property which is the subject of an order under this section such powers as appear to the court to be necessary or expedient.

Amendment

Sub-s (1): para (g) inserted by the Civil Partnership Act 2004, s 71, Sch 4, Pt 2, para 16.

Commentary

For the meaning of "net estate" see s 25(1) below. As to periodical payments which may be ordered under sub-s (1)(a), these will cease in relation to a former spouse on his or her remarriage (see s 19(2) below). As to the power of the court to vary an order under sub-s (1)(a), see s 6 below. As to the manner in which a lump sum can be ordered to be paid, see s 7 below. An order made under sub-s (1)(e) cannot be varied, see s 6(9) below, and therefore the court may take into account future contingencies, as in *Re Besterman* [1984] Ch 458. Orders made under sub-s (1)(f) also cannot be varied (see s 6(9) below). Subsection (4) provides the court with powers to decide on the burden of any award as between beneficiaries but also to enable it to give effect to orders it makes under s 10.

[314]

3 Matters to which court is to have regard in exercising powers under s 2

(1) Where an application is made for an order under section 2 of this Act, the court shall, in determining whether the disposition of the deceased's estate effected by his will or the law relating to intestacy, or the combination of his will and that law, is such as to make reasonable financial provision for the applicant and, if the court considers that reasonable financial provision has not been made, in determining whether and in what manner it shall exercise its powers under that section, have regard to the following matters, that is to say—

(a) the financial resources and financial needs which the applicant has or is likely to have in the foreseeable future;
(b) the financial resources and financial needs which any other applicant for an order under section 2 of this Act has or is likely to have in the foreseeable future;
(c) the financial resources and financial needs which any beneficiary of the estate of the deceased has or is likely to have in the foreseeable future;
(d) any obligations and responsibilities which the deceased had towards any applicant for an order under the said section 2 or towards any beneficiary of the estate of the deceased;
(e) the size and nature of the net estate of the deceased;
(f) any physical or mental disability of any applicant for an order under the said section 2 or any beneficiary of the estate of the deceased;
(g) any other matter, including the conduct of the applicant or any other person, which in the circumstances of the case the court may consider relevant.

(2) [This subsection applies, without prejudice to the generality of paragraph (g) of subsection (1) above, where an application for an order under section 2 of this Act is made by virtue of section 1(1)(a) or (b) of this Act.]

The court shall, in addition to the matters specifically mentioned in paragraphs (a) to (f) of that subsection, have regard to—

(a) the age of the applicant and the duration of the marriage [or civil partnership];
(b) the contribution made by the applicant to the welfare of the family of the deceased, including any contribution made by looking after the home or caring for the family.

. . . In the case of an application by the wife or husband of the deceased, the court shall also, unless at the date of death a *decree of judicial separation* [separation order under the Family Law Act 1996] was in force and the separation was continuing, have regard to the provision which the applicant might reasonably have expected to receive if on the day on which the deceased died the marriage, instead of being terminated by death, had been terminated by *a decree of divorce* [a divorce order].

[In the case of an application by the civil partner of the deceased, the court shall also, unless at the date of the death a separation order under Chapter 2 of Part 2 of the Civil Partnership Act 2004 was in force and the separation was continuing, have regard to the provision which the applicant might reasonably have expected to receive if on the day on which the deceased died the civil partnership, instead of being terminated by death, had been terminated by a dissolution order.]

[(2A) Without prejudice to the generality of paragraph (g) of subsection (1) above, where an application for an order under section 2 of this Act is made by virtue of section 1(1)(ba) of this Act, the court shall, in addition to the matters specifically mentioned in paragraphs (a) to (f) of that subsection, have regard to—

(a) the age of the applicant and the length of the period during which the applicant lived as the husband or wife [or civil partner] of the deceased and in the same household as the deceased;

(b) the contribution made by the applicant to the welfare of the family of the deceased, including any contribution made by looking after the home or caring for the family.]

(3) Without prejudice to the generality of paragraph (g) of subsection (1) above, where an application for an order under section 2 of this Act is made by virtue of section 1(1)(c) or 1(1)(d) of this Act, the court shall, in addition to the matters specifically mentioned in paragraphs (a) to (f) of that subsection, have regard to the manner in which the applicant was being or in which he might expect to be educated or trained, and where the application is made by virtue of section 1(1)(d) the court shall also have regard—

(a) to whether the deceased had assumed any responsibility for the applicant's maintenance and, if so, to the extent to which and the basis upon which the deceased assumed that responsibility and to the length of time for which the deceased discharged that responsibility;

(b) to whether in assuming and discharging that responsibility the deceased did so knowing that the applicant was not his own child;

(c) to the liability of any other person to maintain the applicant.

(4) Without prejudice to the generality of paragraph (g) of subsection (1) above, where an application for an order under section 2 of this Act is made by virtue of section 1(1)(e) of this Act, the court shall, in addition to the matters specifically mentioned in paragraphs (a) to (f) of that subsection, have regard to the extent to which and the basis upon which the deceased assumed responsibility for the maintenance of the applicant, and to the length of time for which the deceased discharged that responsibility.

(5) In considering the matters to which the court is required to have regard under this section, the court shall take into account the facts as known to the court at the date of the hearing.

(6) In considering the financial resources of any person for the purposes of this section the court shall take into account his earning capacity and in considering the financial needs of any person for the purposes of this section the court shall take into account his financial obligations and responsibilities.

Amendment

Sub-s (2): words from "This subsection applies," to "of this Act." in square brackets substituted by the Civil Partnership Act 2004, s 71, Sch 4, Pt 2, para 17(1), (2).
Sub-s (2): in para (a) words "or civil partnership" in square brackets inserted by the Civil Partnership Act 2004, s 71, Sch 4, Pt 2, para 17(1), (3).
Sub-s (2): word omitted repealed by the Civil Partnership Act 2004, s 261(4), Sch 30.
Sub-s (2): words "decree of judicial separation" and "a decree of divorce" in italics repealed and subsequent words in square brackets substituted by the Family Law Act 1996, s 66(1), Sch 8, para 27(3), as from a day to be appointed; for savings see s 66(2), Sch 9, para 5 thereof.
Sub-s (2): words from "In the case" to "a dissolution order." in square brackets inserted by the Civil Partnership Act 2004, s 71, Sch 4, Pt 2, para 17(1), (5).
Sub-s (2A): inserted by the Law Reform (Succession) Act 1995, s 2(4).
Sub-s (2A): in para (a) words "or civil partner" in square brackets inserted by the Civil Partnership Act 2004, s 71, Sch 4, Pt 2, para 18.

Commentary

The factors listed in sub-s (1) apply to all applicants and must be taken into account by the court in deciding whether the deceased made reasonable financial provision for the applicant and if not, what provision ought to be made, see *Re Coventry, Coventry v Coventry* [1980] Ch 462. Note that the test of whether reasonable provision has been made having regard to these factors, is an objective one, see *Moody v Stevenson* [1992] Ch 486. Subsection (2) provides for additional factors which must be taken into account where the claimant is the spouse or former spouse of the deceased. As to claims by spouses where the provision which would have been made on divorce has been taken into account, see *Re Bunning, Bunning v Salmon* [1984] Ch 480 and *Re Besterman* [1984] Ch 458, and as to guidance on the approach to provision on divorce see *White v White* [2001] AC 596 applied by the court under this jurisdiction in *Adam v Lewis* [2001] WTLR 493; *McNutty v McNutty* [2002] WTLR 737; P v G [2006] FLR 431 and *Cunliffe v Fielden* [2006] Ch 36. As far as a former spouse is concerned, it has been said that exceptional circumstances must be shown before provision will be made, see *Re Fullard* [1982] Fam 42; *Barass v Harding and Newman* [2001] 1 FLR 138; *Cameron v Treasury Solicitor* [1996] 2 FLR 138 (but see s 14(1) where death takes place within 12 months of a decree of divorce or nullity). There is as yet no case law guidance on civil partners or former civil partners but it is likely the court will follow the cases in relation to spouses and former spouses. As to cohabitees, the additional factors are contained in sub-s (2A). In the case of a child or a person treated as a child of the family, the additional factors are set out in sub-s (3), as to the application of which see *Re Leach, Leach v Linderman* [1986] Ch 226 and *Re Callaghan [1985*] Fam 1. Claims by adult children seem to have undergone something of a sea change of late, from *Re Coventry, Coventry v Coventry* [1980] Ch 462 where the fact that an adult so was in necessitous circumstances was not enough, to cases such as: *Re Goodchild* [1997] 1 WLR 1216; *Re Abram* [1996] 2 FLR 379; *Re Pearce* [1998] 2 FLR 705; *Re Hancock* [1999] 2 FLR 346; *Espinosa v Bourke* [1999] 1 FLR 747; and *Marks v Shafier* [2001] All ER (D) 193 (a case on conduct); *Robinson v Fernsby* [2004] WTLR 257; *Gold v Curtis* [2005] WTLR 673; *Re Garland* [2007] EWHC 2 and *Re Myers* [2005] WTLR 851 which contains a helpful review of the authorities. For dependants, the additional factors are set out in sub-s (4) as to the application of which see *Re Beaumont, Martin v Midland Bank Trust Co Ltd* [1980] Ch 444; *Jelley v Iliffe* [1981] Fam 128; *Re B* [2000] Ch 662; *Graham v Murphy* [1997] 1 FLR 860; *Malone v Harrison* [1979] 1 WLR 1353; *Harrington v Gill* (1983) 4 FLR 265; *Bishop v Plumley* [1991] 1 WLR 582.

[315]

4 Time-limit for applications

An application for an order under section 2 of this Act shall not, except with the permission of the court, be made after the end of the period of six months from the date on which representation with respect to the estate of the deceased is first taken out.

Commentary

Application under the I(PFD)A 1975 is by way of a Part 8 claim form and the procedure for such claims is set out in Part 57 of the Civil Procedure Rules 1998, SI 1998/3132 and the Practice Directon thereto. An application cannot be made before a grant of probate or letters of administration have been obtained, see *Re McBroom* [1992] 2 FLR 49. See also s 23 below. Time can be extended under the I(PFD)A 1975 and if such relief is required it should be asked for in the Part 8 claim form. The principles which the court will apply in exercising the discretion to extend time were set out in *Re Salmon, Coard v National Westminster Bank* [1981] Ch 167 and see also *Re Dennis, Dennis v Lloyd's Bank Ltd* [1981] 2 All ER 140 and *Re C* [1995] 2 FLR 24 (where the applicant was a minor) see also *McNutty v McNutty* [2002] WTLR 737. Note that the court has no power to extend time in respect of an application for an order under s 9 below.

[316]

5 Interim orders

(1) Where an application for an order under section 3 of this Act it appears to the court-

(a) that the applicant is in immediate need of financial assistance, but it is not yet possible to determine what order (if any) should be made under that section; and

(b) that property forming part of the net estate of the deceased is or can be made available to meet the need of the applicant;

the court may order that, subject to such conditions or restrictions, if any, as the court may impose and to any further order of the court, there shall be paid to the applicant out of the net estate of the deceased such sum or sums and (if more than one) at such intervals as the court thinks reasonable; and the court may order that, subject to the provisions of this Act, such payments are to be made until such date as the court may specify, not being later than the date on which the court either makes an order under the said section 2 or decides not to exercise its powers under that section.

(2) Subsections (2), (3) and (4) of section 2 of this Act shall apply in relation to an order under this section as they apply in relation to an order under that section.

(3) In determining what order, if any, should be made under this section the court shall, so far as the urgency of the case admits, have regard to the same matters as those to which the court is required to have regard under section 3 of this Act.

(4) An order made under section 2 of this Act may provide that any sum paid to the applicant by virtue of this section shall be treated to such an extent and in such manner as may be provided by that order as having been paid on account of any payment provided for by that order.

Commentary

Application under this section is by way of a Part 23 application notice supported by evidence in accordance with Part 23 of the Civil Procedure Rules 1998, SI 1998/3132. As to the position of a personal representative in respect of orders made under this power see s 20(2) below.

[317]

6 Variation, discharge, etc of orders for periodical payments

(1) Subject to the provisions of this Act, where the court has made an order under section 2(1)(a) of this Act (in this section referred to as "the original order") for the making of periodical payments to any person (in this section referred to as "the original recipient"), the court, on an application under this section, shall have power by order to vary or discharge the original order or to suspend any provision of it temporarily and to revive the operation of any provision so suspended.

(2) Without prejudice to the generality of subsection (1) above, an order made on an application for the variation of the original order may—

(a) provide for the making out of any relevant property of such periodical payments and for such term as may be specified in the order to any person who has applied, or would but for section 4 of this Act be entitled to apply, for an order under section 2 of this Act (whether or not, in the case of any application, an order was made in favour of the applicant);

(b) provide for the payment out of any relevant property of a lump sum of such amount as may be so specified to the original recipient or to any such person as is mentioned in paragraph (a) above;

(c) provide for the transfer of the relevant property, or such part thereof as may be so specified, to the original recipient or to any such person as is so mentioned.

(3) Where the original order provides that any periodical payments payable thereunder to the original recipient are to cease on the occurrence of an event specified in the order [(other than the formation of a subsequent marriage or civil partnership by a former spouse or former civil partner)] or on the expiration of a period so specified, then, if, before the end of the period of six months from the date of the occurrence of that event or of the expiration of that period, an application is

made for an order under this section, the court shall have power to make any order which it would have had power to make if the application had been made before the date (whether in favour of the original recipient or any such person as is mentioned in subsection (2)(a) above and whether having effect from that date or from such later date as the court may specify).

(4) Any reference in this section to the original order shall include a reference to an order made under this section and any reference in this section to the original recipient shall include a reference to any person to whom periodical payments are required to be made by virtue of an order under this section.

(5) An application under this section may be made by any of the following persons, that is to say—

(a) any person who by virtue of section 1(1) of this Act has applied, or would but for section 4 of this Act be entitled to apply, for an order under section 2 of this Act,
(b) the personal representatives of the deceased,
(c) the trustees of any relevant property, and
(d) any beneficiary of the estate of the deceased.

(6) An order under this section may only affect—

(a) property the income of which is at the date of the order applicable wholly or in part for the making of periodical payments to any person who has applied for an order under this Act, or
(b) in the case of an application under subsection (3) above in respect of payments which have ceased to be payable on the occurrence of an event or the expiration of a period, property the income of which was so applicable immediately before the occurrence of that event or the expiration of that period, as the case may be,

and any such property as is mentioned in paragraph (a) or (b) above is in subsections (2) and (5) above referred to as "relevant property".

(7) In exercising the powers conferred by this section the court shall have regard to all circumstances of the case, including any change in any of the matters to which the court was required to have regard when making the order to which the application relates.

(8) Where the court makes an order under this section, it may give such consequential directions as it thinks necessary or expedient having regard to the provisions of the order.

(9) No such order as is mentioned in section 2(1)(d), (e) or (f), 9, 10 or 11 of this Act shall be made on an application under this section.

(10) For the avoidance of doubt it is hereby declared that, in relation to an order which provides for the making of periodical payments which are to cease on the occurrence of an event specified in the order [(other than the formation of a subsequent marriage or civil partnership by a former spouse or former civil partner)] or on the expiration of a period so specified, the power to vary an order includes power to provide for the making of periodical payments after the expiration of that period or the occurrence of that event.

Amendment

Sub-s (3): words "(other than the formation of a subsequent marriage or civil partnership by a former spouse or former civil partner)" in square brackets substituted by the Civil Partnership Act 2004, s 71, Sch 4, Pt 2, para 19.
Sub-s (10): words "(other than the formation of a subsequent marriage or civil partnership by a former spouse or former civil partner)" in square brackets substituted by the Civil Partnership Act 2004, s 71, Sch 4, Pt 2, para 19.

Commentary

The apparently wide discretion set out in sub-s (1) is in fact confined by the definition of "relevant property" in sub-s (6) which has the effect that it is only if income of the estate increases, or another recipient of periodical payments dies, that the sum payable can be increased; see *Re Fricker* (1982) 3 FLR 228. Note the restrictions also contained in s 6(9) preventing certain orders being made under this section, and see the commentary to s 2. As to those who can apply to vary, sub-s (5)(a) includes those who fall within s 1 even if they did not make an application within time. For the meaning of "beneficiary" in sub-s (5)(d) see s 25(1) below. This section applies to civil partners and former civil partners.

[318]

7 Payment of lump sums by instalments

(1) An order under section 2(1)(b) or 6(2)(b) of this Act for the payment of a lump sum may provide for the payment of that sum by instalments of such amount as may be specified in the order.

(2) Where an order is made by virtue of subsection (1) above, the court shall have power, on an application made by the person to whom the lump sum is payable, by the personal representatives of the deceased or by the trustees of the property out of which the lump sum is payable, to vary that order by varying the number of instalments payable, the amount of any instalment and the date on which any instalment becomes payable.

Commentary

Although the court has no power to vary a lump sum award as such, if there is an order that it be paid by instalments, then it has power to vary the manner in which the instalments are paid.

[319]

PROPERTY AVAILABLE FOR FINANCIAL PROVISION

8 Property treated as part of "net estate"

(1) Where a deceased person has in accordance with the provisions of any enactment nominated any person to receive any sum of money or other property on his death and that nomination is in force at the time of his death, that sum of money, after deducting therefrom any inheritance tax payable in respect thereof, or that other property, to the extent of the value thereof at the date of the death of the deceased after deducting therefrom any inheritance tax so payable, shall be treated for the purposes of this Act as part of the net estate of the deceased; but this subsection shall not render any person liable for having paid that sum or transferred that other property to the person named in the nomination in accordance with the directions given in the nomination.

(2) Where any sum of money or other property is received by any person as a donatio mortis causa made by a deceased person, that sum of money, after deducting therefrom any inheritance tax payable thereon, or that other property, to the extent of the value thereof at the date of the death of the deceased after deducting therefrom any inheritance tax so payable, shall be treated for the purposes of this Act as part of the net estate of the deceased; but this subsection shall not render any person liable for having paid that sum or transferred that other property in order to give effect to that donatio mortis causa.

(3) The amount of inheritance tax to be deducted for the purposes of this section shall not exceed the amount of that tax which has been borne by the person nominated by the deceased or, as the case may be, the person who has received a sum of money or other property as a donatio mortis causa.

Commentary
For the meaning of "net estate" see s 25(1). This section is intended to maximise the amount in the net estate. Benefits nominated within a private pension scheme were not within sub-s (1), see *Re Cairnes, Howard v Cairnes* (1982) 4 FLR 225. As to sub-s (2) a donatio mortis causa (which occurs only rarely) is where a gift is made by delivery of the subject of the gift, or something representing it, in imminent expectation of death on terms that make the gift absolute on death.

[320]

9 Property held on a joint tenancy

(1) Where a deceased person was immediately before his death beneficially entitled to a joint tenancy of any property, then, if, before the end of the period of six months from the date on which representation with respect to the estate of the deceased was first taken out, an application is made for an order under section 2 of this Act, the court for the purpose of facilitating the making of financial provision for the applicant under this Act may order that the deceased's severable share of that property, at the value thereof immediately before his death, shall, to such extent as appears to the court to be just in all the circumstances of the case, be treated for the purposes of this Act as part of the net estate of the deceased.

(2) In determining the extent to which any severable share is to be treated as part of the net estate of the deceased by virtue of an order under subsection (1) above, the court shall have regard to any inheritance tax payable in respect of that severable share.

(3) Where an order is made under subsection (1) above, the provisions of this section shall not render any person liable for anything done by him before the order was made.

(4) For the avoidance of doubt it is hereby declared that for the purposes of this section there may be a joint tenancy of a chose in action.

Commentary
Time cannot be extended for an application for an order made under this section, which has to be made within six months of the grant, see: *Dingmar v Dingmar* [2006] EWCA Civ 942. As to guidance on the exercise of the court's discretion under this section, see *Kourkgy v Lusher* (1981) 4 FLR 65; *Re Crawford* (1982) 4 FLR 273 (joint bank account); *Jessop v Jessop* [1992] 2 FLR 591; *Powell v Osborne* [1993] 1 FLR 1001 (property subject to a mortgage secured by an endowment policy). The value of the share which is taken into account by the Court is the value at the date of the trial although that is not immediately apparent from the wording of the section, see: *Dingmar v Dingmar* [2006] EWCA Civ 942.

[321]

POWERS OF COURT IN RELATION TO TRANSACTIONS INTENDED TO DEFEAT APPLICATIONS FOR FINANCIAL PROVISION

10 Dispositions intended to defeat applications for financial provision

(1) Where an application is made to the court for an order under section 2 of this Act, the applicant may, in the proceedings on that application, apply to the court for an order under subsection (2) below.

(2) Where on an application under subsection (1) above the court is satisfied—

- (a) that, less than six years before the date of the death of the deceased, the deceased with the intention of defeating an application for financial provision under this Act made a disposition, and
- (b) that full valuable consideration for that disposition was not given by the person to whom or for the benefit of whom the disposition was made (in this section referred to as "the donee") or by any other person, and

(c) that the exercise of the powers conferred by this section would facilitate the making of financial provision for the applicant under this Act,

then, subject to the provisions of this section and of sections 12 and 13 of this Act, the court may order the donee (whether or not at the date of the order he holds any interest in the property disposed of to him or for his benefit by the deceased) to provide, for the purpose of the making of that financial provision, such sum of money or other property as may be specified in the order.

(3) Where an order is made under subsection (2) above as respects any disposition made by the deceased which consisted of the payment of money to or for the benefit of the donee, the amount of any sum of money or the value of any property ordered to be provided under that subsection shall not exceed the amount of the payment made by the deceased after deducting therefrom any inheritance tax borne by the donee in respect of that payment.

(4) Where an order is made under subsection (2) above as respects any disposition made by the deceased which consisted of the transfer of property (other than a sum of money) to or for the benefit of the donee, the amount of any sum of money or the value of any property ordered to be provided under that subsection shall not exceed the value at the date of the death of the deceased of the property disposed of by him to or for the benefit of the donee (or if that property has been disposed of by the person to whom it was transferred by the deceased, the value at the date of that disposal thereof) after deducting therefrom any inheritance tax borne by the donee in respect of the transfer of that property by the deceased.

(5) Where an application (in this subsection referred to as "the original application") is made for an order under subsection (2) above in relation to any disposition, then, if on an application under this subsection by the donee or by any applicant for an order under section 2 of this Act the court is satisfied—

(a) that, less than six years before the date of the death of the deceased, the deceased with the intention of defeating an application for financial provision under this Act made a disposition other than the disposition which is the subject of the original application, and

(b) that full valuable consideration for that other disposition was not given by the person to whom or for the benefit of whom that other disposition was made or by any other person,

the court may exercise in relation to the person to whom or for the benefit of whom that other disposition was made the powers which the court would have had under subsection (2) above if the original application had been made in respect of that other disposition and the court had been satisfied as to the matters set out in paragraphs (a), (b) and (c) of that subsection; and where any application is made under this subsection, any reference in this section (except in subsection (2)(b)) to the donee shall include a reference to the person to whom or for the benefit of whom that other disposition was made.

(6) In determining whether and in what manner to exercise its powers under this section, the court shall have regard to the circumstances in which any disposition was made and any valuable consideration which was given therefor, the relationship, if any, of the donee to the deceased, the conduct and financial resources of the donee and all the other circumstances of the case.

(7) In this section "disposition" does not include—

(a) any provision in a will, any such nomination as is mentioned in section 8(1) of this Act or any donatio mortis causa, or

(b) any appointment of property made, otherwise than by will, in the exercise of a special power of appointment,

but, subject to these exceptions, includes any payment of money (including the payment of a premium under a policy of assurance) and any conveyance, assurance, appointment or gift of property of any description, whether made by an instrument or otherwise.

(8) The provisions of this section do not apply to any disposition made before the commencement of this Act.

Commentary

For the meaning of "full valuable consideration" in sub-s (2)(b), see s 25(1) below. See s 13 for the orders which can be made under this section. Reported decisions under this section are few and far between but see *Re Dawkins, Dawkins v Judd* [1986] 2 FLR 360; *Clifford v Tanner* [1987] CLY 3881; *Re Kennedy, Kennedy v the Official Solicitor* [1980] CLY 2820. See also the provisions of s 12 below. A clause in a will forfeiting a gift in the event of a claim under the Act is not void, see: *Nathan v Leonard* [2003] 1 WLR 827. The section does not confer on the claimant any type of proprietary remedy.

[322]

11 Contracts to leave property by will

(1) Where an application is made to a court for an order under section 2 of this Act, the applicant may, in the proceedings on that application, apply to the court for an order under this section.

(2) Where on an application under subsection (1) above the court is satisfied—

(a) that the deceased made a contract by which he agreed to leave by his will a sum of money or other property to any person or by which he agreed that a sum of money or other property would be paid or transferred to any person out of his estate, and

(b) that the deceased made that contract with the intention of defeating an application for financial provision under this Act, and

(c) that when the contract was made full valuable consideration for that contract was not given or promised by the person with whom or for the benefit of whom the contract was made (in this section referred to as "the donee") or by any other person, and

(d) that the exercise of the powers conferred by this section would facilitate the making of financial provision for the applicant under this Act,

then, subject to the provisions of this section and of sections 12 and 13 of this Act, the court may make any one or more of the following orders, that is to say—

(i) if any money has been paid or any other property has been transferred to or for the benefit of the donee in accordance with the contract, an order directing the donee to provide, for the purpose of the making of that financial provision, such sum of money or other property as may be specified in the order;

(ii) if the money or all the money has not been paid or the property or all the property has not been transferred in accordance with the contract, an order directing the personal representatives not to make any payment or transfer any property, or not to make any further payment or transfer any further property, as the case may be, in accordance therewith or directing the personal representatives only to make such payment or transfer such property as may be specified in the order.

(3) Notwithstanding anything in subsection (2) above, the court may exercise its powers thereunder in relation to any contract made by the deceased only to the extent that the court considers that the amount of any sum of money paid or to be paid or the value of any property transferred or to be transferred in accordance with the contract exceeds the value of any valuable consideration given or to be given for that contract, and for this purpose the court shall have regard to the value of property at the date of the hearing.

(4) In determining whether and in what manner to exercise its powers under this section, the court shall have regard to the circumstances in which the contract was made, the relationship, if any, of the donee to the deceased, the conduct and financial resources of the donee and all the other circumstances of the case.

(5) Where an order has been made under subsection (2) above in relation to any contract the rights of any person to enforce that contract or to recover damages or to obtain other relief for the breach thereof shall be subject to any adjustment made by the court under section 12(3) of this Act and shall survive to such extent only as is consistent with giving effect to the terms of that order.

(6) The provisions of this section do not apply to a contract made before the commencement of this Act.

Commentary

For the meaning of "full valuable consideration" in sub-s (2)(c), see s 25(1) below. This section was enacted to avoid the mischief demonstrated in *Schaefer v Schuhmann* [1972] AC 573, which showed how a contract made in the deceased's lifetime could be used to defeat applications under the I(PFD)A 1975. The section only applies to contracts made after 21 April 1976 when the I(PFD)A 1975 came into force. Note there is no time limit as to when the contract was made because the property does not leave the ownership of the deceased until death. There has to be a binding contract complying with any formalities, see: *Irani v Irani and others* [2006] EWHC 1811. See also the provisions of s 12 below.

[323]

12 Provisions supplementary to ss 10 and 11

(1) Where the exercise of any of the powers conferred by section 10 or 11 of this Act is conditional on the court being satisfied that a disposition or contract was made by a deceased person with the intention of defeating an application for financial provision under this Act, that condition shall be fulfilled if the court is of the opinion that, on a balance of probabilities, the intention of the deceased (though not necessarily his sole intention) in making the disposition or contract was to prevent an order for financial provision being made under this Act or to reduce the amount of the provision which might otherwise be granted by an order thereunder.

(2) Where an application is made under section 11 of this Act with respect to any contract made by the deceased and no valuable consideration was given or promised by any person for that contract then, notwithstanding anything in subsection (1) above, it shall be presumed, unless the contrary is shown, that the deceased made that contract with the intention of defeating an application for financial provision under this Act.

(3) Where the court makes an order under section 10 or 11 of this Act it may give such consequential directions as it thinks fit (including directions requiring the making of any payment or the transfer of any property) for giving effect to the order or for securing a fair adjustment of the rights of the persons affected thereby.

(4) Any power conferred on the court by the said section 10 or 11 to order the donee, in relation to any disposition or contract, to provide any sum of money or other property shall be exercisable in like manner in relation to the personal representative of the donee, and—

- (a) any reference in section 10(4) to the disposal of property by the donee shall include a reference to disposal by the personal representative of the donee, and
- (b) any reference in section 10(5) to an application by the donee under that subsection shall include a reference to an application by the personal representative of the donee;

but the court shall not have power under the said section 10 or 11 to make an order in respect of any property forming part of the estate of the donee which has been distributed by the personal representative; and the personal representative shall not be liable for having distributed any such property before he has notice of the making of an application under the said section 10 or 11 on the ground that he ought to have taken into account the possibility that such an application would be made.

Commentary
This section supplements ss 10 and 11 and should be read with those sections. As to proving intention under sub-s (1) for the purposes of s 10, see *Re Kennedy, Kennedy v the Official Solicitor* [1980] CLY 2820. Note that there is an easier test in respect of contracts within s 11 contained in sub-s (2).

[324]

13 Provisions as to trustees in relation to ss 10 and 11

(1) Where an application is made for—

- (a) an order under section 10 of this Act in respect of a disposition made by the deceased to any person as a trustee, or
- (b) an order under section 11 of this Act in respect of any payment made or property transferred, in accordance with a contract made by the deceased, to any person as a trustee,

the powers of the court under the said section 10 or 11 to order that trustee to provide a sum of money or other property shall be subject to the following limitation (in addition, in a case of an application under section 10, to any provision regarding the deduction of inheritance tax) namely, that the amount of any sum of money or the value of any property ordered to be provided—

- (i) in the case of an application in respect of a disposition which consisted of the payment of money or an application in respect of the payment of money in accordance with a contract, shall not exceed the aggregate of so much of that money as is at the date of the order in the hands of the trustee and the value at that date of any property which represents that money or is derived therefrom and is at that date in the hands of the trustee;
- (ii) in the case of an application in respect of a disposition which consisted of the transfer of property (other than a sum of money) or an application in respect of the transfer of property (other than a sum of money) in accordance with a contract, shall not exceed the aggregate of the value at the date of the order of so much of that property as is at that date in the hands of the trustee and the value at that date of any property which represents the first mentioned property or is derived therefrom and is at that date in the hands of the trustee.

(2) Where any such application is made in respect of a disposition made to any person as a trustee or in respect of any payment made or property transferred in pursuance of a contract to any person as a trustee, the trustee shall not be liable for having distributed any money or other property on the ground that he ought to have taken into account the possibility that such an application would be made.

(3) Where any such application is made in respect of a disposition made to any person as a trustee or in respect of any payment made or property transferred in accordance with a contract to any person as a trustee, any reference in the said section 10 or 11 to the donee shall be construed as including a reference to the trustee or trustees for the time being of the trust in question and any reference in subsection (1) or (2) above to a trustee shall be construed in the same way.

Commentary
This section supplements the provisions of ss 10 and 11 and should be read with them. It applies to cases where the disposition under s 10 is to trustees or where the contract is with trustees but is limited to property actually in the hands of the trustees and they are not liable if they have distributed before an application is made (sub-s (2)).

[325]

SPECIAL PROVISIONS RELATING TO CASES OF DIVORCE, SEPARATION, ETC

14 Provision as to cases where no financial relief was granted in divorce proceedings, etc

(1) Where, within twelve months from the date on which *a decree of divorce or nullity of marriage has been made absolute or a decree of judicial separation has been granted* [a divorce order or separation order has been made under the Family Law Act 1996 in relation to a marriage or a decree of nullity of marriage has been made absolute], a party to the marriage dies and—

(a) an application for a financial provision order under *section 23* [section 22A or 23] of the Matrimonial Causes Act 1973 or a property adjustment order under *section 24* [section 23A or 24] of that Act has not been made by the other party to that marriage, or

(b) such an application has been made but the proceedings thereon have not been determined at the time of the death of the deceased,

then, if an application for an order under section 2 of this Act is made by that other party, the court shall, notwithstanding anything in section 1 or section 3 of this Act, have power, if it thinks it just to do so, to treat that party for the purposes of that application as if *the decree of divorce or nullity of marriage had not been made absolute or the decree of judicial separation had not been granted, as the case may be* [, as the case may be, the divorce order or separation order had not been made or the decree of nullity had not been made absolute].

(2) This section shall not apply in relation to a *decree of judicial separation* [separation order] unless at the date of the death of the deceased *the decree* [the order] was in force and the separation was continuing.

Amendment
Sub-ss (1), (2): words in italics prospectively repealed with savings and subsequent words in square brackets prospectively substituted with savings by the Family Law Act 1996, s 66(1), Sch 8, para 27(4), as from a day to be appointed; for savings see s 66(2), Sch 9, para 5 thereof.

Commentary
As stated above, former spouses have tended not to do well under the I(PFD)A 1975 (see the commentary to s 3). This section enables the court to take the more generous approach which it would take to a spouse in cases where death follows within 12 months of a decree of divorce, or nullity, or separation. Note the jurisdiction is discretionary.

[326]

[14A Provision as to cases where no financial relief was granted in proceedings for the dissolution etc of a civil partnership]

[(1) Subsection (2) below applies where—

(a) a dissolution order, nullity order, separation order or presumption of death order has been made under Chapter 2 of Part 2 of the Civil Partnership Act 2004 in relation to a civil partnership,

(b) one of the civil partners dies within twelve months from the date on which the order is made, and

(c) either—
  (i) an application for a financial provision order under Part 1 of Schedule 5 to that Act or a property adjustment order under Part 2 of that Schedule has not been made by the other civil partner, or
  (ii) such an application has been made but the proceedings on the application have not been determined at the time of the death of the deceased.

(2) If an application for an order under section 2 of this Act is made by the surviving civil partner, the court shall, notwithstanding anything in section 1 or section 3 of this Act, have power, if it thinks it just to do so, to treat the surviving civil partner as if the order mentioned in subsection (1)(a) above had not been made.

(3) This section shall not apply in relation to a separation order unless at the date of the death of the deceased the separation order was in force and the separation was continuing.]

Amendment

Inserted by the Civil Partnership Act 2004, s 71, Sch 4, Pt 2, para 20.

Commentary

This section mirrors the provisions of section 14 in respect of spouses for those where death occurs within 12 months of a civil partnership being dissolved, or a nullity order being made or a separation order. For the definitions of these please see the Civil Partnership Act 2004 **[Appendix VI]**. See also the notes to section 14 above.

[327]

15 Restriction imposed in divorce proceedings, etc on application under this Act

[(1) *On the grant of a decree of divorce, a decree of nullity of marriage or a decree of judicial separation or at any time thereafter* [At any time when the court—
  (a) has jurisdiction under section 23A or 24 of the Matrimonial Causes Act 1973 to make a property adjustment order in relation to a marriage; or
  (b) would have such jurisdiction if either the jurisdiction had not already been exercised or an application for such an order were made with the leave of the court,]

the court, if it considers it just to do so, may, on the application of either party to the marriage, order that the other party to the marriage shall not on the death of the applicant be entitled to apply for an order under section 2 of this Act.

In this subsection "the court" means the High Court or, where a county court has jurisdiction by virtue of Part V of the Matrimonial and Family Proceedings Act 1984, a county court.]

(2) In the case of a decree of divorce or nullity of marriage an order may be made under subsection (1) above before or after the decree is made absolute, but if it is made before the decree is made absolute it shall not take effect unless the decree is made absolute.

(3) Where an order made under subsection (1) above on the grant of a decree of divorce or nullity of marriage has come into force with respect to a party to a marriage, then, on the death of the other party to that marriage, the court shall not entertain any application for an order under section 2 of this Act made by the first-mentioned party.

(4) Where an order made under subsection (1) above on the grant of a decree of judicial separation has come into force with respect to any party to a marriage, then, if the other party to that marriage dies while the decree is in force and the separation is continuing, the court shall not entertain any application for an order under section 2 of this Act made by the first-mentioned party.

[(2) An order made under subsection (1) above with respect to any party to a marriage has effect in accordance with subsection (3) below at any time—

(a) after the marriage has been dissolved;

(b) after a decree of nullity has been made absolute in relation to the marriage; and

(c) while a separation order under the Family Law Act 1996 is in force in relation to the marriage and the separation is continuing.

(3) If at any time when an order made under subsection (1) above with respect to any party to a marriage has effect the other party to the marriage dies, the court shall not entertain any application made by the surviving party to the marriage for an order under section 2 of this Act.]

Amendment

Sub-s (1): substituted by the Matrimonial and Family Proceedings Act 1984, s 8; words in italics prospectively repealed with savings and subsequent words in square brackets prospectively substituted with savings by the Family Law Act 1996, s 66(1), Sch 8, para 27(5), as from a day to be appointed, for savings see s 66(2), Sch 9, para 5 thereof.
Sub-ss (2)-(4): prospectively substituted with savings, by subsequent sub-ss (2), (3), by the Family Law Act 1996, s 66(1), Sch 8, para 27(6), as from a day to be appointed; for savings see s 66(2), Sch 9, para 5 thereof.

Commentary

Before a court exercising its discretion under this section in matrimonial proceedings, makes an order, the court should have some information before it, persuading it that it is just to do so, see *Whiting v Whiting* [1988] 1 WLR 565.

[328]

[15ZA Restriction imposed in proceedings for the dissolution etc of a civil partnership on application under this Act]

[(1) On making a dissolution order, nullity order, separation order or presumption of death order under Chapter 2 of Part 2 of the Civil Partnership Act 2004, or at any time after making such an order, the court, if it considers it just to do so, may, on the application of either of the civil partners, order that the other civil partner shall not on the death of the applicant be entitled to apply for an order under section 2 of this Act.

(2) In subsection (1) above "the court" means the High Court or, where a county court has jurisdiction by virtue of Part 5 of the Matrimonial and Family Proceedings Act 1984, a county court.

(3) In the case of a dissolution order, nullity order or presumption of death order ("the main order") an order may be made under subsection (1) above before (as well as after) the main order is made final, but if made before the main order is made final it shall not take effect unless the main order is made final.

(4) Where an order under subsection (1) above made in connection with a dissolution order, nullity order or presumption of death order has come into force with respect to a civil partner, then, on the death of the other civil partner, the court shall not entertain any application for an order under section 2 of this Act made by the surviving civil partner.

(5) Where an order under subsection (1) above made in connection with a separation order has come into force with respect to a civil partner, then, if the other civil partner dies while the separation order is in force and the separation is continuing, the court shall not entertain any application for an order under section 2 of this Act made by the surviving civil partner.]

Amendment

Inserted by the Civil Partnership Act 2004, s 71, Sch 4, Pt 2, para 21.

Commentary
This section mirrors the provisions of section 14 in respect of spouses for those where death occurs within 12 months of a civil partnership being dissolved, or a nullity order being made or a separation order. For the definitions of these please see the Civil Partnership Act 2004 **[Appendix VI]**. See also the notes to section 15 above.

[329]

[15A Restriction imposed in proceedings under Matrimonial and Family Proceedings Act 1984 on application under this Act]

[(1) On making an order under section 17 of the Matrimonial and Family Proceedings Act 1984 (orders for financial provision and property adjustment following overseas divorces, etc) the court, if it considers it just to do so, may, on the application of either party to the marriage, order that the other party to the marriage shall not on the death of the applicant be entitled to apply for an order under section 2 of this Act.

In this subsection "the court" means the High Court or, where a county court has jurisdiction by virtue of Part V of the Matrimonial and Family Proceedings Act 1984, a county court.

(2) Where an order under subsection (1) above has been made with respect to a party to a marriage which has been dissolved or annulled, then, on the death of the other party to that marriage, the court shall not entertain an application under section 2 of this Act made by the first-mentioned party.

(3) Where an order under subsection (1) above has been made with respect to a party to a marriage the parties to which have been legally separated, then, if the other party to the marriage dies while the legal separation is in force, the court shall not entertain an application under section 2 of this Act made by the first-mentioned party.]

Amendment
Inserted by the Matrimonial and Family Proceedings Act 1984, s 25.

Commentary
See the notes to s 15.

[330]

[15B Restriction imposed in proceedings under Schedule 7 to the Civil Partnership Act 2004 on application under this Act]

[(1) On making an order under paragraph 9 of Schedule 7 to the Civil Partnership Act 2004 (orders for financial provision, property adjustment and pension-sharing following overseas dissolution etc of civil partnership) the court, if it considers it just to do so, may, on the application of either of the civil partners, order that the other civil partner shall not on the death of the applicant be entitled to apply for an order under section 2 of this Act.

(2) In subsection (1) above "the court" means the High Court or, where a county court has jurisdiction by virtue of Part 5 of the Matrimonial and Family Proceedings Act 1984, a county court.

(3) Where an order under subsection (1) above has been made with respect to one of the civil partners in a case where a civil partnership has been dissolved or annulled, then, on the death of the other civil partner, the court shall not entertain an application under section 2 of this Act made by the surviving civil partner.

(4) Where an order under subsection (1) above has been made with respect to one of the civil partners in a case where civil partners have been legally separated, then, if

the other civil partner dies while the legal separation is in force, the court shall not entertain an application under section 2 of this Act made by the surviving civil partner.]

Amendment

Inserted by the Civil Partnership Act 2004, s 71, Sch 4, Pt 2, para 22.

Commentary

This section mirrors the provisions of section15 in respect of spouses. For the definitions of these please see the Civil Partnership Act 2004 **[Appendix VI]**. See also the notes to section 15A above.

[331]

16 Variation and discharge of secured periodical payments orders made under Matrimonial Causes Act 1973

(1) Where an application for an order under section 2 of this Act is made to the court by any person who was at the time of the death of the deceased entitled to payments from the deceased under a secured periodical payments order made under the Matrimonial Causes Act 1973 [or Schedule 5 to the Civil Partnership Act 2004], then, in the proceedings on that application, the court shall have power, if an application is made under this section by that person or by the personal representative of the deceased, to vary or discharge that periodical payments order or to revive the operation of any provision thereof which has been suspended under section 31 of that Act [of 1973 or Part 11 of that Schedule].

(2) In exercising the powers conferred by this section the court shall have regard to all the circumstances of the case, including any order which the court proposes to make under section 2 or section 5 of this Act and any change (whether resulting from the death of the deceased or otherwise) in any of the matters to which the court was required to have regard when making the secured periodical payments order.

(3) The powers exercisable by the court under this section in relation to an order shall be exercisable also in relation to any instrument executed in pursuance of the order.

Amendment

Sub-s (1): words "or Schedule 5 to the Civil Partnership Act 2004" in square brackets inserted by the Civil Partnership Act 2004, s 71, Sch 4, Pt 2, para 23(a).
Sub-s (1): words "of 1973 or Part 11 of that Schedule" in square brackets inserted by the Civil Partnership Act 2004, s 71, Sch 4, Pt 2, para 23(b).

Commentary

This section enables the court to vary orders made under the Matrimonial Causes Act 1973. As to the treatment of former spouses under the I(PFD)A 1975 see the commentary to s 3. As to orders made under this section and its predecessor, see *Eyre v Eyre* [1968] 1 WLR 530 and *Re Crawford* (1982) 4 FLR 273.

[332]

17 Variation and revocation of maintenance agreements

(1) Where an application for an order under section 2 of this Act is made to the court by any person who was at the time of the death of the deceased entitled to payments from the deceased under a maintenance agreement which provided for the continuation of payments under the agreement after the death of the deceased, then, in the proceedings on that application, the court shall have power, if an application is made under this section by that person or by the personal representative of the deceased, to vary or revoke that agreement.

(2) In exercising the powers conferred by this section the court shall have regard to all the circumstances of the case, including any order which the court proposes to make under section 2 or section 5 of this Act and any change (whether resulting from the death of the deceased or otherwise) in any of the circumstances in the light of which the agreement was made.

(3) If a maintenance agreement is varied by the court under this section the like consequences shall ensue as if the variation had been made immediately before the death of the deceased by agreement between the parties and for valuable consideration.

(4) In this section "maintenance agreement", in relation to a deceased person, means any agreement made, whether in writing or not and whether before or after the commencement of this Act, by the deceased with any person with whom he [formed a marriage or civil partnership], being an agreement which contained provisions governing the rights and liabilities towards one another when living separately of the parties to that marriage [or of the civil partners] (whether or not the marriage [or civil partnership] has been dissolved or annulled) in respect of the making or securing of payments or the disposition or use of any property, including such rights and liabilities with respect to the maintenance or education of any child, whether or not a child of the deceased or a person who was treated by the deceased as a child of the family in relation to that marriage [or civil partnership].

Amendment

Sub-s (4): words "formed a marriage or civil partnership" in square brackets substituted by the Civil Partnership Act 2004, s 71, Sch 4, Pt 2, para 24(a).

Sub-s (4): words "or of the civil partners" in square brackets inserted by the Civil Partnership Act 2004, s 71, Sch 4, Pt 2, para 24(b).

Sub-s (4): words "or civil partnership" in square brackets in both places they occur inserted by the Civil Partnership Act 2004, s 71, Sch 4, Pt 2, para 24(c).

Commentary

The court is given like powers as under s 16 where there is no order but an agreement between the parties as to maintenance which is defined in sub-s (4).

[333]

18 Availability of court's powers under this Act in applications under ss 31and36 of the Matrimonial Causes Act 1973

(1) Where—

(a) a person against whom a secured periodical payments order was made under the Matrimonial Causes Act 1973 has died and an application is made under section 31(6) of that Act for the variation or discharge of that order or for the revival of the operation of any provision thereof which has been suspended, or

(b) a party to a maintenance agreement within the meaning of section 34 of that Act has died, the agreement being one which provides for the continuation of payments thereunder after the death of one of the parties, and an application is made under section 36(1) of that Act for the alteration of the agreement under section 35 thereof.

the court shall have power to direct that the application made under the said section 31(6) or 36(1) shall be deemed to have been accompanied by an application for an order under section 2 of this Act.

(2) Where the court gives a direction under subsection (1) above it shall have power, in the proceedings on the application under the said section 31(6) or 36(1), to make any order which the court would have had power to make under the provisions of this Act if the application under the said section 31(6) or 36(1), as the case may be, had

been made jointly with an application for an order under the said section 2; and the court shall have power to give such consequential directions as may be necessary for enabling the court to exercise any of the powers available to the court under this Act in the case of an application for an order under section 2.

(3) Where an order made under section 15(1) of this Act is in force with respect to a party to a marriage, the court shall not give a direction under subsection (1) above with respect to any application made under the said section 31(6) or 36(1) by that party on the death of the other party.

Commentary

This section enables a court, sitting in its matrimonial jurisdiction, to treat an application to vary or discharge a secured periodical payments order or a maintenance agreement as an application under the I(PFD)A 1975, s 2 so that it can consider whether reasonable financial provision should be granted and how. Note that no order under this section will be made if there is an order in force under the I(PFD)A 1975, s 15 (as to which see above).

[334]

[18A Availability of court's powers under this Act in applications under paragraphs 60 and 73 of Schedule 5 to the Civil Partnership Act 2004]

[(1) Where—

(a) a person against whom a secured periodical payments order was made under Schedule 5 to the Civil Partnership Act 2004 has died and an application is made under paragraph 60 of that Schedule for the variation or discharge of that order or for the revival of the operation of any suspended provision of the order, or

(b) a party to a maintenance agreement within the meaning of Part 13 of that Schedule has died, the agreement being one which provides for the continuation of payments under the agreement after the death of one of the parties, and an application is made under paragraph 73 of that Schedule for the alteration of the agreement under paragraph 69 of that Schedule,

the court shall have power to direct that the application made under paragraph 60 or 73 of that Schedule shall be deemed to have been accompanied by an application for an order under section 2 of this Act.

(2) Where the court gives a direction under subsection (1) above it shall have power, in the proceedings on the application under paragraph 60 or 73 of that Schedule, to make any order which the court would have had power to make under the provisions of this Act if the application under that paragraph had been made jointly with an application for an order under section 2 of this Act; and the court shall have power to give such consequential directions as may be necessary for enabling the court to exercise any of the powers available to the court under this Act in the case of an application for an order under section 2.

(3) Where an order made under section 15ZA(1) of this Act is in force with respect to a civil partner, the court shall not give a direction under subsection (1) above with respect to any application made under paragraph 60 or 73 of that Schedule by that civil partner on the death of the other civil partner.]

Amendment

Inserted by the Civil Partnership Act 2004, s 71, Sch 4, Pt 2, para 25.

Commentary

This section mirrors the provisions of section 18 in respect of spouses For the references to the Civil Partnership Act 2004; see **[Appendix VI]**. See also the notes to section 18 above.

[335]

MISCELLANEOUS AND SUPPLEMENTARY PROVISIONS

19 Effect, duration and form of orders

(1) Where an order is made under section 2 of this Act then for all purposes, including the purposes of the enactments relating to inheritance tax, the will or the law relating to intestacy, or both the will and the law relating to intestacy, as the case may be, shall have effect and be deemed to have had effect as from the deceased's death subject to the provisions of the order.

(2) Any order made under section 2 or 5 of this Act in favour of—

(a) an applicant who was the [former spouse or former civil partner] of the deceased, or

(b) an applicant who was the husband or wife of the deceased in a case where *the marriage with the deceased was the subject of a decree of judicial separation and at the date of death the decree was in force*[, at the date of death, a separation order under the Family Law Act 1996 was in force in relation to the marriage with the deceased] and the separation was continuing, [or

(c) an applicant who was the civil partner of the deceased in a case where, at the date of death, a separation order under Chapter 2 of Part 2 of the Civil Partnership Act 2004 was in force in relation to their civil partnership and the separation was continuing,]

shall, in so far as it provides for the making of periodical payments, cease to have effect [on the formation by the applicant of a subsequent marriage or civil partnership, except in relation to any arrears due under the order on the date of the formation of the subsequent marriage or civil partnership].

(3) A copy of every order made under this Act [other than an order made under section 15(1) [or 15ZA(1)] of this Act] shall be sent to the principal registry of the Family Division for entry and filing, and a memorandum of the order shall be endorsed on, or permanently annexed to, the probate or letters of administration under which the estate is being administered.

Amendment

Sub-s (2): in para (a) words "former spouse or former civil partner" in square brackets substituted by the Civil Partnership Act 2004, s 71, Sch 4, Pt 2, para 26(1), (2).
Sub-s (2): in para (b) words from "the marriage with" to "was in force" in italics repealed and subsequent words in square brackets substituted by the Family Law Act 1996, s 66(1), Sch 8, para 27(7), as from a day to be appointed; for savings see s 66(2), Sch 9, para 5 thereof.
Sub-s (2): para (c) and word "or" immediately preceding it inserted by the Civil Partnership Act 2004, s 71, Sch 4, Pt 2, para 26(1), (3).
Sub-s (2): words from "on the formation" to "or civil partnership" in square brackets substituted by the Civil Partnership Act 2004, s 71, Sch 4, Pt 2, para 26(1), (4).
Sub-s (3): words from "other than an order" to "of this Act" in square brackets inserted by the Administration of Justice Act 1982, s 52.
Sub-s (3): words "or 15ZA(1)" in square brackets inserted by the Civil Partnership Act 2004, s 71, Sch 4, Pt 2, para 26(1), (5).

Commentary

Section 19(1) is reflected for inheritance tax purposes in the Inheritance Tax Act 1984, s 146(1). However this section applies for all tax purposes and not just inheritance tax. Therefore inheritance tax may be saved if provision is made for the surviving spouse. Subsection (2) now also covers civil partnerships. As to sub-s (3) the procedure is set out in the Civil Procedure Rules 1998, SI 1998/3132, paragraph 18.2 of the Practice Direction to Part 57 in respect of claims after 2 December 2002.

[336]

20 Provisions as to personal representatives

(1) The provisions of this Act shall not render the personal representative of a deceased person liable for having distributed any part of the estate of the deceased,

after the end of the period of six months from the date on which representation with respect to the estate of the deceased is first taken out, on the ground that he ought to have taken into account the possibility—

(a) that the court might permit the making of an application for an order under section 2 of this Act after the end of that period, or

(b) that, where an order has been made under the said section 2, the court might exercise in relation thereto the powers conferred on it by section 6 of this Act,

but this subsection shall not prejudice any power to recover, by reason of the making of an order under this Act, any part of the estate so distributed.

(2) Where the personal representative of a deceased person pays any sum directed by an order under section 5 of this Act to be paid out of the deceased's net estate, he shall not be under any liability by reason of that estate not being sufficient to make the payment, unless at the time of making the payment he has reasonable cause to believe that the estate is not sufficient.

(3) Where a deceased person entered into a contract by which he agreed to leave by his will any sum of money or other property to any person or by which he agreed that a sum of money or other property would be paid or transferred to any person out of his estate, then, if the personal representative of the deceased has reason to believe that the deceased entered into the contract with the intention of defeating an application for financial provision under this Act, he may, notwithstanding anything in that contract, postpone the payment of that sum of money or the transfer of that property until the expiration of the period of six months from the date on which representation with respect to the estate of the deceased is first taken out or, if during that period an application is made for an order under section 2 of this Act, until the determination of the proceedings on that application.

Commentary

Subsection (1) has the effect that personal representatives can distribute without having to worry about the court extending time for an application or varying an order under s 6. Even if an application is made within the six-month time limit, there is no hard and fast rule that the personal representatives cannot distribute. Everything will depend on the circumstances and they can seek the consent of the beneficiaries and the applicant to distribute part of the estate, or can apply to the court for directions, see *Re Ralphs* [1968] 1 WLR 1522. Subsection (3) protects the personal representatives from failing to distribute where there is a contract which might be intended to defeat the application of the I(PFD)A 1975 (as to which see s 11 above).

[337]

21, 22 . . .

. . .

Amendment

Section 21 repealed by the Civil Evidence Act 1995, s 15(2), Sch 2.
Section 22 repealed by the Administration of Justice Act 1982, s 75, Sch 9, Pt I.

[338]

23 Determination of date on which representation was first taken out

In considering for the purposes of this Act when representation with respect to the estate of a deceased person was first taken out, a grant limited to settled land or to trust property shall be left out of account, and a grant limited to real estate or to personal estate shall be left out of account unless a grant limited to the remainder of the estate has previously been made or is made at the same time.

Commentary

Other grants which are limited and do not permit distribution are left out of account for the purposes of the I(PFD)A 1975, see *Re Johnson* [1987] CLY 3882.

[339]

24 Effect of this Act on s 46(1)(vi)of Administration of Estates Act 1925

Section 46(1)(vi) of the Administration of Estates Act 1925, in so far as it provides for the devolution of property on the Crown, the Duchy of Lancaster or the Duke of Cornwall as bona vacantia, shall have effect subject to the provisions of this Act.

Commentary

For an example of a case where the estate passed as bona vacantia and an application was made under the I(PFD)A 1975, see *Cameron v Treasury Solicitor* [1996] 2 FLR 138. For Administration of Estates Act 1925, s 46(i)(iv) see **[221]**.

[340]

25 Interpretation

(1) In this Act—

"beneficiary", in relation to the estate of a deceased person, means—

(a) a person who under the will of the deceased or under the law relating to intestacy is beneficially interested in the estate or would be so interested if an order had not been made under this Act, and

(b) a person who has received any sum of money or other property which by virtue of section 8(1) or 8(2) of this Act is treated as part of the net estate of the deceased or would have received that sum or other property if an order had not been made under this Act;

"child" includes an illegitimate child and a child en ventre sa mere at the death of the deceased;

"the court" [unless the context otherwise requires] means the High Court, or where a county court has jurisdiction by virtue of section 22 of this Act, a county court;

["former civil partner" means a person whose civil partnership with the deceased was during the lifetime of the deceased either—

(a) dissolved or annulled by an order made under the law of any part of the British Islands, or

(b) dissolved or annulled in any country or territory outside the British Islands by a dissolution or annulment which is entitled to be recognised as valid by the law of England and Wales;]

[["former spouse"] means a person whose marriage with the deceased was during the lifetime of the deceased either—

(a) dissolved or annulled by *a decree* [an order or decree] of divorce or a decree of nullity of marriage granted under the law of any part of the British Islands, or

(b) dissolved or annulled in any country or territory outside the British Islands by a divorce or annulment which is entitled to be recognised as valid by the law of England and Wales;]

"net estate", in relation to a deceased person, means—

(a) all property of which the deceased had power to dispose by his will (otherwise than by virtue of a special power of appointment) less the amount of his funeral, testamentary and administration expenses, debts and liabilities, including any inheritance tax payable out of his estate on his death;

(b) any property in respect of which the deceased held a general power of appointment (not being a power exercisable by will) which has not been exercised;

(c) any sum of money or other property which is treated for the purposes of this Act as part of the net estate of the deceased by virtue of section 8(1) or (2) of this Act;

(d) any property which is treated for the purposes of this Act as part of the net estate of the deceased by virtue of an order made under section 9 of the Act;

(e) any sum of money or other property which is, by reason of a disposition or contract made by the deceased, ordered under section 10 or 11 of this Act to be provided for the purpose of the making of financial provision under this Act;

"property" includes any chose in action;

"reasonable financial provision" has the meaning assigned to it by section 1 of this Act;

"valuable consideration" does not include marriage or a promise of marriage;

"will" includes codicil.

(2) For the purposes of paragraph (a) of the definition of "net estate" in subsection (1) above a person who is not of full age and capacity shall be treated as having power to dispose by will of all property of which he would have had power to dispose by will if he had been of full age and capacity.

(3) Any reference in this Act to provision out of the net estate of a deceased person includes a reference to provision extending to the whole of that estate.

(4) For the purposes of this Act any reference to a [spouse,] wife or husband shall be treated as including a reference to a person who in good faith entered into a void marriage with the deceased unless either—

(a) the marriage of the deceased and that person was dissolved or annulled during the lifetime of the deceased and the dissolution or annulment is recognised by the law of England and Wales, or

(b) that person has during the lifetime of the deceased [formed a subsequent marriage or civil partnership].

[(4A) For the purposes of this Act any reference to a civil partner shall be treated as including a reference to a person who in good faith formed a void civil partnership with the deceased unless either—

(a) the civil partnership between the deceased and that person was dissolved or annulled during the lifetime of the deceased and the dissolution or annulment is recognised by the law of England and Wales, or

(b) that person has during the lifetime of the deceased formed a subsequent civil partnership or marriage.

(5) Any reference in this Act to the formation of, or to a person who has formed, a subsequent marriage or civil partnership includes (as the case may be) a reference to the formation of, or to a person who has formed, a marriage or civil partnership which is by law void or voidable.

(5A) The formation of a marriage or civil partnership shall be treated for the purposes of this Act as the formation of a subsequent marriage or civil partnership, in relation to either of the spouses or civil partners, notwithstanding that the previous marriage or civil partnership of that spouse or civil partner was void or voidable.]

(6) Any reference in this Act to an order or decree made under the Matrimonial Causes Act 1973 or under any section of that Act shall be construed as including a reference to an order or decree which is deemed to have been made under that Act or under that section thereof, as the case may be.

[(6A) Any reference in this Act to an order made under, or under any provision of, the Civil Partnership Act 2004 shall be construed as including a reference to anything which is deemed to be an order made (as the case may be) under that Act or provision.]

(7) Any reference in this Act to any enactment is a reference to that enactment as amended by or under any subsequent enactment.

Amendment

Sub-s (1): in definition "the court" words "unless the context otherwise requires" in square brackets inserted by the Matrimonial and Family Proceedings Act 1984, s 8.
Sub-s (1): definition "former civil partner" inserted by the Civil Partnership Act 2004, s 71, Sch 4, Pt 2, para 27(1), (3).
Sub-s (1): definition "former spouse" (previously ""former wife" or "former husband"") substituted by the Matrimonial and Family Proceedings Act 1984, s 25.
Sub-s (1): in definition "former spouse" (previously ""former wife" and "former husband"") words ""former spouse"" in square brackets substituted by the Civil Partnership Act 2004, s 71, Sch 4, Pt 2, para 27(1), (2).
Sub-s (1): in definition "former spouse" in para (a) words "a decree" in italics repealed and subsequent words in square brackets substituted by the Family Law Act 1996, s 66(1), Sch 8, para 27(8), as from a day to be appointed; for savings see s 66(2), Sch 9, para 5 thereof.
Sub-s (4): word "spouse," in square brackets inserted by the Civil Partnership Act 2004, s 71, Sch 4, Pt 2, para 27(1), (4)(a).
Sub-s (4): in para (b) words "formed a subsequent marriage or civil partnership" in square brackets substituted by the Civil Partnership Act 2004, s 71, Sch 4, Pt 2, para 27(1), (4)(b).
Sub-ss (4A), (5), (5A): substituted, for sub-s (5) as originally enacted, by the Civil Partnership Act 2004, s 71, Sch 4, Pt 2, para 27(1), (5).
Sub-s (6A): inserted by the Civil Partnership Act 2004, s 71, Sch 4, Pt 2, para 27(1), (6).

Commentary

As to the definition of the Court in sub-s (1) County Courts now have unlimited jurisdiction in respect of applications under the Act. As for the High Court, proceedings can be brought in either the Chancery or Family Divisions.
As to a void marriage entered into in good faith under sub-s (4) see *Gandhi v Patel* [2002] 1 FLR 603.

[341]

26 Consequential amendments, repeals and transitional provisions

(1) . . .

(2) Subject to the provisions of this section, the enactments specified in the Schedule to this Act are hereby repealed to the extent specified in the third column of the Schedule; . . .

(3) The repeal of the said enactment shall not affect their operation in relation to any application made thereunder (whether before or after the commencement of this Act) with reference to the death of any person who died before the commencement of this Act.

(4) Without prejudice to the provisions of section 38 of the Interpretation Act 1889 (which relates to the effect of repeals) nothing in any repeal made by this Act shall affect any order made or direction given under any enactment repealed by this Act, and, subject to the provisions of this Act, every such order or direction (other than an order made under section 4A of the Inheritance (Family Provision) Act 1938 or section 28A of the Matrimonial Causes Act 1965) shall, if it is in force at the commencement of this Act or is made by virtue of subsection (2) above, continue in force as if it had been made under section 2(1)(a) of this Act, and for the purposes of section 6(7) of this Act the court in exercising its powers under that section in relation to an order continued in force by this subsection shall be required to have regard to any change in any of the circumstances to which the court would have

been required to have regard when making that order if the order had been made with reference to the death of any person who died after the commencement of this Act.

Amendment
Sub-ss (1), (2): words omitted amend the Matrimonial Causes Act 1973, s 36, Sch 2, para 5(2).

27 Short title, commencement and extent

(1) This Act may be cited as the Inheritance (Provision for Family and Dependants) Act 1975.

(2) This Act does not extend to Scotland or Northern Ireland.

(3) This Act shall come into force on 1st April 1976.

[342]

SCHEDULE
ENACTMENTS REPEALED

Section 26

Chapter	*Short Title*	*Extent of Repeal*
1938 c 72	The Inheritance (Family Provision) Act 1938	The whole Act.
1952 c 64	The Intestates' Estates Act 1952	Section 7 and Schedule 3.
1965 c 72	The Matrimonial Causes Act 1965	Section 26 to 28(A) and section 25(4) and (5) as applied by section 28(2).
1966 c 35	The Family Provision Act 1966	The whole Act, except section 1 and subsections (1) and (3) of section 10.
1969 c 46	The Family Law Reform Act 1969	Sections 5(1) and 18.
1970 c 31	The Administration of Justice Act 1970	In Schedule 2, paragraph 16.
1970 c 33	The Law Reform (Miscellaneous Provisions) Act 1970	Section 6.
1970 c 45	The Matrimonial Proceedings and Property Act 1970	Section 36.
1971 c 23	The Courts Act 1971	Section 45(1)(a).
1973 c 18	The Matrimonial Causes Act 1973	In section 50, in subsection (1)(a) the words from "and sections 26" to the end of the paragraph, in subsection (1)(d) the words "or sections 26 to 28A of the Matrimonial Causes Act 1965" and in subsection (2)(a) the words "or under section 26 or 27 of the Matrimonial Causes Act 1965".
		In Schedule 2, paragraph 5(1) and in paragraph 12 the words "(a) sections 26 to 28A of the Matrimonial Causes Act 1965".
1975 c 7	The Finance Act 1975	In Schedule 12, paragraph 6.

[343]

SUPREME COURT ACT 1981 [SENIOR COURTS ACT 1981]

1981 Chapter 54

ARRANGEMENT OF SECTIONS

PART V
PROBATE CAUSES AND MATTERS

An Act to consolidate with amendments the Supreme Court of Judicature (Consolidation) Act 1925 and other enactments relating to the Supreme Court in England and Wales and the administration of justice therein; to repeal certain obsolete or unnecessary enactments so relating; to amend Part VIII of the Mental Health Act 1959, the Courts-Martial (Appeals) Act 1968, the Arbitration Act 1979 and the law relating to county courts; and for connected purposes

[28th July 1981]

General Note
The following sections establish the probate jurisdiction of the High Court.

Amendment
Words "Supreme Court Act 1981" in italics repealed and subsequent words in square brackets substituted, from a date to be appointed, by the Constitutional Reform Act 2005, s 59(5), Sch 11, Pt 1, para 1.

PART V
PROBATE CAUSES AND MATTERS

PROCEDURE IN PROBATE REGISTRIES IN RELATION TO GRANTS OF REPRESENTATION

105 Applications

Applications for grants of probate or administration and for the revocation of grants may be made to—

(a) the Principal Registry of the Family Division (in this Part referred to as "the Principal Registry"); or

(b) a district probate registry.

Commentary

For the procedure on applying for grants see the Non-Contentious Probate Rules 1987, SI 1987/2024 **[Appendix V].**

[344]

106 Grants by district probate registrars

(1) Any grant made by a district probate registrar shall be made in the name of the High Court under the seal used in the registry.

(2)–(4) . . .

Amendment

Sub-ss (2)–(4): repealed by the Administration of Justice Act 1985, ss 51, 67(2), Sch 8, Part III.

Commentary

There is no territorial limit to the jurisdiction of the district probate registries and application for a grant can be made to any of them, except that grants pending suit can only be issued by the Principal Registry.

[345]

107 No grant where conflicting applications

Subject to probate rules, no grant in respect of the estate, or part of the estate, of a deceased person shall be made out of the Principal Registry or any district probate registry on any application if, at any time before the making of a grant, it appears to the registrar concerned that some other application has been made in respect of that estate or, as the case may be, that part of it and has not been either refused or withdrawn.

Commentary

If there is a dispute as to who should take a grant then a summons can come before the Registrar under the Non-Contentious Probate Rules 1987, SI 1987/2024, r 27(6) **[Appendix V]**. In the event that there is no other good reason for refusing a grant to an applicant and both are equally entitled, the first to apply in point of time will usually prevail.

[346]

108 Caveats

(1) A caveat against a grant of probate or administration may be entered in the Principal Registry or in any district probate registry.

(2) On a caveat being entered in a district probate registry, the district probate registrar shall immediately send a copy of it to the Principal Registry to be entered among the caveats in that Registry.

Commentary

A caveat is a notice in writing lodged at the Principal Registry, or one of the district registries, which prevents a grant being issued and is often the opening salvo in a contentious probate dispute. For the practice in relation to caveats, see the Non-Contentious Probate Rules 1987, SI 1987/2024, r 44 **[Appendix V]**. A caveat prevents any grant apart from a grant ad colligenda bona or a grant pending suit being sealed.

[347]

109 Refusal of grant where inheritance tax unpaid

[(1) No grant shall be made, and no grant made outside the United Kingdom shall be resealed, except—

(a) on the production of information or documents under regulations under section 256(1)(aa) of the Inheritance Tax Act 1984 (excepted estates); or

(b) on the production of an account prepared in pursuance of that Act showing by means of such receipt or certification as may be prescribed by the Commissioners either—

(i) that the inheritance tax payable on the delivery of the account has been paid; or

(ii) that no such tax is so payable.]

(2) Arrangements may be made between the President of the Family Division and the Commissioners providing for the purposes of [subsection (1)(b)] in such cases as may be specified in the arrangements that the receipt or certification of an account may be dispensed with or that some other document may be substituted for the account required by [the Inheritance Tax Act 1984].

[(2A) In this section and the following section, "the Commissioners" means the Commissioners of Inland Revenue.]

(3) . . .

Amendment

Sub-s (1): substituted by the Finance Act 2004, s 294(1)(a).
Sub-s (2): words "subsection (1)(b)" in square brackets substituted by the Finance Act 2004, s 294(1)(b).
Sub-s (2): words "the Inheritance Tax Act 1984" in square brackets substituted by the Inheritance Tax Act 1984, ss 274, 276, Sch 8, para 20.
Sub-s (2A): inserted by the Finance Act 2004, s 294(1)(c).
Sub-s (3): repealed by the Finance Act 2004, ss 294(1)(d), 326, Sch 42, Pt 4(1).

Commentary

The Inheritance Tax Act 1984, s 216 provides for an account to be delivered to the Commissioners of Inland Revenue. Regulations have been made under the Inheritance Tax Act 1984, s 256 dispensing with the need for an account in certain cases (see the Inheritance Tax (Delivery of Accounts)(Excepted Estates) Regulations 2004, SI 2004/2543, as amended by SI 2006/2141). A return does not have to be delivered if the estate is below the inheritance tax threshold (in most cases the nil rate band which is £312,000 for 2008/09).

[348]

110 Documents to be delivered to Commissioners of Inland Revenue

Subject to any arrangements which may from time to time be made between the President of the Family Division and the Commissioners, the Principal Registry and every district probate registry shall, within such period after a grant as the President may direct, deliver to the Commissioners or their proper officer the following documents—

(a) in the case of a grant of probate or of administration with the will annexed, a copy of the will;

(b) in every case, such certificate or note of the grant as the Commissioners may require.

Commentary

This section and the previous one establish the link between the obtaining of a grant and the delivery of the inheritance tax account.

[349]

111 Records of grants

(1) There shall continue to be kept records of all grants which are made in the Principal Registry or in any district probate registry.

(2) Those records shall be in such form, and shall contain such particulars, as the President of the Family Division may direct.

Commentary

A calendar of grants made is available for public inspection. It details the full name of the deceased, date of death and last address, the type of grant, the registry at which it was made and the gross value of the estate.

[350]

POWERS OF COURT IN RELATION TO PERSONAL REPRESENTATIVES

112 Summons to executor to prove or renounce

The High Court may summon any person named as executor in a will to prove, or renounce probate of, the will, and to do such other things concerning the will as the court had power to order such a person to do immediately before the commencement of this Act.

Commentary

If the court uses this procedure to cite an executor to take a grant and if he does not enter an appearance to the citation, his executorship automatically ceases, see the Administration of Estates Act 1925, s 5 **[185].**

[351]

113 Power of court to sever grant

(1) Subject to subsection (2), the High Court may grant probate or administration in respect of any part of the estate of a deceased person, limited in any way the court thinks fit.

(2) Where the estate of a deceased person is known to be insolvent, the grant of representation to it shall not be severed under subsection (1) except as regards a trust estate in which he had no beneficial interest.

Commentary

This section provides the jurisdiction for the court to make limited grants and to deal with situations where the deceased has appointed different executors for different parts of his estate. See also the Administration of Estates Act 1925, s 22 **[197]** in relation to special executors for settled land.

[352]

114 Number of personal representatives

(1) Probate or administration shall not be granted by the High Court to more than four persons in respect of the same part of the estate of a deceased person.

(2) Where under a will or intestacy any beneficiary is a minor or a life interest arises, any grant of administration by the High Court shall be made either to a trust corporation (with or without an individual) or to not less than two individuals, unless it appears to the court to be expedient in all the circumstances to appoint an individual as sole administrator.

(3) For the purpose of determining whether a minority or life interest arises in any particular case, the court may act on such evidence as may be prescribed.

(4) If at any time during the minority of a beneficiary or the subsistence of a life interest under a will or intestacy there is only one personal representative (not being a trust corporation), the High Court may, on the application of any person interested or the guardian or receiver of any such person, and in accordance with probate rules,

appoint one or more additional personal representatives to act while the minority or life interest subsists and until the estate is fully administered.

(5) An appointment of an additional personal representative under subsection (4) to act with an executor shall not have the effect of including him in any chain of representation.

Commentary

Compare with the maximum number of trustees allowed under the Trustee Act 1925, s 34 **[103]**. Where a will appoints more than four executors, the first four named usually prove with power reserved to the others. Note that where there is a minority or life interest arising the court still has discretion to appoint a single executor (sub-s (2)) and can appoint an additional personal representative during the administration.

[353]

115 Grants to trust corporations

(1) The High Court may—

(a) where a trust corporation is named in a will as executor, grant probate to the corporation either solely or jointly with any other person named in the will as executor, as the case may require; or

(b) grant administration to a trust corporation, either solely or jointly with another person;

and the corporation may act accordingly as executor or administrator, as the case may be.

(2) Probate or administration shall not be granted to any person as nominee of a trust corporation.

(3) Any officer authorised for the purpose by a trust corporation or its directors or governing body may, on behalf of the corporation, swear affidavits, give security and do any other act which the court may require with a view to the grant to the corporation of probate or administration; and the acts of an officer so authorised shall be binding on the corporation.

[(4) Subsections (1) to (3) shall also apply in relation to any body which is exempt from the provisions of section 23(1) of the Solicitors Act 1974 (unqualified persons not to prepare papers for probate etc) by virtue of any of paragraphs (e) to (h) of subsection (2) of that section.]

Amendment

Sub-s (4): prospectively inserted by the Courts and Legal Services Act 1990, s 54(2), as from a day to be appointed.

Commentary

For the meaning of "trust corporation" in this context see s 128 below. For the procedure on the application of a grant by a trust corporation see the Non-Contentious Probate Rules 1987, SI 1987/2024, r 36 **[Appendix V]**. Corporations which are not trust corporations cannot take a grant of probate in their own name. The Bank of Ireland was held to be a trust corporation for these purposes in accordance with EEC law, see *Re Barlow* [1977] 2 WLR 773.

[354]

116 Power of court to pass over prior claims to grant

(1) If by reason of any special circumstances it appears to the High Court to be necessary or expedient to appoint as administrator some person other than the person who, but for this section, would in accordance with probate rules have been entitled to the grant, the court may in its discretion appoint as administrator such person as it thinks expedient.

(2) Any grant of administration under this section may be limited in any way the court thinks fit.

Commentary
Examples of special circumstances include where the person entitled to the grant cannot be found: *Re Hall* [1950] P 302; where the person entitled has murdered the deceased: *Re Crippen's Estate* [1911] P 108; where the person entitled is in prison: *Re S's Estate* [1968] P 302; where the person is bankrupt: *Re Mathew* [1984] 1 WLR 1011.

[355]

117 Administration pending suit

(1) Where any legal proceedings concerning the validity of the will of a deceased person, or for obtaining, recalling or revoking any grant, are pending, the High Court may grant administration of the estate of the deceased person in question to an administrator pending suit, who shall, subject to subsection (2), have all the rights, duties and powers of a general administrator.

(2) An administrator pending suit shall be subject to the immediate control of the court and act under its direction; and, except in such circumstances as may be prescribed, no distribution of the estate, or any part of the estate, of the deceased person in question shall be made by such an administrator without the leave of the court.

(3) The court may, out of the estate of the deceased, assign an administrator pending suit such reasonable remuneration as it thinks fit.

Commentary
The application for an administrator pending suit is made in the proceedings which are pending. A caveat is not pending proceedings for these purposes, see *Salter v Salter* [1896] P 291. The procedure on an application can be found in the Civil Procedure Rules 1998, SI 1998/3132, Pt 57 PD 8.

[356]

118 Effect of appointment of minor as executor

Where a testator by his will appoints a minor to be an executor, the appointment shall not operate to vest in the minor the estate, or any part of the estate, of the testator, or to constitute him a personal representative for any purpose, unless and until probate is granted to him in accordance with probate rules.

Commentary
See Non-Contentious Probate Rules 1987, SI 1987/2024, rr 32 and 33 **[Appendix V]**.

[357]

119 Administration with will annexed

(1) Administration with the will annexed shall be granted, subject to and in accordance with probate rules, in every class of case in which the High Court had power to make such a grant immediately before the commencement of this Act.

(2) Where administration with the will annexed is granted, the will of the deceased shall be performed and observed in the same manner as if probate of it had been granted to an executor.

Commentary
This section applies where the deceased died testate but with no one to prove the will, either because they have renounced or predeceased. See Non-Contentious Probate Rules 1987, SI 1987/2024, r 20 for the practice and who is entitled to apply **[Appendix V]**.

[358]

120 Power to require administrators to produce sureties

(1) As a condition of granting administration to any person the High Court may, subject to the following provisions of this section and subject to and in accordance with probate rules, require one or more sureties to guarantee that they will make good, within any limit imposed by the court on the total liability of the surety or sureties, any loss which any person interested in the administration of the estate of the deceased may suffer in consequence of a breach by the administrator of his duties as such.

(2) A guarantee given in pursuance of any such requirement shall enure for the benefit of every person interested in the administration of the estate of the deceased as if contained in a contract under seal made by the surety or sureties with every such person and, where there are two or more sureties, as if they had bound themselves jointly and severally.

(3) No action shall be brought on any such guarantee without the leave of the High Court.

(4) Stamp duty shall not be chargeable on any such guarantee.

(5) This section does not apply where administration is granted to the Treasury Solicitor, the Official Solicitor, the Public Trustee, the Solicitor for the affairs of the Duchy of Lancaster or the Duchy of Cornwall or the Crown Solicitor for Northern Ireland, or to the consular officer of a foreign state to which section 1 of the Consular Conventions Act 1949 applies, or in such other cases as may be prescribed.

Commentary

Although this statutory jurisdiction remains, the former r 38 of the Non-Contentious Probate Rules 1954, SI 1954/796, which required sureties to guarantee the performance of an administrator's duties, was revoked by the Non-Contentious Probate Rules 1987, SI 1987/2024, r 69 **[Appendix V]** as from 1 January 1988 and has not been reinstated.

[359]

REVOCATION OF GRANTS AND CANCELLATION OF RESEALING AT INSTANCE OF COURT

121 Revocation of grants and cancellation of resealing at instance of court

(1) Where it appears to the High Court that a grant either ought not to have been made or contains an error, the court may call in the grant and, if satisfied that it would be revoked at the instance of a party interested, may revoke it.

(2) A grant may be revoked under subsection (1) without being called in, if it cannot be called in.

(3) Where it appears to the High Court that a grant resealed under the Colonial Probates Acts 1892 and 1927 ought not to have been resealed, the court may call in the relevant document and, if satisfied that the resealing would be cancelled at the instance of a party interested, may cancel the resealing.

In this and the following subsection "the relevant document" means the original grant or, where some other document was sealed by the court under those Acts, that document.

(4) A resealing may be cancelled under subsection (3) without the relevant document being called in, if it cannot be called in.

Commentary

Usually a grant will be revoked on the application of a person interested usually with the consent of the grantee or after a probate claim, but the court here has power to revoke of its own motion. As to resealing of grants referred to in sub-ss (4) and (5) see the Colonial Probates Acts 1892 and 1927 **[45, 237]**.

[360]

ANCILLARY POWERS OF COURT

122 Examination of person with knowledge of testamentary document

(1) Where it appears that there are reasonable grounds for believing that any person has knowledge of any document which is or purports to be a testamentary document, the High Court may, whether or not any legal proceedings are pending, order him to attend for the purpose of being examined in open court.

(2) The court may—

- (a) require any person who is before it in compliance with an order under subsection (1) to answer any question relating to the document concerned; and
- (b) if appropriate, order him to bring in the document in such manner as the court may direct.

(3) Any person who, having been required by the court to do so under this section, fails to attend for examination, answer any question or bring in any document shall be guilty of contempt of court.

Commentary

Application for an order under this section if there are not proceedings pending is made in accordance with Non-Contentious Probate Rules 1987, SI 1987/2024, r 50(2) **[Appendix V]**. If proceedings are pending, then application is by application notice in accordance with the Civil Procedure Rules 1998, SI 1998/2024, Pt 23 and should be served on the person against whom the order is sought (see Civil Procedure Rules 1998, SI 1998/2024, Pt 57 PD 7.1 for the procedure generally).

[361]

123 Subpoena to bring in testamentary document

Where it appears that any person has in his possession, custody or power any document which is or purports to be a testamentary document, the High Court may, whether or not any legal proceedings are pending, issue a subpoena requiring him to bring in the document in such manner as the court may in the subpoena direct.

Commentary

A subpoena is now known under the Civil Procedure Rules 1998, SI 1998/2024 as a witness summons. Application for an order under this section if there are not proceedings pending is made in accordance with Non-Contentious Probate Rules 1987, SI 1987/3132, r 50(2) **[Appendix V]**. If proceedings are pending, then application is by application notice in accordance with the Civil Procedure Rules 1998, SI 1998/2024, Pt 23 and without notice (see the Civil Procedure Rules 1998, SI 1998/2024, Pt 57, PD.7.2 and for the procedure generally).

[362]

PROVISIONS AS TO DOCUMENTS

124 Place for deposit of original wills and other documents

All original wills and other documents which are under the control of the High Court in the Principal Registry or in any district probate registry shall be deposited and preserved in such places [as may be provided for in directions given in accordance with Part 1 of Schedule 2 to the Constitutional Reform Act 2005]; and any wills or other documents so deposited shall, subject to the control of the High Court and to probate rules, be open to inspection.

Amendment

Words from "as may be" to "Constitutional Reform Act 2005" in square brackets substituted by the Constitutional Reform Act 2005, s 13(2), Sch 2, Pt 2, para 5.

Commentary
A will was not allowed out of the jurisdiction even in the custody of an official of the Supreme Court because of the duty to "preserve" under this section, see *Re Greer* (1929) 45 TLR 362. This section does not simply enable the Attorney-General to apply for a will to be unsealed by a member of the public, see: *Brown v HM Queen Elizabeth the Queen Mother* [2008] EWCA Civ 56 where the Court of Appeal described the process under this section as not transparent.

[363]

125 Copies of wills and grants

An office copy, or a sealed and certified copy, of any will or part of a will open to inspection under section 124 or of any grant may, on payment of [the fee prescribed by an order under section 92 of the Courts Act 2003 (fees)], be obtained—

(a) from the registry in which in accordance with section 124 the will or documents relating to the grant are preserved; or

(b) where in accordance with that section the will or such documents are preserved in some place other than a registry, from the Principal Registry; or

(c) subject to the approval of the Senior Registrar of the Family Division, from the Principal Registry in any case where the will was proved in or the grant was issued from a district probate registry.

Amendment
Words "the fee prescribed by an order under section 92 of the Courts Act 2003 (fees)" in square brackets substituted by the Courts Act 2003, s 109(1), Sch 8, para 262(a).

Commentary
Application can be made in person or by post to the Principal Registry which holds all grants whether issued by it or a district registry. If by post the request will be forwarded to the York district sub-registry, see *Practice Direction* [1990] 3 All ER 734. Application can be made by post to the district registries if it is known that the grant emanated from there. See the limit on the right to inspect in the commentary to s 124.

[364]

126 Depositories for wills of living persons

(1) There shall be provided, under the control and direction of the High Court, safe and convenient depositories for the custody of the wills of living persons; and any person may deposit his will in such a depository on payment of [the fee prescribed by an order under section 92 of the Courts Act 2003 (fees)] and subject to such conditions as may be prescribed by regulations made by the President of the Family Division with the concurrence of the Lord Chancellor.

(2) Any regulations made under this section shall be made by statutory instrument which shall be laid before Parliament after being made; and the Statutory Instruments Act 1946 shall apply to a statutory instrument containing regulations under this section in like manner as if they had been made by a Minister of the Crown.

Amendment
Prospectively repealed by the Administration of Justice Act 1982, s 75, Sch 9, Part I, as from a day to be appointed.
Sub-s (1): words "the fee prescribed by an order under section 92 of the Courts Act 2003 (fees)" in square brackets substituted by the Courts Act 2003, s 109(1), Sch 8, para 262(b).

Commentary
Current regulations are the Wills (Deposit for Safe Custody) Regulations 1978, SI 1978/3032. Wills can be deposited at the Principal Registry in person or by post or at the district registries in person by the testator or his agent.

[365]

PROBATE RULES

127 Probate rules

(1) [Rules of court (in this Part referred to as "probate rules") may be made in accordance with Part 1 of Schedule 1 to the Constitutional Reform Act 2005 for regulating] and prescribing the practice and procedure of the High Court with respect to non-contentious or common form probate business.

(2) Without prejudice to the generality of subsection (1), probate rules may make provision for regulating the classes of persons entitled to grants of probate or administration in particular circumstances and the relative priorities of their claims thereto.

(3) . . .

Amendment

Sub-s (1): words from "Rules of court" to "Constitutional Reform Act 2005 for regulating" in square brackets substituted by the Constitutional Reform Act 2005, s 12(2), Sch 1, Pt 2, paras 11, 12(1), (2).

Sub-s (3): repealed by the Constitutional Reform Act 2005, ss 12(2), 146, Sch 1, Pt 2, paras 11, 12(1), (3), Sch 18, Pt 1.

Commentary

Currently Non-Contentious Probate Rules 1987, SI 1987/2024, as amended **[Appendix V]**.

[366]

INTERPRETATION OF PART V AND OTHER PROBATE PROVISIONS

128 Interpretation of Part V and other probate provisions

In this Part, and in the other provisions of this Act relating to probate causes and matters, unless the context otherwise requires—

"administration" includes all letters of administration of the effects of deceased persons, whether with or without a will annexed, and whether granted for general, special or limited purposes;

"estate" means real and personal estate, and "real estate" includes—

(a) chattels real and land in possession, remainder or reversion and every interest in or over land to which the deceased person was entitled at the time of his death, and

(b) real estate held on trust or by way of mortgage or security, but not . . . money secured or charged on land;

"grant" means a grant of probate or administration;

"non-contentious or common form probate business" means the business of obtaining probate and administration where there is no contention as to the right thereto, including—

(a) the passing of probates and administrations through the High Court in contentious cases where the contest has been terminated,

(b) all business of a non-contentious nature in matters of testacy and intestacy not being proceedings in any action, and

(c) the business of lodging caveats against the grant of probate or administration;

"Principal Registry" means the Principal Registry of the Family Division;

"probate rules" means rules of court made under section 127;

"trust corporation" means the Public Trustee or a corporation either appointed by the court in any particular case to be a trustee or authorised by rules made under section 4(3) of the Public Trustee Act 1906 to act as a custodian trustee;

"will" includes a nuncupative will and any testamentary document of which probate may be granted.

Amendment

In definition "real estate" words omitted repealed by the Trusts of Land and Appointment of Trustees Act 1996, s 25(2), Sch 4; for savings in relation to entailed interests created before the commencement of that Act, and savings consequential upon the abolition of the doctrine of conversion, see s 25(4), (5) thereof.

[367]

FORFEITURE ACT 1982

1982 Chapter 34

ARRANGEMENT OF SECTIONS

An Act to provide for relief for persons guilty of unlawful killing from forfeiture of inheritance and other rights; to enable such persons to apply for financial provision out of the deceased's estate; to provide for the question whether pension and social security benefits have been forfeited to be determined by the Social Security commissioners; and for connected purposes

[13th July 1982]

General Note

The Forfeiture Act 1982 (FA 1982) was introduced to provide relief against the rule that a person who is guilty of a criminal act which causes the death of another cannot benefit under his estate. It also deals with the question of the forfeiture of social security benefits.

1 The "forfeiture rule"

(1) In this Act, the "forfeiture rule" means the rule of public policy which in certain circumstances precludes a person who has unlawfully killed another from acquiring a benefit in consequence of the killing.

(2) References in this Act to a person who has unlawfully killed another include a reference to a person who has unlawfully aided, abetted, counselled or procured the death of that other and references in this Act to unlawful killing shall be interpreted accordingly.

Commentary

There are numerous examples in the case law of the application of the rule but see *Re Sigsworth Bedford v Bedford* [1935] Ch 89; *Royse v Royse* [1985] Ch 22 and *Dunbar v Plant* [1997] 4 All ER 289 (aiding and abetting a suicide). It seems clear now that, contrary to some authorities, violence is not needed before the rule applies.

[368]

2 Power to modify the rule

(1) Where a court determines that the forfeiture rule has precluded a person (in this section referred to as "the offender") who has unlawfully killed another from

acquiring any interest in property mentioned in subsection (4) below, the court may make an order under this section modifying the effect of that rule.

(2) The court shall not make an order under this section modifying the effect of the forfeiture rule in any case unless it is satisfied that, having regard to the conduct of the offender and of the deceased and to such other circumstances as appear to the court to be material, the justice of the case requires the effect of the rule to be so modified in that case.

(3) In any case where a person stands convicted of an offence of which unlawful killing is an element, the court shall not make an order under this section modifying the effect of the forfeiture rule in that case unless proceedings for the purpose are brought before the expiry of the period of three months beginning with his conviction.

(4) The interests in property referred to in subsection (1) above are—

- (a) any beneficial interest in property which (apart from the forfeiture rule) the offender would have acquired—
  - (i) under the deceased's will (including, as respects Scotland, any writing having testamentary effect) or the law relating to intestacy or by way of ius relicti, ius relictae or legitim;
  - (ii) on the nomination of the deceased in accordance with the provisions of any enactment;
  - (iii) as a donatio mortis causa made by the deceased; or
  - (iv) under a special destination (whether relating to heritable or moveable property); or
- (b) any beneficial interest in property which (apart from the forfeiture rule) the offender would have acquired in consequence of the death of the deceased, being property which, before the death, was held on trust for any person.

(5) An order under this section may modify the effect of the forfeiture rule in respect of any interest in property to which the determination referred to in subsection (1) above relates and may do so in either or both of the following ways, that is—

- (a) where there is more than one such interest, by excluding the application of the rule in respect of any (but not all) of those interests; and
- (b) in the case of any such interest in property, by excluding the application of the rule in respect of part of the property.

(6) On the making of an order under this section, the forfeiture rule shall have effect for all purposes (including purposes relating to anything done before the order is made) subject to the modifications made by the order.

(7) The court shall not make an order under this section modifying the effect of the forfeiture rule in respect of any interest in property which, in consequence of the rule, has been acquired before the coming into force of this section by a person other than the offender or a person claiming through him.

(8) In this section—

"property" includes any chose in action or incorporeal moveable property; and
"will" includes codicil.

Commentary

The discretion in sub-s (2) above is of the widest kind, see *Dunbar v Plant* [1997] 4 All ER 289. There the Court of Appeal modified the rule in relation to the whole of the property which the applicant would have inherited but note sub-s (5). For other cases where the court has considered its discretion under this section see: *Re K* [1986] Ch 180; *Re H* [1991] 1 FLR 144 and *Re S* [1996] 1 WLR 235 all of which were unopposed. For a case where the court refused to modify the rule see *Dalton v Latham* [2003] NPC 1009. The jurisdiction cannot be exercised if the property has been acquired by someone other than the offender (sub-s (7)). As to the property covered, a putative right to be considered under public service pension scheme was not included and there was not other residual jurisdiction in the court to modify the forfeiture rule apart from under this Act, see: *Glover v Staffordshire Police Authority* (2007) ICR 661. The time limit for an application is strict and it is not a breach of human rights legislation for it to be so, see: *Land v Land* [2007] 1 WLR 1009.

[369]

3 Application for financial provision not affected by the rule

(1) The forfeiture rule shall not be taken to preclude any person from making any application under a provision mentioned in subsection (2) below or the making of any order on the application.

(2) The provisions referred to in subsection (1) above are—

(a) any provision of the Inheritance (Provision for Family and Dependants) Act 1975;

[(b) sections 31(6) and 36(1) of the Matrimonial Causes Act 1973 (variation by court in England and Wales of periodical payments orders and maintenance agreements in respect of marriages);

(c) paragraphs 60(2) and 73(2) of Schedule 5 to the Civil Partnership Act 2004 (variation by court in England and Wales of periodical payments orders and maintenance agreements in respect of civil partnerships); and

(d) section 13(4) of the Family Law (Scotland) Act 1985 (variation etc of periodical allowances in respect of marriages and civil partnerships)].

Amendment

Sub-s (2): paras (b)-(d) substituted, for para (b) as originally enacted, by the Civil Partnership Act 2004, s 261(1), Sch 27, para 79.

Commentary

This section was recently considered in *Land v Land* [2007] 1 WLR 1009 where it was held that in the case of someone who loses their right to benefit from the estate of the deceased because of the forfeiture rule and who fails to make an application under the 1982 Act in time, they will still be able to apply under the 1975 Act.

[370]

4 Commissioner to decide whether rule applies to social security benefits

(1) Where a question arises as to whether, if a person were otherwise entitled to or eligible for any benefit or advantage under a relevant enactment, he would be precluded by virtue of the forfeiture rule from receiving the whole or part of the benefit or advantage, that question shall (notwithstanding anything in any relevant enactment) be determined by a Commissioner.

[(1A) Where a Commissioner determines that the forfeiture rule has precluded a person (in this section referred to as "the offender") who has unlawfully killed another from receiving the whole or part of any such benefit or advantage, the Commissioner may make a decision under this subsection modifying the effect of that rule and may do so whether the unlawful killing occurred before or after the coming into force of this subsection.

(1B) The Commission shall not make a decision under subsection (1A) above modifying the effect of the forfeiture rule in any case unless he is satisfied that, having regard to the conduct of the offender and of the deceased and to such other circumstances as appear to the Commissioner to be material, the justice of the case requires the effect of the rule to be so modified in that case.

(1C) Subject to subsection (1D) below, a decision under subsection (1A) above may modify the effect of the forfeiture rule in either or both of the following ways—

(a) so that it applies only in respect of a specified proportion of the benefit or advantage;

(b) so that it applies in respect of the benefit or advantage only for a specified period of time.

(1D) Such a decision may not modify the effect of the forfeiture rule so as to allow any person to receive the whole or any part of a benefit or advantage in respect of any period before the commencement of this subsection.

(1E) If the Commissioner thinks it expedient to do so, he may direct that his decision shall apply to any future claim for a benefit or advantage under a relevant enactment, on which a question such as is mentioned in subsection (1) above arises by reason of the same unlawful killing.

(1F) It is immaterial for the purposes of subsection (1E) above whether the claim is in respect of the same or a different benefit or advantage.

(1G) For the purpose of obtaining a decision whether the forfeiture rule should be modified the Secretary of State may refer to a Commissioner for review any determination of a question such as is mentioned in subsection (1) above that was made before the commencement of subsections (1A) to (1F) above (whether by a Commissioner or not) and shall do so if the offender requests him to refer such a determination.

(1H) Subsections (1A) to (1F) above shall have effect on a reference under subsection (1G) above as if in subsection (1A) the words "it has been determined" were substituted for the words "a Commissioner determines".]

(2) Regulations under this section may make such provision as appears to [the Lord Chancellor] to be necessary or expedient for carrying this section into effect; and (without prejudice to the generality of that) the regulations may, in relation to the question mentioned in subsection (1) above or any determination under that subsection [or any decision under subsection (1A) above]—

(a) apply any provision of any relevant enactment, with or without modifications, or exclude or contain provision corresponding to any such provision; and

(b) make provision for purposes corresponding to those for which provision may be made by regulations under *[section 59 of the Social Security Administration Act 1992]* [section 16 of the Social Security Act 1998] (matters relating to adjudication).

(3) The power to make regulations under this section shall be exercisable by statutory instrument which shall be subject to annulment in pursuance of a resolution of either House of Parliament.

(4) [Section 175(3) to (5) of the Social Security Contributions and Benefits Act 1992] (provision about extent of power to make regulations) shall apply to the power to make regulations conferred by this section as it applies to the power to make regulations conferred by that Act, but as if for references to that Act there were substituted references to this section.

(5) In this section—

"Commissioner" has the same meaning as in the *[Social Security Administration Act 1992]* [Chapter II of Part I of the Social Security Act 1998]; and

"relevant enactment" means any provision of the following and any instrument made by virtue of such a provision:

the Personal Injuries (Emergency Provisions) Act 1939,
the Pensions (Navy, Army, Air Force and Mercantile Marine) Act 1939,
the Polish Resettlement Act 1947,
[the Child Benefit Act 1975,
[the Social Security Acts 1975 to 1991]],
[the Social Security Contributions and Benefits Act 1992],

[section 1 of the Armed Forces (Pensions and Compensation) Act 2004,]
[the Pension Schemes Act 1993],

and any other enactment relating to pensions or social security prescribed by regulations under this section.

Amendment

Sub-ss (1A)-(1H): inserted by the Social Security Act 1986, s 76(2).
Sub-s (2): words "the Lord Chancellor" in square brackets substituted by SI 1984/1818, art 3.
Sub-s (2): words "or any decision under subsection (1A) above" in square brackets inserted by the Social Security Act 1986, s 76(3).
Sub-s (2): in para (b) words "section 59 of the Social Security Administration Act 1992" in square brackets substituted by the Social Security (Consequential Provisions) Act 1992, s 4, Sch 2, para 63(1).
Sub-s (2): in para (b) words "section 59 of the Social Security Administration Act 1992" in italics repealed and subsequent words in square brackets substituted by the Social Security Act 1998, s 86(1), Sch 7, para 11(1).
Sub-s (4): words in square brackets substituted by the Social Security (Consequential Provisions) Act 1992, s 4, Sch 2, para 63(2).
Sub-s (5): in definition "Commissioner" words "Social Security Administration Act 1992" in square brackets substituted by the Social Security (Consequential Provisions) Act 1992, s 4, Sch 2, para 63(3).
Sub-s (5): in definition "Commissioner" words "Social Security Administration Act 1992" in italics repealed and subsequent words in square brackets substituted by the Social Security Act 1998, s 86(1), Sch 7, para 11(2).
Sub-s (5): in definition "relevant enactment" words in square brackets beginning with the words "the Child Benefit Act 1975," substituted by the Social Security Act 1986, s 86, Sch 10, para 108(b).
Sub-s (5): in definition "relevant enactment" words "the Social Security Acts 1975 to 1991" in square brackets substituted by the Statutory Sick Pay Act 1991, s 3(1).
Sub-s (5): in definition "relevant enactment" words "the Social Security Contributions and Benefits Act 1992" in square brackets inserted by the Social Security (Consequential Provisions) Act 1992, s 4, Sch 2, para 63(3).
Sub-s (5): in definition "relevant enactment" words "section 1 of the Armed Forces (Pensions and Compensation) Act 2004," in square brackets inserted by the Armed Forces (Pensions and Compensation) Act 2004, s 7(1).
Sub-s (5): in definition "relevant enactment" words "the Pension Schemes Act 1993" in square brackets inserted by the Pension Schemes Act 1993, s 190, Sch 8, para 15.

Commentary

The forfeiture rule will preclude someone who has unlawfully killed someone from benefiting on their death, and this has an impact on social security benefits which this section is designed to alleviate. The Social Security Commissioners must first decide if there has been an unlawful killing (R(G) 2/90). It appears that the power under this section is to modify and not to relieve totally against the rule (R(G)3/90(T)).

[371]

5 Exclusion of murderers

Nothing in this Act or in any order made under section 2 or referred to in section 3(1) of this Act [or in any decision made under section 4(1A) of this Act] shall affect the application of the forfeiture rule in the case of a person who stands convicted of murder.

Amendment

Words in square brackets inserted by the Social Security Act 1986, s 76(4).

Commentary

The FA 1982 does not apply to a person who is convicted of murder, which reflects the public policy considerations behind the original forfeiture rule. It could never be right to relieve in such circumstances.

[372]

6 Corresponding provision for Northern Ireland

An Order in Council under paragraph 1(1)(b) of Schedule 1 to the Northern Ireland Act 1974 (legislation for Northern Ireland in the interim period) which contains a statement that it is made only for purposes corresponding to the purposes of this Act—

(a) shall not be subject to paragraph 1(4) and (5) of that Schedule (affirmative resolution of both Houses of Parliament); but

(b) shall be subject to annulment in pursuance of a resolution of either House.

[373]

7 Short title, etc

(1) This Act may be cited as the Forfeiture Act 1982.

(2) Section 4 of this Act shall come into force on such day as the Secretary of State may appoint by order made by statutory instrument; and sections 1 to 3 and 5 of this Act shall come into force on the expiry of the period of three months beginning with the day on which it is passed.

(3) This Act, except section 6, does not extend to Northern Ireland.

(4) Subject to section 2(7) of this Act, an order under section 2 of this Act or an order referred to in section 3(1) of this Act and made in respect of a person who has unlawfully killed another may be made whether the unlawful killing occurred before or after the coming into force of those sections.

[374]

ADMINISTRATION OF JUSTICE ACT 1982

1982 Chapter 53

ARRANGEMENT OF SECTIONS

PART IV
WILLS

PART IX
GENERAL AND SUPPLEMENTARY

An Act to make further provision with respect to the administration of justice and matters connected therewith; to amend the law relating to actions for damages for personal injuries, including injuries resulting in death, and to abolish certain actions for loss of services; to amend the law relating to wills; to make further provision with respect to funds in court, statutory deposits and schemes for the common investment of such funds and deposits and certain other funds; to amend the law relating to deductions by employers under attachment of earnings orders; to make further provision with regard to penalties that may be awarded by the Solicitors' Disciplinary Tribunal under section 47 of the Solicitors Act 1974; to make further provision for the appointment of justices of the peace in England and Wales and in relation to temporary vacancies in the membership of the Law Commission; to enable the title register kept by the Chief Land Registrar to be kept otherwise than in documentary form; and to authorise the payment of travelling, subsistence and financial loss allowances for justices of the peace in Northern Ireland

[28th October 1982]

General Note

The following sections are those which relate to wills. The bulk of the Act is outside the scope of this work.

RECTIFICATION AND INTERPRETATION OF WILLS

20 Rectification

(1) If a court is satisfied that a will is so expressed that it fails to carry out the testator's intentions, in consequence—

(a) of a clerical error; or
(b) of a failure to understand his instructions,

it may order that the will shall be rectified so as to carry out his intentions.

(2) An application for an order under this section shall not, except with the permission of the court, be made after the end of the period of six months from the date on which representation with respect to the estate of the deceased is first taken out.

(3) The provisions of this section shall not render the personal representatives of a deceased person liable for having distributed any part of the estate of the deceased, after the end of the period of six months from the date on which representation with respect to the estate of the deceased is first taken out, on the ground that they ought to have taken into account the possibility that the court might permit the making of an application for an order under this section after the end of that period; but this subsection shall not prejudice any power to recover, by reason of the making of an order under this section, any part of the estate so distributed.

(4) In considering for the purposes of this section when representation with respect to the estate of a deceased person was first taken out, a grant limited to settled land or to trust property shall be left out of account, and a grant limited to real estate or to

personal estate shall be left out of account unless a grant limited to the remainder of the estate has previously been made or is made at the same time.

Commentary

This section only applies to wills of testators who die after 1 January 1983 (Administration of Justice Act 1982 (AJA 1982), ss 73(6)(c) and 76(11)). The old law which still applies to deaths before that date was that, although the probate court had a limited ability to admit wills to probate with words omitted, in general wills could not be rectified (see *Re Reynette-James, Wightman v Reynette-James* [1975] 1 WLR 161). A clerical error in sub-s (1)(a) has been defined as an inadvertent error in drafting or transcribing the instructions of the testator, as in omitting a clause, see *Wordingham v Royal Exchange Trust Co Ltd* [1992] Ch 412, and where the draftsman had not applied his mind to the significance or effect of a clause, see *Re Segeleman* [1995] 3 All ER 676; *Re Martin* [2006] EWHC 2939; *Price v Craig* [2006] EWHC 2561. As far as failure to understand instructions is concerned (sub-s (1)(b)) a distinction has to be drawn between a failure to understand the client's instructions and a failure to understand the legal effect of a clause. The court will rectify in the case of the former but not the latter. For cases where the draftsman failed to understand the testator's intentions, see: *Lily v Pegram* [2002] All ER (D) 265 and *Goodman v Goodman* [2006] WHC 1757. The claim will fail if it cannot be established on a balance of probabilities what the intention of the testator was, see: *Bell v Georgiou* [2002] EWHC 1080 [2002] WTLR 1105. This jurisdiction ought to be used rather than suing a solicitor for negligence if the allegation is that the draftsman failed to understand the instructions of the testator and an intended beneficiary was thereby disappointed, see *Walker v Geo Medlicott & Sons Ltd* [1999] 1 All ER 685, but not where the claim to rectification is not an easy one, see *Horsfall v Haywards* [2000] WTLR 29. Note that the application must be made within six months of the grant, although the court does have power to extend time and it appears will do so on similar principles as it applies in extending time for applications under the Inheritance (Provision for Family and Dependants) Act 1975, see *Re Salmon* [1981] Ch 167. For the procedure on an application to rectify a will, see the Civil Procedure Rules 1998, SI 1998/2024, r 57.12 **[Appendix VII]** and paras 9, 10 and 11 of the Practice Direction to Part 57.

[375]

21 Interpretation of wills—general rules as to evidence

(1) This section applies to a will—

- (a) in so far as any part of it is meaningless;
- (b) in so far as the language used in any part of it is ambiguous on the face of it;
- (c) in so far as evidence, other than evidence of the testator's intention, shows that the language used in any part of it is ambiguous in the light of surrounding circumstances.

(2) In so far as this section applies to a will extrinsic evidence, including evidence of the testator's intention, may be admitted to assist in its interpretation.

Commentary

This section only applies to wills of testators who die after 1 January 1983 (AJA 1982, ss 73(6)(c) and 76(11)). For wills of testators dying before that time, the old law applies. In general, that prevented the admissibility of evidence outside the will as an aid to construing it if the words in the will were plain on the face of it (see *Higgins v Dawson* [1902] AC 1). Of course, words as to the surrounding circumstances of the testator, his family and the property he owns are admitted (the so called "armchair principle"). However, extrinsic evidence was in general only admitted when the words in the will were meaningless (*Re Glassington, Glassington v Follett* [1906] 2 Ch 305) or where there was an ambiguity on the face of the will (a patent ambiguity). In the case of a latent ambiguity (ie where the description in the will when looked at in the light of material circumstances, could refer to one or more items or people or to nobody or thing, see, for example, *Re Alexander's Will Trusts* [1948] 2 All ER 1111), the court admitted extrinsic evidence including if necessary evidence of the testator's intention to construe the will. The effect of this section is to permit the court to admit extrinsic evidence and evidence of the testator's intention in the three cases in sub-s (1)(a)–(c). Evidence of the testator's intention was under the old law admissible in category (c) (which covers latent ambiguities) but not categories (a) and (b).

[376]

22 Presumption as to effect of gifts to spouses

Except where a contrary intention is shown it shall be presumed that if a testator devises or bequeaths property to his spouse in terms which in themselves would give an absolute interest to the spouse, but by the same instrument purports to give his issue an interest in the same property, the gift to the spouse is absolute notwithstanding the purported gift to the issue.

Commentary

This section only applies to wills of testators who die after 1 January 1983 (AJA 1982, ss 73(6)(c) and 76(11)). The provision is designed to cover the case where a testator uses words in his will to the effect "I leave everything to my wife and then to my children" which might otherwise be construed as a life interest to the testator's wife. For a case where on the construction of the will as a whole the Court held that the section did not apply because the terms were not in themselves such as to give an absolute interest to the spouse, see: *Harrison v Gibson* [2006] 1 WLR 1212.

[377]

REGISTRATION OF WILLS

23 Deposit and registration of wills of living persons

(1) The following, namely—
- (a) the Principal Registry of the Family Division of the High Court of Justice;
- (b) the Keeper of the Registers of Scotland; and
- (c) the Probate and Matrimonial Office of the *Supreme Court* [Court of Judicature] of Northern Ireland,

shall be registering authorities for the purposes of this section.

(2) Each registering authority shall provide and maintain safe and convenient depositories for the custody of the wills of living persons.

(3) Any person may deposit his will in such a depository in accordance with regulations under section 25 below and on payment of the prescribed fee.

(4) It shall be the duty of a registering authority to register in accordance with regulations under section 25 below—
- (a) any will deposited in a depository maintained by the authority; and
- (b) any other will whose registration is requested under Article 6 of the Registration Convention.

(5) A will deposited in a depository provided—
- (a) under section 172 of the Supreme Court of Judicature (Consolidation) Act 1925 or section 126 of the *Supreme Court Act 1981* [Senior Courts Act 1981]; or
- (b) under Article 27 of the Administration of Estates (Northern Ireland) Order 1979,

shall be treated for the purposes of this section as if it had been deposited under this section.

(6) In this section "prescribed" means—
- (a) in the application of this section to England and Wales, prescribed by an order under [section 92 of the Courts Act 2003];
- (b) in its application to Scotland, prescribed by an order under section 26 below; and
- (c) in its application to Northern Ireland, prescribed by an order under section 116 of the Judicature (Northern Ireland) Act 1978.

Amendment

Sub-s (1): in para (c) words "Supreme Court" in italics repealed and subsequent words in square brackets substituted, from a date to be appointed, by the Constitutional Reform Act 2005, s 59(5), Sch 11, Pt 4, para 27(1), (2)(a).

Sub-s (5): in para (a) words "Supreme Court Act 1981" in italics repealed and subsequent words in square brackets substituted, from a date to be appointed, by the Constitutional Reform Act 2005, s 59(5), Sch 11, Pt 1, para 1(2).
Sub-s (6): in para (a) words "section 92 of the Courts Act 2003" in square brackets substituted by the Courts Act 2003, s 109(1), Sch 8, para 270.

Commentary
This provision and the following ss 24 and 25 provide for a system of deposit and registration of wills in accordance with a European Convention on a scheme for the registration of wills (concluded at Basel on 6 May 1972). They are not yet in force and the system has not yet been established. For the current system of depositing of wills, see the Supreme Court Act 1981, s 126 **[365]**.

[378]

24 Designation of Principal Registry as national body under Registration Convention

(1) The Principal Registry of the Family Division of the High Court of Justice shall be the national body for the purposes of the Registration Convention, and shall accordingly have the functions assigned to the national body by the Registration Convention including, without prejudice to the general application of the Convention to the Principal Registry by virtue of this section, the functions—

- (a) of arranging for the registration of wills in other Contracting States as provided for in Article 6 of the Convention;
- (b) of receiving and answering requests for information arising from the national bodies of other Contracting States.

(2) In this Part of this Act "the Registration Convention" means the Convention on the Establishment of a Scheme of Registration of Wills concluded at Basle on 16th May 1972.

Commentary
See the notes to s 23 above.

[379]

25 Regulations as to deposit and registration of wills

(1) Regulations may make provision—

- (a) as to the conditions for the deposit of a will;
- (b) as to the manner of and procedure for—
  - (i) the deposit and registration of a will; and
  - (ii) the withdrawal of a will which has been deposited; and
  - (iii) the cancellation of the registration of a will; and
- (c) as to the manner in which the Principal Registry of the Family Division is to perform its functions as the national body under the Registration Convention.

(2) Regulations under this section may contain such incidental or supplementary provisions as the authority making the regulations considers appropriate.

(3) Any such regulations are to be made—

- (a) for England and Wales, by the President of the Family Division of the High Court of Justice, with the concurrence of the Lord Chancellor;
- (b) for Scotland, by the Secretary of State after consultation with the Lord President of the Court of Session; and
- (c) for Northern Ireland, by the Northern Ireland *Supreme Court* [Court of Judicature] Rules Committee, with the concurrence of the Lord Chancellor.

(4) Regulations made by virtue of subsection (1)(c) above shall be made by the Lord Chancellor [after consulting the Lord Chief Justice of England and Wales].

(5) Subject to subsection (6) below, regulations under this section shall be made by statutory instrument and shall be laid before Parliament after being made.

(6) Regulations for Northern Ireland shall be statutory rules for the purposes of the Statutory Rules (Northern Ireland) Order 1979; and any such statutory rule shall be laid before Parliament after being made in like manner as a statutory instrument and section 4 of the Statutory Instruments Act 1946 shall apply accordingly.

(7) The Statutory Instruments Act 1946 shall apply to a statutory instrument containing regulations made in accordance with subsection (3)(a) or (c) above as if the regulations had been made by a Minister of the Crown.

(8) Any regulations made under section 172 of the Supreme Court of Judicature (Consolidation) Act 1925 or section 126 of the *Supreme Court Act 1981* [Senior Courts Act 1981] shall have effect for the purposes of this Part of this Act as they have effect for the purposes of the enactment under which they were made.

[(9) The Lord Chief Justice may nominate a judicial office holder (as defined in section 109(4) of the Constitutional Reform Act 2005) to exercise his functions under subsection (4).]

Amendment

Sub-s (3): in para (c) words "Supreme Court" in italics repealed and subsequent words in square brackets substituted, from a date to be appointed, by the Constitutional Reform Act 2005, s 59(5), Sch 11, Pt 4, para 27(1), (2)(b).

Sub-s (4): words "after consulting the Lord Chief Justice of England and Wales" in square brackets inserted by the Constitutional Reform Act 2005, s 15(1), Sch 4, Pt 1, paras 147, 148(1), (2).

Sub-s (8): words "Supreme Court Act 1981" in italics repealed and subsequent words in square brackets substituted, from a date to be appointed, by the Constitutional Reform Act 2005, s 59(5), Sch 11, Pt 1, para 1(2).

Sub-s (9): inserted by the Constitutional Reform Act 2005, s 15(1), Sch 4, Pt 1, paras 147, 148(1), (3).

Commentary

See the notes to s 23 above.

[380]

INTERNATIONAL WILLS

27 The form of an international will

(1) The Annex to the Convention on International Wills shall have the force of law in the United Kingdom.

(2) The Annex is set out in Schedule 2 to this Act.

(3) In this Part of this Act—

"international will" means a will made in accordance with the requirements of the Annex, as set out in Schedule 2 to this Act; and

"the Convention on International Wills" means the Convention providing a Uniform Law on the Form of an International Will concluded at Washington on 26th October 1973.

[381]

28 International wills—procedure

(1) The persons authorised to act in the United Kingdom in connection with international wills are—

(a) solicitors; and
(b) notaries public.

(2) A person who is authorised under section 6(1) of the Commissioners for Oaths Act 1889 to do notarial acts in any foreign country or place is authorised to act there in connection with international wills.

(3) An international will certified by virtue of subsection (1) or (2) above may be deposited in a depository provided under section 23 above.

(4) Section 23 above shall accordingly have effect in relation to such international wills.

(5) Subject to subsection (6) below, regulations under section 25 above shall have effect in relation to such international wills as they have effect in relation to wills deposited under section 23 above.

(6) Without prejudice to the generality of section 25 above, regulations under that section may make special provision with regard to such international wills.

(7) . . .

Amendment

Sub-s (7): amends the Consular Relations Act 1968, s 10.

[382]

PART IX
GENERAL AND SUPPLEMENTARY

73 Transitional provisions and savings

(1) Subject to subsections (2) and (3) below, nothing in Part I of this Act or paragraphs 2 to 10 of Schedule 6 to this Act applies to causes of action which accrue before its commencement.

(2) Section 6 above and paragraph 10 of Schedule 6 to this Act shall apply to actions whenever commenced, including actions commenced before the passing of this Act.

(3) The provisions to which this subsection applies have effect where a person has died after the commencement of Part I of this Act.

(4) The provisions of this Act to which subsection (3) above applies are—
- (a) section 1;
- (b) section 4(2); and
- (c) paragraph 9(2) of Schedule 6.

(5) Without prejudice to the provisions of Parts II and III of the Prescription and Limitation (Scotland) Act 1973, Part II of this Act shall apply to rights of action which accrued before, as well as rights of action which accrue after, the coming into operation of that Part of this Act; but nothing in Part II of this Act other than the repeal of section 5 of the Damages (Scotland) Act 1976 shall affect any proceedings commenced before that Part of this Act comes into operation.

(6) Nothing in the following provisions of this Act—
- (a) section 17;
- (b) section 18(2);
- (c) sections 19 to 22;
- (d) section 75, so far as it relates—
  - (i) to the Wills Act Amendment Act 1852; and
  - (ii) to the Family Law Reform Act 1969,

affects the will of a testator who dies before the commencement of the provision in question.

(7) Neither section 18(1) above nor the repeal by this Act of section 177 of the Law of Property Act 1925 affects a will made before the commencement of section 18(1) above.

(8) . . .

(9) Nothing in paragraph 1 of Schedule 6 to this Act affects a cause of action accruing before that paragraph comes into force if an action in respect thereof has been begun before the paragraph comes into force.

Amendment

Sub-s (8): repealed by the Statute Law (Repeals) Act 2004.

[383]

74 . . .

. . .

Amendment

Repealed by the Income and Corporation Taxes Act 1988, s 844, Sch 31.

[384]

75 Repeals and revocations

(1) The enactments specified in Part I of Schedule 9 to this Act (which include enactments already obsolete or unnecessary) are repealed to the extent specified in the third column of that Part of that Schedule.

(2) The instruments specified in Part II of that Schedule are revoked to the extent specified in the third column of that Part of that Schedule.

[385]

76 Commencement

(1) The provisions of this Act specified in subsection (2) below shall come into operation on such day as the Lord Chancellor may by order appoint.

(2) The provisions of this Act mentioned in subsection (1) above are—

- (a) section 6;
- (b) Part III;
- (c) sections 34 and 35;
- (d) sections 38 to 47;
- (e) section 54;
- (f) section 57;
- (g) section 69;
- (h) section 73(8);
- (j) section 75, so far as it relates—
  - (i) to the Judicial Trustees Act 1896;
  - (ii) to section 17 of the Law Reform (Miscellaneous Provisions) Act (Northern Ireland) 1937;
  - (iii) to the Prevention of Fraud (Investments) Act 1958;
  - (iv) to sections 99(3), 168 to 174A and 176 of the County Courts Act 1959;
  - (v) to sections 1 to 16 of the Administration of Justice Act 1965 and Schedule 1 to that Act;
  - (vi) to the Administration of Justice Act 1977; and
  - (vii) to the Judicature (Northern Ireland) Act 1978;
- (k) paragraph 10 of Schedule 6; and
- (l) paragraphs 6 to 8 of Schedule 8.

(3) The provisions of this Act specified in subsection (4) below shall come into operation on such day as the Secretary of State may by order appoint.

(4) The provisions of this Act mentioned in subsection (3) above are—

(a) section 12;

(b) section 14(2);

(c) section 48; and

(d) section 75 above, so far as it relates to the Damages (Scotland) Act 1976.

(5) The provisions of this Act specified in subsection (6) below shall come into operation on such day as the Lord Chancellor and the Secretary of State may by order jointly appoint.

(6) The provisions of this Act mentioned in subsection (5) above are—

(a) sections 23 to 25;

(b) sections 27 and 28;

(c) section 75, so far as it relates—

(i) to section 126 of the *Supreme Court Act 1981* [Senior Courts Act 1981]; and

(ii) to Article 27 of the Administration of Estates (Northern Ireland) Order 1979.

(7) Any order under this section shall be made by statutory instrument.

(8) Any such order may appoint different days for different provisions and for different purposes.

(9) The provisions of this Act specified in subsection (10) below shall come into operation on the day this Act is passed.

(10) The provisions of this Act mentioned in subsection (9) above are—

(a) section 32;

(b) section 36;

(c) section 52;

(d) section 60;

(e) section 64;

(f) section 65;

(g) this section;

(h) section 77; and

(i) section 78.

(11) Subject to the foregoing provisions of this section, this Act shall come into operation on 1st January 1983.

Amendment

Sub-s (6): in para (c)(i) words "Supreme Court Act 1981" in italics repealed and subsequent words in square brackets substituted, from a date to be appointed, by the Constitutional Reform Act 2005, s 59(5), Sch 11, Pt 1, para 1(2).

[386]

77 Extent

(1) Subject to subsection (6) below, the following provisions of this Act—

(a) sections 3, 4 and 6;

(b) Part III;

(c) sections 17 to 22;

(d) Part V;

(e) sections 49 to 57;

(f) sections 65 to 67,

extend to England and Wales only.

(2) Sections 1, 2, 5, 39, 42 to 47, 64 and 74 above extend to England and Wales and Northern Ireland.

(3) Part II of this Act and section 26 above extend to Scotland only and Part VI of this Act applies to Scotland only to the extent specified in section 48 above.

(4) Part VIII of this Act extends to Northern Ireland only.

(5) . . .

(6) Subject to subsection (5) above, where any enactment repealed or amended or instrument revoked by this Act extends to any part of the United Kingdom, the repeal, amendment or revocation extends to that part.

Amendment

Sub-s (5): repealed by the Statute Law (Repeals) Act 2004.

[387]

78 Citation

This Act may be cited as the Administration of Justice Act 1982.

[388]

SCHEDULE 2
THE ANNEX TO THE CONVENTION ON INTERNATIONAL WILLS

Section 27

UNIFORM LAW ON THE FORM OF AN INTERNATIONAL WILL

ARTICLE 1

1 A will shall be valid as regards form, irrespective particularly of the place where it is made, of the location of the assets and of the nationality, domicile or residence of the testator, if it is made in the form of an international will complying with the provisions set out in Articles 2 to 5 hereinafter.

2 The invalidity of the will as an international will shall not affect its formal validity as a will of another kind.

ARTICLE 2

This law shall not apply to the form of testamentary dispositions made by two or more persons in one instrument.

ARTICLE 3

1 The will shall be made in writing.

2 It need not be written by the testator himself.

3 It may be written in any language, by hand or by any other means.

ARTICLE 4

1 The testator shall declare in the presence of two witnesses and of a person authorized to act in connection with international wills that the document is his will and that he knows the contents thereof.

2 The testator need not inform the witnesses, or the authorized person, of the contents of the will.

ARTICLE 5

1 In the presence of the witnesses and of the authorized persons, the testator shall sign the will or, if he has previously signed it, shall acknowledge his signature.

2 When the testator is unable to sign, he shall indicate the reason therefor to the authorized person who shall make note of this on the will. Moreover, the testator may be authorized by the law under which the authorized person was designated to direct another person to sign on his behalf.

3 The witnesses and the authorized person shall there and then attest the will by signing in the presence of the testator.

ARTICLE 6

1 The signatures shall be placed at the end of the will.

2 If the will consists of several sheets, each sheet shall be signed by the testator or, if he is unable to sign, by the person signing on his behalf or, if there is no such person, by the authorized person. In addition, each sheet shall be numbered.

ARTICLE 7

1 The date of the will shall be the date of its signature by the authorized person.

2 This date shall be noted at the end of the will by the authorized person.

ARTICLE 8

In the absence of any mandatory rule pertaining to the safekeeping of the will, the authorized person shall ask the testator whether he wishes to make a declaration concerning the safekeeping of his will. If so and at the express request of the testator the place where he intends to have his will kept shall be mentioned in the certificate provided for in Article 9.

ARTICLE 9

The authorized person shall attach to the will a certificate in the form prescribed in Article 10 establishing that the obligations of this law have been complied with.

ARTICLE 10

The certificate drawn up by the authorized person shall be in the following form or in a substantially similar form:

CERTIFICATE

(Convention of October 26th, 1973)

1. I, ... (name, address and capacity), a person authorized to act in connection with international wills

2. Certify that on .... (date) at .... (place)

3. (testator) .... (name, address, date and place of birth)

in my presence and that of the witnesses

4.

(a) .... (name, address, date and place of birth)
(b) .... (name, address, date and place of birth)

has declared that the attached document is his will and that he knows the contents thereof.

5. I furthermore certify that:

6. (a) in my presence and in that of the witnesses

(1) the testator has signed the will or has acknowledged his signature previously affixed.

*(2) following a declaration of the testator stating that he was unable to sign his will for the following reason ....

—I have mentioned this declaration on the will

*—the signature has been affixed by .... (name, address)

7. (b) the witnesses and I have signed the will;

8. *(c) each page of the will has been signed by .... and numbered:

9. (d) I have satisfied myself as to the identity of the testator and of the witnesses as designated above;

10. (e) the witnesses met the conditions requisite to act as such according to the law under which I am acting;

11. *(f) the testator has requested me to include the following statement concerning the safekeeping of his will:

....

....

12. PLACE

13. DATE

14. SIGNATURE and, if necessary, SEAL

***To be completed if appropriate.**

ARTICLE 11

The authorized person shall keep a copy of the certificate and deliver another to the testator.

ARTICLE 12

In the absence of evidence to the contrary, the certificate of the authorized person shall be conclusive of the formal validity of the instrument as a will under this Law.

ARTICLE 13

The absence or irregularity of a certificate shall not affect the formal validity of a will under this Law.

ARTICLE 14

The international will shall be subject to the ordinary rules of revocation of wills.

ARTICLE 15

In interpreting and applying the provisions of this law, regard shall be had to its international origin and to the need for uniformity in its interpretation.

[389]

SCHEDULE 3
MONETARY LIMITS OF COUNTY COURT JURISDICTION

Section 37

PART I

. . .

. . .

Amendment
Repealed by the County Courts Act 1984, s 148(3), Sch 4.

PART II
AMENDMENTS OF ENACTMENTS SPECIFYING MONETARY LIMITS

. . .

Amendment
Repealed in part by the County Courts Act 1984, s 148(3), Sch 4.
Repealed in part by the Statute Law (Repeals) Act 2004.

Commentary
This Schedule contains amendments to the Consumer Credit Act 1974, s 139, the Solicitors Act 1974, s 69 and the Charging Orders Act 1979, s 1.

PART III

. . .

. . .

Amendment
Repealed by the Statute Law (Repeals) Act 2004.

PART IV
HIGHWAYS

8 (1) Sums recoverable under section 59 of the Highways Act 1980 (expenses due to extraordinary traffic) shall be recoverable in the county court . . .

(2) . . .

Amendment
Sub-para (1): words omitted repealed by SI 1991/724, art 2(8), Schedule, Part I.
Sub-para (2): contains amendments to the Highways Act 1980, s 59(4).

[390]

SCHEDULE 4
ATTACHMENT OF DEBTS

Section 55

PART I
SECTION INSERTED IN SUPREME COURT ACT 1981

. . .

Commentary
This Part sets out the Supreme Court Act 1981, s 40A.

PART II

. . .

. . .

Amendment
Repealed by the County Courts Act 1984, s 148(3), Sch 4.

[391]

SCHEDULE 5

. . .

. . .

Amendment
Repealed by the Land Registration Act 2002, s 135, Sch 13.

[392]

SCHEDULE 6
DAMAGES FOR PERSONAL INJURIES ETC

Section 68

ABOLITION OF ACTIONS FOR ENTICEMENT, SEDUCTION AND HARBOURING OF CHILD

1 No person shall be liable in tort under the law of Northern Ireland—
- (a) to a parent (or person standing in the place of a parent) on the ground only of his having deprived the parent (or other person) of the services of his or her child by raping, seducing or enticing that child; or
- (b) to any other person for harbouring the child of that other person.

2–9

. . .

Commentary
Paras 2–8: contain amendments to the Fatal Accidents (Northern Ireland) Order 1977, SI 1977/1251.
Para 9: contains amendments to the Law Reform (Miscellaneous Provisions) Act (Northern Ireland) 1937, s 14.

ORDERS FOR PROVISIONAL DAMAGES FOR PERSONAL INJURY

10 (1) This paragraph applies to an action under the law of Northern Ireland for damages for personal injuries in which there is proved or admitted to be a chance that at some definite or indefinite time in the future the injured person will, as a result of the act or omission which gave rise to the cause of action, develop some serious disease or suffer some serious deterioration in his physical or mental condition.

(2) Subject to sub-paragraph (4) below, as regards any action for damages to which this paragraph applies in which a judgment is given in the High Court, provision may be made by rules of court for enabling the court, in such circumstances as may be prescribed, to award the injured person—
- (a) damages assessed on the assumption that the injured person will not develop the disease or suffer deterioration in his condition; and

(b) further damages at a further date if he develops the disease or suffers the deterioration.

(3) Any rules made by virtue of this paragraph may include such incidental, supplementary and consequential provisions as the rule-making authority may consider necessary or expedient.

(4) Nothing in this paragraph shall be construed—

(a) as affecting the exercise of any power relating to costs, including any power to make rules of court relating to costs; or

(b) as prejudicing any duty of the court under any enactment or rule of law to reduce or limit the total damages which would have been recoverable apart from any such duty.

(5) This paragraph shall have effect in relation to county courts in Northern Ireland as it has effect in relation to the High Court as if references in it to rules of court included references to county court rules.

(6) In this paragraph "personal injuries" includes any disease and any impairment of a person's physical or mental condition.

[393]

SCHEDULE 7
INTEREST ON DEBTS AND DAMAGES

Section 69

PART I
SECTION INSERTED IN JUDICATURE

. . .

Commentary
This Part sets out the Judicature (Northern Ireland) Act 1978, s 33A.

PART II
ARTICLE INSERTED IN COUNTY COURTS

. . .

Commentary
This Part sets out the County Courts (Northern Ireland) Order 1980, SI 1980/397, art 45A.

PART III
AMENDMENTS CONSEQUENTIAL ON SECTION 69

CROWN PROCEEDINGS ACT

1 In section 24(3) of the Crown Proceedings Act 1947 as it applies in Northern Ireland in relation to Her Majesty's Government in the United Kingdom and in relation to Her Majesty's Government in Northern Ireland for the words from the beginning to "damages)" there shall be substituted the words "Section 33A of the Judicature (Northern Ireland) Act 1978 and Article 45A of the County Courts (Northern Ireland) Order 1980 (which respectively empower the High Court and county courts to award interest on debts and damages)".

2, 3

. . .

Commentary
Para 2: contains amendments to the Judicature (Northern Ireland) Act 1978, s 31(9)(c).

Para 3: contains amendments to the County Courts (Northern Ireland) Order 1980, SI 1980/397, art 2(4).

[394]

SCHEDULE 8
AMENDMENTS OFJUDICATURE (NORTHERN IRELAND) ACT 1978

Section 70

1

. . .

2

. . .

3

. . .

4

. . .

5

. . .

6

. . .

7

. . .

8

. . .

9

. . .

10

. . .

11

. . .

12

. . .

Commentary
This Schedule contains amendments to the Judicature (Northern Ireland) Act 1978.

Amendment
Para 2: repealed by the Justice (Northern Ireland) Act 2002, s 86, Sch 13.
Para 3: repealed by the Statute Law (Repeals) Act 2004.

[395]

SCHEDULE 9
REPEALS AND REVOCATIONS

Section 75

PART I
REPEALS

Chapter	*Short Title*	*Extent of Repeal*
15 & 16 Vict c 24	Wills Act Amendment Act 1852	The whole Act.
23 & 24 Vict c 115	Crown Debts and Judgments Act 1860	The whole Act.
59 & 60 Vict c 35	Judicial Trustees Act 1896	In section 1(6), the words from the beginning to "and", in the second place where it occurs.
4 & 5 Geo 5 c 59	Bankruptcy Act 1914	In section 16(13) and in section 28(1)(c), the words "under a judgment against him in an action for seduction, or".
15 & 16 Geo 5 c 20	Law of Property Act 1925	Section 177.
24 & 25 Geo 5 c 41	Law Reform (Miscellaneous Provisions) Act 1934	In section 1(1), the words "or seduction".
1 Edw 8 & 1 Geo 6 c 9(NI)	Law Reform (Miscellaneous Provisions) Act (Northern Ireland) 1937	In section 14(1), the words "or seduction".
		Section 17.
6 & 7 Eliz 2 c 45	Prevention of Fraud (Investments) Act 1958	Section 4(3).
7 & 8 Eliz 2 c 22	County Courts Act 1959	Section 2.
		Section 20.
		Section 25.
		Section 99(3).
		Section 102(3)(e).
		In section 148, in subsection (1)(a), the words "in a county court", and subsection (2).
		Sections 168 to 174.
		Section 174A.
		Section 176.
7 & 8 Eliz 2 c 72	Mental Health Act 1959	In section 103(1)(h), the words from "so however" to the end of the paragraph.
1965 c 2	Administration of Justice Act 1965	Sections 1 to 16.
		Section 18.
		In section 20, subsections (1) and (2), and in subsection (7), the words from "and" to the end.
		In Schedule 1, the entry relating to the Prevention of Fraud (Investments) Act 1958.
1969 c 46	Family Law Reform Act 1969	Section 16.
1969 c 58	Administration of Justice Act 1969	Section 10.
1974 c 4	Legal Aid Act 1974	In Part II of Schedule 1, paragraph 2.
1975 c 63	Inheritance (Provision for Family and Dependants) Act 1975	Section 22.
1976 c 13	Damages (Scotland) Act 1976	Section 5.

Chapter	Short Title	Extent of Repeal
1976 c 30	Fatal Accidents Act 1976	In section 5, the words "brought for the benefit of the dependants of that person". In Schedule 1, in paragraph 2(2) the entry relating to the Deposit of Poisonous Waste Act 1972.
1977 c 38	Administration of Justice Act 1977	Section 11.
1978 c 23	Judicature (Northern Ireland) Act 1978	Section 83.
1979 c 2	Customs and Excise Management Act 1979	In Schedule 4, in the Table to paragraph 12, the entry relating to the Crown Debts and Judgments Act 1960.
1981 c 54	Supreme Court Act 1981	Section 126. Section 143. In Schedule 3, paragraphs 23 to 26. In Schedule 5, the paragraphs relating to the Bankruptcy Act 1914 and the Companies Act 1948.

PART II
REVOCATIONS

Reference	Title	Extent of revocation
SI 1967 No 761	Land Registration Rules 1967	The whole instrument.
SI 1977 No 1251 (NI 18)	Fatal Accidents (Northern Ireland) Order 1977	In Article 7, the words "brought for the benefit of the dependants of that person".
SI 1979 No 1575 (NI 14)	Administration of Estates (Northern Ireland) Order 1979	Article 27.

[396]

ADMINISTRATION OF JUSTICE ACT 1985

1985 Chapter 61

ARRANGEMENT OF SECTIONS

PART IV
THE SUPREME COURT AND COUNTY COURTS

An Act to make further provision with respect to the administration of justice and matters connected therewith; to amend the Solicitors Act 1974; to regulate the provision of solicitors' services in the case of incorporated practices; to regulate the provision of conveyancing services by persons practising as licensed conveyancers; to make further provision with respect to complaints relating to the provision of legal aid services; to amend the law relating to time limits for actions for libel and slander; and to make further provision with respect to arbitrations and proceedings in connection with European patents

[30th October 1985]

General Note
The sections of this Act reproduced below are of immense practical importance.

PART IV
THE SUPREME COURT AND COUNTY COURTS

48 Power of High Court to authorise action to be taken in reliance on counsel's opinion

(1) Where—
 (a) any question of construction has arisen out of the terms of a will or a trust; and
 (b) an opinion in writing given by a [person who has a 10 year High Court qualification, within the meaning of section 71 of the Courts and Legal Services Act 1990,] has been obtained on that question by the personal representatives or trustees under the will or trust,

the High Court may, on the application of the personal representatives or trustees and without hearing argument, make an order authorising those persons to take such steps in reliance on the said opinion as are specified in the order.

(2) The High Court shall not make an order under subsection (1) if it appears to the court that a dispute exists which would make it inappropriate for the court to make the order without hearing argument.

Amendment
Sub-s (1): words in square brackets substituted by the Courts and Legal Services Act 1990, s 71(2), Sch 10, para 63.

Commentary
For the meaning of a ten year High Court qualification see: Courts and Legal Services Act 1990 s. 71(2) Schedule 10 paragraph 63. Application under this section is made under Part 8 rule 8.2A of the Civil Procedure Rules 1998, SI 1998/2024 **[Appendix VII]**, for the procedure see paragraph 5 to the Practice Direction to Part 64 of the Civil Procedure Rules

[397]

49 Powers of High Court on compromise of probate action

(1) Where on a compromise of a probate action in the High Court—
 (a) the court is invited to pronounce for the validity of one or more wills, or against the validity of one or more wills, or for the validity of one or more wills and against the validity of one or more other wills; and
 (b) the court is satisfied that consent to the making of the pronouncement or, as the case may be, each of the pronouncements in question has been given by or on behalf of every relevant beneficiary,

the court may without more pronounce accordingly.

(2) In this section—

"probate action" means an action for the grant of probate of the will, or letters of administration of the estate, of a deceased person or for the revocation of such a grant or for a decree pronouncing for or against the validity of an alleged will, not being an action which is non-contentious or common form probate business; and

"relevant beneficiary", in relation to a pronouncement relating to any will or wills of a deceased person, means—
 (a) a person who under any such will is beneficially interested in the deceased's estate; and

(b) where the effect of the pronouncement would be to cause the estate to devolve as on an intestacy (or partial intestacy), or to prevent it from so devolving, a person who under the law relating to intestacy is beneficially interested in the estate.

Commentary
This is a very useful method of obtaining an order compromising a probate action (see sub-s (2)) where all the "relevant beneficiaries" consent. As to the meaning of relevant beneficiary see sub-s (2). Applications may be heard by a Master or District Judge (although they do not have to be) and must be supported by written evidence identifying the relevant beneficiaries, and exhibiting their consents. Written evidence of testamentary documents required by the Civil Procedure Rules 1998, SI 1998/2024, r 57.5 is necessary **[Appendix VII]**. As to the practice see the Civil Procedure Rules 1998, Pt 57 PD 6.2.

[398]

50 Power of High Court to appoint substitute for, or to remove, personal representative

(1) Where an application relating to the estate of a deceased person is made to the High Court under this subsection by or on behalf of a personal representative of the deceased or a beneficiary of the estate, the court may in its discretion—

(a) appoint a person (in this section called a substituted personal representative) to act as personal representative of the deceased in place of the existing personal representative or representatives of the deceased or any of them; or

(b) if there are two or more existing personal representatives of the deceased, terminate the appointment of one or more, but not all, of those persons.

(2) Where the court appoints a person to act as a substituted personal representative of a deceased person, then—

(a) if that person is appointed to act with an executor or executors the appointment shall (except for the purpose of including him in any chain of representation) constitute him executor of the deceased as from the date of the appointment; and

(b) in any other case the appointment shall constitute that person administrator of the deceased's estate as from the date of the appointment.

(3) The court may authorise a person appointed as a substituted personal representative to charge remuneration for his services as such, on such terms (whether or not involving the submission of bills of charges for taxation by the court) as the court may think fit.

(4) Where an application relating to the estate of a deceased person is made to the court under subsection (1), the court may, if it thinks fit, proceed as if the application were, or included, an application for the appointment under the Judicial Trustees Act 1896 of a judicial trustee in relation to that estate.

(5) In this section "beneficiary", in relation to the estate of a deceased person, means a person who under the will of the deceased or under the law relating to intestacy is beneficially interested in the estate.

(6) . . .

Amendment
Sub-s (6): amends the Judicial Trustees Act 1896, s 1.

Commentary
Under the Trustee Act 1925, s 41 **[110]** the court has no power to replace or remove a personal representative. Before this section the only method of achieving this was by the appointment of a judicial trustee (which route the court can still take on an application under this section, see sub-s (4)). For the Judicial Trustee Act 1896 see **[53]**. Under sub-s (1)(b) the court can terminate an appointment but only if it leaves at least one personal representative in office. Otherwise the court has to substitute under sub-s (1)(a). The power to allow a personal

representative to charge (sub-s (3)) is widely used. Note that the definition of beneficiary in sub-s (5) is quite narrow and would not include a person interested in the due administration of the estate such as a creditor. However, a personal representative can apply to have himself removed and that provides a way in which he can retire. Application under this section should be made by way of a Part 8 claim form in the Chancery Division or the county court if it has jurisdiction, or it can be made by way of a Part 23 application in ongoing proceedings relating to the administration of the estate. For the procedure see Part 57 of the Civil Procedure Rules 1998, SI 1998/ 2024 **[Appendix VII]** and the Practice Direction to that Part. An application can also be made by summons in the probate registry. There is little reported guidance on the way in which the court will exercise its jurisdiction under this section as many cases are dealt with in chambers, but see: *Perotti v Watson* [2001] EWCA Civ 116 and [2001] All ER (D) 26 where the Court of Appeal held that there was no jurisdiction to remove a non-proving executor. A beneficiary of an agreement to maintain mutual wills is not a beneficiary within sub-s (5), see: *Thomas and Agnes Carvel Foundation v Carvel* [2007] 4 All ER 81.

[399]

RECOGNITION OF TRUSTS ACT 1987

1987 Chapter 14

ARRANGEMENT OF SECTIONS

An Act to enable the United Kingdom to ratify the Convention on the law applicable to trusts and on their recognition which was signed on behalf of the United Kingdom on 10th January 1986

[9th April 1987]

General Note

This statute was enacted to give effect to the Hague Convention on the Recognition of Trusts.

1 Applicable law and recognition of trusts

(1) The provisions of the Convention set out in the Schedule to this Act shall have the force of law in the United Kingdom.

(2) Those provisions shall, so far as applicable, have effect not only in relation to the trusts described in Articles 2 and 3 of the Convention but also in relation to any other trusts of property arising under the law of any part of the United Kingdom or by virtue of a judicial decision whether in the United Kingdom or elsewhere.

(3) In accordance with Articles 15 and 16 such provisions of the law as are there mentioned shall, to the extent there specified, apply to the exclusion of the other provisions of the Convention.

(4) In Article 17 the reference to a State includes a reference to any country or territory (whether or not a party to the Convention and whether or not forming part of the United Kingdom) which has its own system of law.

(5) Article 22 shall not be construed as affecting the law to be applied in relation to anything done or omitted before the coming into force of this Act.

Commentary

For the trusts to which the RTA 1987 and the Convention apply, see arts 2 and 3 in the Schedule below. Note, however, that the somewhat restrictive definition in those articles is extended by sub-s (2) in relation to trusts of property under United Kingdom law and all trusts created by a foreign judgment (so that the English courts can in this way enforce the judgment of a foreign court which establishes a trust). The Convention which is set out in the Schedule to this Act will not affect the rules applicable before the RTA 1987 came into force on 1 August 1987 (sub-s (5)).

[400]

2 Extent

(1) This Act extends to Northern Ireland.

(2) Her Majesty may by Order in Council direct that this Act shall also form part of the law of the Isle of Man, any of the Channel Islands or any colony.

(3) An Order in Council under subsection (2) above may modify this Act in its application to any of the territories there mentioned and may contain such supplementary provisions as Her Majesty considers appropriate.

(4) An Order in Council under subsection (2) above shall be subject to annulment in pursuance of a resolution of either House of Parliament.

[401]

3 Short title, commencement and application to the Crown

(1) This Act may be cited as the Recognition of Trusts Act 1987.

(2) This Act shall come into force on such date as the Lord Chancellor and the Lord Advocate may appoint by an order made by statutory instrument.

(3) This Act binds the Crown.

Transfer of Functions
By virtue of the Scotland Act 1998, s 44(1)(c), the Lord Advocate ceased, on 20 May 1999 (see SI 1998/3178), to be a Minister of the Crown and became a member of the Scottish Executive. Accordingly, certain functions of the Lord Advocate are transferred to the Secretary of State (or as the case may be the Secretary of State for Scotland), or the Advocate General for Scotland: see the Transfer of Functions (Lord Advocate and Secretary of State) Order 1999, SI 1999/678 and the Transfer of Functions (Lord Advocate and Advocate General for Scotland) Order 1999, SI 1999/679.

[402]

SCHEDULE
CONVENTION ON THE LAW APPLICABLE TO TRUSTS AND ON THEIR RECOGNITION

Section 1

CHAPTER I
SCOPE

ARTICLE 1

This Convention specifies the law applicable to trusts and governs their recognition.

ARTICLE 2

For the purposes of this Convention, the term "trust" refers to the legal relationship created— inter vivos or on death— by a person, the settlor, when assets have been placed under the control of a trustee for the benefit of a beneficiary or for a specified purpose.

A trust has the following characteristics—

(a) the assets constitute a separate fund and are not a part of the trustee's own estate;

(b) title to the trust assets stands in the name of the trustee or in the name of another person on behalf of the trustee;
(c) the trustee has the power and the duty, in respect of which he is accountable, to manage, employ or dispose of the assets in accordance with the terms of the trust and the special duties imposed upon him by law.

The reservation by the settlor of certain rights and powers, and the fact that the trustee may himself have rights as a beneficiary, are not necessarily inconsistent with the existence of a trust.

Commentary

This article should be read together with art 3 below as to the definition of a trust. Note that constructive trusts would seem to be excluded from this definition (by use of the term "created") but also note the extension of the definition in this and the following article by s 1(2) above. The definition also seems to require a transfer of assets, and quaere whether a declaration of trust by the owner of assets would fall within this definition save of course that all UK trusts are caught by s 1(2). It is questionable whether rules such as those against excessive accumulation can be avoided by choosing a foreign law where the rule does not apply.

ARTICLE 3

The Convention applies only to trusts created voluntarily and evidenced in writing.

Commentary

Note that the trust is not required to be in writing, simply evidenced by it. Note that s 1(2) extends the definition in this and the preceding article to all UK trusts and trusts imposed by a foreign judgment (which will of course be in writing but not voluntary).

ARTICLE 4

The Convention does not apply to preliminary issues relating to the validity of wills or of other acts by virtue of which assets are transferred to the trustee.

Commentary

The validity of wills in a foreign context is dealt with in this work in the Wills Act 1968 **[295]**. Reference must be made to common law rules for the validity of transfers into inter vivos trusts. The Act does apply to the law expressly chosen to govern a will trust, see: *Tod v Barton* [2002] EWHC 264

ARTICLE 5

The Convention does not apply to the extent that the law specified by Chapter II does not provide for trusts or the category of trusts involved.

Commentary

See arts 6 and 7 below

CHAPTER II
APPLICABLE LAW

ARTICLE 6

A trust shall be governed by the law chosen by the settlor. The choice must be express or be implied in the terms of the instrument creating or the writing evidencing the trust, interpreted, if necessary, in the light of the circumstances of the case.

Where the law chosen under the previous paragraph does not provide for trusts or the category of trust involved, the choice shall not be effective and the law specified in Article 7 shall apply.

Commentary
The settlor can choose any law to govern the settlement and is not constrained by choosing a law with which he or the settlement has no connection (but do see arts 16 and 18 below which modify this rule), but if he chooses a law which does not recognise trusts or the type of trust he is creating, then the default provisions of art 7 will apply. A choice of law might be implied if a provision of a system of law is included in the terms of the settlement, see *Chellaram v Chellaram* [1985] Ch 409. See also *Tod v Barton* [2002] EWHC 264.

ARTICLE 7

Where no applicable law has been chosen, a trust shall be governed by the law with which it is most closely connected.

In ascertaining the law with which a trust is most closely connected reference shall be made in particular to—

(a) the place of administration of the trust designated by the settlor;
(b) the situs of the assets of the trust;
(c) the place of residence or business of the trustee;
(d) the objects of the trust and the places where they are to be fulfilled.

Commentary
The list of factors to which the court should have regard is not exhaustive. Note also that there is no specific reference to immovable property so there would be nothing to stop a trust of English land (which would traditionally be governed by its lex situs) being governed by some other system of law, if, applying the factors in this article that was the result. For a case where Jersey law clearly applied to a settlement but the Court held that it had jurisdiction in England to vary it under the Matrimonial Causes Act 1973, see *C v C* [2004] Fam 250.

ARTICLE 8

The law specified by Article 6 or 7 shall govern the validity of the trust, its construction, its effects and the administration of the trust. In particular that law shall govern—

(a) the appointment, resignation and removal of trustees, the capacity to act as a trustee, and the devolution of the office of trustee;
(b) the rights and duties of trustees among themselves;
(c) the right of trustees to delegate in whole or in part the discharge of their duties or the exercise of their powers;
(d) the power of trustees to administer or to dispose of trust assets, to create security interests in the trust assets, or to acquire new assets;
(e) the powers of investment of trustees;
(f) restrictions upon the duration of the trust, and upon the power to accumulate the income of the trust;
(g) the relationships between the trustees and the beneficiaries including the personal liability of the trustees to the beneficiaries;
(h) the variation or termination of the trust;
(i) the distribution of the trust assets;
(j) the duty of trustees to account for their administration.

Commentary
But see art 9 to the effect that parts of the administration which can be severed might be governed by a different law.

ARTICLE 9

In applying this Chapter a severable aspect of the trust, particularly matters of administration, may be governed by a different law.

Commentary
Note that in English law the possibility of separating off aspects of the administration of the trust has been doubted, see *Chellaram v Chellaram* [1985] Ch 409. However, there would seem to be no reason why a settlor could not choose different aspects of law to govern different parts of the trust.

ARTICLE 10

The law applicable to the validity of the trust shall determine whether that law or the law governing a severable aspect of the trust may be replaced by another law.

Commentary
Under English law the applicable law to a trust can only, it seems, be changed by an application under the Variation of Trusts Act 1958 **[256]** (see *Duke of Marlborough v A-G* [1945] Ch 78) and it is therefore common to include an express provision in trust deeds enabling the trustees to change the law governing the settlement. See also *Chellaram v Chellaram* [2002] WTLR 675.

CHAPTER III
RECOGNITION

ARTICLE 11

A trust created in accordance with the law specified by the preceding Chapter shall be recognised as a trust.

Such recognition shall imply, as a minimum, that the trust property constitutes a separate fund, that the trustee may sue and be sued in his capacity as trustee, and that he may appear or act in this capacity before a notary or any person acting in an official capacity.

In so far as the law applicable to the trust requires or provides, such recognition shall imply in particular—

(a) that personal creditors of the trustee shall have no recourse against the trust assets;
(b) that the trust assets shall not form part of the trustee's estate upon his insolvency or bankruptcy;
(c) that the trust assets shall not form part of the matrimonial property of the trustee or his spouse nor part of the trustee's estate upon his death;
(d) that the trust assets may be recovered when the trustee, in breach of trust, has mingled trust assets with his own property or has alienated trust assets. However, the rights and obligations of any third party holder of the assets shall remain subject to the law determined by the choice of law rules of the forum.

Commentary
Strictly there was little need for this provision but it emphasises that a trust which falls within the preceding provisions will be recognised in other states. However, it must be read subject to arts 15 and 16 below.

ARTICLE 12

Where the trustee desires to register assets, movable or immovable, or documents of title to them, he shall be entitled, in so far as this is not prohibited by or inconsistent with the law of the State where registration is sought, to do so in his capacity as trustee or in such other way that the existence of the trust is disclosed.

Commentary
Note that this is not a mandatory requirement and the trustee can register ownership without disclosing the trust if he wishes and the system of law applicable to it allows.

(English law does not incorporate art 13 of the Convention which gives states a discretion as to whether or not to recognise trusts where they are more closely connected with states which do not have a law of trusts.)

ARTICLE 14

The Convention shall not prevent the application of rules of law more favourable to the recognition of trusts.

Commentary
This Article preserves the common law conflicts of laws rules as they apply to trusts.

CHAPTER IV
GENERAL CLAUSES

ARTICLE 15

The Convention does not prevent the application of provisions of the law designated by the conflicts rules of the forum, in so far as those provisions cannot be derogated from by voluntary act, relating in particular to the following matters—

- (a) the protection of minors and incapable parties;
- (b) the personal and proprietary effects of marriage;
- (c) succession rights, testate and intestate, especially the indefeasible shares of spouses and relatives;
- (d) the transfer of title property and security interests in property;
- (e) the protection of creditors in matters of insolvency;
- (f) the protection, in other respects, of third parties acting in good faith.

If recognition of a trust is prevented by application of the preceding paragraph, the court shall try to give effect to the objects of the trust by other means.

Commentary
The effect of this article is that where there are mandatory rules which no voluntary act can overcome (eg the forced heirship rules which many jurisdictions impose), the normal conflicts of laws rules applied by the state in question must be applied rather than the provisions of this Convention. The final sentence empowers a court which does not recognise a trust because of a mandatory rule, to give effect to it in some other way. It is not at all clear how this would apply in English law.

ARTICLE 16

The Convention does not prevent the application of those provisions of the law of the forum which must be applied even to international situations, irrespective of rules of conflict of laws.

Commentary
This article preserves the rules of forum in respect of what are known as overriding rules—rules of a country which have extra-territorial effect. The old exchange control legislation in England might be an example.

ARTICLE 17

In the Convention the word "law" means the rules of law in force in a State other than its rules of conflict of laws.

ARTICLE 18

The provisions of the Convention may be disregarded when their application would be manifestly incompatible with public policy.

Commentary
If the effect of applying foreign law under the Convention is to offend against English public policy (eg discrimination on the grounds of race, or human rights) then the law can be ignored.

ARTICLE 22

The Convention applies to trusts regardless of the date on which they were created.

Commentary
Note s 1(5) above.

[403]

FAMILY LAW REFORM ACT 1987

1987 Chapter 42

ARRANGEMENT OF SECTIONS

PART I GENERAL PRINCIPLE

PART III PROPERTY RIGHTS

PART VI MISCELLANEOUS AND SUPPLEMENTAL

An Act to reform the law relating to the consequences of birth outside marriage; to make further provision with respect to the rights and duties of parents and the determination of parentage; and for connected purposes

[15th May 1987]

General Note
Only the sections of and Schedules to the Family Law Reform Act 1987 (FLRA 1987) which are directly relevant to trusts and estates are reproduced here. These provisions took the law on illegitimate children one step further, repealing the provisions of the Family Law Reform Act 1969 and ensuring as far as possible that illegitimate children are on a par with legitimate children for the purposes of succession and the construction trusts and wills.

PART I
GENERAL PRINCIPLE

1 General principle

(1) In this Act and enactments passed and instruments made after the coming into force of this section, references (however expressed) to any relationship between two

persons shall, unless the contrary intention appears, be construed without regard to whether or not the father and mother of either of them, or the father and mother of any person through whom the relationship is deduced, have or had been married to each other at any time.

(2) In this Act and enactments passed after the coming into force of this section, unless the contrary intention appears—

(a) references to a person whose father and mother were married to each other at the time of his birth include; and

(b) references to a person whose father and mother were not married to each other at the time of his birth do not include,

references to any person to whom subsection (3) below applies, and cognate references shall be construed accordingly.

(3) This subsection applies to any person who—

(a) is treated as legitimate by virtue of section 1 of the Legitimacy Act 1976;

(b) is a legitimated person within the meaning of section 10 of that Act;

[(c) is an adopted person within the meaning of Chapter 4 of Part 1 of the Adoption and Children Act 2002]; or

(d) is otherwise treated in law as legitimate.

(4) For the purpose of construing references falling within subsection (2) above, the time of a person's birth shall be taken to include any time during the period beginning with—

(a) the insemination resulting in his birth; or

(b) where there was no such insemination, his conception,

and (in either case) ending with his birth.

Amendment

Sub-s (3): para (c) substituted by the Adoption and Children Act 2002, s 139(1), Sch 3, paras 50, 51.

Commentary

In the case of wills executed before 1 January 1970, references to children at common law in general (with some exceptions) were construed as references to legitimate children only. For wills executed after that date but before 4 April 1988 (when the FLRA 1987 came into force) the Family Law Reform Act 1969 provided that references to children in a will should, unless there was a contrary intention, be construed as references to the illegitimate children of the testator. For wills executed after 4 April 1988 the fundamental principle set out in this section is that there is, in construing any instrument or enactment, no concept of illegitimacy. The Act does not apply retrospectively and that is not contrary to the European Convention on Human Rights, see: *Upton v National Westminster Bank plc* unreported 9 August 2004. See s 19(1) below as to the specific application of this principle to wills. Note that sub-s (3) preserves the special status of adopted and legitimated persons and reference should be made to the relevant legislation (outside the scope of this work) where that is dealt with.

[404]

PART III
PROPERTY RIGHTS

18 Succession on intestacy

(1) In Part IV of the Administration of Estates Act 1925 (which deals with the distribution of the estate of an intestate), references (however expressed) to any relationship between two persons shall be construed in accordance with section 1 above.

(2) For the purposes of subsection (1) above and that Part of that Act, a person whose father and mother were not married to each other at the time of his birth shall be

presumed not to have been survived by his father, or by any person related to him only through his father, unless the contrary is shown.

(3) In section 50(1) of that Act (which relates to the construction of documents), the reference to Part IV of that Act, or to the foregoing provisions of that Part, shall in relation to an instrument inter vivos made, or a will or codicil coming into operation, after the coming into force of this section (but not in relation to instruments inter vivos made or wills or codicils coming into operation earlier) be construed as including references to this section.

(4) This section does not affect any rights under the intestacy of a person dying before the coming into force of this section.

Commentary

This section only applies to deaths after 3 April 1988 when the FLRA 1987 came into force (and see the commentary under s 1). For persons dying before that date but after 1 January 1970 when the Family Law Reform Act 1969 came into force, the rule was that illegitimate children could take on the intestacy of either parent and his parents had rights on his intestacy. However, other relatives did not take. This section which should be read in the light of the general principle set out in s 1, effectively treats illegitimate children in the same way as all other children. Subsection (2) (which reflects a similar but more restrictive provision in the Family Law Reform Act 1969) deals with the fact that identifying the father of an illegitimate child may prove difficult, but the presumption does not prevent the father of the deceased child and his relatives establishing paternity. For the references in sub-ss (1) and (3) to the Administration of Estates Act 1925 see **[181]**.

[405]

19 Dispositions of property

(1) In the following dispositions, namely—

(a) dispositions inter vivos made on or after the date on which this section comes into force; and

(b) dispositions by will or codicil where the will or codicil is made on or after that date,

references (whether express or implied) to any relationship between two persons shall be construed in accordance with section 1 above.

(2) It is hereby declared that the use, without more, of the word "heir" or "heirs" or any expression [purporting to create] an entailed interest in real or personal property does not show a contrary intention for the purposes of section 1 as applied by subsection (1) above.

(3) In relation to the dispositions mentioned in subsection (1) above, section 33 of the Trustee Act 1925 (which specifies the trust implied by a direction that income is to be held on protective trusts for the benefit of any person) shall have effect as if any reference (however expressed) to any relationship between two persons were construed in accordance with section 1 above.

(4) Where under any disposition of real or personal property, any interest in such property is limited (whether subject to any preceding limitation or charge or not) in such a way that it would, apart from this section, devolve (as nearly as the law permits) along with a dignity or title of honour, then—

(a) whether or not the disposition contains an express reference to the dignity or title of honour; and

(b) whether or not the property or some interest in the property may in some event become severed from it,

nothing in this section shall operate to sever the property or any interest in it from the dignity or title, but the property or interest shall devolve in all respects as if this section had not been enacted.

(5) This section is without prejudice to section 42 of the Adoption Act 1976 [or section 69 of the Adoption and Children Act 2002] (construction of dispositions in cases of adoption).

(6) In this section "disposition" means a disposition, including an oral disposition, of real or personal property whether inter vivos or by will or codicil.

(7) Notwithstanding any rule of law, a disposition made by will or codicil executed before the date on which this section comes into force shall not be treated for the purposes of this section as made on or after that date by reason only that the will or codicil is confirmed by a codicil executed on or after that date.

Amendment

Sub-s (2): words in square brackets substituted by the Trusts of Land and Appointment of Trustees Act 1996, s 25(1), Sch 3, para 25; for savings in relation to entailed interests created before the commencement of that Act, and savings consequential upon the abolition of the doctrine of conversion, see s 25(4), (5) thereof.
Sub-s (5): words "or section 69 of the Adoption and Children Act 2002" in square brackets inserted by the Adoption and Children Act 2002, s 139(1), Sch 3, paras 50, 52.

Commentary

This section must be read together with the general principles set out in s 1 and the commentary thereon. Before the commencement of the FLRA 1987 on 4 April 1988, the Family Law Reform Act 1969, s 15 applied so that references to children included references to illegitimate children, which in turn reversed the common law rule. This rule of construction admits to a contrary intention. Subsection (2) means that the use of the word "heirs" will not on its own constitute that intention, but note that the position was different under the Family Law Reform Act 1969. Subsection (3) refers to statutory protective trusts under the Trustee Act 1925, s 33 as to which see **[102]**. For the meaning of disposition in sub-s (5) see *Re Hoff* [1942] Ch 298 and *Re Brinkley's Will Trusts* [1968] Ch 407. The FLRA 1987 applies to wills executed after its commencement regardless of the date of death (sub-s (7)).

[406]

20 No special protection for trustees and personal representatives

. . .

Commentary

This section repeals the Family Law Reform Act 1969, s 17.
The effect of this repeal is that trustees must rely on the general protection afforded to them under the Trustee Act 1925, s 27 **[97]**.

[407]

21 Entitlement to grant of probate etc

(1) For the purpose of determining the person or persons who would in accordance with probate rules be entitled to a grant of probate or administration in respect of the estate of a deceased person, the deceased shall be presumed, unless the contrary is shown, not to have been survived—

- (a) by any person related to him whose father and mother were not married to each other at the time of his birth; or
- (b) by any person whose relationship with him is deduced through such a person as is mentioned in paragraph (a) above.

(2) In this section "probate rules" means rules of court made under section 127 of the *Supreme Court Act 1981* [Senior Courts Act 1981].

(3) This section does not apply in relation to the estate of a person dying before the coming into force of this section.

Amendment
Sub-s (2): words "Supreme Court Act 1981" in italics repealed and subsequent words in square brackets substituted, from a date to be appointed, by the Constitutional Reform Act 2005, s 59(5), Sch 11, Pt 1, para 1(2).

Commentary
The presumption in this section can be rebutted by the applicant for a grant swearing an oath (see *Practice Direction* [1988] 1 WLR 610). The current probate rules referred to in sub-s (2) are the Non-Contentious Probate Rules 1987, SI 1987/2024 **[Appendix V]**.

[408]

PART VI
MISCELLANEOUS AND SUPPLEMENTAL

MISCELLANEOUS

27 Artificial insemination

(1) Where after the coming into force of this section a child is born in England and Wales as the result of the artificial insemination of a woman who—

(a) was at the time of the insemination a party to a marriage (being a marriage which had not at that time been dissolved or annulled); and

(b) was artificially inseminated with the semen of some person other than the other party to that marriage,

then, unless it is proved to the satisfaction of any court by which the matter has to be determined that the other party to that marriage did not consent to the insemination, the child shall be treated in law as the child of the parties to that marriage and shall not be treated as the child of any person other than the parties to that marriage.

(2) Any reference in this section to a marriage includes a reference to a void marriage if at the time of the insemination resulting in the birth of the child both or either of the parties reasonably believed that the marriage was valid; and for the purposes of this section it shall be presumed, unless the contrary is shown, that one of the parties so believed at that time that the marriage was valid.

(3) Nothing in this section shall affect the succession to any dignity or title of honour or render any person capable of succeeding to or transmitting a right to succeed to any such dignity or title.

Commentary
This section deals with the problem of a child conceived as a result of artificial insemination where the mother is married to someone other than the donor. At common law her husband would not be the father of the child, see *Re M (Child Support Act: Parentage)* [1997] 2 FLR 90. This section must be read together with the Human Fertilisation and Embryology Act 1990, s 49 **[417]** which disapplies this section to artificial inseminations carried out after 1 August 1991. The crucial date is that of the insemination and not the birth of the child, see: *Re J v C* [2007] Fam 1. That latter case was also authority for the proposition that a party to a marriage which is void because he was of the same gender as the mother, is not a marriage within the meaning of the Act. This section has been replaced by similar but more wide-ranging provisions contained in the Human Fertilisation and Embryology Act 1990 which apply to children born outside as well as within England and Wales.

[409]

34 Short title, commencement and extent

(1) This Act may be cited as the Family Law Reform Act 1987.

(2) This Act shall come into force on such day as the Lord Chancellor may by order made by statutory instrument appoint; and different days may be so appointed for different provisions or different purposes.

(3) Without prejudice to the transitional provisions contained in Schedule 3 to this Act, an order under subsection (2) above may make such further transitional provisions as appear to the Lord Chancellor to be necessary or expedient in connection with the provisions brought into force by the order, including—

(a) such adaptations of the provisions so brought into force; and

(b) such adaptations of any provisions of this Act then in force,

as appear to him necessary or expedient in consequence of the partial operation of this Act.

(4) The following provisions of this Act extend to Scotland and Northern Ireland, namely—

(a) section 33(1) and paragraphs 12, 13 and 74 of Schedule 2;

(b) section 33(2) and paragraph 7 of Schedule 3 so far as relating to the operation of the Maintenance Orders Act 1950;

(c) section 33(4) and Schedule 4 so far as relating to that Act and the Interpretation Act 1978; and

(d) this section.

(5) Subject to subsection (4) above, this Act extends to England and Wales only.

[410]

SCHEDULE 3
TRANSITIONAL PROVISIONS AND SAVINGS

Section 33(2)

APPLICATIONS PENDING UNDER AMENDED OR REPEALED ENACTMENTS

1 This Act (including the repeals and amendments made by it) shall not have effect in relation to any application made under any enactment repealed or amended by this Act if that application is pending at the time when the provision of this Act which repeals or amends that enactment comes into force.

. . .

2–5

. . .

AFFILIATION ORDERS

6 (1) Neither section 17 of this Act nor any associated amendment or repeal shall affect, or affect the operation of any enactment in relation to—

(a) any affiliation order made under the Affiliation Proceedings Act 1957 which is in force immediately before the coming into force of that section; or

(b) any affiliation order made under that Act by virtue of paragraph 1 above.

(2) Any reference in this paragraph or paragraph 7 below to an affiliation order made under the Affiliation Proceedings Act 1957 includes a reference to—

(a) an affiliation order made, by virtue of section 44 of the National Assistance Act 1948, section 19 of the Supplementary Benefits Act 1976, section 49 or

50 of the Child Care Act 1980 or section 25 of the Social Security Act 1986; and

(b) any order made in relation to such an order.

7 Where—

(a) an application is made to the High Court or a county court for an order under section 11B of the 1971 Act in respect of a child whose parents were not married to each other at the time of his birth, and

(b) an affiliation order made under the Affiliation Proceedings Act 1957 and providing for periodical payments is in force in respect of the child by virtue of this Schedule,

the court may, if it thinks fit, direct that the affiliation order shall cease to have effect on such date as may be specified in the direction.

PROPERTY RIGHTS

8 The repeal by this Act of section 14 of the Family Law Reform Act 1969 shall not affect any rights arising under the intestacy of a person dying before the coming into force of the repeal.

9 The repeal by this Act of section 15 of the Family Law Reform Act 1969 shall not affect, or affect the operation of section 33 of the Trustee Act 1925 in relation to—

(a) any disposition inter vivos made before the date on which the repeal comes into force; or

(b) any disposition by will or codicil executed before that date.

10 The repeal by this Act of section 17 of the Family Law Reform Act 1969 shall not affect the liability of trustees or personal representatives in respect of any conveyance or distribution made before the coming into force of the repeal.

REGISTRATION OF BIRTHS

11, 12

. . .

Amendment

Paras 2–5: repealed by the Adoption and Children Act 2002, s 139(3), Sch 5.
Paras 11, 12: repealed by the Children Act 1989, s 108(7), Sch 15.

Commentary

Only the paragraphs in this Schedule directly relating to trusts and estates are reproduced here. Note that para 8 preserves the rights of any person who becomes entitled on intestacy under the Family Law Reform Act 1969, s 14 (now the FLRA 1987, s 18). The reference in para 9 is to protective trusts, now dealt with by the FLRA 1987, s 19(3). For the Trustee Act 1925, s 33 see **[102]**. The Family Law Reform Act 1969, s 17 referred to in para 10 provided protection to trustees and personal representatives who distributed in ignorance of the existence of someone who was illegitimate. See the commentary on s 21 above.

[411]

SCHEDULE 4
REPEALS

Section 33(4)

Chapter	*Short Title*	*Extent of Repeal*
11 & 12 Geo. 6 c 29	The National Assistance Act 1948	Section 42(2).
		Section 44.
14 Geo. 6 c 37	The Maintenance Orders Act 1950	Section 3.
		In section 16(2)(a)—
		(a) sub-paragraph (iv);
		(b) the sub-paragraph (vi) inserted by the Children Act 1975;
		(c) in the sub-paragraph (vi) inserted by the Supplementary Benefits Act 1976, the words from "or section 4 of the Affiliation Proceedings Act 1957" to the end;
		(d) in sub-paragraph (viii), the words from "or section 4 of the Affiliation Proceedings Act 1957" to the end.
3 & 4 Eliz. 2 c 18	The Army Act 1955	In section 150(5), the words from "references to a sum ordered to be paid" to the end.
3 & 4 Eliz. 2 c 19	The Air Force Act 1955	In section 150(5), the words "references to a sum ordered to be paid" to the end.
5 & 6 Eliz. 2 c 53	The Naval Discipline Act 1957	In section 101(5), the words "and includes an affiliation order within the meaning of the Affiliation Orders Act 1914".
5 & 6 Eliz. 2 c 55	The Affiliation Proceedings Act 1957	The whole Act.
6 & 7 Eliz. 2 c 39	The Maintenance Orders Act 1958	In section 21(1), the words "affiliation order".
7 & 8 Eliz. 2 c 73	The Legitimacy Act 1959	The whole Act.
1968 c 63	The Domestic and Appellate Proceedings (Restriction of Publicity) Act 1968	In section 2(1), the word "and" following paragraph (c).
1969 c 46	The Family Law Reform Act 1969	Sections 14 and 15.
		Section 17.
		Section 27.
1970 c 31	The Administration of Justice Act 1970	In Schedule 8, paragraph 5.
1971 c 3	The Guardianship of Minors Act 1971	In section 12B, in subsection (1), the words "in maintaining the minor" and, in subsection (3), the words "of a minor".
		Section 14 and the heading preceding that section.
1971 c 32	The Attachment of Earnings Act 1971	In Schedule 1, paragraph 6.
1972 c 18	The Maintenance Orders (Reciprocal Enforcement) Act 1972	Section 3(3).
		In section 27(9), the words "section 5(5) of the Affiliation Proceedings Act 1957".

Chapter	*Short Title*	*Extent of Repeal*
		In section 30— (a) in subsection (3), the words "the Affiliation Proceedings Act 1957 or", the words "paragraph (b) of section 2(1) of the said Act of 1957 (time for making complaint) or", the words "(provision to the like effect), as the case may be", the words "three years (or" and the words "in the case of a complaint under the said Act of 1924)"; (b) in subsection (5), the words "the said Act of 1957" and the words "as the case may be"; (c) in subsection (6), the words "or an affiliation order under the said Act of 1957".
		In section 41— (a) subsection (1); (b) in subsection (2A), paragraph (a); (c) in subsection (2B), paragraph (a).
1972 c 49	The Affiliation Proceedings (Amendment) Act 1972	The whole Act.
1973 c 29	The Guardianship Act 1973	Section 2(6).
		Section 4(3D).
1974 c 4	The Legal Aid Act 1974	In Schedule 1, in Part I, paragraph 2.
1975 c 72	The Children Act 1975	In section 34, subsections (3) and (4).
		Section 36(5A).
		Section 45.
		In section 85(2), the words "(which relate to separation agreements between husband and wife)".
		In section 93, subsections (1) and (2).
		In Schedule 3, paragraphs 14 and 75(1).
1976 c 36	The Adoption Act 1976	In Schedule 3, paragraph 16.
1978 c 22	The Domestic Proceedings and Magistrates' Courts Act 1978	In section 20, subsections (10) and (13).
		In section 36(1), paragraph (c).
		Section 38(2).
		Section 41.
		In section 45, subsections (2) and (3).
		In Schedule 2, paragraphs 30 and 44.
1978 c 30	The Interpretation Act 1978	In Schedule 2, in paragraph 4, the words "earlier than the commencement of this Act".
1980 c 5	The Child Care Act 1980	Sections 49 and 50.
		In section 52(1), paragraph (b).
		In section 54, in subsections (1) and (2), the words "49, 50".
		In section 55, subsection (3) and, in subsection (5), the words from "and any jurisdiction conferred by this section in affiliation proceedings" to the end.

Chapter	Short Title	Extent of Repeal
		In section 87(1), in the definition of "relative", the words from "and includes" to the end. In Schedule 2, paragraphs 4 and 5 and, in paragraph 7, the words "49, 50". In Schedule 5, paragraphs 6 to 8.
1980 c 43	The Magistrates' Courts Act 1980	In section 59(2), the words "an affiliation order". In section 65(1)— (a) in paragraph (b), the words "or section 44"; (b) paragraph (d); (c) in paragraph (i), the words "or section 19"; (d) in paragraph (k), the words "49 or 50". Section 92(3). In section 150(1), the definition of "affiliation order".
1981 c 54	The Supreme Court Act 1981	In Schedule 1, in paragraph 3(b)(iii), the words "affiliation or".
1982 c 24	The Social Security and Housing Benefits Act 1982	In Schedule 4, paragraph 1.
1986 c 50	The Social Security Act 1986	In section 24, subsections (2) and (3). Section 25.

[412]

HUMAN FERTILISATION AND EMBRYOLOGY ACT 1990

1990 Chapter 37

ARRANGEMENT OF SECTIONS

An Act to make provision in connection with human embryos and any subsequent development of such embryos; to prohibit certain practices in connection with embryos and gametes; to establish a Human Fertilisation and Embryology Authority; to make provision about the persons who in certain circumstances are to be treated in law as the parents of a child; and to amend the Surrogacy Arrangements Act 1985

[1st November 1990]

General Note

The provisions of the Human Fertilisation and Embryology Act 1990 (HFEA 1990) which are set out below are those which have relevance to succession. Before the coming into force of the HFEA 1990 the position of children conceived by artificial insemination was governed by the Family Reform Act 1987, s 27 which is included in this work **[409]**. However, that Act does not apply to artificial insemination taking place after 1 August 1991.

27 Meaning of "mother"

(1) The woman who is carrying or has carried a child as a result of the placing in her of an embryo or of sperm and eggs, and no other woman, is to be treated as the mother of the child.

(2) Subsection (1) above does not apply to any child to the extent that the child is treated by virtue of adoption as not being the [woman's child].

(3) Subsection (1) above applies whether the woman was in the United Kingdom or elsewhere at the time of the placing in her of the embryo or the sperm and eggs.

Amendment

Sub-s (2): words "woman's child" in square brackets substituted by the Adoption and Children Act 2002, s 139(1), Sch 3, paras 76, 77.

Modification

Modification: sub-s (2) modified, in relation to parental orders, to read as a reference to the child being treated by virtue of a parental order as not being the child of any person other than the husband and wife within the meaning of section 30 of this Act, by the Parental Orders (Human Fertilisation and Embryology) Regulations 1994, SI 1994/2767, reg 4, Sch 3 and the Parental Orders (Human Fertilisation and Embryology) (Scotland) Regulations 1994, SI 1994/2804, reg 3, Sch 2, para 6.

Commentary

This section deals with the problem when fertilisation takes place as a result of eggs being donated by another woman, and makes it clear that it is the woman giving birth to the child who is the mother, and not the egg donor.

[413]

28 Meaning of "father"

(1) [Subject to subsections (5A) to (5I) below,] this section applies in the case of a child who is being or has been carried by a woman as the result of the placing in her of an embryo or of sperm and eggs or her artificial insemination.

(2) If—

(a) at the time of the placing in her of the embryo or the sperm and eggs or of her insemination, the woman was a party to a marriage, and

(b) the creation of the embryo carried by her was not brought about with the sperm of the other party to the marriage,

then, subject to subsection (5) below, the other party to the marriage shall be treated as the father of the child unless it is shown that he did not consent to the placing in her of the embryo or the sperm and eggs or to her insemination (as the case may be).

(3) If no man is treated, by virtue of subsection (2) above, as the father of the child but—

(a) the embryo or the sperm and eggs were placed in the woman, or she was artificially inseminated, in the course of treatment services provided for her and a man together by a person to whom a licence applies, and

(b) the creation of the embryo carried by her was not brought about with the sperm of that man,

then, subject to subsection (5) below, that man shall be treated as the father of the child.

(4) Where a person is treated as the father of the child by virtue of subsection (2) or (3) above, no other person is to be treated as the father of the child.

(5) Subsections (2) and (3) above do not apply—

(a) in relation to England and Wales and Northern Ireland, to any child who, by virtue of the rules of common law, is treated as the legitimate child of the parties to a marriage,

(b) in relation to Scotland, to any child who, by virtue of any enactment or other rule of law, is treated as the child of the parties to a marriage, or

(c) to any child to the extent that the child is treated by virtue of adoption as not being the [man's child].

[(5A) If—

(a) a child has been carried by a woman as the result of the placing in her of an embryo or of sperm and eggs or her artificial insemination,

(b) the creation of the embryo carried by her was brought about by using the sperm of a man after his death, or the creation of the embryo was brought about using the sperm of a man before his death but the embryo was placed in the woman after his death,

(c) the woman was a party to a marriage with the man immediately before his death,

(d) the man consented in writing (and did not withdraw the consent)—

(i) to the use of his sperm after his death which brought about the creation of the embryo carried by the woman or (as the case may be) to the placing in the woman after his death of the embryo which was brought about using his sperm before his death, and

(ii) to being treated for the purpose mentioned in subsection (5I) below as the father of any resulting child,

(e) the woman has elected in writing not later than the end of the period of 42 days from the day on which the child was born for the man to be treated for the purpose mentioned in subsection (5I) below as the father of the child, and

(f) no-one else is to be treated as the father of the child by virtue of subsection (2) or (3) above or by virtue of adoption or the child being treated as mentioned in paragraph (a) or (b) of subsection (5) above,

then the man shall be treated for the purpose mentioned in subsection (5I) below as the father of the child.

(5B) If—

(a) a child has been carried by a woman as the result of the placing in her of an embryo or of sperm and eggs or her artificial insemination,

(b) the creation of the embryo carried by her was brought about by using the sperm of a man after his death, or the creation of the embryo was brought about using the sperm of a man before his death but the embryo was placed in the woman after his death,

(c) the woman was not a party to a marriage with the man immediately before his death but treatment services were being provided for the woman and the man together before his death either by a person to whom a licence applies or outside the United Kingdom,

(d) the man consented in writing (and did not withdraw the consent)—

(i) to the use of his sperm after his death which brought about the creation of the embryo carried by the woman or (as the case may be) to the placing in the woman after his death of the embryo which was brought about using his sperm before his death, and

(ii) to being treated for the purpose mentioned in subsection (5I) below as the father of any resulting child,

(e) the woman has elected in writing not later than the end of the period of 42 days from the day on which the child was born for the man to be treated for the purpose mentioned in subsection (5I) below as the father of the child, and

(f) no-one else is to be treated as the father of the child by virtue of subsection (2) or (3) above or by virtue of adoption or the child being treated as mentioned in paragraph (a) or (b) of subsection (5) above,

then the man shall be treated for the purpose mentioned in subsection (5I) below as the father of the child.

(5C) If—

(a) a child has been carried by a woman as the result of the placing in her of an embryo,

(b) the embryo was created at a time when the woman was a party to a marriage,

(c) the creation of the embryo was not brought about with the sperm of the other party to the marriage,

(d) the other party to the marriage died before the placing of the embryo in the woman,

(e) the other party to the marriage consented in writing (and did not withdraw the consent)—

(i) to the placing of the embryo in the woman after his death, and

(ii) to being treated for the purpose mentioned in subsection (5I) below as the father of any resulting child,

(f) the woman has elected in writing not later than the end of the period of 42 days from the day on which the child was born for the other party to the marriage to be treated for the purpose mentioned in subsection (5I) below as the father of the child, and

(g) no-one else is to be treated as the father of the child by virtue of subsection (2) or (3) above or by virtue of adoption or the child being treated as mentioned in paragraph (a) or (b) of subsection (5) above,

then the other party to the marriage shall be treated for the purpose mentioned in subsection (5I) below as the father of the child.

(5D) If—

(a) a child has been carried by a woman as the result of the placing in her of an embryo,

(b) the embryo was not created at a time when the woman was a party to a marriage but was created in the course of treatment services provided for the woman and a man together either by a person to whom a licence applies or outside the United Kingdom,

(c) the creation of the embryo was not brought about with the sperm of that man,

(d) the man died before the placing of the embryo in the woman,

(e) the man consented in writing (and did not withdraw the consent)—

(i) to the placing of the embryo in the woman after his death, and

(ii) to being treated for the purpose mentioned in subsection (5I) below as the father of any resulting child,

(f) the woman has elected in writing not later than the end of the period of 42 days from the day on which the child was born for the man to be treated for the purpose mentioned in subsection (5I) below as the father of the child, and

(g) no-one else is to be treated as the father of the child by virtue of subsection (2) or (3) above or by virtue of adoption or the child being treated as mentioned in paragraph (a) or (b) of subsection (5) above, then the man shall be treated for the purpose mentioned in subsection (5I) below as the father of the child.

(5E) In the application of subsections (5A) to (5D) above to Scotland, for any reference to a period of 42 days there shall be substituted a reference to a period of 21 days.

(5F) The requirement under subsection (5A), (5B), (5C) or (5D) above as to the making of an election (which requires an election to be made either on or before the day on which the child was born or within the period of 42 or, as the case may be, 21 days from that day) shall nevertheless be treated as satisfied if the required election is made after the end of that period but with the consent of the Registrar General under subsection (5G) below.

(5G) The Registrar General may at any time consent to the making of an election after the end of the period mentioned in subsection (5F) above if, on an application made to him in accordance with such requirements as he may specify, he is satisfied that there is a compelling reason for giving his consent to the making of such an election.

(5H) In subsections (5F) and (5G) above "the Registrar General" means the Registrar General for England and Wales, the Registrar General of Births, Deaths and Marriages for Scotland or (as the case may be) the Registrar General for Northern Ireland.

(5I) The purpose referred to in subsections (5A) to (5D) above is the purpose of enabling the man's particulars to be entered as the particulars of the child's father in (as the case may be) a register of live-births or still-births kept under the Births and Deaths Registration Act 1953 or the Births and Deaths Registration (Northern Ireland) Order 1976 or a register of births or still-births kept under the Registration of Births, Deaths and Marriages (Scotland) Act 1965.]

(6) Where—

(a) the sperm of a man who had given such consent as is required by paragraph 5 of Schedule 3 to this Act was used for a purpose for which such consent was required, or

(b) the sperm of a man, or any embryo the creation of which was brought about with his sperm, was used after his death,

he is not[, subject to subsections (5A) and (5B) above,] to be treated as the father of the child.

(7) The references in subsection (2) above [and subsections (5A) to (5D) above] to the parties to a marriage at the time there referred to—

(a) are to the parties to a marriage subsisting at that time, unless a judicial separation was then in force, but

(b) include the parties to a void marriage if either or both of them reasonably believed at that time that the marriage was valid; and for the purposes of this subsection it shall be presumed, unless the contrary is shown, that one of them reasonably believed at that time that the marriage was valid.

(8) This section applies whether the woman was in the United Kingdom or elsewhere at the time of the placing in her of the embryo or the sperm and eggs or her artificial insemination.

(9) In subsection (7)(a) above, "judicial separation" includes a legal separation obtained in a country outside the British Islands and recognised in the United Kingdom.

Amendment

Sub-s (1): words "Subject to subsections (5A) to (5I) below," in square brackets inserted by the Human Fertilisation and Embryology (Deceased Fathers) Act 2003, s 2(1), Schedule, para 13.

Sub-s (5): in para (c) words "man's child" in square brackets substituted by the Adoption and Children Act 2002, s 139(1), Sch 3, paras 76, 78.
Sub-ss (5A)-(5I): inserted by the Human Fertilisation and Embryology (Deceased Fathers) Act 2003, s 1(1).
Sub-s (6): words ", subject to subsections (5A) and (5B) above," in square brackets inserted by the Human Fertilisation and Embryology (Deceased Fathers) Act 2003, s 2(1), Schedule, para 14.
Sub-s (7): words "and subsections (5A) to (5D) above" in square brackets inserted by the Human Fertilisation and Embryology (Deceased Fathers) Act 2003, s 2(1), Schedule, para 15.

Modification
Modification: sub-s (5)(c) modified, in relation to parental orders, to read as a reference to the child being treated by virtue of a parental order as not being the child of any person other than the husband and wife within the meaning of section 30 of this Act, by the Parental Orders (Human Fertilisation and Embryology) Regulations 1994, SI 1994/2767, reg 4, Sch 3 and Parental Orders (Human Fertilisation and Embryology) (Scotland) Regulations 1994, SI 1994/2804, reg 3, Sch 2, para 6.

Commentary
These provisions deal with the problem of fertilisation occurring by the use of sperm from a sperm donor, who will usually not be known to the children concerned, and deals with the problem of a child conceived as a result of artificial insemination where the mother is married to someone other than the donor, or has been treated together with a partner. At common law her husband would not be the father of the child, see *Re M (Child Support Act: Parentage)* [1997] 2 FLR 90. As to sub-s (3) and the meaning of treatment services, see *Re B (Parentage)* [1996] 2 FLR 15 and *Re Q (Parental Order)* [1996] 1 FLR 369 and *Re D* [2005] 2 AC 621 for the time at which the matter is to be assessed. As to the use of sperm after the death of the donor within sub-s (6)(b), see *R v Human Fertilisation and Embryology Authority, ex p Blood* [1997] 2 All ER 687 now dealt with by subsections (5A) onwards.

[414]

29 Effect of sections 27 and 28

(1) Where by virtue of section 27 or 28 of this Act a person is to be treated as the mother or father of a child, that person is to be treated in law as the mother or, as the case may be, father of the child for all purposes.

(2) Where by virtue of section 27 or 28 of this Act a person is not to be treated as the mother or father of a child, that person is to be treated in law as not being the mother or, as the case may be, father of the child for any purpose.

(3) Where subsection (1) or (2) above has effect, references to any relationship between two people in any enactment, deed or other instrument or document (whenever passed or made) are to be read accordingly.

[(3A) Subsections (1) to (3) above do not apply in relation to the treatment in law of a deceased man in a case to which section 28(5A), (5B), (5C) or (5D) of this Act applies.

(3B) Where subsection (5A), (5B), (5C) or (5D) of section 28 of this Act applies, the deceased man—

- (a) is to be treated in law as the father of the child for the purpose referred to in that subsection, but
- (b) is to be treated in law as not being the father of the child for any other purpose.

(3C) Where subsection (3B) above has effect, references to any relationship between two people in any enactment, deed or other instrument or document (whenever passed or made) are to be read accordingly.

(3D) In subsection (3C) above "enactment" includes an enactment comprised in, or in an instrument made under, an Act of the Scottish Parliament or Northern Ireland legislation.]

(4) In relation to England and Wales and Northern Ireland, nothing in the provisions of section 27(1) or 28(2) to (4) [or (5A) to (5I)], read with this section, affects—

- (a) the succession to any dignity or title of honour or renders any person capable of succeeding to or transmitting a right to succeed to any such dignity or title, or
- (b) the devolution of any property limited (expressly or not) to devolve (as nearly as the law permits) along with any dignity or title of honour.

(5) In relation to Scotland—

- (a) those provisions do not apply to any title, coat of arms, honour or dignity transmissible on the death of the holder thereof or affect the succession thereto or the devolution thereof, and
- (b) where the terms of any deed provide that any property or interest in property shall devolve along with a title, coat of arms, honour or dignity, nothing in those provisions shall prevent that property or interest from so devolving.

Amendment

Sub-ss (3A)-(3D): inserted by the Human Fertilisation and Embryology (Deceased Fathers) Act 2003, s 1(2).

Sub-s (4): words "or (5A) to (5I)" in square brackets inserted by the Human Fertilisation and Embryology (Deceased Fathers) Act 2003, s 2(1), Schedule, para 16.

Commentary

These provisions make it clear that if a child is treated under ss 27 and 28 as the child of a particular person, then on their death they will have all the rights to succeed to their property as any other child (as to which see the Administration of Estates Act 1925, s 46 **[221]**) but as with the provisions of the Family Law Reform Act 1987 **[404]**, these rules do not affect titles of honour and their passing.

[415]

30 Parental orders in favour of gamete donors

(1) The court may make an order providing for a child to be treated in law as the child of the parties to a marriage (referred to in this section as "the husband" and "the wife") if—

- (a) the child has been carried by a woman other than the wife as the result of the placing in her of an embryo or sperm and eggs or her artificial insemination.
- (b) the gametes of the husband or the wife, or both, were used to bring about the creation of the embryo, and
- (c) the conditions in subsections (2) to (7) below are satisfied.

(2) The husband and the wife must apply for the order within six months of the birth of the child or, in the case of a child born before the coming into force of this Act, within six months of such coming into force.

(3) At the time of the application and of the making of the order—

- (a) the child's home must be with the husband and the wife, and
- (b) the husband or the wife, or both of them, must be domiciled in a part of the United Kingdom or in the Channel Islands or the Isle of Man.

(4) At the time of the making of the order both the husband and the wife must have attained the age of eighteen.

(5) The court must be satisfied that both the father of the child (including a person who is the father by virtue of section 28 of this Act), where he is not the husband, and the woman who carried the child have freely, and with full understanding of what is involved, agreed unconditionally to the making of the order.

(6) Subsection (5) above does not require the agreement of a person who cannot be found or is incapable of giving agreement and the agreement of the woman who carried the child is ineffective for the purposes of that subsection if given by her less than six weeks after the child's birth.

(7) The court must be satisfied that no money or other benefit (other than for expenses reasonably incurred) has been given or received by the husband or the wife for or in consideration of—

- (a) the making of the order,
- (b) any agreement required by subsection (5) above,
- (c) the handing over of the child to the husband and the wife, or
- (d) the making of any arrangements with a view to the making of the order,

unless authorised by the court.

(8) For the purposes of an application under this section—

- (a) in relation to England and Wales, section 92(7) to (10) of, and Part I of Schedule 11 to, the Children Act 1989 (jurisdiction of courts) shall apply for the purposes of this section to determine the meaning of "the court" as they apply for the purposes of that Act and proceedings on the application shall be "family proceedings" for the purposes of that Act,
- (b) in relation to Scotland, "the court" means the Court of Session or the sheriff court of the sheriffdom within which the child is, and
- (c) in relation to Northern Ireland, "the court" means the High Court or any county court within whose division the child is.

(9) Regulations may provide—

- (a) for any provision of the enactments about adoption to have effect, with such modifications (if any) as may be specified in the regulations, in relation to orders under this section, and applications for such orders, as it has effect in relation to adoption, and applications for adoption orders, and
- (b) for references in any enactment to adoption, an adopted child or an adoptive relationship to be read (respectively) as references to the effect of an order under this section, a child to whom such an order applies and a relationship arising by virtue of the enactments about adoption, as applied by the regulations, and for similar expressions in connection with adoption to be read accordingly,

and the regulations may include such incidental or supplemental provision as appears to the Secretary of State necessary or desirable in consequence of any provision made by virtue of paragraph (a) or (b) above.

(10) In this section "the enactments about adoption" means the *Adoption Act 1976* [Adoption and Children Act 2002], the Adoption (Scotland) Act 1978, *and* the Adoption (Northern Ireland) Order 1987 [and the Adoption and Children (Scotland) Act 2007 (asp 4)].

(11) Subsection (1)(a) above applies whether the woman was in the United Kingdom or elsewhere at the time of the placing in her of the embryo or the sperm and eggs or her artificial insemination.

Amendment

Sub-s (10): words "Adoption Act 1976" in italics repealed and subsequent words in square brackets substituted, from a date to be appointed, by the Adoption and Children Act 2002, s 139(1), Sch 3, paras 76, 79.
Sub-s (10): word "and" in italics repealed, from a date to be appointed, by the Adoption and Children (Scotland) Act 2007, s 120(2), Sch 3.
Sub-s (10): words "and the Adoption and Children (Scotland) Act 2007 (asp 4)" in square brackets inserted, from a date to be appointed, by the Adoption and Children (Scotland) Act 2007, s 120(1), Sch 2, para 6.

Modification

The reference to "any enactment" in sub-s (9)(b) above shall be read as including a reference to any enactment contained in s 28(5A)-(5I) hereof: see the Human Fertilisation and Embryology (Deceased Fathers) Act 2003, s 2(1), Schedule, para 17; for retrospective, transitional and transitory provision see s 3 thereof.

Commentary

These provisions deal with situations where a surrogate mother has been used. The section only applies to married couples. See further: *Re B (Parentage)* [1996] 2 FLR 15; *Re Q (Parental Order)* [1996] 1 FLR 369; and *U v W (Attorney General Intervening)* [1997] 2 FLR 282.

[416]

49 Short title, commencement, etc

(1) This Act may be cited as the Human Fertilisation and Embryology Act 1990.

(2) This Act shall come into force on such day as the Secretary of State may by order made by statutory instrument appoint and different days may be appointed for different provisions and for different purposes.

(3) Sections 27 to 29 of this Act shall have effect only in relation to children carried by women as a result of the placing in them of embryos or of sperm and eggs, or of their artificial insemination (as the case may be), after the commencement of those sections.

(4) Section 27 of the Family Law Reform Act 1987 (artificial insemination) does not have effect in relation to children carried by women as the result of their artificial insemination after the commencement of sections 27 to 29 of this Act.

(5) Schedule 4 to this Act (which makes minor and consequential amendments) shall have effect.

(6) An order under this section may make such transitional provision as the Secretary of State considers necessary or desirable and, in particular, may provide that where activities are carried on under the supervision of a particular individual, being activities which are carried on under the supervision of that individual at the commencement of sections 3 and 4 of this Act, those activities are to be treated, during such period as may be specified in or determined in accordance with the order, as authorised by a licence (having, in addition to the conditions required by this Act, such conditions as may be so specified or determined) under which that individual is the person responsible.

(7) Her Majesty may by Order in Council direct that any of the provisions of this Act shall extend, with such exceptions, adaptations and modifications (if any) as may be specified in the Order, to any of the Channel Islands.

Commentary

Subsections (3) and (4) make it clear that in the case of inseminations or implantation of embryos before 1 August 1991, the provisions of the Family Law Reform Act 1987, s 27 **[409]** will apply and see: *J v C* [2007] Fam 1. After that the provisions of ss 27–29 above will apply. In essence the new provisions are wider in scope and do not just apply to treatment which has taken place in England and Wales.

[417]

LAW OF PROPERTY (MISCELLANEOUS PROVISIONS) ACT 1994

1994 Chapter 36

ARRANGEMENT OF SECTIONS

PART II MATTERS ARISING IN CONNECTION WITH DEATH

PART III GENERAL PROVISIONS

An Act to provide for new covenants for title to be implied on dispositions of property; to amend the law with respect to certain matters arising in connection with the death of the owner of property; and for connected purposes

[3rd November 1994]

General Note

Only Pt II of the Law of Property (Miscellaneous Provisions) Act 1994 is relevant to trusts and estates, and Pt I has therefore not been reproduced. Part II changes the way in which the estate of an intestate vests—now in the Public Trustee rather than the President of the Family Division—and makes other changes to acts done after someone's death.

PART II
MATTERS ARISING IN CONNECTION WITH DEATH

14 Vesting of estate in case of intestacy or lack of executors

(1) . . .

(2) Any real or personal estate of a person dying before the commencement of this section shall, if it is property to which this subsection applies, vest in the Public Trustee on the commencement of this section.

(3) Subsection (2) above applies to any property—

(a) if it was vested in the Probate Judge under section 9 of the Administration of Estates Act 1925 immediately before the commencement of this section, or

(b) if it was not so vested but as at commencement there has been no grant of representation in respect of it and there is no executor with power to obtain such a grant.

(4) Any property vesting in the Public Trustee by virtue of subsection (2) above shall—

(a) if the deceased died intestate, be treated as vesting in the Public Trustee under section 9(1) of the Administration of Estates Act 1925 (as substituted by subsection (1) above); and

(b) otherwise be treated as vesting in the Public Trustee under section 9(2) of that Act (as so substituted).

(5) Anything done by or in relation to the Probate Judge with respect to property vested in him as mentioned in subsection (3)(a) above shall be treated as having been done by or in relation to the Public Trustee.

(6) So far as may be necessary in consequence of the transfer to the Public Trustee of the functions of the Probate Judge under section 9 of the Administration of Estates Act 1925, any reference in an enactment or instrument to the Probate Judge shall be construed as a reference to the Public Trustee.

Amendment

Sub-s (1): substitutes the Administration of Estates Act 1925, s 9.

Commentary

This section should be read together with the Administration of Estates Act 1925, s 9 **[189]** which sub-s (1) amends. Section 9 provided for the estate of a deceased dying intestate to vest in the Probate Judge, that is, the President of the Family Division. Henceforth, that function will be assumed by the Public Trustee whose office is established by the Public Trustee Act 1906 **[59]**. The Public Trustee has no duties to discharge in this role, nor is he a trustee within the meaning of the Trustee Act 1925 **[81]** (see *Re Deans* [1954] 1 WLR 332 and *Earnshaw v Hartley* [2000] Ch 155). However, notices to terminate the deceased's tenancy can be served on him and land charges registered against him (*Smith v Mather* [1948] 2 KB 212; *Wirral v Smith* (1982) 43 P & CR 312).

[418]

15 Registration of land charges after death

(1)–(4) . . .

(5) The amendments made by this section do not apply where the application for registration was made before the commencement of this section, but without prejudice to a person's right to make a new application after commencement.

Amendment

Sub-ss (1)–(4): insert the Land Charges Act 1972, ss 3(1A), 5(4A), 6(2A).

Commentary

Before this section, if an estate owner died having created a land charge in someone's favour before it was registered under the Land Charges Act, he had to register against the names of the personal representatives (whom he might not know), or in the case of an intestacy, the Probate Judge (as to which see the commentary under s 1 above). This section amends the Land Charges Act 1972 to enable registration against the name of the deceased. As unregistered land disappears this will have less and less relevance. The relevant amended sections are:

Section 3(1A): "[Where a person has died and a land charge created before his death would apart from his death have been registered in his name, it shall be so registered notwithstanding his death.]"

Section 5(4A): "Where a person has died and a pending land action would apart from his death have been registered in his name, it shall be so registered notwithstanding his death."

Section 6(2A) "Where a person has died and any such writ or order as is mentioned in subsection (1)(a) or (b) above would apart from his death have been registered in his name, it shall be so registered notwithstanding his death."

[419]

16 Concurrence of personal representatives in dealings with interests in land

(1), (2) . . .

(3) The amendments made by subsection (1) apply to contracts made after the commencement of this section . . .

Amendment

Sub-s (1): amends the Administration of Estates Act 1925, s 2(2).
Sub-s (2): repealed by the Trusts of Land and Appointment of Trustees Act 1996, s 25(2), Sch 4; for savings in relation to entailed interests created before the commencement of that Act, and savings consequential upon the abolition of the doctrine of conversion, see s 25(4), (5) thereof.
Sub-s (3): words omitted repealed by the Trusts of Land and Appointment of Trustees Act 1996, s 25(2), Sch 4; for savings in relation to entailed interests created before the commencement of that Act, and savings consequential upon the abolition of the doctrine of conversion, see s 25(4), (5) thereof.

Commentary

See the Administration of Estates Act 1925 **[182]** for the amendments made by this section.

[420]

17 Notices affecting land: absence of knowledge of intended recipient's death

(1) Service of a notice affecting land which would be effective but for the death of the intended recipient is effective despite his death if the person serving the notice has no reason to believe that he has died.

(2) Where the person serving a notice affecting land has no reason to believe that the intended recipient has died, the proper address for the purposes of section 7 of the Interpretation Act 1978 (service of documents by post) shall be what would be the proper address apart from his death.

(3) The above provisions do not apply to a notice authorised or required to be served for the purposes of proceedings before—

(a) any court,

(b) any tribunal specified in Schedule 1 to the Tribunals and Inquiries Act 1992 (tribunals within general supervision of Council on Tribunals), or

[(b) any tribunal that is (to any extent) a listed tribunal for, or for any of, the purposes of Schedule 7 to the Tribunals, Courts and Enforcement Act 2007 (functions etc of Administrative Justice and Tribunals Council), or]

(c) the Chief Land Registrar or [the Adjudicator to Her Majesty's Land Registry];

but this is without prejudice to the power to make provision in relation to such proceedings by rules of court, procedural rules *within the meaning of section 8 of the Tribunals and Inquiries Act 1992* [within the meaning given by paragraph 28 of Schedule 7 to the Tribunals, Courts and Enforcement Act 2007] or rules under [the Land Registration Act 2002].

Amendment

Sub-s (3): para (b) substituted, from a date to be appointed, by the Tribunals, Courts and Enforcement Act 2007, s 48(1), Sch 8, para 33(1), (2).
Sub-s (3): in para (c) words "the Adjudicator to Her Majesty's Land Registry" in square brackets substituted by the Land Registration Act 2002, s 133, Sch 11, para 31(1), (3)(a).
Sub-s (3): words "within the meaning of section 8 of the Tribunals and Inquiries Act 1992" in italics repealed and subsequent words in square brackets substituted, from a date to be appointed, by the Tribunals, Courts and Enforcement Act 2007, s 48(1), Sch 8, para 33(1), (3).
Sub-s (3): words "the Land Registration Act 2002" in square brackets substituted by the Land Registration Act 2002, s 133, Sch 11, para 31(1), (3)(b).

Commentary

Before this section a notice could be invalid if the recipient had unknown to the sender died. The address for the purposes of the Interpretation Act 1978, s 7 referred to in sub-s (2) is the last known address of the deceased. The section does not apply to court or tribunal proceedings or those brought under the land registration legislation.

[421]

18 Notices affecting land: service on personal representatives before filing of grant

(1) A notice affecting land which would have been authorised or required to be served on a person but for his death shall be sufficiently served before a grant of representation has been filed if—

(a) it is addressed to "The Personal Representatives of" the deceased (naming him) and left at or sent by post to his last known place of residence or business in the United Kingdom, and

(b) a copy of it, similarly addressed, is served on the Public Trustee.

(2) The reference in subsection (1) to the filing of a grant of representation is to the filing at the Principal Registry of the Family Division of the High Court of a copy of a grant of representation in respect of the deceased's estate or, as the case may be, the part of his estate which includes the land in question.

(3) The method of service provided for by this section is not available where provision is made—

(a) by or under any enactment, or

(b) by an agreement in writing,

requiring a different method of service, or expressly prohibiting the method of service provided for by this section, in the circumstances.

Commentary

For the filing of grants of representation see the Supreme Court Act 1981, s 111 **[350].**

[422]

19 Functions of Public Trustee in relation to notices, etc

(1) The Public Trustee may give directions as to the office or offices at which documents may be served on him—

(a) by virtue of section 9 of the Administration of Estates Act 1925 (as substituted by section 14(1) above), or

(b) in pursuance of section 18(1)(b) above (service on Public Trustee of copy of certain notices affecting land);

and he shall publish such directions in such manner as he considers appropriate.

(2) The Lord Chancellor may by regulations make provision with respect to the functions of the Public Trustee in relation to such documents; and the regulations may make different provision in relation to different descriptions of document or different circumstances.

(3) The regulations may, in particular, make provision requiring the Public Trustee—

(a) to keep such documents for a specified period and thereafter to keep a copy or record of their contents in such form as may be specified;

(b) to keep such documents, copies and records available for inspection at such reasonable hours as may be specified; and

(c) to supply copies to any person on request.

In this subsection "specified" means specified by or under the regulations.

(4) Regulations under this section shall be made by statutory instrument which shall be subject to annulment in pursuance of a resolution of either House of Parliament.

(5) The following provisions of the Public Trustee Act 1906, namely—

(a) section 8(5) (payment of expenses out of money provided by Parliament), and

(b) section 9(1) [and (3)] (provisions as to fees),

apply in relation to the functions of the Public Trustee in relation to documents to which this section applies as in relation to his functions under that Act.

Amendment

Sub-s (5): in para (b) words "and (3)" in square brackets substituted by the Public Trustee (Liability and Fees) Act 2002, s 2(4).

Commentary

For the role of the Public Trustee in relation to intestate estates, see the Administration of Estates Act 1925, s 9 as amended by s 14 above **[189]**. For the office of the Public Trustee, see the Public Trustee Act 1906 **[59]** and in particular ss 8 and 9 as to the payment of fees. The main regulations under this section are the Public Trustee (Notices Affecting Land) (Title on Death) Regulations 1995, SI 1995/1330 which provide for the Public Trustee to maintain a register of notices served on him under s 18 with search facilities available on application.

[423]

PART III
GENERAL PROVISIONS

20 Crown application

This Act binds the Crown.

[424]

21 Consequential amendments and repeals

(1) The enactments specified in Schedule 1 are amended in accordance with that Schedule, the amendments being consequential on the provisions of this Act.

(2) The enactments specified in Schedule 2 are repealed to the extent specified.

(3) In the case of section 76 of the Law of Property Act 1925 and section 24(1)(a) of the Land Registration Act 1925, those provisions are repealed in accordance with section 10(1) above (general saving for covenants in old form).

(4) The amendments consequential on Part I of this Act (namely those in paragraphs 1, 2, 3, 5, 7, 9 and 12 of Schedule 1) shall not have effect in relation to any disposition of property to which, by virtue of section 10(1) or 11 above (transitional provisions), section 76 of the Law of Property Act 1925 or section 24(1)(a) of the Land Registration Act 1925 continues to apply.

[425]

22 Extent

(1) The provisions of this Act extend to England and Wales.

(2) In addition—

(a) the provisions of Schedules 1 and 2 (consequential amendments and repeals) extend to Scotland so far as they relate to enactments which so extend; and

(b) the provisions of Schedule 1 extend to Northern Ireland so far as they relate to enactments which so extend.

[426]

23 Commencement

(1) The provisions of this Act come into force on such day as the Lord Chancellor may appoint by order made by statutory instrument.

(2) Different days may be appointed for different provisions and for different purposes.

[427]

24 Short title

This Act may be cited as the Law of Property (Miscellaneous Provisions) Act 1994.

[428]

SCHEDULE 1
CONSEQUENTIAL AMENDMENTS

Section 21(1)

. . .

Amendment

Repealed in part by the Land Registration Act 2002, s 135, Sch 13.
Repealed in part by the Statute Law (Repeals) Act 1998.

Commentary

This Schedule amends the Law of Property Act 1925, s 77(1), the Law of Property (Joint Tenants) Act 1964, s 1(1), the Land Commission Act 1967, Sch 12, para 10, the Leasehold Reform Act 1967, ss 10, 15, Sch 1, the Consumer Credit Act 1974, s 176, the Rentcharges Act 1977, s 11, the Rent Act 1977, Sch 2, para 1, the Housing Act 1985, Sch 6, Parts I, II, the Financial Services Act 1986, s 45, the Housing Act 1988, Sch 1, para 17, and the Leasehold Reform, Housing and Urban Development Act 1993, ss 34, 57, Schs 7, 9.

[429]

SCHEDULE 2
REPEALS

Section 21(2)

Chapter	*Short title*	*Extent of repeal*
15 & 16 Geo 5 c 20.	Law of Property Act 1925.	Section 76.
		In Schedule 2, Parts I to VI.
15 & 16 Geo 5 c 21.	Land Registration Act 1925.	Section 24(1)(a).
15 & 16 Geo 5 c 23.	Administration of Estates Act 1925.	In section 2(2), the words ", save as otherwise provided as respects trust estates including settled land,".
		Section 36(3).
		In section 55(1), paragraph (xv).
1964 c 63.	Law of Property (Joint Tenants) Act 1964.	In section 1(1), the words "he conveys as beneficial owner or".
1967 c 1.	Land Commission Act 1967.	In Schedule 12, paragraph 10(2).
1967 c 88.	Leasehold Reform Act 1967.	In section 10(1), from the words "nor to enter into any covenant for title" to the end.
1970 c 31.	Administration of Justice Act 1970.	In Schedule 2, paragraph 5.
1985 c 6.	Companies Act 1985.	Section 209(10)(d).
1985 c 68.	Housing Act 1985.	In Schedule 6, paragraph 10.

[430]

TRUSTS OF LAND AND APPOINTMENT OF TRUSTEES ACT 1996

1996 Chapter 47

ARRANGEMENT OF SECTIONS

PART I
TRUSTS OF LAND

PART II
APPOINTMENT AND RETIREMENT OF TRUSTEES

PART III
SUPPLEMENTARY

An Act to make new provision about trusts of land including provision phasing out the Settled Land Act 1925, abolishing the doctrine of conversion and otherwise amending the law about trusts for sale of land; to amend the law about the appointment and retirement of trustees of any trust; and for connected purposes

[24th July 1996]

General Note
The Trusts of Land and Appointment of Trustees Act 1996 (TLATA 1996) altered the way in which land is held on trust by abolishing strict settlements for the future and conferring new powers on trustees of land and rights on the beneficiaries under the trust. The Act also quite distinctly deals with the appointment of trustees.

PART I
TRUSTS OF LAND

INTRODUCTORY

1 Meaning of "trust of land"

(1) In this Act—

(a) "trust of land" means (subject to subsection (3)) any trust of property which consists of or includes land, and

(b) "trustees of land" means trustees of a trust of land.

(2) The reference in subsection (1)(a) to a trust—

(a) is to any description of trust (whether express, implied, resulting or constructive), including a trust for sale and a bare trust, and

(b) includes a trust created, or arising, before the commencement of this Act.

(3) The reference to land in subsection (1)(a) does not include land which (despite section 2) is settled land or which is land to which the Universities and College Estates Act 1925 applies.

Commentary
For the meaning of "land" see s 23(2) below. "Trust" in sub-s (2) has a very wide meaning and a distinction is drawn in some sections with "a trust created by a disposition" which does not seem to encompass an implied or constructive trust. The inclusion of bare trusts resolves a difficulty before TLATA 1996 that if a beneficiary under a trust for sale became absolutely entitled as against the trustees, their statutory powers would cease, see *Re Wakeman* [1945] Ch 177. The Act applies to (and does not abolish as appears to be widely believed) trusts for sale. The trust does not have to be solely of land but must include land. Note that the Act does not apply to settled land (although see s 17(3) below) or land to which the Universities and College Estates Act 1925 applies (that is land held on a similar regime to the Settled Land Act 1925 **[Appendix II]** by the universities of Oxford, Cambridge and Durham).

[431]

SETTLEMENTS AND TRUSTS FOR SALE AS TRUSTS OF LAND

2 Trusts in place of settlements

(1) No settlement created after the commencement of this Act is a settlement for the purposes of the Settled Land Act 1925; and no settlement shall be deemed to be made under that Act after that commencement.

(2) Subsection (1) does not apply to a settlement created on the occasion of an alteration in any interest in, or of a person becoming entitled under, a settlement which—

(a) is in existence at the commencement of this Act, or

(b) derives from a settlement within paragraph (a) or this paragraph.

(3) But a settlement created as mentioned in subsection (2) is not a settlement for the purposes of the Settled Land Act 1925 if provision to the effect that it is not is made in the instrument, or any of the instruments, by which it is created.

(4) Where at any time after the commencement of this Act there is in the case of any settlement which is a settlement for the purposes of the Settled Land Act 1925 no relevant property which is, or is deemed to be, subject to the settlement, the

settlement permanently ceases at that time to be a settlement for the purposes of that Act.

In this subsection "relevant property" means land and personal chattels to which section 67(1) of the Settled Land Act 1925 (heirlooms) applies.

(5) No land held on charitable, ecclesiastical or public trusts shall be or be deemed to be settled land after the commencement of this Act, even if it was or was deemed to be settled land before that commencement.

(6) Schedule 1 has effect to make provision consequential on this section (including provision to impose a trust in circumstances in which, apart from this section, there would be a settlement for the purposes of the Settled Land Act 1925 (and there would not otherwise be a trust)).

Commentary

Subsection (1) places a ban on the creation of settlements under the Settled Land Act 1925 **[Appendix II]** from the date on which the TLATA 1996 commenced (1 January 1997). Old settlements will remain subject to the Settled Land Act regime and will be gradually phased out. Subsection (2) covers the position where there is a resettlement of an existing settlement and that will be preserved under the Settled Land Act 1925 unless it is decided to opt out in the resettlement under sub-s (3). For the machinery for achieving this, see Sch 3, para 2(6). Subsection (4) brings to an end strict settlements where there is no land or personal chattels falling within the Settled Land Act 1925 held, ie if it is all sold, and see Sch 1, para 6 below in this regard. As to "charitable ecclesiastical or public trusts" referred to in sub-s (5) it is not clear what is meant by a "public trust" if it is not charitable.

[432]

3 Abolition of doctrine of conversion

(1) Where land is held by trustees subject to a trust for sale, the land is not to be regarded as personal property; and where personal property is subject to a trust for sale in order that the trustees may acquire land, the personal property is not to be regarded as land.

(2) Subsection (1) does not apply to a trust created by a will if the testator died before the commencement of this Act.

(3) Subject to that, subsection (1) applies to a trust whether it is created, or arises, before or after that commencement.

Commentary

The doctrine of conversion meant that if land was held on a trust for sale, it was treated as money, and if money was held on trust for sale to purchase land, it was treated as land. The courts had begun to mitigate the artificial effect of this doctrine and the Act now abolishes it with consequential amendments made to many statutes set out in Schs 3 and 4. Note that while the section has retroactive effect in general terms, it will not apply to the will of a testator dying before 1 January 1997 when the Act came into force.

[433]

4 Express trusts for sale as trusts of land

(1) In the case of every trust for sale of land created by a disposition there is to be implied, despite any provision to the contrary made by the disposition, a power for the trustees to postpone sale of the land; and the trustees are not liable in any way for postponing sale of the land, in the exercise of their discretion, for an indefinite period.

(2) Subsection (1) applies to a trust whether it is created, or arises, before or after the commencement of this Act.

(3) Subsection (1) does not affect any liability incurred by trustees before that commencement.

Commentary
For the meaning of "trust for sale" see s 23(2) below which incorporates the Law of Property Act 1925 **[180]**, s 205(xxi), as that section is amended by s 25 and Sch 4 of this Act. For the meaning of "created by disposition" see s 23(2) below which incorporates the Law of Property Act 1925 **[180]**, s 205(1)(ii). As to a power to postpone, a mere failure to sell is not a conscious exercise of the power to postpone, see *Re Guinness's Settlement* [1966] 1 WLR 1355. Note that nothing in the disposition creating the trust for sale can override this implied power, whereas the statutory power contained in the Law of Property Act 1925, s 25 was subject to a contrary intention.

[434]

5 Implied trusts for sale as trusts of land

(1) Schedule 2 has effect in relation to statutory provisions which impose a trust for sale of land in certain circumstances so that in those circumstances there is instead a trust of the land (without a duty to sell).

(2) Section 1 of the Settled Land Act 1925 does not apply to land held on any trust arising by virtue of that Schedule (so that any such land is subject to a trust of land).

Commentary
Numerous statutory provisions imposed trusts for sale in certain circumstances, see, for example the Law of Property Act 1925, ss 34 and 36 **[153, 154]** (land conveyed to persons in undivided shares or held in trust for persons entitled as beneficial joint tenants) and Administration of Trusts Act 1925 s 33 **[208]**. These provisions are repealed and modified in Sch 2 to ensure that these statutory trusts become trusts of land and not trusts for sale. The major difference of course is that the trustees are not under a duty to sell the land but have a power to do so. Subsection (2) prevents there becoming settled land once there is no immediate binding trust for sale

[435]

FUNCTIONS OF TRUSTEES OF LAND

6 General powers of trustees

(1) For the purpose of exercising their functions as trustees, the trustees of land have in relation to the land subject to the trust all the powers of an absolute owner.

(2) Where in the case of any land subject to a trust of land each of the beneficiaries interested in the land is a person of full age and capacity who is absolutely entitled to the land, the powers conferred on the trustees by subsection (1) include the power to convey the land to the beneficiaries even though they have not required the trustees to do so; and where land is conveyed by virtue of this subsection—

- (a) the beneficiaries shall do whatever is necessary to secure that it vests in them, and
- (b) if they fail to do so, the court may make an order requiring them to do so.

(3) The trustees of land have power to [acquire land under the power conferred by section 8 of the Trustee Act 2000].

(4) . . .

(5) In exercising the powers conferred by this section trustees shall have regard to the rights of the beneficiaries.

(6) The powers conferred by this section shall not be exercised in contravention of, or of any order made in pursuance of, any other enactment or any rule of law or equity.

(7) The reference in subsection (6) to an order includes an order of any court or of the [Charity Commission].

(8) Where any enactment other than this section confers on trustees authority to act subject to any restriction, limitation or condition, trustees of land may not exercise the powers conferred by this section to do any act which they are prevented from doing under the other enactment by reason of the restriction, limitation or condition.

[(9) The duty of care under section 1 of the Trustee Act 2000 applies to trustees of land when exercising the powers conferred by this section.]

Amendment

Sub-s (3): words "acquire land under the power conferred by section 8 of the Trustee Act 2000" in square brackets substituted by the Trustee Act 2000, s 40(1), Sch 2, Pt II, para 45(1).
Sub-s (4): repealed by the Trustee Act 2000, s 40(1), (3), Sch 2, Pt II, para 45(2), Sch 4, Pt II.
Sub-s (7): words "Charity Commission" in square brackets substituted by the Charities Act 2006, s 75(1), Sch 8, para 182.
Sub-s (9): inserted by the Trustee Act 2000, s 40(1), Sch 2, Pt II, para 45(3).

Commentary

Subsection (1) confers wide powers of management of the land on the trustees. The purpose of s 6(2) is not entirely clear but it would seem to enable the trustees to foist the legal title upon beneficiaries (as to the meaning of which see s 22). Although not clear, it would seem that if there is more than one beneficiary, they would need to be concurrently absolutely entitled. As to sub-s (3) see the Trustee Act 2000, s 8 and the notes thereto **[483]**. Note that the trustees must take into account the rights of the beneficiaries under sub-s (5) although they should in any event do so in exercising what are clearly fiduciary powers. Subsection (6) applies only to this section and not to other parts of the Act, in particular section 14, see: *Avis v Hamilton Turner* [2007] 48 EG 146. As to the reference to the statutory duty of care in sub-s (9) see Trustee Act 2000 s 1 **[476]**.

[436]

7 Partition by trustees

(1) The trustees of land may, where beneficiaries of full age are absolutely entitled in undivided shares to land subject to the trust, partition the land, or any part of it, and provide (by way of mortgage or otherwise) for the payment of any equality money.

(2) The trustees shall give effect to any such partition by conveying the partitioned land in severalty (whether or not subject to any legal mortgage created for raising equality money), either absolutely or in trust, in accordance with the rights of those beneficiaries.

(3) Before exercising their powers under subsection (2) the trustees shall obtain the consent of each of those beneficiaries.

(4) Where a share in the land is affected by an incumbrance, the trustees may either give effect to it or provide for its discharge from the property allotted to that share as they think fit.

(5) If a share in the land is absolutely vested in a minor, subsections (1) to (4) apply as if he were of full age, except that the trustees may act on his behalf and retain land or other property representing his share in trust for him.

[(6) Subsection (1) is subject to sections 21 (part-unit: interests) and 22 (part-unit: charging) of the Commonhold and Leasehold Reform Act 2002.]

Amendment

Sub-s (6): inserted by the Commonhold and Leasehold Reform Act 2002, s 68, Sch 5, para 8.

Commentary

This section follows closely its predecessor—the Law of Property Act 1925, s 28(3). The main difference would seem to be the use of "beneficiaries" rather than "each of the beneficiaries" in s 6(2) which implies that if only one or some of the beneficiaries were of full age and absolutely entitled, they could partition the land to them. Note that the consent which is required under sub-s (3) can be overridden by the court under ss 14 and 15 below.

[437]

8 Exclusion and restriction of powers

(1) Sections 6 and 7 do not apply in the case of a trust of land created by a disposition in so far as provision to the effect that they do not apply is made by the disposition.

(2) If the disposition creating such a trust makes provision requiring any consent to be obtained to the exercise of any power conferred by section 6 or 7, the power may not be exercised without that consent.

(3) Subsection (1) does not apply in the case of charitable, ecclesiastical or public trusts.

(4) Subsections (1) and (2) have effect subject to any enactment which prohibits or restricts the effect of provision of the description mentioned in them.

Commentary

Note that this section only applies where the trust was created by "disposition". For the meaning of "created by disposition" see s 23(2) below which incorporates the Law of Property Act 1925 **[180]**, s 205(1)(ii). Rather surprisingly the section has the effect that the instrument creating the trust can exclude the power to sell which arises under s 6. Note that consent can be required to the exercise of the powers by charitable ecclesiastical or public trusts (as to the difficulty with the meaning of which, see the notes to s 2 above) but the powers cannot be excluded in relation to such trusts (sub-s (3)).

[438]

9 Delegation by trustees

(1) The trustees of land may, by power of attorney, delegate to any beneficiary or beneficiaries of full age and beneficially entitled to an interest in possession in land subject to the trust any of their functions as trustees which relate to the land.

(2) Where trustees purport to delegate to a person by a power of attorney under subsection (1) functions relating to any land and another person in good faith deals with him in relation to the land, he shall be presumed in favour of that other person to have been a person to whom the functions could be delegated unless that other person has knowledge at the time of the transaction that he was not such a person.

And it shall be conclusively presumed in favour of any purchaser whose interest depends on the validity of that transaction that that other person dealt in good faith and did not have such knowledge if that other person makes a statutory declaration to that effect before or within three months after the completion of the purchase.

(3) A power of attorney under subsection (1) shall be given by all the trustees jointly and (unless expressed to be irrevocable and to be given by way of security) may be revoked by any one or more of them; and such a power is revoked by the appointment as a trustee of a person other than those by whom it is given (though not by any of those persons dying or otherwise ceasing to be a trustee).

(4) Where a beneficiary to whom functions are delegated by a power of attorney under subsection (1) ceases to be a person beneficially entitled to an interest in possession in land subject to the trust—

(a) if the functions are delegated to him alone, the power is revoked,

(b) if the functions are delegated to him and to other beneficiaries to be exercised by them jointly (but not separately), the power is revoked if each of the other beneficiaries ceases to be so entitled (but otherwise functions exercisable in accordance with the power are so exercisable by the remaining beneficiary or beneficiaries), and

(c) if the functions are delegated to him and to other beneficiaries to be exercised by them separately (or either separately or jointly), the power is revoked in so far as it relates to him.

(5) A delegation under subsection (1) may be for any period or indefinite.

(6) A power of attorney under subsection (1) cannot be [an enduring power of attorney or lasting power of attorney within the meaning of the Mental Capacity Act 2005].

(7) Beneficiaries to whom functions have been delegated under subsection (1) are, in relation to the exercise of the functions, in the same position as trustees (with the same duties and liabilities); but such beneficiaries shall not be regarded as trustees for any other purposes (including, in particular, the purposes of any enactment permitting the delegation of functions by trustees or imposing requirements relating to the payment of capital money).

(8) . . .

(9) Neither this section nor the repeal by this Act of section 29 of the Law of Property Act 1925 (which is superseded by this section) affects the operation after the commencement of this Act of any delegation effected before that commencement.

Amendment

Sub-s (6): words from "an enduring power" to the end substituted by the Mental Capacity Act 2005, s 67(1), Sch 6, para 42(1), (2).
Sub-s (8): repealed by the Trustee Act 2000, s 40(1), (3), Sch 2, Pt II, para 46, Sch 4, Pt II.

Commentary

For the meaning of "beneficiary" see s 22 below. "In possession" is defined in accordance with the Law of Property Act 1925 **[180]**, s 205(1)(xx), incorporated into the TLATA 1996 by s 23(2) below and includes a person in receipt of rents and profits. The aim of this section was to ensure that the trustees' powers could be delegated to beneficiaries so as to preserve some of the features of a strict settlement where powers are vested in the tenant for life. The major difference of course is that the legal estate will remain in the trustees. Nowhere is there any provision whereby this power can be excluded. The reference in sub-s (6) to an enduring power of attorney is to those created before the Enduring Powers of Attorney Act 1985 was repealed by the Mental Capacity Act 2005 **[562]**. That latter Act introduced lasting powers of attorney **[567]**. See s 9A below for the duties of trustees when delegating under this section. For powers of trustees to delegate generally, see the Trustee Act 2000, s 11 **[486]**.

[439]

[9A Duties of trustees in connection with delegation etc]

[(1) The duty of care under section 1 of the Trustee Act 2000 applies to trustees of land in deciding whether to delegate any of their functions under section 9.

(2) Subsection (3) applies if the trustees of land—
- (a) delegate any of their functions under section 9, and
- (b) the delegation is not irrevocable.

(3) While the delegation continues, the trustees—
- (a) must keep the delegation under review,
- (b) if circumstances make it appropriate to do so, must consider whether there is a need to exercise any power of intervention that they have, and
- (c) if they consider that there is a need to exercise such a power, must do so.

(4) "Power of intervention" includes—
- (a) a power to give directions to the beneficiary;
- (b) a power to revoke the delegation.

(5) The duty of care under section 1 of the 2000 Act applies to trustees in carrying out any duty under subsection (3).

(6) A trustee of land is not liable for any act or default of the beneficiary, or beneficiaries, unless the trustee fails to comply with the duty of care in deciding to

delegate any of the trustees' functions under section 9 or in carrying out any duty under subsection (3).

(7) Neither this section nor the repeal of section 9(8) by the Trustee Act 2000 affects the operation after the commencement of this section of any delegation effected before that commencement.]

Amendment

Inserted by the Trustee Act 2000, s 40(1), Sch 2, Pt II, para 47.

Commentary

This provision mirrors the provisions of the Trustee Act 2000, ss 21–23 **[496–498]** and reference should be made to the notes to those sections. For references to the statutory duty of care in sub-ss (1) and (5) see the Trustee Act 2000, s 1, Sch 1 and the notes thereto **[476, 519]**.

[440]

10 Consents

(1) If a disposition creating a trust of land requires the consent of more than two persons to the exercise by the trustees of any function relating to the land, the consent of any two of them to the exercise of the function is sufficient in favour of a purchaser.

(2) Subsection (1) does not apply to the exercise of a function by trustees of land held on charitable, ecclesiastical or public trusts.

(3) Where at any time a person whose consent is expressed by a disposition creating a trust of land to be required to the exercise by the trustees of any function relating to the land is not of full age—

- (a) his consent is not, in favour of a purchaser, required to the exercise of the function, but
- (b) the trustees shall obtain the consent of a parent who has parental responsibility for him (within the meaning of the Children Act 1989) or of a guardian of his.

Commentary

This provision follows closely its predecessor, the Law of Property Act 1925 s 26. Note it applies only where the trust is created by a "disposition". It is a section designed to protect a purchaser. Note the difficulties with the term "charitable, ecclesiastical and public trusts" referred to in the notes to s 2. This section does not apply to land held on trust by personal representatives, see s 18(1) below.

[441]

11 Consultation with beneficiaries

(1) The trustees of land shall in the exercise of any function relating to land subject to the trust—

- (a) so far as practicable, consult the beneficiaries of full age and beneficially entitled to an interest in possession in the land, and
- (b) so far as consistent with the general interest of the trust, give effect to the wishes of those beneficiaries, or (in case of dispute) of the majority (according to the value of their combined interests).

(2) Subsection (1) does not apply—

- (a) in relation to a trust created by a disposition in so far as provision that it does not apply is made by the disposition,
- (b) in relation to a trust created or arising under a will made before the commencement of this Act, or
- (c) in relation to the exercise of the power mentioned in section 6(2).

(3) Subsection (1) does not apply to a trust created before the commencement of this Act by a disposition, or a trust created after that commencement by reference to such a trust, unless provision to the effect that it is to apply is made by a deed executed—

(a) in a case in which the trust was created by one person and he is of full capacity, by that person, or

(b) in a case in which the trust was created by more than one person, by such of the persons who created the trust as are alive and of full capacity.

(4) A deed executed for the purposes of subsection (3) is irrevocable.

Commentary

Under sub-s (1)(b) the value of the beneficiaries' interests must be taken into account, presumably on an actuarial basis if they are life interests. Subsection (2)(a), which allows this section to be excluded, has resulted in the very common practice of providing that this section should not apply in family trust deeds. Unlike other provisions of the Act subsection (2) provides that it does not apply to trusts or wills made before 1 January 1997 (the commencement of the Act) but note the opting in provisions contained in sub-ss (3) and (4). See also the notes to s 6(2) above in respect of sub-s (2)(c). It has been held that the service of a notice to quit by one of two joint tenants does not require consultation under this section, see *Notting Hill Housing Trust v Brackley* [2001] EWCA Civ 1543. This section does not apply to land held on trust by personal representatives, see s 18(1) below

[442]

RIGHT OF BENEFICIARIES TO OCCUPY TRUST LAND

12 The right to occupy

(1) A beneficiary who is beneficially entitled to an interest in possession in land subject to a trust of land is entitled by reason of his interest to occupy the land at any time if at that time—

(a) the purposes of the trust include making the land available for his occupation (or for the occupation of beneficiaries of a class of which he is a member or of beneficiaries in general), or

(b) the land is held by the trustees so as to be so available.

(2) Subsection (1) does not confer on a beneficiary a right to occupy land if it is either unavailable or unsuitable for occupation by him.

(3) This section is subject to section 13.

Commentary

For the meaning of "beneficiary" see s 22 below. "In possession" is defined in accordance with the Law of Property Act 1925 **[180]**, s 205(1)(xx) incorporated into the TLATA 1996 by s 23(2) below and includes in receipt of rents and profits. Co-owners have always had the right to occupy (see *Dennis v MacDonald* [1982] Fam 63) but this section makes it clear. The concept of the purpose of the trust was something which the old law took into account when deciding whether to order a sale under the Law of Property Act 1925, s 30 (see *Re Buchanan-Wallaston's Conveyance* [1939] Ch 738 and *Jones v Challenger* [1961] 1 QB 176). As to the question of suitability in sub-s (2) see *Chan v Leung* [2002] EWCA Civ 1075. Issues such as whether an occupation rent should be paid should be determined in accordance with this and the following sections, see: *Stack v Dowden* [2007] 2 AC 432 and *Murphy v Gooch* [2007] 2 FLR 934.

[443]

13 Exclusion and restriction of right to occupy

(1) Where two or more beneficiaries are (or apart from this subsection would be) entitled under section 12 to occupy land, the trustees of land may exclude or restrict the entitlement of any one or more (but not all) of them.

(2) Trustees may not under subsection (1)—

(a) unreasonably exclude any beneficiary's entitlement to occupy land, or

(b) restrict any such entitlement to an unreasonable extent.

(3) The trustees of land may from time to time impose reasonable conditions on any beneficiary in relation to his occupation of land by reason of his entitlement under section 12.

(4) The matters to which trustees are to have regard in exercising the powers conferred by this section include—

(a) the intentions of the person or persons (if any) who created the trust,
(b) the purposes for which the land is held, and
(c) the circumstances and wishes of each of the beneficiaries who is (or apart from any previous exercise by the trustees of those powers would be) entitled to occupy the land under section 12.

(5) The conditions which may be imposed on a beneficiary under subsection (3) include, in particular, conditions requiring him—

(a) to pay any outgoings or expenses in respect of the land, or
(b) to assume any other obligation in relation to the land or to any activity which is or is proposed to be conducted there.

(6) Where the entitlement of any beneficiary to occupy land under section 12 has been excluded or restricted, the conditions which may be imposed on any other beneficiary under subsection (3) include, in particular, conditions requiring him to—

(a) make payments by way of compensation to the beneficiary whose entitlement has been excluded or restricted, or
(b) forgo any payment or other benefit to which he would otherwise be entitled under the trust so as to benefit that beneficiary.

(7) The powers conferred on trustees by this section may not be exercised—

(a) so as prevent any person who is in occupation of land (whether or not by reason of an entitlement under section 12) from continuing to occupy the land, or
(b) in a manner likely to result in any such person ceasing to occupy the land,

unless he consents or the court has given approval.

(8) The matters to which the court is to have regard in determining whether to give approval under subsection (7) include the matters mentioned in subsection (4)(a) to (c).

Commentary

The vague nature of the matters set out in sub-s (2) do seem to invite litigation. As to the factors set out in sub-s (4)(a) and (b) see the old cases deciding whether to order a sale under the Law of Property Act 1925, s 30 on the question of "purpose": *Re Buchanan-Wallaston's Conveyance* [1939] Ch 738 and *Jones v Challenger* [1961] 1 QB 176. Subsection (6) contemplates a beneficiary in occupation paying an occupation rent to a beneficiary whose occupation has been excluded, and such issues should be determined in accordance with this the previous and following sections, see: *Stack v Dowden* [2007] 2 AC 432 and *Murphy v Gooch* [2007] 2 FLR 934. On the extent of the court's powers under this section to partition land, allow beneficiaries to occupy separate parts and pay for the conversion, see *Rodway v Landy* [2001] Ch 703.

[444]

POWERS OF COURT

14 Applications for order

(1) Any person who is a trustee of land or has an interest in a property subject to a trust of land may make an application to the court for an order under this section.

(2) On an application for an order under this section the court may make any such order—

(a) relating to the exercise by the trustees of any of their functions (including an order relieving them of any obligation to obtain the consent of, or to consult, any person in connection with the exercise of any of their functions), or

(b) declaring the nature or extent of a person's interest in property subject to the trust,

as the court thinks fit.

(3) The court may not under this section make any order as to the appointment or removal of trustees.

(4) The powers conferred on the court by this section are exercisable on an application whether it is made before or after the commencement of this Act.

Commentary

The jurisdiction under this section confers on the court a wider discretion than the old Law of Property Act 1925, s 30, see *Mortgage Corporation v Shaire* [2001] Ch 743. The appointment and removal of trustees is dealt with under the Trustee Act 1925, s 41 **[110]**. There have been a number of reported cases on the exercise of this discretion by the court which are noted after s 15 below. Often applications (which in cases where there is no dispute of fact should be by way of Part 8 claim form, but in other cases by way of Part 7 claim) will be for an order that the trustees exercise their power to sell. Note that any person who has an interest in the property can apply (eg a chargee of the land, see *Bank of Ireland Home Mortgages Ltd v Bell* [2001] 3 FCR 134). This section does not apply to land held on trust by personal representatives, see s 18(1) below. See also *Dear v Robsinon* [2001] EWCA Civ. 1543 where the wishes of the majority of the beneficiaries were taken into account, and *Chun v Ho* [2003] 1 FLR 23, [2003] 1 PC & R 15, where the Court of Appeal discussed the principles applicable in exercising its jurisdiction under this section.

[445]

15 Matters relevant in determining applications

(1) The matters to which the court is to have regard in determining an application for an order under section 14 include—

(a) the intentions of the person or persons (if any) who created the trust,

(b) the purposes for which the property subject to the trust is held,

(c) the welfare of any minor who occupies or might reasonably be expected to occupy any land subject to the trust as his home, and

(d) the interests of any secured creditor of any beneficiary.

(2) In the case of an application relating to the exercise in relation to any land of the powers conferred on the trustees by section 13, the matters to which the court is to have regard also include the circumstances and wishes of each of the beneficiaries who is (or apart from any previous exercise by the trustees of those powers would be) entitled to occupy the land under section 12.

(3) In the case of any other application, other than one relating to the exercise of the power mentioned in section 6(2), the matters to which the court is to have regard also include the circumstances and wishes of any beneficiaries of full age and entitled to an interest in possession in property subject to the trust or (in case of dispute) of the majority (according to the value of their combined interests).

(4) This section does not apply to an application if section 335A of the Insolvency Act 1986 (which is inserted by Schedule 3 and relates to applications by a trustee of a bankrupt) applies to it.

Commentary

As to examples of the way in which the court has applied the principles set out in this section, see *Pickering v Wells* [2002] All ER (D) 281 (May) (application by chargee to enforce charging order); *Dear v Robinson* [2001] EWCA Civ 1543 (application for order for sale where right of pre-emption); *Mortgage Corporation v Shaire* [2001] Ch 743 (application by chargee); *Bank of Ireland Home Mortgages Ltd v Bell* [2001] 3 FCR 134; *Tee v Tee* [1999] 3 FCR 409 (dispute between husband and wife on divorce); *Murphy v Gooch* [2007] 2 FLR 934 and *Avis v*

Hamilton Turner [2007] 48 EG 146 (trustee in bankruptcy application). In *Mortgage Corporation v Shaire* it was made clear that the interests of secured creditors are only one of the factors which the court should take into account and will not automatically prevail over the beneficiaries.

[446]

PURCHASER PROTECTION

16 Protection of purchasers

(1) A purchaser of land which is or has been subject to a trust need not be concerned to see that any requirement imposed on the trustees by section 6(5), 7(3) or 11(1) has been complied with.

(2) Where—
- (a) trustees of land who convey land which (immediately before it is conveyed) is subject to the trust contravene section 6(6) or (8), but
- (b) the purchaser of the land from the trustees has no actual notice of the contravention,

the contravention does not invalidate the conveyance.

(3) Where the powers of trustees of land are limited by virtue of section 8—
- (a) the trustees shall take all reasonable steps to bring the limitation to the notice of any purchaser of the land from them, but
- (b) the limitation does not invalidate any conveyance by the trustees to a purchaser who has no actual notice of the limitation.

(4) Where trustees of land convey land which (immediately before it is conveyed) is subject to the trust to persons believed by them to be beneficiaries absolutely entitled to the land under the trust and of full age and capacity—
- (a) the trustees shall execute a deed declaring that they are discharged from the trust in relation to that land, and
- (b) if they fail to do so, the court may make an order requiring them to do so.

(5) A purchaser of land to which a deed under subsection (4) relates is entitled to assume that, as from the date of the deed, the land is not subject to the trust unless he has actual notice that the trustees were mistaken in their belief that the land was conveyed to beneficiaries absolutely entitled to the land under the trust and of full age and capacity.

(6) Subsections (2) and (3) do not apply to land held on charitable, ecclesiastical or public trusts.

(7) This section does not apply to registered land.

Commentary

It is important to note that these provisions protecting purchasers do not apply to registered land (sub-s (7)) and will therefore be of less and less importance. The definition of "purchaser" is incorporated from the Law of Property Act 1925 **[180]**, s 205(1)(xxi), by s 23(1) below, and means that to be a purchaser the person has to act in good faith and give money or money's worth. The definition includes mortgagees, chargees and lessees. Subsection (1) relieves a purchaser from trustees of land from having to investigate whether they have had regard to the rights of the beneficiaries, obtained their consent before partitioning land, or consulted them. The wording "need not be concerned" follows that used in the Law of Property Act 1925 **[150]**, s 27. Subsection (2) ensures that where a purchaser has no notice of any breach of law the conveyance to him will not be invalidated. Note in sub-s (3) that the duty of the trustees ought to be discharged if a proper investigation of title would put the purchaser on notice. Subsection (4) provides a method of recording on the title that the property has been conveyed to the beneficiaries, similar to the provisions in the Settled Land Act 1925, ss 27 and 100 **[Appendix II]**. Note the problems with the terms charitable, ecclesiastical, or public trusts noted after s 2.

[447]

SUPPLEMENTARY

17 Application of provisions to trusts of proceeds of sale

(1) . . .

(2) Section 14 applies in relation to a trust of proceeds of sale of land and trustees of such a trust as in relation to a trust of land and trustees of land.

(3) In this section "trust of proceeds of sale of land" means (subject to subsection (5)) any trust of property (other than a trust of land) which consists of or includes—

- (a) any proceeds of a disposition of land held in trust (including settled land), or
- (b) any property representing any such proceeds.

(4) The references in subsection (3) to a trust—

- (a) are to any description of trust (whether express, implied, resulting or constructive), including a trust for sale and a bare trust, and
- (b) include a trust created, or arising, before the commencement of this Act.

(5) A trust which (despite section 2) is a settlement for the purposes of the Settled Land Act 1925 cannot be a trust of proceeds of sale of land.

(6) In subsection (3)—

- (a) "disposition" includes any disposition made, or coming into operation, before the commencement of this Act, and
- (b) the reference to settled land includes personal chattels to which section 67(1) of the Settled Land Act 1925 (heirlooms) applies.

Amendment

Sub-s (1): repealed by the Trustee Act 2000, s 40(1), (3), Sch 2, Pt II, para 48, Sch 4, Pt II.

Commentary

Subsection (1) was unnecessary in light of the wide powers to acquire land conferred on all trustees by the Trustee Act 2000, s 8 **[483]**. Although the section does not apply to strict settlements under the Settled Land Act 1925 (sub-s (5)) each case should be looked at to see if the settlement has ceased to be governed by the Settled Land Act 1925 [**Appendix II]**.

[448]

18 Application of Part to personal representatives

(1) The provisions of this Part relating to trustees, other than sections 10, 11 and 14, apply to personal representatives, but with appropriate modifications and without prejudice to the functions of personal representatives for the purposes of administration.

(2) The appropriate modifications include—

- (a) the substitution of references to persons interested in the due administration of the estate for references to beneficiaries, and
- (b) the substitution of references to the will for references to the disposition creating the trust.

(3) Section 3(1) does not apply to personal representatives if the death occurs before the commencement of this Act.

Commentary

The provisions in relation to consents, consultation and orders of the court do not apply to personal representatives but the rest of this part of the Act does. References to "beneficiaries" in this section are to be construed as references to a person interested in the due administration of the estate (sub-s (2)(a)). That means not only those beneficially entitled but also creditors of the estate who could bring an administration action. Subsection (3) has the effect that the doctrine of conversion will still apply to the wills and estates of those dying before 1 January 1997.

[449]

PART II
APPOINTMENT AND RETIREMENT OF TRUSTEES

19 Appointment and retirement of trustee at instance of beneficiaries

(1) This section applies in the case of a trust where—
- (a) there is no person nominated for the purpose of appointing new trustees by the instrument, if any, creating the trust, and
- (b) the beneficiaries under the trust are of full age and capacity and (taken together) are absolutely entitled to the property subject to the trust.

(2) The beneficiaries may give a direction or directions of either or both of the following descriptions—
- (a) a written direction to a trustee or trustees to retire from the trust, and
- (b) a written direction to the trustees or trustee for the time being (or, if there are none, to the personal representative of the last person who was a trustee) to appoint by writing to be a trustee or trustees the person or persons specified in the direction.

(3) Where—
- (a) a trustee has been given a direction under subsection (2)(a),
- (b) reasonable arrangements have been made for the protection of any rights of his in connection with the trust,
- (c) after he has retired there will be either a trust corporation or at least two persons to act as trustees to perform the trust, and
- (d) either another person is to be appointed to be a new trustee on his retirement (whether in compliance with a direction under subsection (2)(b) or otherwise) or the continuing trustees by deed consent to his retirement,

he shall make a deed declaring his retirement and shall be deemed to have retired and be discharged from the trust.

(4) Where a trustee retires under subsection (3) he and the continuing trustees (together with any new trustee) shall (subject to any arrangements for the protection of his rights) do anything necessary to vest the trust property in the continuing trustees (or the continuing and new trustees).

(5) This section has effect subject to the restrictions imposed by the Trustee Act 1925 on the number of trustees.

Commentary

This part of the Act applies to *all* trusts and not just those of land. Before this section was enacted beneficiaries of full age and capacity, even if absolutely entitled and therefore able to be break the trusts, could not force a trustee to retire in the absence of some express provision in the trust instrument, or an application to the court. The requirement under s 19(1)(a) would seem to mirror the provisions in Trustee Act 1925 s 36(1)(a) as to a person nominated to appoint new trustees **[105]**. For the meaning of "beneficiary" see s 22(1). It is not clear whether objects of a discretionary trust, who together would be entitled to the property, could qualify as beneficiaries. As to the meaning of "reasonable arrangements" in sub-s 19(3)(b) there is no guidance as yet, but trustees retiring voluntarily usually require any unpaid remuneration to be paid and an indemnity, although the justification for the latter is a matter of debate. Note that unlike removal under the Trustee Act 1925, s 36(1) **[105]** the co-operation of the trustee is required in executing the deed under sub-s (3). As to restrictions on the number of trustees mentioned in sub-s (5) see the Trustee Act 1925, s 34 **[103]**. See the supplementary provisions in s 21 below.

[450]

[20 Appointment of substitute for trustee who lacks capacity]

(1) This section applies where—
- (a) a trustee [lacks capacity (within the meaning of the Mental Capacity Act 2005) to exercise] his functions as trustee,

(b) there is no person who is both entitled and willing and able to appoint a trustee in place of him under section 36(1) of the Trustee Act 1925, and

(c) the beneficiaries under the trust are of full age and capacity and (taken together) are absolutely entitled to the property subject to the trust.

(2) The beneficiaries may give to—

[(a) a deputy appointed for the trustee by the Court of Protection,]

(b) an attorney acting for him under the authority of [an enduring power of attorney or lasting power of attorney registered under the Mental Capacity Act 2005], or

(c) a person authorised for the purpose by [the Court of Protection],

a written direction to appoint by writing the person or persons specified in the direction to be a trustee or trustees in place of the incapable trustee.

Amendment

Section heading: substituted by the Mental Capacity Act 2005, s 67(1), Sch 6, para 42(1), (3).
Sub-s (1): in para (a) words from "lacks capacity" to "to exercise" substituted by the Mental Capacity Act 2005, s 67(1), Sch 6, para 42(1), (3)(a).
Sub-s (2): para (a) substituted by the Mental Capacity Act 2005, s 67(1), Sch 6, para 42(1), (3)(i).
Sub-s (2): in para (b) words from "an enduring power" to the end substituted by the Mental Capacity Act 2005, s 67(1), Sch 6, para 42(1), (3)(b)(ii).
Sub-s (2): in para (c) words "the Court of Protection" substituted by the Mental Capacity Act 2005, s 67(1), Sch 6, para 42(1), (3)(b)(iii).

Commentary

This section applies (unlike s 19) where there is someone nominated for the purpose of appointing new trustees. If only one of two or more trustees lacks capacity, the co-trustee or trustees can remove the incapable trustee and appoint a substitute under the Trustee Act 1925, s 36(1) **[105]** so it is only if this power cannot be exercised that the alternative in this section can be used. See the supplementary provisions in s 21 below. The Mental Capacity Act 2005 **[562]** introduced deputies rather than receivers and lasting powers of attorney replace enduring powers, although those entered into before 31 October 2007 will continue to have effect in the future.

[451]

21 Supplementary

(1) For the purposes of section 19 or 20 a direction is given by beneficiaries if—

(a) a single direction is jointly given by all of them, or

(b) (subject to subsection (2)) a direction is given by each of them (whether solely or jointly with one or more, but not all, of the others),

and none of them by writing withdraws the direction given by him before it has been complied with.

(2) Where more than one direction is given each must specify for appointment or retirement the same person or persons.

(3) Subsection (7) of section 36 of the Trustee Act 1925 (powers of trustees appointed under that section) applies to a trustee appointed under section 19 or 20 as if he were appointed under that section.

(4) A direction under section 19 or 20 must not specify a person or persons for appointment if the appointment of that person or those persons would be in contravention of section 35(1) of the Trustee Act 1925 or section 24(1) of the Law of Property Act 1925 (requirements as to identity of trustees).

(5) Sections 19 and 20 do not apply in relation to a trust created by a disposition in so far as provision that they do not apply is made by the disposition.

(6) Sections 19 and 20 do not apply in relation to a trust created before the commencement of this Act by a disposition in so far as provision to the effect that they do not apply is made by a deed executed—

(a) in a case in which the trust was created by one person and he is of full capacity, by that person, or

(b) in a case in which the trust was created by more than one person, by such of the persons who created the trust as are alive and of full capacity.

(7) A deed executed for the purposes of subsection (6) is irrevocable.

(8) Where a deed is executed for the purposes of subsection (6)—

(a) it does not affect anything done before its execution to comply with a direction under section 19 or 20, but

(b) a direction under section 19 or 20 which has been given but not complied with before its execution shall cease to have effect.

Commentary

For the Trustee Act 1925, s 36(7) referred to in sub-s (3) see **[105]**. As to sub-s (4) the provisions referred to (in the Trustee Act 1925, s 35(1)) can be found at **[104]**) and ensure that if there is a trust of land and a trust of the proceeds of sale of land, the same persons are appointed as trustees of both. Subsection (5) enables a contrary intention to be shown in the "disposition" which bears the same meaning as in s 205(1)(ii), see s 23 below. Subsection (6) offers the chance for opting out of these provisions in pre-1 January 1997 trusts, but note that the settlor must execute the deed and so must still be alive and capable.

[452]

PART III
SUPPLEMENTARY

22 Meaning of "beneficiary"

(1) In this Act "beneficiary", in relation to a trust, means any person who under the trust has an interest in property subject to the trust (including a person who has such an interest as a trustee or a personal representative).

(2) In this Act references to a beneficiary who is beneficially entitled do not include a beneficiary who has an interest in property subject to the trust only by reason of being a trustee or personal representative.

(3) For the purposes of this Act a person who is a beneficiary only by reason of being an annuitant is not to be regarded as entitled to an interest in possession in land subject to the trust.

Commentary

The term "interest in property" in sub-s (1) is not entirely clear and it is not clear whether the Act would apply, for example, to a beneficiary under a discretionary trust who has been held not to have an interest in the trust property (see *Gartside v IRC* [1968] AC 553). Subsection (2) presumably means a beneficiary with a present right to present enjoyment (see *Pearson v IRC* [1981] AC 753). The subsection clearly contemplates that trustees of a sub-trust could be beneficiaries for the purpose of sub-s (1). Annuitants under pension trusts would be excluded from the definition of beneficiary under sub-s (3).

[453]

23 Other interpretation provisions

(1) In this Act "purchaser" has the same meaning as in Part I of the Law of Property Act 1925.

(2) Subject to that, where an expression used in this Act is given a meaning by the Law of Property Act 1925 it has the same meaning as in that Act unless the context otherwise requires.

(3) In this Act "the court" means—
(a) the High Court, or
(b) a county court.

Commentary
The definitions in the Law of Property Act 1925 **[180]** can be found in the in s 205(1) of that Act.

[454]

24 Application to Crown

(1) Subject to subsection (2), this Act binds the Crown.

(2) This Act (except so far as it relates to undivided shares and joint ownership) does not affect or alter the descent, devolution or nature of the estates and interests of or in—
(a) land for the time being vested in Her Majesty in right of the Crown or of the Duchy of Lancaster, or
(b) land for the time being belonging to the Duchy of Cornwall and held in right or respect of the Duchy.

[455]

25 Amendments, repeals etc

(1) The enactments mentioned in Schedule 3 have effect subject to the amendments specified in that Schedule (which are minor or consequential on other provisions of this Act).

(2) The enactments mentioned in Schedule 4 are repealed to the extent specified in the third column of that Schedule.

(3) Neither section 2(5) nor the repeal by this Act of section 29 of the Settled Land Act 1925 applies in relation to the deed of settlement set out in the Schedule to the Chequers Estate Act 1917 or the trust instrument set out in the Schedule to the Chevening Estate Act 1959.

(4) The amendments and repeals made by this Act do not affect any entailed interest created before the commencement of this Act.

(5) The amendments and repeals made by this Act in consequence of section 3—
(a) do not affect a trust created by a will if the testator died before the commencement of this Act, and
(b) do not affect personal representatives of a person who died before that commencement;

and the repeal of section 22 of the Partnership Act 1890 does not apply in any circumstances involving the personal representatives of a partner who died before that commencement.

Commentary
As to future entailed interests (sub-s (4)), see Sch 1, para 5 below.

[456]

26 Power to make consequential provision

(1) The Lord Chancellor may by order made by statutory instrument make any such supplementary, transitional or incidental provision as appears to him to be appropriate for any of the purposes of this Act or in consequence of any of the provisions of this Act.

(2) An order under subsection (1) may, in particular, include provision modifying any enactment contained in a public general or local Act which is passed before, or in the same Session as, this Act.

(3) A statutory instrument made in the exercise of the power conferred by this section is subject to annulment in pursuance of a resolution of either House of Parliament.

Commentary
No orders have yet been made.

[457]

27 Short title, commencement and extent

(1) This Act may be cited as the Trusts of Land and Appointment of Trustees Act 1996.

(2) This Act comes into force on such day as the Lord Chancellor appoints by order made by statutory instrument.

(3) Subject to subsection (4), the provisions of this Act extend only to England and Wales.

(4) The repeal in section 30(2) of the Agriculture Act 1970 extends only to Northern Ireland.

[458]

SCHEDULE 1
PROVISIONS CONSEQUENTIAL ON SECTION 2

Section 2

MINORS

1 (1) Where after the commencement of this Act a person purports to convey a legal estate in land to a minor, or two or more minors, alone, the conveyance—

(a) is not effective to pass the legal estate, but
(b) operates as a declaration that the land is held in trust for the minor or minors (or if he purports to convey it to the minor or minors in trust for any persons, for those persons).

(2) Where after the commencement of this Act a person purports to convey a legal estate in land to—

(a) a minor or two or more minors, and
(b) another person who is, or other persons who are, of full age,

the conveyance operates to vest the land in the other person or persons in trust for the minor or minors and the other person or persons (or if he purports to convey it to them in trust for any persons, for those persons).

(3) Where immediately before the commencement of this Act a conveyance is operating (by virtue of section 27 of the Settled Land Act 1925) as an agreement to execute a settlement in favour of a minor or minors—

(a) the agreement ceases to have effect on the commencement of this Act, and
(b) the conveyance subsequently operates instead as a declaration that the land is held in trust for the minor or minors.

2 Where after the commencement of this Act a legal estate in land would, by reason of intestacy or in any other circumstances not dealt with in paragraph 1, vest in a person who is a minor if he were a person of full age, the land is held in trust for the minor.

FAMILY CHARGES

3 Where, by virtue of an instrument coming into operation after the commencement of this Act, land becomes charged voluntarily (or in consideration of marriage [or the formation of a civil partnership]) or by way of family arrangement, whether immediately or after an interval, with the payment of—

(a) a rentcharge for the life of a person or a shorter period, or

(b) capital, annual or periodical sums for the benefit of a person,

the instrument operates as a declaration that the land is held in trust for giving effect to the charge.

CHARITABLE, ECCLESIASTICAL AND PUBLIC TRUSTS

4 (1) This paragraph applies in the case of land held on charitable, ecclesiastical or public trusts (other than land to which the Universities and College Estates Act 1925 applies).

(2) Where there is a conveyance of such land—

(a) if neither section 37(1) nor section 39(1) of the Charities Act 1993 applies to the conveyance, it shall state that the land is held on such trusts, and

(b) if neither section 37(2) nor section 39(2) of that Act has been complied with in relation to the conveyance and a purchaser has notice that the land is held on such trusts, he must see that any consents or orders necessary to authorise the transaction have been obtained.

(3) Where any trustees or the majority of any set of trustees have power to transfer or create any legal estate in the land, the estate shall be transferred or created by them in the names and on behalf of the persons in whom it is vested.

ENTAILED INTERESTS

5 (1) Where a person purports by an instrument coming into operation after the commencement of this Act to grant to another person an entailed interest in real or personal property, the instrument—

(a) is not effective to grant an entailed interest, but

(b) operates instead as a declaration that the property is held in trust absolutely for the person to whom an entailed interest in the property was purportedly granted.

(2) Where a person purports by an instrument coming into operation after the commencement of this Act to declare himself a tenant in tail of real or personal property, the instrument is not effective to create an entailed interest.

PROPERTY HELD ON SETTLEMENT CEASING TO EXIST

6 Where a settlement ceases to be a settlement for the purposes of the Settled Land Act 1925 because no relevant property (within the meaning of section 2(4)) is, or is deemed to be, subject to the settlement, any property which is or later becomes subject to the settlement is held in trust for the persons interested under the settlement.

Amendment

Para 3: words "or the formation of a civil partnership" in square brackets inserted by the Civil Partnership Act 2004, s 261(1), Sch 27, para 153.

Commentary

These provisions are necessary as a result of the abolition after the commencement of this Act of strict settlements. Paragraphs 1 and 2 deal with transfers to minors formerly dealt with by the Settled Land Act 1925, s 27 **[Appendix II]** and the Law of Property Act 1925, s 19. Essentially land cannot be held by minors and must be held in trust for them and these paragraphs codify the law on that. Land charged with family charges is dealt with by para 3. That formerly took effect as a strict settlement under the Settled Land Act 1925, s 1(1)(v). Paragraph 4 in relation to charitable, ecclesiastical or public trusts replaces the Settled Land Act 1925, s 29. See the notes to s 2 above as to the difficulties with this definition. Paragraph 5 deals with the fact that it is no longer possible to create entailed interests, although existing entails are preserved (see s 24(4) above).

[459]

SCHEDULE 2
AMENDMENTS OF STATUTORY PROVISIONS IMPOSING TRUST FOR SALE

Section 5

MORTGAGED PROPERTY HELD BY TRUSTEES AFTER REDEMPTION BARRED

1 (1)–(6) . . .

(7) The amendments made by this paragraph—

(a) apply whether the right of redemption is discharged before or after the commencement of this Act, but

(b) are without prejudice to any dealings or arrangements made before the commencement of this Act.

Commentary

Para 1: sub-paras (1)–(6) amend the Law of Property Act 1925, s 31.

LAND PURCHASED BY TRUSTEES OF PERSONAL PROPERTY ETC

2 (1) . . .

(2) The repeal made by this paragraph applies in relation to land purchased after the commencement of this Act whether the trust or will in pursuance of which it is purchased comes into operation before or after the commencement of this Act.

Commentary

Para 2: sub-para (1) repeals the Law of Property Act 1925, s 32.

DISPOSITIONS TO TENANTS IN COMMON

3 (1)–(5) . . .

(6) The amendments made by this paragraph apply whether the disposition is made, or comes into operation, before or after the commencement of this Act.

Commentary

Para 3: sub-paras (1)–(5) amend the Law of Property Act 1925, s 34.

JOINT TENANCIES

4 (1)–(3) . . .

(4) The amendments made by this paragraph apply whether the legal estate is limited, or becomes held in trust, before or after the commencement of this Act.

Commentary

Para 4: sub-paras (1)–(3) amend the Law of Property Act 1925, s 36(1), (2).

INTESTACY

5 (1)–(4) . . .

(5) The amendments made by this paragraph apply whether the death occurs before or after the commencement of this Act.

Commentary
Para 5: sub-paras (1)–(4) amend the Administration of Estates Act 1925, s 33.

REVERTER OF SITES

6 (1)–(5) . . .

(6) The amendments made by this paragraph apply whether the trust arises before or after the commencement of this Act.

Commentary
Para 6: sub-paras (1)-(5) amend the Reverter of Sites Act 1987, s 1.

TRUSTS DEEMED TO ARISE IN 1926

7 Where at the commencement of this Act any land is held on trust for sale, or on the statutory trusts, by virtue of Schedule 1 to the Law of Property Act 1925 (transitional provisions), it shall after that commencement be held in trust for the persons interested in the land; and references in that Schedule to trusts for sale or trustees for sale or to the statutory trusts shall be construed accordingly.

Commentary
These are the various statutory provisions which imposed a trust for sale and which now, instead, impose a trust of land.

[460]

SCHEDULE 3
MINOR AND CONSEQUENTIAL AMENDMENTS

Section 25(1)

. . .

Amendment
Repealed in part by the Land Registration Act 2002, s 135, Sch 13.
Repealed in part by the Trustee Act 2000, s 40(1), (3), Sch 2, Pt II, para 49, Sch 4, Pt II.
Repealed in part by the Countryside and Rights of Way Act 2000, s 102, Sch 16, Pt III.

Commentary
This Schedule contains amendments only.

[461]

SCHEDULE 4
REPEALS

Section 25(2)

Chapter	*Short title*	*Extent of repeal*
3 & 4 Will 4 c 74	The Fines and Recoveries Act 1833	In section 1, the words ", and any undivided share thereof", in both places.
7 Will 4 & 1 Vict c 26	The Wills Act 1837	In section 1, the words "and to any undivided share thereof,".
		Section 32.
53 & 54 Vict c 39	The Partnership Act 1890	Section 22.

Chapter	*Short title*	*Extent of repeal*
12 & 13 Geo 5 c 16	The Law of Property Act 1922	In section 188–
		in subsection (1), the words "but not an undivided share in land;" and the words "but not an undivided share thereof", and
		subsection (30).
15 & 16 Geo 5 c 18	The Settled Land Act 1925	Section 27.
		Section 29.
15 & 16 Geo 5 c 19	The Trustee Act 1925	In section 10(2)–
		in the first paragraph, the words "by trustees or" and the words "the trustees, or ", and
		in the second paragraph, the words from the beginning to "mortgage; and".
		In section 19(1), the words "building or", in the second place.
		In section 68–
		in subsection (6), the words ", but not an undivided share in land" and the words ", but not an undivided share thereof", and
		in subsection (19), the word "binding", the words ", and with or without power at discretion to postpone the sale" and the definition of "trustees for sale".
15 & 16 Geo 5 c 20	The Law of Property Act 1925	In section 3–
		subsections (1)(b) and (2), and
		in subsection (5), the words "trustees for sale or other".
		In section 7(3), the second paragraph.
		In section 18–
		in subsection (1), the words from ", and personal estate" to "payable", in the second place, and the words "or is capable of being", and
		in subsection (2), the words "of the settlement or the trustees for sale", in both places.
		Section 19.
		Section 23 (and the heading immediately preceding it).
		Sections 25 and 26.
		Sections 28 to 30.
		Section 31(3).
		Section 32.
		In section 34–
		in subsection (3), the words from "the trustees (if any)" to "then to" and the words "in each case", and
		subsection (4).
		Section 35.
		Section 42(6).

Chapter	*Short title*	*Extent of repeal*
		In section 60, paragraphs (b) and (c) of the proviso to subsection (4). In section 130, subsections (1) to (3) and (6) (and the words "Creation of" in the sidenote). Section 201(3). In section 205(1)– in paragraph (ix), the words "but not an undivided share in land;" and the words "but not an undivided share thereof", in paragraph (x), the words "or in the proceeds of sale thereof", and in paragraph (xxix), the word "binding", the words ", and with or without a power at discretion to postpone the sale" and the words "and "power" onwards.
15 & 16 Geo 5 c 21	The Land Registration Act 1925	In section 3– in paragraph (viii), the words "but not an undivided share in land;", in paragraph (xi), the words "or in the proceeds of sale thereof", in paragraph (xiv), the words ", but not an undivided share thereof", and paragraphs (xxviii) and (xxix).
15 & 16 Geo 5 c 23	The Administration of Estates Act 1925	In section 3(1)(ii), the words "money to arise under a trust for sale of land, nor". In section 39(1)(i), the words from ", and such power" to "legal mortgage". In section 51– in subsection (3), the word "settled", and subsection (4). In section 55(1)– in paragraph (vii), the words "or in the proceeds of sale thereof", in paragraph (xxiv), the word ""land"", and paragraph (xxvii).
15 & 16 Geo 5 c 24	The Universities and College Estates Act 1925	In section 43(iv), the words ", but not an undivided share in land".
16 & 17 Geo 5 c 11	The Law of Property (Amendment) Act 1926	In the Schedule, the entries relating to section 3 of the Settled Land Act 1925 and sections 26, 28 and 35 of the Law of Property Act 1925.
17 & 18 Geo 5 c 36	The Landlord and Tenant Act 1927	In section 13– in subsection (1), the words from "(either" to "Property Act, 1925)", in subsection (2), the words ", trustee for sale, or personal representative", and in subsection (3), the words ", and "settled land"" onwards.

Chapter	*Short title*	*Extent of repeal*
22 & 23 Geo 5 c 27	The Law of Property (Entailed Interests) Act 1932	Section 1.
2 & 3 Geo 6 c 72	The Landlord and Tenant (War Damage) Act 1939	Section 3(c).
9 & 10 Geo 6 c 73	The Hill Farming Act 1946	Section 11(2).
12 & 13 Geo 6 c 74	The Coast Protection Act 1949	In section 11(2)(a)–
		the words ", by that section as applied by section twenty-eight of the Law of Property Act, 1925, in relation to trusts for sale,", and
		the words ", by that section as applied as aforesaid,".
2 & 3 Eliz 2 c 56	The Landlord and Tenant Act 1954	In the Second Schedule, in paragraph 6–
		the words ", by that section as applied by section twenty-eight of the Law of Property Act, 1925, in relation to trusts for sale,", and
		the words ", by that section as applied as aforesaid,".
7 & 8 Eliz 2 c 72	The Mental Health Act 1959	In Schedule 7, in Part I, the entries relating to sections 26 and 28 of the Law of Property Act 1925.
1964 No 2	The Incumbents and Churchwardens (Trusts) Measure 1964	In section 1, in the definition of "land", the words "nor an undivided share in land".
1967 c 10	The Forestry Act 1967	In Schedule 2, paragraph 1(4).
1967 c 88	The Leasehold Reform Act 1967	In section 6(5)–
		the words ", or by that section as applied by section 28 of the Law of Property Act 1925 in relation to trusts for sale,"
		the words "or by that section as applied as aforesaid", and
		the words "or by trustees for sale".
		In Schedule 2, in paragraph 9(1)–
		the words ", or by that section as applied by section 28 of the Law of Property Act 1925 in relation to trusts for sale, and the words "or by that section as applied as aforesaid".
1969 c 10	The Mines and Quarries (Tips) Act 1969	In section 32(2)(a) and (b), the words ", by that section as applied by section 28 of the Law of Property Act 1925 in relation to trusts for sale".
1970 c 40	The Agriculture Act 1970	In section 30
		in subsection (1), the words "(including those provisions as extended to trusts for sale by section 28 of the Law of Property Act 1925)", and
		in subsection (2), the words "the words from "(including those provisions" to "Law of Property Act 1925)" and".
1972 c 61	The Land Charges Act 1972	In section 17(1), the definition of "trust for sale".

Chapter	*Short title*	*Extent of repeal*
1976 c 31	The Legitimacy Act 1976	Section 10(4).
1976 c 36	The Adoption Act 1976	Section 46(5).
1977 c 42	The Rent Act 1977	In Schedule 2, in Part I, in paragraph 2(b), the words "or, if it is held on trust for sale, the proceeds of its sale are".
1980 c58	The Limitation Act 1980	In section 18–
		in subsection (1), the words ", including interests in the proceeds of the sale of land held upon trust for sale, ", and
		in subsections (3) and (4), the words "(including a trust for sale)" and the words "or in the proceeds of sale".
		In section 38(1)–
		in the definition of "land", the words ", including an interest in the proceeds of the sale of land held upon trust for sale,", and
		the definition of "trust for sale".
		In Schedule 1, in Part I, in paragraph 9–
		the words "or in the proceeds of sale",
		the words "or the proceeds", and
		the words "or the proceeds of sale".
1981 c 54	The Supreme Court Act 1981	In section 128, in the definition of "real estate", in paragraph (b), the words "money to arise under a trust for sale of land, nor".
1983 c 41	The Health and Social Services and Social Security Adjudications Act 1983	Section 22(3).
1984 c 28	The County Courts Act 1984	In Schedule 2, in Part II, in paragraph 2–
		in sub-paragraph (1), the entry relating to section 30 of the Law of Property Act 1925,
		sub-paragraph (2), and
		in sub-paragraph (3), "30(2),".
1984 c 51	The Inheritance Tax Act 1984	In section 237(3), the words "and undivided shares in land held on trust for sale, whether statutory or not,".
1986 c 5	The Agricultural Holdings Act 1986	In section 89(1), the words "or the Law of Property Act 1925".
1986 c 45	The Insolvency Act 1986	In section 336–
		subsection (3), and
		in subsection (4), the words "or (3)" and the words "or section 30 of the Act of 1925".
1988 c 50	The Housing Act 1988	In Schedule 1, in Part III, in paragraph 18(1)(b), the words "or, if it is held on trust for sale, the proceeds of its sale are".
1989 c 34	The Law of Property (Miscellaneous Provisions) Act 1989	In sections 1(6) and 2(6), the words " or in or over the proceeds of sale of land".

Chapter	*Short title*	*Extent of repeal*
1990 c 8	The Town and Country Planning Act 1990	In section 328–
1991 c 31		in subsection (1)(a), the words "and by that section as applied by section 28 of the Law of Property Act 1925 in relation to trusts for sale", and
		in subsection (2)(a), the words "and by that section as so applied".
1991 c 31	The Finance Act 1991	Section 110(5)(b).
1993 c 10	The Charities Act 1993	Section 37(6).
		Section 39(5).
1993 c 28	The Leasehold Reform, Housing and Urban Development Act 1993	In section 93A(4)–
		the words ", or by that section as applied by section 28 of the Law of Property Act 1925 in relation to trusts for sale",
		the words ", or by that section as so applied,", and
		the words "or by trustees for sale".
		In Schedule 2, paragraph 5(2)(b) and the word "and" immediately preceding it.
1994 c 36	The Law of Property (Miscellaneous Provisions) Act 1994	In section 16–
		subsection (2), and
		in subsection (3), the words "; and subsection (2)" onwards.
1995 c 8	The Agricultural Tenancies Act 1995	In section 33–
		in subsections (1) and (2), the words from "(either " to "Property Act 1925)" and
		in subsection (4), the definition of "settled land" and the word "and" immediately preceding it.
1996 c 53	The Housing Grants, Construction and Regeneration Act 1996	Section 55(4)(b).
		Section 73(3)(b).
		In section 98(2)(a), the words "or to the proceeds of sale of the dwelling".

[462]

TRUSTEE DELEGATION ACT 1999

1999 Chapter 15

ARRANGEMENT OF SECTIONS

An Act to amend the law relating to the delegation of trustee functions by power of attorney and the exercise of such functions by the donee of a power of attorney; and to make provision about the authority of the donee of a power of attorney to act in relation to land.

[15th July 1999]

General Note

The Trustee Delegation Act 1999 (TDA 1999) amends the law in relation to individual delegation by trustees of their function, previously dealt with in the Trustee Act 1925, s 25 **[95]** and circumvents a problem which prevented donors who were trustees of land but also beneficiaries, from delegating their functions as trustees successfully.

ATTORNEY OF TRUSTEE WITH BENEFICIAL INTEREST IN LAND

1 Exercise of trustee functions by attorney

(1) The donee of a power of attorney is not prevented from doing an act in relation to—

- (a) land,
- (b) capital proceeds of a conveyance of land, or
- (c) income from land,

by reason only that the act involves the exercise of a trustee function of the donor if, at the time when the act is done, the donor has a beneficial interest in the land, proceeds or income.

(2) In this section—

- (a) "conveyance" has the same meaning as in the Law of Property Act 1925, and
- (b) references to a trustee function of the donor are to a function which the donor has as trustee (either alone or jointly with any other person or persons).

(3) Subsection (1) above—

- (a) applies only if and so far as a contrary intention is not expressed in the instrument creating the power of attorney, and
- (b) has effect subject to the terms of that instrument.

(4) The donor of the power of attorney—

- (a) is liable for the acts or defaults of the donee in exercising any function by virtue of subsection (1) above in the same manner as if they were acts or defaults of the donor, but
- (b) is not liable by reason only that a function is exercised by the donee by virtue of that subsection.

(5) Subsections (1) and (4) above—

- (a) apply only if and so far as a contrary intention is not expressed in the instrument (if any) creating the trust, and
- (b) have effect subject to the terms of such an instrument.

(6) The fact that it appears that, in dealing with any shares or stock, the donee of the power of attorney is exercising a function by virtue of subsection (1) above does not affect with any notice of any trust a person in whose books the shares are, or stock is, registered or inscribed.

(7) In any case where (by way of exception to section 3(1) of the Trusts of Land and Appointment of Trustees Act 1996) the doctrine of conversion continues to operate, any person who, by reason of the continuing operation of that doctrine, has a beneficial interest in the proceeds of sale of land shall be treated for the purposes of this section and section 2 below as having a beneficial interest in the land.

(8) The donee of a power of attorney is not to be regarded as exercising a trustee function by virtue of subsection (1) above if he is acting under a trustee delegation power; and for this purpose a trustee delegation power is a power of attorney given under—

(a) a statutory provision, or
(b) a provision of the instrument (if any) creating a trust,

under which the donor of the power is expressly authorised to delegate the exercise of all or any of his trustee functions by power of attorney.

(9) Subject to section 4(6) below, this section applies only to powers of attorney created after the commencement of this Act.

Commentary

For the meaning of "conveyance" in sub-s (2) see the Law of Property Act 1925 **[180]**, s 205 (1)(ii). "Land" has the same meaning as in the Trustee Act 1925, s 68(1)(6) **[138]**. The power enables someone who is, for example, a beneficial co-owner of land, the ability by power of attorney to delegate his functions as trustee. All this is subject to the terms of the instrument creating the power of attorney (sub-s (3)) and the instrument creating the trust (sub-s (5)). As to sub-s (7), the doctrine of conversion has been abolished but still applies to trusts and wills predating the commencement of the Trusts of Land and Appointment of Trustees Act 1996. For the Trusts of Land and Appointment of Trustees Act 1996, s 3(1) see **[433]**. Subsection (8) appears at first somewhat obscure but would seem to mean that if the power of attorney is granted under the Trustee Act 1925, s 25 **[95]** or under an express power in the trust instrument, then the power derives from that rather than sub-s (1).

[463]

2 Evidence of beneficial interest

(1) This section applies where the interest of a purchaser depends on the donee of a power of attorney having power to do an act in relation to any property by virtue of section 1(1) above.

In this subsection "purchaser" has the same meaning as in Part I of the Law of Property Act 1925.

(2) Where this section applies an appropriate statement is, in favour of the purchaser, conclusive evidence of the donor of the power having a beneficial interest in the property at the time of the doing of the act.

(3) In this section "an appropriate statement" means a signed statement made by the donee—

(a) when doing the act in question, or
(b) at any other time within the period of three months beginning with the day on which the act is done,

that the donor has a beneficial interest in the property at the time of the donee doing the act.

(4) If an appropriate statement is false, the donee is liable in the same way as he would be if the statement were contained in a statutory declaration.

Commentary
The definition of "purchaser" as incorporated from the Law of Property Act 1925 **[180]**, s 205(1)(xxi) means that to be a purchaser the person has to act in good faith and give money or money's worth. As to the liability for making a false statutory declaration, see the Perjury Act 1911, s 5.

[464]

3 General powers in specified form

In section 10(2) of the Powers of Attorney Act 1971 (which provides that a general power of attorney in the form set out in Schedule 1 to that Act, or a similar form, does not confer on the donee of the power any authority to exercise functions of the donor as trustee etc), for the words "This section" substitute "Subject to section 1 of the Trustee Delegation Act 1999, this section".

Commentary
This makes a necessary amendment to the Powers of Attorney Act 1971 so that delegation of trust functions can take place in accordance with that Act to the limited extent permitted by s 1 above.

[465]

4 . . .

. . .

Amendment
Repealed by the Mental Capacity Act 2005, s 67(2), Sch 7.

[466]

TRUSTEE DELEGATION UNDER SECTION 25 OF THE TRUSTEE ACT 1925

5 Delegation under section 25 of the Trustee Act 1925

(1) For section 25 of the Trustee Act 1925 substitute—

"25 Delegation of trustee's functions by power of attorney

(1) Notwithstanding any rule of law or equity to the contrary, a trustee may, by power of attorney, delegate the execution or exercise of all or any of the trusts, powers and discretions vested in him as trustee either alone or jointly with any other person or persons.

(2) A delegation under this section—
- (a) commences as provided by the instrument creating the power or, if the instrument makes no provision as to the commencement of the delegation, with the date of the execution of the instrument by the donor; and
- (b) continues for a period of twelve months or any shorter period provided by the instrument creating the power.

(3) The persons who may be donees of a power of attorney under this section include a trust corporation.

(4) Before or within seven days after giving a power of attorney under this section the donor shall give written notice of it (specifying the date on which the power comes into operation and its duration, the donee of the power, the reason why the power is given and, where some only are delegated, the trusts, powers and discretions delegated) to—
- (a) each person (other than himself), if any, who under any instrument creating the trust has power (whether alone or jointly) to appoint a new trustee; and
- (b) each of the other trustees, if any;

but failure to comply with this subsection shall not, in favour of a person dealing with the donee of the power, invalidate any act done or instrument executed by the donee.

(5) A power of attorney given under this section by a single donor—

(a) in the form set out in subsection (6) of this section; or

(b) in a form to the like effect but expressed to be made under this subsection,

shall operate to delegate to the person identified in the form as the single donee of the power the execution and exercise of all the trusts, powers and discretions vested in the donor as trustee (either alone or jointly with any other person or persons) under the single trust so identified.

(6) The form referred to in subsection (5) of this section is as follows—

"THIS GENERAL TRUSTEE POWER OF ATTORNEY is made on [*date*] by [*name of one donor*] of [*address of donor*] as trustee of [*name or details of one trust*].

I appoint [*name of one donee*] of [*address of donee*] to be my attorney [*if desired, the date on which the delegation commences or the period for which it continues (or both)*] in accordance with section 25(5) of the Trustee Act 1925.

[*To be executed as a deed*]".

(7) The donor of a power of attorney given under this section shall be liable for the acts or defaults of the donee in the same manner as if they were the acts or defaults of the donor.

(8) For the purpose of executing or exercising the trusts or powers delegated to him, the donee may exercise any of the powers conferred on the donor as trustee by statute or by the instrument creating the trust, including power, for the purpose of the transfer of any inscribed stock, himself to delegate to an attorney power to transfer, but not including the power of delegation conferred by this section.

(9) The fact that it appears from any power of attorney given under this section, or from any evidence required for the purposes of any such power of attorney or otherwise, that in dealing with any stock the donee of the power is acting in the execution of a trust shall not be deemed for any purpose to affect any person in whose books the stock is inscribed or registered with any notice of the trust.

(10) This section applies to a personal representative, tenant for life and statutory owner as it applies to a trustee except that subsection (4) shall apply as if it required the notice there mentioned to be given—

(a) in the case of a personal representative, to each of the other personal representatives, if any, except any executor who has renounced probate;

(b) in the case of a tenant for life, to the trustees of the settlement and to each person, if any, who together with the person giving the notice constitutes the tenant for life; and

(c) in the case of a statutory owner, to each of the persons, if any, who together with the person giving the notice constitute the statutory owner and, in the case of a statutory owner by virtue of section 23(1)(a) of the Settled Land Act 1925, to the trustees of the settlement."

(2) Subsection (1) above has effect in relation to powers of attorney created after the commencement of this Act.

(3) In section 34(2)(b) of the Pensions Act 1995 (delegation by trustees of trustee scheme under section 25 of the Trustee Act 1925), for "during absence abroad" substitute "for period not exceeding twelve months".

Commentary

See the notes to the Trustee Act 1925, s 25 in its amended form at **[95]**.

[467]

6 . . .

. . .

Amendment
Repealed by the Mental Capacity Act 2005, s 67(2), Sch 7.

[468]

MISCELLANEOUS PROVISIONS ABOUT ATTORNEY ACTING FOR TRUSTEE

7 Two-trustee rules

(1) A requirement imposed by an enactment—

(a) that capital money be paid to, or dealt with as directed by, at least two trustees or that a valid receipt for capital money be given otherwise than by a sole trustee, or

(b) that, in order for an interest or power to be overreached, a conveyance or deed be executed by at least two trustees,

is not satisfied by money being paid to or dealt with as directed by, or a receipt for money being given by, a relevant attorney or by a conveyance or deed being executed by such an attorney.

(2) In this section "relevant attorney" means a person (other than a trust corporation within the meaning of the Trustee Act 1925) who is acting either—

(a) both as a trustee and as attorney for one or more other trustees, or

(b) as attorney for two or more trustees,

and who is not acting together with any other person or persons.

(3) This section applies whether a relevant attorney is acting under a power created before or after the commencement of this Act (but in the case of such an attorney acting under an enduring power created before that commencement is without prejudice to any continuing application of section 3(3) of the Enduring Powers of Attorney Act 1985 to the enduring power after that commencement . . .).

Amendment
Sub-s (3): words omitted repealed by the Mental Capacity Act 2005, s 67(2), Sch 7.

Commentary
Two trustees or a trust corporation are required by the Law of Property Act 1925 **[150]**, s 27(2) (as amended) and the Settled Land Act 1925, s 94(1) **[Appendix II]**. As to the meaning of "trust corporation" see the Trustee Act 1925, s 68(1)(18) **[138]** and see s 14 of that Act **[84]**.

[469]

8 Appointment of additional trustee by attorney

(1) In section 36 of the Trustee Act 1925 (appointment of trustees), after subsection (6) (additional trustees) insert—

"(6A) A person who is either—

(a) both a trustee and attorney for the other trustee (if one other), or for both of the other trustees (if two others), under a registered power; or

(b) attorney under a registered power for the trustee (if one) or for both or each of the trustees (if two or three),

may, if subsection (6B) of this section is satisfied in relation to him, make an appointment under subsection (6)(b) of this section on behalf of the trustee or trustees.

(6B) This subsection is satisfied in relation to an attorney under a registered power for one or more trustees if (as attorney under the power)—

(a) he intends to exercise any function of the trustee or trustees by virtue of section 1(1) of the Trustee Delegation Act 1999; or

(b) he intends to exercise any function of the trustee or trustees in relation to any land, capital proceeds of a conveyance of land or income from land by virtue of its delegation to him under section 25 of this Act or the instrument (if any) creating the trust.

(6C) In subsections (6A) and (6B) of this section "registered power" means a power of attorney created by an instrument which is for the time being registered under section 6 of the Enduring Powers of Attorney Act 1985.

(6D) Subsection (6A) of this section—

(a) applies only if and so far as a contrary intention is not expressed in the instrument creating the power of attorney (or, where more than one, any of them) or the instrument (if any) creating the trust; and

(b) has effect subject to the terms of those instruments."

(2) The amendment made by subsection (1) above has effect only where the power, or (where more than one) each of them, is created after the commencement of this Act.

Commentary

See the notes to the Trustee Act 1925, s 36(6)(A)–(D) **[105]**.

[470]

9 Attorney acting for incapable trustee

(1) In section 22 of the Law of Property Act 1925 (requirement, before dealing with legal estate vested in trustee who is incapable by reason of mental disorder, to appoint new trustee or discharge incapable trustee), after subsection (2) insert—

"(3) Subsection (2) of this section does not prevent a legal estate being dealt with without the appointment of a new trustee, or the discharge of the incapable trustee, at a time when the donee of an enduring power (within the meaning of the Enduring Powers of Attorney Act 1985) is entitled to act for the incapable trustee in the dealing."

The amendment made by subsection (1) above has effect whether the enduring power was created before or after the commencement of this Act.

Commentary

This amendment to the Law of Property Act 1925 **[148]** is necessitated because it might otherwise conflict with the TDA 1999, s 1. Indeed the provisions probably conflicted with the Enduring Powers of Attorney Act 1985, s 3(3) before its repeal. Since the commencement of the Mental Capacity Act 2005 on 1 October 2007 no new enduring powers of attorney can be created.

[471]

AUTHORITY OF ATTORNEY TO ACT IN RELATION TO LAND

10 Extent of attorney's authority to act in relation to land

(1) Where the donee of a power of attorney is authorised by the power to do an act of any description in relation to any land, his authority to do an act of that description at any time includes authority to do it with respect to any estate or interest in the land which is held at that time by the donor (whether alone or jointly with any other person or persons).

(2) Subsection (1) above—

(a) applies only if and so far as a contrary intention is not expressed in the instrument creating the power of attorney, and

(b) has effect subject to the terms of that instrument.

(3) This section applies only to powers of attorney created after the commencement of this Act.

Commentary

Note that the instrument creating the power of attorney can restrict the ambit of the power.

[472]

SUPPLEMENTARY

11 Interpretation

(1) In this Act—

"land" has the same meaning as in the Trustee Act 1925, and

"enduring power" has the same meaning as in the Enduring Powers of Attorney Act 1985.

(2) References in this Act to the creation of a power of attorney are to the execution by the donor of the instrument creating it.

Commentary

For the definition of "land" in the Trustee Act 1925, see s 68(1) **[138]**. The Enduring Powers of Attorney Act 1985 has been repealed by the Mental Capacity Act 2005 and no new powers can be created after 1 October 2007.

[473]

12 Repeals

The enactments specified in the Schedule to this Act are repealed to the extent specified in the third column, but subject to the note at the end.

13 Commencement, extent and short title

(1) The preceding provisions of this Act shall come into force on such day as the Lord Chancellor may by order made by statutory instrument appoint.

(2) This Act extends to England and Wales only.

(3) This Act may be cited as the Trustee Delegation Act 1999.

[474]

SCHEDULE
REPEALS

Section 12

Chapter	*Short title*	*Extent of repeal*
1971 c 27	The Powers of Attorney Act 1971	Section 9
1985 c 29	The Enduring Powers of Attorney Act 1985	Section 2(8)
		Section 3(3)

The repeal of section 3(3) of the Enduring Powers of Attorney Act 1985 has effect in accordance with section 4 of this Act and the remaining repeals have effect in relation to powers of attorney created after the commencement of this Act.

[475]

TRUSTEE ACT 2000

2000 Chapter 29

ARRANGEMENT OF SECTIONS

PART I
THE DUTY OF CARE

PART II
INVESTMENT

PART III
ACQUISITION OF LAND

PART IV
AGENTS, NOMINEES AND CUSTODIANS

PART V
REMUNERATION

PART VI
MISCELLANEOUS AND SUPPLEMENTARY

An Act to amend the law relating to trustees and persons having the investment powers of trustees; and for connected purposes.

[23rd November 2000]

General Note

The Trustee Act 2000 (TA 2000) extended the powers of trustees to invest and delegate and reformed other areas of a trustee's powers.

PART I
THE DUTY OF CARE

1 The duty of care

(1) Whenever the duty under this subsection applies to a trustee, he must exercise such care and skill as is reasonable in the circumstances, having regard in particular—

(a) to any special knowledge or experience that he has or holds himself out as having, and

(b) if he acts as trustee in the course of a business or profession, to any special knowledge or experience that it is reasonable to expect of a person acting in the course of that kind of business or profession.

(2) In this Act the duty under subsection (1) is called "the duty of care".

Commentary

This section introduces the new statutory duty of care. Subsection (1)(a) and (b) set out the standard of care imposed on trustees. The first limb of the circumstances to which the court will have regard in deciding whether a trustee has fulfilled his duty is a subjective one: what particular expertise does this particular trustee have? The second limb is objective: what standard is to be expected from a trustee who is, for example, a solicitor or an accountant? It appears that the intention of the TA 2000 (according to the guidance notes to the Bill) where it applies to trustees acting in the course of a profession or business, was to impose a basic standard on professional trustees which might be uplifted if the trustee in question has special expertise. Note that the duty applies to all trusts whenever created but can be excluded or restricted, see Sch 1, para 7.

[476]

2 Application of duty of care

Schedule 1 makes provision about when the duty of care applies to a trustee.

Commentary
This duty does not replace the common law duty imposed on trustees to take care and only applies in the circumstances set out in Sch 1. Those circumstances generally apply to trustees carrying out their powers and not where they do not exercise them at all.

[477]

PART II
INVESTMENT

3 General power of investment

(1) Subject to the provisions of this Part, a trustee may make any kind of investment that he could make if he were absolutely entitled to the assets of the trust.

(2) In this Act the power under subsection (1) is called "the general power of investment".

(3) The general power of investment does not permit a trustee to make investments in land other than in loans secured on land (but see also section 8).

(4) A person invests in a loan secured on land if he has rights under any contract under which—
- (a) one person provides another with credit, and
- (b) the obligation of the borrower to repay is secured on land.

(5) "Credit" includes any cash loan or other financial accommodation.

(6) "Cash" includes money in any form.

Commentary
This section confers on trustees a wide power to invest. While it does not permit trustees to invest in land (sub-s (3)) this exclusion is illusory as a power to acquire land is contained in s 8. However, it is clear that trustees can make loans on land which are widely defined in sub-s (4). It should be noted that nowhere in the TA 2000 is there any definition of the term "investment" although it is considered unlikely now that it would have the restricted meaning of an asset which produced income, see *Re Wragg* [1919] 2 Ch 58. Any asset which produced income or capital profit for the trust would almost certainly be an investment in modern parlance.

[478]

4 Standard investment criteria

(1) In exercising any power of investment, whether arising under this Part or otherwise, a trustee must have regard to the standard investment criteria.

(2) A trustee must from time to time review the investments of the trust and consider whether, having regard to the standard investment criteria, they should be varied.

(3) The standard investment criteria, in relation to a trust, are—
- (a) the suitability to the trust of investments of the same kind as any particular investment proposed to be made or retained and of that particular investment as an investment of that kind, and
- (b) the need for diversification of investments of the trust, in so far as is appropriate to the circumstances of the trust.

Commentary
Trustees must have regard to the standard investment criteria, not only when exercising the power of investment conferred by the TA 2000, but *any* power of investment, so that express powers will be covered too. There is some doubt as to whether the standard investment criteria can be excluded but it is becoming increasingly common for wills and settlements to attempt to do so.
In fact there is nothing new about these provisions. The standard investment criteria are lifted almost verbatim from the Trustee Investment Act 1961, s 6 and that Act too extended them to the exercise of all powers of investment.

The first criteria which has to be fulfilled by the trustees, either when making an investment or reviewing investments (which is a duty imposed on the trustees by s 4(2)) is to have regard to the suitability of the investment. As with the Trustee Investment Act 1961, this involves trustees in a twofold test: they must look first of all at the type of investment in question to decide whether it would be a good investment for the trust, and then look at the specific investment of that type, taking into account matters such as performance.

The requirement of diversification mirrors the modern portfolio approach to investment, but it is not an absolute criteria. It will only apply so far as appropriate to the circumstances of the trust.

[479]

5 Advice

(1) Before exercising any power of investment, whether arising under this Part or otherwise, a trustee must (unless the exception applies) obtain and consider proper advice about the way in which, having regard to the standard investment criteria, the power should be exercised.

(2) When reviewing the investments of the trust, a trustee must (unless the exception applies) obtain and consider proper advice about whether, having regard to the standard investment criteria, the investments should be varied.

(3) The exception is that a trustee need not obtain such advice if he reasonably concludes that in all the circumstances it is unnecessary or inappropriate to do so.

(4) Proper advice is the advice of a person who is reasonably believed by the trustee to be qualified to give it by his ability in and practical experience of financial and other matters relating to the proposed investment.

Commentary

The need to seek advice imposed by this section on trustees, whether exercising their powers under the TA 2000, or express or other statutory powers, is more stringent than the previous law. Under the Trustee Investment Act 1961, trustees could invest in certain assets without the need for advice. Advice must be sought not only when the initial investment is made but also when the trustees review investments (sub-s (2)).

There is an exception contained in sub-s (3) which demands that the trustee act reasonably in concluding that advice is inappropriate or unnecessary. Everything will depend on the circumstances as to whether a trustee should seek advice.

[480]

6 Restriction or exclusion of this Part etc

(1) The general power of investment is—

(a) in addition to powers conferred on trustees otherwise than by this Act, but

(b) subject to any restriction or exclusion imposed by the trust instrument or by any enactment or any provision of subordinate legislation.

(2) For the purposes of this Act, an enactment or a provision of subordinate legislation is not to be regarded as being, or as being part of, a trust instrument.

(3) In this Act "subordinate legislation" has the same meaning as in the Interpretation Act 1978.

Commentary

This provision makes it clear that what is being conferred on trustees are default powers of investment. Therefore if the trust instrument (see section 39(2) for a definition) provides express powers, then the powers under the TA 2000 will be an addition to those.

It will also be possible for the trust instrument to exclude or restrict the default powers, although the circumstances where this will be desirable must be rare. As to exclusion of the power in existing trusts, see s 7 below.

For these purposes "subordinate legislation" means Orders in Council, orders, rules, regulations, schemes, warrants, byelaws and other instruments made or to be made under any Act, including any local, personal or private acts.

[481]

7 Existing trusts

(1) This Part applies in relation to trusts whether created before or after its commencement.

(2) No provision relating to the powers of a trustee contained in a trust instrument made before 3rd August 1961 is to be treated (for the purposes of section 6(1)(b)) as restricting or excluding the general power of investment.

(3) A provision contained in a trust instrument made before the commencement of this Part which—

- (a) has effect under section 3(2) of the Trustee Investments Act 1961 as a power to invest under that Act, or
- (b) confers power to invest under that Act,

is to be treated as conferring the general power of investment on a trustee.

Commentary

The TA 2000 applies to all trusts whether created before or after the Act. The special provisions contained in sub-s (2) relate to the coming into effect of the Trustee Investments Act 1961. That legislation overrode any restriction contained in a trust instrument which would have restricted or excluded the operation of the Trustee Investments Act 1961. This provision prevents the resurrection of exclusions and restrictions from those trust instruments. On the other hand if trust instruments after that date restrict or exclude the Act, then that will be effective.

Subsection (3) ensures that where a trust instrument empowers the trustees to invest in accordance with the Trustee Investments Act 1961, that provision will now be construed as conferring on the trustees the general power of investment which is of course much wider in terms than the default powers under the Trustee Investments Act 1961.

[482]

PART III
ACQUISITION OF LAND

8 Power to acquire freehold and leasehold land

(1) A trustee may acquire freehold or leasehold land in the United Kingdom—

- (a) as an investment,
- (b) for occupation by a beneficiary, or
- (c) for any other reason.

(2) "Freehold or leasehold land" means—

- (a) in relation to England and Wales, a legal estate in land,
- (b) in relation to Scotland—
  - (i) the estate or interest of the proprietor of the dominium utile or, in the case of land not held on feudal tenure, the estate or interest of the owner, or
  - (ii) a tenancy, and
- (c) in relation to Northern Ireland, a legal estate in land, including land held under a fee farm grant.

(3) For the purpose of exercising his functions as a trustee, a trustee who acquires land under this section has all the powers of an absolute owner in relation to the land.

Commentary

While s 3 excluded from the general power of investment any power to invest in land, s 8 introduces default powers which enable trustees not just to invest in land, but also to acquire it for occupation by a beneficiary (which would not otherwise constitute investment, see *Re Power* [1947] Ch 572) and for any other purpose. It seems this last provision is designed so that charity trustees can acquire functional land.

It should be noted that the power is narrower than might at first sight appear. It does not permit the acquisition of anything other than the legal estate in land, and as the general power of investment does not extend to investment in land, trustees cannot invest in equitable interests in land, or legal interests such as rentcharges (although if they hold any they can retain them, see **[521]**). The power is also restricted to land in the UK, which may be a very serious impediment where there are worldwide beneficiaries.

Subsection (3) effectively re-enacts the Trusts of Land and Appointment of Trustees Act 1996, s 6 **[436]** and confers on trustees all the powers of an absolute owner. Apart from the obvious, this power gets around the inconvenient rule that trustees cannot hold land jointly with or in common with others, see *Webb v Jonas* (1888) 39 Ch D 6.

[483]

9 Restriction or exclusion of this Part etc

The powers conferred by this Part are—

(a) in addition to powers conferred on trustees otherwise than by this Part, but

(b) subject to any restriction or exclusion imposed by the trust instrument or by any enactment or any provision of subordinate legislation.

Commentary

Again the TA 2000 makes it clear that these are default powers and are in addition to express powers and can be restricted or excluded by the trust instrument. Note that even pre-3 August 1963 trust instruments can exclude or restrict these powers if they contain the appropriate clauses to that effect.

[484]

10 Existing trusts

(1) This Part does not apply in relation to—

(a) a trust of property which consists of or includes land which (despite section 2 of the Trusts of Land and Appointment of Trustees Act 1996) is settled land, or

(b) a trust to which the Universities and College Estates Act 1925 applies.

(2) Subject to subsection (1), this Part applies in relation to trusts whether created before or after its commencement.

Commentary

The TA 2000 does not apply to strict settlements in existence on 1 January 1997, and preserved by the Trusts of Land and Appointment of Trustees Act 1996 **[432]** which abolished them for the future. Therefore, the power to invest capital arising under a strict settlement will still depend on the Settled Land Act 1925, s 73 **[Appendix II]**. The Universities and College Estates Act 1925 confers on Oxford, Cambridge and Durham powers similar to those of a tenant for life under the Settled Land Act 1925.

[485]

PART IV
AGENTS, NOMINEES AND CUSTODIANS

AGENTS

11 Power to employ agents

(1) Subject to the provisions of this Part, the trustees of a trust may authorise any person to exercise any or all of their delegable functions as their agent.

(2) In the case of a trust other than a charitable trust, the trustees' delegable functions consist of any function other than—

(a) any function relating to whether or in what way any assets of the trust should be distributed,

(b) any power to decide whether any fees or other payment due to be made out of the trust funds should be made out of income or capital,

(c) any power to appoint a person to be a trustee of the trust, or
(d) any power conferred by any other enactment or the trust instrument which permits the trustees to delegate any of their functions or to appoint a person to act as a nominee or custodian.

(3) In the case of a charitable trust, the trustees' delegable functions are—
(a) any function consisting of carrying out a decision that the trustees have taken;
(b) any function relating to the investment of assets subject to the trust (including, in the case of land held as an investment, managing the land and creating or disposing of an interest in the land);
(c) any function relating to the raising of funds for the trust otherwise than by means of profits of a trade which is an integral part of carrying out the trust's charitable purpose;
(d) any other function prescribed by an order made by the Secretary of State.

(4) For the purposes of subsection (3)(c) a trade is an integral part of carrying out a trust's charitable purpose if, whether carried on in the United Kingdom or elsewhere, the profits are applied solely to the purposes of the trust and either—
(a) the trade is exercised in the course of the actual carrying out of a primary purpose of the trust, or
(b) the work in connection with the trade is mainly carried out by beneficiaries of the trust.

(5) The power to make an order under subsection (3)(d) is exercisable by statutory instrument which shall be subject to annulment in pursuance of a resolution of either House of Parliament.

Commentary

Before the TA 2000 it was clear that the scope of trustees' powers to delegate collectively was, in the absence of an express power in the trust instrument, severely limited. The provisions of this section differentiate between trustees of a charitable trust and other trustees and the approach in respect of both is quite different.

In the case of non-charitable trusts the trustees can delegate all their functions, except those listed in sub-s (2)(a)–(b), which in essence are fiduciary functions relating to distribution of trust property and delegation itself.

As far as charitable trusts are concerned, the trustees can only delegate the functions which are set out in sub-s (3)(a)–(c) with power vested in the Secretary of State to prescribe further delegable functions but subject to Parliament (see sub-s (5)).

Charitable trustees cannot delegate a fund-raising function which involves a trade integral to the charitable purposes. In other words if the purpose of the charity is to run a business employing disabled persons, then the function of running that trade cannot be delegated. On the other hand a charity shop run to raise funds for a charity will not be an integral part of the charitable purposes of a charity whose objects are cancer research.

[486]

12 Persons who may act as agents

(1) Subject to subsection (2), the persons whom the trustees may under section 11 authorise to exercise functions as their agent include one or more of their number.

(2) The trustees may not authorise two (or more) persons to exercise the same function unless they are to exercise the function jointly.

(3) The trustees may not under section 11 authorise a beneficiary to exercise any function as their agent (even if the beneficiary is also a trustee).

(4) The trustees may under section 11 authorise a person to exercise functions as their agent even though he is also appointed to act as their nominee or custodian (whether under section 16, 17 or 18 or any other power).

Commentary
The Trustees may delegate to their co-trustees which may be very helpful, for example for signing documents when one is unavailable. They can also delegate to persons appointed to act as their nominees or custodians, but trustees cannot however delegate their functions to beneficiaries.
Delegation must be to agents jointly and not jointly and severally, so they must act together.

[487]

13 Linked functions etc

(1) Subject to subsections (2) and (5), a person who is authorised under section 11 to exercise a function is (whatever the terms of the agency) subject to any specific duties or restrictions attached to the function.

For example, a person who is authorised under section 11 to exercise the general power of investment is subject to the duties under section 4 in relation to that power.

(2) A person who is authorised under section 11 to exercise a power which is subject to a requirement to obtain advice is not subject to the requirement if he is the kind of person from whom it would have been proper for the trustees, in compliance with the requirement, to obtain advice.

(3) Subsections (4) and (5) apply to a trust to which section 11(1) of the Trusts of Land and Appointment of Trustees Act 1996 (duties to consult beneficiaries and give effect to their wishes) applies.

(4) The trustees may not under section 11 authorise a person to exercise any of their functions on terms that prevent them from complying with section 11(1) of the 1996 Act.

(5) A person who is authorised under section 11 to exercise any function relating to land subject to the trust is not subject to section 11(1) of the 1996 Act.

Commentary
Subsection (1) is such an unclear piece of drafting that the draftsman thought it necessary to provide an example to illustrate it. Essentially if a function such as investment is delegated to an agent, he will be subject to duties which go with that function, such as having regard to the standard investment criteria and taking advice. How far the agent would be subject to other fiduciary duties remains unclear.
Subsection (2) softens the requirement to seek advice if there has been delegation to the sort of person from whom advice would be sought, eg an investment manager.
Subsections (3), (4) and (5) apply where there is a duty to consult beneficiaries under the Trusts of Land and Appointment of Trustees Act 1996 **[431]**. This is a duty which is now often excluded. However, if it does apply, the duty remains in the trustees and not on the agent and the trustees cannot delegate so as to prevent their compliance with s 11. In the case of trusts of land where s 11 still applies, this may severely hamper the ability of trustees to delegate their functions.

[488]

14 Terms of agency

(1) Subject to subsection (2) and sections 15(2) and 29 to 32, the trustees may authorise a person to exercise functions as their agent on such terms as to remuneration and other matters as they may determine.

(2) The trustees may not authorise a person to exercise functions as their agent on any of the terms mentioned in subsection (3) unless it is reasonably necessary for them to do so.

(3) The terms are—
- (a) a term permitting the agent to appoint a substitute;
- (b) a term restricting the liability of the agent or his substitute to the trustees or any beneficiary;

(c) a term permitting the agent to act in circumstances capable of giving rise to a conflict of interest.

Commentary

These provisions apply to all delegation, and not just it would seem delegation under the TA 2000. It is notable that the terms which are prohibited under s 15(3) are very commonly found in documents appointing agents. It remains to be seen whether it will be regarded as "reasonably necessary" (sub-s (2)) to include those terms because market forces demand it.

[489]

15 Asset management: special restrictions

(1) The trustees may not authorise a person to exercise any of their asset management functions as their agent except by an agreement which is in or evidenced in writing.

(2) The trustees may not authorise a person to exercise any of their asset management functions as their agent unless—

- (a) they have prepared a statement that gives guidance as to how the functions should be exercised ("a policy statement"), and
- (b) the agreement under which the agent is to act includes a term to the effect that he will secure compliance with—
  - (i) the policy statement, or
  - (ii) if the policy statement is revised or replaced under section 22, the revised or replacement policy statement.

(3) The trustees must formulate any guidance given in the policy statement with a view to ensuring that the functions will be exercised in the best interests of the trust.

(4) The policy statement must be in or evidenced in writing.

(5) The asset management functions of trustees are their functions relating to—

- (a) the investment of assets subject to the trust,
- (b) the acquisition of property which is to be subject to the trust, and
- (c) managing property which is subject to the trust and disposing of, or creating or disposing of an interest in, such property.

Commentary

The most common form of delegation is asset management or investment functions to an investment manager. Again this section applies not only to delegation under the TA 2000 but also to delegation under express powers and it is not clear how far it can be excluded. Asset management functions are defined in sub-s (5).

There are two main requirements under this provision. The first is that the agreement delegating asset management functions is evidenced in writing. Note that delegation of functions other than asset management functions need not be evidenced in writing.

The second requirement is that of the policy statement which also must be evidenced in writing.

[490]

NOMINEES AND CUSTODIANS

16 Power to appoint nominees

(1) Subject to the provisions of this Part, the trustees of a trust may—

- (a) appoint a person to act as their nominee in relation to such of the assets of the trust as they determine (other than settled land), and
- (b) take such steps as are necessary to secure that those assets are vested in a person so appointed.

(2) An appointment under this section must be in or evidenced in writing.

(3) This section does not apply to any trust having a custodian trustee or in relation to any assets vested in the official custodian for charities.

Commentary

A custodian trustee referred to in sub-s(3) is defined by the Public Trustee Act 1906 **[62]**.

[491]

17 Power to appoint custodians

(1) Subject to the provisions of this Part, the trustees of a trust may appoint a person to act as a custodian in relation to such of the assets of the trust as they may determine.

(2) For the purposes of this Act a person is a custodian in relation to assets if he undertakes the safe custody of the assets or of any documents or records concerning the assets.

(3) An appointment under this section must be in or evidenced in writing.

(4) This section does not apply to any trust having a custodian trustee or in relation to any assets vested in the official custodian for charities.

Commentary

Note the restrictions on who can act as a custodian imposed by s 19.

[492]

18 Investment in bearer securities

(1) If trustees retain or invest in securities payable to bearer, they must appoint a person to act as a custodian of the securities.

(2) Subsection (1) does not apply if the trust instrument or any enactment or provision of subordinate legislation contains provision which (however expressed) permits the trustees to retain or invest in securities payable to bearer without appointing a person to act as a custodian.

(3) An appointment under this section must be in or evidenced in writing.

(4) This section does not apply to any trust having a custodian trustee or in relation to any securities vested in the official custodian for charities.

Commentary

The power to appoint a custodian becomes a duty in the circumstances set out in sub-s (1). This section replaces the Trustee Act 1925, s 7(1) but with a wider class of persons who can be appointed as custodian (as to which see s 19 below). The duties imposed under this section do not apply to a trustee which is a trust corporation (see s 24).

[493]

19 Persons who may be appointed as nominees or custodians

(1) A person may not be appointed under section 16, 17 or 18 as a nominee or custodian unless one of the relevant conditions is satisfied.

(2) The relevant conditions are that—

(a) the person carries on a business which consists of or includes acting as a nominee or custodian;

(b) the person is a body corporate which is controlled by the trustees;

(c) the person is a body corporate recognised under section 9 of the Administration of Justice Act 1985.

(3) The question whether a body corporate is controlled by trustees is to be determined in accordance with section 840 of the Income and Corporation Taxes Act 1988.

(4) The trustees of a charitable trust which is not an exempt charity must act in accordance with any guidance given by the [Charity Commission] concerning the selection of a person for appointment as a nominee or custodian under section 16, 17 or 18.

(5) Subject to subsections (1) and (4), the persons whom the trustees may under section 16, 17 or 18 appoint as a nominee or custodian include—

- (a) one of their number, if that one is a trust corporation, or
- (b) two (or more) of their number, if they are to act as joint nominees or joint custodians.

(6) The trustees may under section 16 appoint a person to act as their nominee even though he is also—

- (a) appointed to act as their custodian (whether under section 17 or 18 or any other power), or
- (b) authorised to exercise functions as their agent (whether under section 11 or any other power).

(7) Likewise, the trustees may under section 17 or 18 appoint a person to act as their custodian even though he is also—

- (a) appointed to act as their nominee (whether under section 16 or any other power), or
- (b) authorised to exercise functions as their agent (whether under section 11 or any other power).

Amendment

Sub-s (4): words "Charity Commission" in square brackets substituted by the Charities Act 2006, s 75(1), Sch 8, para 197.

Commentary

This section restricts those who can act as custodian or nominees basically to those in the business of acting as such or to a company controlled by the trustees (as defined in the Income and Corporation Taxes Act 1998, s 840) (now Income Tax Act 2007, s 995). The trustees themselves, if they fulfil the relevant conditions, can be appointed and the same person or persons can be appointed to act both as custodians, nominees or agents.

[494]

20 Terms of appointment of nominees and custodians

(1) Subject to subsection (2) and sections 29 to 32, the trustees may under section 16, 17 or 18 appoint a person to act as a nominee or custodian on such terms as to remuneration and other matters as they may determine.

(2) The trustees may not under section 16, 17 or 18 appoint a person to act as a nominee or custodian on any of the terms mentioned in subsection (3) unless it is reasonably necessary for them to do so.

(3) The terms are—

- (a) a term permitting the nominee or custodian to appoint a substitute;
- (b) a term restricting the liability of the nominee or custodian or his substitute to the trustees or to any beneficiary;
- (c) a term permitting the nominee or custodian to act in circumstances capable of giving rise to a conflict of interest.

Commentary

It will be noted that there are similar restrictions on the terms on which custodians and nominees can be appointed as agents generally (see s 14). Again the prohibited terms are not unusual in the market place.

[495]

REVIEW OF AND LIABILITY FOR AGENTS, NOMINEES AND CUSTODIANS ETC

21 Application of sections 22 and 23

(1) Sections 22 and 23 apply in a case where trustees have, under section 11, 16, 17 or 18—

(a) authorised a person to exercise functions as their agent, or

(b) appointed a person to act as a nominee or custodian.

(2) Subject to subsection (3), sections 22 and 23 also apply in a case where trustees have, under any power conferred on them by the trust instrument or by any enactment or any provision of subordinate legislation—

(a) authorised a person to exercise functions as their agent, or

(b) appointed a person to act as a nominee or custodian.

(3) If the application of section 22 or 23 is inconsistent with the terms of the trust instrument or the enactment or provision of subordinate legislation, the section in question does not apply.

Commentary

This section introduces the provisions which relate to the liability of agents, custodians and nominees and the duty on the trustees to review their performance. It should be noted that while ss 22 and 23 will apply in all cases to the exercise by the trustees of the powers conferred by the TA 2000, they will only apply to other powers conferred by the trust instrument or by statute or subordinate legislation, insofar as the trust instrument is not inconsistent with them. Therefore, if the draftsman wishes to exclude the provisions of ss 22 and 23 it is certainly possible for him to do so.

[496]

22 Review of agents, nominees and custodians etc

(1) While the agent, nominee or custodian continues to act for the trust, the trustees—

(a) must keep under review the arrangements under which the agent, nominee or custodian acts and how those arrangements are being put into effect,

(b) if circumstances make it appropriate to do so, must consider whether there is a need to exercise any power of intervention that they have, and

(c) if they consider that there is a need to exercise such a power, must do so.

(2) If the agent has been authorised to exercise asset management functions, the duty under subsection (1) includes, in particular—

(a) a duty to consider whether there is any need to revise or replace the policy statement made for the purposes of section 15,

(b) if they consider that there is a need to revise or replace the policy statement, a duty to do so, and

(c) a duty to assess whether the policy statement (as it has effect for the time being) is being complied with.

(3) Subsections (3) and (4) of section 15 apply to the revision or replacement of a policy statement under this section as they apply to the making of a policy statement under that section.

(4) "Power of intervention" includes—

(a) a power to give directions to the agent, nominee or custodian;

(b) a power to revoke the authorisation or appointment.

Commentary

Note that this section only applies to the review of agents, nominees or custodians appointed under the powers conferred by the TA 2000, and to those appointed under express powers, insofar as the terms of the trust instrument are not inconsistent (see the commentary to s 21).

The duty imposed on trustees by this section is twofold: (1) they must review; and (2) they must intervene if appropriate to do so, and sub-s (4) sets out the powers of intervention. Failure to carry out this duty properly may amount to a breach of the statutory duty of care (see Sch 1, para 3(1)(e)), although failure to review in the first place is probably not a breach of the statutory duty, although it may be a breach of the common law duty of care.

[497]

23 Liability for agents, nominees and custodians etc

(1) A trustee is not liable for any act or default of the agent, nominee or custodian unless he has failed to comply with the duty of care applicable to him, under paragraph 3 of Schedule 1—

- (a) when entering into the arrangements under which the person acts as agent, nominee or custodian, or
- (b) when carrying out his duties under section 22.

(2) If a trustee has agreed a term under which the agent, nominee or custodian is permitted to appoint a substitute, the trustee is not liable for any act or default of the substitute unless he has failed to comply with the duty of care applicable to him, under paragraph 3 of Schedule 1—

- (a) when agreeing that term, or
- (b) when carrying out his duties under section 22 in so far as they relate to the use of the substitute.

Commentary

The liability of the trustees for the acts of their agents is circumscribed by this section. They will only be liable for the defaults of their agent when they have been in breach of their statutory duty of care on appointment, and when they are in breach of their statutory duty of care in carrying out a review of the agent. It seems, however, that if the trustees fail to review the agent's activities they will not be in breach of their statutory duty of care (see the wording of Sch 1) and therefore not liable. While this is the most natural construction of the section, it gives rise to a most unfortunate result.

[498]

SUPPLEMENTARY

24 Effect of trustees exceeding their powers

A failure by the trustees to act within the limits of the powers conferred by this Part—

- (a) in authorising a person to exercise a function of theirs as an agent, or
- (b) in appointing a person to act as a nominee or custodian,

does not invalidate the authorisation or appointment.

Commentary

This section ensures that trustees who fail to follow the provisions as to appointing agents, custodians or nominees will nevertheless have made a valid appointment. So, for example, if trustees delegating their asset management functions fail to evidence the appointment in writing (as required by s 15), the appointment will be valid although the trustees will be in breach of their statutory duty of care.

[499]

25 Sole trustees

(1) Subject to subsection (2), this Part applies in relation to a trust having a sole trustee as it applies in relation to other trusts (and references in this Part to trustees—except in sections 12(1) and (3) and 19(5)—are to be read accordingly).

(2) Section 18 does not impose a duty on a sole trustee if that trustee is a trust corporation.

Commentary
This part refers throughout to "trustees" but this section makes it clear that the powers to delegate are available to sole trustees too. It is also made clear that trust corporations are relieved of the duties in relation to custodians holding bearer securities imposed by s 18.

[500]

26 Restriction or exclusion of this Part etc

The powers conferred by this Part are—

(a) in addition to powers conferred on trustees otherwise than by this Act, but
(b) subject to any restriction or exclusion imposed by the trust instrument or by any enactment or any provision of subordinate legislation.

Commentary
See the notes to s 9.

[501]

27 Existing trusts

This Part applies in relation to trusts whether created before or after its commencement.

Commentary
See the notes to s 9.

[502]

PART V
REMUNERATION

28 Trustee's entitlement to payment under trust instrument

(1) Except to the extent (if any) to which the trust instrument makes inconsistent provision, subsections (2) to (4) apply to a trustee if—

(a) there is a provision in the trust instrument entitling him to receive payment out of trust funds in respect of services provided by him to or on behalf of the trust, and
(b) the trustee is a trust corporation or is acting in a professional capacity.

(2) The trustee is to be treated as entitled under the trust instrument to receive payment in respect of services even if they are services which are capable of being provided by a lay trustee.

(3) Subsection (2) applies to a trustee of a charitable trust who is not a trust corporation only—

(a) if he is not a sole trustee, and
(b) to the extent that a majority of the other trustees have agreed that it should apply to him.

(4) Any payments to which the trustee is entitled in respect of services are to be treated as remuneration for services (and not as a gift) for the purposes of—

(a) section 15 of the Wills Act 1837 (gifts to an attesting witness to be void), and
(b) section 34(3) of the Administration of Estates Act 1925 (order in which estate to be paid out).

(5) For the purposes of this Part, a trustee acts in a professional capacity if he acts in the course of a profession or business which consists of or includes the provision of services in connection with—

(a) the management or administration of trusts generally or a particular kind of trust, or
(b) any particular aspect of the management or administration of trusts generally or a particular kind of trust,

and the services he provides to or on behalf of the trust fall within that description.

(6) For the purposes of this Part, a person acts as a lay trustee if he—
(a) is not a trust corporation, and
(b) does not act in a professional capacity.

Commentary

The crucial point to note in respect of the main provisions of s 28 is that they apply only where there is an express charging clause in the trust instrument and there is no contrary intention in the trust instrument (sub-s (1)). They also only apply to charitable trustees in certain circumstances—that is, where the charitable trustee is a trust corporation or where he is not a sole trustee and his co-trustees agree.

The first of the main provisions is that professional trustees (note the definition of a trustee acting in a professional capacity in sub-s (5) which applies for this whole part) with the benefit of a charging clause can charge for items which a lay trustee could have performed (the definition of which is contained for the whole of this Part of the TA 2000 in sub-s (6)). Most well-drafted charging clauses already provide for this to be the case.

The second change made to the law was to characterise fees to which the trustee was entitled under the charging clause as remuneration and not as a gift, which was the previous position. This had the effect that if a solicitor, who was to be the executor of a will where there was an express charging clause, witnessed the will, the "gift" of the charging clause payments to him would be void. Similarly for the purposes of marshalling debts and assets of an estate under the Administration of Estates Act 1925, s 34(3) **[209]**, remuneration to which an executor was entitled under a charging clause was treated not as a debt but as a pecuniary legacy, thus postponing it. This section does away with such anomalies in the future where it applies.

[503]

29 Remuneration of certain trustees

(1) Subject to subsection (5), a trustee who—
(a) is a trust corporation, but
(b) is not a trustee of a charitable trust,

is entitled to receive reasonable remuneration out of the trust funds for any services that the trust corporation provides to or on behalf of the trust.

(2) Subject to subsection (5), a trustee who—
(a) acts in a professional capacity, but
(b) is not a trust corporation, a trustee of a charitable trust or a sole trustee,

is entitled to receive reasonable remuneration out of the trust funds for any services that he provides to or on behalf of the trust if each other trustee has agreed in writing that he may be remunerated for the services.

(3) "Reasonable remuneration" means, in relation to the provision of services by a trustee, such remuneration as is reasonable in the circumstances for the provision of those services to or on behalf of that trust by that trustee and for the purposes of subsection (1) includes, in relation to the provision of services by a trustee who is an authorised institution under the Banking Act 1987 and provides the services in that capacity, the institution's reasonable charges for the provision of such services.

(4) A trustee is entitled to remuneration under this section even if the services in question are capable of being provided by a lay trustee.

(5) A trustee is not entitled to remuneration under this section if any provision about his entitlement to remuneration has been made—
(a) by the trust instrument, or
(b) by any enactment or any provision of subordinate legislation.

(6) This section applies to a trustee who has been authorised under a power conferred by Part IV or the trust instrument—

(a) to exercise functions as an agent of the trustees, or

(b) to act as a nominee or custodian,

as it applies to any other trustee.

Commentary

This section will only apply where there is no express charging clause in the trust instrument or anything showing that the trustee should not be entitled to remuneration (see sub-s (5)). The position in relation to a trust corporation is straightforward—where it is not a trustee of a charitable trust it will be entitled to reasonable remuneration which is defined in sub-s (3). The closing words of that subsection are to enable the bank trust companies to charge in respect of banking services they may provide to the trust or estate.

In the case of other trustees, it should be noted that they can charge only if: (a) they are acting in a professional capacity, as to which see s 28(5); (b) they are not a trust corporation; (c) they are not a sole trustee; (d) they are not a charitable trustee; and (e) their co-trustee or trustees agree in writing.

Although only trustees acting in a professional capacity qualify, they can charge for services which could have been performed by a lay trustee (sub-s (4)). The section will also apply to trustees to whom functions have been delegated under the TA 2000, Pt IV who can accordingly charge for those services. See s 32 as to remuneration for agents, nominees and custodians generally.

[504]

30 Remuneration of trustees of charitable trusts

(1) The Secretary of State may by regulations make provision for the remuneration of trustees of charitable trusts who are trust corporations or act in a professional capacity.

(2) The power under subsection (1) includes power to make provision for the remuneration of a trustee who has been authorised under a power conferred by Part IV or any other enactment or any provision of subordinate legislation, or by the trust instrument—

(a) to exercise functions as an agent of the trustees, or

(b) to act as a nominee or custodian.

(3) Regulations under this section may—

(a) make different provision for different cases;

(b) contain such supplemental, incidental, consequential and transitional provision as the Secretary of State considers appropriate.

(4) The power to make regulations under this section is exercisable by statutory instrument, but no such instrument shall be made unless a draft of it has been laid before Parliament and approved by a resolution of each House of Parliament.

Commentary

As yet there have been no regulations. The reason for no express provision being made in the TA 2000 is that the proposal for charitable trustees to be remunerated was controversial and more consultation with the charitable sector was considered necessary.

[505]

31 Trustees' expenses

(1) A trustee—

(a) is entitled to be reimbursed from the trust funds, or

(b) may pay out of the trust funds,

expenses properly incurred by him when acting on behalf of the trust.

(2) This section applies to a trustee who has been authorised under a power conferred by Part IV or any other enactment or any provision of subordinate legislation, or by the trust instrument—

(a) to exercise functions as an agent of the trustees, or

(b) to act as a nominee or custodian,

as it applies to any other trustee.

Commentary

Subsection (1) confirms the position which has always obtained, ie that trustees are entitled to reimburse themselves out of the trust fund for out of pocket expenses. It remains the position that they must show those expenses were properly incurred. Subsection (2) applies the rule to trustees who have been authorised to act as agent of the body of trustees.

[506]

32 Remuneration and expenses of agents, nominees and custodians

(1) This section applies if, under a power conferred by Part IV or any other enactment or any provision of subordinate legislation, or by the trust instrument, a person other than a trustee has been—

(a) authorised to exercise functions as an agent of the trustees, or

(b) appointed to act as a nominee or custodian.

(2) The trustees may remunerate the agent, nominee or custodian out of the trust funds for services if—

(a) he is engaged on terms entitling him to be remunerated for those services, and

(b) the amount does not exceed such remuneration as is reasonable in the circumstances for the provision of those services by him to or on behalf of that trust.

(3) The trustees may reimburse the agent, nominee or custodian out of the trust funds for any expenses properly incurred by him in exercising functions as an agent, nominee or custodian.

Commentary

The new wide powers conferred on trustees to delegate clearly needed this section to enable trustees to remunerate agents, nominees or custodians. Note that the section is of wider application in that it applies also where the power to delegate comes from some other source, including the trust instrument. What is reasonable remuneration (sub-s (2)(b)) will depend on the agent engaged and the market rates applicable.

[507]

33 Application

(1) Subject to subsection (2), sections 28, 29, 31 and 32 apply in relation to services provided to or on behalf of, or (as the case may be) expenses incurred on or after their commencement on behalf of, trusts whenever created.

(2) Nothing in section 28 or 29 is to be treated as affecting the operation of—

(a) section 15 of the Wills Act 1837, or

(b) section 34(3) of the Administration of Estates Act 1925,

in relation to any death occurring before the commencement of section 28 or (as the case may be) section 29.

Commentary

It is made clear that trustees cannot take advantage of the provisions as to remuneration contained in this part of the TA 2000, in relation to services provided before the commencement of the TA 2000 or expenses incurred. Subsection (2) means that in relation to any death which occurred before the commencement of the TA 2000, the personal representatives are still bound by the somewhat anomalous rules explained in the notes to ss 28 and 29 above.

[508]

PART VI
MISCELLANEOUS AND SUPPLEMENTARY

34 Power to insure

(1) For section 19 of the Trustee Act 1925 (power to insure) substitute—

"19 Power to insure

(1) A trustee may—

(a) insure any property which is subject to the trust against risks of loss or damage due to any event, and

(b) pay the premiums out of the trust funds.

(2) In the case of property held on a bare trust, the power to insure is subject to any direction given by the beneficiary or each of the beneficiaries—

(a) that any property specified in the direction is not to be insured;

(b) that any property specified in the direction is not to be insured except on such conditions as may be so specified.

(3) Property is held on a bare trust if it is held on trust for—

(a) a beneficiary who is of full age and capacity and absolutely entitled to the property subject to the trust, or

(b) beneficiaries each of whom is of full age and capacity and who (taken together) are absolutely entitled to the property subject to the trust.

(4) If a direction under subsection (2) of this section is given, the power to insure, so far as it is subject to the direction, ceases to be a delegable function for the purposes of section 11 of the Trustee Act 2000 (power to employ agents).

(5) In this section "trust funds" means any income or capital funds of the trust."

(2) In section 20(1) of the Trustee Act 1925 (application of insurance money) omit "whether by fire or otherwise".

(3) The amendments made by this section apply in relation to trusts whether created before or after its commencement.

Commentary

This section replaces the Trustee Act 1925, s 19 **[89]** which was rarely relied upon as a default power as a matter of choice as it was both hard to decipher and unsatisfactory in practice. Now trustees can insure the trust property as they see fit and can use either capital or income of the trust fund to pay for that insurance. They are subject to a direction by beneficiaries under a bare trust (explained in sub-s (3)) not to insure, which is interesting as it suggests that the TA 2000 would otherwise apply to bare trustees which is not immediately obvious. Note that there is no duty imposed on the trustees to insure (and as a matter of law it not clear whether such a duty exists).

[509]

35 Personal representatives

(1) Subject to the following provisions of this section, this Act applies in relation to a personal representative administering an estate according to the law as it applies to a trustee carrying out a trust for beneficiaries.

(2) For this purpose this Act is to be read with the appropriate modifications and in particular—

(a) references to the trust instrument are to be read as references to the will,
(b) references to a beneficiary or to beneficiaries, apart from the reference to a beneficiary in section 8(1)(b), are to be read as references to a person or the persons interested in the due administration of the estate, and
(c) the reference to a beneficiary in section 8(1)(b) is to be read as a reference to a person who under the will of the deceased or under the law relating to intestacy is beneficially interested in the estate.

(3) Remuneration to which a personal representative is entitled under section 28 or 29 is to be treated as an administration expense for the purposes of—
(a) section 34(3) of the Administration of Estates Act 1925 (order in which estate to be paid out), and
(b) any provision giving reasonable administration expenses priority over the preferential debts listed in Schedule 6 to the Insolvency Act 1986.

(4) Nothing in subsection (3) is to be treated as affecting the operation of the provisions mentioned in paragraphs (a) and (b) of that subsection in relation to any death occurring before the commencement of this section.

Commentary
This section is of huge practical importance because it applies the TA 2000 to personal representatives. References to "beneficiaries" in the TA 2000 are to be construed as references to a person interested in the due administration of the estate. That means not only those beneficially entitled but also creditors of the estate who could bring an administration action. This is the case except in respect of the power to acquire land for the occupation of any beneficiary. In that case, it is only those beneficially interested in the estate, true beneficiaries, in whose favour the power can be exercised. For deaths occurring after the TA 2000, any remuneration to which a personal representative becomes entitled, will be treated as an administration expense (and therefore paid out before any beneficiaries under the Administration of Estates Act 1925, s 34(3)) **[209]** and when the estate is being administered as an insolvent estate in accordance with the Insolvency Act 1986, Sch 6.

[510]

36 Pension schemes

(1) In this section "pension scheme" means an occupational pension scheme (within the meaning of the Pension Schemes Act 1993) established under a trust and subject to the law of England and Wales.

(2) Part I does not apply in so far as it imposes a duty of care in relation to—
(a) the functions described in paragraphs 1 and 2 of Schedule 1, or
(b) the functions described in paragraph 3 of that Schedule to the extent that they relate to trustees—
(i) authorising a person to exercise their functions with respect to investment, or
(ii) appointing a person to act as their nominee or custodian.

(3) Nothing in Part II or III applies to the trustees of any pension scheme.

(4) Part IV applies to the trustees of a pension scheme subject to the restrictions in subsections (5) to (8).

(5) The trustees of a pension scheme may not under Part IV authorise any person to exercise any functions relating to investment as their agent.

(6) The trustees of a pension scheme may not under Part IV authorise a person who is—
(a) an employer in relation to the scheme, or
(b) connected with or an associate of such an employer,

to exercise any of their functions as their agent.

(7) For the purposes of subsection (6)—

(a) "employer", in relation to a scheme, has the same meaning as in the Pensions Act 1995;

(b) sections 249 and 435 of the Insolvency Act 1986 apply for the purpose of determining whether a person is connected with or an associate of an employer.

(8) Sections 16 to 20 (powers to appoint nominees and custodians) do not apply to the trustees of a pension scheme.

Commentary

What the draftsman clearly intended to do was to disapply certain parts of the TA 2000 to trustees of occupational pension schemes. Subsection (3) clearly does this, so that pension trustees do not have the powers of investment and acquiring land in the TA 2000, Pts II and III as they have their own default powers under the Pensions Act 1995. However, remarkably, sub-s (2), if read literally, disapplies large sections of the TA 2000, Pt I (duty of care) to all trustees! It seems most unlikely that the section would be construed in this unfortunate way, but that is what it says. The powers to delegate subject to the provisions restricting their exercise contained in sub-ss (5)–(8) do apply to pension trustees.

[511]

37 Authorised unit trusts

(1) Parts II to IV do not apply to trustees of authorised unit trusts.

(2) "Authorised unit trust" means a unit trust scheme in the case of which an order under section 78 of the Financial Services Act 1986 is in force.

Commentary

Note that although the powers in Pts II–IV are not conferred on trustees of unit trusts, the duty of care (contained in Pt I) is.

[512]

38 Common investment schemes for charities etc

Parts II to IV do not apply to—

(a) trustees managing a fund under a common investment scheme made, or having effect as if made, under section 24 of the Charities Act 1993, other than such a fund the trusts of which provide that property is not to be transferred to the fund except by or on behalf of a charity the trustees of which are the trustees appointed to manage the fund, or

(b) trustees managing a fund under a common deposit scheme made, or having effect as if made, under section 25 of that Act.

Commentary

Reference should be made to works on the Charities Act 1993 for these schemes.

[513]

39 Interpretation

(1) In this Act—

"asset" includes any right or interest;

"charitable trust" means a trust under which property is held for charitable purposes and "charitable purposes" has the same meaning as in the Charities Act 1993;

"custodian trustee" has the same meaning as in the Public Trustee Act 1906;

"enactment" includes any provision of a Measure of the Church Assembly or of the General Synod of the Church of England;

"exempt charity" has the same meaning as in the Charities Act 1993;

"functions" includes powers and duties;
"legal mortgage" has the same meaning as in the Law of Property Act 1925;
"personal representative" has the same meaning as in the Trustee Act 1925;
"settled land" has the same meaning as in the Settled Land Act 1925;
"trust corporation" has the same meaning as in the Trustee Act 1925;
"trust funds" means income or capital funds of the trust.

(2) In this Act the expressions listed below are defined or otherwise explained by the provisions indicated—

asset management functions	section 15(5)
custodian	section 17(2)
the duty of care	section 1(2)
the general power of investment	section 3(2)
lay trustee	section 28(6)
power of intervention	section 22(4)
the standard investment criteria	section 4(3)
subordinate legislation	section 6(3)
trustee acting in a professional capacity	section 28(5)
trust instrument	sections 6(2) and 35(2)(a)

Commentary
The TA 2000 is somewhat short on definitions. For example "trustee" is never defined (could it include a bare or constructive trustee?), and there is no definition of terms such as "investment" and "land". However, this section does provide some limited definitions and guidance on where to look in the TA 2000 for explanations.

[514]

40 Minor and consequential amendments etc

(1) Schedule 2 (minor and consequential amendments) shall have effect.

(2) Schedule 3 (transitional provisions and savings) shall have effect.

(3) Schedule 4 (repeals) shall have effect.

Commentary
See the notes to Schs 2, 3 and 4.

[515]

41 Power to amend other Acts

(1) A Minister of the Crown may by order make such amendments of any Act, including an Act extending to places outside England and Wales, as appear to him appropriate in consequence of or in connection with Part II or III.

(2) Before exercising the power under subsection (1) in relation to a local, personal or private Act, the Minister must consult any person who appears to him to be affected by any proposed amendment.

(3) An order under this section may—
  (a) contain such transitional provisions and savings as the Minister thinks fit;
  (b) make different provision for different purposes.

(4) The power to make an order under this section is exercisable by statutory instrument which shall be subject to annulment in pursuance of a resolution of either House of Parliament.

(5) "Minister of the Crown" has the same meaning as in the Ministers of the Crown Act 1975.

Commentary

A considerable amount of legislation relied on the Trustee Investments Act 1961, which is almost wholly repealed by the TA 2000, and this preserves the power of a Minister of the Crown to make further consequential amendments.

[516]

42 Commencement and extent

(1) Section 41, this section and section 43 shall come into force on the day on which this Act is passed.

(2) The remaining provisions of this Act shall come into force on such day as the Lord Chancellor may appoint by order made by statutory instrument; and different days may be so appointed for different purposes.

(3) An order under subsection (2) may contain such transitional provisions and savings as the Lord Chancellor considers appropriate in connection with the order.

(4) Subject to section 41(1) and subsection (5), this Act extends to England and Wales only.

(5) An amendment or repeal in Part II or III of Schedule 2 or Part II of Schedule 4 has the same extent as the provision amended or repealed.

Commentary

The TA 2000 was passed on 23 November 2000 and brought into effect on 1 February 2001.

[517]

43 Short title

This Act may be cited as the Trustee Act 2000.

[518]

SCHEDULE 1
APPLICATION OF DUTY OF CARE

Section 2

INVESTMENT

1 The duty of care applies to a trustee—
- (a) when exercising the general power of investment or any other power of investment, however conferred;
- (b) when carrying out a duty to which he is subject under section 4 or 5 (duties relating to the exercise of a power of investment or to the review of investments).

ACQUISITION OF LAND

2 The duty of care applies to a trustee—
- (a) when exercising the power under section 8 to acquire land;
- (b) when exercising any other power to acquire land, however conferred;
- (c) when exercising any power in relation to land acquired under a power mentioned in sub-paragraph (a) or (b).

AGENTS, NOMINEES AND CUSTODIANS

3 (1) The duty of care applies to a trustee—
- (a) when entering into arrangements under which a person is authorised under section 11 to exercise functions as an agent;

(b) when entering into arrangements under which a person is appointed under section 16 to act as a nominee;
(c) when entering into arrangements under which a person is appointed under section 17 or 18 to act as a custodian;
(d) when entering into arrangements under which, under any other power, however conferred, a person is authorised to exercise functions as an agent or is appointed to act as a nominee or custodian;
(e) when carrying out his duties under section 22 (review of agent, nominee or custodian, etc).

(2) For the purposes of sub-paragraph (1), entering into arrangements under which a person is authorised to exercise functions or is appointed to act as a nominee or custodian includes, in particular—
(a) selecting the person who is to act,
(b) determining any terms on which he is to act, and
(c) if the person is being authorised to exercise asset management functions, the preparation of a policy statement under section 15.

COMPOUNDING OF LIABILITIES

4 The duty of care applies to a trustee—
(a) when exercising the power under section 15 of the Trustee Act 1925 to do any of the things referred to in that section;
(b) when exercising any corresponding power, however conferred.

INSURANCE

5 The duty of care applies to a trustee—
(a) when exercising the power under section 19 of the Trustee Act 1925 to insure property;
(b) when exercising any corresponding power, however conferred.

REVERSIONARY INTERESTS, VALUATIONS AND AUDIT

6 The duty of care applies to a trustee—
(a) when exercising the power under section 22(1) or (3) of the Trustee Act 1925 to do any of the things referred to there;
(b) when exercising any corresponding power, however conferred.

EXCLUSION OF DUTY OF CARE

7 The duty of care does not apply if or in so far as it appears from the trust instrument that the duty is not meant to apply.

Commentary
Schedule 1, paras 1–6 set out the circumstances where trustees will be subject to the duty of care imposed on them by the TA 2000, s 1. It does not apply in any other circumstances, and it should be noted that it applies where the trustees are exercising the various powers referred to and not where they fail to exercise powers. In such a case the common law duties will apply. It should also be noted that it applies not just to powers which are conferred by the TA 2000 but express powers conferred by the trust instrument or other legislation. Schedule 1, para 7 means that the trust instrument can effectively exclude the statutory duty of power imposed by the TA 2000.

[519]

SCHEDULE 2
MINOR AND CONSEQUENTIAL AMENDMENTS

Section 40

PART I
THE TRUSTEE INVESTMENTS ACT 1961 AND THE CHARITIES ACT 1993

THE TRUSTEE INVESTMENTS ACT 1961 (C 62)

1 (1) Sections 1, 2, 5, 6, 12, 13 and 15 shall cease to have effect, except in so far as they are applied by or under any other enactment.

(2) Section 3 and Schedules 2 and 3 shall cease to have effect, except in so far as they relate to a trustee having a power of investment conferred on him under an enactment—

(a) which was passed before the passing of the 1961 Act, and

(b) which is not amended by this Schedule.

(3) Omit—

(a) sections 8 and 9,

(b) paragraph 1(1) of Schedule 4, and

(c) section 16(1), in so far as it relates to paragraph 1(1) of Schedule 4.

THE CHARITIES ACT 1993 (C 10)

2 (1) Omit sections 70 and 71.

(2) In section 86(2) in paragraph (a)—

(a) omit "70", and

(b) at the end insert "or".

(3) Omit section 86(2)(b).

PART II
OTHER PUBLIC GENERAL ACTS

THE PLACES OF WORSHIP SITES ACT 1873 (C 50)

3 In section 2 (payment of purchase money, etc) for "shall be invested upon such securities or investments as would for the time being be authorised by statute or the Court of Chancery" substitute "shall be invested under the general power of investment in section 3 of the Trustee Act 2000".

THE TECHNICAL AND INDUSTRIAL INSTITUTIONS ACT 1892 (C 29)

4 In section 9 (investment powers relating to proceeds of sale of land acquired under the Act) for subsection (5) substitute—

"(5) Money arising by sale may, until reinvested in the purchase of land, be invested—

(a) in the names of the governing body, in any investments in which trustees may invest under the general power of investment in section 3 of the Trustee Act 2000 (as restricted by sections 4 and 5 of that Act), or

(b) under the general power of investment in section 3 of that Act, by trustees for the governing body or by a person authorised by the trustees under that Act to invest as an agent of the trustees.

(6) Any profits from investments under subsection (5) shall be invested in the same way and added to capital until the capital is reinvested in the purchase of land."

THE DUCHY OF CORNWALL MANAGEMENT ACT 1893 (C 20)

5 The 1893 Act is hereby repealed.

THE DUCHY OF LANCASTER ACT 1920 (C 51)

6 In section 1 (extension of powers of investment of funds of Duchy of Lancaster) for "in any of the investments specified in paragraph (a) of section one of the Trustees Act 1893 and any enactment amending or extending that paragraph" substitute "under the general power of investment in section 3 of the Trustee Act 2000 (as restricted by sections 4 and 5 of that Act)".

THE SETTLED LAND ACT 1925 (C 18)

7 In section 21 (absolute owners subject to certain interests to have the powers of tenant for life), in subsection (1)(d) for "income thereof" substitute "resultant profits".

8 In section 39 (regulations respecting sales), in subsection (2), in the proviso, for the words from "accumulate" to the end of the subsection substitute "accumulate the profits from the capital money by investing them and any resulting profits under the general power of investment in section 3 of the Trustee Act 2000 and shall add the accumulations to capital."

9 In section 73 (modes of investment or application), in subsection (1) for paragraph (i) substitute—

"(i) In investment in securities either under the general power of investment in section 3 of the Trustee Act 2000 or under a power to invest conferred on the trustees of the settlement by the settlement;".

10 (1) In section 75 (regulations respecting investment, devolution, and income of securities etc), for subsection (2) substitute—

"(2) Subject to Part IV of the Trustee Act 2000, to section 75A of this Act and to the following provisions of this section—

(a) the investment or other application by the trustees shall be made according to the discretion of the trustees, but subject to any consent required or direction given by the settlement with respect to the investment or other application by the trustees of trust money of the settlement, and
(b) any investment shall be in the names or under the control of the trustees."

(2) For subsection (4) of that section substitute—

"(4) The trustees, in exercising their power to invest or apply capital money, shall—

(a) so far as practicable, consult the tenant for life; and
(b) so far as consistent with the general interest of the settlement, give effect to his wishes.

(4A) Any investment or other application of capital money under the direction of the court shall not during the subsistence of the beneficial interest of the tenant for life be altered without his consent.

(4B) The trustees may not under section 11 of the Trustee Act 2000 authorise a person to exercise their functions with respect to the investment or application of capital money on terms that prevent them from complying with subsection (4) of this section.

(4C) A person who is authorised under section 11 of the Trustee Act 2000 to exercise any of their functions with respect to the investment or application of capital money is not subject to subsection (4) of this section."

(3) Nothing in this paragraph affects the operation of section 75 in relation to directions of the tenant for life given, but not acted upon by the trustees, before the commencement of this paragraph.

11 After section 75 insert—

"75A Power to accept charge as security for part payment for land sold

(1) Where—

(a) land subject to the settlement is sold by the tenant for life or statutory owner, for an estate in fee simple or a term having at least five hundred years to run, and

(b) the proceeds of sale are liable to be invested,

the tenant for life or statutory owner may, with the consent of the trustees of the settlement, contract that the payment of any part, not exceeding two-thirds, of the purchase money shall be secured by a charge by way of legal mortgage of the land sold, with or without the security of any other property.

(2) If any buildings are comprised in the property secured by the charge, the charge must contain a covenant by the mortgagor to keep them insured for their full value against loss or damage due to any event.

(3) A person exercising the power under subsection (1) of this section, or giving consent for the purposes of that subsection—

(a) is not required to comply with section 5 of the Trustee Act 2000 before giving his consent, and

(b) is not liable for any loss incurred merely because the security is insufficient at the date of the charge.

(4) The power under subsection (1) of this section is exercisable subject to the consent of any person whose consent to a change of investment is required by the instrument, if any, creating the trust.

(5) Where the sale referred to in subsection (1) of this section is made under the order of the court, the power under that subsection applies only if and as far as the court may by order direct."

12 Omit section 96 (protection of each trustee individually).

13 In section 98 (protection of trustees in particular cases), omit subsections (1) and (2).

14 Omit section 100 (trustees' reimbursements).

15 In section 102 (management of land during minority or pending contingency), in subsection (2) for paragraph (e) substitute—

"(e) to insure against risks of loss or damage due to any event under section 19 of the Trustee Act 1925;".

16 (1) In section 104 (powers of tenant for life not assignable etc)—

(a) in subsection (3)(b) omit "authorised by statute for the investment of trust money", and

(b) in subsection (4)(b) for the words from "no investment" to "trust money;" substitute "the consent of the assignee shall be required to an investment of capital money for the time being affected by the assignment in investments other than securities, and to any application of such capital money;".

(2) Sub-paragraph (1) applies to the determination on or after the commencement of that sub-paragraph of whether an assignee's consent is required to the investment or application of capital money.

17 In section 107 (tenant for life deemed to be in the position and to have the duties and liabilities of a trustee, etc) after subsection (1) insert—

"(1A) The following provisions apply to the tenant for life as they apply to the trustees of the settlement—

(a) sections 11, 13 to 15 and 21 to 23 of the Trustee Act 2000 (power to employ agents subject to certain restrictions),
(b) section 32 of that Act (remuneration and expenses of agents etc),
(c) section 19 of the Trustee Act 1925 (power to insure), and
(d) in so far as they relate to the provisions mentioned in paragraphs (a) and (c), Part I of, and Schedule 1 to, the Trustee Act 2000 (the duty of care)."

THE TRUSTEE ACT 1925 (C 19)

18 Omit Part I (investments).

19 In section 14 (power of trustees to give receipts) in subsection (1) after "securities," insert "investments".

20 In section 15 (power to compound liabilities), for "in good faith" substitute "if he has or they have discharged the duty of care set out in section 1(1) of the Trustee Act 2000".

21 Omit section 21 (deposit of documents for safe custody).

22 In section 22 (reversionary interests, valuations, and audit)—

(a) in subsection (1), for "in good faith" substitute "if they have discharged the duty of care set out in section 1(1) of the Trustee Act 2000", and
(b) in subsection (3), omit "in good faith" and at the end insert "if the trustees have discharged the duty of care set out in section 1(1) of the Trustee Act 2000".

23 Omit section 23 (power to employ agents).

24 Omit section 30 (implied indemnity of trustees).

25 In section 31(2) (power to invest income during minority) for "in the way of compound interest by investing the same and the resulting income thereof" substitute "by investing it, and any profits from so investing it".

. . .

26 . . .

THE ADMINISTRATION OF ESTATES ACT 1925 (C 23)

27 In section 33, in subsection (3) (investment during minority of beneficiary or the subsistence of a life interest) for the words from "in any investments for the time being authorised by statute" to the end of the subsection substitute "under the Trustee Act 2000."

28 In section 39 (powers of management) after subsection (1) insert—

"(1A) Subsection (1) of this section is without prejudice to the powers conferred on personal representatives by the Trustee Act 2000."

THE UNIVERSITIES AND COLLEGE ESTATES ACT 1925 (C 24)

29 In section 26 (modes of application of capital money) in subsection (1) for paragraph (i) substitute—

"(i) In investments in which trustees may invest under the general power of investment in section 3 of the Trustee Act 2000 (as restricted by sections 4 and 5 of that Act);".

THE REGIMENTAL CHARITABLE FUNDS ACT 1935 (C 11)

30 In section 2(1) (application of funds held on account of regimental charitable funds)—

(a) in paragraph (a) for "in some manner" to "trusts" substitute "under the general power of investment in section 3 of the Trustee Act 2000";
(b) in paragraph (b) after "the income" insert "or the other profits".

THE AGRICULTURAL MARKETING ACT 1958 (C 47)

31 (1) In section 16 (investment of surplus funds of boards) for paragraph (a) substitute—

"(a) the moneys of the board not for the time being required by them for the purposes of their functions are not, except with the approval of the Minister, invested otherwise than in investments in which trustees may invest under the general power of investment in section 3 of the Trustee Act 2000 (as restricted by sections 4 and 5 of that Act); and".

(2) Any scheme made under the 1958 Act and in effect before the day on which sub-paragraph (1) comes into force shall be treated, in relation to the making of investments on and after that day, as including provision permitting investment by the board in accordance with section 16(a) of the 1958 Act as amended by sub-paragraph (1).

THE HORTICULTURE ACT 1960 (C 22)

32 In section 13 (miscellaneous financial powers of organisations promoting home-grown produce) for subsection (3) substitute—

"(3) A relevant organisation may invest any of its surplus money which is not for the time being required for any other purpose in any investments in which trustees may invest under the general power of investment in section 3 of the Trustee Act 2000 (as restricted by sections 4 and 5 of that Act)".

THE HOUSE OF COMMONS MEMBERS' FUND ACT 1962 (C 53)

33 (1) In section 1 (powers of investment of trustees of House of Commons Members' Fund)—

(a) in subsection (2) omit "Subject to the following provisions of this section";
(b) omit subsections (3) to (5).

(2) In section 2 (interpretation etc) omit subsection (1).

THE BETTING, GAMING AND LOTTERIES ACT 1963 (C 2)

***34** In section 25(1) (general powers and duties of the Horserace Betting Levy Board) for paragraph (e) substitute—*

"(e) to make such other investments as—

(i) they judge desirable for the proper conduct of their affairs, and

(ii) a trustee would be able to make under the general power of investment in section 3 of the Trustee Act 2000 (as restricted by sections 4 and 5 of that Act);".

THE CEREALS MARKETING ACT 1965 (C 14)

35 (1) In section 18, in subsection (2) (Home-Grown Cereals Authority's power to invest reserve funds) for "in accordance with the next following subsection" substitute "in any investments in which trustees may invest under the general power of investment in section 3 of the Trustee Act 2000 (as restricted by sections 4 and 5 of that Act)."

(2) Omit section 18(3).

THE AGRICULTURE ACT 1967 (C 22)

36 (1) In section 18, in subsection (2) (Meat and Livestock Commission's power to invest reserve fund) for "in accordance with the next following subsection" substitute "in any investments in which trustees may invest under the general power of investment in section 3 of the Trustee Act 2000 (as restricted by sections 4 and 5 of that Act)."

(2) Omit section 18(3).

THE SOLICITORS ACT 1974 (C 47)

37 In Schedule 2, for paragraph 3 (power of Law Society to invest) substitute—

"**3** The Society may invest any money which forms part of the fund in any investments in which trustees may invest under the general power of investment in section 3 of the Trustee Act 2000 (as restricted by sections 4 and 5 of that Act)."

THE POLICYHOLDERS PROTECTION ACT 1975 (C 75)

38 In Schedule 1, in paragraph 7, for sub-paragraph (1) (power of Policyholders Protection Board to invest) substitute—

"(1) The Board may invest any funds held by them which appear to them to be surplus to their requirements for the time being—

(a) in any investments in which trustees may invest under the general power of investment in section 3 of the Trustee Act 2000 (as restricted by sections 4 and 5 of that Act); or

(b) in any investment approved for the purpose by the Treasury."

THE NATIONAL HERITAGE ACT 1980 (C 17)

39 In section 6 for subsection (3) (powers of investment of Trustees of National Heritage Memorial Fund) substitute—

"(3) The Trustees may invest any sums to which subsection (2) does not apply in any investments in which trustees may invest under the general power of investment in section 3 of the Trustee Act 2000 (as restricted by sections 4 and 5 of that Act)."

THE LICENSING (ALCOHOL EDUCATION AND RESEARCH) ACT 1981 (C 28)

40 In section 7 (powers of investment of Alcohol Education and Research Council) for subsection (5) substitute—

"(5) Any sums in the Fund which are not immediately required for any other purpose may be invested by the Council in any investments in which trustees may invest under the general power of investment in section 3 of the Trustee Act 2000 (as restricted by sections 4 and 5 of that Act)."

THE FISHERIES ACT 1981 (C 29)

41 For section 10 (powers of investment of Sea Fish Industry Authority) substitute—

10 "Investment of reserve funds

Any money of the Authority which is not immediately required for any other purpose may be invested by the Authority in any investments in which trustees may invest under the general power of investment in section 3 of the Trustee Act 2000 (as restricted by sections 4 and 5 of that Act)".

THE DUCHY OF CORNWALL MANAGEMENT ACT 1982 (C 47)

42 For section 1 (powers of investment of Duchy property) substitute—

1 "Powers of investment of Duchy property

The power of investment conferred by the Duchy of Cornwall Management Act 1863 includes power to invest in any investments in which trustees may invest under the general power of investment in section 3 of the Trustee Act 2000 (as restricted by sections 4 and 5 of that Act)."

43 In—

(a) section 6(3) (Duchy of Cornwall Management Acts extended in relation to banking), and

(b) section 11(2) (collective citation of Duchy of Cornwall Management Acts),

for "Duchy of Cornwall Management Acts 1868 to 1893" substitute "Duchy of Cornwall Management Acts 1863 to 1868".

THE ADMINISTRATION OF JUSTICE ACT 1982 (C 53)

44 In section 42 (common investment schemes) in subsection (6) for paragraph (a) substitute—

"(a) he may invest trust money in shares in the fund without obtaining and considering advice on whether to make such an investment; and".

THE TRUSTS OF LAND AND APPOINTMENT OF TRUSTEES ACT 1996 (C 47)

45 (1) In section 6 (general powers of trustees), in subsection (3) for "purchase a legal estate in any land in England and Wales" substitute "acquire land under the power conferred by section 8 of the Trustee Act 2000."

(2) Omit subsection (4) of that section.

(3) After subsection (8) of that section insert—

"(9) The duty of care under section 1 of the Trustee Act 2000 applies to trustees of land when exercising the powers conferred by this section."

46 In section 9 (delegation by trustees) omit subsection (8).

47 After section 9 insert—

"9A Duties of trustees in connection with delegation etc

(1) The duty of care under section 1 of the Trustee Act 2000 applies to trustees of land in deciding whether to delegate any of their functions under section 9.

(2) Subsection (3) applies if the trustees of land—
  (a) delegate any of their functions under section 9, and
  (b) the delegation is not irrevocable.

(3) While the delegation continues, the trustees—
  (a) must keep the delegation under review,
  (b) if circumstances make it appropriate to do so, must consider whether there is a need to exercise any power of intervention that they have, and
  (c) if they consider that there is a need to exercise such a power, must do so.

(4) "Power of intervention" includes—
  (a) a power to give directions to the beneficiary;
  (b) a power to revoke the delegation.

(5) The duty of care under section 1 of the 2000 Act applies to trustees in carrying out any duty under subsection (3).

(6) A trustee of land is not liable for any act or default of the beneficiary, or beneficiaries, unless the trustee fails to comply with the duty of care in deciding to delegate any of the trustees' functions under section 9 or in carrying out any duty under subsection (3).

(7) Neither this section nor the repeal of section 9(8) by the Trustee Act 2000 affects the operation after the commencement of this section of any delegation effected before that commencement."

48 Omit section 17(1) (application of section 6(3) in relation to trustees of proceeds of sale of land).

49 In Schedule 3 (consequential amendments) omit paragraph 3(4) (amendment of section 19(1) and (2) of Trustee Act 1925).

Amendment
Para 26: repealed by the Land Registration Act 2002, s 135, Sch 13.
Para 34: repealed, from a date to be appointed, by the Horserace Betting and Olympic Lottery Act 2004, s 38, Sch 6.

PART III
MEASURES

THE ECCLESIASTICAL DILAPIDATIONS MEASURE 1923 (NO 3)

50 In section 52, in subsection (5) (investment of sums held in relation to repair of chancels)—
  (a) for "in any investment permitted by law for the investment of trust funds, and the yearly income resulting therefrom shall be applied," substitute "in

any investments in which trustees may invest under the general power of investment in section 3 of the Trustee Act 2000, and the annual profits from the investments shall be applied"; and

(b) in paragraph (iii) for "any residue of the said income not applied as aforesaid in any year" substitute "any residue of the profits from the investments not applied in any year."

THE DIOCESAN STIPENDS FUNDS MEASURE 1953 (NO 2)

51 In section 4 (application of moneys credited to capital accounts) in subsection (1) for paragraph (bc) substitute—

"(bc) investment in any investments in which trustees may invest under the general power of investment in section 3 of the Trustee Act 2000 (as restricted by sections 4 and 5 of that Act);".

THE CHURCH FUNDS INVESTMENT MEASURE 1958 (NO 1)

52 In the Schedule, in paragraph 21 (range of investments of deposit fund) for paragraphs (a) to (d) of sub-paragraph (1) substitute—

"(aa) In any investments in which trustees may invest under the general power of investment in section 3 of the Trustee Act 2000 (as restricted by sections 4 and 5 of that Act);".

THE CLERGY PENSIONS MEASURE 1961 (NO 3)

53 (1) In section 32 (investment powers of Board), in subsection (1), for paragraph (a) substitute—

"(a) in any investments in which trustees may invest under the general power of investment in section 3 of the Trustee Act 2000 (as restricted by sections 4 and 5 of that Act);".

(2) Omit subsection (3) of that section.

THE REPAIR OF BENEFICE BUILDINGS MEASURE 1972 (NO 2)

54 In section 17, in subsection (2) (diocesan parsonages fund's power of investment), for "who shall have the same powers of investment as trustees of trust funds:" substitute "who shall have the same power as trustees to invest in any investments in which trustees may invest under the general power of investment in section 3 of the Trustee Act 2000 (as restricted by sections 4 and 5 of that Act)."

THE PASTORAL MEASURE 1983 (NO 1)

55 In section 44, for subsection (6) (Redundant Churches Fund's power of investment) substitute—

"(6) The powers to invest any such sums are—

(a) power to invest in investments in which trustees may invest under the general power of investment in section 3 of the Trustee Act 2000 (as restricted by sections 4 and 5 of that Act); and

(b) power to invest in the investments referred to in paragraph 21(1)(e) and (f) of the Schedule to the Church Funds Investment Measure 1958."

THE CHURCH OF ENGLAND (PENSIONS) MEASURE 1988 (NO 4)

56 Omit section 14(b) (amendment of section 32(3) of the Clergy Pensions Measure 1961).

THE CATHEDRALS MEASURE 1999 (NO 1)

57 In section 16 (cathedral moneys: investment powers, etc), in subsection (1)—

(a) for paragraph (c) substitute—

"(c) power to invest in any investments in which trustees may invest under the general power of investment in section 3 of the Trustee Act 2000 (as restricted by sections 4 and 5 of that Act),", and

(b) omit the words from "and the powers" to the end of the subsection.

Commentary

The Trustee Investments Act 1961 is almost wholly repealed by the TA 2000. There is also some significant amendment to parts of the Charities Act 1993.

[520]

SCHEDULE 3
TRANSITIONAL PROVISIONS AND SAVINGS

Section 40

THE TRUSTEE ACT 1925 (C 19)

1 (1) Sub-paragraph (2) applies if, immediately before the day on which Part IV of this Act comes into force, a banker or banking company holds any bearer securities deposited with him under section 7(1) of the 1925 Act (investment in bearer securities).

(2) On and after the day on which Part IV comes into force, the banker or banking company shall be treated as if he had been appointed as custodian of the securities under section 18.

2 The repeal of section 8 of the 1925 Act (loans and investments by trustees not chargeable as breaches of trust) does not affect the operation of that section in relation to loans or investments made before the coming into force of that repeal.

3 The repeal of section 9 of the 1925 Act (liability for loss by reason of improper investment) does not affect the operation of that section in relation to any advance of trust money made before the coming into force of that repeal.

4 (1) Sub-paragraph (2) applies if, immediately before the day on which Part IV of this Act comes into force, a banker or banking company holds any documents deposited with him under section 21 of the 1925 Act (deposit of documents for safe custody).

(2) On and after the day on which Part IV comes into force, the banker or banking company shall be treated as if he had been appointed as custodian of the documents under section 17.

5 (1) Sub-paragraph (2) applies if, immediately before the day on which Part IV of this Act comes into force, a person has been appointed to act as or be an agent or attorney under section 23(1) or (3) of the 1925 Act (general power to employ agents etc).

(2) On and after the day on which Part IV comes into force, the agent shall be treated as if he had been authorised to exercise functions as an agent under section 11 (and, if appropriate, as if he had also been appointed under that Part to act as a custodian or nominee).

6 The repeal of section 23(2) of the 1925 Act (power to employ agents in respect of property outside the United Kingdom) does not affect the operation after the commencement of the repeal of an appointment made before that commencement.

THE TRUSTEE INVESTMENTS ACT 1961 (C 62)

7 (1) A trustee shall not be liable for breach of trust merely because he continues to hold an investment acquired by virtue of paragraph 14 of Part II of Schedule 1 to the 1961 Act (perpetual rent-charges etc).

(2) A person who—

(a) is not a trustee,

(b) before the commencement of Part II of this Act had powers to invest in the investments described in paragraph 14 of Part II of Schedule 1 to the 1961 Act, and

(c) on that commencement acquired the general power of investment,

shall not be treated as exceeding his powers of investment merely because he continues to hold an investment acquired by virtue of that paragraph.

THE CATHEDRALS MEASURE 1963 (NO 2)

8 While section 21 of the Cathedrals Measure 1963 (investment powers, etc of capitular bodies) continues to apply in relation to any cathedral, that section shall have effect as if—

(a) in subsection (1), for paragraph (c) and the words from "and the powers" to the end of the subsection there were substituted—

"(c) power to invest in any investments in which trustees may invest under the general power of investment in section 3 of the Trustee Act 2000 (as restricted by sections 4 and 5 of that Act).", and

(b) in subsection (5), for "subsections (2) and (3) of section six of the Trustee Investments Act 1961" there were substituted "section 5 of the Trustee Act 2000".

Commentary

Most of the amendments made by this Schedule are to ensure that, in legislation where a power of investment is required, the default powers of investment contained in the TA 2000, Pt II will apply. However, tucked away in these are substantial and far reaching amendments to the Settled Land Act 1925 **[Appendix II]**. The first major change is that the investment or other application of capital monies is no longer to be at the direction of the tenant for life, and in default according to the discretion of the trustees. Instead, the discretion as to how the trust fund should be invested is vested in the trustees, and any investment is to be in the names, or under the control, of the trustees. Furthermore the requirement that the consent of the tenant for life must be obtained before any investment or application of capital monies was altered during the currency of his beneficial interest, has been dispensed with. Instead, the trustees in exercising their power to invest or apply capital money must consult the tenant for life.

[521]

SCHEDULE 4
REPEALS

Section 40

PART I
THE TRUSTEE INVESTMENTS ACT 1961 AND THE CHARITIES ACT 1993

Chapter	*Short title*	*Extent of repeal*
1961 c 62.	The Trustee Investments Act 1961.	Sections 1 to 3, 5, 6, 8, 9, 12, 13, 15 and 16(1).
		Schedules 2 and 3.
		In Schedule 4, paragraph 1(1).
1993 c 10.	The Charities Act 1993.	Sections 70 and 71.
		In section 86(2) in paragraph (a), "70" and paragraph (b).

Note: the repeals in this Part of this Schedule have effect in accordance with Part I of Schedule 2.

PART II
OTHER REPEALS

Chapter	*Short title*	*Extent of repeal*
1893 c 20.	The Duchy of Cornwall Management Act 1893.	The whole Act.
1925 c 18.	The Settled Land Act 1925.	Section 96.
		Section 98(1) and (2).
		Section 100.
		In section 104(3)(b) the words "authorised by statute for the investment of trust money".
1925 c 19.	The Trustee Act 1925.	Part I.
		In section 20(1) the words "whether by fire or otherwise".
		Sections 21, 23 and 30.
1961 No 3.	The Clergy Pensions Measure 1961.	Section 32(3).
1962 c 53.	The House of Commons Members' Fund Act 1962.	In section 1, in subsection (2) the words "Subject to the following provisions of this section" and subsections (3) to (5).
		Section 2(1).
1965 c 14.	The Cereals Marketing Act 1965.	Section 18(3).
1967 c 22.	The Agriculture Act 1967.	Section 18(3).
1988 No 4.	The Church of England (Pensions) Measure 1988.	Section 14(b).
1996 c 47.	The Trusts of Land and Appointment of Trustees Act 1996.	Section 6(4).
		Section 9(8). Section 17(1).
		In Schedule 3, paragraph 3(4).
1999 No 1.	The Cathedrals Measure 1999.	In section 16(1), the words from "and the powers" to the end of the subsection.

Commentary
This Schedule prevents trustees finding themselves in a difficult position as a result of the TA 2000 being passed. So for example, trustees who have relied on the Trustee Act 1925, s 9 in lending money on land before the TA 2000 can still rely on it after, notwithstanding its repeal. Further, the TA 2000 is surprisingly in some respects more restrictive than the Trustee Investments Act 1961, and does not permit investment in rentcharges. However, trustees holding them when the TA 2000 commences, can continue to do so.

[522]

PUBLIC TRUSTEE (LIABILITY AND FEES) ACT 2002

2002 Chapter 35

ARRANGEMENT OF SECTIONS

An Act to amend the Public Trustee Act 1906 in respect of the liability and fees of the Public Trustee; and for connected purposes.

[7th November 2002]

General Note
This Act amends a number of statutes in this work and is included so that the reader can see the precise amendments made. Reference should be made to the statues in question for commentary on substance.

1 Liability

(1) Section 7 of the Public Trustee Act 1906 (c 55) (liability of Consolidated Fund) is repealed.

(2) In section 40(2)(h) of the Crown Proceedings Act 1947 (c 44) (saving for liability imposed by the 1906 Act), the words "or on the Consolidated Fund of the United Kingdom" are repealed.

(3) Paragraph (a) of section 3(6) of the Public Trustee and Administration of Funds Act 1986 (c 57) (section 7 of the 1906 Act not to apply) is repealed.

[523]

2 Fees

(1) In section 9 of the Public Trustee Act 1906 (fees charged by public trustee)—

(a) in subsection (1), for the words from "as the Treasury with" to the end there is substituted "as the Lord Chancellor may fix.",

(b) in subsection (3) the words ", under the regulations of the Treasury," are repealed, and

(c) subsection (4) is repealed.

(2) In section 138 of the Law of Property Act 1925 (c 20) (power to nominate a trust corporation to receive notices), in subsection (11) for "by the Treasury, with the sanction of the Lord Chancellor," there is substituted "by the Lord Chancellor".

(3) In section 1(1) of the Public Trustee (Fees) Act 1957 (c 12) (orders fixing fees under section 9(1) of the 1906 Act)—

(a) for "Treasury" in each place there is substituted "Lord Chancellor", and
(b) the words ", with the sanction of the Lord Chancellor," are repealed.

(4) In section 19(5)(b) of the Law of Property (Miscellaneous Provisions) Act 1994 (c 36) (application of section 9(1), (3) and (4) of the 1906 Act), for ", (3) and (4)" there is substituted "and (3)".

Commentary
See section 9 of the Public Trustee Act 1906 **[67]** and the notes thereto for the amendments made by section (1). For the amendments made to section 138 of the Law of Property Act 1925 in subsection (2) see **[163]**. For the amendments made to the Public Trustee (Fees) Act 1957 in subsection (3) see **[252]**. The reference to the Lord Chancellor in subsections (1), (2),(3) and (4) should be read in the light of constitutional changes. For the amendments to the Law of Property (Miscellaneous Provisions) Act 1994 in subsection (4) see **[423]**.

[524]

3 Short Title and extent

(1) This Act may be cited as the Public Trustee (Liability and Fees) Act 2002.

(2) This Act does not extend to Scotland or Northern Ireland.

[525]

GENDER RECOGNITION ACT 2004

2004 Chapter 7

ARRANGEMENT OF SECTIONS

An Act to make provision for and in connection with change of gender.

[1st July 2004]

General Note

Before the passing of this Act, a person's gender was determined in accordance with the circumstances at their birth regardless of subsequent events. This Act changes that position and has an impact in relation to wills and trusts and the manner in which they are interpreted. Although the whole Act is included for sake of completeness, only those sections which have some bearing on the subject matter of this work are annotated.

APPLICATIONS FOR GENDER RECOGNITION CERTIFICATE

1 Applications

(1) A person of either gender who is aged at least 18 may make an application for a gender recognition certificate on the basis of—
- (a) living in the other gender, or
- (b) having changed gender under the law of a country or territory outside the United Kingdom.

(2) In this Act "the acquired gender", in relation to a person by whom an application under subsection (1) is or has been made, means—
- (a) in the case of an application under paragraph (a) of that subsection, the gender in which the person is living, or
- (b) in the case of an application under paragraph (b) of that subsection, the gender to which the person has changed under the law of the country or territory concerned.

(3) An application under subsection (1) is to be determined by a Gender Recognition Panel.

(4) Schedule 1 (Gender Recognition Panels) has effect.

Commentary

Before this Act, a person's gender was fixed at birth and could not be changed, see: *Bellinger v Bellinger* [2003] 2 AC 467. Under this Act once a full gender recognition certificate has been issued the person's gender becomes for all purposes the acquired gender subject to the provisions in respect of wills and trusts set out below under section 15. The provisions which apply to the acquisition of a full certificate are set out in his section and the following to section 8.

[526]

2 Determination of applications

(1) In the case of an application under section 1(1)(a), the Panel must grant the application if satisfied that the applicant—
- (a) has or has had gender dysphoria,
- (b) has lived in the acquired gender throughout the period of two years ending with the date on which the application is made,
- (c) intends to continue to live in the acquired gender until death, and
- (d) complies with the requirements imposed by and under section 3.

(2) In the case of an application under section 1(1)(b), the Panel must grant the application if satisfied—

(a) that the country or territory under the law of which the applicant has changed gender is an approved country or territory, and

(b) that the applicant complies with the requirements imposed by and under section 3.

(3) The Panel must reject an application under section 1(1) if not required by subsection (1) or (2) to grant it.

(4) In this Act "approved country or territory" means a country or territory prescribed by order made by the Secretary of State after consulting the Scottish Ministers and the Department of Finance and Personnel in Northern Ireland.

[527]

3 Evidence

(1) An application under section 1(1)(a) must include either—

(a) a report made by a registered medical practitioner practising in the field of gender dysphoria and a report made by another registered medical practitioner (who may, but need not, practise in that field), or

(b) a report made by a chartered psychologist practising in that field and a report made by a registered medical practitioner (who may, but need not, practise in that field).

(2) But subsection (1) is not complied with unless a report required by that subsection and made by—

(a) a registered medical practitioner, or

(b) a chartered psychologist,

practising in the field of gender dysphoria includes details of the diagnosis of the applicant's gender dysphoria.

(3) And subsection (1) is not complied with in a case where—

(a) the applicant has undergone or is undergoing treatment for the purpose of modifying sexual characteristics, or

(b) treatment for that purpose has been prescribed or planned for the applicant,

unless at least one of the reports required by that subsection includes details of it.

(4) An application under section 1(1)(a) must also include a statutory declaration by the applicant that the applicant meets the conditions in section 2(1)(b) and (c).

(5) An application under section 1(1)(b) must include evidence that the applicant has changed gender under the law of an approved country or territory.

(6) Any application under section 1(1) must include—

(a) a statutory declaration as to whether or not the applicant is married [or a civil partner],

(b) any other information or evidence required by an order made by the Secretary of State, and

(c) any other information or evidence which the Panel which is to determine the application may require,

and may include any other information or evidence which the applicant wishes to include.

(7) The Secretary of State may not make an order under subsection (6)(b) without consulting the Scottish Ministers and the Department of Finance and Personnel in Northern Ireland.

(8) If the Panel which is to determine the application requires information or evidence under subsection (6)(c) it must give reasons for doing so.

Amendment
Sub-s (6): in para (a) words "or a civil partner" in square brackets inserted by the Civil Partnership Act 2004, s 250(1), (2)(a).

[528]

4 Successful applications

(1) If a Gender Recognition Panel grants an application under section 1(1) it must issue a gender recognition certificate to the applicant.

(2) Unless the applicant is married [or a civil partner], the certificate is to be a full gender recognition certificate.

(3) If the applicant is married [or a civil partner], the certificate is to be an interim gender recognition certificate.

(4) Schedule 2 (annulment or dissolution of marriage after issue of interim gender recognition certificate) has effect.

(5) The Secretary of State may, after consulting the Scottish Ministers and the Department of Finance and Personnel in Northern Ireland, specify the content and form of gender recognition certificates.

Amendment
Sub-s (2): words "or a civil partner" in square brackets inserted by the Civil Partnership Act 2004, s 250(1), (2)(b).
Sub-s (3): words "or a civil partner" in square brackets inserted by the Civil Partnership Act 2004, s 250(1), (2)(b).

[529]

[5 Issue of full certificates where applicant has been married]

(1) A court which—

(a) makes absolute a decree of nullity granted on the ground that an interim gender recognition certificate has been issued to a party to the marriage, or

(b) (in Scotland) grants a decree of divorce on that ground,

must, on doing so, issue a full gender recognition certificate to that party and send a copy to the Secretary of State.

(2) If an interim gender recognition certificate has been issued to a person and either—

(a) the person's marriage is dissolved or annulled (otherwise than on the ground mentioned in subsection (1)) in proceedings instituted during the period of six months beginning with the day on which it was issued, or

(b) the person's spouse dies within that period,

the person may make an application for a full gender recognition certificate at any time within the period specified in subsection (3) (unless the person is again married [or is a civil partner]).

(3) That period is the period of six months beginning with the day on which the marriage is dissolved or annulled or the death occurs.

(4) An application under subsection (2) must include evidence of the dissolution or annulment of the marriage and the date on which proceedings for it were instituted, or of the death of the spouse and the date on which it occurred.

(5) An application under subsection (2) is to be determined by a Gender Recognition Panel.

(6) The Panel—

(a) must grant the application if satisfied that the applicant [is neither married nor a civil partner], and

(b) otherwise must reject it.

(7) If the Panel grants the application it must issue a full gender recognition certificate to the applicant.

Amendment
Section heading: substituted by the Civil Partnership Act 2004, s 250(1), (3)(c).
Sub-s (2): words "or is a civil partner" in square brackets inserted by the Civil Partnership Act 2004, s 250(1), (3)(a).
Sub-s (6): in para (a) words "is neither married nor a civil partner" in square brackets substituted by the Civil Partnership Act 2004, s 250(1), (3)(b).

[530]

[5A Issue of full certificates where applicant has been a civil partner]

[(1) A court which—

(a) makes final a nullity order made on the ground that an interim gender recognition certificate has been issued to a civil partner, or

(b) (in Scotland) grants a decree of dissolution on that ground,

must, on doing so, issue a full gender recognition certificate to that civil partner and send a copy to the Secretary of State.

(2) If an interim gender recognition certificate has been issued to a person and either—

(a) the person's civil partnership is dissolved or annulled (otherwise than on the ground mentioned in subsection (1)) in proceedings instituted during the period of six months beginning with the day on which it was issued, or

(b) the person's civil partner dies within that period,

the person may make an application for a full gender recognition certificate at any time within the period specified in subsection (3) (unless the person is again a civil partner or is married).

(3) That period is the period of six months beginning with the day on which the civil partnership is dissolved or annulled or the death occurs.

(4) An application under subsection (2) must include evidence of the dissolution or annulment of the civil partnership and the date on which proceedings for it were instituted, or of the death of the civil partner and the date on which it occurred.

(5) An application under subsection (2) is to be determined by a Gender Recognition Panel.

(6) The Panel—

(a) must grant the application if satisfied that the applicant is neither a civil partner nor married, and

(b) otherwise must reject it.

(7) If the Panel grants the application it must issue a full gender recognition certificate to the applicant.]

Amendment
Inserted by the Civil Partnership Act 2004, s 250(1), (4).

[531]

6 Errors in certificates

(1) Where a gender recognition certificate has been issued to a person, the person or the Secretary of State may make an application for a corrected certificate on the ground that the certificate which has been issued contains an error.

(2) If the certificate was issued by a court the application is to be determined by the court but in any other case it is to be determined by a Gender Recognition Panel.

(3) The court or Panel—

(a) must grant the application if satisfied that the gender recognition certificate contains an error, and

(b) otherwise must reject it.

(4) If the court or Panel grants the application it must issue a corrected gender recognition certificate to the applicant.

[532]

7 Applications: supplementary

(1) An application to a Gender Recognition Panel under section 1(1), 5(2)[, 5A(2)] or 6(1) must be made in a form and manner specified by the Secretary of State after consulting the Scottish Ministers and the Department of Finance and Personnel in Northern Ireland.

(2) The applicant must pay to the Secretary of State a non-refundable fee of an amount prescribed by order made by the Secretary of State unless the application is made in circumstances in which, in accordance with provision made by the order, no fee is payable; and fees of different amounts may be prescribed for different circumstances.

Amendment

Sub-s (1): reference to ", 5A(2)" in square brackets inserted by the Civil Partnership Act 2004, s 250(1), (5)(a).

[533]

8 Appeals etc

(1) An applicant to a Gender Recognition Panel under section 1(1), 5(2)[, 5A(2)] or 6(1) may appeal to the High Court or Court of Session on a point of law against a decision by the Panel to reject the application.

(2) An appeal under subsection (1) must be heard in private if the applicant so requests.

(3) On such an appeal the court must—

(a) allow the appeal and issue the certificate applied for,

(b) allow the appeal and refer the matter to the same or another Panel for re-consideration, or

(c) dismiss the appeal.

(4) If an application under section 1(1) is rejected, the applicant may not make another application before the end of the period of six months beginning with the date on which it is rejected.

(5) If an application under section 1(1), 5(2)[, 5A(2)] or 6(1) is granted but the Secretary of State considers that its grant was secured by fraud, the Secretary of State may refer the case to the High Court or Court of Session.

(6) On a reference under subsection (5) the court—

(a) must either quash or confirm the decision to grant the application, and

(b) if it quashes it, must revoke the gender recognition certificate issued on the grant of the application and may make any order which it considers appropriate in consequence of, or otherwise in connection with, doing so.

Amendment

Sub-s (1): reference to ", 5A(2)" in square brackets inserted by the Civil Partnership Act 2004, s 250(1), (5)(b).

Sub-s (5): reference to ", 5A(2)" in square brackets inserted by the Civil Partnership Act 2004, s 250(1), (5)(b).

[534]

CONSEQUENCES OF ISSUE OF GENDER RECOGNITION CERTIFICATE ETC

9 General

(1) Where a full gender recognition certificate is issued to a person, the person's gender becomes for all purposes the acquired gender (so that, if the acquired gender is the male gender, the person's sex becomes that of a man and, if it is the female gender, the person's sex becomes that of a woman).

(2) Subsection (1) does not affect things done, or events occurring, before the certificate is issued; but it does operate for the interpretation of enactments passed, and instruments and other documents made, before the certificate is issued (as well as those passed or made afterwards).

(3) Subsection (1) is subject to provision made by this Act or any other enactment or any subordinate legislation.

Commentary

This section must be read subject to the specific provisions in respect of wills and trusts set out below in s 15. The Act will not affect any steps taken before it came into force on 4 April 2005. However, it will affect the interpretation of instruments and documents made before the certificate is issued. It seems clear that if an interest is not vested under a trust or will and is dependent on someone's gender (eg to a son) and before it vests, a person acquires a gender which would qualify them as a son, then they can take. The position is not clear if a gift is subject to a contingency—for example to my daughters on attaining 25 and before satisfying that contingency a daughter acquires male gender under the Act. Similarly it is not clear if a gift is vested and is linked to gender, whether a change of gender will terminate that vested interest. The answer in the latter case would seem to be not, but the matter is not clear.

[535]

10 Registration

(1) Where there is a UK birth register entry in relation to a person to whom a full gender recognition certificate is issued, the Secretary of State must send a copy of the certificate to the appropriate Registrar General.

(2) In this Act "UK birth register entry", in relation to a person to whom a full gender recognition certificate is issued, means—

- (a) an entry of which a certified copy is kept by a Registrar General, or
- (b) an entry in a register so kept,

containing a record of the person's birth or adoption (or, if there would otherwise be more than one, the most recent).

(3) "The appropriate Registrar General" means whichever of—

- (a) the Registrar General for England and Wales,
- (b) the Registrar General for Scotland, or
- (c) the Registrar General for Northern Ireland,

keeps a certified copy of the person's UK birth register entry or the register containing that entry.

(4) Schedule 3 (provisions about registration) has effect.

[536]

11 Marriage

Schedule 4 (amendments of marriage law) has effect.

[537]

12 Parenthood

The fact that a person's gender has become the acquired gender under this Act does not affect the status of the person as the father or mother of a child.

[538]

13 Social security benefits and pensions

Schedule 5 (entitlement to benefits and pensions) has effect.

[539]

14 Discrimination

Schedule 6 (amendments of Sex Discrimination Act 1975 (c 65) and Sex Discrimination (Northern Ireland) Order 1976 (SI 1976/1042 (NI 15))) has effect.

[540]

15 Succession etc

The fact that a person's gender has become the acquired gender under this Act does not affect the disposal or devolution of property under a will or other instrument made before the appointed day.

Commentary

What is important is not when the disposition was made but when the will or other instrument was made. The appointed day is 4 April 2005. In respect of instruments made after that date, then expressions descriptive of gender will be interpreted in accordance with any full certificates granted. If a will refers to the 'eldest daughter', and a person who was previously a son becomes the 'eldest daughter' following recognition in the acquired gender, that person (subject to section 18) will inherit as the 'eldest daughter'. If an appointment is made out of a settlement which pre-dates 4 April 2005 but is made after the appointed day, then it must be interpreted on the basis of this Act, even if the settlement would not be so interpreted.

[541]

16 Peerages etc

The fact that a person's gender has become the acquired gender under this Act—

(a) does not affect the descent of any peerage or dignity or title of honour, and

(b) does not affect the devolution of any property limited (expressly or not) by a will or other instrument to devolve (as nearly as the law permits) along with any peerage or dignity or title of honour unless an intention that it should do so is expressed in the will or other instrument.

Commentary

This section provides an exception to the general rule applied by this Act. If a person acquires a full certificate it will not enable him or her to succeed to a title which devolves according to gender and conversely will not disentitle someone. Subsection (b) provides property which devolves with a title will continue to do so unless the Will expresses a contrary intention.

[542]

17 Trustees and personal representatives

(1) A trustee or personal representative is not under a duty, by virtue of the law relating to trusts or the administration of estates, to enquire, before conveying or distributing any property, whether a full gender recognition certificate has been issued to any person or revoked (if that fact could affect entitlement to the property).

(2) A trustee or personal representative is not liable to any person by reason of a conveyance or distribution of the property made without regard to whether a full gender recognition certificate has been issued to any person or revoked if the trustee or personal representative has not received notice of the fact before the conveyance or distribution.

(3) This section does not prejudice the right of a person to follow the property, or any property representing it, into the hands of another person who has received it unless that person has purchased it for value in good faith and without notice.

Commentary

This section provides protection to trustees and personal representatives who distribute without knowledge of a gender recognition certificate having been issued and indeed relieves them from the duty to inquire as to whether one has been issued. They will, however be liable on normal principles if they distribute with notice of a certificate. Subsection (3) does preserves the right of the personal representatives/trustees or beneficiaries to follow the property if it has been wrongly distributed.

[543]

18 Orders where expectations defeated

(1) This section applies where the disposition or devolution of any property under a will or other instrument (made on or after the appointed day) is different from what it would be but for the fact that a person's gender has become the acquired gender under this Act.

(2) A person may apply to the High Court or Court of Session for an order on the ground of being adversely affected by the different disposition or devolution of the property.

(3) The court may, if it is satisfied that it is just to do so, make in relation to any person benefiting from the different disposition or devolution of the property such order as it considers appropriate.

(4) An order may, in particular, make provision for—

- (a) the payment of a lump sum to the applicant,
- (b) the transfer of property to the applicant,
- (c) the settlement of property for the benefit of the applicant,
- (d) the acquisition of property and either its transfer to the applicant or its settlement for the benefit of the applicant.

(5) An order may contain consequential or supplementary provisions for giving effect to the order or for ensuring that it operates fairly as between the applicant and the other person or persons affected by it; and an order may, in particular, confer powers on trustees.

Commentary

The principles which will govern such applications and the procedure for them are as yet wholly unclear.

[544]

19 Sport

(1) A body responsible for regulating the participation of persons as competitors in an event or events involving a gender-affected sport may, if subsection (2) is satisfied, prohibit or restrict the participation as competitors in the event or events of persons whose gender has become the acquired gender under this Act.

(2) This subsection is satisfied if the prohibition or restriction is necessary to secure—

(a) fair competition, or

(b) the safety of competitors,

at the event or events.

(3) "Sport" means a sport, game or other activity of a competitive nature.

(4) A sport is a gender-affected sport if the physical strength, stamina or physique of average persons of one gender would put them at a disadvantage to average persons of the other gender as competitors in events involving the sport.

(5) This section does not affect—

(a) section 44 of the Sex Discrimination Act 1975 (c 65) (exception from Parts 2 to 4 of that Act for acts related to sport), or

(b) Article 45 of the Sex Discrimination (Northern Ireland) Order 1976 (SI 1976/1042 (NI 15)) (corresponding provision for Northern Ireland).

[545]

20 Gender-specific offences

(1) Where (apart from this subsection) a relevant gender-specific offence could be committed or attempted only if the gender of a person to whom a full gender recognition certificate has been issued were not the acquired gender, the fact that the person's gender has become the acquired gender does not prevent the offence being committed or attempted.

(2) An offence is a "relevant gender-specific offence" if—

(a) either or both of the conditions in subsection (3) are satisfied, and

(b) the commission of the offence involves the accused engaging in sexual activity.

(3) The conditions are—

(a) that the offence may be committed only by a person of a particular gender, and

(b) that the offence may be committed only on, or in relation to, a person of a particular gender,

and the references to a particular gender include a gender identified by reference to the gender of the other person involved.

[546]

21 Foreign gender change and marriage

(1) A person's gender is not to be regarded as having changed by reason only that it has changed under the law of a country or territory outside the United Kingdom.

(2) Accordingly, a person is not to be regarded as being married by reason of having entered into a foreign post-recognition marriage.

(3) But if a full gender recognition certificate is issued to a person who has entered into a foreign post-recognition marriage, after the issue of the certificate the marriage is no longer to be regarded as being void on the ground that (at the time when it was entered into) the parties to it were not respectively male and female.

(4) However, subsection (3) does not apply to a foreign post-recognition marriage if a party to it has entered into a later (valid) marriage [or civil partnership] before the issue of the full gender recognition certificate.

(5) For the purposes of this section a person has entered into a foreign post-recognition marriage if (and only if)—

(a) the person has entered into a marriage in accordance with the law of a country or territory outside the United Kingdom,
(b) before the marriage was entered into the person had changed gender under the law of that or any other country or territory outside the United Kingdom,
(c) the other party to the marriage was not of the gender to which the person had changed under the law of that country or territory, and
(d) by virtue of subsection (1) the person's gender was not regarded as having changed under the law of any part of the United Kingdom.

(6) Nothing in this section prevents the exercise of any enforceable Community right.

Amendment

Sub-s (4): words "or civil partnership" in square brackets inserted by the Civil Partnership Act 2004, s 250(1), (6).

[547]

SUPPLEMENTARY

22 Prohibition on disclosure of information

(1) It is an offence for a person who has acquired protected information in an official capacity to disclose the information to any other person.

(2) "Protected information" means information which relates to a person who has made an application under section 1(1) and which—
(a) concerns that application or any application by the person under section 5(2)[, 5A(2)] or 6(1), or
(b) if the application under section 1(1) is granted, otherwise concerns the person's gender before it becomes the acquired gender.

(3) A person acquires protected information in an official capacity if the person acquires it—
(a) in connection with the person's functions as a member of the civil service, a constable or the holder of any other public office or in connection with the functions of a local or public authority or of a voluntary organisation,
(b) as an employer, or prospective employer, of the person to whom the information relates or as a person employed by such an employer or prospective employer, or
(c) in the course of, or otherwise in connection with, the conduct of business or the supply of professional services.

(4) But it is not an offence under this section to disclose protected information relating to a person if—
(a) the information does not enable that person to be identified,
(b) that person has agreed to the disclosure of the information,
(c) the information is protected information by virtue of subsection (2)(b) and the person by whom the disclosure is made does not know or believe that a full gender recognition certificate has been issued,
(d) the disclosure is in accordance with an order of a court or tribunal,
(e) the disclosure is for the purpose of instituting, or otherwise for the purposes of, proceedings before a court or tribunal,
(f) the disclosure is for the purpose of preventing or investigating crime,
(g) the disclosure is made to the Registrar General for England and Wales, the Registrar General for Scotland or the Registrar General for Northern Ireland,
(h) the disclosure is made for the purposes of the social security system or a pension scheme,

(i) the disclosure is in accordance with provision made by an order under subsection (5), or

(j) the disclosure is in accordance with any provision of, or made by virtue of, an enactment other than this section.

(5) The Secretary of State may by order make provision prescribing circumstances in which the disclosure of protected information is not to constitute an offence under this section.

(6) The power conferred by subsection (5) is exercisable by the Scottish Ministers (rather than the Secretary of State) where the provision to be made is within the legislative competence of the Scottish Parliament.

(7) An order under subsection (5) may make provision permitting—

(a) disclosure to specified persons or persons of a specified description,

(b) disclosure for specified purposes,

(c) disclosure of specified descriptions of information, or

(d) disclosure by specified persons or persons of a specified description.

(8) A person guilty of an offence under this section is liable on summary conviction to a fine not exceeding level 5 on the standard scale.

Amendment

Sub-s (2): in para (a) reference to ", 5A(2)" in square brackets inserted by the Civil Partnership Act 2004, s 250(1), (5)(c).

[548]

23 Power to modify statutory provisions

(1) The Secretary of State may by order make provision for modifying the operation of any enactment or subordinate legislation in relation to—

(a) persons whose gender has become the acquired gender under this Act, or

(b) any description of such persons.

(2) The power conferred by subsection (1) is exercisable by the Scottish Ministers (rather than the Secretary of State) where the provision to be made is within the legislative competence of the Scottish Parliament.

(3) The appropriate Northern Ireland department may by order make provision for modifying the operation of any enactment or subordinate legislation which deals with a transferred matter in relation to—

(a) persons whose gender has become the acquired gender under this Act, or

(b) any description of such persons.

(4) In subsection (3)—

"the appropriate Northern Ireland department", in relation to any enactment or subordinate legislation which deals with a transferred matter, means the Northern Ireland department which has responsibility for that matter,

"deals with" is to be construed in accordance with section 98(2) and (3) of the Northern Ireland Act 1998 (c 47), and

"transferred matter" has the meaning given by section 4(1) of that Act.

(5) Before an order is made under this section, appropriate consultation must be undertaken with persons likely to be affected by it.

[549]

24 Orders and regulations

(1) Any power of the Secretary of State . . ., the Scottish Ministers or a Northern Ireland department to make an order under this Act includes power to make any

appropriate incidental, supplementary, consequential or transitional provision or savings.

(2) Any power of the Secretary of State . . . or the Scottish Ministers to make an order under this Act, and any power of the Registrar General for England and Wales or the Registrar General for Scotland to make regulations under this Act, is exercisable by statutory instrument.

(3) No order may be made under section 2 . . . unless a draft of the statutory instrument containing the order has been laid before, and approved by a resolution of, each House of Parliament.

(4) A statutory instrument containing an order made by the Secretary of State under section 7, 22 or 23 is subject to annulment in pursuance of a resolution of either House of Parliament.

(5) A statutory instrument containing an order made by the Scottish Ministers under section 22 or 23 is subject to annulment in pursuance of a resolution of the Scottish Parliament.

(6) Any power of a Northern Ireland department to make an order or regulations under this Act is exercisable by statutory rule for the purposes of the Statutory Rules (Northern Ireland) Order 1979 (SI 1979/1573 (NI 12)).

(7) Orders and regulations made by a Northern Ireland department under this Act are subject to negative resolution (within the meaning of section 41(6) of the Interpretation Act (Northern Ireland) 1954 (c 33 (NI))).

Amendment

Sub-s (1): words omitted repealed by the Legislative and Regulatory Reform Act 2006, s 30(1), Schedule.
Sub-s (2): words omitted repealed by the Legislative and Regulatory Reform Act 2006, s 30(1), Schedule.
Sub-s (3): words omitted repealed by the Legislative and Regulatory Reform Act 2006, s 30(1), Schedule.

[550]

25 Interpretation

In this Act—

"the acquired gender" is to be construed in accordance with section 1(2),

"approved country or territory" has the meaning given by section 2(4),

"the appointed day" means the day appointed by order under section 26,

"chartered psychologist" means a person for the time being listed in the British Psychological Society's Register of Chartered Psychologists,

"enactment" includes an enactment contained in an Act of the Scottish Parliament or in any Northern Ireland legislation,

"full gender recognition certificate" and "interim gender recognition certificate" mean the certificates issued as such under section 4[, 5 or 5A] and "gender recognition certificate" means either of those sorts of certificate,

"gender dysphoria" means the disorder variously referred to as gender dysphoria, gender identity disorder and transsexualism,

"Gender Recognition Panel" (and "Panel") is to be construed in accordance with Schedule 1,

"subordinate legislation" means an Order in Council, an order, rules, regulations, a scheme, a warrant, bye-laws or any other instrument made under an enactment, and

"UK birth register entry" has the meaning given by section 10(2).

Amendment

In definition ""full gender recognition certificate" and "interim gender recognition certificate"" words ", 5 or 5A" in square brackets substituted by the Civil Partnership Act 2004, s 250(1), (7).

[551]

26 Commencement

Apart from sections 23 to 25, this section and sections 28 and 29, this Act does not come into force until such day as the Secretary of State may appoint by order made after consulting the Scottish Ministers and the Department of Finance and Personnel in Northern Ireland.

[552]

27 Applications within two years of commencement

(1) This section applies where applications are made under section 1(1)(a) during the period of two years beginning with the appointed day ("the initial period").

(2) Section 2(1)(a) has effect as if there were inserted at the end "or has undergone surgical treatment for the purpose of modifying sexual characteristics,".

(3) In the case of an application which—

(a) is made during the first six months of the initial period, or

(b) is made during the rest of the initial period and is based on the applicant having undergone surgical treatment for the purpose of modifying sexual characteristics,

section 2(1)(b) has effect as if for "two" there were substituted "six".

(4) Subsections (5) and (6) apply in the case of an application to which subsection (3) applies and in the case of an application—

(a) made during the rest of the initial period,

(b) based on the applicant having or having had gender dysphoria, and

(c) including a statutory declaration by the applicant that the applicant has lived in the acquired gender throughout the period of six years ending with the date on which the application is made.

(5) Section 3 has effect as if for subsections (1) to (3) there were substituted—

"(1) An application under section 1(1)(a) must include either—

(a) a report made by a registered medical practitioner, or

(b) a report made by a chartered psychologist practising in the field of gender dysphoria.

(2) Where the application is based on the applicant having or having had gender dysphoria—

(a) the reference in subsection (1) to a registered medical practitioner is to one practising in the field of gender dysphoria, and

(b) that subsection is not complied with unless the report includes details of the diagnosis of the applicant's gender dysphoria.

(3) Subsection (1) is not complied with in a case where—

(a) the applicant has undergone or is undergoing treatment for the purpose of modifying sexual characteristics, or

(b) treatment for that purpose has been prescribed or planned for the applicant,

unless the report required by that subsection includes details of it."

(6) Paragraph 4(2) of Schedule 1 has effect with the omission of paragraph (b).

[553]

28 Extent

(1) The following provisions extend only to England and Wales—
- (a) Part 1 of Schedule 2,
- (b) Part 1 of Schedule 3, and
- (c) Part 1 of Schedule 4.

(2) The following provisions extend only to Scotland—
- (a) section 24(5),
- (b) Part 2 of Schedule 2,
- (c) Part 2 of Schedule 3, and
- (d) Part 2 of Schedule 4.

(3) The following provisions extend only to England and Wales and Scotland—
- (a) paragraphs 12, 14 and 16 of Schedule 5, and
- (b) Part 1 of Schedule 6.

(4) The following provisions extend only to Northern Ireland—
- (a) section 23(3) and (4),
- (b) section 24(6) and (7),
- (c) Part 3 of Schedule 2,
- (d) Part 3 of Schedule 3,
- (e) Part 3 of Schedule 4,
- (f) paragraphs 13, 15 and 17 of Schedule 5, and
- (g) Part 2 of Schedule 6.

(5) Subject to subsections (1) to (4), this Act extends to Northern Ireland (as well as to England and Wales and Scotland).

[554]

29 Short title

This Act may be cited as the Gender Recognition Act 2004.

[555]

SCHEDULE 1
GENDER RECOGNITION PANELS

Section 1

LIST OF PERSONS ELIGIBLE TO SIT

1 (1) [Subject to sub-paragraph (1A), the Lord Chancellor] must, after consulting the Scottish Ministers and the Department of Finance and Personnel in Northern Ireland, make appointments to a list of persons eligible to sit as members of Gender Recognition Panels.

[(1A) The Lord Chancellor may appoint a person under sub-paragraph (1) only with the concurrence of all of the following—
- (a) the Lord Chief Justice of England and Wales;
- (b) the Lord President of the Court of Session;
- (c) the Lord Chief Justice of Northern Ireland.]

(2) The only persons who may be appointed to the list are persons who—
- (a) have a relevant legal qualification ("legal members"), or
- (b) are registered medical practitioners or chartered psychologists ("medical members").

(3) The following have a relevant legal qualification—
(a) a person who has a 7 year general qualification within the meaning of section 71 of the Courts and Legal Services Act 1990 (c 41),
(b) an advocate or solicitor in Scotland of at least seven years' standing, and
(c) a member of the Bar of Northern Ireland or *solicitor of the Supreme Court of Northern Ireland* [solicitor of the Court of Judicature of Northern Ireland] of at least seven years' standing.

PRESIDENT

2 (1) [Subject to sub-paragraph (1A), the Lord Chancellor] must, after consulting the Scottish Ministers and the Department of Finance and Personnel in Northern Ireland—
(a) appoint one of the legal members to be the President of Gender Recognition Panels ("the President"), and
(b) appoint another of the legal members to be the Deputy President of Gender Recognition Panels ("the Deputy President").

[(1A) The Lord Chancellor may appoint a person under sub-paragraph (1) only with the concurrence of all of the following—
(a) the Lord Chief Justice of England and Wales;
(b) the Lord President of the Court of Session;
(c) the Lord Chief Justice of Northern Ireland.]

(2) The Deputy President has the functions of the President—
(a) if the President is unavailable, and
(b) during any vacancy in the office of President.

TENURE OF PERSONS APPOINTED TO LIST

3 Persons on the list—
(a) hold and vacate their appointments in accordance with the terms on which they are appointed, and
(b) are eligible for re-appointment at the end of their period of appointment.

MEMBERSHIP OF PANELS

4 (1) The President must make arrangements for determining the membership of Panels.

(2) The arrangements must ensure that a Panel determining an application under section 1(1)(a) includes—
(a) at least one legal member, and
(b) at least one medical member.

5 The arrangements must ensure that a Panel determining an application under section 1(1)(b), 5(2)[, 5A(2)] or 6(1) includes at least one legal member.

PROCEDURE

6 (1) Where a Panel consists of more than one member, either the President or Deputy President or another legal member nominated by the President must preside.

(2) Decisions of a Panel consisting of more than one member may be taken by majority vote (and, if its members are evenly split, the member presiding has a casting vote).

(3) Panels are to determine applications in private.

(4) A Panel must determine an application without a hearing unless the Panel considers that a hearing is necessary.

(5) The President may, after consulting the *Council on Tribunals* [Administrative Justice and Tribunals Council], give directions about the practice and procedure of Panels.

(6) Panels must give reasons for their decisions.

(7) Where a Panel has determined an application, the Secretary of State must communicate to the applicant the Panel's decision and its reasons for making its decision.

STAFF AND FACILITIES

7 The Secretary of State may make staff and other facilities available to Panels.

MONEY

8 (1) The Secretary of State may pay sums by way of remuneration, allowances and expenses to members of Panels.

(2) The Secretary of State may pay compensation to a person who ceases to be on the list if the Secretary of State thinks it appropriate to do so because of special circumstances.

[DELEGATION

8A (1) The Lord Chief Justice of England and Wales may nominate a judicial office holder (as defined in section 109(4) of the Constitutional Reform Act 2005) to exercise any of his functions under this Schedule.

(2) The Lord President of the Court of Session may nominate a judge of the Court of Session who is a member of the First or Second Division of the Inner House of that Court to exercise his functions under this Schedule.

(3) The Lord Chief Justice of Northern Ireland may nominate any of the following to exercise his functions under this Schedule—

(a) the holder of one of the offices listed in Schedule 1 to the Justice (Northern Ireland) Act 2002;

(b) a Lord Justice of Appeal (as defined in section 88 of that Act).]

COUNCIL ON TRIBUNALS

9 In Schedule 1 to the Tribunals and Inquiries Act 1992 (c 53) (tribunals under supervision of Council on Tribunals), before paragraph 22 insert—

"Gender Recognition	21AA Gender Recognition Panels constituted under Schedule 1 to the Gender Recognition Act 2004 (c 7)."

DISQUALIFICATION

10 In Part 3 of Schedule 1 to the House of Commons Disqualification Act 1975 (c 24) (offices disqualifying person from membership of House of Commons), at the appropriate place insert—

"Person on the list of those eligible to sit as members of a Gender Recognition Panel."

11 In Part 3 of Schedule 1 to the Northern Ireland Assembly Disqualification Act 1975 (c 25) (offices disqualifying persons from membership of Northern Ireland Assembly), at the appropriate place insert—

"Person on the list of those eligible to sit as members of a Gender Recognition Panel."

Amendment

Para 1: in sub-para (1) words "Subject to sub-paragraph (1A), the Lord Chancellor" in square brackets substituted by SI 2006/1016, art 2, Sch 1, paras 12, 13.
Para 1: sub-para (1A) inserted by SI 2006/1016, art 2, Sch 1, paras 12, 14.
Para 1: in sub-para (3)(c) words "solicitor of the Supreme Court of Northern Ireland" in italics repealed and subsequent words in square brackets substituted, from a date to be appointed, by the Constitutional Reform Act 2005, s 59(5), Sch 11, Pt 3, para 5.
Para 2: in sub-para (1) words "Subject to sub-paragraph (1A), the Lord Chancellor" in square brackets substituted by SI 2006/1016, art 2, Sch 1, paras 12, 15.
Para 2: sub-para (1A) inserted by SI 2006/1016, art 2, Sch 1, paras 12, 16.
Para 5: reference to ", 5A(2)" in square brackets inserted by the Civil Partnership Act 2004, s 250(1), (8).
Para 6: in sub-para (5) words "Council on Tribunals" in italics repealed and subsequent words in square brackets substituted, from a date to be appointed, by the Tribunals, Courts and Enforcement Act 2007, s 48(1), Sch 8, para 60.
Para 8A: inserted by SI 2006/1016, art 2, Sch 1, paras 12, 17.

[556]

SCHEDULE 2
INTERIM CERTIFICATES: MARRIAGE

Section 4

PART 1
ENGLAND AND WALES

1 The Matrimonial Causes Act 1973 (c 18) is amended as follows.

2 In section 12 (grounds on which a marriage celebrated after 31st July 1971 is voidable), after paragraph (f) insert—

"(g) that an interim gender recognition certificate under the Gender Recognition Act 2004 has, after the time of the marriage, been issued to either party to the marriage;" .

3 In section 13 (bars to relief), after subsection (2) insert—

"(2A) Without prejudice to subsection (1) above, the court shall not grant a decree of nullity by virtue of section 12 above on the ground mentioned in paragraph (g) of that section unless it is satisfied that proceedings were instituted within the period of six months from the date of issue of the interim gender recognition certificate."

4 (1) Paragraph 11 of Schedule 1 (grounds on which a marriage celebrated before 1st August 1971 is voidable) is amended as follows.

(2) In sub-paragraph (1), after paragraph (d) insert

"or

(e) that an interim gender recognition certificate under the Gender Recognition Act 2004 has been issued to either party to the marriage;" .

(3) After sub-paragraph (3) insert—

"(3A) The court shall not grant a decree of nullity in a case falling within sub-paragraph (1)(e) above unless it is satisfied that proceedings were instituted within six months from the date of issue of the interim gender recognition certificate."

PART 2
SCOTLAND

5 The Divorce (Scotland) Act 1976 (c 39) is amended as follows.

6 (1) In subsection (1) of section 1 (grounds on which decree of divorce may be granted)—

(a) the words "the marriage has broken down irretrievably" become paragraph (a), and

(b) after that paragraph insert

"or

(b) an interim gender recognition certificate under the Gender Recognition Act 2004 has, after the date of the marriage, been issued to either party to the marriage."

(2) Accordingly, the title of that section becomes "Grounds of divorce".

7 In section 2(1) (encouragement of reconciliation), for "in an action for divorce" substitute "under paragraph (a) of section 1(1)".

PART 3
NORTHERN IRELAND

8 The Matrimonial Causes (Northern Ireland) Order 1978 (SI 1978/1045 (NI 15)) is amended as follows.

9 In Article 14 (grounds on which a marriage celebrated after the commencement of that Article is voidable), after paragraph (f) insert—

"(g) that an interim gender recognition certificate under the Gender Recognition Act 2004 has, after the time of the marriage, been issued to either party to the marriage;" .

10 In Article 16 (bars to relief), after paragraph (2) insert—

"(2A) Without prejudice to paragraph (1), the court shall not grant a decree of nullity by virtue of Article 14 on the ground mentioned in paragraph (g) of that Article unless it is satisfied that proceedings were instituted within the period of six months from the date of issue of the interim gender recognition certificate."

11 (1) Paragraph 18 of Schedule 3 (grounds on which a marriage celebrated before the commencement of Article 14 is voidable) is amended as follows.

(2) In sub-paragraph (1), after paragraph (d) insert

"or

(e) that an interim gender recognition certificate under the Gender Recognition Act 2004 has been issued to either party to the marriage;" .

(3) After sub-paragraph (4) insert—

"(4A) The court shall not grant a decree of nullity in a case falling within sub-paragraph (1)(e) unless it is satisfied that proceedings were instituted within six months from the date of issue of the interim gender recognition certificate."

SCHEDULE 3
REGISTRATION

Section 10

PART 1
ENGLAND AND WALES

INTRODUCTORY

1 In this Part—

"the Registrar General" means the Registrar General for England and Wales, and
"the 1953 Act" means the Births and Deaths Registration Act 1953 (c 20).

GENDER RECOGNITION REGISTER

2 (1) The Registrar General must maintain, in the General Register Office, a register to be called the Gender Recognition Register.

(2) In this Part "the Gender Recognition Register" means the register maintained under sub-paragraph (1).

(3) The form in which the Gender Recognition Register is maintained is to be determined by the Registrar General.

(4) The Gender Recognition Register is not to be open to public inspection or search.

ENTRIES IN GENDER RECOGNITION REGISTER AND MARKING OF EXISTING BIRTH REGISTER ENTRIES

3 (1) If the Registrar General receives under section 10(1) a copy of a full gender recognition certificate issued to a person, the Registrar General must—

- (a) make an entry in the Gender Recognition Register containing such particulars as may be prescribed in relation to the person's birth and any other prescribed matter,
- (b) secure that the UK birth register entry is marked in such manner as may be prescribed, and
- (c) make traceable the connection between the entry in the Gender Recognition Register and the UK birth register entry.

(2) Sub-paragraph (1) does not apply if the certificate was issued after an application under section 6(1) and that sub-paragraph has already been complied with in relation to the person.

(3) No certified copy of the UK birth register entry and no short certificate of birth compiled from that entry is to include anything marked by virtue of sub-paragraph (1)(b).

(4) Information kept by the Registrar General for the purposes of sub-paragraph (1)(c) is not to be open to public inspection or search.

(5) "Prescribed" means prescribed by regulations made by the Registrar General with the approval of the Chancellor of the Exchequer.

INDEXING OF ENTRIES IN GENDER RECOGNITION REGISTER

4 (1) The Registrar General must make arrangements for each entry made in the Gender Recognition Register to be included in the relevant index kept in the General Register Office.

(2) Any right to search the relevant index includes the right to search entries included in it by virtue of sub-paragraph (1).

(3) Where by virtue of sub-paragraph (1) an index includes entries in the Gender Recognition Register, the index must not disclose that fact.

(4) "The relevant index", in relation to an entry made in the Gender Recognition Register in relation to a person, means the index of the certified copies of entries in registers, or of entries in registers, which includes the person's UK birth register entry.

CERTIFIED COPIES OF ENTRIES IN GENDER RECOGNITION REGISTER

5 (1) Anyone who may have a certified copy of the UK birth register entry of a person issued with a full gender recognition certificate may have a certified copy of the entry made in relation to the person in the Gender Recognition Register.

(2) Any fee which would be payable for a certified copy of the person's UK birth register entry is payable for a certified copy of the entry made in relation to the person in the Gender Recognition Register.

(3) If the person's UK birth register entry is an entry in the Gender Recognition Register, sub-paragraph (1) applies as if the person's UK birth register entry were the most recent entry within section 10(2)(a) or (b) containing a record of the person's birth or adoption which is not an entry in the Gender Recognition Register.

(4) A certified copy of an entry in the Gender Recognition Register must not disclose the fact that the entry is contained in the Gender Recognition Register.

(5) A certified copy of an entry in the Gender Recognition Register must be sealed or stamped with the seal of the General Register Office.

SHORT CERTIFICATES OF BIRTH COMPILED FROM GENDER RECOGNITION REGISTER

6 Where a short certificate of birth under section 33 of the 1953 Act is compiled from the Gender Recognition Register, the certificate must not disclose that fact.

GENDER RECOGNITION REGISTER: RE-REGISTRATION

7 (1) Section 10A of the 1953 Act (re-registration where parents not married) applies where an entry relating to a person's birth has been made in the Gender Recognition Register as where the birth of a child has been registered under that Act.

(2) In its application by virtue of sub-paragraph (1) section 10A has effect—
- (a) as if the reference to the registrar in subsection (1) were to the Registrar General, and
- (b) with the omission of subsection (2).

(3) Sections 14 and 14A of the 1953 Act (re-registration in cases of legitimation and after declaration of parentage) apply where an entry relating to a person's birth has been made in the Gender Recognition Register as if the references in those sections to the Registrar General authorising re-registration of the person's birth were to the Registrar General's re-registering it.

CORRECTION ETC OF GENDER RECOGNITION REGISTER

8 (1) Any power or duty of the Registrar General or any other person to correct, alter, amend, mark or cancel the marking of a person's UK birth register entry is exercisable, or falls to be performed, by the Registrar General in relation to an entry in the Gender Recognition Register which—
- (a) relates to that person, and
- (b) under paragraph 4(1) is included in the index which includes the person's UK birth register entry.

(2) If the person's UK birth register entry is an entry in the Gender Recognition Register, the references in sub-paragraph (1) to the person's UK birth register entry are to the most recent entry within section 10(2)(a) or (b) containing a record of the person's birth or adoption which is not an entry in the Gender Recognition Register.

(3) The Registrar General may correct the Gender Recognition Register by entry in the margin (without any alteration of the original entry) in consequence of the issue of a full gender recognition certificate after an application under section 6(1).

REVOCATION OF GENDER RECOGNITION CERTIFICATE ETC

9 (1) This paragraph applies if, after an entry has been made in the Gender Recognition Register in relation to a person, the High Court or the Court of Session makes an order under section 8(6) quashing the decision to grant the person's application under section 1(1)[, 5(2) or 5A(2)].

(2) The High Court or the Court of Session must inform the Registrar General.

(3) Subject to any appeal, the Registrar General must—
- (a) cancel the entry in the Gender Recognition Register, and
- (b) cancel, or secure the cancellation, of any marking of an entry relating to the person made by virtue of paragraph 3(1)(b).

EVIDENCE

10 (1) Section 34(5) of the 1953 Act (certified copy of entry in register under that Act deemed to be true copy) applies in relation to the Gender Recognition Register as if it were a register under that Act.

(2) A certified copy of an entry made in the Gender Recognition Register in relation to a person is to be received, without further or other proof, as evidence—
- (a) if the relevant index is the index of the Adopted Children Register, of the matters of which a certified copy of an entry in that Register is evidence,
- (b) if the relevant index is the index of the Parental Order Register, of the matters of which a certified copy of an entry in that Register is evidence, and
- (c) otherwise, of the person's birth.

(3) And any certified copy which is receivable in evidence of any matter in Northern Ireland by virtue of paragraph 31(2)(a) or (b) of this Schedule is also receivable as evidence of that matter in England and Wales.

. . .

11 . . .

Amendment

Para 9: in sub-para (1) words ", 5(2) or 5A(2)" in square brackets substituted by the Civil Partnership Act 2004, s 250(1), (9).

Para 11: repealed by the Legislative and Regulatory Reform Act 2006, s 30(1), Schedule.

PART 2
SCOTLAND

INTRODUCTORY

12 In this Part—

"the Registrar General" means the Registrar General for Scotland, and

"the 1965 Act" means the Registration of Births, Deaths and Marriages (Scotland) Act 1965 (c 49).

GENDER RECOGNITION REGISTER

13 (1) The Registrar General must maintain, in the General Register Office of Births, Deaths and Marriages in Scotland, a register to be called the Gender Recognition Register.

(2) In this Part "the Gender Recognition Register" means the register maintained under sub-paragraph (1).

(3) The form in which the Gender Recognition Register is maintained is to be determined by the Registrar General.

(4) The Gender Recognition Register is not to be open to public inspection or search.

ENTRIES IN GENDER RECOGNITION REGISTER

14 (1) If the Registrar General receives under section 10(1) a copy of a full gender recognition certificate issued to a person, the Registrar General must—

- (a) make an entry in the Gender Recognition Register containing such particulars as may be prescribed in relation to the person's birth and any other prescribed matter, and
- (b) otherwise than by annotating in any way the birth register, make traceable the connection between the UK birth register entry and the entry in the Gender Recognition Register.

(2) Sub-paragraph (1) does not apply if the gender recognition certificate was issued after an application under section 6(1) and that sub-paragraph has already been complied with in relation to the person.

(3) Information kept by the Registrar General for the purposes of sub-paragraph (1)(b) is not to be open to public inspection or search.

(4) "Prescribed" means prescribed by regulations made by the Registrar General with the approval of the Scottish Ministers.

INDEXING OF ENTRIES IN GENDER RECOGNITION REGISTER

15 (1) The Registrar General must make arrangements for each entry made in the Gender Recognition Register to be included in an index of such entries kept in the General Register Office of Births, Deaths and Marriages in Scotland.

(2) Whenever the Registrar General causes a search to be made under subsection (2)(a) of section 38 of the 1965 Act (search of indexes of entries in the registers of births, deaths and marriages) on behalf of any person, he must also, without payment of any fee additional to the fee or fees prescribed under that section—

- (a) cause a search to be made of the index of entries in the Gender Recognition Register on behalf of that person, and
- (b) issue to that person an extract of any such entry provided that (disregarding, for the purposes of subsection (4)(j) of section 22, this paragraph) disclosure of the entry to the person would not constitute an offence under that section.

EXTRACTS OF ENTRIES IN GENDER RECOGNITION REGISTER

16 (1) This paragraph applies in respect of an extract issued under paragraph 15(2)(b).

(2) Except as regards the sex and name of the person to whom it relates, the extract must have the form and content it would have had had it been an extract from the register of births of the entry relating to that person.

(3) The extract must not disclose the fact that the entry is contained in the Gender Recognition Register.

[ABBREVIATED EXTRACTS OF BIRTH COMPILED FROM GENDER RECOGNITION REGISTER

17 Where an abbreviated extract of birth under section 39E of the 1965 Act is compiled from the Gender Recognition Register, the extract must not disclose that fact.]

GENDER RECOGNITION REGISTER: CORRECTION, RE-REGISTRATION ETC

18 Section 18A(2) (decrees of parentage and non-parentage), [section 20(1)] (re-registration in certain cases), section 42(1) and (5) (correction of errors), section 43(1), (2) and (5) to (9) (recording change of name or surname) and section 44 (Register of Corrections etc) of the 1965 Act apply in relation to the Gender Recognition Register as they apply in relation to the register of births.

REVOCATION OF GENDER RECOGNITION CERTIFICATE ETC

19 (1) This paragraph applies if, after an entry has been made in the Gender Recognition Register in relation to a person, the High Court or the Court of Session makes an order under section 8(6) quashing the decision to grant the person's application under section 1(1)[, 5(2) or 5A(2)].

(2) The High Court or the Court of Session must inform the Registrar General.

(3) Subject to any appeal, the Registrar General must cancel the entry in the Gender Recognition Register.

AUTHENTICATION AND ADMISSIBILITY

20 [Sections 41 and 41A] of the 1965 Act (authentication of extracts etc and their admissibility as evidence) [apply] in relation to the Gender Recognition Register as in relation to the registers kept under the provisions of that Act.

Amendment

Para 17: substituted by SSI 2006/596, art 2(1), (2).
Para 18: words "section 20(1)" in square brackets substituted by SSI 2006/596, art 2(1), (3).
Para 19: in sub-para (1) words ", 5(2) or 5A(2)" in square brackets substituted by the Civil Partnership Act 2004, s 250(1), (9).
Para 20: words "Sections 41 and 41A" in square brackets substituted by SSI 2006/596, art 2(1), (4)(a).
Para 20: word "apply" in square brackets substituted by SSI 2006/596, art 2(1), (4)(b).

PART 3
NORTHERN IRELAND

INTRODUCTORY

21 In this Part—

"the Registrar General" means the Registrar General for Northern Ireland, and
"the 1976 Order" means the Births and Deaths Registration (Northern Ireland) Order 1976 (SI 1976/1041 (NI 14)).

GENDER RECOGNITION REGISTER

22 (1) The Registrar General must maintain, in the General Register Office in Northern Ireland, a register to be called the Gender Recognition Register.

(2) In this Part "the Gender Recognition Register" means the register maintained under sub-paragraph (1).

(3) The form in which the Gender Recognition Register is maintained is to be determined by the Registrar General.

(4) The Gender Recognition Register is not to be open to public inspection or search.

ENTRIES IN GENDER RECOGNITION REGISTER AND MARKING OF EXISTING BIRTH REGISTER ENTRIES

23 (1) If the Registrar General receives under section 10(1) a copy of a full gender recognition certificate issued to a person, the Registrar General must—

- (a) make an entry in the Gender Recognition Register containing such particulars as may be prescribed in relation to the person's birth and any other prescribed matter,
- (b) secure that the UK birth register entry is marked in such manner as may be prescribed, and
- (c) make traceable the connection between the entry in the Gender Recognition Register and the UK birth register entry.

(2) Sub-paragraph (1) does not apply if the gender recognition certificate was issued after an application under section 6(1) and that sub-paragraph has already been complied with in relation to the person.

(3) No certified copy of the UK birth register entry and no short certificate of birth compiled from that entry is to include anything marked by virtue of sub-paragraph (1)(b).

(4) Information kept by the Registrar General for the purposes of sub-paragraph (1)(c) is not to be open to public inspection or search.

(5) "Prescribed" means prescribed by regulations made by the Department of Finance and Personnel.

INDEXING OF ENTRIES IN GENDER RECOGNITION REGISTER

24 (1) The Registrar General must make arrangements for each entry made in the Gender Recognition Register to be included in the relevant index kept in the General Register Office in Northern Ireland.

(2) Any right to search the relevant index includes the right to search entries included in it by virtue of sub-paragraph (1).

(3) Where by virtue of sub-paragraph (1) an index includes entries in the Gender Recognition Register, the index must not disclose that fact.

(4) "The relevant index", in relation to an entry made in the Gender Recognition Register in relation to a person, means the index of the entries in registers which includes the UK birth register entry.

CERTIFIED COPIES OF ENTRIES IN GENDER RECOGNITION REGISTER

25 (1) Anyone who may have a certified copy of the UK birth register entry of a person issued with a full gender recognition certificate may have a certified copy of the entry made in relation to the person in the Gender Recognition Register.

(2) Any fee which would be payable for a certified copy of the person's UK birth register entry is payable for a certified copy of the entry made in relation to the person in the Gender Recognition Register.

(3) If the person's UK birth register entry is an entry in the Gender Recognition Register, sub-paragraph (1) applies as if the person's UK birth register entry were the most recent entry within section 10(2)(a) or (b) containing a record of the person's birth or adoption which is not an entry in the Gender Recognition Register.

(4) A certified copy of an entry in the Gender Recognition Register must not disclose the fact that the entry is contained in the Gender Recognition Register.

(5) A certified copy of an entry in the Gender Recognition Register must be sealed or stamped with the seal of the General Register Office in Northern Ireland.

SHORT CERTIFICATES OF BIRTH COMPILED FROM GENDER RECOGNITION REGISTER

26 Where a short certificate of birth under Article 40 of the 1976 Order is compiled from the Gender Recognition Register, the certificate must not disclose that fact.

GENDER RECOGNITION REGISTER: RE-REGISTRATION

27 Articles 18, 19 and 19A of the 1976 Order (re-registration of births) apply where an entry relating to a person's birth has been made in the Gender Recognition Register as if the references in those Articles to the Registrar General authorising re-registration of the person's birth were to the Registrar General's re-registering it.

CORRECTION OF ERRORS IN GENDER RECOGNITION REGISTER

28 (1) Any power or duty of the Registrar General to correct, alter, amend, mark or cancel the marking of a person's UK birth register entry is exercisable, or falls to be performed, by the Registrar General in relation to an entry in the Gender Recognition Register which—

(a) relates to that person, and
(b) under paragraph 24(1) is included in the index which includes the person's UK birth register entry.

(2) If the person's UK birth register entry is an entry in the Gender Recognition Register, the references in sub-paragraph (1) to the person's UK birth register entry are to the most recent entry within section 10(2)(a) or (b) containing a record of the person's birth or adoption which is not an entry in the Gender Recognition Register.

(3) The Registrar General may correct the Gender Recognition Register by entry in the margin (without any alteration of the original entry) in consequence of the issue of a full gender recognition certificate after an application under section 6(1).

REVOCATION OF GENDER RECOGNITION CERTIFICATE ETC

29 (1) This paragraph applies if, after an entry has been made in the Gender Recognition Register in relation to a person, the High Court or the Court of Session makes an order under section 8(6) quashing the decision to grant the person's application under section 1(1)[, 5(2) or 5A(2)].

(2) The High Court or the Court of Session must inform the Registrar General.

(3) Subject to any appeal, the Registrar General must—

(a) cancel the entry in the Gender Recognition Register, and
(b) cancel, or secure the cancellation of, any marking of an entry relating to the person made by virtue of paragraph 23(1)(b).

CHANGE OF NAME

30 Paragraphs (4) to (6) of Article 37 of the 1976 Order (change of name) apply in relation to the Gender Recognition Register as they apply in relation to a register under that Order.

EVIDENCE

31 (1) Article 42 of the 1976 Order (proof of age or death) applies in relation to the Gender Recognition Register as it applies in relation to a register under that Order.

(2) A certified copy of an entry made in the Gender Recognition Register in relation to a person is to be received, without further or other proof, as evidence—
- (a) if the relevant index is the index of the Adopted Children Register, of the matters of which a certified copy of an entry in that Register is evidence,
- (b) if the relevant index is the index of the Parental Order Register, of the matters of which a certified copy of an entry in that Register is evidence, and
- (c) otherwise, of the person's birth.

(3) And any certified copy which is receivable in evidence of any matter in England and Wales by virtue of paragraph 10(2)(a) or (b) of this Schedule is also receivable as evidence of that matter in Northern Ireland.

FEES

32 Article 47 of the 1976 Order (fees for searches, certificates etc) applies in relation to the Gender Recognition Register as it applies in relation to a register under that Order.

Amendment
Para 29: in sub-para (1) words ", 5(2) or 5A(2)" in square brackets substituted by the Civil Partnership Act 2004, s 250(1), (9).

[558]

SCHEDULE 4
EFFECT ON MARRIAGE

Section 11

PART 1
ENGLAND AND WALES

MARRIAGE ACT 1949 (C 76)

1 The Marriage Act 1949 is amended as follows.

2 . . .

3 After section 5A insert—

"5B Marriages involving person of acquired gender

(1) A clergyman is not obliged to solemnise the marriage of a person if the clergyman reasonably believes that the person's gender has become the acquired gender under the Gender Recognition Act 2004.

(2) A clerk in Holy Orders of the Church in Wales is not obliged to permit the marriage of a person to be solemnised in the church or chapel of which the clerk is the minister if the clerk reasonably believes that the person's gender has become the acquired gender under that Act."

MATRIMONIAL CAUSES ACT 1973 (C 18)

4 The Matrimonial Causes Act 1973 is amended as follows.

5 In section 12 (grounds on which a marriage celebrated after 31st July 1971 is voidable), insert at the end—

"(h) that the respondent is a person whose gender at the time of the marriage had become the acquired gender under the Gender Recognition Act 2004."

6 In section 13(2), (3) and (4) (bars to relief), for "or (f)" substitute ", (f) or (h)".

Amendment

Para 2: repealed by the Civil Partnership Act 2004, s 261(4), Sch 30.

PART 2
SCOTLAND

MARRIAGE (SCOTLAND) ACT 1977 (C 15

7 In section 2 of the Marriage (Scotland) Act 1977 (marriage of related persons), insert at the end—

"(6) Subsections (1A) and (1B) above and paragraphs 2 and 2A of Schedule 1 to this Act have effect subject to the following modifications in the case of a party to a marriage whose gender has become the acquired gender under the Gender Recognition Act 2004 ("the relevant person").

(7) Any reference in those provisions to a former wife or former husband of the relevant person includes (respectively) any former husband or former wife of the relevant person.

(8) And—

(a) the reference in paragraph (b) of subsection (1B) above to the relevant person's son's mother is to the relevant person's son's father if the relevant person is the son's mother; and

(b) the reference in paragraph (d) of that subsection to the relevant person's daughter's father is to the relevant person's daughter's mother if the relevant person is the daughter's father."

PART 3
NORTHERN IRELAND

. . .

8 . . .

MATRIMONIAL CAUSES (NORTHERN IRELAND) ORDER 1978 (SI 1978/1045 (NI 15))

9 The Matrimonial Causes (Northern Ireland) Order 1978 is amended as follows.

10 In Article 14 (grounds on which a marriage celebrated after the commencement of that Article is voidable), insert at the end—

"(h) that the respondent is a person whose gender at the time of the marriage had become the acquired gender under the Gender Recognition Act 2004."

11 In Article 16(2), (3) and (4) (bars to relief), for "or (f)" substitute ", (f) or (h)".

Amendment
Para 8: repealed by the Law Reform (Miscellaneous Provisions) (Northern Ireland) Order 2006, SI 2006/1945, art 5(c).

[559]

SCHEDULE 5
BENEFITS AND PENSIONS

Section 13

PART 1
INTRODUCTORY

1 This Schedule applies where a full gender recognition certificate is issued to a person.

PART 2
STATE BENEFITS

INTRODUCTORY

2 (1) In this Part of this Schedule "the 1992 Act" means—

(a) in England and Wales and Scotland, the Social Security Contributions and Benefits Act 1992 (c 4), and

(b) in Northern Ireland, the Social Security Contributions and Benefits (Northern Ireland) Act 1992 (c 7).

(2) In this Part of this Schedule "the Administration Act" means—

(a) in England and Wales and Scotland, the Social Security Administration Act 1992 (c 5), and

(b) in Northern Ireland, the Social Security Administration (Northern Ireland) Act 1992 (c 8).

(3) Expressions used in this Part of this Schedule and in Part 2 of the 1992 Act have the same meaning in this Part of this Schedule as in Part 2 of the 1992 Act.

WIDOWED MOTHER'S ALLOWANCE

3 (1) If (immediately before the certificate is issued) the person is, or but for section 1 of the Administration Act would be, entitled to a widowed mother's allowance under section 37 of the 1992 Act (allowance for woman whose husband died before 9th April 2001)—

(a) the person is not entitled to that allowance afterwards, but

(b) (instead) subsections (2) to (5) of section 39A of the 1992 Act (widowed parent's allowance) apply in relation to the person.

(2) If (immediately before the certificate is issued) the person is (actually) entitled to a widowed mother's allowance, the entitlement to widowed parent's allowance conferred by sub-paragraph (1) is not subject to section 1 of the Administration Act.

WIDOW'S PENSION

4 If (immediately before the certificate is issued) the person is entitled to a widow's pension under section 38 of the 1992 Act (pension for woman whose husband died before 9th April 2001), the person is not entitled to that pension afterwards.

WIDOWED PARENT'S ALLOWANCE

5 If (immediately before the certificate is issued) the person is, or but for section 1 of the Administration Act would be, entitled to a widowed parent's allowance by virtue of subsection (1)(b) of section 39A of the 1992 Act (allowance for man whose wife died before 9th April 2001), subsections (2) to (5) of that section continue to apply in relation to the person afterwards.

LONG-TERM INCAPACITY BENEFIT ETC

6 If (immediately before the certificate is issued) the person is entitled to incapacity benefit, or a Category A retirement pension, under—

(a) section 40 of the 1992 Act (long-term incapacity benefit etc for woman whose husband died before 9th April 2001), or

(b) section 41 of the 1992 Act (long-term incapacity benefit etc for man whose wife died before that date),

the person is not so entitled afterwards.

CATEGORY A RETIREMENT PENSION

7 (1) Any question—

(a) whether the person is entitled to a Category A retirement pension (under section 44 of the 1992 Act) for any period after the certificate is issued, and

(b) (if so) the rate at which the person is so entitled for the period,

is to be decided as if the person's gender had always been the acquired gender.

(2) Accordingly, if (immediately before the certificate is issued) the person—

(a) is a woman entitled to a Category A retirement pension, but

(b) has not attained the age of 65,

the person ceases to be so entitled when it is issued.

(3) And, conversely, if (immediately before the certificate is issued) the person—

(a) is a man who has attained the age at which a woman of the same age attains pensionable age, but

(b) has not attained the age of 65,

the person is to be treated for the purposes of section 44 of the 1992 Act as attaining pensionable age when it is issued.

(4) But sub-paragraph (1) does not apply if and to the extent that the decision of any question to which it refers is affected by—

(a) the payment or crediting of contributions, or the crediting of earnings, in respect of a period ending before the certificate is issued, or

(b) preclusion from regular employment by responsibilities at home for such a period.

(5) Paragraph 10 makes provision about deferment of Category A retirement pensions.

CATEGORY B RETIREMENT PENSION ETC

8 (1) Any question whether the person is entitled to—

(a) a Category B retirement pension (under section 48A, 48B, 48BB or 51 of the 1992 Act), or

(b) an increase in a Category A retirement pension under section 51A or 52 of the 1992 Act (increase in Category A retirement pension by reference to amount of Category B retirement pension), for any period after the certificate is issued is (in accordance with section 9(1)) to be decided as if the person's gender were the acquired gender (but subject to sub-paragraph (4)).

(2) Accordingly, if (immediately before the certificate is issued) the person is a woman entitled to—

- (a) a Category B retirement pension, or
- (b) an increase in a Category A retirement pension under section 51A or 52 of the 1992 Act,

the person may cease to be so entitled when it is issued.

(3) And, conversely, if (immediately before the certificate is issued) the person—

- (a) is a man who has attained the age at which a woman of the same age attains pensionable age, but
- (b) has not attained the age of 65,

the person is to be treated for the purposes of sections 48A, 48B and 48BB of the 1992 Act as attaining pensionable age when it is issued.

(4) But a person who is a man (immediately before the certificate is issued) is not entitled to a Category B retirement pension under section 48B of the 1992 Act for any period after it is issued if the person—

- (a) attains (or has attained) the age of 65 before 6th April 2010, and
- (b) would not have been entitled to a Category B retirement pension under section 51 of the 1992 Act for that period if still a man.

(5) Paragraph 10 makes provision about deferment of Category B retirement pensions.

SHARED ADDITIONAL PENSION

9 (1) Any question—

- (a) whether the person is entitled to a shared additional pension (under section 55A of the 1992 Act) for any period after the certificate is issued, and
- (b) (if so) the rate at which the person is so entitled for the period,

is to be decided on the basis of the person attaining pensionable age on the same date as someone of the acquired gender (and the same age).

(2) Accordingly, if (immediately before the certificate is issued) the person—

- (a) is a woman entitled to a shared additional pension, but
- (b) has not attained the age of 65,

the person ceases to be so entitled when it is issued.

(3) And, conversely, if (immediately before the certificate is issued) the person—

- (a) is a man who has attained the age at which a woman of the same age attains pensionable age, but
- (b) has not attained the age of 65,

the person is to be treated for the purposes of section 55A of the 1992 Act as attaining pensionable age when it is issued.

(4) Paragraph 10 makes provision about deferment of shared additional pensions.

DEFERMENT OF PENSIONS

10 (1) The person's entitlement to—

- (a) a Category A retirement pension,
- (b) a Category B retirement pension, or
- (c) a shared additional pension,

is not to be taken to have been deferred for any period ending before the certificate is issued unless the condition in sub-paragraph (2) is satisfied.

(2) The condition is that the entitlement both—

(a) was actually deferred during the period, and
(b) would have been capable of being so deferred had the person's gender been the acquired gender.

CATEGORY C RETIREMENT PENSION FOR WIDOWS

11 If (immediately before the certificate is issued) the person is entitled to a Category C retirement pension under section 78(2) of the 1992 Act, the person is not entitled to that pension afterwards.

GRADUATED RETIREMENT BENEFIT: GREAT BRITAIN

12 (1) The provision that may be made by regulations under paragraph 15 of Schedule 3 to the Social Security (Consequential Provisions) Act 1992 (c 6) (power to retain provisions repealed by Social Security Act 1973 (c 38), with or without modification, for transitional purposes) includes provision modifying the preserved graduated retirement benefit provisions in consequence of this Act.

(2) "The preserved graduated retirement benefit provisions" are the provisions of the National Insurance Act 1965 (c 51) relating to graduated retirement benefit continued in force, with or without modification, by regulations having effect as if made under that paragraph.

GRADUATED RETIREMENT BENEFIT: NORTHERN IRELAND

13 (1) The provision that may be made by regulations under paragraph 15 of Schedule 3 to the Social Security (Consequential Provisions) (Northern Ireland) Act 1992 (c 9) (corresponding power for Northern Ireland) includes provision modifying the Northern Ireland preserved graduated retirement benefit provisions in consequence of this Act.

(2) "The Northern Ireland preserved graduated retirement benefit provisions" are the provisions of the National Insurance Act (Northern Ireland) 1966 (c 6 (NI)) relating to graduated retirement benefit continued in force, with or without modification, by regulations having effect as if made under that paragraph.

PART 3
OCCUPATIONAL PENSION SCHEMES

GUARANTEED MINIMUM PENSIONS ETC: GREAT BRITAIN

14 (1) In this paragraph "the 1993 Act" means the Pension Schemes Act 1993 (c 48); and expressions used in this paragraph and in that Act have the same meaning in this paragraph as in that Act.

(2) The fact that the person's gender has become the acquired gender does not affect the operation of section 14 of the 1993 Act (guaranteed minimum) in relation to the person, except to the extent that its operation depends on section 16 of the 1993 Act (revaluation); and sub-paragraphs (3) and (5) have effect subject to that.

(3) If (immediately before the certificate is issued) the person is a woman who is entitled to a guaranteed minimum pension but has not attained the age of 65—

(a) the person is for the purposes of section 13 of the 1993 Act and the guaranteed minimum pension provisions to be treated after it is issued as not having attained pensionable age (so that the entitlement ceases) but as attaining pensionable age on subsequently attaining the age of 65, and
(b) in a case where the person's guaranteed minimum pension has commenced before the certificate is issued, it is to be treated for the purposes of Chapter 3 of Part 4 of the 1993 Act (anti-franking) as if it had not.

(4) But sub-paragraph (3)(a) does not—
- (a) affect any pension previously paid to the person, or
- (b) prevent section 15 of the 1993 Act (increase of guaranteed minimum where commencement of guaranteed minimum pension postponed) operating to increase the person's guaranteed minimum by reason of a postponement of the commencement of the person's guaranteed minimum pension for a period ending before the certificate is issued.

(5) If (immediately before the certificate is issued) the person is a man who—
- (a) has attained the age of 60, but
- (b) has not attained the age of 65,

the person is to be treated for the purposes of section 13 of the 1993 Act and the guaranteed minimum pension provisions as attaining pensionable age when it is issued.

(6) If at that time the person has attained the age of 65, the fact that the person's gender has become the acquired gender does not affect the person's pensionable age for those purposes.

(7) The fact that the person's gender has become the acquired gender does not affect any guaranteed minimum pension to which the person is entitled as a widow or widower immediately before the certificate is issued (except in consequence of the operation of the previous provisions of this Schedule).

(8) If a transaction to which section 19 of the 1993 Act applies which is carried out before the certificate is issued discharges a liability to provide a guaranteed minimum pension for or in respect of the person, it continues to do so afterwards.

(9) "The guaranteed minimum pension provision" means so much of the 1993 Act (apart from section 13) and of any other enactment as relates to guaranteed minimum pensions.

GUARANTEED MINIMUM PENSIONS ETC: NORTHERN IRELAND

15 (1) In this paragraph "the 1993 Act" means the Pension Schemes (Northern Ireland) Act 1993 (c 49); and expressions used in this paragraph and in that Act have the same meaning in this paragraph as in that Act.

(2) The fact that the person's gender has become the acquired gender does not affect the operation of section 10 of the 1993 Act (guaranteed minimum) in relation to the person, except to the extent that its operation depends on section 12 of the 1993 Act (revaluation); and sub-paragraphs (3) and (5) have effect subject to that.

(3) If (immediately before the certificate is issued) the person is a woman who is entitled to a guaranteed minimum pension but has not attained the age of 65—
- (a) the person is for the purposes of section 9 of the 1993 Act and the guaranteed minimum pension provisions to be treated after it is issued as not having attained pensionable age (so that the entitlement ceases) but as attaining pensionable age on subsequently attaining the age of 65, and
- (b) in a case where the person's guaranteed minimum pension has commenced before the certificate is issued, it is to be treated for the purposes of Chapter 3 of Part 4 of the 1993 Act (anti-franking) as if it had not.

(4) But sub-paragraph (3)(a) does not—
- (a) affect any pension previously paid to the person, or
- (b) prevent section 11 of the 1993 Act (increase of guaranteed minimum where commencement of guaranteed minimum pension postponed) operating to increase the person's guaranteed minimum by reason of a postponement of the commencement of the person's guaranteed minimum pension for a period ending before the certificate is issued.

(5) If (immediately before the certificate is issued) the person is a man who—

(a) has attained the age of 60, but

(b) has not attained the age of 65,

the person is to be treated for the purposes of section 9 of the 1993 Act and the guaranteed minimum pension provisions as attaining pensionable age when it is issued.

(6) If at that time the person has attained the age of 65, the fact that the person's gender has become the acquired gender does not affect the person's pensionable age for those purposes.

(7) The fact that the person's gender has become the acquired gender does not affect any guaranteed minimum pension to which the person is entitled as a widow or widower immediately before the certificate is issued (except in consequence of the operation of the previous provisions of this Schedule).

(8) If a transaction to which section 15 of the 1993 Act applies which is carried out before the certificate is issued discharges a liability to provide a guaranteed minimum pension for or in respect of the person, it continues to do so afterwards.

(9) "The guaranteed minimum pension provision" means so much of the 1993 Act (apart from section 9) and of any other enactment as relates to guaranteed minimum pensions.

EQUIVALENT PENSION BENEFITS: GREAT BRITAIN

16 (1) The provision that may be made by regulations under paragraph 15 of Schedule 3 to the Social Security (Consequential Provisions) Act 1992 (c 6) (power to retain provisions repealed by Social Security Act 1973 (c 38), with or without modification, for transitional purposes) includes provision modifying the preserved equivalent pension benefits provisions in consequence of this Act.

(2) "The preserved equivalent pension benefits provisions" are the provisions of the National Insurance Act 1965 (c 51) relating to equivalent pension benefits continued in force, with or without modification, by regulations having effect as if made under that paragraph.

EQUIVALENT PENSION BENEFITS: NORTHERN IRELAND

17 (1) The provision that may be made by regulations under paragraph 15 of Schedule 3 to the Social Security (Consequential Provisions) (Northern Ireland) Act 1992 (c 9) (corresponding power for Northern Ireland) includes provision modifying the Northern Ireland preserved equivalent pension benefits provisions in consequence of this Act.

(2) "The Northern Ireland preserved equivalent pension benefits provisions" are the provisions of the National Insurance Act (Northern Ireland) 1966 (c 6 (NI)) relating to equivalent pension benefits continued in force, with or without modification, by regulations having effect as if made under that paragraph.

[560]

SCHEDULE 6
SEX DISCRIMINATION

Section 14

PART 1
GREAT BRITAIN

1 The Sex Discrimination Act 1975 (c 65) is amended as follows.

2 In section 7A (gender reassignment: exception for genuine occupational qualification), insert at the end—

"(4) Subsection (1) does not apply in relation to discrimination against a person whose gender has become the acquired gender under the Gender Recognition Act 2004."

3 In section 7B (supplementary exceptions relating to gender reassignment), for subsection (3) substitute—

"(3) Subsection (2) does not apply in relation to discrimination against a person whose gender has become the acquired gender under the Gender Recognition Act 2004."

4 In section 9 (discrimination against contract workers), after subsection (3C) insert—

"(3D) Subsections (3B) and (3C) do not apply in relation to discrimination against a person whose gender has become the acquired gender under the Gender Recognition Act 2004."

5 In section 11 (partnerships), after subsection (3C) insert—

"(3D) Subsections (3B) and (3C) do not apply in relation to discrimination against a person whose gender has become the acquired gender under the Gender Recognition Act 2004."

PART 2
NORTHERN IRELAND

6 The Sex Discrimination (Northern Ireland) Order 1976 (SI 1976/1042 (NI 15)) is amended as follows.

7 In Article 10A (gender reassignment: exception for genuine occupational qualification), insert at the end—

"(4) Paragraph (1) does not apply in relation to discrimination against a person whose gender has become the acquired gender under the Gender Recognition Act 2004."

8 In Article 10B (supplementary exceptions relating to gender reassignment), for paragraph (3) substitute—

"(3) Paragraph (2) does not apply in relation to discrimination against a person whose gender has become the acquired gender under the Gender Recognition Act 2004."

9 In Article 12 (discrimination against contract workers), after paragraph (3C) insert—

"(3D) Paragraphs (3B) and (3C) do not apply in relation to discrimination against a person whose gender has become the acquired gender under the Gender Recognition Act 2004."

10 In Article 14 (partnerships), after paragraph (3C) insert—

"(3D) Paragraphs (3B) and (3C) do not apply in relation to discrimination against a person whose gender has become the acquired gender under the Gender Recognition Act 2004."

[561]

MENTAL CAPACITY ACT 2005

2005 Chapter 9

ARRANGEMENT OF SECTIONS

PART 1
PERSONS WHO LACK CAPACITY

PART 2
THE COURT OF PROTECTION AND THE PUBLIC GUARDIAN

PART 3
MISCELLANEOUS AND GENERAL

An Act to make new provision relating to persons who lack capacity; to establish a superior court of record called the Court of Protection in place of the office of the Supreme Court called by that name; to make provision in connection with the Convention on the International Protection of Adults signed at the Hague on 13th January 2000; and for connected purposes.

[7th April 2005]

General Note

The Mental Capacity Act 2005 introduces a new framework for dealing with those who lack capacity and establishes a new Court of Protection as well as Lasting Powers of Attorney which replace Enduring Powers of Attorney. There are a number of substantial prospective amendments made by the Mental Health Act 2007 which are not yet in force and which are strictly outside the ambit of this work. Only those parts of the Act which relate to the subject matter of this work are included. The Act introduces for the first time powers to deal with the care and treatment of a person. *F v West Berkshire Health Authority* [1989] 2 All ER 545 drew public attention to the fact that English law possessed no procedure whereby a family member, a health authority, or even a court could make medical decisions on behalf of an incapacitated adult who was unable to make such decisions personally. However, those parts of the Act are not included as they do no impact on the ability of a person lacking capacity to deal with his property and affairs.

PART 1
PERSONS WHO LACK CAPACITY

THE PRINCIPLES

1 The principles

(1) The following principles apply for the purposes of this Act.

(2) A person must be assumed to have capacity unless it is established that he lacks capacity.

(3) A person is not to be treated as unable to make a decision unless all practicable steps to help him to do so have been taken without success.

(4) A person is not to be treated as unable to make a decision merely because he makes an unwise decision.

(5) An act done, or decision made, under this Act for or on behalf of a person who lacks capacity must be done, or made, in his best interests.

(6) Before the act is done, or the decision is made, regard must be had to whether the purpose for which it is needed can be as effectively achieved in a way that is less restrictive of the person's rights and freedom of action.

Commentary

This section introduces a new approach to the assessment of a person's capacity. Everyone is presumed to have capacity unless established otherwise. Note in subsection (3) the requirement for steps to help the person to make a decision have been taken. The impact that this provision will have on day to day legal transactions such as making a Will are not entirely clear. Subsection (5) sets out the principle that acts done and decisions made on behalf of those lacking capacity must in their best interests as to which see s 4 below.

[562]

PRELIMINARY

2 People who lack capacity

(1) For the purposes of this Act, a person lacks capacity in relation to a matter if at the material time he is unable to make a decision for himself in relation to the matter because of an impairment of, or a disturbance in the functioning of, the mind or brain.

(2) It does not matter whether the impairment or disturbance is permanent or temporary.

(3) A lack of capacity cannot be established merely by reference to—
  (a) a person's age or appearance, or
  (b) a condition of his, or an aspect of his behaviour, which might lead others to make unjustified assumptions about his capacity.

(4) In proceedings under this Act or any other enactment, any question whether a person lacks capacity within the meaning of this Act must be decided on the balance of probabilities.

(5) No power which a person ("D") may exercise under this Act—
  (a) in relation to a person who lacks capacity, or
  (b) where D reasonably thinks that a person lacks capacity,
is exercisable in relation to a person under 16.

(6) Subsection (5) is subject to section 18(3).

Commentary
Subsection (1) sets out the statutory test of capacity. It is clear that the test is issue specific which mirrors the common law position as set out in cases such as *Masterman-Lister v Bruton & Co.* [2003] 3 All ER 162. The statutory test applies to all acts and decisions but it seems likely that the common law tests such as the *Banks v Goodfellow* test for making a Will will continue to apply. In *Carlo Saulle v Olivier Nouvet* [2007] EWHC 2902 (QB) it was held that the test in this section applied only to decisions made by the Court of Protection but there may be doubt as to whether that is correct. In many cases the issue will be academic because the common law tests for capacity are indistinguishable from the statutory test, see: *Local Authority X v (1) MM (by her litigation friend the official solicitor) (2) KM* [2007] EWHC 2003 (Fam). The inability must be caused by an impairment or disturbance of the mind—a diagnostic test. Subsection (5) should be read subject to s 18(3) below which provides that in respect of the powers which the Court of Protection has to manage property and affairs, may be exercised even though a person has not reached 16, if the court considers it likely that he will still lack capacity to make decisions in respect of that matter when he reaches 18. The subsection introduces the concept of "D"—the person making the decision in relation to a person who lacks capacity.

[563]

3 Inability to make decisions

(1) For the purposes of section 2, a person is unable to make a decision for himself if he is unable—
  (a) to understand the information relevant to the decision,
  (b) to retain that information,
  (c) to use or weigh that information as part of the process of making the decision, or

(d) to communicate his decision (whether by talking, using sign language or any other means).

(2) A person is not to be regarded as unable to understand the information relevant to a decision if he is able to understand an explanation of it given to him in a way that is appropriate to his circumstances (using simple language, visual aids or any other means).

(3) The fact that a person is able to retain the information relevant to a decision for a short period only does not prevent him from being regarded as able to make the decision.

(4) The information relevant to a decision includes information about the reasonably foreseeable consequences of—

(a) deciding one way or another, or

(b) failing to make the decision.

Commentary

This section provides specific guidance on how capacity is to be assessed and again follows the approach which the courts have tended to apply in cases such as *Masterman-Lister v Bruton & Co.* [2003] 3 All ER 162. Subsection 1(d) covers a small category of persons with locked in syndrome. The emphasis again is on a person being provided with assistance to reach a decision.

[564]

4 Best interests

(1) In determining for the purposes of this Act what is in a person's best interests, the person making the determination must not make it merely on the basis of—

(a) the person's age or appearance, or

(b) a condition of his, or an aspect of his behaviour, which might lead others to make unjustified assumptions about what might be in his best interests.

(2) The person making the determination must consider all the relevant circumstances and, in particular, take the following steps.

(3) He must consider—

(a) whether it is likely that the person will at some time have capacity in relation to the matter in question, and

(b) if it appears likely that he will, when that is likely to be.

(4) He must, so far as reasonably practicable, permit and encourage the person to participate, or to improve his ability to participate, as fully as possible in any act done for him and any decision affecting him.

(5) Where the determination relates to life-sustaining treatment he must not, in considering whether the treatment is in the best interests of the person concerned, be motivated by a desire to bring about his death.

(6) He must consider, so far as is reasonably ascertainable—

(a) the person's past and present wishes and feelings (and, in particular, any relevant written statement made by him when he had capacity),

(b) the beliefs and values that would be likely to influence his decision if he had capacity, and

(c) the other factors that he would be likely to consider if he were able to do so.

(7) He must take into account, if it is practicable and appropriate to consult them, the views of—

(a) anyone named by the person as someone to be consulted on the matter in question or on matters of that kind,

(b) anyone engaged in caring for the person or interested in his welfare,

(c) any donee of a lasting power of attorney granted by the person, and
(d) any deputy appointed for the person by the court,

as to what would be in the person's best interests and, in particular, as to the matters mentioned in subsection (6).

(8) The duties imposed by subsections (1) to (7) also apply in relation to the exercise of any powers which—

(a) are exercisable under a lasting power of attorney, or
(b) are exercisable by a person under this Act where he reasonably believes that another person lacks capacity.

(9) In the case of an act done, or a decision made, by a person other than the court, there is sufficient compliance with this section if (having complied with the requirements of subsections (1) to (7)) he reasonably believes that what he does or decides is in the best interests of the person concerned.

(10) "Life-sustaining treatment" means treatment which in the view of a person providing health care for the person concerned is necessary to sustain life.

(11) "Relevant circumstances" are those—

(a) of which the person making the determination is aware, and
(b) which it would be reasonable to regard as relevant.

Commentary

This section explains the concept of best interests. The test does not involve substituted judgment i.e. what the person would have wanted if he had capacity but is an objective test. Note the involvement of P in the decision making process even if lacking capacity. See: *Local Authority X v (1) MM (by her litigation friend the official solicitor) (2) KM* [2007] EWHC 2003 (Fam) for an example of the application of these principles.

[565]

7 Payment for necessary goods and services

(1) If necessary goods or services are supplied to a person who lacks capacity to contract for the supply, he must pay a reasonable price for them.

(2) "Necessary" means suitable to a person's condition in life and to his actual requirements at the time when the goods or services are supplied.

Commentary

This section revises and extends the statutory rule contained in s 3(2) of the Sale of Good Act 1979 which applies to necessary goods. In general terms a contract entered into by a person who lacks capacity to contract is voidable if the other person knew or must be taken to have known of the lack of capacity but that rule does not apply to the supply of "necessaries".

[566]

LASTING POWERS OF ATTORNEY

9 Lasting powers of attorney

(1) A lasting power of attorney is a power of attorney under which the donor ("P") confers on the donee (or donees) authority to make decisions about all or any of the following—

(a) P's personal welfare or specified matters concerning P's personal welfare, and
(b) P's property and affairs or specified matters concerning P's property and affairs,

and which includes authority to make such decisions in circumstances where P no longer has capacity.

(2) A lasting power of attorney is not created unless—

(a) section 10 is complied with,
(b) an instrument conferring authority of the kind mentioned in subsection (1) is made and registered in accordance with Schedule 1, and
(c) at the time when P executes the instrument, P has reached 18 and has capacity to execute it.

(3) An instrument which—
(a) purports to create a lasting power of attorney, but
(b) does not comply with this section, section 10 or Schedule 1,

confers no authority.

(4) The authority conferred by a lasting power of attorney is subject to—
(a) the provisions of this Act and, in particular, sections 1 (the principles) and 4 (best interests), and
(b) any conditions or restrictions specified in the instrument.

Commentary
Lasting Powers of Attorney replace Enduring Powers of Attorney. No new Enduring Powers of Attorney can be created after this Act came into force on 1 October 2007, There are transitional provisions which provide for the operation and registration of all Enduring Powers of Attorney created before the Act comes into force and these will remain important for some time, as to which see Sch 4. Note that Lasting Powers have to be in the form set out in Sch 1 which makes detailed provisions about the making and registration of the instrument and see the notes to that schedule. See also the Lasting Power of Attorney, Enduring Powers of Attorney and Public Guardian Regulations 2007 (SI 2007/1253) **[Appendix VIII]** and in particular Part 2.

[567]

10 Appointment of donees

(1) A donee of a lasting power of attorney must be—
(a) an individual who has reached 18, or
(b) if the power relates only to P's property and affairs, either such an individual or a trust corporation.

(2) An individual who is bankrupt may not be appointed as donee of a lasting power of attorney in relation to P's property and affairs.

(3) Subsections (4) to (7) apply in relation to an instrument under which two or more persons are to act as donees of a lasting power of attorney.

(4) The instrument may appoint them to act—
(a) jointly,
(b) jointly and severally, or
(c) jointly in respect of some matters and jointly and severally in respect of others.

(5) To the extent to which it does not specify whether they are to act jointly or jointly and severally, the instrument is to be assumed to appoint them to act jointly.

(6) If they are to act jointly, a failure, as respects one of them, to comply with the requirements of subsection (1) or (2) or Part 1 or 2 of Schedule 1 prevents a lasting power of attorney from being created.

(7) If they are to act jointly and severally, a failure, as respects one of them, to comply with the requirements of subsection (1) or (2) or Part 1 or 2 of Schedule 1—
(a) prevents the appointment taking effect in his case, but
(b) does not prevent a lasting power of attorney from being created in the case of the other or others.

(8) An instrument used to create a lasting power of attorney—
(a) cannot give the donee (or, if more than one, any of them) power to appoint a substitute or successor, but

(b) may itself appoint a person to replace the donee (or, if more than one, any of them) on the occurrence of an event mentioned in section 13(6)(a) to (d) which has the effect of terminating the donee's appointment.

Commentary

This section provides the restrictions on who can be a donee. Note that a trust corporation can only act if the power is limited to property and affairs and not about what might be termed welfare decisions. For the meaning of trust corporation see section 68(1) of the Trustee Act 1925 **[138]**. This section provides the donees can be appointed to act jointly, or jointly and severally and in relation to specific matters. The default position (subsection (5) is that they will be assumed to be appointed jointly. The donor cannot delegate the power of appointing a successor to the donee but can himself specify who should succeed him in the event of termination of the attorneyship.

[568]

12 Scope of lasting powers of attorney: gifts

(1) Where a lasting power of attorney confers authority to make decisions about P's property and affairs, it does not authorise a donee (or, if more than one, any of them) to dispose of the donor's property by making gifts except to the extent permitted by subsection (2).

(2) The donee may make gifts—

(a) on customary occasions to persons (including himself) who are related to or connected with the donor, or

(b) to any charity to whom the donor made or might have been expected to make gifts,

if the value of each such gift is not unreasonable having regard to all the circumstances and, in particular, the size of the donor's estate.

(3) "Customary occasion" means—

(a) the occasion or anniversary of a birth, a marriage or the formation of a civil partnership, or

(b) any other occasion on which presents are customarily given within families or among friends or associates.

(4) Subsection (2) is subject to any conditions or restrictions in the instrument.

Commentary

This section mirrors section 3(5) of the Enduring Powers of Attorney Act 1985 and is an important restriction on the use of the power. Under section 3(5) it was commented that the power is very limited and does not extend to inheritance tax planning (see *Re W (Enduring Power of Attorney)* [2000] Ch 233 on appeal at [2001] Ch 609) and see *Brown Shipley Trust Co. v Holland* [2004] WTLR 321.

[569]

13 Revocation of lasting powers of attorney etc

(1) This section applies if—

(a) P has executed an instrument with a view to creating a lasting power of attorney, or

(b) a lasting power of attorney is registered as having been conferred by P,

and in this section references to revoking the power include revoking the instrument.

(2) P may, at any time when he has capacity to do so, revoke the power.

(3) P's bankruptcy revokes the power so far as it relates to P's property and affairs.

(4) But where P is bankrupt merely because an interim bankruptcy restrictions order has effect in respect of him, the power is suspended, so far as it relates to P's property and affairs, for so long as the order has effect.

(5) The occurrence in relation to a donee of an event mentioned in subsection (6)—
- (a) terminates his appointment, and
- (b) except in the cases given in subsection (7), revokes the power.

(6) The events are—
- (a) the disclaimer of the appointment by the donee in accordance with such requirements as may be prescribed for the purposes of this section in regulations made by the Lord Chancellor,
- (b) subject to subsections (8) and (9), the death or bankruptcy of the donee or, if the donee is a trust corporation, its winding-up or dissolution,
- (c) subject to subsection (11), the dissolution or annulment of a marriage or civil partnership between the donor and the donee,
- (d) the lack of capacity of the donee.

(7) The cases are—
- (a) the donee is replaced under the terms of the instrument,
- (b) he is one of two or more persons appointed to act as donees jointly and severally in respect of any matter and, after the event, there is at least one remaining donee.

(8) The bankruptcy of a donee does not terminate his appointment, or revoke the power, in so far as his authority relates to P's personal welfare.

(9) Where the donee is bankrupt merely because an interim bankruptcy restrictions order has effect in respect of him, his appointment and the power are suspended, so far as they relate to P's property and affairs, for so long as the order has effect.

(10) Where the donee is one of two or more appointed to act jointly and severally under the power in respect of any matter, the reference in subsection (9) to the suspension of the power is to its suspension in so far as it relates to that donee.

(11) The dissolution or annulment of a marriage or civil partnership does not terminate the appointment of a donee, or revoke the power, if the instrument provided that it was not to do so.

Commentary

This section specifies the circumstances in which a Lasting Power of Attorney will come to an end whether before or after registration. Bankruptcy includes in respect of an individual any time when a bankruptcy restriction order is in force in relation to him within the meaning of Sch 4A to the Insolvency Act 1986 (see s 64(3)) whereas interim bankruptcy restriction orders have suspensory effect (see sub-s (4) and (9).

[570]

14 Protection of donee and others if no power created or power revoked

(1) Subsections (2) and (3) apply if—
- (a) an instrument has been registered under Schedule 1 as a lasting power of attorney, but
- (b) a lasting power of attorney was not created,

whether or not the registration has been cancelled at the time of the act or transaction in question.

(2) A donee who acts in purported exercise of the power does not incur any liability (to P or any other person) because of the non-existence of the power unless at the time of acting he—
- (a) knows that a lasting power of attorney was not created, or
- (b) is aware of circumstances which, if a lasting power of attorney had been created, would have terminated his authority to act as a donee.

(3) Any transaction between the donee and another person is, in favour of that person, as valid as if the power had been in existence, unless at the time of the transaction that person has knowledge of a matter referred to in subsection (2).

(4) If the interest of a purchaser depends on whether a transaction between the donee and the other person was valid by virtue of subsection (3), it is conclusively presumed in favour of the purchaser that the transaction was valid if—

(a) the transaction was completed within 12 months of the date on which the instrument was registered, or

(b) the other person makes a statutory declaration, before or within 3 months after the completion of the purchase, that he had no reason at the time of the transaction to doubt that the donee had authority to dispose of the property which was the subject of the transaction.

(5) In its application to a lasting power of attorney which relates to matters in addition to P's property and affairs, section 5 of the Powers of Attorney Act 1971 (c 27) (protection where power is revoked) has effect as if references to revocation included the cessation of the power in relation to P's property and affairs.

(6) Where two or more donees are appointed under a lasting power of attorney, this section applies as if references to the donee were to all or any of them.

Commentary

This section provides some protection to donees of a lasting power and purchasers in the event that the power is not in fact valid unless they have knowledge that is the case.

[571]

GENERAL POWERS OF THE COURT AND APPOINTMENT OF DEPUTIES

15 Power to make declarations

(1) The court may make declarations as to—

(a) whether a person has or lacks capacity to make a decision specified in the declaration;

(b) whether a person has or lacks capacity to make decisions on such matters as are described in the declaration;

(c) the lawfulness or otherwise of any act done, or yet to be done, in relation to that person.

(2) "Act" includes an omission and a course of conduct.

Commentary

This section will probably be used mostly in respect of welfare decisions but there is no reason why in principle it could not be used to obtain a declaration as to a person's testamentary capacity or capacity to enter into any legal transaction. The difficulties in using the section in that way are more practical ones—Who would make the application? Who would be joined to it?

[572]

16 Powers to make decisions and appoint deputies: general

(1) This section applies if a person ("P") lacks capacity in relation to a matter or matters concerning—

(a) P's personal welfare, or

(b) P's property and affairs.

(2) The court may—

(a) by making an order, make the decision or decisions on P's behalf in relation to the matter or matters, or

(b) appoint a person (a "deputy") to make decisions on P's behalf in relation to the matter or matters.

(3) The powers of the court under this section are subject to the provisions of this Act and, in particular, to sections 1 (the principles) and 4 (best interests).

(4) When deciding whether it is in P's best interests to appoint a deputy, the court must have regard (in addition to the matters mentioned in section 4) to the principles that—

(a) a decision by the court is to be preferred to the appointment of a deputy to make a decision, and

(b) the powers conferred on a deputy should be as limited in scope and duration as is reasonably practicable in the circumstances.

(5) The court may make such further orders or give such directions, and confer on a deputy such powers or impose on him such duties, as it thinks necessary or expedient for giving effect to, or otherwise in connection with, an order or appointment made by it under subsection (2).

(6) Without prejudice to section 4, the court may make the order, give the directions or make the appointment on such terms as it considers are in P's best interests, even though no application is before the court for an order, directions or an appointment on those terms.

(7) An order of the court may be varied or discharged by a subsequent order.

(8) The court may, in particular, revoke the appointment of a deputy or vary the powers conferred on him if it is satisfied that the deputy—

(a) has behaved, or is behaving, in a way that contravenes the authority conferred on him by the court or is not in P's best interests, or

(b) proposes to behave in a way that would contravene that authority or would not be in P's best interests.

Commentary

The system of the Court of Protection appointing receivers to manage the property and affairs of someone incapable of doing so has been replaced by the power of the Court to appoint a deputy not just to manage the property and affairs of P but also to make welfare decisions. Existing receivers appointed under Part VII of the Mental Health Act 1983 will be converted to deputies (Sch 5). As to the nature of such decisions see section 17 below. The power is also conferred by this section on the Court of Protection to make welfare decisions on P's behalf which is an entirely new power. These powers cannot be exercised so as to be inconsistent with Article 8 of the ECHR and the Act does not allow a person to be detained or physically transported to a particular place and see: *Local Authority X v (1) MM (by her litigation friend the official solicitor) (2) KM* [2007] EWHC 2003 (Fam). The Court may therefore decide where a person is to live, but it remains unclear what powers the Court will have to bring a person to that particular place. The preference set out in subsection 4(a) is for the Court of Protection to make decisions on behalf of someone who is incapable to doing so, thus reflecting the issue specific nature of deciding whether someone has capacity in any particular case. However this procedure recognises that there may be circumstances where the Court should albeit to a limited extent delegate its powers to a deputy. As to who can be a deputy see section 19. The limits to which its powers can be delegated are set out in section 20. Sub-s (7) is subject to para 6 of Sch 2.

[573]

18 Section 16 powers: property and affairs

(1) The powers under section 16 as respects P's property and affairs extend in particular to—

(a) the control and management of P's property;

(b) the sale, exchange, charging, gift or other disposition of P's property;

(c) the acquisition of property in P's name or on P's behalf;

(d) the carrying on, on P's behalf, of any profession, trade or business;

(e) the taking of a decision which will have the effect of dissolving a partnership of which P is a member;
(f) the carrying out of any contract entered into by P;
(g) the discharge of P's debts and of any of P's obligations, whether legally enforceable or not;
(h) the settlement of any of P's property, whether for P's benefit or for the benefit of others;
(i) the execution for P of a will;
(j) the exercise of any power (including a power to consent) vested in P whether beneficially or as trustee or otherwise;
(k) the conduct of legal proceedings in P's name or on P's behalf.

(2) No will may be made under subsection (1)(i) at a time when P has not reached 18.

(3) The powers under section 16 as respects any other matter relating to P's property and affairs may be exercised even though P has not reached 16, if the court considers it likely that P will still lack capacity to make decisions in respect of that matter when he reaches 18.

(4) Schedule 2 supplements the provisions of this section.

(5) Section 16(7) (variation and discharge of court orders) is subject to paragraph 6 of Schedule 2.

(6) Subsection (1) is subject to section 20 (restrictions on deputies).

Commentary

The powers contained in section 18 are broadly similar to those contained in section 96 of the Mental Health Act 1983. The Court's powers under section 18 can be exercised by the Court as "one off" decisions, whether or not a deputy has been appointed or a Lasting Power of Attorney has been created. However a deputy cannot be authorised to settle any of P's property, whether for P's benefit or for the benefit of others, execute a will for P or exercise any power (including a power to consent) vested in P whether beneficially or as trustee or otherwise (see section 20). Those matters have to be dealt with by the Court of Protection. One of the most frequently used powers under the old regime was the power of the Court of Protection to make a statutory will for someone lacking testamentary capacity and it is anticipated the principles applicable to that will remain.

[574]

19 Appointment of deputies

(1) A deputy appointed by the court must be—
(a) an individual who has reached 18, or
(b) as respects powers in relation to property and affairs, an individual who has reached 18 or a trust corporation.

(2) The court may appoint an individual by appointing the holder for the time being of a specified office or position.

(3) A person may not be appointed as a deputy without his consent.

(4) The court may appoint two or more deputies to act—
(a) jointly,
(b) jointly and severally, or
(c) jointly in respect of some matters and jointly and severally in respect of others.

(5) When appointing a deputy or deputies, the court may at the same time appoint one or more other persons to succeed the existing deputy or those deputies—
(a) in such circumstances, or on the happening of such events, as may be specified by the court;
(b) for such period as may be so specified.

(6) A deputy is to be treated as P's agent in relation to anything done or decided by him within the scope of his appointment and in accordance with this Part.

(7) The deputy is entitled—
- (a) to be reimbursed out of P's property for his reasonable expenses in discharging his functions, and
- (b) if the court so directs when appointing him, to remuneration out of P's property for discharging them.

(8) The court may confer on a deputy powers to—
- (a) take possession or control of all or any specified part of P's property;
- (b) exercise all or any specified powers in respect of it, including such powers of investment as the court may determine.

(9) The court may require a deputy—
- (a) to give to the Public Guardian such security as the court thinks fit for the due discharge of his functions, and
- (b) to submit to the Public Guardian such reports at such times or at such intervals as the court may direct.

Commentary

For the meaning of trust corporation see s 68(1) of the Trustee Act 1925 **[138]**. Trust corporations can only be appointed as deputies in respect of P's property and affairs. A successor can be appointed by the Court (sub-s (5)). Sub-s (6) reflects the case law in respect of receivers appointed under the Mental health Act 1983.

[575]

20 Restrictions on deputies

(1) A deputy does not have power to make a decision on behalf of P in relation to a matter if he knows or has reasonable grounds for believing that P has capacity in relation to the matter.

(2) Nothing in section 16(5) or 17 permits a deputy to be given power—
- (a) to prohibit a named person from having contact with P;
- (b) to direct a person responsible for P's health care to allow a different person to take over that responsibility.

(3) A deputy may not be given powers with respect to—
- (a) the settlement of any of P's property, whether for P's benefit or for the benefit of others,
- (b) the execution for P of a will, or
- (c) the exercise of any power (including a power to consent) vested in P whether beneficially or as trustee or otherwise.

(4) A deputy may not be given power to make a decision on behalf of P which is inconsistent with a decision made, within the scope of his authority and in accordance with this Act, by the donee of a lasting power of attorney granted by P (or, if there is more than one donee, by any of them).

(5) A deputy may not refuse consent to the carrying out or continuation of life-sustaining treatment in relation to P.

(6) The authority conferred on a deputy is subject to the provisions of this Act and, in particular, sections 1 (the principles) and 4 (best interests).

(7) A deputy may not do an act that is intended to restrain P unless four conditions are satisfied.

(8) The first condition is that, in doing the act, the deputy is acting within the scope of an authority expressly conferred on him by the court.

(9) The second is that P lacks, or the deputy reasonably believes that P lacks, capacity in relation to the matter in question.

(10) The third is that the deputy reasonably believes that it is necessary to do the act in order to prevent harm to P.

(11) The fourth is that the act is a proportionate response to—

(a) the likelihood of P's suffering harm, *or* [and]

(b) the seriousness of that harm.

(12) For the purposes of this section, a deputy restrains P if he—

(a) uses, or threatens to use, force to secure the doing of an act which P resists, or

(b) restricts P's liberty of movement, whether or not P resists,

or if he authorises another person to do any of those things.

(13) But a deputy does more than merely restrain P if he deprives P of his liberty within the meaning of Article 5(1) of the Human Rights Convention (whether or not the deputy is a public authority).

Amendment

Sub-s (11): word "or" in italics repealed and subsequent word in square brackets substituted, from a date to be appointed, by Mental Health Act 2007, s 51.
Sub-s (13): repealed, from a date to be appointed, by Mental Health Act 2007, ss 50(1), (4)(c), 55, Sch 11, Pt 10.

Commentary

The first and important point a deputy needs to take into account is whether P had capacity to make a particular decision (sub-s (1). The section then circumscribes the decisions which a deputy can take. Subsection (5) prevents a deputy from making life and death decisions about the treatment of P. Those issues are reserved to the Court of Protection and Rule 86 of the Court of Protection Rules 2007 (SI 2007/1744 (L 12)) provides that the court will consider whether the application is of a type specified in the relevant practice direction as being one which must be dealt with by the President, the Vice-President, or one of the nominated puisne judges of the High Court. See also Practice Direction 09E.

[576]

21 Transfer of proceedings relating to people under 18

[(1)] The [Lord Chief Justice, with the concurrence of the Lord Chancellor,] may by order make provision as to the transfer of proceedings relating to a person under 18, in such circumstances as are specified in the order—

(a) from the Court of Protection to a court having jurisdiction under the Children Act 1989 (c 41), or

(b) from a court having jurisdiction under that Act to the Court of Protection.

[(2) The Lord Chief Justice may nominate any of the following to exercise his functions under this section—

(a) the President of the Court of Protection;

(b) a judicial office holder (as defined in section 109(4) of the Constitutional Reform Act 2005).]

Amendment

Sub-s (1): numbered as such by SI 2006/1016, art 2, Sch 1, paras 30, 31(1), (2).
Sub-s (1): words "Lord Chief Justice, with the concurrence of the Lord Chancellor," in square brackets substituted by SI 2006/1016, art 2, Sch 1, paras 30, 31(1), (3).
Sub-s (2): inserted by SI 2006/1016, art 2, Sch 1, paras 30, 31(1), (4).

Commentary

See the Mental Capacity Act 2005 (Transfer of Proceedings Order) 2007 (SI 2007/1899) **[Appendix VIII]**.

[577]

[POWERS OF THE COURT IN RELATION TO SCHEDULE A1]

POWERS OF THE COURT IN RELATION TO LASTING POWERS OF ATTORNEY

22 Powers of court in relation to validity of lasting powers of attorney

(1) This section and section 23 apply if—
- (a) a person ("P") has executed or purported to execute an instrument with a view to creating a lasting power of attorney, or
- (b) an instrument has been registered as a lasting power of attorney conferred by P.

(2) The court may determine any question relating to—
- (a) whether one or more of the requirements for the creation of a lasting power of attorney have been met;
- (b) whether the power has been revoked or has otherwise come to an end.

(3) Subsection (4) applies if the court is satisfied—
- (a) that fraud or undue pressure was used to induce P—
  - (i) to execute an instrument for the purpose of creating a lasting power of attorney, or
  - (ii) to create a lasting power of attorney, or
- (b) that the donee (or, if more than one, any of them) of a lasting power of attorney—
  - (i) has behaved, or is behaving, in a way that contravenes his authority or is not in P's best interests, or
  - (ii) proposes to behave in a way that would contravene his authority or would not be in P's best interests.

(4) The court may—
- (a) direct that an instrument purporting to create the lasting power of attorney is not to be registered, or
- (b) if P lacks capacity to do so, revoke the instrument or the lasting power of attorney.

(5) If there is more than one donee, the court may under subsection (4)(b) revoke the instrument or the lasting power of attorney so far as it relates to any of them.

(6) "Donee" includes an intended donee.

Commentary

Unlike Enduring Powers of Attorney the registration took place when the donor was becoming incapable. Lasting Powers of Attorney are registered at any time and the donor can apply as well as the donee. This section enables the Court of Protection to direct that an invalidly created power should not be registered or should be revoked. Some of the grounds such as fraud and undue pressure were grounds for objection to the registration of Enduring Powers.

[578]

23 Powers of court in relation to operation of lasting powers of attorney

(1) The court may determine any question as to the meaning or effect of a lasting power of attorney or an instrument purporting to create one.

(2) The court may—
- (a) give directions with respect to decisions—
  - (i) which the donee of a lasting power of attorney has authority to make, and
  - (ii) which P lacks capacity to make;
- (b) give any consent or authorisation to act which the donee would have to obtain from P if P had capacity to give it.

(3) The court may, if P lacks capacity to do so—

(a) give directions to the donee with respect to the rendering by him of reports or accounts and the production of records kept by him for that purpose;

(b) require the donee to supply information or produce documents or things in his possession as donee;

(c) give directions with respect to the remuneration or expenses of the donee;

(d) relieve the donee wholly or partly from any liability which he has or may have incurred on account of a breach of his duties as donee.

(4) The court may authorise the making of gifts which are not within section 12(2) (permitted gifts).

(5) Where two or more donees are appointed under a lasting power of attorney, this section applies as if references to the donee were to all or any of them.

Commentary

This section defines the functions of the Court of Protection once a Lasting Power is in place and these are similar to those which the Court of Protection exercised (and indeed will continue to exercise) in respect Enduring Powers of Attorney once registered. As under the old section the court can relieve the restrictions on making gifts under s 12(2), but the old principle will almost certainly apply that it cannot override any restriction contained in the power itself, see *Re R (Enduring Power of Attorney)* [1991] 1 FLR 128.

[579]

MISCELLANEOUS AND SUPPLEMENTARY

42 Codes of practice

(1) The Lord Chancellor must prepare and issue one or more codes of practice—

(a) for the guidance of persons assessing whether a person has capacity in relation to any matter,

(b) for the guidance of persons acting in connection with the care or treatment of another person (see section 5),

(c) for the guidance of donees of lasting powers of attorney,

(d) for the guidance of deputies appointed by the court,

(e) for the guidance of persons carrying out research in reliance on any provision made by or under this Act (and otherwise with respect to sections 30 to 34),

(f) for the guidance of independent mental capacity advocates,

[(fa) for the guidance of persons exercising functions under Schedule A1,

(fb) for the guidance of representatives appointed under Part 10 of Schedule A1,]

(g) with respect to the provisions of sections 24 to 26 (advance decisions and apparent advance decisions), and

(h) with respect to such other matters concerned with this Act as he thinks fit.

(2) The Lord Chancellor may from time to time revise a code.

(3) The Lord Chancellor may delegate the preparation or revision of the whole or any part of a code so far as he considers expedient.

(4) It is the duty of a person to have regard to any relevant code if he is acting in relation to a person who lacks capacity and is doing so in one or more of the following ways—

(a) as the donee of a lasting power of attorney,

(b) as a deputy appointed by the court,

(c) as a person carrying out research in reliance on any provision made by or under this Act (see sections 30 to 34),

(d) as an independent mental capacity advocate,

[(da) in the exercise of functions under Schedule A1,
(db) as a representative appointed under Part 10 of Schedule A1,]
(e) in a professional capacity,
(f) for remuneration.

(5) If it appears to a court or tribunal conducting any criminal or civil proceedings that—

(a) a provision of a code, or
(b) a failure to comply with a code,

is relevant to a question arising in the proceedings, the provision or failure must be taken into account in deciding the question.

(6) A code under subsection (1)(d) may contain separate guidance for deputies appointed by virtue of paragraph 1(2) of Schedule 5 (functions of deputy conferred on receiver appointed under the Mental Health Act).

(7) In this section and in section 43, "code" means a code prepared or revised under this section.

Amendment
Sub-s (1): sub-paras (fa), (fb) inserted, as from a date to be appointed, by the Mental Health Act 2007, s 50(7), Sch 9, Pt 1, paras 1, 8.
Sub-s (4): sub-paras (da), (db) inserted, as from a date to be appointed, by the Mental Health Act 2007, s 50(7), Sch 9, Pt 1, paras 1, 8.

Commentary
Reference should be made to the Mental Capacity Act 2005 Code of Practice.

[580]

43 Codes of practice: procedure

(1) Before preparing or revising a code, the Lord Chancellor must consult—

(a) the National Assembly for Wales, and
(b) such other persons as he considers appropriate.

(2) The Lord Chancellor may not issue a code unless—

(a) a draft of the code has been laid by him before both Houses of Parliament, and
(b) the 40 day period has elapsed without either House resolving not to approve the draft.

(3) The Lord Chancellor must arrange for any code that he has issued to be published in such a way as he considers appropriate for bringing it to the attention of persons likely to be concerned with its provisions.

(4) "40 day period", in relation to the draft of a proposed code, means—

(a) if the draft is laid before one House on a day later than the day on which it is laid before the other House, the period of 40 days beginning with the later of the two days;
(b) in any other case, the period of 40 days beginning with the day on which it is laid before each House.

(5) In calculating the period of 40 days, no account is to be taken of any period during which Parliament is dissolved or prorogued or during which both Houses are adjourned for more than 4 days.

Commentary
See the notes to s 42.

[581]

PART 2
THE COURT OF PROTECTION AND THE PUBLIC GUARDIAN

THE COURT OF PROTECTION

45 The Court of Protection

(1) There is to be a superior court of record known as the Court of Protection.

(2) The court is to have an official seal.

(3) The court may sit at any place in England and Wales, on any day and at any time.

(4) The court is to have a central office and registry at a place appointed by the Lord Chancellor[, after consulting the Lord Chief Justice].

(5) The Lord Chancellor may[, after consulting the Lord Chief Justice,] designate as additional registries of the court any district registry of the High Court and any county court office.

[(5A) The Lord Chief Justice may nominate any of the following to exercise his functions under this section—

(a) the President of the Court of Protection;

(b) a judicial office holder (as defined in section 109(4) of the Constitutional Reform Act 2005).]

(6) The office of the Supreme Court called the Court of Protection ceases to exist.

Amendment

Sub-s (4): words ", after consulting the Lord Chief Justice" in square brackets inserted by SI 2006/1016, art 2, Sch 1, paras 30, 32(1), (2).
Sub-s (5) words ", after consulting the Lord Chief Justice," in square brackets inserted by SI 2006/1016, art 2, Sch 1, paras 30, 32(1), (3).
Sub-s (5A): inserted by SI 2006/1016, art 2, Sch 1, paras 30, 32(1), (4).

Commentary

This crucial section established the new Court of Protection which came into being on 1 October 2007. The new Court of Protection is a superior court of record, which will have the same powers, rights, privileges and authority as the High Court as opposed to the old Court which was a creature of statute. For the rules governing procedure see the Court of Protection Rules 2007 (SI 2007/1744). The Court is enabled to sit anywhere in England and Wales whereas formerly there was Court sittings in London and Preston. The following venues have been designated for Court of Protection hearings with effect from 1 October 2007: Birmingham, Bristol, Cardiff, Manchester, Newcastle-upon-Tyne and Preston. More may be added in the future.

[582]

46 The judges of the Court of Protection

(1) Subject to Court of Protection Rules under section 51(2)(d), the jurisdiction of the court is exercisable by a judge nominated for that purpose by—

(a) the [Lord Chief Justice], or

[(b) where nominated by the Lord Chief Justice to act on his behalf under this subsection—

(i) the President of the Court of Protection; or

(ii) a judicial office holder (as defined in section 109(4) of the Constitutional Reform Act 2005)].

(2) To be nominated, a judge must be—

(a) the President of the Family Division,

(b) the Vice-Chancellor,

(c) a puisne judge of the High Court,

(d) a circuit judge, or

(e) a district judge.

(3) The [Lord Chief Justice, after consulting the Lord Chancellor,] must—

(a) appoint one of the judges nominated by virtue of subsection (2)(a) to (c) to be President of the Court of Protection, and

(b) appoint another of those judges to be Vice-President of the Court of Protection.

(4) The [Lord Chief Justice, after consulting the Lord Chancellor,] must appoint one of the judges nominated by virtue of subsection (2)(d) or (e) to be Senior Judge of the Court of Protection, having such administrative functions in relation to the court as the Lord Chancellor[, after consulting the Lord Chief Justice,] may direct.

Amendment

Sub-s (1): in para (a) words "Lord Chief Justice" in square brackets substituted by SI 2006/1016, art 2, Sch 1, paras 30, 33(1), (2).
Sub-s (1): para (b) substituted by SI 2006/1016, art 2, Sch 1, paras 30, 33(1), (3).
Sub-s (3): words "Lord Chief Justice, after consulting the Lord Chancellor," in square brackets substituted by SI 2006/1016, art 2, Sch 1, paras 30, 33(1), (4).
Sub-s (4): words "Lord Chief Justice, after consulting the Lord Chancellor," in square brackets substituted by SI 2006/1016, art 2, Sch 1, paras 30, 33(1), (5)(a).
Sub-s (4): words ", after consulting the Lord Chief Justice," in square brackets inserted by SI 2006/1016, art 2, Sch 1, paras 30, 33(1), (5)(b).

Commentary

The Court's judiciary is currently: President – Sir Mark Potter (President of Family Division); Vice-President – Sir Andrew Morritt (Chancellor of the High Court); Senior Judge – HHJ Denzil Lush; Nominated High Court Judges (in practice these will be from the Chancery and Family Divisions); Nominated Circuit Judges; Nominated District Judges.

[583]

SUPPLEMENTARY POWERS

47 General powers and effect of orders etc

(1) The court has in connection with its jurisdiction the same powers, rights, privileges and authority as the High Court.

(2) Section 204 of the Law of Property Act 1925 (c 20) (orders of High Court conclusive in favour of purchasers) applies in relation to orders and directions of the court as it applies to orders of the High Court.

(3) Office copies of orders made, directions given or other instruments issued by the court and sealed with its official seal are admissible in all legal proceedings as evidence of the originals without any further proof.

Commentary

This makes it clear that the new Court is a superior court of record and has the status of the High Court.

[584]

48 Interim orders and directions

The court may, pending the determination of an application to it in relation to a person ("P"), make an order or give directions in respect of any matter if—

(a) there is reason to believe that P lacks capacity in relation to the matter,

(b) the matter is one to which its powers under this Act extend, and

(c) it is in P's best interests to make the order, or give the directions, without delay.

Commentary

This confers on the Court jurisdiction to act as a matter of urgency if necessary. In practice the old Court of Protection did so.

[585]

49 Power to call for reports

(1) This section applies where, in proceedings brought in respect of a person ("P") under Part 1, the court is considering a question relating to P.

(2) The court may require a report to be made to it by the Public Guardian or by a Court of Protection Visitor.

(3) The court may require a local authority, or an NHS body, to arrange for a report to be made—

(a) by one of its officers or employees, or
(b) by such other person (other than the Public Guardian or a Court of Protection Visitor) as the authority, or the NHS body, considers appropriate.

(4) The report must deal with such matters relating to P as the court may direct.

(5) Court of Protection Rules may specify matters which, unless the court directs otherwise, must also be dealt with in the report.

(6) The report may be made in writing or orally, as the court may direct.

(7) In complying with a requirement, the Public Guardian or a Court of Protection Visitor may, at all reasonable times, examine and take copies of—

(a) any health record,
(b) any record of, or held by, a local authority and compiled in connection with a social services function, and
(c) any record held by a person registered under Part 2 of the Care Standards Act 2000 (c 14),

so far as the record relates to P.

(8) If the Public Guardian or a Court of Protection Visitor is making a visit in the course of complying with a requirement, he may interview P in private.

(9) If a Court of Protection Visitor who is a Special Visitor is making a visit in the course of complying with a requirement, he may if the court so directs carry out in private a medical, psychiatric or psychological examination of P's capacity and condition.

(10) "NHS body" has the meaning given in section 148 of the Health and Social Care (Community Health and Standards) Act 2003 (c 43).

(11) "Requirement" means a requirement imposed under subsection (2) or (3).

Commentary

A great deal of the work carried out by the Court of Protection will involve taking into account medical and other evidence and this enables the Court to call for reports. For the appointment of Visitors see s 61 below.

[586]

PRACTICE AND PROCEDURE

50 Applications to the Court of Protection

(1) No permission is required for an application to the court for the exercise of any of its powers under this Act—

(a) by a person who lacks, or is alleged to lack, capacity,
(b) if such a person has not reached 18, by anyone with parental responsibility for him,
(c) by the donor or a donee of a lasting power of attorney to which the application relates,
(d) by a deputy appointed by the court for a person to whom the application relates, or

(e) by a person named in an existing order of the court, if the application relates to the order.

[(1A) Nor is permission required for an application to the court under section 21A by the relevant person's representative.]

(2) But, subject to Court of Protection Rules and to paragraph 20(2) of Schedule 3 (declarations relating to private international law), permission is required for any other application to the court.

(3) In deciding whether to grant permission the court must, in particular, have regard to—

(a) the applicant's connection with the person to whom the application relates,
(b) the reasons for the application,
(c) the benefit to the person to whom the application relates of a proposed order or directions, and
(d) whether the benefit can be achieved in any other way.

(4) "Parental responsibility" has the same meaning as in the Children Act 1989 (c 41).

Amendment
Sub-s (1A) inserted, as from a date to be appointed, by the Mental Health Act 2007, s 50(7), Sch 9, Pt 1, paras 1, 9.

Commentary
Permission is not needed for most applications in respect of property and affairs nor where it is by a deputy or donee of a Lasting or Enduring Power of Attorney. Part 8 of the Court of Protection Rules 2007 (SI 2007/1744) governs the procedure for obtaining permission.

[587]

51 Court of Protection Rules

[(1) Rules of court with respect to the practice and procedure of the court (to be called "Court of Protection Rules") may be made in accordance with Part 1 of Schedule 1 to the Constitutional Reform Act 2005.]

(2) Court of Protection Rules may, in particular, make provision—

(a) as to the manner and form in which proceedings are to be commenced;
(b) as to the persons entitled to be notified of, and be made parties to, the proceedings;
(c) for the allocation, in such circumstances as may be specified, of any specified description of proceedings to a specified judge or to specified descriptions of judges;
(d) for the exercise of the jurisdiction of the court, in such circumstances as may be specified, by its officers or other staff;
(e) for enabling the court to appoint a suitable person (who may, with his consent, be the Official Solicitor) to act in the name of, or on behalf of, or to represent the person to whom the proceedings relate;
(f) for enabling an application to the court to be disposed of without a hearing;
(g) for enabling the court to proceed with, or with any part of, a hearing in the absence of the person to whom the proceedings relate;
(h) for enabling or requiring the proceedings or any part of them to be conducted in private and for enabling the court to determine who is to be admitted when the court sits in private and to exclude specified persons when it sits in public;
(i) as to what may be received as evidence (whether or not admissible apart from the rules) and the manner in which it is to be presented;
(j) for the enforcement of orders made and directions given in the proceedings.

(3) Court of Protection Rules may, instead of providing for any matter, refer to provision made or to be made about that matter by directions.

(4) Court of Protection Rules may make different provision for different areas.

Amendment
Sub-s (1): substituted by SI 2006/1016, art 2, Sch 1, paras 30, 34.

Commentary
The rules are the Court of Protection Rules 2007 (SI 2007/1744) which extend to about 202 rules.

[588]

[52 Practice directions

(1) Directions as to the practice and procedure of the court may be given in accordance with Part 1 of Schedule 2 to the Constitutional Reform Act 2005.

(2) Practice directions given otherwise than under subsection (1) may not be given without the approval of—

(a) the Lord Chancellor, and
(b) the Lord Chief Justice.

(3) The Lord Chief Justice may nominate any of the following to exercise his functions under this section—

(a) the President of the Court of Protection;
(b) a judicial office holder (as defined in section 109(4) of the Constitutional Reform Act 2005).]

Amendment
Substituted by SI 2006/1016, art 2, Sch 1, paras 30, 35.

Commentary
The Lord Chief Justice has nominated the President to exercise his functions to give practice directions under section 52 of the Act and Practice Directions have been made.

[589]

53 Rights of appeal

(1) Subject to the provisions of this section, an appeal lies to the Court of Appeal from any decision of the court.

(2) Court of Protection Rules may provide that where a decision of the court is made by—

(a) a person exercising the jurisdiction of the court by virtue of rules made under section 51(2)(d),
(b) a district judge, or
(c) a circuit judge,

an appeal from that decision lies to a prescribed higher judge of the court and not to the Court of Appeal.

(3) For the purposes of this section the higher judges of the court are—

(a) in relation to a person mentioned in subsection (2)(a), a circuit judge or a district judge;
(b) in relation to a person mentioned in subsection (2)(b), a circuit judge;
(c) in relation to any person mentioned in subsection (2), one of the judges nominated by virtue of section 46(2)(a) to (c).

(4) Court of Protection Rules may make provision—

(a) that, in such cases as may be specified, an appeal from a decision of the court may not be made without permission;

(b) as to the person or persons entitled to grant permission to appeal;
(c) as to any requirements to be satisfied before permission is granted;
(d) that where a higher judge of the court makes a decision on an appeal, no appeal may be made to the Court of Appeal from that decision unless the Court of Appeal considers that—
  (i) the appeal would raise an important point of principle or practice, or
  (ii) there is some other compelling reason for the Court of Appeal to hear it;
(e) as to any considerations to be taken into account in relation to granting or refusing permission to appeal.

Commentary

This section enables court rules to provide that an appeal in respect of a decision of the Court of Protection may be heard by a higher judge of the Court of Protection, rather than being heard by the Court of Appeal. Rule 180 of the Court of Protection Rules 2007 (SI 2007/1744) provides that an appeal from a decision of a district judge shall be heard by a circuit judge, and that a first instance decision of a circuit judge shall be heard by the President, Vice-President, or a puisne judge of the High Court. Rule 181 provides that, where the decision sought to be appealed is a decision of the President, Vice-President, or a puisne judge, an appeal will lie only to the Court of Appeal. Rule 182 provides that a decision of a judge which was itself made on appeal from a judge of the court may only be appealed further to the Court of Appeal.

[590]

FEES AND COSTS

54 Fees

(1) The Lord Chancellor may with the consent of the Treasury by order prescribe fees payable in respect of anything dealt with by the court.

(2) An order under this section may in particular contain provision as to—
  (a) scales or rates of fees;
  (b) exemptions from and reductions in fees;
  (c) remission of fees in whole or in part.

(3) Before making an order under this section, the Lord Chancellor must consult—
  (a) the President of the Court of Protection,
  (b) the Vice-President of the Court of Protection, and
  (c) the Senior Judge of the Court of Protection.

(4) The Lord Chancellor must take such steps as are reasonably practicable to bring information about fees to the attention of persons likely to have to pay them.

(5) Fees payable under this section are recoverable summarily as a civil debt.

Commentary

Fees for applications and appeals are currently set at £400 and the fee for a final hearing is £500. The fees do not apply to applications by the Public Guardian, and certain applications by the donees of Lasting Powers of Attorney and those entitled to be notified of their registration who are objecting, see the Court of Protection Fees Order 2007 (SI 2007/1745).

[591]

55 Costs

(1) Subject to Court of Protection Rules, the costs of and incidental to all proceedings in the court are in its discretion.

(2) The rules may in particular make provision for regulating matters relating to the costs of those proceedings, including prescribing scales of costs to be paid to legal or other representatives.

(3) The court has full power to determine by whom and to what extent the costs are to be paid.

(4) The court may, in any proceedings—

(a) disallow, or

(b) order the legal or other representatives concerned to meet,

the whole of any wasted costs or such part of them as may be determined in accordance with the rules.

(5) "Legal or other representative", in relation to a party to proceedings, means any person exercising a right of audience or right to conduct litigation on his behalf.

(6) "Wasted costs" means any costs incurred by a party—

(a) as a result of any improper, unreasonable or negligent act or omission on the part of any legal or other representative or any employee of such a representative, or

(b) which, in the light of any such act or omission occurring after they were incurred, the court considers it is unreasonable to expect that party to pay.

Commentary

Costs are dealt with in Part 19 of the Court of Protection Rules 2007 (SI 2007/1744). The general rule is that in proceedings relating to P's property and affairs, everyone's costs will be paid out of P's estate and that in proceedings relating to P's personal welfare there will be no order for costs. Where the proceedings relate to both, the costs will be apportioned. The court may depart from the general rules if it is justified in doing so in all the circumstances. The rules as to assessment of costs are similar to the Civil Procedure Rules 1998. It should be noted that there can now be a summary assessment even where P is the paying party.

[592]

56 Fees and costs: supplementary

(1) Court of Protection Rules may make provision—

(a) as to the way in which, and funds from which, fees and costs are to be paid;

(b) for charging fees and costs upon the estate of the person to whom the proceedings relate;

(c) for the payment of fees and costs within a specified time of the death of the person to whom the proceedings relate or the conclusion of the proceedings.

(2) A charge on the estate of a person created by virtue of subsection (1)(b) does not cause any interest of the person in any property to fail or determine or to be prevented from recommencing.

Commentary

See the notes to s 55 above.

[593]

THE PUBLIC GUARDIAN

57 The Public Guardian

(1) For the purposes of this Act, there is to be an officer, to be known as the Public Guardian.

(2) The Public Guardian is to be appointed by the Lord Chancellor.

(3) There is to be paid to the Public Guardian out of money provided by Parliament such salary as the Lord Chancellor may determine.

(4) The Lord Chancellor may, after consulting the Public Guardian—

(a) provide him with such officers and staff, or

(b) enter into such contracts with other persons for the provision (by them or their sub-contractors) of officers, staff or services, as the Lord Chancellor thinks necessary for the proper discharge of the Public Guardian's functions.

(5) Any functions of the Public Guardian may, to the extent authorised by him, be performed by any of his officers.

Commentary

This section establishes the new office of the Public Guardian who is assisted by Visitors (appointed under s 61 below). The Office of the Public Guardian (OPG) is an executive agency of the Ministry of Justice.

[594]

58 Functions of the Public Guardian

(1) The Public Guardian has the following functions—

- (a) establishing and maintaining a register of lasting powers of attorney,
- (b) establishing and maintaining a register of orders appointing deputies,
- (c) supervising deputies appointed by the court,
- (d) directing a Court of Protection Visitor to visit—
  - (i) a donee of a lasting power of attorney,
  - (ii) a deputy appointed by the court, or
  - (iii) the person granting the power of attorney or for whom the deputy is appointed ("P"),

  and to make a report to the Public Guardian on such matters as he may direct,
- (e) receiving security which the court requires a person to give for the discharge of his functions,
- (f) receiving reports from donees of lasting powers of attorney and deputies appointed by the court,
- (g) reporting to the court on such matters relating to proceedings under this Act as the court requires,
- (h) dealing with representations (including complaints) about the way in which a donee of a lasting power of attorney or a deputy appointed by the court is exercising his powers,
- (i) publishing, in any manner the Public Guardian thinks appropriate, any information he thinks appropriate about the discharge of his functions.

(2) The functions conferred by subsection (1)(c) and (h) may be discharged in co-operation with any other person who has functions in relation to the care or treatment of P.

(3) The Lord Chancellor may by regulations make provision—

- (a) conferring on the Public Guardian other functions in connection with this Act;
- (b) in connection with the discharge by the Public Guardian of his functions.

(4) Regulations made under subsection (3)(b) may in particular make provision as to—

- (a) the giving of security by deputies appointed by the court and the enforcement and discharge of security so given;
- (b) the fees which may be charged by the Public Guardian;
- (c) the way in which, and funds from which, such fees are to be paid;
- (d) exemptions from and reductions in such fees;
- (e) remission of such fees in whole or in part;
- (f) the making of reports to the Public Guardian by deputies appointed by the court and others who are directed by the court to carry out any transaction for a person who lacks capacity.

(5) For the purpose of enabling him to carry out his functions, the Public Guardian may, at all reasonable times, examine and take copies of—

(a) any health record,

(b) any record of, or held by, a local authority and compiled in connection with a social services function, and

(c) any record held by a person registered under Part 2 of the Care Standards Act 2000 (c 14),

so far as the record relates to P.

(6) The Public Guardian may also for that purpose interview P in private.

Commentary

This sets out the function of the Public Guardian. The Lasting Powers of Attorney, Enduring Powers of Attorney and Public Guardian Regulations 2007 (SI 2007/1253), came into force on 1 October 2007 and deal with functions in Part 4. One of the important functions of the Public Guardian is in relation to the registration of Lasting Powers of Attorney and it is his task to maintain the registers. His role is to decide whether such powers are technically invalid and refuse to register them if he considers them to be. Issues as to the substantive validity of such powers are dealt with by the Court of Protection.

[595]

59 Public Guardian Board

(1) There is to be a body, to be known as the Public Guardian Board.

(2) The Board's duty is to scrutinise and review the way in which the Public Guardian discharges his functions and to make such recommendations to the Lord Chancellor about that matter as it thinks appropriate.

(3) The Lord Chancellor must, in discharging his functions under sections 57 and 58, give due consideration to recommendations made by the Board.

(4) . . .

(5) The Board must have—

(a) at least one member who is a judge of the court, and

(b) at least four members who are persons appearing to the Lord Chancellor to have appropriate knowledge or experience of the work of the Public Guardian.

[(5A) Where a person to be appointed as a member of the Board is a judge of the court, the appointment is to be made by the Lord Chief Justice after consulting the Lord Chancellor.

(5B) In any other case, the appointment of a person as a member of the Board is to be made by the Lord Chancellor.]

(6) The Lord Chancellor may by regulations make provision as to—

(a) the appointment of members of the Board (and, in particular, the procedures to be followed in connection with appointments);

(b) the selection of one of the members to be the chairman;

(c) the term of office of the chairman and members;

(d) their resignation, suspension or removal;

(e) the procedure of the Board (including quorum);

(f) the validation of proceedings in the event of a vacancy among the members or a defect in the appointment of a member.

(7) Subject to any provision made in reliance on subsection (6)(c) or (d), a person is to hold and vacate office as a member of the Board in accordance with the terms of the instrument appointing him.

(8) The Lord Chancellor may make such payments to or in respect of members of the Board by way of reimbursement of expenses, allowances and remuneration as he may determine.

(9) The Board must make an annual report to the Lord Chancellor about the discharge of its functions.

[(10) The Lord Chief Justice may nominate any of the following to exercise his functions under this section—

(a) the President of the Court of Protection;

(b) a judicial office holder (as defined in section 109(4) of the Constitutional Reform Act 2005).]

Amendment

Sub-s (4): repealed by SI 2006/1016, art 2, Sch 1, paras 30, 36(1), (2).
Sub-ss (5A), (5B): inserted by SI 2006/1016, art 2, Sch 1, paras 30, 36(1), (3).
Sub-s (10): inserted by SI 2006/1016, art 2, Sch 1, paras 30, 36(1), (4).

Commentary

Regulations made under this section are the Public Guardian Board Regulations 2007 (SI 2007/1770). They provide that the members of the Board shall be appointed for a fixed term of office not exceeding four years (reg 4(1)); on the expiry of a member's term of office, the Lord Chancellor (or the Lord Chief Justice, as the case may be) may re-appoint that member to serve a further fixed term not exceeding four years (reg 4(2)), but a member may not be re-appointed more than once (reg 4(3)); the Lord Chancellor shall select one of the members of the Board to be its chairman (reg 3) for a fixed term not exceeding four years (reg 5(1)). Regulation 6 makes provision for the resignation, suspension and removal of members of the Board who are not judges of the Court of Protection. Regulation 7 makes provision about the procedure of the Board, including quorum and voting. Regulation 8 provides for the validity of proceedings notwithstanding a vacancy in the membership or a defect in a member's appointment or in the chairman's selection. Regulation 9 provides that the Board must hold at least one meeting each year that is open to members of the public to attend.

[596]

60 Annual report

(1) The Public Guardian must make an annual report to the Lord Chancellor about the discharge of his functions.

(2) The Lord Chancellor must, within one month of receiving the report, lay a copy of it before Parliament.

Commentary

This is an important check on the role of the Public Guardian.

[597]

COURT OF PROTECTION VISITORS

61 Court of Protection Visitors

(1) A Court of Protection Visitor is a person who is appointed by the Lord Chancellor to—

(a) a panel of Special Visitors, or

(b) a panel of General Visitors.

(2) A person is not qualified to be a Special Visitor unless he—

(a) is a registered medical practitioner or appears to the Lord Chancellor to have other suitable qualifications or training, and

(b) appears to the Lord Chancellor to have special knowledge of and experience in cases of impairment of or disturbance in the functioning of the mind or brain.

(3) A General Visitor need not have a medical qualification.

(4) A Court of Protection Visitor—

(a) may be appointed for such term and subject to such conditions, and

(b) may be paid such remuneration and allowances,

as the Lord Chancellor may determine.

(5) For the purpose of carrying out his functions under this Act in relation to a person who lacks capacity ("P"), a Court of Protection Visitor may, at all reasonable times, examine and take copies of—

(a) any health record,
(b) any record of, or held by, a local authority and compiled in connection with a social services function, and
(c) any record held by a person registered under Part 2 of the Care Standards Act 2000 (c 14),

so far as the record relates to P.

(6) A Court of Protection Visitor may also for that purpose interview P in private.

Commentary
The Court of Protection Special Visitors replace the Lord Chancellor's Medical Visitors, who were appointed under section 102 of the Mental Health Act 1983. The panel of General Court of Protection Visitors replaces the panel of Lord Chancellor's General Visitors. In light of the important regulatory function of the Public Guardian general visitors will become very important in ensuring that this Act is working on a day to day basis.

[598]

PART 3
MISCELLANEOUS AND GENERAL

DECLARATORY PROVISION

62 Scope of the Act

For the avoidance of doubt, it is hereby declared that nothing in this Act is to be taken to affect the law relating to murder or manslaughter or the operation of section 2 of the Suicide Act 1961 (c 60) (assisting suicide)

Commentary
This provision is necessary to make clear that decisions taken as to the medical treatment of P will still be susceptible to these crimes.

[599]

PRIVATE INTERNATIONAL LAW

63 International protection of adults

Schedule 3—

(a) gives effect in England and Wales to the Convention on the International Protection of Adults signed at the Hague on 13th January 2000 (Cm 5881) (in so far as this Act does not otherwise do so), and
(b) makes related provision as to the private international law of England and Wales.

Commentary
See Schedule 3.

[600]

GENERAL

64 Interpretation

(1) In this Act—

"the 1985 Act" means the Enduring Powers of Attorney Act 1985 (c 29),

"advance decision" has the meaning given in section 24(1),

["authorisation under Schedule A1" means either—

(a) a standard authorisation under that Schedule, or

(b) an urgent authorisation under that Schedule.]

"the court" means the Court of Protection established by section 45,

"Court of Protection Rules" has the meaning given in section 51(1),

"Court of Protection Visitor" has the meaning given in section 61,

"deputy" has the meaning given in section 16(2)(b),

"enactment" includes a provision of subordinate legislation (within the meaning of the Interpretation Act 1978 (c 30)),

"health record" has the meaning given in section 68 of the Data Protection Act 1998 (c 29) (as read with section 69 of that Act),

"the Human Rights Convention" has the same meaning as "the Convention" in the Human Rights Act 1998 (c 42),

"independent mental capacity advocate" has the meaning given in section 35(1),

"lasting power of attorney" has the meaning given in section 9,

"life-sustaining treatment" has the meaning given in section 4(10),

"local authority"[, except in Schedule A1,] means—

(a) the council of a county in England in which there are no district councils,

(b) the council of a district in England,

(c) the council of a county or county borough in Wales,

(d) the council of a London borough,

(e) the Common Council of the City of London, or

(f) the Council of the Isles of Scilly,

"Mental Health Act" means the Mental Health Act 1983 (c 20),

"prescribed", in relation to regulations made under this Act, means prescribed by those regulations,

"property" includes any thing in action and any interest in real or personal property,

"public authority" has the same meaning as in the Human Rights Act 1998,

"Public Guardian" has the meaning given in section 57,

"purchaser" and "purchase" have the meaning given in section 205(1) of the Law of Property Act 1925 (c 20),

"social services function" has the meaning given in section 1A of the Local Authority Social Services Act 1970 (c 42),

"treatment" includes a diagnostic or other procedure,

"trust corporation" has the meaning given in section 68(1) of the Trustee Act 1925 (c 19), and

"will" includes codicil.

(2) In this Act, references to making decisions, in relation to a donee of a lasting power of attorney or a deputy appointed by the court, include, where appropriate, acting on decisions made.

(3) In this Act, references to the bankruptcy of an individual include a case where a bankruptcy restrictions order under the Insolvency Act 1986 (c 45) has effect in respect of him.

(4) "Bankruptcy restrictions order" includes an interim bankruptcy restrictions order.

[(5) In this Act, references to deprivation of a person's liberty have the same meaning as in Article 5(1) of the Human Rights Convention.

(6) For the purposes of such references, it does not matter whether a person is deprived of his liberty by a public authority or not.]

Amendment

Sub-s (1): definition "authorisation under Schedule A1" inserted, as from a date to be appointed, by the Mental Health Act 2007, s 50(7), Sch 9, Pt 1, paras 1, 10.
Sub-s (1): in definition "local authority" words ", except in Schedule A1," in square brackets inserted, as from a date to be appointed, by the Mental Health Act 2007, s 50(7), Sch 9, Pt 1, paras 1, 10.
Sub-ss (4), (5) inserted, as from a date to be appointed, by the Mental Health Act 2007, s 50(7), Sch 9, Pt 1, paras 1, 10.

Commentary

These are the definitions to be found throughout the Act.

[601]

65 Rules, regulations and orders

(1) Any power to make rules, regulations or orders under this Act[, other than the power in section 21]—

(a) is exercisable by statutory instrument;
(b) includes power to make supplementary, incidental, consequential, transitional or saving provision;
(c) includes power to make different provision for different cases.

(2) Any statutory instrument containing rules, regulations or orders made by the Lord Chancellor or the Secretary of State under this Act, other than—

(a) regulations under section 34 (loss of capacity during research project),
(b) regulations under section 41 (adjusting role of independent mental capacity advocacy service),
(c) regulations under paragraph 32(1)(b) of Schedule 3 (private international law relating to the protection of adults),
(d) an order of the kind mentioned in section 67(6) (consequential amendments of primary legislation), or
(e) an order under section 68 (commencement),

is subject to annulment in pursuance of a resolution of either House of Parliament.

(3) A statutory instrument containing an Order in Council under paragraph 31 of Schedule 3 (provision to give further effect to Hague Convention) is subject to annulment in pursuance of a resolution of either House of Parliament.

(4) A statutory instrument containing regulations made by the Secretary of State under section 34 or 41 or by the Lord Chancellor under paragraph 32(1)(b) of Schedule 3 may not be made unless a draft has been laid before and approved by resolution of each House of Parliament.

[(4A) Subsection (2) does not apply to a statutory instrument containing regulations made by the Secretary of State under Schedule A1.

(4B) If such a statutory instrument contains regulations under paragraph 42(2)(b), 129, 162 or 164 of Schedule A1 (whether or not it also contains other regulations), the instrument may not be made unless a draft has been laid before and approved by resolution of each House of Parliament.

(4C) Subject to that, such a statutory instrument is subject to annulment in pursuance of a resolution of either House of Parliament.]

[(5) An order under section 21—

(a) may include supplementary, incidental, consequential, transitional or saving provision;
(b) may make different provision for different cases;
(c) is to be made in the form of a statutory instrument to which the Statutory Instruments Act 1946 applies as if the order were made by a Minister of the Crown; and
(d) is subject to annulment in pursuance of a resolution of either House of Parliament.]

Amendment

Sub-s (1): words ", other than the power in section 21" in square brackets inserted by SI 2006/1016, art 2, Sch 1, paras 30, 37(1), (2).
Sub-ss (4A)–(4C) inserted, as from a date to be appointed, by the Mental Health Act 2007, s 50(7), Sch 9, Pt 1, paras 1, 11.
Sub-s (5): inserted by SI 2006/1016, art 2, Sch 1, paras 30, 37(1), (3).

Commentary

The following regulations have been made under the Act: The Court of Protection Rules 2007 (SI 2007/1744); The Lasting Powers of Attorney, Enduring Powers of Attorney and Public Guardian Regulations 2007 (SI 2007/1253 amended by SI 2007/2051 and by SI 2007/2161); The Mental Capacity Act 2005 (Transitional and Consequential Provisions) Order 2007 (SI 2007/1898); The Mental Capacity Act 2005 (Transfer of Proceedings Order) 2007 (SI 2007/1899); The Court of Protection Fees Order 2007 (SI 2007/1745); The Public Guardian (Fees etc) Regulations 2007 (SI 2007/2051).

[602]

66 Existing receivers and enduring powers of attorney etc

(1) The following provisions cease to have effect—
(a) Part 7 of the Mental Health Act,
(b) the Enduring Powers of Attorney Act 1985 (c 29).

(2) No enduring power of attorney within the meaning of the 1985 Act is to be created after the commencement of subsection (1)(b).

(3) Schedule 4 has effect in place of the 1985 Act in relation to any enduring power of attorney created before the commencement of subsection (1)(b).

(4) Schedule 5 contains transitional provisions and savings in relation to Part 7 of the Mental Health Act and the 1985 Act.

Commentary

No Enduring Power of Attorney can be granted after 1 October 2007 but of course there are many in existence created before that date and these are now governed by the transitional provisions contained in Sch 4.

[603]

67 Minor and consequential amendments and repeals

(1) Schedule 6 contains minor and consequential amendments.

(2) Schedule 7 contains repeals.

(3) The Lord Chancellor may by order make supplementary, incidental, consequential, transitional or saving provision for the purposes of, in consequence of, or for giving full effect to a provision of this Act.

(4) An order under subsection (3) may, in particular—
(a) provide for a provision of this Act which comes into force before another provision of this Act has come into force to have effect, until the other provision has come into force, with specified modifications;
(b) amend, repeal or revoke an enactment, other than one contained in an Act or Measure passed in a Session after the one in which this Act is passed.

(5) The amendments that may be made under subsection (4)(b) are in addition to those made by or under any other provision of this Act.

(6) An order under subsection (3) which amends or repeals a provision of an Act or Measure may not be made unless a draft has been laid before and approved by resolution of each House of Parliament.

[604]

68 Commencement and extent

(1) This Act, other than sections 30 to 41, comes into force in accordance with provision made by order by the Lord Chancellor.

(2) Sections 30 to 41 come into force in accordance with provision made by order by—

(a) the Secretary of State, in relation to England, and
(b) the National Assembly for Wales, in relation to Wales.

(3) An order under this section may appoint different days for different provisions and different purposes.

(4) Subject to subsections (5) and (6), this Act extends to England and Wales only.

(5) The following provisions extend to the United Kingdom—

(a) paragraph 16(1) of Schedule 1 (evidence of instruments and of registration of lasting powers of attorney),
(b) paragraph 15(3) of Schedule 4 (evidence of instruments and of registration of enduring powers of attorney).

(6) Subject to any provision made in Schedule 6, the amendments and repeals made by Schedules 6 and 7 have the same extent as the enactments to which they relate.

Commentary

Some provisions of the Act came in on 1 April 2007 but the bulk came into force on 1 October 2007 when the new Court of Protection was established.

[605]

69 Short title

This Act may be cited as the Mental Capacity Act 2005.

[606]

SCHEDULE 1
LASTING POWERS OF ATTORNEY: FORMALITIES

Section 9

PART 1
MAKING INSTRUMENTS

GENERAL REQUIREMENTS AS TO MAKING INSTRUMENTS

1 (1) An instrument is not made in accordance with this Schedule unless—

(a) it is in the prescribed form,
(b) it complies with paragraph 2, and
(c) any prescribed requirements in connection with its execution are satisfied.

(2) Regulations may make different provision according to whether—

(a) the instrument relates to personal welfare or to property and affairs (or to both);

(b) only one or more than one donee is to be appointed (and if more than one, whether jointly or jointly and severally).

(3) In this Schedule—

(a) "prescribed" means prescribed by regulations, and

(b) "regulations" means regulations made for the purposes of this Schedule by the Lord Chancellor.

Commentary

A Lasting Power of Attorney ("LPA") which is not in the correct form will be invalid (see section 9 above) and its registration will be rejected by the Public Guardian. For the prescribed forms see Parts 1 and 2 of Sch 1 to the Lasting Powers of Attorney, Enduring Powers of Attorney and Public Guardian Regulations 2007 (SI 2007/1253) **[Appendix VIII]**, as for the execution of the Lasting Power see reg 9 of the above regulations.

REQUIREMENTS AS TO CONTENT OF INSTRUMENTS

2 (1) The instrument must include—

(a) the prescribed information about the purpose of the instrument and the effect of a lasting power of attorney,

(b) a statement by the donor to the effect that he—

(i) has read the prescribed information or a prescribed part of it (or has had it read to him), and

(ii) intends the authority conferred under the instrument to include authority to make decisions on his behalf in circumstances where he no longer has capacity,

(c) a statement by the donor—

(i) naming a person or persons whom the donor wishes to be notified of any application for the registration of the instrument, or

(ii) stating that there are no persons whom he wishes to be notified of any such application,

(d) a statement by the donee (or, if more than one, each of them) to the effect that he—

(i) has read the prescribed information or a prescribed part of it (or has had it read to him), and

(ii) understands the duties imposed on a donee of a lasting power of attorney under sections 1 (the principles) and 4 (best interests), and

(e) a certificate by a person of a prescribed description that, in his opinion, at the time when the donor executes the instrument—

(i) the donor understands the purpose of the instrument and the scope of the authority conferred under it,

(ii) no fraud or undue pressure is being used to induce the donor to create a lasting power of attorney, and

(iii) there is nothing else which would prevent a lasting power of attorney from being created by the instrument.

(2) Regulations may—

(a) prescribe a maximum number of named persons;

(b) provide that, where the instrument includes a statement under sub-paragraph (1)(c)(ii), two persons of a prescribed description must each give a certificate under sub-paragraph (1)(e).

(3) The persons who may be named persons do not include a person who is appointed as donee under the instrument.

(4) In this Schedule, "named person" means a person named under sub-paragraph (1)(c).

(5) A certificate under sub-paragraph (1)(e)—
(a) must be made in the prescribed form, and
(b) must include any prescribed information.

(6) The certificate may not be given by a person appointed as donee under the instrument.

Commentary
This sets out some of the more important requirements for a Lasting Power of Attorney. Note that it is a requirement that the donor reads the required information or has it read to him which is a greater burden than for the creation of an Enduring Power. The other major differences are that the donor can specify those he wishes to be notified of the application for registration or specify that nobody should be notified. Regulation 6 of the Lasting Powers of Attorney, Enduring Powers of Attorney and Public Guardian Regulations 2007 (SI 2007/1253) **[Appendix VIII]** specifies the maximum number of persons to be notified as 5 (sub-para (2) above). As to the certification procedure those regulations provide that there need to be two certificates in the event that no persons are specified to be notified (reg 7) and reg 8 provides detailed guidance on those who can and cannot certify.

FAILURE TO COMPLY WITH PRESCRIBED FORM

3 (1) If an instrument differs in an immaterial respect in form or mode of expression from the prescribed form, it is to be treated by the Public Guardian as sufficient in point of form and expression.

(2) The court may declare that an instrument which is not in the prescribed form is to be treated as if it were, if it is satisfied that the persons executing the instrument intended it to create a lasting power of attorney.

Commentary
While the rules as to the LPA being in the prescribed form are strict, this provides some relaxation for minor defects. For the prescribed forms see Parts 1 and 2 of Sch 1 to the Lasting Powers of Attorney, Enduring Powers of Attorney and Public Guardian Regulations 2007 (SI 2007/1253) **[Appendix VIII]**.

PART 2
REGISTRATION

APPLICATIONS AND PROCEDURE FOR REGISTRATION

4 7(1) An application to the Public Guardian for the registration of an instrument intended to create a lasting power of attorney—
(a) must be made in the prescribed form, and
(b) must include any prescribed information.

(2) The application may be made—
(a) by the donor,
(b) by the donee or donees, or
(c) if the instrument appoints two or more donees to act jointly and severally in respect of any matter, by any of the donees.

(3) The application must be accompanied by—
(a) the instrument, and
(b) any fee provided for under section 58(4)(b).

(4) A person who, in an application for registration, makes a statement which he knows to be false in a material particular is guilty of an offence and is liable—
(a) on summary conviction, to imprisonment for a term not exceeding 12 months or a fine not exceeding the statutory maximum or both;
(b) on conviction on indictment, to imprisonment for a term not exceeding 2 years or a fine or both.

5 Subject to paragraphs 11 to 14, the Public Guardian must register the instrument as a lasting power of attorney at the end of the prescribed period.

Commentary
For the detailed procedure see regs 10 to 17 of the Lasting Powers of Attorney, Enduring Powers of Attorney and Public Guardian Regulations 2007 (SI 2007/1253) **[Appendix VIII]**. In summary with reference to the relevant forms provided by the regulation: LPA created; donee decides to register power; donee notifies named persons (LPA001); Registration application made (LPA002 - £150 fee); Public Guardian notifies donor of application (LPA003B); objection made to court on ground that LPA not validly created; notice of objection must also be give to Public Guardian by objector; objection dealt with by court. Assuming there are no objections the Public Guardian has 6 weeks to register the LPA (reg 12 of the above regulations).

NOTIFICATION REQUIREMENTS

6 (1) A donor about to make an application under paragraph 4(2)(a) must notify any named persons that he is about to do so.

(2) The donee (or donees) about to make an application under paragraph 4(2)(b) or (c) must notify any named persons that he is (or they are) about to do so.

7 As soon as is practicable after receiving an application by the donor under paragraph 4(2)(a), the Public Guardian must notify the donee (or donees) that the application has been received.

8 (1) As soon as is practicable after receiving an application by a donee (or donees) under paragraph 4(2)(b), the Public Guardian must notify the donor that the application has been received.

(2) As soon as is practicable after receiving an application by a donee under paragraph 4(2)(c), the Public Guardian must notify—

- (a) the donor, and
- (b) the donee or donees who did not join in making the application,

that the application has been received.

9 (1) A notice under paragraph 6 must be made in the prescribed form.

(2) A notice under paragraph 6, 7 or 8 must include such information, if any, as may be prescribed.

Commentary
See regs 10 to 17 of the Lasting Powers of Attorney, Enduring Powers of Attorney and Public Guardian Regulations 2007 (SI 2007/1253) **[Appendix VIII]**, as amended by the Lasting Powers of Attorney, Enduring Powers of Attorney and Public Guardian (Amendment) Regulations 2007 (SI 2007/2161), and the summary above.

POWER TO DISPENSE WITH NOTIFICATION REQUIREMENTS

10 The court may—

- (a) on the application of the donor, dispense with the requirement to notify under paragraph 6(1), or
- (b) on the application of the donee or donees concerned, dispense with the requirement to notify under paragraph 6(2),

if satisfied that no useful purpose would be served by giving the notice.

Commentary
This enables the requirements as to notification to be relaxed.

INSTRUMENT NOT MADE PROPERLY OR CONTAINING INEFFECTIVE PROVISION

11 (1) If it appears to the Public Guardian that an instrument accompanying an application under paragraph 4 is not made in accordance with this Schedule, he must not register the instrument unless the court directs him to do so.

(2) Sub-paragraph (3) applies if it appears to the Public Guardian that the instrument contains a provision which—

(a) would be ineffective as part of a lasting power of attorney, or
(b) would prevent the instrument from operating as a valid lasting power of attorney.

(3) The Public Guardian—

(a) must apply to the court for it to determine the matter under section 23(1), and
(b) pending the determination by the court, must not register the instrument.

(4) Sub-paragraph (5) applies if the court determines under section 23(1) (whether or not on an application by the Public Guardian) that the instrument contains a provision which—

(a) would be ineffective as part of a lasting power of attorney, or
(b) would prevent the instrument from operating as a valid lasting power of attorney.

(5) The court must—

(a) notify the Public Guardian that it has severed the provision, or
(b) direct him not to register the instrument.

(6) Where the court notifies the Public Guardian that it has severed a provision, he must register the instrument with a note to that effect attached to it.

Commentary
The Public Guardian can object to registration on technical grounds but must refer any concerns he has under this sub-paragraph to the Court of Protection.

DEPUTY ALREADY APPOINTED

12 (1) Sub-paragraph (2) applies if it appears to the Public Guardian that—

(a) there is a deputy appointed by the court for the donor, and
(b) the powers conferred on the deputy would, if the instrument were registered, to any extent conflict with the powers conferred on the attorney.

(2) The Public Guardian must not register the instrument unless the court directs him to do so.

Commentary
This sub-paragraph prevents the automatic registration of an LPA where there is already a deputy appointed.

OBJECTION BY DONEE OR NAMED PERSON

13 (1) Sub-paragraph (2) applies if a donee or a named person—

(a) receives a notice under paragraph 6, 7 or 8 of an application for the registration of an instrument, and
(b) before the end of the prescribed period, gives notice to the Public Guardian of an objection to the registration on the ground that an event mentioned in section 13(3) or (6)(a) to (d) has occurred which has revoked the instrument.

(2) If the Public Guardian is satisfied that the ground for making the objection is established, he must not register the instrument unless the court, on the application of the person applying for the registration—

(a) is satisfied that the ground is not established, and

(b) directs the Public Guardian to register the instrument.

(3) Sub-paragraph (4) applies if a donee or a named person—

(a) receives a notice under paragraph 6, 7 or 8 of an application for the registration of an instrument, and

(b) before the end of the prescribed period—

(i) makes an application to the court objecting to the registration on a prescribed ground, and

(ii) notifies the Public Guardian of the application.

(4) The Public Guardian must not register the instrument unless the court directs him to do so.

Commentary

See reg 14 of the Lasting Powers of Attorney, Enduring Powers of Attorney and Public Guardian Regulations 2007 (SI 2007/1253) **[Appendix VIII],** as amended by the Lasting Powers of Attorney, Enduring Powers of Attorney and Public Guardian (Amendment) Regulations 2007 (SI 2007/2161). The period specified for objection is 5 weeks.

OBJECTION BY DONOR

14 (1) This paragraph applies if the donor—

(a) receives a notice under paragraph 8 of an application for the registration of an instrument, and

(b) before the end of the prescribed period, gives notice to the Public Guardian of an objection to the registration.

(2) The Public Guardian must not register the instrument unless the court, on the application of the donee or, if more than one, any of them—

(a) is satisfied that the donor lacks capacity to object to the registration, and

(b) directs the Public Guardian to register the instrument.

Commentary

The procedure is set out in reg 14A of the Lasting Powers of Attorney, Enduring Powers of Attorney and Public Guardian Regulations 2007 (SI 2007/1253) **[Appendix VIII],** as amended by the Lasting Powers of Attorney, Enduring Powers of Attorney and Public Guardian (Amendment) Regulations 2007 (SI 2007/2161). The period for objection is 5 weeks.

NOTIFICATION OF REGISTRATION

15 Where an instrument is registered under this Schedule, the Public Guardian must give notice of the fact in the prescribed form to—

(a) the donor, and

(b) the donee or, if more than one, each of them.

Commentary

See reg 17 of the Lasting Powers of Attorney, Enduring Powers of Attorney and Public Guardian Regulations 2007 (SI 2007/1253) **[Appendix VIII]**. The prescribed form is in Sch 5 to the regulations (LPA004).

EVIDENCE OF REGISTRATION

16 (1) A document purporting to be an office copy of an instrument registered under this Schedule is, in any part of the United Kingdom, evidence of—

(a) the contents of the instrument, and
(b) the fact that it has been registered.

(2) Sub-paragraph (1) is without prejudice to—
(a) section 3 of the Powers of Attorney Act 1971 (c 27) (proof by certified copy), and
(b) any other method of proof authorised by law.

Commentary
This provides the method whereby LPAs in practice can be proved.

PART 3
CANCELLATION OF REGISTRATION AND NOTIFICATION OF SEVERANCE

17 (1) The Public Guardian must cancel the registration of an instrument as a lasting power of attorney on being satisfied that the power has been revoked—
(a) as a result of the donor's bankruptcy, or
(b) on the occurrence of an event mentioned in section 13(6)(a) to (d).

(2) If the Public Guardian cancels the registration of an instrument he must notify—
(a) the donor, and
(b) the donee or, if more than one, each of them.

Commentary
See the notes to section 13 for the events which will revoke an LPA.

18 The court must direct the Public Guardian to cancel the registration of an instrument as a lasting power of attorney if it—
(a) determines under section 22(2)(a) that a requirement for creating the power was not met,
(b) determines under section 22(2)(b) that the power has been revoked or has otherwise come to an end, or
(c) revokes the power under section 22(4)(b) (fraud etc).

Commentary
See the notes to section 22.

19 (1) Sub-paragraph (2) applies if the court determines under section 23(1) that a lasting power of attorney contains a provision which—
(a) is ineffective as part of a lasting power of attorney, or
(b) prevents the instrument from operating as a valid lasting power of attorney.

(2) The court must—
(a) notify the Public Guardian that it has severed the provision, or
(b) direct him to cancel the registration of the instrument as a lasting power of attorney.

Commentary
See the notes to section 23.

20 On the cancellation of the registration of an instrument, the instrument and any office copies of it must be delivered up to the Public Guardian to be cancelled.

Commentary
Regulation 19 of the Lasting Powers of Attorney, Enduring Powers of Attorney and Public Guardian Regulations 2007 (SI 2007/1253) **[Appendix VIII]** deals with the position if the document which is to be delivered up has been lost or destroyed.

PART 4
RECORDS OF ALTERATIONS IN REGISTERED POWERS

PARTIAL REVOCATION OR SUSPENSION OF POWER AS A RESULT OF BANKRUPTCY

21 If in the case of a registered instrument it appears to the Public Guardian that under section 13 a lasting power of attorney is revoked, or suspended, in relation to the donor's property and affairs (but not in relation to other matters), the Public Guardian must attach to the instrument a note to that effect.

Commentary
For the procedure see reg 18 of the Lasting Powers of Attorney, Enduring Powers of Attorney and Public Guardian Regulations 2007 (SI 2007/1253) **[Appendix VIII]**.

TERMINATION OF APPOINTMENT OF DONEE WHICH DOES NOT REVOKE POWER

22 If in the case of a registered instrument it appears to the Public Guardian that an event has occurred—

(a) which has terminated the appointment of the donee, but
(b) which has not revoked the instrument,

the Public Guardian must attach to the instrument a note to that effect.

Commentary
For the procedure see regulation 18 of the Lasting Powers of Attorney, Enduring Powers of Attorney and Public Guardian Regulations 2007 (SI 2007/1253) **[Appendix VIII]**.

REPLACEMENT OF DONEE

23 If in the case of a registered instrument it appears to the Public Guardian that the donee has been replaced under the terms of the instrument the Public Guardian must attach to the instrument a note to that effect.

Commentary
For the procedure see reg 18 of the Lasting Powers of Attorney, Enduring Powers of Attorney and Public Guardian Regulations 2007 (SI 2007/1253) **[Appendix VIII]**.

SEVERANCE OF INEFFECTIVE PROVISIONS

24 If in the case of a registered instrument the court notifies the Public Guardian under paragraph 19(2)(a) that it has severed a provision of the instrument, the Public Guardian must attach to it a note to that effect.

Commentary
For the procedure see reg 18 of the Lasting Powers of Attorney, Enduring Powers of Attorney and Public Guardian Regulations 2007 (SI 2007/1253) **[Appendix VIII]**.

NOTIFICATION OF ALTERATIONS

25 If the Public Guardian attaches a note to an instrument under paragraph 21, 22, 23 or 24 he must give notice of the note to the donee or donees of the power (or, as the case may be, to the other donee or donees of the power).

Commentary
For the procedure see reg 18(2) of the Lasting Powers of Attorney, Enduring Powers of Attorney and Public Guardian Regulations 2007 (SI 2007/1253) **[Appendix VIII]**.

SCHEDULE 2
PROPERTY AND AFFAIRS: SUPPLEMENTARY PROVISIONS

Section 18(4)

WILLS: GENERAL

1 Paragraphs 2 to 4 apply in relation to the execution of a will, by virtue of section 18, on behalf of P.

Commentary
One of the frequent exercises of the jurisdiction of the Court of Protection is in making what have been known as statutory wills for those who lack capacity. There is no reason to believe the principles the Court will apply have changed for which see: *Re D(J)* [1982] Ch 237.

PROVISION THAT MAY BE MADE IN WILL

2 The will may make any provision (whether by disposing of property or exercising a power or otherwise) which could be made by a will executed by P if he had capacity to make it.

Commentary
This confirms that the court's powers are to make a will which P could have made and see the notes to para 1 above.

WILLS: REQUIREMENTS RELATING TO EXECUTION

3 (1) Sub-paragraph (2) applies if under section 16 the court makes an order or gives directions requiring or authorising a person ("the authorised person") to execute a will on behalf of P.

(2) Any will executed in pursuance of the order or direction—
- (a) must state that it is signed by P acting by the authorised person,
- (b) must be signed by the authorised person with the name of P and his own name, in the presence of two or more witnesses present at the same time,
- (c) must be attested and subscribed by those witnesses in the presence of the authorised person, and
- (d) must be sealed with the official seal of the court.

Commentary
This reflects the previous law under the Mental Health Act 1983.

WILLS: EFFECT OF EXECUTION

4 (1) This paragraph applies where a will is executed in accordance with paragraph 3.

(2) The Wills Act 1837 (c 26) has effect in relation to the will as if it were signed by P by his own hand, except that—
- (a) section 9 of the 1837 Act (requirements as to signing and attestation) does not apply, and
- (b) in the subsequent provisions of the 1837 Act any reference to execution in the manner required by the previous provisions is to be read as a reference to execution in accordance with paragraph 3.

(3) The will has the same effect for all purposes as if—
- (a) P had had the capacity to make a valid will, and
- (b) the will had been executed by him in the manner required by the 1837 Act.

(4) But sub-paragraph (3) does not have effect in relation to the will—
- (a) in so far as it disposes of immovable property outside England and Wales, or
- (b) in so far as it relates to any other property or matter if, when the will is executed—
  - (i) P is domiciled outside England and Wales, and
  - (ii) the condition in sub-paragraph (5) is met.

(5) The condition is that, under the law of P's domicile, any question of his testamentary capacity would fall to be determined in accordance with the law of a place outside England and Wales.

Commentary
For the Wills Act 1837 see **[1]**. A will made under this jurisdiction does not have to comply with section 9 of the Wills Act 1837 **[7]** and takes effect as if P had capacity. However note the provisions of sub-ss (4) and (5). In general the law of succession in relation to movables is governed by the law of the domicile of the testator. The law of succession in relation to immovables on the other is governed by where they are situated. As to capacity, in relation to *movables* this is governed by the law of the domicile of the testator. In relation to *immovables* however, the law governing capacity is the law applicable to the territory in which the assets are situated. The Court of Protection cannot make a will where the issue of capacity if governed by the law of another domicile or where the will purports to dispose of foreign immovables.

VESTING ORDERS ANCILLARY TO SETTLEMENT ETC

5 (1) If provision is made by virtue of section 18 for—
- (a) the settlement of any property of P, or
- (b) the exercise of a power vested in him of appointing trustees or retiring from a trust,

the court may also make as respects the property settled or the trust property such consequential vesting or other orders as the case may require.

(2) The power under sub-paragraph (1) includes, in the case of the exercise of such a power, any order which could have been made in such a case under Part 4 of the Trustee Act 1925 (c 19).

Commentary
Part 4 of the Trustee Act 1925 **[110]** confers on the court power to make vesting orders in respect of trust property. This sub-paragraph confers that jurisdiction on the Court of Protection as well when settling P's property.

VARIATION OF SETTLEMENTS

6 (1) If a settlement has been made by virtue of section 18, the court may by order vary or revoke the settlement if—
- (a) the settlement makes provision for its variation or revocation,
- (b) the court is satisfied that a material fact was not disclosed when the settlement was made, or
- (c) the court is satisfied that there has been a substantial change of circumstances.

(2) Any such order may give such consequential directions as the court thinks fit.

Commentary
Note the wider jurisdiction under the Variation of Trusts Act 1958 **[256]** will also be available. However, the grounds of change of circumstance provides a useful power and may obviate a need to apply to the Court for an order for rectification or setting aside by mistake.

VESTING OF STOCK IN CURATOR APPOINTED OUTSIDE ENGLAND AND WALES

7 (1) Sub-paragraph (2) applies if the court is satisfied—
- (a) that under the law prevailing in a place outside England and Wales a person ("M") has been appointed to exercise powers in respect of the property or affairs of P on the ground (however formulated) that P lacks capacity to make decisions with respect to the management and administration of his property and affairs, and
- (b) that, having regard to the nature of the appointment and to the circumstances of the case, it is expedient that the court should exercise its powers under this paragraph.

(2) The court may direct—
- (a) any stocks standing in the name of P, or
- (b) the right to receive dividends from the stocks,

to be transferred into M's name or otherwise dealt with as required by M, and may give such directions as the court thinks fit for dealing with accrued dividends from the stocks.

(3) "Stocks" includes—
- (a) shares, and
- (b) any funds, annuity or security transferable in the books kept by any body corporate or unincorporated company or society or by an instrument of transfer either alone or accompanied by other formalities,

and "dividends" is to be construed accordingly.

Commentary

This sub-paragraph empowers the Court of Protection to transfer stocks to the equivalent of a deputy appointed under a foreign jurisdiction. It re-enacts the power in s 100 of the Mental Health Act 1983.

PRESERVATION OF INTERESTS IN PROPERTY DISPOSED OF ON BEHALF OF PERSON LACKING CAPACITY

8 (1) Sub-paragraphs (2) and (3) apply if—
- (a) P's property has been disposed of by virtue of section 18,
- (b) under P's will or intestacy, or by a gift perfected or nomination taking effect on his death, any other person would have taken an interest in the property but for the disposal, and
- (c) on P's death, any property belonging to P's estate represents the property disposed of.

(2) The person takes the same interest, if and so far as circumstances allow, in the property representing the property disposed of.

(3) If the property disposed of was real property, any property representing it is to be treated, so long as it remains part of P's estate, as if it were real property.

(4) The court may direct that, on a disposal of P's property—
- (a) which is made by virtue of section 18, and
- (b) which would apart from this paragraph result in the conversion of personal property into real property,

property representing the property disposed of is to be treated, so long as it remains P's property or forms part of P's estate, as if it were personal property.

(5) References in sub-paragraphs (1) to (4) to the disposal of property are to—
- (a) the sale, exchange, charging of or other dealing (otherwise than by will) with property other than money;

(b) the removal of property from one place to another;
(c) the application of money in acquiring property;
(d) the transfer of money from one account to another;

and references to property representing property disposed of are to be construed accordingly and as including the result of successive disposals.

(6) The court may give such directions as appear to it necessary or expedient for the purpose of facilitating the operation of sub-paragraphs (1) to (3), including the carrying of money to a separate account and the transfer of property other than money.

Commentary
Normally if the subject matter of a specific gift in a Will is sold during the lifetime of a Testator the gift adeems. Section 101 of the Mental Health Act 1983 prevented that happening as does this section albeit in somewhat wider terms. Sub-paragraph (6) recognises the practice of the Master of the Court of Protection under the old regime who sometimes when a patient's house was sold in these circumstances would direct that they be kept in a separate account.

9 (1) Sub-paragraph (2) applies if the court has ordered or directed the expenditure of money—
(a) for carrying out permanent improvements on any of P's property, or
(b) otherwise for the permanent benefit of any of P's property.

(2) The court may order that—
(a) the whole of the money expended or to be expended, or
(b) any part of it,

is to be a charge on the property either without interest or with interest at a specified rate.

(3) An order under sub-paragraph (2) may provide for excluding or restricting the operation of paragraph 8(1) to (3).

(4) A charge under sub-paragraph (2) may be made in favour of such person as may be just and, in particular, where the money charged is paid out of P's general estate, may be made in favour of a person as trustee for P.

(5) No charge under sub-paragraph (2) may confer any right of sale or foreclosure during P's lifetime.

Commentary
See the notes to sub-para 8 as the Court can vary the operation of that paragraph if it decides to charge property which is the subject of a specific gift.

POWERS AS PATRON OF BENEFICE

10 (1) Any functions which P has as patron of a benefice may be discharged only by a person ("R") appointed by the court.

(2) R must be an individual capable of appointment under section 8(1)(b) of the 1986 Measure (which provides for an individual able to make a declaration of communicant status, a clerk in Holy Orders, etc to be appointed to discharge a registered patron's functions).

(3) The 1986 Measure applies to R as it applies to an individual appointed by the registered patron of the benefice under section 8(1)(b) or (3) of that Measure to discharge his functions as patron.

(4) "The 1986 Measure" means the Patronage (Benefices) Measure 1986 (No 3).

Commentary
A benefice is a freehold office in the Church of England. A patron has the right to present someone to that benefice and the Court may appoint a person to exercise those functions if the patron lacks capacity.

SCHEDULE 3
INTERNATIONAL PROTECTION OF ADULTS

Section 63

PART 1
PRELIMINARY

INTRODUCTION

1 This Part applies for the purposes of this Schedule.

THE CONVENTION

2 (1) "Convention" means the Convention referred to in section 63.

(2) "Convention country" means a country in which the Convention is in force.

(3) A reference to an Article or Chapter is to an Article or Chapter of the Convention.

(4) An expression which appears in this Schedule and in the Convention is to be construed in accordance with the Convention.

COUNTRIES, TERRITORIES AND NATIONALS

3 (1) "Country" includes a territory which has its own system of law.

(2) Where a country has more than one territory with its own system of law, a reference to the country, in relation to one of its nationals, is to the territory with which the national has the closer, or the closest, connection.

ADULTS WITH INCAPACITY

4 "Adult" means a person who—

- (a) as a result of an impairment or insufficiency of his personal faculties, cannot protect his interests, and
- (b) has reached 16.

PROTECTIVE MEASURES

5 (1) "Protective measure" means a measure directed to the protection of the person or property of an adult; and it may deal in particular with any of the following—

- (a) the determination of incapacity and the institution of a protective regime,
- (b) placing the adult under the protection of an appropriate authority,
- (c) guardianship, curatorship or any corresponding system,
- (d) the designation and functions of a person having charge of the adult's person or property, or representing or otherwise helping him,
- (e) placing the adult in a place where protection can be provided,
- (f) administering, conserving or disposing of the adult's property,
- (g) authorising a specific intervention for the protection of the person or property of the adult.

(2) Where a measure of like effect to a protective measure has been taken in relation to a person before he reaches 16, this Schedule applies to the measure in so far as it has effect in relation to him once he has reached 16.

CENTRAL AUTHORITY

6 (1) Any function under the Convention of a Central Authority is exercisable in England and Wales by the Lord Chancellor.

(2) A communication may be sent to the Central Authority in relation to England and Wales by sending it to the Lord Chancellor.

PART 2
JURISDICTION OF COMPETENT AUTHORITY

SCOPE OF JURISDICTION

7 (1) The court may exercise its functions under this Act (in so far as it cannot otherwise do so) in relation to—

(a) an adult habitually resident in England and Wales,
(b) an adult's property in England and Wales,
(c) an adult present in England and Wales or who has property there, if the matter is urgent, or
(d) an adult present in England and Wales, if a protective measure which is temporary and limited in its effect to England and Wales is proposed in relation to him.

(2) An adult present in England and Wales is to be treated for the purposes of this paragraph as habitually resident there if—

(a) his habitual residence cannot be ascertained,
(b) he is a refugee, or
(c) he has been displaced as a result of disturbance in the country of his habitual residence.

8 (1) The court may also exercise its functions under this Act (in so far as it cannot otherwise do so) in relation to an adult if sub-paragraph (2) or (3) applies in relation to him.

(2) This sub-paragraph applies in relation to an adult if—

(a) he is a British citizen,
(b) he has a closer connection with England and Wales than with Scotland or Northern Ireland, and
(c) Article 7 has, in relation to the matter concerned, been complied with.

(3) This sub-paragraph applies in relation to an adult if the Lord Chancellor, having consulted such persons as he considers appropriate, agrees to a request under Article 8 in relation to the adult.

EXERCISE OF JURISDICTION

9 (1) This paragraph applies where jurisdiction is exercisable under this Schedule in connection with a matter which involves a Convention country other than England and Wales.

(2) Any Article on which the jurisdiction is based applies in relation to the matter in so far as it involves the other country (and the court must, accordingly, comply with any duty conferred on it as a result).

(3) Article 12 also applies, so far as its provisions allow, in relation to the matter in so far as it involves the other country.

10 A reference in this Schedule to the exercise of jurisdiction under this Schedule is to the exercise of functions under this Act as a result of this Part of this Schedule.

PART 3
APPLICABLE LAW

APPLICABLE LAW

11 In exercising jurisdiction under this Schedule, the court may, if it thinks that the matter has a substantial connection with a country other than England and Wales, apply the law of that other country.

12 Where a protective measure is taken in one country but implemented in another, the conditions of implementation are governed by the law of the other country.

LASTING POWERS OF ATTORNEY, ETC

13 (1) If the donor of a lasting power is habitually resident in England and Wales at the time of granting the power, the law applicable to the existence, extent, modification or extinction of the power is—

(a) the law of England and Wales, or

(b) if he specifies in writing the law of a connected country for the purpose, that law.

(2) If he is habitually resident in another country at that time, but England and Wales is a connected country, the law applicable in that respect is—

(a) the law of the other country, or

(b) if he specifies in writing the law of England and Wales for the purpose, that law.

(3) A country is connected, in relation to the donor, if it is a country—

(a) of which he is a national,

(b) in which he was habitually resident, or

(c) in which he has property.

(4) Where this paragraph applies as a result of sub-paragraph (3)(c), it applies only in relation to the property which the donor has in the connected country.

(5) The law applicable to the manner of the exercise of a lasting power is the law of the country where it is exercised.

(6) In this Part of this Schedule, "lasting power" means—

(a) a lasting power of attorney (see section 9),

(b) an enduring power of attorney within the meaning of Schedule 4, or

(c) any other power of like effect.

14 (1) Where a lasting power is not exercised in a manner sufficient to guarantee the protection of the person or property of the donor, the court, in exercising jurisdiction under this Schedule, may disapply or modify the power.

(2) Where, in accordance with this Part of this Schedule, the law applicable to the power is, in one or more respects, that of a country other than England and Wales, the court must, so far as possible, have regard to the law of the other country in that respect (or those respects).

15 Regulations may provide for Schedule 1 (lasting powers of attorney: formalities) to apply with modifications in relation to a lasting power which comes within paragraph 13(6)(c) above.

PROTECTION OF THIRD PARTIES

16 (1) This paragraph applies where a person (a "representative") in purported exercise of an authority to act on behalf of an adult enters into a transaction with a third party.

(2) The validity of the transaction may not be questioned in proceedings, nor may the third party be held liable, merely because—

- (a) where the representative and third party are in England and Wales when entering into the transaction, sub-paragraph (3) applies;
- (b) where they are in another country at that time, sub-paragraph (4) applies.

(3) This sub-paragraph applies if—

- (a) the law applicable to the authority in one or more respects is, as a result of this Schedule, the law of a country other than England and Wales, and
- (b) the representative is not entitled to exercise the authority in that respect (or those respects) under the law of that other country.

(4) This sub-paragraph applies if—

- (a) the law applicable to the authority in one or more respects is, as a result of this Part of this Schedule, the law of England and Wales, and
- (b) the representative is not entitled to exercise the authority in that respect (or those respects) under that law.

(5) This paragraph does not apply if the third party knew or ought to have known that the applicable law was—

- (a) in a case within sub-paragraph (3), the law of the other country;
- (b) in a case within sub-paragraph (4), the law of England and Wales.

MANDATORY RULES

17 Where the court is entitled to exercise jurisdiction under this Schedule, the mandatory provisions of the law of England and Wales apply, regardless of any system of law which would otherwise apply in relation to the matter.

PUBLIC POLICY

18 Nothing in this Part of this Schedule requires or enables the application in England and Wales of a provision of the law of another country if its application would be manifestly contrary to public policy.

PART 4
RECOGNITION AND ENFORCEMENT

RECOGNITION

19 (1) A protective measure taken in relation to an adult under the law of a country other than England and Wales is to be recognised in England and Wales if it was taken on the ground that the adult is habitually resident in the other country.

(2) A protective measure taken in relation to an adult under the law of a Convention country other than England and Wales is to be recognised in England and Wales if it was taken on a ground mentioned in Chapter 2 (jurisdiction).

(3) But the court may disapply this paragraph in relation to a measure if it thinks that—

(a) the case in which the measure was taken was not urgent,
(b) the adult was not given an opportunity to be heard, and
(c) that omission amounted to a breach of natural justice.

(4) It may also disapply this paragraph in relation to a measure if it thinks that—
(a) recognition of the measure would be manifestly contrary to public policy,
(b) the measure would be inconsistent with a mandatory provision of the law of England and Wales, or
(c) the measure is inconsistent with one subsequently taken, or recognised, in England and Wales in relation to the adult.

(5) And the court may disapply this paragraph in relation to a measure taken under the law of a Convention country in a matter to which Article 33 applies, if the court thinks that that Article has not been complied with in connection with that matter.

20 (1) An interested person may apply to the court for a declaration as to whether a protective measure taken under the law of a country other than England and Wales is to be recognised in England and Wales.

(2) No permission is required for an application to the court under this paragraph.

21 For the purposes of paragraphs 19 and 20, any finding of fact relied on when the measure was taken is conclusive.

ENFORCEMENT

22 (1) An interested person may apply to the court for a declaration as to whether a protective measure taken under the law of, and enforceable in, a country other than England and Wales is enforceable, or to be registered, in England and Wales in accordance with Court of Protection Rules.

(2) The court must make the declaration if—
(a) the measure comes within sub-paragraph (1) or (2) of paragraph 19, and
(b) the paragraph is not disapplied in relation to it as a result of sub-paragraph (3), (4) or (5).

(3) A measure to which a declaration under this paragraph relates is enforceable in England and Wales as if it were a measure of like effect taken by the court.

MEASURES TAKEN IN RELATION TO THOSE AGED UNDER 16

23 (1) This paragraph applies where—
(a) provision giving effect to, or otherwise deriving from, the Convention in a country other than England and Wales applies in relation to a person who has not reached 16, and
(b) a measure is taken in relation to that person in reliance on that provision.

(2) This Part of this Schedule applies in relation to that measure as it applies in relation to a protective measure taken in relation to an adult under the law of a Convention country other than England and Wales.

SUPPLEMENTARY

24 The court may not review the merits of a measure taken outside England and Wales except to establish whether the measure complies with this Schedule in so far as it is, as a result of this Schedule, required to do so.

25 Court of Protection Rules may make provision about an application under paragraph 20 or 22.

PART 5
CO-OPERATION

PROPOSAL FOR CROSS-BORDER PLACEMENT

26 (1) This paragraph applies where a public authority proposes to place an adult in an establishment in a Convention country other than England and Wales.

(2) The public authority must consult an appropriate authority in that other country about the proposed placement and, for that purpose, must send it—

(a) a report on the adult, and
(b) a statement of its reasons for the proposed placement.

(3) If the appropriate authority in the other country opposes the proposed placement within a reasonable time, the public authority may not proceed with it.

27 A proposal received by a public authority under Article 33 in relation to an adult is to proceed unless the authority opposes it within a reasonable time.

ADULT IN DANGER ETC

28 (1) This paragraph applies if a public authority is told that an adult—

(a) who is in serious danger, and
(b) in relation to whom the public authority has taken, or is considering taking, protective measures,

is, or has become resident, in a Convention country other than England and Wales.

(2) The public authority must tell an appropriate authority in that other country about—

(a) the danger, and
(b) the measures taken or under consideration.

29 A public authority may not request from, or send to, an appropriate authority in a Convention country information in accordance with Chapter 5 (co-operation) in relation to an adult if it thinks that doing so—

(a) would be likely to endanger the adult or his property, or
(b) would amount to a serious threat to the liberty or life of a member of the adult's family.

PART 6
GENERAL

CERTIFICATES

30 A certificate given under Article 38 by an authority in a Convention country other than England and Wales is, unless the contrary is shown, proof of the matters contained in it.

POWERS TO MAKE FURTHER PROVISION AS TO PRIVATE INTERNATIONAL LAW

31 Her Majesty may by Order in Council confer on the Lord Chancellor, the court or another public authority functions for enabling the Convention to be given effect in England and Wales.

32 (1) Regulations may make provision—
(a) giving further effect to the Convention, or
(b) otherwise about the private international law of England and Wales in relation to the protection of adults.

(2) The regulations may—
(a) confer functions on the court or another public authority;
(b) amend this Schedule;
(c) provide for this Schedule to apply with specified modifications;
(d) make provision about countries other than Convention countries.

EXCEPTIONS

33 Nothing in this Schedule applies, and no provision made under paragraph 32 is to apply, to any matter to which the Convention, as a result of Article 4, does not apply.

REGULATIONS AND ORDERS

34 A reference in this Schedule to regulations or an order (other than an Order in Council) is to regulations or an order made for the purposes of this Schedule by the Lord Chancellor.

COMMENCEMENT

35 The following provisions of this Schedule have effect only if the Convention is in force in accordance with Article 57—
(a) paragraph 8,
(b) paragraph 9,
(c) paragraph 19(2) and (5),
(d) Part 5,
(e) paragraph 30.

Commentary

These provisions give effect in England and Wales to the Convention on the International Protection of Adults which was signed on 13 January 2000. The Convention will only come into force if ratified by three States and so far only Scotland has ratified. However, this schedule in effect governs the jurisdictional rules which will apply between Scotland and England and Wales which may be important in practice and regardless of whether the Convention is in force or not. Part 2 of this schedule deals with the cases which the Court of Protection will deal with when there is an international element. Part 3 deals with the law applicable.

[609]

SCHEDULE 4
PROVISIONS APPLYING TO EXISTING ENDURING POWERS OF ATTORNEY

Section 66(3)

PART 1
ENDURING POWERS OF ATTORNEY

ENDURING POWER OF ATTORNEY TO SURVIVE MENTAL INCAPACITY OF DONOR

1 (1) Where an individual has created a power of attorney which is an enduring power within the meaning of this Schedule—
(a) the power is not revoked by any subsequent mental incapacity of his, but

(b) upon such incapacity supervening, the donee of the power may not do anything under the authority of the power except as provided by sub-paragraph (2) unless or until the instrument creating the power is registered under paragraph 13, and

(c) if and so long as paragraph (b) operates to suspend the donee's authority to act under the power, section 5 of the Powers of Attorney Act 1971 (c 27) (protection of donee and third persons), so far as applicable, applies as if the power had been revoked by the donor's mental incapacity,

and, accordingly, section 1 of this Act does not apply.

(2) Despite sub-paragraph (1)(b), where the attorney has made an application for registration of the instrument then, until it is registered, the attorney may take action under the power—

(a) to maintain the donor or prevent loss to his estate, or

(b) to maintain himself or other persons in so far as paragraph 3(2) permits him to do so.

(3) Where the attorney purports to act as provided by sub-paragraph (2) then, in favour of a person who deals with him without knowledge that the attorney is acting otherwise than in accordance with sub-paragraph (2)(a) or (b), the transaction between them is as valid as if the attorney were acting in accordance with sub-paragraph (2)(a) or (b).

Commentary

Enduring Powers of Attorney ("EPAs") can no longer be created and the Enduring Powers of Attorney Act 1985 has been revoked. However, this schedule provides the transitional provision for those EPAs in existence on 1 October 2007. Whereas a normal power of attorney would be revoked if the donor became incapable of managing his affairs an enduring power will continue.

CHARACTERISTICS OF AN ENDURING POWER OF ATTORNEY

2 (1) Subject to sub-paragraphs (5) and (6) and paragraph 20, a power of attorney is an enduring power within the meaning of this Schedule if the instrument which creates the power—

(a) is in the prescribed form,

(b) was executed in the prescribed manner by the donor and the attorney, and

(c) incorporated at the time of execution by the donor the prescribed explanatory information.

(2) In this paragraph, "prescribed" means prescribed by such of the following regulations as applied when the instrument was executed—

(a) the Enduring Powers of Attorney (Prescribed Form) Regulations 1986 (SI 1986/126),

(b) the Enduring Powers of Attorney (Prescribed Form) Regulations 1987 (SI 1987/1612),

(c) the Enduring Powers of Attorney (Prescribed Form) Regulations 1990 (SI 1990/1376),

(d) the Enduring Powers of Attorney (Welsh Language Prescribed Form) Regulations 2000 (SI 2000/289).

(3) An instrument in the prescribed form purporting to have been executed in the prescribed manner is to be taken, in the absence of evidence to the contrary, to be a document which incorporated at the time of execution by the donor the prescribed explanatory information.

(4) If an instrument differs in an immaterial respect in form or mode of expression from the prescribed form it is to be treated as sufficient in point of form and expression.

(5) A power of attorney cannot be an enduring power unless, when he executes the instrument creating it, the attorney is—

(a) an individual who has reached 18 and is not bankrupt, or

(b) a trust corporation.

(6) A power of attorney which gives the attorney a right to appoint a substitute or successor cannot be an enduring power.

(7) An enduring power is revoked by the bankruptcy of the donor or attorney.

(8) But where the donor or attorney is bankrupt merely because an interim bankruptcy restrictions order has effect in respect of him, the power is suspended for so long as the order has effect.

(9) An enduring power is revoked if the court—

(a) exercises a power under sections 16 to 20 in relation to the donor, and

(b) directs that the enduring power is to be revoked.

(10) No disclaimer of an enduring power, whether by deed or otherwise, is valid unless and until the attorney gives notice of it to the donor or, where paragraph 4(6) or 15(1) applies, to the Public Guardian.

Commentary

The form of an enduring power of attorney and its execution are governed by the Enduring Powers of Attorney (Prescribed Forms) Regulations 1990 (SI 1990/1376), and use of the form is mandatory. The use of the form was extended to 1 October 2007. As to the meaning of "trust corporation" see s 68(1) of the Trustee Act 1925 **[138]**.

SCOPE OF AUTHORITY ETC OF ATTORNEY UNDER ENDURING POWER

3 (1) If the instrument which creates an enduring power of attorney is expressed to confer general authority on the attorney, the instrument operates to confer, subject to—

(a) the restriction imposed by sub-paragraph (3), and

(b) any conditions or restrictions contained in the instrument,

authority to do on behalf of the donor anything which the donor could lawfully do by an attorney at the time when the donor executed the instrument.

(2) Subject to any conditions or restrictions contained in the instrument, an attorney under an enduring power, whether general or limited, may (without obtaining any consent) act under the power so as to benefit himself or other persons than the donor to the following extent but no further—

(a) he may so act in relation to himself or in relation to any other person if the donor might be expected to provide for his or that person's needs respectively, and

(b) he may do whatever the donor might be expected to do to meet those needs.

(3) Without prejudice to sub-paragraph (2) but subject to any conditions or restrictions contained in the instrument, an attorney under an enduring power, whether general or limited, may (without obtaining any consent) dispose of the property of the donor by way of gift to the following extent but no further—

(a) he may make gifts of a seasonal nature or at a time, or on an anniversary, of a birth, a marriage or the formation of a civil partnership, to persons (including himself) who are related to or connected with the donor, and

(b) he may make gifts to any charity to whom the donor made or might be expected to make gifts,

provided that the value of each such gift is not unreasonable having regard to all the circumstances and in particular the size of the donor's estate.

Commentary
Even an attorney with general authority under sub-para (1) does not have power to make decisions about the personal welfare or health of the donor, see *Re F (Sterilisation: Mental Patient)* [1989] 2 FLR 376 whereas the donee of a LPA might have. Neither can an attorney do anything which requires evidence of the donor's signature, see *Clauss v Pir* [1988] 1 Ch 267 (swearing an affidavit). Neither can an attorney take over as personal representative for the donor, but note the Non-Contentious Probate Rules 1985, SI 1985/3132, r 35(2) **[Appendix V]** and see *Practice Direction Enduring Powers of Attorney: Grants of Administration* [1986] 1 FLR 627. As to the power of the attorney to make gifts under sub-para (3), it has been commented that the power is very limited and does not extend to inheritance tax planning (see *Re W (Enduring Power of Attorney)* [2000] Ch 233 on appeal at [2001] Ch 609) but see s 8(2)(e) below.

PART 2
ACTION ON ACTUAL OR IMPENDING INCAPACITY OF DONOR

DUTIES OF ATTORNEY IN EVENT OF ACTUAL OR IMPENDING INCAPACITY OF DONOR

4 (1) Sub-paragraphs (2) to (6) apply if the attorney under an enduring power has reason to believe that the donor is or is becoming mentally incapable.

(2) The attorney must, as soon as practicable, make an application to the Public Guardian for the registration of the instrument creating the power.

(3) Before making an application for registration the attorney must comply with the provisions as to notice set out in Part 3 of this Schedule.

(4) An application for registration—
- (a) must be made in the prescribed form, and
- (b) must contain such statements as may be prescribed.

(5) The attorney—
- (a) may, before making an application for the registration of the instrument, refer to the court for its determination any question as to the validity of the power, and
- (b) must comply with any direction given to him by the court on that determination.

(6) No disclaimer of the power is valid unless and until the attorney gives notice of it to the Public Guardian; and the Public Guardian must notify the donor if he receives a notice under this sub-paragraph.

(7) A person who, in an application for registration, makes a statement which he knows to be false in a material particular is guilty of an offence and is liable—
- (a) on summary conviction, to imprisonment for a term not exceeding 12 months or a fine not exceeding the statutory maximum or both;
- (b) on conviction on indictment, to imprisonment for a term not exceeding 2 years or a fine or both.

(8) In this paragraph, "prescribed" means prescribed by regulations made for the purposes of this Schedule by the Lord Chancellor.

Commentary
The procedure for registration is contained in Part 3 of the Lasting Powers of Attorney, Enduring Powers of Attorney and Public Guardian Regulations 2007 (SI 2007/1253) **[Appendix VIII]**. The prescribed form of application is in Sch 8 to those regulations. The application is now made to the Public Guardian.

PART 3
NOTIFICATION PRIOR TO REGISTRATION

DUTY TO GIVE NOTICE TO RELATIVES

5 Subject to paragraph 7, before making an application for registration the attorney must give notice of his intention to do so to all those persons (if any) who are entitled to receive notice by virtue of paragraph 6.

Commentary

The prescribed form of notice is in Sch 7 to the Lasting Powers of Attorney, Enduring Powers of Attorney and Public Guardian Regulations 2007 (SI 2007/1253) **[Appendix VIII]**, as amended by the Public Guardian (Fees etc) Regulations 2007 (SI 2007/2051), and see reg 23.

6 (1) Subject to sub-paragraphs (2) to (4), persons of the following classes ("relatives") are entitled to receive notice under paragraph 5—

(a) the donor's spouse or civil partner,
(b) the donor's children,
(c) the donor's parents,
(d) the donor's brothers and sisters, whether of the whole or half blood,
(e) the widow, widower or surviving civil partner of a child of the donor,
(f) the donor's grandchildren,
(g) the children of the donor's brothers and sisters of the whole blood,
(h) the children of the donor's brothers and sisters of the half blood,
(i) the donor's uncles and aunts of the whole blood,
(j) the children of the donor's uncles and aunts of the whole blood.

(2) A person is not entitled to receive notice under paragraph 5 if—

(a) his name or address is not known to the attorney and cannot be reasonably ascertained by him, or
(b) the attorney has reason to believe that he has not reached 18 or is mentally incapable.

(3) Except where sub-paragraph (4) applies—

(a) no more than 3 persons are entitled to receive notice under paragraph 5, and
(b) in determining the persons who are so entitled, persons falling within the class in sub-paragraph (1)(a) are to be preferred to persons falling within the class in sub-paragraph (1)(b), those falling within the class in sub-paragraph (1)(b) are to be preferred to those falling within the class in sub-paragraph (1)(c), and so on.

(4) Despite the limit of 3 specified in sub-paragraph (3), where—

(a) there is more than one person falling within any of classes (a) to (j) of sub-paragraph (1), and
(b) at least one of those persons would be entitled to receive notice under paragraph 5,

then, subject to sub-paragraph (2), all the persons falling within that class are entitled to receive notice under paragraph 5.

Commentary

The effect of these provisions in relation to relatives is that each category must be exhausted before turning to the next and if one member of a particular group has to be notified to make up the minimum of three relatives notified, then all members of that group have to be notified.

7 (1) An attorney is not required to give notice under paragraph 5—

(a) to himself, or
(b) to any other attorney under the power who is joining in making the application,

even though he or, as the case may be, the other attorney is entitled to receive notice by virtue of paragraph 6.

(2) In the case of any person who is entitled to receive notice by virtue of paragraph 6, the attorney, before applying for registration, may make an application to the court to be dispensed from the requirement to give him notice; and the court must grant the application if it is satisfied—

(a) that it would be undesirable or impracticable for the attorney to give him notice, or

(b) that no useful purpose is likely to be served by giving him notice.

Commentary

If the donee falls within one of the categories of relatives he does not have to give notice to himself.

DUTY TO GIVE NOTICE TO DONOR

8 (1) Subject to sub-paragraph (2), before making an application for registration the attorney must give notice of his intention to do so to the donor.

(2) Paragraph 7(2) applies in relation to the donor as it applies in relation to a person who is entitled to receive notice under paragraph 5.

Commentary

The donor has to be served with notice unless it would be undesirable or no useful purpose would be served.

CONTENTS OF NOTICES

9 A notice to relatives under this Part of this Schedule must—

(a) be in the prescribed form,

(b) state that the attorney proposes to make an application to the Public Guardian for the registration of the instrument creating the enduring power in question,

(c) inform the person to whom it is given of his right to object to the registration under paragraph 13(4), and

(d) specify, as the grounds on which an objection to registration may be made, the grounds set out in paragraph 13(9).

Commentary

The prescribed form of notice is in Sch 7 to the Lasting Powers of Attorney, Enduring Powers of Attorney and Public Guardian Regulations 2007 (SI 2007/1253) **[Appendix VIII]**, as amended by the Public Guardian (Fees etc) Regulations 2007 (SI 2007/2051).

10 A notice to the donor under this Part of this Schedule—

(a) must be in the prescribed form,

(b) must contain the statement mentioned in paragraph 9(b), and

(c) must inform the donor that, while the instrument remains registered, any revocation of the power by him will be ineffective unless and until the revocation is confirmed by the court.

Commentary

Regulation 23 also requires that the attorney provide or arrange for the provision of an explanation to the donor of the notice and what its effect is and why it is being brought to his attention and that must be provided to the donor personally and in a way that is appropriate to the donor's circumstances (for example using simple language, visual aids or other appropriate means).

DUTY TO GIVE NOTICE TO OTHER ATTORNEYS

11 (1) Subject to sub-paragraph (2), before making an application for registration an attorney under a joint and several power must give notice of his intention to do so to any other attorney under the power who is not joining in making the application; and paragraphs 7(2) and 9 apply in relation to attorneys entitled to receive notice by virtue of this paragraph as they apply in relation to persons entitled to receive notice by virtue of paragraph 6.

(2) An attorney is not entitled to receive notice by virtue of this paragraph if—

(a) his address is not known to the applying attorney and cannot reasonably be ascertained by him, or

(b) the applying attorney has reason to believe that he has not reached 18 or is mentally incapable.

Commentary

The notification under this section protects joint and several attorneys.

SUPPLEMENTARY

12 Despite section 7 of the Interpretation Act 1978 (c 30) (construction of references to service by post), for the purposes of this Part of this Schedule a notice given by post is to be regarded as given on the date on which it was posted.

Commentary

The 1978 Act provides for a notice to be regarded as served on the day after it is posted and this varies that rule.

PART 4
REGISTRATION

REGISTRATION OF INSTRUMENT CREATING POWER

13 (1) If an application is made in accordance with paragraph 4(3) and (4) the Public Guardian must, subject to the provisions of this paragraph, register the instrument to which the application relates.

(2) If it appears to the Public Guardian that—

(a) there is a deputy appointed for the donor of the power created by the instrument, and

(b) the powers conferred on the deputy would, if the instrument were registered, to any extent conflict with the powers conferred on the attorney,

the Public Guardian must not register the instrument except in accordance with the court's directions.

(3) The court may, on the application of the attorney, direct the Public Guardian to register an instrument even though notice has not been given as required by paragraph 4(3) and Part 3 of this Schedule to a person entitled to receive it, if the court is satisfied—

(a) that it was undesirable or impracticable for the attorney to give notice to that person, or

(b) that no useful purpose is likely to be served by giving him notice.

(4) Sub-paragraph (5) applies if, before the end of the period of 5 weeks beginning with the date (or the latest date) on which the attorney gave notice under paragraph 5 of an application for registration, the Public Guardian receives a valid notice of objection to the registration from a person entitled to notice of the application.

(5) The Public Guardian must not register the instrument except in accordance with the court's directions.

(6) Sub-paragraph (7) applies if, in the case of an application for registration—

(a) it appears from the application that there is no one to whom notice has been given under paragraph 5, or

(b) the Public Guardian has reason to believe that appropriate inquiries might bring to light evidence on which he could be satisfied that one of the grounds of objection set out in sub-paragraph (9) was established.

(7) The Public Guardian—

(a) must not register the instrument, and

(b) must undertake such inquiries as he thinks appropriate in all the circumstances.

(8) If, having complied with sub-paragraph (7)(b), the Public Guardian is satisfied that one of the grounds of objection set out in sub-paragraph (9) is established—

(a) the attorney may apply to the court for directions, and

(b) the Public Guardian must not register the instrument except in accordance with the court's directions.

(9) A notice of objection under this paragraph is valid if made on one or more of the following grounds—

(a) that the power purported to have been created by the instrument was not valid as an enduring power of attorney,

(b) that the power created by the instrument no longer subsists,

(c) that the application is premature because the donor is not yet becoming mentally incapable,

(d) that fraud or undue pressure was used to induce the donor to create the power,

(e) that, having regard to all the circumstances and in particular the attorney's relationship to or connection with the donor, the attorney is unsuitable to be the donor's attorney.

(10) If any of those grounds is established to the satisfaction of the court it must direct the Public Guardian not to register the instrument, but if not so satisfied it must direct its registration.

(11) If the court directs the Public Guardian not to register an instrument because it is satisfied that the ground in sub-paragraph (9)(d) or (e) is established, it must by order revoke the power created by the instrument.

(12) If the court directs the Public Guardian not to register an instrument because it is satisfied that any ground in sub-paragraph (9) except that in paragraph (c) is established, the instrument must be delivered up to be cancelled unless the court otherwise directs.

Commentary

The requirement that the court register in sub-para (1) is mandatory if all the formalities have been complied with and there is no objection. As to the grounds for objection, see *Re W (Enduring Power of Attorney)* [2001] Ch 609. As to the unsuitability in sub-para 9(e) see also *Re E (Enduring Power of Attorney)* [2001] Ch 364. The contents of a notice of objection are provided for by reg 25 of the Lasting Powers of Attorney, Enduring Powers of Attorney and Public Guardian Regulations 2007 (SI 2007/1253) **[Appendix VIII]**.

REGISTER OF ENDURING POWERS

14 The Public Guardian has the function of establishing and maintaining a register of enduring powers for the purposes of this Schedule.

Commentary
In practice this is one of the most important functions of the Public Guardian. See reg 30 of the the Lasting Powers of Attorney, Enduring Powers of Attorney and Public Guardian Regulations 2007 (SI 2007/1253) **[Appendix VIII]**.

PART 5
LEGAL POSITION AFTER REGISTRATION

EFFECT AND PROOF OF REGISTRATION

15 (1) The effect of the registration of an instrument under paragraph 13 is that—
- (a) no revocation of the power by the donor is valid unless and until the court confirms the revocation under paragraph 16(3);
- (b) no disclaimer of the power is valid unless and until the attorney gives notice of it to the Public Guardian;
- (c) the donor may not extend or restrict the scope of the authority conferred by the instrument and no instruction or consent given by him after registration, in the case of a consent, confers any right and, in the case of an instruction, imposes or confers any obligation or right on or creates any liability of the attorney or other persons having notice of the instruction or consent.

(2) Sub-paragraph (1) applies for so long as the instrument is registered under paragraph 13 whether or not the donor is for the time being mentally incapable.

(3) A document purporting to be an office copy of an instrument registered under this Schedule is, in any part of the United Kingdom, evidence of—
- (a) the contents of the instrument, and
- (b) the fact that it has been so registered.

(4) Sub-paragraph (3) is without prejudice to section 3 of the Powers of Attorney Act 1971 (c 27) (proof by certified copies) and to any other method of proof authorised by law.

Commentary
Before registration there is nothing to prevent a donor revoking the power in the normal way. However, after registration the requirements of this section apply. Clearly if the donor lacks mental capacity he cannot revoke, but of course a power can be registered while a donor is becoming mentally incapable. Note that a later enduring power will not necessarily revoke an earlier one, see *Re E (Enduring Power of Attorney)* [2001] Ch 364. See also para 16(4) below.

FUNCTIONS OF COURT WITH REGARD TO REGISTERED POWER

16 (1) Where an instrument has been registered under paragraph 13, the court has the following functions with respect to the power and the donor of and the attorney appointed to act under the power.

(2) The court may—
- (a) determine any question as to the meaning or effect of the instrument;
- (b) give directions with respect to—
  - (i) the management or disposal by the attorney of the property and affairs of the donor;
  - (ii) the rendering of accounts by the attorney and the production of the records kept by him for the purpose;
  - (iii) the remuneration or expenses of the attorney whether or not in default of or in accordance with any provision made by the instrument, including directions for the repayment of excessive or the payment of additional remuneration;

(c) require the attorney to supply information or produce documents or things in his possession as attorney;
(d) give any consent or authorisation to act which the attorney would have to obtain from a mentally capable donor;
(e) authorise the attorney to act so as to benefit himself or other persons than the donor otherwise than in accordance with paragraph 3(2) and (3) (but subject to any conditions or restrictions contained in the instrument);
(f) relieve the attorney wholly or partly from any liability which he has or may have incurred on account of a breach of his duties as attorney.

(3) On application made for the purpose by or on behalf of the donor, the court must confirm the revocation of the power if satisfied that the donor—
(a) has done whatever is necessary in law to effect an express revocation of the power, and
(b) was mentally capable of revoking a power of attorney when he did so (whether or not he is so when the court considers the application).

(4) The court must direct the Public Guardian to cancel the registration of an instrument registered under paragraph 13 in any of the following circumstances—
(a) on confirming the revocation of the power under sub-paragraph (3),
(b) on directing under paragraph 2(9)(b) that the power is to be revoked,
(c) on being satisfied that the donor is and is likely to remain mentally capable,
(d) on being satisfied that the power has expired or has been revoked by the mental incapacity of the attorney,
(e) on being satisfied that the power was not a valid and subsisting enduring power when registration was effected,
(f) on being satisfied that fraud or undue pressure was used to induce the donor to create the power,
(g) on being satisfied that, having regard to all the circumstances and in particular the attorney's relationship to or connection with the donor, the attorney is unsuitable to be the donor's attorney.

(5) If the court directs the Public Guardian to cancel the registration of an instrument on being satisfied of the matters specified in sub-paragraph (4)(f) or (g) it must by order revoke the power created by the instrument.

(6) If the court directs the cancellation of the registration of an instrument under sub-paragraph (4) except paragraph (c) the instrument must be delivered up to the Public Guardian to be cancelled, unless the court otherwise directs.

Commentary

The functions set out in sub-para (2) are there because after registration the donor can no longer give instructions or authorise the attorney to act and therefore the Court of Protection takes on that role, while not having as much involvement as if a deputy were appointed. Note that although the court can relieve the restrictions on making gifts under para 3(3), by using sub-para (2)(e) it cannot override any restriction contained in the power itself, see *Re R (Enduring Power of Attorney)* [1991] 1 FLR 128. A cancellation on the basis of sub-para (4)(c) (donor mentally capable and likely to remain so) will have the effect that the power will remain operative until revoked but will not be registered.

CANCELLATION OF REGISTRATION BY PUBLIC GUARDIAN

17 The Public Guardian must cancel the registration of an instrument creating an enduring power of attorney—
(a) on receipt of a disclaimer signed by the attorney;
(b) if satisfied that the power has been revoked by the death or bankruptcy of the donor or attorney or, if the attorney is a body corporate, by its winding up or dissolution;

(c) on receipt of notification from the court that the court has revoked the power;
(d) on confirmation from the court that the donor has revoked the power.

Commentary
While the substantive validity of an EPA is within the remit of the Court of Protection the Public Guardian can cancel the registration in clear cases.

PART 6
PROTECTION OF ATTORNEY AND THIRD PARTIES

PROTECTION OF ATTORNEY AND THIRD PERSONS WHERE POWER IS INVALID OR REVOKED

18 (1) Sub-paragraphs (2) and (3) apply where an instrument which did not create a valid power of attorney has been registered under paragraph 13 (whether or not the registration has been cancelled at the time of the act or transaction in question).

(2) An attorney who acts in pursuance of the power does not incur any liability (either to the donor or to any other person) because of the non-existence of the power unless at the time of acting he knows—

(a) that the instrument did not create a valid enduring power,
(b) that an event has occurred which, if the instrument had created a valid enduring power, would have had the effect of revoking the power, or
(c) that, if the instrument had created a valid enduring power, the power would have expired before that time.

(3) Any transaction between the attorney and another person is, in favour of that person, as valid as if the power had then been in existence, unless at the time of the transaction that person has knowledge of any of the matters mentioned in sub-paragraph (2).

(4) If the interest of a purchaser depends on whether a transaction between the attorney and another person was valid by virtue of sub-paragraph (3), it is conclusively presumed in favour of the purchaser that the transaction was valid if—

(a) the transaction between that person and the attorney was completed within 12 months of the date on which the instrument was registered, or
(b) that person makes a statutory declaration, before or within 3 months after the completion of the purchase, that he had no reason at the time of the transaction to doubt that the attorney had authority to dispose of the property which was the subject of the transaction.

(5) For the purposes of section 5 of the Powers of Attorney Act 1971 (c 27) (protection where power is revoked) in its application to an enduring power the revocation of which by the donor is by virtue of paragraph 15 invalid unless and until confirmed by the court under paragraph 16—

(a) knowledge of the confirmation of the revocation is knowledge of the revocation of the power, but
(b) knowledge of the unconfirmed revocation is not.

Commentary
Reference should be made to the protection offered both to attorneys and purchasers under the Powers of Attorney Act 1971 (which is outside the scope of this work). That protection will not assist if there was never a valid power of attorney created in the first place and sub-para (2) fills that gap.

FURTHER PROTECTION OF ATTORNEY AND THIRD PERSONS

19 (1) If—

(a) an instrument framed in a form prescribed as mentioned in paragraph 2(2) creates a power which is not a valid enduring power, and
(b) the power is revoked by the mental incapacity of the donor,

sub-paragraphs (2) and (3) apply, whether or not the instrument has been registered.

(2) An attorney who acts in pursuance of the power does not, by reason of the revocation, incur any liability (either to the donor or to any other person) unless at the time of acting he knows—

(a) that the instrument did not create a valid enduring power, and
(b) that the donor has become mentally incapable.

(3) Any transaction between the attorney and another person is, in favour of that person, as valid as if the power had then been in existence, unless at the time of the transaction that person knows—

(a) that the instrument did not create a valid enduring power, and
(b) that the donor has become mentally incapable.

(4) Paragraph 18(4) applies for the purpose of determining whether a transaction was valid by virtue of sub-paragraph (3) as it applies for the purpose or determining whether a transaction was valid by virtue of paragraph 18(3).

Commentary

For protection in general see para 18 above. These provisions protect an attorney and third parties in circumstances where a valid power of attorney has been created but it is not a valid enduring power. While the attorney is ignorant of the fact that the power is not an enduring one and of the mental incapacity of the donor, he will not be personally liable.

PART 7
JOINT AND JOINT AND SEVERAL ATTORNEYS

APPLICATION TO JOINT AND JOINT AND SEVERAL ATTORNEYS

20 (1) An instrument which appoints more than one person to be an attorney cannot create an enduring power unless the attorneys are appointed to act—

(a) jointly, or
(b) jointly and severally.

(2) This Schedule, in its application to joint attorneys, applies to them collectively as it applies to a single attorney but subject to the modifications specified in paragraph 21.

(3) This Schedule, in its application to joint and several attorneys, applies with the modifications specified in sub-paragraphs (4) to (7) and in paragraph 22.

(4) A failure, as respects any one attorney, to comply with the requirements for the creation of enduring powers—

(a) prevents the instrument from creating such a power in his case, but
(b) does not affect its efficacy for that purpose as respects the other or others or its efficacy in his case for the purpose of creating a power of attorney which is not an enduring power.

(5) If one or more but not both or all the attorneys makes or joins in making an application for registration of the instrument—

(a) an attorney who is not an applicant as well as one who is may act pending the registration of the instrument as provided in paragraph 1(2),
(b) notice of the application must also be given under Part 3 of this Schedule to the other attorney or attorneys, and

(c) objection may validly be taken to the registration on a ground relating to an attorney or to the power of an attorney who is not an applicant as well as to one or the power of one who is an applicant.

(6) The Public Guardian is not precluded by paragraph 13(5) or (8) from registering an instrument and the court must not direct him not to do so under paragraph 13(10) if an enduring power subsists as respects some attorney who is not affected by the ground or grounds of the objection in question; and where the Public Guardian registers an instrument in that case, he must make against the registration an entry in the prescribed form.

(7) Sub-paragraph (6) does not preclude the court from revoking a power in so far as it confers a power on any other attorney in respect of whom the ground in paragraph 13(9)(d) or (e) is established; and where any ground in paragraph 13(9) affecting any other attorney is established the court must direct the Public Guardian to make against the registration an entry in the prescribed form.

(8) In sub-paragraph (4), "the requirements for the creation of enduring powers" means the provisions of—

(a) paragraph 2 other than sub-paragraphs (8) and (9), and
(b) the regulations mentioned in paragraph 2.

Commentary

The aim of sub-para(1) is to prevent the appointment of successive attorneys or to enable an attorney to appoint a substitute (although quaere whether the appointment of A to act if B cannot is the appointment of more than one attorney). Note also that if the power gives the attorney the right to appoint an alternative or successor, it cannot be an enduring power (see s 2(6) above). Where joint attorneys are appointed, the wording makes it clear that they will be treated collectively. The position is different if joint and several attorneys are appointed. Sub-para (4) makes it clear that some validity affecting one attorney on the creation of the power will not invalidate the appointment of the others. Nor do all joint and several attorneys have to apply for registration although note the requirements for service of notice and objection (sub-para (5)). Sub-paras (6) and (7) enable the registration of the EPA if the objection or revocation takes effect against one of the attorneys only. As to the prescribed form of entry in the register see reg 28 of the Lasting Powers of Attorney, Enduring Powers of Attorney and Public Guardian Regulations 2007 (SI 2007/1253) **[Appendix VIII].**

JOINT ATTORNEYS

21 (1) In paragraph 2(5), the reference to the time when the attorney executes the instrument is to be read as a reference to the time when the second or last attorney executes the instrument.

(2) In paragraph 2(6) to (8), the reference to the attorney is to be read as a reference to any attorney under the power.

(3) Paragraph 13 has effect as if the ground of objection to the registration of the instrument specified in sub-paragraph (9)(e) applied to any attorney under the power.

(4) In paragraph 16(2), references to the attorney are to be read as including references to any attorney under the power.

(5) In paragraph 16(4), references to the attorney are to be read as including references to any attorney under the power.

(6) In paragraph 17, references to the attorney are to be read as including references to any attorney under the power.

Commentary

These provisions make it clear that in respect of joint attorneys (as to which see para 20 above), the Act treats them collectively, and if, for example, one of them becomes bankrupt, that will revoke the power in respect of all of them (para 2). Contrast the treatment of joint and several attorneys under para 22 of this Schedule.

JOINT AND SEVERAL ATTORNEYS

22 (1) In paragraph 2(7), the reference to the bankruptcy of the attorney is to be read as a reference to the bankruptcy of the last remaining attorney under the power; and the bankruptcy of any other attorney under the power causes that person to cease to be an attorney under the power.

(2) In paragraph 2(8), the reference to the suspension of the power is to be read as a reference to its suspension in so far as it relates to the attorney in respect of whom the interim bankruptcy restrictions order has effect.

(3) The restriction upon disclaimer imposed by paragraph 4(6) applies only to those attorneys who have reason to believe that the donor is or is becoming mentally incapable.

Commentary
Contrast the treatment of joint attorneys under para 21 and see para 20. Where there are joint and several attorneys the policy of the Act is to treat them as individuals, and therefore the bankruptcy of one will not have the effect of revoking the power, just revoking the authority of the bankrupt attorney, unless he is the last one left.

PART 8
INTERPRETATION

23 (1) In this Schedule—

"enduring power" is to be construed in accordance with paragraph 2,

"mentally incapable" or "mental incapacity", except where it refers to revocation at common law, means in relation to any person, that he is incapable by reason of mental disorder *(within the meaning of the Mental Health Act)* of managing and administering his property and affairs and "mentally capable" and "mental capacity" are to be construed accordingly,

"notice" means notice in writing, and

"prescribed", except for the purposes of paragraph 2, means prescribed by regulations made for the purposes of this Schedule by the Lord Chancellor.

[(1A) In sub-paragraph (1), "mental disorder" has the same meaning as in the Mental Health Act but disregarding the amendments made to that Act by the Mental Health Act 2007.]

(2) Any question arising under or for the purposes of this Schedule as to what the donor of the power might at any time be expected to do is to be determined by assuming that he had full mental capacity at the time but otherwise by reference to the circumstances existing at that time.

Amendment
Para 23: in sub-para (1) the words "(within the meaning of the Mental Health Act)" in italics repealed, as from a date to be appointed, by the Mental Health Act 2007, s 55, Sch 1, Pt 2, para 23(1), (2), Sch 11, Pt 1.
Para 23: sub-para (1A) inserted, as from a date to be appointed, by the Mental Health Act 2007, s 1(4), Sch 1, Pt 2, para 23(1), (3).

Commentary
Not all the definitions contained in the Enduring Powers of Attorney Act 1985 have survived into this paragraph. Note for the purpose of these provisions the concept of mental capacity is not that contained in section 1 of the Act but remains the test under the Mental Health Act 1983. As to the meaning of mental disorder as set out in section 1(2) of the Mental Health Act 1983, that means "mental illness, arrested or incomplete development of mind, psychopathic disorder and any other disorder or disability of mind".

[610]

SCHEDULE 5
TRANSITIONAL PROVISIONS AND SAVINGS

Section 66(4)

PART 1
REPEAL OF PART 7 OF THE MENTAL HEALTH ACT 1983

EXISTING RECEIVERS

1 (1) This paragraph applies where, immediately before the commencement day, there is a receiver ("R") for a person ("P") appointed under section 99 of the Mental Health Act.

(2) On and after that day—

(a) this Act applies as if R were a deputy appointed for P by the court, but with the functions that R had as receiver immediately before that day, and

(b) a reference in any other enactment to a deputy appointed by the court includes a person appointed as a deputy as a result of paragraph (a).

(3) On any application to it by R, the court may end R's appointment as P's deputy.

(4) Where, as a result of section 20(1), R may not make a decision on behalf of P in relation to a relevant matter, R must apply to the court.

(5) If, on the application, the court is satisfied that P is capable of managing his property and affairs in relation to the relevant matter—

(a) it must make an order ending R's appointment as P's deputy in relation to that matter, but

(b) it may, in relation to any other matter, exercise in relation to P any of the powers which it has under sections 15 to 19.

(6) If it is not satisfied, the court may exercise in relation to P any of the powers which it has under sections 15 to 19.

(7) R's appointment as P's deputy ceases to have effect if P dies.

(8) "Relevant matter" means a matter in relation to which, immediately before the commencement day, R was authorised to act as P's receiver.

(9) In sub-paragraph (1), the reference to a receiver appointed under section 99 of the Mental Health Act includes a reference to a person who by virtue of Schedule 5 to that Act was deemed to be a receiver appointed under that section.

Commentary

Sub-para (2) provides for receivers appointed under the Mental health Act 1983 to be converted into deputies on 1 October 2007. He will only have the powers he had as a receiver and the Court can curtail them if in respect of a particular matter P has capacity (sub-para (5)) thereby emphasising the issue specific nature of the test.

ORDERS, APPOINTMENTS ETC

2 (1) Any order or appointment made, direction or authority given or other thing done which has, or by virtue of Schedule 5 to the Mental Health Act was deemed to have, effect under Part 7 of the Act immediately before the commencement day is to continue to have effect despite the repeal of Part 7.

(2) In so far as any such order, appointment, direction, authority or thing could have been made, given or done under sections 15 to 20 if those sections had then been in force—

(a) it is to be treated as made, given or done under those sections, and

(b) the powers of variation and discharge conferred by section 16(7) apply accordingly.

(3) Sub-paragraph (1)—

(a) does not apply to nominations under section 93(1) or (4) of the Mental Health Act, and

(b) as respects receivers, has effect subject to paragraph 1.

(4) This Act does not affect the operation of section 109 of the Mental Health Act (effect and proof of orders etc) in relation to orders made and directions given under Part 7 of that Act.

(5) This paragraph is without prejudice to section 16 of the Interpretation Act 1978 (c 30) (general savings on repeal).

PENDING PROCEEDINGS

3 (1) Any application for the exercise of a power under Part 7 of the Mental Health Act which is pending immediately before the commencement day is to be treated, in so far as a corresponding power is exercisable under sections 16 to 20, as an application for the exercise of that power.

(2) For the purposes of sub-paragraph (1) an application for the appointment of a receiver is to be treated as an application for the appointment of a deputy.

Commentary

This converts pending applications o the Court of Protection on 1 October 2007 into applications which can be made under this Act.

APPEALS

4 (1) Part 7 of the Mental Health Act and the rules made under it are to continue to apply to any appeal brought by virtue of section 105 of that Act which has not been determined before the commencement day.

(2) If in the case of an appeal brought by virtue of section 105(1) (appeal to nominated judge) the judge nominated under section 93 of the Mental Health Act has begun to hear the appeal, he is to continue to do so but otherwise it is to be heard by a puisne judge of the High Court nominated under section 46.

FEES

5 All fees and other payments which, having become due, have not been paid to the former Court of Protection before the commencement day, are to be paid to the new Court of Protection.

COURT RECORDS

6 (1) The records of the former Court of Protection are to be treated, on and after the commencement day, as records of the new Court of Protection and are to be dealt with accordingly under the Public Records Act 1958 (c 51).

(2) On and after the commencement day, the Public Guardian is, for the purpose of exercising any of his functions, to be given such access as he may require to such of the records mentioned in sub-paragraph (1) as relate to the appointment of receivers under section 99 of the Mental Health Act.

EXISTING CHARGES

7 This Act does not affect the operation in relation to a charge created before the commencement day of—

(a) so much of section 101(6) of the Mental Health Act as precludes a charge created under section 101(5) from conferring a right of sale or foreclosure during the lifetime of the patient, or

(b) section 106(6) of the Mental Health Act (charge created by virtue of section 106(5) not to cause interest to fail etc).

PRESERVATION OF INTERESTS ON DISPOSAL OF PROPERTY

8 Paragraph 8(1) of Schedule 2 applies in relation to any disposal of property (within the meaning of that provision) by a person living on 1st November 1960, being a disposal effected under the Lunacy Act 1890 (c 5) as it applies in relation to the disposal of property effected under sections 16 to 20.

ACCOUNTS

9 Court of Protection Rules may provide that, in a case where paragraph 1 applies, R is to have a duty to render accounts—

(a) while he is receiver;

(b) after he is discharged.

INTERPRETATION

10 In this Part of this Schedule—

(a) "the commencement day" means the day on which section 66(1)(a) (repeal of Part 7 of the Mental Health Act) comes into force,

(b) "the former Court of Protection" means the office abolished by section 45, and

(c) "the new Court of Protection" means the court established by that section.

PART 2
REPEAL OF THE ENDURING POWERS OF ATTORNEY ACT 1985

ORDERS, DETERMINATIONS, ETC

11 (1) Any order or determination made, or other thing done, under the 1985 Act which has effect immediately before the commencement day continues to have effect despite the repeal of that Act.

(2) In so far as any such order, determination or thing could have been made or done under Schedule 4 if it had then been in force—

(a) it is to be treated as made or done under that Schedule, and

(b) the powers of variation and discharge exercisable by the court apply accordingly.

(3) Any instrument registered under the 1985 Act is to be treated as having been registered by the Public Guardian under Schedule 4.

(4) This paragraph is without prejudice to section 16 of the Interpretation Act 1978 (c 30) (general savings on repeal).

PENDING PROCEEDINGS

12 (1) An application for the exercise of a power under the 1985 Act which is pending immediately before the commencement day is to be treated, in so far as a corresponding power is exercisable under Schedule 4, as an application for the exercise of that power.

(2) For the purposes of sub-paragraph (1)—

- (a) a pending application under section 4(2) of the 1985 Act for the registration of an instrument is to be treated as an application to the Public Guardian under paragraph 4 of Schedule 4 and any notice given in connection with that application under Schedule 1 to the 1985 Act is to be treated as given under Part 3 of Schedule 4,
- (b) a notice of objection to the registration of an instrument is to be treated as a notice of objection under paragraph 13 of Schedule 4, and
- (c) pending proceedings under section 5 of the 1985 Act are to be treated as proceedings on an application for the exercise by the court of a power which would become exercisable in relation to an instrument under paragraph 16(2) of Schedule 4 on its registration.

APPEALS

13 (1) The 1985 Act and, so far as relevant, the provisions of Part 7 of the Mental Health Act and the rules made under it as applied by section 10 of the 1985 Act are to continue to have effect in relation to any appeal brought by virtue of section 10(1)(c) of the 1985 Act which has not been determined before the commencement day.

(2) If, in the case of an appeal brought by virtue of section 105(1) of the Mental Health Act as applied by section 10(1)(c) of the 1985 Act (appeal to nominated judge), the judge nominated under section 93 of the Mental Health Act has begun to hear the appeal, he is to continue to do so but otherwise the appeal is to be heard by a puisne judge of the High Court nominated under section 46.

EXERCISE OF POWERS OF DONOR AS TRUSTEE

14 (1) Section 2(8) of the 1985 Act (which prevents a power of attorney under section 25 of the Trustee Act 1925 (c 19) as enacted from being an enduring power) is to continue to apply to any enduring power—

- (a) created before 1st March 2000, and
- (b) having effect immediately before the commencement day.

(2) Section 3(3) of the 1985 Act (which entitles the donee of an enduring power to exercise the donor's powers as trustee) is to continue to apply to any enduring power to which, as a result of the provision mentioned in sub-paragraph (3), it applies immediately before the commencement day.

(3) The provision is section 4(3)(a) of the Trustee Delegation Act 1999 (c 15) (which provides for section 3(3) of the 1985 Act to cease to apply to an enduring power when its registration is cancelled, if it was registered in response to an application made before 1st March 2001).

(4) Even though section 4 of the 1999 Act is repealed by this Act, that section is to continue to apply in relation to an enduring power—

- (a) to which section 3(3) of the 1985 Act applies as a result of sub-paragraph (2), or
- (b) to which, immediately before the repeal of section 4 of the 1999 Act, section 1 of that Act applies as a result of section 4 of it.

(5) The reference in section 1(9) of the 1999 Act to section 4(6) of that Act is to be read with sub-paragraphs (2) to (4).

INTERPRETATION

15 In this Part of this Schedule, "the commencement day" means the day on which section 66(1)(b) (repeal of the 1985 Act) comes into force.

[611]

SCHEDULE 6
MINOR AND CONSEQUENTIAL AMENDMENTS

Section 67(1)

FINES AND RECOVERIES ACT 1833 (C 74)

1 (1) The Fines and Recoveries Act 1833 (c 74) is amended as follows.

(2) In section 33 (case where protector of settlement lacks capacity to act), for the words from "shall be incapable" to "is incapable as aforesaid" substitute "lacks capacity (within the meaning of the Mental Capacity Act 2005) to manage his property and affairs, the Court of Protection is to take his place as protector of the settlement while he lacks capacity".

(3) In sections 48 and 49 (mental health jurisdiction), for each reference to the judge having jurisdiction under Part 7 of the Mental Health Act substitute a reference to the Court of Protection.

IMPROVEMENT OF LAND ACT 1864 (C 114)

2 In section 68 of the Improvement of Land Act 1864 (c 114) (apportionment of rentcharges)—

(a) for ", curator, or receiver of" substitute "or curator of, or a deputy with powers in relation to property and affairs appointed by the Court of Protection for,", and

(b) for "or patient within the meaning of Part VII of the Mental Health Act 1983" substitute "person who lacks capacity (within the meaning of the Mental Capacity Act 2005) to receive the notice".

Trustee Act 1925 (c 19)

3 (1) The Trustee Act 1925 (c 19) is amended as follows.

(2) In section 36 (appointment of new trustee)—

(a) in subsection (6C), for the words from "a power of attorney" to the end, substitute "an enduring power of attorney or lasting power of attorney registered under the Mental Capacity Act 2005", and

(b) in subsection (9)—

(i) for the words from "is incapable" to "exercising" substitute "lacks capacity to exercise", and

(ii) for the words from "the authority" to the end substitute "the Court of Protection".

(3) In section 41(1) (power of court to appoint new trustee) for the words from "is incapable" to "exercising" substitute "lacks capacity to exercise".

(4) In section 54 (mental health jurisdiction)—

(a) for subsection (1) substitute—

"(1) Subject to subsection (2), the Court of Protection may not make an order, or give a direction or authority, in relation to a person who lacks capacity to exercise his functions as trustee, if the High Court may make an order to that effect under this Act.",

(b) in subsection (2)—

(i) for the words from the beginning to "of a receiver" substitute "Where a person lacks capacity to exercise his functions as a trustee and a deputy is appointed for him by the Court of Protection or an application for the appointment of a deputy",

(ii) for "the said authority", in each place, substitute "the Court of Protection", and

(iii) for "the patient", in each place, substitute "the person concerned", and

(c) omit subsection (3).

(5) In section 55 (order made on particular allegation to be conclusive evidence of it)—

(a) for the words from "Part VII" to "Northern Ireland" substitute "sections 15 to 20 of the Mental Capacity Act 2005 or any corresponding provisions having effect in Northern Ireland", and

(b) for paragraph (a) substitute—

"(a) that a trustee or mortgagee lacks capacity in relation to the matter in question;".

(6) In section 68 (definitions), at the end add—

"(3) Any reference in this Act to a person who lacks capacity in relation to a matter is to a person—

(a) who lacks capacity within the meaning of the Mental Capacity Act 2005 in relation to that matter, or

(b) in respect of whom the powers conferred by section 48 of that Act are exercisable and have been exercised in relation to that matter.".

LAW OF PROPERTY ACT 1925 (C 20)

4 (1) The Law of Property Act 1925 (c 20) is amended as follows.

(2) In section 22 (conveyances on behalf of persons who lack capacity)—

(a) in subsection (1)—

(i) for the words from "in a person suffering" to "is acting" substitute ", either solely or jointly with any other person or persons, in a person lacking capacity (within the meaning of the Mental Capacity Act 2005) to convey or create a legal estate, a deputy appointed for him by the Court of Protection or (if no deputy is appointed", and

(ii) for "the authority having jurisdiction under Part VII of the Mental Health Act 1983" substitute "the Court of Protection",

(b) in subsection (2), for "is incapable, by reason of mental disorder, of exercising" substitute "lacks capacity (within the meaning of that Act) to exercise", and

(c) in subsection (3), for the words from "an enduring power" to the end substitute "an enduring power of attorney or lasting power of attorney (within the meaning of the 2005 Act) is entitled to act for the trustee who lacks capacity in relation to the dealing.".

(3) In section 205(1) (interpretation), omit paragraph (xiii).

ADMINISTRATION OF ESTATES ACT 1925 (C 23)

5 (1) The Administration of Estates Act 1925 (c 23) is amended as follows.

(2) In section 41(1) (powers of personal representatives to appropriate), in the proviso—

(a) in paragraph (ii)—

(i) for the words from "is incapable" to "the consent" substitute "lacks capacity (within the meaning of the Mental Capacity Act 2005) to give the consent, it", and

(ii) for "or receiver" substitute "or a person appointed as deputy for him by the Court of Protection", and

(b) in paragraph (iv), for "no receiver is acting for a person suffering from mental disorder" substitute "no deputy is appointed for a person who lacks capacity to consent".

(3) Omit section 55(1)(viii) (definitions of "person of unsound mind" and "defective").

NATIONAL ASSISTANCE ACT 1948 (C 29)

6 In section 49 of the National Assistance Act 1948 (c 29) (expenses of council officers acting for persons who lack capacity)—

(a) for the words from "applies" to "affairs of a patient" substitute "applies for appointment by the Court of Protection as a deputy", and

(b) for "such functions" substitute "his functions as deputy".

USA VETERANS' PENSIONS (ADMINISTRATION) ACT 1949 (C 45)

7 In section 1 of the USA Veterans' Pensions (Administration) Act 1949 (c 45) (administration of pensions)—

(a) in subsection (4), omit the words from "or for whom" to "1983", and

(b) after subsection (4), insert—

"(4A) An agreement under subsection (1) is not to be made in relation to a person who lacks capacity (within the meaning of the Mental Capacity Act 2005) for the purposes of this Act if—

(a) there is a donee of an enduring power of attorney or lasting power of attorney (within the meaning of the 2005 Act), or a deputy appointed for the person by the Court of Protection, and

(b) the donee or deputy has power in relation to the person for the purposes of this Act.

(4B) The proviso at the end of subsection (4) also applies in relation to subsection (4A).".

INTESTATES' ESTATES ACT 1952 (C 64)

8 In Schedule 2 to the Intestates' Estates Act 1952 (c 64) (rights of surviving spouse or civil partner in relation to home), for paragraph 6(1) substitute—

"(1) Where the surviving spouse or civil partner lacks capacity (within the meaning of the Mental Capacity Act 2005) to make a requirement or give a consent under this Schedule, the requirement or consent may be made or given by a deputy appointed by the Court of Protection with power in that respect or, if no deputy has that power, by that court.".

VARIATION OF TRUSTS ACT 1958 (C 53)

9 In section 1 of the Variation of Trusts Act 1958 (c 53) (jurisdiction of courts to vary trusts)—

(a) in subsection (3), for the words from "shall be determined" to the end substitute "who lacks capacity (within the meaning of the Mental Capacity Act 2005) to give his assent is to be determined by the Court of Protection", and

(b) in subsection (6), for the words from "the powers" to the end substitute "the powers of the Court of Protection".

ADMINISTRATION OF JUSTICE ACT 1960 (C 65)

10 In section 12(1)(b) of the Administration of Justice Act 1960 (c 65) (contempt of court to publish information about proceedings in private relating to persons with incapacity) for the words from "under Part VIII" to "that Act" substitute "under the Mental Capacity Act 2005, or under any provision of the Mental Health Act 1983".

INDUSTRIAL AND PROVIDENT SOCIETIES ACT 1965 (C 12)

11 In section 26 of the Industrial and Provident Societies Act 1965 (c 12) (payments for mentally incapable people), for subsection (2) substitute—

"(2) Subsection (1) does not apply where the member or person concerned lacks capacity (within the meaning of the Mental Capacity Act 2005) for the purposes of this Act and—

(a) there is a donee of an enduring power of attorney or lasting power of attorney (within the meaning of the 2005 Act), or a deputy appointed for the member or person by the Court of Protection, and

(b) the donee or deputy has power in relation to the member or person for the purposes of this Act.".

COMPULSORY PURCHASE ACT 1965 (C 56)

12 In Schedule 1 to the Compulsory Purchase Act 1965 (c 56) (persons without power to sell their interests), for paragraph 1(2)(b) substitute—

"(b) do not have effect in relation to a person who lacks capacity (within the meaning of the Mental Capacity Act 2005) for the purposes of this Act if—

(i) there is a donee of an enduring power of attorney or lasting power of attorney (within the meaning of the 2005 Act), or a deputy appointed for the person by the Court of Protection, and

(ii) the donee or deputy has power in relation to the person for the purposes of this Act.".

LEASEHOLD REFORM ACT 1967 (C 88)

13 (1) For section 26(2) of the Leasehold Reform Act 1967 (c 88) (landlord lacking capacity) substitute—

"(2) Where a landlord lacks capacity (within the meaning of the Mental Capacity Act 2005) to exercise his functions as a landlord, those functions are to be exercised—

(a) by a donee of an enduring power of attorney or lasting power of attorney (within the meaning of the 2005 Act), or a deputy appointed for him by the Court of Protection, with power to exercise those functions, or

(b) if no donee or deputy has that power, by a person authorised in that respect by that court.".

(2) That amendment does not affect any proceedings pending at the commencement of this paragraph in which a receiver or a person authorised under Part 7 of the Mental Health Act is acting on behalf of the landlord.

MEDICINES ACT 1968 (C 67)

14 In section 72 of the Medicines Act 1968 (c 67) (pharmacist lacking capacity)—

(a) in subsection (1)(c), for the words from "a receiver" to "1959" substitute "he becomes a person who lacks capacity (within the meaning of the Mental Capacity Act 2005) to carry on the business",

(b) after subsection (1) insert—

"(1A) In subsection (1)(c), the reference to a person who lacks capacity to carry on the business is to a person—

(a) in respect of whom there is a donee of an enduring power of attorney or lasting power of attorney (within the meaning of the Mental Capacity Act 2005), or

(b) for whom a deputy is appointed by the Court of Protection,

and in relation to whom the donee or deputy has power for the purposes of this Act.",

(c) in subsection (3)(d)—

(i) for "receiver" substitute "deputy", and

(ii) after "guardian" insert "or from the date of registration of the instrument appointing the donee", and

(d) in subsection (4)(c), for "receiver" substitute "donee, deputy".

FAMILY LAW REFORM ACT 1969 (C 46)

15 For section 21(4) of the Family Law Reform Act 1969 (c 46) (consent required for taking of bodily sample from person lacking capacity), substitute—

"(4) A bodily sample may be taken from a person who lacks capacity (within the meaning of the Mental Capacity Act 2005) to give his consent, if consent is given by the court giving the direction under section 20 or by—

(a) a donee of an enduring power of attorney or lasting power of attorney (within the meaning of that Act), or

(b) a deputy appointed, or any other person authorised, by the Court of Protection,

with power in that respect.".

LOCAL AUTHORITY SOCIAL SERVICES ACT 1970 (C 42)

16 (1) Schedule 1 to the Local Authority Social Services Act 1970 (c 42) (enactments conferring functions assigned to social services committee) is amended as follows.

(2) In the entry for section 49 of the National Assistance Act 1948 (expenses of local authority officer appointed for person who lacks capacity) for "receiver" substitute "deputy".

(3) At the end, insert—

"Mental Capacity Act 2005	
Section 39	Instructing independent mental capacity advocate before providing accommodation for person lacking capacity.
Section 49	Reports in proceedings.".

COURTS ACT 1971 (C 23)

17 In Part 1A of Schedule 2 to the Courts Act 1971 (c 23) (office-holders eligible for appointment as circuit judges), omit the reference to a Master of the Court of Protection.

LOCAL GOVERNMENT ACT 1972 (C 70)

18 (1) Omit section 118 of the Local Government Act 1972 (c 70) (payment of pension etc where recipient lacks capacity).

(2) Sub-paragraph (3) applies where, before the commencement of this paragraph, a local authority has, in respect of a person referred to in that section as "the patient", made payments under that section—

(a) to an institution or person having the care of the patient, or
(b) in accordance with subsection (1)(a) or (b) of that section.

(3) The local authority may, in respect of the patient, continue to make payments under that section to that institution or person, or in accordance with subsection (1)(a) or (b) of that section, despite the repeal made by sub-paragraph (1).

MATRIMONIAL CAUSES ACT 1973 (C 18)

19 In section 40 of the Matrimonial Causes Act 1973 (c 18) (payments to person who lacks capacity) (which becomes subsection (1))—

(a) for the words from "is incapable" to "affairs" substitute "("P") lacks capacity (within the meaning of the Mental Capacity Act 2005) in relation to the provisions of the order",
(b) for "that person under Part VIII of that Act" substitute "P under that Act",
(c) for the words from "such persons" to the end substitute "such person ("D") as it may direct", and
(d) at the end insert—

"(2) In carrying out any functions of his in relation to an order made under subsection (1), D must act in P's best interests (within the meaning of that Act).".

JURIES ACT 1974 (C 23)

20 In Schedule 1 to the Juries Act 1974 (c 23) (disqualification for jury service), for paragraph 3 substitute—

"**3** A person who lacks capacity, within the meaning of the Mental Capacity Act 2005, to serve as a juror.".

CONSUMER CREDIT ACT 1974 (C 39)

21 For section 37(1)(c) of the Consumer Credit Act 1974 (c 39) (termination of consumer credit licence if holder lacks capacity) substitute—

"(c) becomes a person who lacks capacity (within the meaning of the Mental Capacity Act 2005) to carry on the activities covered by the licence.".

SOLICITORS ACT 1974 (C 47)

22 (1) The Solicitors Act 1974 (c 47) is amended as follows.

(2) For section 12(1)(j) (application for practising certificate by solicitor lacking capacity) substitute—

"(j) while he lacks capacity (within the meaning of the Mental Capacity Act 2005) to act as a solicitor and powers under sections 15 to 20 or section 48 of that Act are exercisable in relation to him;".

(3) In section 62(4) (contentious business agreements made by clients) for paragraphs (c) and (d) substitute—

"(c) as a deputy for him appointed by the Court of Protection with powers in relation to his property and affairs, or

(d) as another person authorised under that Act to act on his behalf.".

(4) In paragraph 1(1) of Schedule 1 (circumstances in which Law Society may intervene in solicitor's practice), for paragraph (f) substitute—

"(f) a solicitor lacks capacity (within the meaning of the Mental Capacity Act 2005) to act as a solicitor and powers under sections 15 to 20 or section 48 of that Act are exercisable in relation to him;".

LOCAL GOVERNMENT (MISCELLANEOUS PROVISIONS) ACT 1976 (C 57)

23 In section 31 of the Local Government (Miscellaneous Provisions) Act 1976 (c 57) (the title to which becomes "Indemnities for local authority officers appointed as deputies or administrators"), for the words from "as a receiver" to "1959" substitute "as a deputy for a person by the Court of Protection".

SALE OF GOODS ACT 1979 (C 54)

24 In section 3(2) of the Sale of Goods Act 1979 (c 54) (capacity to buy and sell) the words "mental incapacity or" cease to have effect in England and Wales.

LIMITATION ACT 1980 (C 58)

25 In section 38 of the Limitation Act 1980 (c 58) (interpretation) substitute—

(a) in subsection (2) for "of unsound mind" substitute "lacks capacity (within the meaning of the Mental Capacity Act 2005) to conduct legal proceedings", and

(b) omit subsections (3) and (4).

PUBLIC PASSENGER VEHICLES ACT 1981 (C 14)

26 In section 57(2)(c) of the Public Passenger Vehicles Act 1981 (c 14) (termination of public service vehicle licence if holder lacks capacity) for the words from "becomes a patient" to "or" substitute "becomes a person who lacks capacity (within the meaning of the Mental Capacity Act 2005) to use a vehicle under the licence, or".

JUDICIAL PENSIONS ACT 1981 (C 20)

27 In Schedule 1 to the Judicial Pensions Act 1981 (c 20) (pensions of Supreme Court officers, etc), in paragraph 1, omit the reference to a Master of the Court of Protection except in the case of a person holding that office immediately before the commencement of this paragraph or who had previously retired from that office or died.

SUPREME COURT ACT 1981 [SENIOR COURTS ACT 1981] (C 54)

28 In Schedule 2 to the *Supreme Court Act 1981* [Senior Courts Act 1981] (c 54) (qualifications for appointment to office in Supreme Court), omit paragraph 11 (Master of the Court of Protection).

MENTAL HEALTH ACT 1983 (C 20)

29 (1) The Mental Health Act is amended as follows.

(2) In section 134(3) (cases where correspondence of detained patients may not be withheld) for paragraph (b) substitute—

"(b) any judge or officer of the Court of Protection, any of the Court of Protection Visitors or any person asked by that Court for a report under section 49 of the Mental Capacity Act 2005 concerning the patient;".

(3) In section 139 (protection for acts done in pursuance of 1983 Act), in subsection (1), omit from "or in, or in pursuance" to "Part VII of this Act,".

(4) Section 142 (payment of pension etc where recipient lacks capacity) ceases to have effect in England and Wales.

(5) Sub-paragraph (6) applies where, before the commencement of sub-paragraph (4), an authority has, in respect of a person referred to in that section as "the patient", made payments under that section—

(a) to an institution or person having the care of the patient, or
(b) in accordance with subsection (2)(a) or (b) of that section.

(6) The authority may, in respect of the patient, continue to make payments under that section to that institution or person, or in accordance with subsection (2)(a) or (b) of that section, despite the amendment made by sub-paragraph (4).

(7) In section 145(1) (interpretation), in the definition of "patient", omit " (except in Part VII of this Act)".

(8) In section 146 (provisions having effect in Scotland), omit from "104(4)" to "section),".

(9) In section 147 (provisions having effect in Northern Ireland), omit from "104(4)" to "section),".

ADMINISTRATION OF JUSTICE ACT 1985 (C 61)

30 In section 18(3) of the Administration of Justice Act 1985 (c 61) (licensed conveyancer who lacks capacity), for the words from "that person" to the end substitute "he becomes a person who lacks capacity (within the meaning of the Mental Capacity Act 2005) to practise as a licensed conveyancer.".

INSOLVENCY ACT 1986 (C 45)

31 (1) The Insolvency Act 1986 (c 45) is amended as follows.

(2) In section 389A (people not authorised to act as nominee or supervisor in voluntary arrangement), in subsection (3)—

(a) omit the "or" immediately after paragraph (b),

(b) in paragraph (c), omit "Part VII of the Mental Health Act 1983 or", and

(c) after that paragraph, insert

", or

(d) he lacks capacity (within the meaning of the Mental Capacity Act 2005) to act as nominee or supervisor".

(3) In section 390 (people not qualified to be insolvency practitioners), in subsection (4)—

(a) omit the "or" immediately after paragraph (b),

(b) in paragraph (c), omit "Part VII of the Mental Health Act 1983 or", and

(c) after that paragraph, insert

", or

(d) he lacks capacity (within the meaning of the Mental Capacity Act 2005) to act as an insolvency practitioner.".

BUILDING SOCIETIES ACT 1986 (C 53)

32 In section 102D(9) of the Building Societies Act 1986 (c 53) (references to a person holding an account on trust for another)—

(a) in paragraph (a), for "Part VII of the Mental Health Act 1983" substitute "the Mental Capacity Act 2005", and

(b) for paragraph (b) substitute—

"(b) to an attorney holding an account for another person under—

(i) an enduring power of attorney or lasting power of attorney registered under the Mental Capacity Act 2005, or

(ii) an enduring power registered under the Enduring Powers of Attorney (Northern Ireland) Order 1987;".

PUBLIC TRUSTEE AND ADMINISTRATION OF FUNDS ACT 1986 (C 57)

33 In section 3 of the Public Trustee and Administration of Funds Act 1986 (c 57) (functions of the Public Trustee)—

(a) for subsections (1) to (5) substitute—

"(1) The Public Trustee may exercise the functions of a deputy appointed by the Court of Protection.",

(b) in subsection (6), for "the 1906 Act" substitute "the Public Trustee Act 1906", and

(c) omit subsection (7).

PATRONAGE (BENEFICES) MEASURE 1986 (NO 3)

34 (1) The Patronage (Benefices) Measure 1986 (No 3) is amended as follows.

(2) In section 5 (rights of patronage exercisable otherwise than by registered patron), after subsection (3) insert—

"(3A) The reference in subsection (3) to a power of attorney does not include an enduring power of attorney or lasting power of attorney (within the meaning of the Mental Capacity Act 2005)."

(3) In section 9 (information to be sent to designated officer when benefice becomes vacant), after subsection (5) insert—

"(5A) Subsections (5B) and (5C) apply where the functions of a registered patron are, as a result of paragraph 10 of Schedule 2 to the Mental Capacity Act 2005 (patron's loss of capacity to discharge functions), to be discharged by an individual appointed by the Court of Protection.

(5B) If the individual is a clerk in Holy Orders, subsection (5) applies to him as it applies to the registered patron.

(5C) If the individual is not a clerk in Holy Orders, subsection (1) (other than paragraph (b)) applies to him as it applies to the registered patron."

COURTS AND LEGAL SERVICES ACT 1990 (C 41)

35 (1) The Courts and Legal Services Act 1990 (c 41) is amended as follows.

(2) In Schedule 11 (judges etc barred from legal practice), for the reference to a Master of the Court of Protection substitute a reference to each of the following—

(a) Senior Judge of the Court of Protection,
(b) President of the Court of Protection,
(c) Vice-President of the Court of Protection.

(3) In paragraph 5(3) of Schedule 14 (exercise of powers of intervention in registered foreign lawyer's practice), for paragraph (f) substitute—

"(f) he lacks capacity (within the meaning of the Mental Capacity Act 2005) to act as a registered foreign lawyer and powers under sections 15 to 20 or section 48 are exercisable in relation to him;".

CHILD SUPPORT ACT 1991 (C 48)

36 In section 50 of the Child Support Act 1991 (c 48) (unauthorised disclosure of information)—

(a) in subsection (8)—
  (i) immediately after paragraph (a), insert "or",
  (ii) omit paragraphs (b) and (d) and the "or" immediately after paragraph (c), and
  (iii) for ", receiver, custodian or appointee" substitute "or custodian", and
(b) after that subsection, insert—

"(9) Where the person to whom the information relates lacks capacity (within the meaning of the Mental Capacity Act 2005) to consent to its disclosure, the appropriate person is—

(a) a donee of an enduring power of attorney or lasting power of attorney (within the meaning of that Act), or
(b) a deputy appointed for him, or any other person authorised, by the Court of Protection,

with power in that respect.".

SOCIAL SECURITY ADMINISTRATION ACT 1992 (C 5)

37 In section 123 of the Social Security Administration Act 1992 (c 5) (unauthorised disclosure of information)—

(a) in subsection (10), omit—

(i) in paragraph (b), "a receiver appointed under section 99 of the Mental Health Act 1983 or",

(ii) in paragraph (d)(i), "sub-paragraph (a) of rule 41(1) of the Court of Protection Rules 1984 or",

(iii) in paragraph (d)(ii), "a receiver ad interim appointed under sub-paragraph (b) of the said rule 41(1) or", and

(iv) "receiver,", and

(b) after that subsection, insert—

"(11) Where the person to whom the information relates lacks capacity (within the meaning of the Mental Capacity Act 2005) to consent to its disclosure, the appropriate person is—

(a) a donee of an enduring power of attorney or lasting power of attorney (within the meaning of that Act), or

(b) a deputy appointed for him, or any other person authorised, by the Court of Protection,

with power in that respect.".

JUDICIAL PENSIONS AND RETIREMENT ACT 1993 (C 8)

38 (1) The Judicial Pensions and Retirement Act 1993 (c 8) is amended as follows.

(2) In Schedule 1 (qualifying judicial offices), in Part 2, under the cross-heading "Court officers", omit the reference to a Master of the Court of Protection except in the case of a person holding that office immediately before the commencement of this sub-paragraph or who had previously retired from that office or died.

(3) In Schedule 5 (retirement: the relevant offices), omit the entries relating to the Master and Deputy or temporary Master of the Court of Protection, except in the case of a person holding any of those offices immediately before the commencement of this sub-paragraph.

(4) In Schedule 7 (retirement: transitional provisions), omit paragraph 5(5)(i)(g) except in the case of a person holding office as a deputy or temporary Master of the Court of Protection immediately before the commencement of this sub-paragraph.

LEASEHOLD REFORM, HOUSING AND URBAN DEVELOPMENT ACT 1993 (C 28)

39 (1) For paragraph 4 of Schedule 2 to the Leasehold Reform, Housing and Urban Development Act 1993 (c 28) (landlord under a disability), substitute—

"**4** (1) This paragraph applies where a Chapter I or Chapter II landlord lacks capacity (within the meaning of the Mental Capacity Act 2005) to exercise his functions as a landlord.

(2) For the purposes of the Chapter concerned, the landlord's place is to be taken—

(a) by a donee of an enduring power of attorney or lasting power of attorney (within the meaning of the 2005 Act), or a deputy appointed for him by the Court of Protection, with power to exercise those functions, or

(b) if no deputy or donee has that power, by a person authorised in that respect by that court.".

(2) That amendment does not affect any proceedings pending at the commencement of this paragraph in which a receiver or a person authorised under Part 7 of the Mental Health Act 1983 (c 20) is acting on behalf of the landlord.

GOODS VEHICLES (LICENSING OF OPERATORS) ACT 1995 (C 23)

40 (1) The Goods Vehicles (Licensing of Operators) Act 1995 (c 23) is amended as follows.

(2) In section 16(5) (termination of licence), for "he becomes a patient within the meaning of Part VII of the Mental Health Act 1983" substitute "he becomes a person who lacks capacity (within the meaning of the Mental Capacity Act 2005) to use a vehicle under the licence".

(3) In section 48 (licence not to be transferable, etc)—

(a) in subsection (2)—

(i) for "or become a patient within the meaning of Part VII of the Mental Health Act 1983" substitute ", or become a person who lacks capacity (within the meaning of the Mental Capacity Act 2005) to use a vehicle under the licence,", and

(ii) in paragraph (a), for "became a patient" substitute "became a person who lacked capacity in that respect", and

(b) in subsection (5), for "a patient within the meaning of Part VII of the Mental Health Act 1983" substitute "a person lacking capacity".

DISABILITY DISCRIMINATION ACT 1995 (C 50)

41 In section 20(7) of the Disability Discrimination Act 1995 (c 50) (regulations to disapply provisions about incapacity), in paragraph (b), for "Part VII of the Mental Health Act 1983" substitute "the Mental Capacity Act 2005".

TRUSTS OF LAND AND APPOINTMENT OF TRUSTEES ACT 1996 (C 47)

42 (1) The Trusts of Land and Appointment of Trustees Act 1996 (c 47) is amended as follows.

(2) In section 9 (delegation by trustees), in subsection (6), for the words from "an enduring power" to the end substitute "an enduring power of attorney or lasting power of attorney within the meaning of the Mental Capacity Act 2005".

(3) In section 20 (the title to which becomes "Appointment of substitute for trustee who lacks capacity")—

(a) in subsection (1)(a), for "is incapable by reason of mental disorder of exercising" substitute "lacks capacity (within the meaning of the Mental Capacity Act 2005) to exercise", and

(b) in subsection (2)—

(i) for paragraph (a) substitute—

"(a) a deputy appointed for the trustee by the Court of Protection,",

(ii) in paragraph (b), for the words from "a power of attorney" to the end substitute "an enduring power of attorney or lasting power of attorney registered under the Mental Capacity Act 2005", and

(iii) in paragraph (c), for the words from "the authority" to the end substitute "the Court of Protection".

HUMAN RIGHTS ACT 1998 (C 42)

43 In section 4(5) of the Human Rights Act 1998 (c 42) (courts which may make declarations of incompatibility), after paragraph (e) insert—

"(f) the Court of Protection, in any matter being dealt with by the President of the Family Division, the Vice-Chancellor or a puisne judge of the High Court."

ACCESS TO JUSTICE ACT 1999 (C 22)

44 In paragraph 1 of Schedule 2 to the Access to Justice Act 1999 (c 22) (services excluded from the Community Legal Service), after paragraph (e) insert—

"(ea) the creation of lasting powers of attorney under the Mental Capacity Act 2005,

(eb) the making of advance decisions under that Act,".

ADOPTION AND CHILDREN ACT 2002 (C 38)

45 In section 52(1)(a) of the Adoption and Children Act 2002 (c 38) (parental consent to adoption), for "is incapable of giving consent" substitute "lacks capacity (within the meaning of the Mental Capacity Act 2005) to give consent".

LICENSING ACT 2003 (C 17)

46 (1) The Licensing Act 2003 (c 17) is amended as follows.

(2) In section 27(1) (lapse of premises licence), for paragraph (b) substitute—

"(b) becomes a person who lacks capacity (within the meaning of the Mental Capacity Act 2005) to hold the licence,".

(3) In section 47 (interim authority notice in relation to premises licence)—

(a) in subsection (5), for paragraph (b) substitute—

"(b) the former holder lacks capacity (within the meaning of the Mental Capacity Act 2005) to hold the licence and that person acts for him under an enduring power of attorney or lasting power of attorney registered under that Act,", and

(b) in subsection (10), omit the definition of "mentally incapable".

COURTS ACT 2003 (C 39)

47 (1) The Courts Act 2003 (c 39) is amended as follows.

(2) In section 1(1) (the courts in relation to which the Lord Chancellor must discharge his general duty), after paragraph (a) insert—

"(aa) the Court of Protection,".

(3) In section 64(2) (judicial titles which the Lord Chancellor may by order alter)—

(a) omit the reference to a Master of the Court of Protection, and

(b) at the appropriate place insert a reference to each of the following—

(i) Senior Judge of the Court of Protection,

(ii) President of the Court of Protection,

(iii) Vice-president of the Court of Protection.

Amendment

Para 28 heading: words "Supreme Court Act 1981" in italics repealed and subsequent words in square brackets substituted, from a date to be appointed, by the Constitutional Reform Act 2005, s 59(5), Sch 11, Pt 1, para 1(2).

Para 28: words "Supreme Court Act 1981" in italics repealed and subsequent words in square brackets substituted, from a date to be appointed, by the Constitutional Reform Act 2005, s 59(5), Sch 11, Pt 1, para 1(2).

[612]

SCHEDULE 7
REPEALS

Section 67(2)

Short title and chapter	*Extent of repeal*
Trustee Act 1925 (c 19)	Section 54(3).
Law of Property Act 1925 (c 20)	Section 205(1)(xiii).
Administration of Estates Act 1925 (c 23)	Section 55(1)(viii)
USA Veterans' Pensions (Administration) Act 1949 (c 45)	In section 1(4), the words from "or for whom" to "1983".
Mental Health Act 1959 (c 72)	In Schedule 7, in Part 1, the entries relating to— section 33 of the Fines and Recoveries Act 1833, section 68 of the Improvement of Land Act 1864, section 55 of the Trustee Act 1925, section 205(1) of the Law of Property Act 1925, section 49 of the National Assistance Act 1948, and section 1 of the Variation of Trusts Act 1958.
Courts Act 1971 (c 23)	In Schedule 2, in Part 1A, the words "Master of the Court of Protection".
Local Government Act 1972 (c 70)	Section 118.
Limitation Act 1980 (c 58)	Section 38(3) and (4).
Supreme Court Act 1981 [Senior Courts Act 1981] (c 54)	In Schedule 2, in Part 2, paragraph 11.
Mental Health Act 1983 (c 20)	Part 7. In section 139(1) the words from "or in, or in pursuance" to "Part VII of this Act,". In section 145(1), in the definition of "patient" the words "(except in Part VII of this Act)". In sections 146 and 147 the words from "104(4)" to "section),". Schedule 3. In Schedule 4, paragraphs 1, 2, 4, 5, 7, 9, 14, 20, 22, 25, 32, 38, 55 and 56. In Schedule 5, paragraphs 26, 43, 44 and 45.
Enduring Powers of Attorney Act 1985 (c 29)	The whole Act.
Insolvency Act 1986 (c 45)	In section 389A(3)— the "or" immediately after paragraph (b), and in paragraph (c), the words "Part VII of the Mental Health Act 1983 or". In section 390(4)— the "or" immediately after paragraph (b), and in paragraph (c), the words "Part VII of the Mental Health Act 1983 or".
Public Trustee and Administration of Funds Act 1986 (c 57)	Section 2. Section 3(7).
Child Support Act 1991 (c 48)	In section 50(8)— paragraphs (b) and (d), and the "or" immediately after paragraph (c).

Short title and chapter	*Extent of repeal*
Social Security Administration Act 1992 (c 5)	In section 123(10)— in paragraph (b), "a receiver appointed under section 99 of the Mental Health Act 1983 or", in paragraph (d)(i), "sub-paragraph (a) of rule 41(1) of the Court of Protection Rules Act 1984 or", in paragraph (d)(ii), "a receiver ad interim appointed under sub-paragraph (b) of the said rule 41(1) or", and "receiver,".
Trustee Delegation Act 1999 (c 15)	Section 4. Section 6. In section 7(3), the words "in accordance with section 4 above".
Care Standards Act 2000 (c 14)	In Schedule 4, paragraph 8.
Licensing Act 2003 (c 17)	In section 47(10), the definition of "mentally incapable".
Courts Act 2003 (c 64)	In section 64(2), the words "Master of the Court of Protection".

Amendment

In column 1 words "Supreme Court Act 1981" in italics repealed and subsequent words in square brackets substituted, from a date to be appointed, by the Constitutional Reform Act 2005, s 59(5), Sch 11, Pt 1, para 1(2).

[613]

PART II
Appendices

APPENDIX I
PUBLIC TRUSTEE RULES 1912
SI 1912/348

INTERPRETATION

1 In these Rules the expression "the Act" means the Public Trustee Act 1906, and unless there is anything in the context or in the Act inconsistent therewith—

The expression "trust" includes any trust duty or office which the Public Trustee is authorised by the Act or these Rules to accept; and the expression "trustee" shall be construed accordingly.

The expression "trust instrument" includes any instrument, Act of Parliament, or Order of Court by which a trust is created or declared.

The expression "trust property" includes all property subject to a trust, or comprised in an estate, which is proposed to be administered by the Public Trustee.

2 The Interpretation Act 1889, applies for the purpose of the interpretation of these Rules as it applies for the purpose of the interpretation of an Act of Parliament.

OFFICES

3 (1) The Central Office of the Public Trustee shall be situate in London.

(2) Branch Offices may from time to time be established as may be prescribed by the Lord Chancellor by notice in the "London Gazette".

DEPUTY PUBLIC TRUSTEES

4 There shall be Deputy Public Trustees at any branch offices so established who shall be officers of the Public Trustee, and shall have the powers and perform the duties assigned to them by or under these Rules. Their number shall be such as the Lord Chancellor, with the sanction of the Treasury, may from time to time prescribe, and every such appointment shall be notified in the "London Gazette".

SECURITY

5 Security shall be given by such persons employed under the Act as the Treasury may direct for the due performance of their duties, and for the due accounting for and payment of all moneys received by them in pursuance of the Act and these Rules. The security shall be for such sum and shall be given in such manner and form as the Treasury shall order in the case of each such person, and the Treasury may at any time require that the amount or nature of any such security be varied.

AUTHORISED TRUSTS AND DUTIES

6 Subject to the Act and these Rules the Public Trustee is authorised—

- (a) to accept any trust created or declared by any trust instrument or arising upon an intestacy;
- (b) to accept any duty incident to, and to act in, any of the following offices, *viz.*: (i) as incident to the office of Trustee of any trust accepted by him the office of guardian of any infant beneficiary, (ii) the office (where the execution of any trust is involved therein) of agent or attorney for any person;
- (c) to accept by the name of the Public Trustee probate or letters of administration of any kind and either as principal or as agent for any person;
- (d) to accept as custodian Trustee any trust created or declared by any trust instrument;
- (e) to receive any money or damages paid to him in pursuance of the Rules of the Supreme Court, Order 22, Rule 15, or any rule which may be substituted therefor, and to apply the same in accordance with such rule or any directions of the Court or a Judge thereunder.

Provided that he shall not accept the trusts of any instrument made solely by way of security for money.

7 The Public Trustee may if he thinks fit—

(1) act as custodian trustee of a trust which involves the management or carrying on of any business, but upon the conditions that (a) he shall not act in the management or carrying on of such business, and (b) he shall not hold any property of such a nature as will expose the holder thereof to any liability except under exceptional circumstances and when he is satisfied that he is fully indemnified or secured against loss; and

(2) accept as ordinary trustee, under exceptional circumstances, a trust which involves the management or carrying on of any business, but upon the conditions that, except with the consent of the Treasury, he shall only carry on the same (a) for a short time not exceeding eighteen months, and (b) with a view to sale disposition or winding-up, and (c) if satisfied that the same can be carried on without risk of loss.

TRUSTEESHIPS

8 (1) A testator may appoint the Public Trustee to be trustee or custodian trustee under any testamentary instrument without previously applying to him for his consent to act as such.

(2) No such appointment by a testator shall have effect, and no appointment of the Public Trustee to be trustee or custodian trustee shall be made except by a testator, unless and until (in either case) the consent of the Public Trustee to act as such trustee shall have been obtained in accordance with these Rules. Provided that in the case of any such appointment by a testator the Public Trustee shall at any time after the fact of his appointment shall have come to his knowledge be at liberty to act as if an application for his consent had been received by him.

(3) It shall be the duty of any person appointed by a testator to be co-trustee with the Public Trustee, and not renouncing or disclaiming the trust, to give to the Public Trustee notice in writing of such appointment as soon as practicable after the same has come to his knowledge.

9 Upon receiving an application for his consent to act as trustee or as custodian trustee the Public Trustee may require to be produced to him the trust instrument (if any), and may require to be supplied to him a copy of that instrument, and of any other document affecting the trust, and such particulars as to the nature and value of any trust property, and the liabilities (if any) attaching to such property, or the holder thereof, and the names and places of abode of any beneficiaries and trustees under the trust, and such other information relating to the trust as he may consider it desirable to obtain in any particular case.

10 As soon as may be after receiving any such application the Public Trustee shall take into consideration upon such evidence as may appear to him sufficient—

- (a) the gross capital value of the trust property;
- (b) the mode of investment and the condition of the trust property;
- (c) the situation, tenure, and character of any land comprised in the trust property;
- (d) any liabilities attaching to the trust property or the holder thereof;
- (e) the duties incident to the office of trustee of the trust;
- (f) the places of abode and circumstances of any beneficiaries; and
- (g) all the circumstances of the case;

and shall decide whether the application ought to be accepted or refused, and shall give notice to the applicant of such acceptance or refusal, and in case of acceptance shall in writing under his . . . official seal signify his consent to act in the trust.

Amendment
Words omitted revoked by SR & O 1916/489.

11 Upon the appointment of the Public Trustee being completed, the Public Trustee shall consider and determine whether the trust shall be administered from his Central Office or from a Branch Office, and shall give directions accordingly, and any such directions may at any time be rescinded or varied by the Public Trustee at his discretion.

ADMINISTRATION OF SMALL ESTATES

12 Upon receiving an application under section 3(1) of the Act the Public Trustee shall require to be supplied to him such evidence as to the value of the estate, and the circumstances of the persons beneficially entitled, and such other information relating thereto as he may consider it desirable to obtain in any particular case.

13 (1) If it is not proved to the satisfaction of the Public Trustee that the gross capital value of the estate is less than £1,000, or if it does not appear to him that the persons beneficially entitled are persons of small means, or if he sees any other good reason for refusing the application, he shall refuse the same, and shall forthwith give notice to the applicant of such refusal.

(2) In any other case the Public Trustee shall make in respect of the estate the declaration mentioned in section 3 (2) of the Act, and shall give notice to the applicant that the application is accepted, and shall take such other steps as may be necessary or proper to enable him to administer the estate; and any person having the custody of the probate or letters of administration, or other document relating to the estate, shall, upon the request in writing of the Public Trustee, deliver the same to him, or as he shall direct.

(3) A refusal under this Rule shall not prevent the Public Trustee from exercising, with respect to the estate, any powers (other than powers under section 3 of the Act) exercisable by him with respect thereto under the Act or these Rules, if duly appointed to exercise the same.

(4) Upon the acceptance of any application the Public Trustee shall consider and determine whether the estate shall be administered from his Central Office or from a Branch Office, and shall give directions accordingly, and any such directions may at any time be rescinded or varied by the Public Trustee at his discretion.

14 For the purposes of the administration the Public Trustee shall (subject as hereafter provided) have all the administrative powers and authorities exercisable by a Master of the Supreme Court acting in the administration of an estate.

15 (1) The Public Trustee may, . . . without judicial proceedings, take the opinion of the High Court upon any question arising in the course of an administration.

[(2) Any such question shall be submitted—

(a) to such Judge of the Chancery Division as the Vice-Chancellor may specify; and

(b) in such manner as that judge may direct.]

(4) The Judge may, before giving his opinion, require the attendance of, or communicate with any person interested in the estate as trustee or beneficiary, but no such person shall have a right to be heard by the Judge unless he otherwise directs.

(5) The Judge shall give his opinion to the Public Trustee, and the Public Trustee shall act in accordance with such opinion, and shall, upon the request in writing of any such interested person, communicate to him the effect of such opinion.

Amendment

Para (1): words omitted revoked by SI 1983/1050, r 2(1).
Para (2): substituted for original paras (2), (3) by SI 1983/1050, r 2(1).

ADMINISTRATION OF SMALL TRUSTS AND ESTATES

16 There shall be kept at the Central Office in London of the Public Trustee such registers and other books as shall be required for recording or entering in a convenient form as to each trust or estate which the Public Trustee is administering the particulars following—

(a) the date of the acceptance of the trust or of the declaration made under section 3 (2) of the Act;

(b) particulars of the trust property from time to time;

(c) the names and place of abode of the person in receipt of the income of the trust property;

(d) a reference to any notice received of any dealing with any beneficial interest in the trust property, and of any exercise or release of any power relating to the trust or estate;

(e) an entry of any decision or opinion of the High Court in respect of the trust or estate;
(f) such entries of his decisions and such other particulars as the Public Trustee may think fit;

and such particulars shall be recorded or entered accordingly.

ADMINISTRATION OF TRUSTS AND ESTATES

[17] [The Public Trustee may—

(a) invest or retain invested money belonging to any trust or estate and coming into his hands in any mode of investment—
    (i) expressly or implicitly authorised by the trust instrument, or
    (ii) if there is no trust instrument, authorised by law for the investment of trust funds,
(b) pay and deposit such money in court for investment in any manner authorised by rules made under section 38(7) of the Administration of Justice Act 1982,
(c) if authorised by the trust instrument or otherwise by law, retain any investment existing at the date of the commencement of the trust.

Provided that he shall not invest in or hold any investment in such manner as to expose him to liability as the holder thereof, unless he is satisfied that he is fully indemnified or secured against loss.]

Amendment
Substituted by SI 1987/2249, r 2.

18 (1) The securities and documents belonging or relating to a trust or estate which the Public Trustee is administering shall, if under his control, be kept at the bank to the trust or estate or at some other safe place of deposit allowed generally or specially by the Treasury, so far as the convenience of business will admit.

(2) All orders for the withdrawal of securities or documents from any such bank or other place of deposit shall be signed by not less than two persons, *viz.*: (a) by the Public Trustee and a co-trustee, or (b) by the Public Trustee and an officer of the Public Trustee authorised in writing by him to act in that behalf, either generally or in any particular case, or (c) by a co-trustee and one such duly authorised officer, or (d) by two such duly authorised officers.

19 (1) Separate accounts shall be kept for every trust or estate.

(2) A separate account shall be kept of the capital of the trust property and of the mode in which it is from time to time invested, and all dealing with such capital shall be entered in such account.

(3) A separate account shall be kept of the income of the trust property (if received by the Public Trustee), and of the mode in which it is from time to time dealt with by the Public Trustee.

20 All payments of money to or from the capital of the trust property shall be made through the bank to the trust or estate.

[21] [In all cases where any deed or other instrument requires to be executed by the Public Trustee under his Official Seal, the affixing of the Seal may be authenticated by the signature either of the Public Trustee or of some officer of the Public Trustee duly authorised by the Public Trustee in that behalf under his Seal, and any deed or other instrument purporting to be a deed or instrument executed by the Public Trustee and to be sealed with his seal authenticated in manner provided by this Rule shall be received in evidence and be deemed to be a deed or instrument so executed without further proof unless the contrary is shown.]

Amendment
Substituted by SR & O 1916/489.

22 All sums payable out of the income or capital of the trust property shall be made by a cheque [on the Bank of England bearing a signature or a facsimile signature of an officer of the Public Trustee authorised in writing by him to act in that behalf or a cheque] on a bank signed by not less than two persons, *viz*: (a) by the Public Trustee and a co-trustee, or (b) by the Public Trustee and an officer of the Public Trustee authorised in writing by him to act in that behalf either generally or in any particular case, or (c) by a co-trustee and one such duly authorised officer, or (d) by two such duly authorised officers. Provided that in any particular case the Public Trustee may authorise the payment of income by the person liable to pay the same direct to the person entitled to receive the same, or to his bank.

Amendment
Amended by SI 1983/1050, r 2(2).

23 (1) The income of the trust property may be paid to the person for the time being entitled to receive the same either through a bank or direct, and where such person is a married woman may be so paid notwithstanding any restraint on anticipation.

(2) Where authority is given to any Corporation or bank to pay any income to any person, the books of that Corporation or bank showing the payment of that income in accordance with the authority shall be a sufficient discharge to the Public Trustee.

(3) Where authority is given to any person to pay any income to the bank of the person entitled, the certificate of that bank stating the receipt of that income shall be a sufficient discharge to the Public Trustee.

(4) Where any person is solely entitled to receive any income, the Public Trustee may, on the request in writing of that person, and notwithstanding any restraint on anticipation, authorise that person for such period as the Public Trustee may think fit to collect or arrange for the collection of such income. During the continuance of any such authority such request in writing shall be a sufficient discharge to the Public Trustee in respect of such income.

24 The Public Trustee may, if the special circumstances of the case appear to him to render it desirable, pay to any other trustee of the trust or allow him to receive, the income of the trust property or any part thereof, on such trustee undertaking to apply it in manner directed by the trust.

25 The Public Trustee may make advances for the purposes of any trust or estate in course of administration, or about to be administered, by him, out of any moneys which may be placed at his disposal by the Treasury for that purpose, and upon such terms as he may think proper.

26 Subject to the provisions of the Act and of these rules and to the terms of any particular trust, the Public Trustee may, in the administration of any trust or estate, take and use professional advice and assistance in regard to legal and other matters, and may act on credible information (though less than legal evidence) as to matters of fact.

27 The Public Trustee may at any time require a statutory declaration or other sufficient evidence that a person is alive and is the person to whom any money or property is payable or transferable, and may refuse payment or transfer until such declaration or evidence is produced.

28 Where a person appearing to be beneficially entitled to any sum of money under the trust or to be interested in the trust property cannot be found, or it is not known whether he is living or dead, the Public Trustee may apply to the Court for directions as to the course to be taken with reference to such person, and until an Order of the Court is made shall keep any sum payable to such person, and if it is kept for more than six months shall invest the same or deposit the same at interest and shall accumulate the dividends or interest thereof.

29 (1) Upon an application in writing by or with the authority of any person interested in the trust property the Public Trustee—

- (a) shall permit the applicant or his Solicitor or other authorised agent to inspect and take copies of any entry in any Register or book relating to the trust or estate and (so far as the interest of the applicant in the trust property is or may be affected thereby) of any account notice or other document in the custody of the Public Trustee;
- (b) shall at the expense of the applicant supply him or his Solicitor or other authorised agent with a copy of any such entry, account notice or document as aforesaid, or with any extract therefrom;
- (c) shall give to the applicant or his Solicitor or other authorised agent such information respecting the trust or estate and the trust property as shall be reasonably requested in the application and shall be within the power of the Public Trustee.

(2) Subject as aforesaid the Public Trustee shall observe strict secrecy in respect of every trust or estate in course of administration by him.

Modification

References to solicitors etc modified to include references to bodies recognised under the Administration of Justice Act 1985, s 9, by the Solicitors' Incorporated Practices Order 1991, SI 1991/2684, arts 4, 5, Sch 1.

[CORPORATE BODIES AS CUSTODIAN TRUSTEES]

[30] [[(1)] The following corporations shall be entitled to act as custodian trustees—

(a) the Treasury Solicitor;

(b) any corporation which—

(i) is constituted under the law of the United Kingdom or of any part thereof, or under the law of any other Member State of the European Economic Community or of any part thereof;

(ii) is empowered by its constitution to undertake trust business (which for the purpose of this rule means the business of acting as trustee under wills and settlements and as executor and administrator) in England and Wales;

(iii) has one or more places of business in the United Kingdom; and

(iv) is—

a company incorporated by special Act of Parliament or Royal Charter, or

a company registered (with or without limited liability) in the United Kingdom under the Companies Act 1948 or under the Companies Act (Northern Ireland) 1960 or in another Member State of the European Economic Community and having a capital (in stock or shares) for the time being issued of not less than £250,000 (or its equivalent in the currency of the State where the company is registered), of which not less than £100,000 (or its equivalent) has been paid up in cash, or

a company which is registered without limited liability in the United Kingdom under the Companies Act 1948 or the Companies Act (Northern Ireland) 1960 or in another Member State of the European Economic Community and of which one of the members is a company within any of the classes defined in this sub-paragraph;

(c) any corporation which is incorporated by special Act or Royal Charter or under the Charitable Trustees Incorporation Act 1872 which is empowered by its constitution to act as a trustee for any charitable purposes, but only in relation to trusts in which its constitution empowers it to act;

(d) any corporation which is constituted under the law of the United Kingdom or of any part thereof and having its place of business there, and which is either—

(i) established for the purpose of undertaking trust business for the benefit of Her Majesty's Navy, Army, Air Force or Civil Service or of any unit, department, member or association of members thereof, and having among its directors or members any persons appointed or nominated by the Defence Council or any Department of State or any one or more of those Departments, or

(ii) authorised by the Lord Chancellor to act in relation to any charitable, ecclesiastical or public trusts as a trust corporation, but only in connection with any such trust as is so authorised;

[(e) (i) any [Strategic Health Authority, Health Authority] or special health authority, but only in relation to any trust which the authority is authorised to accept or hold by virtue of section 90 of the National Health Service Act 1977;]

(ii) any preserved Board as defined by section 15(6) of [The National Health Reorganisation Act 1973], but only in relation to any trust which the Board is authorised to accept or hold by virtue of an order made under that section;

(f) the British Gas Corporation [or any subsidiary of the British Gas Corporation], but only in relation to a pension scheme or pension fund established or maintained by the Corporation by virtue of section 36 of the Gas Act 1972;

(g) the London Transport Executive, but only in relation to a pension scheme or pension fund—

(i) which is established or administered by the Executive by virtue of section 6 of the Transport (London) Act 1969, or

(ii) in relation to which rights, liabilities and functions have been transferred to the Executive by an order under section 74 of the Transport Act 1962 as applied by section 18 of the Transport (London) Act 1969;

(h) any of the following, namely—

(i) the Greater London Council,

(ii) the corporation of any London borough (acting by the council),

(iii) a county council, district council, parish council or community council,

(iv) the Council of the Isles of Scilly,

[(v) the Common Council of the City of London;]

but only in relation to charitable or public trusts (and not trusts for an ecclesiastical charity or for a charity for the relief of poverty) for the benefit of the inhabitants of the area of the local authority concerned and its neighbourhood, or any part of that area.

[(i) any of the following, namely—

(i) a metropolitan district council or a non-metropolitan county council,

(ii) the corporation of any London borough (acting by the council),

(iii) the Common Council of the City of London,

(iv) the Council of the Isles of Scilly,

but only in relation to any trust under which property devolves for the sole benefit of a person who occupies residential accommodation provided under section 21(1)(a) of the National Assistance Act 1948 by the local authority concerned or is in the care of that authority; and a corporation acting as a custodian trustee by virtue of this paragraph in relation to any trust shall be entitled to continue so to act in relation to that trust until a new custodian trustee is appointed, notwithstanding that the person concerned ceases to occupy such accommodation or to be in the care of that authority, as the case may be;]

[(j) The National Coal Board or any subsidiary of the National Coal Board, but only in relation to a scheme or arrangements established under regulations made under section 37 of the Coal Industry Nationalisation Act 1946;]

[(k) any corporation acting as trustee of the trusts of any pension scheme or pension fund established or maintained by the British Broadcasting Corporation, but only in relation to those trusts];

[(l) any corporation appointed by the Secretary of State as a trustee of any scheme having effect by virtue of regulations made under section 37 of the Coal Industry Nationalisation Act 1946 for purposes relating to pensions, gratuities or other like benefits and in relation to which provision is, or has been, made by regulations made under paragraph 2(1) of Schedule 5 to the Coal Industry Act 1994 for the scheme to continue in force notwithstanding the repeal by the Coal Industry Act 1994 of section 37 of the Coal Industry Nationalisation Act 1946 and of the enactments modifying that section, but only in relation to such a scheme].

(2) In this rule "subsidiary" has the same meaning as in section 154 of the Companies Act 1948]

Amendment

Substituted by SI 1975/1189, r 2.
Para (1): numbered as such by SI 1981/358, r 2(1).
Para (1): sub-para (e)(i) substituted by SI 1984/109, r 2(a).
Para (1): in sub-para (e)(i) words "Strategic Health Authority, Health Authority" in square brackets substituted by SI 2002/2469, reg 4, Sch 1, Pt 2, para 32.
Para (1): in sub-para (e)(ii) words "The National Health Service Reorganisation Act 1973" in square brackets substituted by SI 1984/109, r 2(b).
Para (1): in sub-para (f) words "or any subsidiary of the British Gas Corporation" in square brackets inserted by SI 1985/132, r 2.
Para (1): sub-para (h)(v) inserted by SI 1976/836, r 2(a).
Para (1): sub-para (i) inserted by SI 1976/836, r 2(b).
Para (1): sub-para (j) inserted by SI 1981/358, r 2(2).
Para (1): sub-para (k) inserted by SI 1987/1891, r 2.
Para (1): sub-para (l) inserted by SI 1994/2519, r 2.
Para (2): inserted by SI 1981/358, r 2(3).

INVESTIGATION AND AUDIT OF TRUST ACCOUNTS

31 Any application under section 13 (1) of the Act shall be made to the Public Trustee, and notice thereof shall (unless the Public Trustee otherwise directs) be given by the applicant to every other person being a trustee or beneficiary under the trust.

32 (1) Upon receiving any such application the Public Trustee may in his absolute discretion by notice to the applicant require that before a day to be specified in the notice such security (by deposit of a sum of money) as he shall deem sufficient shall be given to him by the applicant for the payment of any expenses of the investigation and audit which may be ordered by the Public Trustee to be paid by the applicant personally.

(2) Where any such requirement is made no further proceedings shall be taken upon the application until the security has been given, and if the same is not given before the day specified in the notice the application shall be disallowed unless under special circumstances the Public Trustee thinks fit to extend the time for giving the security or to dispense therewith.

(3) Any sum so deposited shall be kept by the Public Trustee on deposit in his name and to a separate account at a Bank until all proceedings in connection with the investigation and audit have been concluded, and thereupon the deposited sum and the interest (if any) allowed thereon by the Bank shall be applied in or towards payment of any expenses of the investigation and audit which may be so ordered to be paid by the applicant personally and the balance (if any) shall be paid to the applicant.

33 The Public Trustee may in his absolute discretion upon the application of any trustee or beneficiary direct that the investigation and audit shall extend only to a specified period of time or to a specified part of the trust property or shall be otherwise restricted.

34 If within one month from the date of the application under section 13(1) of the Act no Solicitor or public accountant shall have been appointed by the applicant and the trustees to conduct the investigation and audit, there shall be deemed to be a default of agreement within the meaning of the said section 13(1) and the applicant may apply to the Public Trustee accordingly.

Modification

References to solicitors etc modified to include references to bodies recognised under the Administration of Justice Act 1985, s 9, by the Solicitors' Incorporated Practices Order 1991, SI 1991/2684, arts 4, 5, Sch 1.

35 The remuneration of the auditor and the other expenses of the investigation and audit shall be such as may be determined by the Public Trustee. Provided that the Public Trustee may refer the costs of any Solicitor (being part of such expenses) for taxation to a Taxing Master of the Supreme Court, and in such case the amount of the said costs when taxed shall be included in such expenses.

Modification

References to solicitors etc modified to include references to bodies recognised under the Administration of Justice Act 1985, s 9, by the Solicitors' Incorporated Practices Order 1991, SI 1991/2684, arts 4, 5, Sch 1.

36 (1) Where any investigation or audit has been made, copies of the report and certificate of the auditor under section 13 (2) of the Act and such copies of accounts and other documents as the Public Trustee may require shall be forwarded to him by the auditor, and shall be considered by the Public Trustee before giving any direction or making any order under section 13 (5) of the Act.

(2) The expense of making and forwarding any such copies as aforesaid and the fee of the Public Trustee (within the limits prescribed by or in pursuance of any order relating to the fees of the Public Trustee for the time being in force) shall for the purpose of section 13 (5) of the Act be part of the expenses of the investigation and audit.

37 (1) Before making any order under section 13(5) of the Act the Public Trustee shall, if any of the parties interested so desire, hear the said parties in such manner as he shall think fit.

(2) Any such order shall specify the person by or to whom any sum is to be paid and the amount of such sum provided that such an order may direct payment of the taxed costs of any solicitor employed in connection with the investigation and audit, and such costs shall be taxed

by a Taxing Master of the Supreme Court, and the amount of such costs when taxed shall be paid as if such amount had been specified in the Order.

(3) Any such Order may be enforced in the same manner as a judgment or order of the Court to the same effect.

Modification

References to solicitors etc modified to include references to bodies recognised under the Administration of Justice Act 1985, s 9, by the Solicitors' Incorporated Practices Order 1991, SI 1991/2684, arts 4, 5, Sch 1.

MISCELLANEOUS

38 The accounts of the Public Trustee shall be audited and the securities held by him verified from time to time by such person or persons as the Treasury may appoint in accordance with regulations made by the Treasury.

39 Any Officer of the Public Trustee who shall be authorised by him in writing in that behalf may take any oath, make any declaration, verify any account and give personal attendance at any Court or place.

40 (1) Any notice or application required to be given or made for the purposes of the Act or these Rules to the Public Trustee may be addressed to the Public Trustee at his Office in London, or if the same relates to a trust or estate in course of administration or proposed to be administered from a Branch Office then at that Branch Office.

(2) Any notice or application required to be given or made for the purpose of the Act or these Rules to any person other than the Public Trustee may be addressed to that person at his last known place of abode or place of business.

(3) Any such notice or application may be delivered at the place to which it is addressed or may be served by post.

41 Where any person who (if not under disability) might have made any application, given any consent, done any act, or been party to any proceeding in pursuance of these Rules is an infant, idiot, or lunatic, the guardian or (as the case may require) the committee or receiver of the estate of such person may make such application, give such consent, do such act, and be party to such proceedings as such person if free from disability might have made, given, done or been party to, and shall otherwise represent such person for the purposes of these Rules. Where there is no guardian or committee or receiver of the estate of any such infant, idiot, or lunatic, or where any person is of unsound mind, or incapable of managing his affairs but has not been found lunatic under any inquisition, it shall be lawful for the Court to appoint a guardian of such person for the purpose of any proceedings under these Rules and from time to time to change such guardian.

42 (1) The Public Trustee may in writing authorise any Deputy Public Trustee to exercise and perform (either generally or in relation to any particular case and subject to such conditions and restrictions (if any) as the Public Trustee may impose) all or any of the powers and duties of the Public Trustee under any of the foregoing Rules except—

- (a) the power or duty of determining whether a trust or estate shall be administered from his Central Office or from a Branch Office; and
- (b) the power of authorising officers of the Public Trustee to transfer securities or assure land or to sign cheques;
- (c) the power of making advances for the purposes of any trust or estate.

(2) Any such authority conditions or restrictions may at any time in like manner be withdrawn or varied by the Public Trustee at his discretion.

43 No Deputy Public Trustee and no firm or member of a firm of Solicitors of which such Deputy is a member shall, except with the consent in writing of the Public Trustee and subject to such conditions as he may impose, act as Solicitor or Solicitors to a trust or estate which is in course of administration by such Deputy.

Modification

References to solicitors etc modified to include references to bodies recognised under the Administration of Justice Act 1985, s 9, by the Solicitors' Incorporated Practices Order 1991, SI 1991/2684, arts 4, 5, Sch 1.

44 The Public Trustee may frame and cause to be printed and circulated or otherwise promulgated such forms and directions and regulations as he may deem requisite or expedient for facilitating proceedings under the Act and these Rules.

45 The Public Trustee Rules 1907, are hereby rescinded.

46 These Rules may be cited as "The Public Trustee Rules 1912", and shall come into operation on the 15th day of April, 1912.

APPENDIX II

SETTLED LAND ACT 1925

1925 Chapter 18

PART I
GENERAL PRELIMINARY PROVISIONS

SETTLEMENTS AND SETTLED LAND

1 What constitutes a settlement

(1) Any deed, will, agreement for a settlement or other agreement, Act of Parliament, or other instrument, or any number of instruments, whether made or passed before or after, or partly before and partly after, the commencement of this Act, under or by virtue of which instrument or instruments any land, after the commencement of this Act, stands for the time being—

- (i) limited in trust for any persons by way of succession; or
- (ii) limited in trust for any person in possession—
  - (a) for an entailed interest whether or not capable of being barred or defeated;
  - (b) for an estate in fee simple or for a term of years absolute subject to an executory limitation, gift, or disposition over on failure of his issue or in any other event;
  - (c) for a base or determinable fee [(other than a fee which is a fee simple absolute by virtue of section 7 of the Law of Property Act 1925)] or any corresponding interest in leasehold land;
  - (d) being an infant, for an estate in fee simple or for a term of years absolute; or
- (iii) limited in trust for any person for an estate in fee simple or for a term of years absolute contingently on the happening of any event; or
- (iv) . . .
- (v) charged, whether voluntarily or in consideration of marriage or by way of family arrangement, and whether immediately or after an interval, with the payment of any rentcharge for the life of any person, or any less period, or of any capital, annual, or periodical sums for the portions, advancement, maintenance, or otherwise for the benefit of any persons, with or without any term of years for securing or raising the same;

creates or is for the purposes of this Act a settlement and is in this Act referred to as a settlement, or as the settlement, as the case requires;

Provided that, where land is the subject of a compound settlement, references in this Act to the settlement shall be construed as meaning such compound settlement, unless the context otherwise requires.

(2) Where an infant is beneficially entitled to land for an estate in fee simple or for a term of years absolute and by reason of an intestacy or otherwise there is no instrument under which the interest of the infant arises or is acquired, a settlement shall be deemed to have been made by the intestate, or by the person whose interest the infant has acquired.

(3) An infant shall be deemed to be entitled in possession notwithstanding any subsisting right of dower (not assigned by metes and bounds) affecting the land, and such a right of dower shall be deemed to be an interest comprised in the subject of the settlement and coming to the dowress under or by virtue of the settlement.

Where dower has been assigned by metes and bounds, the letters of administration or probate granted in respect of the estate of the husband of the dowress shall be deemed a settlement made by the husband.

(4) An estate or interest not disposed of by a settlement and remaining in or reverting to the settlor, or any person deriving title under him, is for the purposes of this Act an estate or interest comprised in the subject of the settlement and coming to the settlor or such person under or by virtue of the settlement.

(5) Where—

(a) a settlement creates an entailed interest which is incapable of being barred or defeated, or a base or determinable fee, whether or not the reversion or right of reverter is in the Crown, or any corresponding interest in leasehold land; or

(b) the subject of a settlement is an entailed interest, or a base or determinable fee, whether or not the reversion or right of reverter is in the Crown, or any corresponding interest in leasehold land;

the reversion or right of reverter upon the cesser of the interest so created or settled shall be deemed to be an interest comprised in the subject of the settlement, and limited by the settlement.

(6) Subsection (4) and (5) of this section bind the Crown.

[(7) This section does not apply to land held upon trust for sale.]

Amendment

Sub-s (1): words in square brackets inserted by the Trusts of Land and Appointment of Trustees Act 1996, s 25(1), Sch 3, para 2(2), for savings in relation to entailed interests created before the commencement of that Act, and savings consequential upon the abolition of the doctrine of conversion, see s 25(4), (5) thereof; words omitted repealed by the Married Women (Restraint upon Anticipation) Act 1949, s 1(4), Sch 2.
Sub-s (7): inserted by the Law of Property (Amendment) Act 1926, s 7, Schedule.

2 What is settled land

Land which is or is deemed to be the subject of a settlement is for the purposes of this Act settled land, and is in relation to the settlement referred to in this Act as the settled land.

3 Duration of settlements

Land [which has been subject to a settlement which is a settlement for the purposes of this Act] shall be deemed for the purposes of this Act to remain and be settled land, and the settlement shall be deemed to be a subsisting settlement for the purposes of this Act so long as—

(a) any limitation, charge, or power of charging under the settlement subsists, or is capable of being exercised; or

(b) the person who, if of full age, would be entitled as beneficial owner to have that land vested in him for a legal estate is an infant.

Amendment

Words in square brackets substituted by the Trusts of Land and Appointment of Trustees Act 1996, s 25(1), Sch 3, para 2(3); for savings in relation to entailed interests created before the commencement of that Act, and savings consequential upon the abolition of the doctrine of conversion, see s 25(4), (5) thereof.

4 Authorised method of settling land inter vivos

(1) Every settlement of a legal estate in land inter vivos shall, save as in this Act otherwise provided, be effected by two deeds, namely, a vesting deed and a trust instrument and if effected in any other way shall not operate to transfer or create a legal estate.

(2) By the vesting deed the land shall be conveyed to the tenant for life or statutory owner (and if more than one as joint tenants) for the legal estate the subject of the intended settlement:

Provided that, where such legal estate is already vested in the tenant for life or statutory owner, it shall be sufficient, without any other conveyance, if the vesting deed declares that the land is vested in him for that estate.

(3) The trust instrument shall—

(a) declare the trusts affecting the settled land;

(b) appoint or constitute trustees of the settlement:

(c) contain the power, if any, to appoint new trustees of the settlement;

(d) set out, either expressly or by reference, any powers intended to be conferred by the settlement in extension of those conferred by this Act;

(e) bear any ad valorem stamp duty which may be payable (whether by virtue of the vesting deed or otherwise) in respect of the settlement.

5 Contents of vesting deeds

(1) Every vesting deed for giving effect to a settlement or for conveying settled land to a tenant for life or statutory owner during the subsistence of the settlement (in this Act referred

to as a "principal vesting deed") shall contain the following statements and particulars, namely—

(a) A description, either specific or general, of the settled land;
(b) A statement that the settled land is vested in the person or persons to whom it is conveyed or in whom it is declared to be vested upon the trusts from time to time affecting the settled Land;
(c) The names of the persons who are the trustees of the settlement;
(d) Any additional or larger powers conferred by the trust instrument relating to the settled land which by virtue of this Act operate and are exercisable as if conferred by this Act on a tenant for life;
(e) The name of any person for the time being entitled under the trust instrument to appoint new trustees of the settlement.

(2) The statements or particulars required by this section may be incorporated by reference to an existing vesting instrument, and, where there is a settlement subsisting at the commencement of this Act, by reference to that settlement and to any instrument whereby land has been conveyed to the uses or upon the trusts of that settlement, but not (save as last aforesaid) by reference to a trust instrument nor by reference to a disentailing deed.

(3) A principal vesting deed shall not be invalidated by reason only of any error in any of the statements or particulars by this Act required to be contained therein.

6 Procedure in the case of settlements by will

Where a settlement is created by the will of an estate owner who dies after the commencement of this Act—

(a) the will is for the purposes of this Act a trust instrument; and
(b) the personal representatives of the testator shall hold the settled land on trust, if and when required so to do, to convey it to the person who, under the will, or by virtue of this Act, is the tenant for life or statutory owner, and, if more than one, as joint tenants.

7 Procedure on change of ownership

(1) If, on the death of a tenant for life or statutory owner, or of the survivor of two or more tenants for life or statutory owners, in whom the settled land was vested, the land remains settled land, his personal representatives shall hold the settled land on trust, if and when required so to do, to convey it to the person who under the trust instrument or by virtue of this Act becomes the tenant for life or statutory owner and, if more than one, as joint tenants.

(2) If a person by reason of attaining full age becomes a tenant for life for the purposes of this Act of settled land, he shall be entitled to require the trustees of the settlement, personal representatives, or other persons in whom the settled land is vested, to convey the land to him.

(3) If a person who, when of full age, will together with another person or other persons constitute the tenant for life for the purposes of this Act of settled land attains that age, he shall be entitled to require the tenant for life, trustees of the settlement, personal representatives or other persons in whom the settled land is vested to convey the land to him and the other person or persons who together with him constitute the tenant for life as joint tenants.

(4) If by reason of forfeiture, surrender, or otherwise the estate owner of any settled land ceases to have the statutory powers of a tenant for life and the land remains settled land, he shall be bound forthwith to convey the settled land to the person who under the trust instrument, or by virtue of this Act, becomes the tenant for life or statutory owner and, if more than one, as joint tenants.

(5) If any person of full age becomes absolutely entitled to the settled land (whether beneficially, or as personal representative, or as [trustee of land], or otherwise) free from all limitations, powers, and charges taking effect under the settlement, he shall be entitled to require the trustees of the settlement, personal representatives, or other persons in whom the settled land is vested, to convey the land to him, and if more persons than one being of full age become so entitled to the settled land they shall be entitled to require such persons as aforesaid to convey the land to them as joint tenants.

Amendment

Sub-s (5): words in square brackets substituted by the Trusts of Land and Appointment of Trustees Act 1996, s 25(1), Sch 3, para 2(4); for savings in relation to entailed interests created before the commencement of that Act, and savings consequential upon the abolition of the doctrine of conversion, see s 25(4), (5) thereof.

8 Mode and costs of conveyance, and saving of rights of personal representative and equitable charges

(1) A conveyance by personal representatives under either of the last two preceding sections may be made by an assent in writing signed by them which shall operate as a conveyance.

(2) Every conveyance under either of the last two preceding sections shall be made at the cost of the trust estate.

(3) The obligations to convey settled land imposed by the last two preceding sections are subject and without prejudice—

- (a) where the settlement is created by a will, to the rights and powers of the personal representatives for purposes of administration; and
- (b) in any case, to the person on whom the obligation is imposed being satisfied that provision has been or will be made for the payment of any unpaid death duties in respect of the land or any interest therein for which he is accountable, and any interest and costs in respect of such duties, or that he is otherwise effectually indemnified against such duties, interest and costs.

(4) Where the land is or remains settled land a conveyance under either of the last two preceding sections shall—

- (a) if by deed, be a principal vesting deed; and
- (b) if by an assent, be a vesting assent, which shall contain the like statements and particulars as are required by this Act in the case of a principal vesting deed.

(5) Nothing contained in either of the last two preceding sections affects the right of personal representatives to transfer or create such legal estates to take effect in priority to a conveyance under either of those sections as may be required for giving effect to the obligations imposed on them by statute.

(6) A conveyance under either of the last two preceding sections, if made by deed, may contain a reservation to the person conveying of a term of years absolute in the land conveyed, upon trusts for indemnifying him against any unpaid death duties in respect of the land conveyed or any interest therein, and any interest and costs in respect of such duties.

(7) Nothing contained in either of the last two preceding sections affects any right which a person entitled to an equitable charge for securing money actually raised, and affecting the whole estate the subject of the settlement, may have to require effect to be given thereto by a legal mortgage, before the execution of a conveyance under either of those sections.

9 Procedure in the case of settlement and of instruments deemed to be trust instruments

(1) Each of the following settlements or instruments shall for the purposes of this Act be deemed to be a trust instrument, and any reference to a trust instrument contained in this Act shall apply thereto, namely—

- (i) An instrument executed, or, in case of a will, coming into operation, after the commencement of this Act which by virtue of this Act is deemed to be a settlement;
- (ii) A settlement which by virtue of this Act is deemed to have been made by any person after the commencement of this Act;
- (iii) An instrument inter vivos intended to create a settlement of a legal estate in land which is executed after the commencement of this Act, and does not comply with the requirements of this Act with respect to the method of effecting such a settlement; and
- (iv) A settlement made after the commencement of this Act (including a settlement by the will of a person who dies after such commencement) of any of the following interests—
  - (a) an equitable interest in land which is capable, when in possession, of subsisting at law; or
  - (b) an entailed interest; or

(c) a base or determinable fee or any corresponding interest in leasehold land,

but only if and when the interest settled takes effect free from all equitable interests and powers under every prior settlement (if any).

(2) As soon as practicable after a settlement, or an instrument which for the purposes of this Act is deemed to be a trust instrument, takes effect as such, the trustees of the settlement may, and on the request of the tenant for life or statutory owner shall, execute a principal vesting deed, containing the proper statements and particulars, declaring that the legal estate in the settled land shall vest or is vested in the person or persons therein named, being the tenant for life or statutory owner, and including themselves if they are the statutory owners, and such deed shall, unless the legal estate is already so vested, operate to convey or vest the legal estate in the settled land to or in the person or persons aforesaid and, if more than one, as joint tenants.

(3) If there are no trustees of the settlement, then (in default of a person able and willing to appoint such trustees) an application under this Act shall be made to the court for the appointment of such trustees.

(4) The provisions of the last preceding section with reference to a conveyance shall apply, so far as they are applicable, to a principal vesting deed under this section.

10 Procedure on acquisition of land to be made subject to a settlement

(1) Where after the commencement of this Act land is acquired with capital money arising under this Act or in exchange for settled land, or a rentcharge is reserved on a grant of settled land, the land shall be conveyed to, and the rentcharge shall by virtue of this Act become vested in, the tenant for life or statutory owner, and such conveyance or grant is in this Act referred to as a subsidiary vesting deed:

Provided that, where an instrument is subsisting at the commencement of this Act, or is made or comes into operation after such commencement, by virtue of which any money or securities are liable under this Act, or the Acts which it replaces, or under a trust or direction contained in the instrument, to be invested in the purchase of land to be conveyed so as to become settled land, but at the commencement of this Act, or when such instrument is made or comes into operation after such commencement, as the case may be, there is no land in respect of which a principal vesting deed is capable of being executed, the first deed after the commencement of this Act by which any land is acquired as aforesaid shall be a principal vesting deed and shall be framed accordingly.

(2) A subsidiary vesting deed executed on the acquisition of land to be made subject to a settlement shall contain the following statements and particulars, namely—

(a) particulars of the last or only principal vesting instrument affecting land subject to the settlement;
(b) a statement that the land conveyed is to be held upon and subject to the same trusts and powers as the land comprised in such last or only principal vesting instrument;
(c) the names of the persons who are the trustees of the settlement;
(d) the name of any person for the time being entitled to appoint new trustees of the settlement.

(3) A subsidiary vesting deed reserving a rentcharge on a grant of settled land shall contain the following statements and particulars—

(a) a statement that the rentcharge is vested in the grantor and is subject to the settlement which, immediately before the grant, was subsisting with respect to the land out of which it was reserved;
(b) particulars of the last or only principal vesting instrument affecting such land.

(4) A subsidiary vesting deed shall not be invalidated by reason only of any error in any of the statements or particulars by this Act required to be contained therein.

(5) The acquisition of the land shall not operate to increase or multiply charges or powers of charging.

11 As to contracts for the settlement of land

(1) A contract made or other liability created or arising after the commencement of this Act for the settlement of land—

(i) by or on the part of an estate owner; or
(ii) by a person entitled to—
(a) an equitable interest which is capable when in possession of subsisting at law; or
(b) an entailed interest; or
(c) a base or determinable fee or any corresponding interest in leasehold land;

shall, but in cases under paragraph (ii) only if and when the interest of the person entitled takes effect free from all equitable interests and powers under every prior settlement, if any, be deemed an estate contract within the meaning of the Land Charges Act 1925, and may be registered as a land charge accordingly, and effect shall be given thereto by a vesting deed and a trust instrument in accordance with this Act.

(2) A contract made or other liability created or arising before the commencement of this Act to make a settlement of land shall be deemed to be sufficiently complied with if effect is given thereto by a vesting deed and a trust instrument in accordance with this Act.

12 Power to make vesting orders as to settled land

(1) If—
(a) any person who is bound under this Part of this Act to execute a conveyance, vesting deed or vesting assent or in whom settled land is wrongly vested refuses or neglects to execute the requisite conveyance, vesting deed or vesting assent within one month after demand in writing; or
(b) any such person is outside the United Kingdom, or cannot be found, or it is not known whether he is alive or dead; or
(c) for any reason the court is satisfied that the conveyance, vesting deed or vesting assent cannot be executed, or cannot be executed without undue delay or expense;

the court may, on the application of any person interested, make an order vesting the settled land in the tenant for life or statutory owner or person, if any, of full age absolutely entitled (whether beneficially or as personal representative or [trustee of land] or otherwise), and, if the land remains settled land, the provisions of this Act relating to a principal vesting deed or a subsidiary vesting deed, as the case may be, shall apply to any order so made and every such order shall contain the like statements and particulars.

(2) No stamp duty shall be payable in respect of a vesting order made in place of a vesting or other assent.

Amendment
Sub-s (1): words in square brackets substituted by the Trusts of Land and Appointment of Trustees Act 1996, s 25(1), Sch 3, para 2(5); for savings in relation to entailed interests created before the commencement of that Act, and savings consequential upon the abolition of the doctrine of conversion, see s 25(4), (5) thereof.

13 Dispositions not to take effect until vesting instrument is made

Where a tenant for life or statutory owner has become entitled to have a principal vesting deed or a vesting assent executed in his favour, then until a vesting instrument is executed or made pursuant to this Act in respect of the settled land, any purported disposition thereof inter vivos by any person, other than a personal representative (not being a disposition which he has power to make in right of his equitable interests or powers under a trust instrument), shall not take effect except in favour of a purchaser of a legal estate [without notice of such tenant for life or statutory owner having become so entitled as aforesaid] but, save as aforesaid, shall operate only as a contract for valuable consideration to carry out the transaction after the requisite vesting instrument has been executed or made, and a purchaser of a legal estate shall not be concerned with such disposition unless the contract is registered as a land charge.

[Nothing in this section affects the creation or transfer of a legal estate by virtue of an order of the court or the Minister or other competent authority.]

Amendment
Amended by the Law of Property (Amendment) Act 1926, ss 6, 7, Schedule.

14 Forfeiture and stamps

(1) Any vesting effected under the powers conferred by this Act in relation to settled land shall not operate as a breach of a covenant or condition against alienation or give rise to a forfeiture.

(2) Nothing in this Act shall operate to impose any stamp duty on a vesting or other assent.

15 . . .

. . .

Amendment
Repealed by the Statute Law (Repeals) Act 2004.

ENFORCEMENT OF EQUITABLE INTERESTS AND POWERS AGAINST ESTATE OWNER AND DISCHARGE ON TERMINATION OF SETTLEMENT

16 Enforcement of equitable interests and powers against estate owner

(1) All equitable interests and powers in or over settled land (whether created before or after the date of any vesting instrument affecting the legal estate) shall be enforceable against the estate owner in whom the settled land is vested (but in the case of personal representatives without prejudice to their rights and powers for purposes of administration) in manner following (that is to say)—

(i) The estate owner shall stand possessed of the settled land and the income thereof upon such trusts and subject to such powers and provisions as may be requisite for giving effect to the equitable interests and powers affecting the settled land or income thereof of which he has notice according to their respective priorities;

(ii) Where any person of full age becomes entitled to require a legal estate in the settled land to be vested in him in priority to the settlement, by reason of a right of reverter, statutory or otherwise, or an equitable right of entry taking effect, or on the ground that his interest ought no longer to be capable of being overreached under the powers of this Act, the estate owner shall be bound, if so requested in writing, to transfer or create such legal estate as may be required for giving legal effect to the rights of the person so entitled;

(iii) Where—

(a) any principal sum is required to be raised on the security of the settled land, by virtue of any trust, or by reason of the exercise of an equitable power affecting the settled land, or by any person or persons who under the settlement is or are entitled or together entitled to or has or have a general power of appointment over the settled land, whether subject to any equitable charges or powers of charging subsisting under the settlement or not; or

(b) the settled land is subject to any equitable charge for securing money actually raised and affecting the whole estate the subject of the settlement;

the estate owner shall be bound, if so requested in writing, to create such legal estate or charge by way of legal mortgage as may be required for raising the money or giving legal effect to the equitable charge:

Provided that, so long as the settlement remains subsisting, any legal estate or charge by way of legal mortgage so created shall take effect and shall be expressed to take effect subject to any equitable charges or powers of charging subsisting under the settlement which have priority to the interests or powers of the person or persons by or on behalf of whom the money is required to be raised or legal effect is required to be given to the equitable charge, unless the persons entitled to the prior charges or entitled to exercise the powers consent in writing to the same being postponed, but it shall not be necessary for such consent to be expressed in the instrument creating such legal estate or charge by way of legal mortgage.

(2) Where a mortgage or charge is expressed to be made by an estate owner pursuant to this section, then, in favour of the mortgagee or chargee and persons deriving title under him, the same shall take effect in priority to all the trusts of the settlement and all equitable interests and powers subsisting or to arise under the settlement except those to which it is expressly made subject, and shall so take effect, whether the mortgagee or chargee has notice of any such trusts, interests, or powers, or not, and the mortgagee or chargee shall not be concerned to see that a case had arisen to authorise the mortgage or charge, or that no more money than was wanted was raised.

(3) Nothing contained in paragraph (iii) of subsection (1) of this section affects the power conferred by this Act on a tenant for life of raising money by mortgage or of directing money to be applied in discharge of incumbrances.

(4) Effect may be given by means of a legal mortgage to an agreement for a mortgage, or a charge or lien, whether or not arising by operation of law, if the agreement charge or lien ought to have priority over the settlement.

(5) Save as hereinbefore expressly provided, no legal estate shall, so long as the settlement is subsisting, be transferred or created by the estate owner for giving effect to any equitable interest or power under the settlement.

(6) If a question arises or a doubt is entertained whether any and what legal estate ought to be transferred or created pursuant to this section, an application may be made to the court for directions as hereinafter provided.

(7) If an estate owner refuses or neglects for one month after demand in writing to transfer or create any such legal estate, or if by reason of his being outside the United Kingdom, or being unable to be found, or by reason of the dissolution of a corporation, or for any other reason, the court is satisfied that the transaction cannot otherwise be effected, or cannot be effected without undue delay or expense, the court may, on the application of any person interested, make a vesting order transferring or creating the requisite legal estate.

(8) This section does not affect a purchaser of a legal estate taking free from any equitable interest or power.

17 Deed of discharge on termination of settlement

(1) Where the estate owner of any settled land holds the land free from all equitable interests and powers under a trust instrument, the persons who in the last or only principal vesting instrument or the last or only endorsement on or annex thereto are declared to be the trustees of the settlement or the survivors of them shall, save as hereinafter mentioned, be bound to execute, at the cost of the trust estate, a deed declaring that they are discharged from the trust so far as regards that land;

Provided that, if the trustees have notice of any derivative settlement, [trust of land] or equitable charge affecting such land, they shall not execute a deed of discharge until—

(a) in the case of a derivative settlement, or [trust of land], a vesting instrument or a conveyance has been executed or made for giving effect thereto; and

(b) in the case of an equitable charge, they are satisfied that the charge is or will be secured by a legal mortgage, or is protected by registration as a land charge, or by deposit of the documents of title, or that the owner thereof consents to the execution of the deed of discharge.

Where the land is affected by a derivative settlement or [trust of land], the deed of discharge shall contain a statement that the land is settled land by virtue of such vesting instrument as aforesaid and the trust instrument therein referred to, or is [subject to a trust of land] by virtue of such conveyance as aforesaid, as the case may require.

(2) If, in the circumstances mentioned in subsection (1) of this section and when the conditions therein mentioned have been complied with, the trustees of a settlement on being requested to execute a deed of discharge—

(a) by the estate owner; or

(b) by a person interested under, or by the trustees of, a derivative settlement; or

(c) by the trustees of [land];

refuse to do so, or if for any reason the discharge cannot be effected without undue delay or expense, the estate owner, person interested, or trustees may apply to the court for an order discharging the first mentioned trustees as respects the whole or any part of the settled land, and the court may make such order as it may think fit.

(3) Where a deed or order of discharge contains no statement to the contrary, a purchaser of a legal estate in the land to which the deed or order relates shall be entitled to assume that the land has ceased to be settled land, and is not subject to [a trust of land].

Amendment

Sub-ss (1)-(3): words in square brackets substituted by the Trusts of Land and Appointment of Trustees Act 1996, s 25(1), Sch 3, para 2(6); for savings in relation to entailed interests created before the commencement of that Act, and savings consequential upon the abolition of the doctrine of conversion, see s 25(4), (5) thereof.

RESTRICTIONS ON DISPOSITIONS OF SETTLED LAND WHERE TRUSTEES HAVE NOT BEEN DISCHARGED

18 Restrictions on dispositions of settled land where trustees have not been discharged

(1) Where land is the subject of a vesting instrument and the trustees of the settlement have not been discharged under this Act, then—

(a) any disposition by the tenant for life or statutory owner of the land, other than a disposition authorised by this Act or any other statute, or made in pursuance of any additional or larger powers mentioned in the vesting instrument, shall be void, except for the purpose of conveying or creating such equitable interests as he has power, in right of his equitable interests and powers under the trust instrument, to convey or create; and

(b) if any capital money is payable in respect of a transaction, a conveyance to a purchaser of the land shall only take effect under this Act if the capital money is paid to or by the direction of the trustees of the settlement or into court; and

(c) notwithstanding anything to the contrary in the vesting instrument, or the trust instrument, capital money shall not, except where the trustee is a trust corporation, be paid to or by the direction of fewer persons than two as trustees of the settlement.

(2) The restrictions imposed by this section do not affect—

(a) the right of a personal representative in whom the settled land may be vested to convey or deal with the land for the purposes of administration;

(b) the right of a person of full age who has become absolutely entitled (whether beneficially or as [trustee of land] or personal representative or otherwise) to the settled land, free from all limitations, powers, and charges taking effect under the trust instrument, to require the land to be conveyed to him;

(c) the power of the tenant for life, statutory owner, or personal representative in whom the settled land is vested to transfer or create such legal estates, to take effect in priority to the settlement, as may be required for giving effect to any obligations imposed on him by statute, but where any capital money is raised or received in respect of the transaction the money shall be paid to or by the direction of the trustees of the settlement or in accordance with an order of the court.

Amendment

Sub-s (2): words in square brackets substituted by the Trusts of Land and Appointment of Trustees Act 1996, s 25(1), Sch 3, para 2(7); for savings in relation to entailed interests created before the commencement of that Act, and savings consequential upon the abolition of the doctrine of conversion, see s 25(4), (5) thereof.

TENANTS FOR LIFE AND PERSONS WITH POWERS OF TENANT FOR LIFE

19 Who is tenant for life

(1) The person of full age who is for the time being beneficially entitled under a settlement to possession of settled land for his life is for the purposes of this Act the tenant for life of that land and the tenant for life under that settlement.

(2) If in any case there are two or more persons of full age so entitled as joint tenants, they together constitute the tenant for life for the purposes of this Act.

(3) If in any case there are two or more persons so entitled as joint tenants and they are not all of full age, such one or more of them as is or are for the time being of full age is or (if more than one) together constitute the tenant for life for the purposes of this Act, but this subsection does not affect the beneficial interests of such of them as are not for the time being of full age.

(4) A person being tenant for life within the foregoing definitions shall be deemed to be such notwithstanding that, under the settlement or otherwise, the settled land, or his estate or interest therein, is incumbered or charged in any manner or to any extent, and notwithstanding any assignment by operation of law or otherwise of his estate or interest under the settlement, whether before or after it came into possession, other than an assurance which extinguishes that estate or interest.

20 Other limited owners having powers of tenant for life

(1) Each of the following persons being of full age shall, when his estate or interest is in possession, have the powers of a tenant for life under this Act, (namely)—

(i) A tenant in tail, including a tenant in tail after possibility of issue extinct, and a tenant in tail who is by Act of Parliament restrained from barring or defeating his estate tail, and although the reversion is in the Crown, but not including such a tenant in tail where the land in respect whereof he is so restrained was purchased with money provided by Parliament in consideration of public services;

(ii) A person entitled to land for an estate in fee simple or for a term of years absolute with or subject to, in any of such cases, an executory limitation, gift, or disposition over on failure of his issue or in any other event;

(iii) A person entitled to a base or determinable fee, although the reversion or right of reverter is in the Crown, or to any corresponding interest in leasehold land;

(iv) A tenant for years determinable on life, not holding merely under a lease at a rent;

(v) A tenant for the life of another, not holding merely under a lease at a rent;

(vi) A tenant for his own or any other life, or for years determinable on life, whose estate is liable to cease in any event during that life, whether by expiration of the estate, or by conditional limitation, or otherwise, or to be defeated by an executory limitation, gift, or disposition over, or is subject to a trust for accumulation of income for any purpose;

(vii) A tenant by the curtesy;

(viii) A person entitled to the income of land under a trust or direction for payment thereof to him during his own or any other life, whether or not subject to expenses of management or to a trust for accumulation of income for any purpose, or until sale of the land, or until forfeiture, cesser or determination by any means of his interest therein, unless the land is subject to [a trust of land];

(ix) A person beneficially entitled to land for an estate in fee simple or for a term of years absolute subject to any estates, interests, charges, or powers of charging, subsisting or capable of being exercised under a settlement;

(x) . . .

(2) In every such case as is mentioned in subsection (1) of this section, the provisions of this Act referring to a tenant for life, either as conferring powers on him or otherwise, shall extend to each of the persons aforesaid, and any reference in this Act to death as regards a tenant for life shall, where necessary, be deemed to refer to the determination by death or otherwise of the estate or interest of the person on whom the powers of a tenant for life are conferred by this section.

(3) For the purposes of this Act the estate or interest of a tenant by the curtesy shall be deemed to be an estate or interest arising under a settlement made by his wife.

(4) Where the reversion of right or reverter or other reversionary right is in the Crown, the exercise by a person on whom the powers of a tenant for life are conferred by this section of his powers under this Act, binds the Crown.

Amendment

Sub-s (1): words in square brackets in para (viii) substituted by the Trusts of Land and Appointment of Trustees Act 1996, s 25(1), Sch 3, para 2(8), for savings in relation to entailed interests created before the commencement of that Act, and savings consequential upon the abolition of the doctrine of conversion, see s 25(4), (5) thereof; para (x) repealed by The Married Women (Restraint upon Anticipation) Act 1949, s 1(4), Sch 2.

21 Absolute owners subject to certain interests to have the powers of tenant for life

(1) Where a person of full age is beneficially entitled in possession to a legal estate subject to any equitable interests or powers, then, for the purpose of overreaching such interests or powers, he may, notwithstanding any stipulation to the contrary, by deed (which shall have effect as a principal vesting deed within the meaning of this Act) declare that the legal estate is vested in him on trust to give effect to all equitable interests and powers affecting the legal estate, and that deed shall be executed by two or more individuals approved or appointed by the court or a trust corporation, who shall be stated to be the trustees of the settlement for the purposes of this Act.

Thereupon so long as any of the equitable interests and powers are subsisting the following provisions shall have effect—

(a) The person so entitled as aforesaid and each of his successors in title being an estate owner shall have the powers of a tenant for life and the land shall be deemed to be settled land;

(b) The instrument (if any) under which his estate arises or is acquired, and the instrument (if any) under which the equitable interests or powers are subsisting or capable of taking effect shall be deemed to be the trust instrument:

Provided that where there is no such instrument as last aforesaid then a deed (which shall take effect as a trust instrument) shall be executed contemporaneously with the vesting deed, and shall declare the trusts affecting the land;

(c) The persons stated in the principal vesting deed to be the trustees of the settlement for the purposes of this Act shall also be the trustees of the trust instrument for those purposes; and

(d) Capital money arising on any disposition of the land shall be paid to or by the direction of the trustees of the settlement or into court, and shall be applicable towards discharging or providing for payment in due order of any principal money payable in respect of such interests or charges as are overreached by such disposition, and until so applied shall be invested or applied as capital money under the trust instrument, and the [resultant profits] shall be applied as the income of such capital money, and be liable for keeping down in due order any annual or periodical sum which may be overreached by the disposition.

(2) The following equitable interests and powers are excepted from the operation of subsection (1) of this section namely—

(i) an equitable interest protected by a deposit of documents relating to the legal estate affected;

(ii) the benefit of a covenant or agreement restrictive of the user of land;

(iii) an easement, liberty or privilege over or affecting land and being merely an equitable interest;

(iv) the benefit of a contract to convey or create a legal estate, including a contract conferring either expressly or by statutory implication a valid option of purchase, a right of pre-emption, or any other like right;

(v) any equitable interest protected by registration under the Land Charges Act 1925, other than—

  (a) an annuity within the meaning of Part II of that Act;

  (b) a limited owner's charge or a general equitable charge within the meaning of that Act.

(3) Subject to the powers conferred by this Act on a tenant for life, nothing contained in this section shall deprive an equitable chargee of any of his rights or of his remedies for enforcing those rights.

Amendment

Sub-s (1): in para (d) words "resultant profits" in square brackets substituted by the Trustee Act 2000, s 40(1), Sch 2, Pt II, para 7.

22 Provisions applicable where interest in settled land is restored

(1) Where by a disentailing assurance settled land is expressed to be limited (whether subject or not to any estates, interests, charges or powers expressly created or conferred thereby) upon the trusts subsisting with respect thereto immediately before the execution of such disentailing assurance, or any of such trusts then, for the purposes of this Act and otherwise, a person entitled to any estate or interest in the settled land under any such previously subsisting trust is entitled thereto after the execution of such disentailing assurance as of his former estate or interest.

(2) Where by a resettlement of settled land any estate or interest therein is expressed to be limited to any person (whether subject or not to any estate, interest, charge or power expressly created or conferred by the resettlement) in restoration or confirmation of his estate or interest under a prior settlement, then, for the purposes of this Act and otherwise, that person is entitled to the estate or interest so restored or confirmed as of his former estate or interest and in

addition to the powers exercisable by him in respect of his former estate or interest, he is capable of exercising all such further powers as he could have exercised by virtue of the resettlement, if his estate or interest under the prior settlement had not been so restored or confirmed, but he had been entitled under the resettlement only.

23 Powers of trustees, etc, when there is no tenant for life

(1) Where under a settlement there is no tenant for life nor, independently of this section, a person having by virtue of this Act the powers of a tenant for life then—

(a) any person of full age on whom such powers are by the settlement expressed to be conferred; and

(b) in any other case the trustees of the settlement;

shall have the powers of a tenant for life under this Act.

(2) This section applies to trustees of settlements of land purchased with money provided by Parliament in consideration of public services where the tenant in tail is restrained from barring or defeating his estate tail, except that, if the tenant in tail is of full age and capacity, the powers shall not be exercised without his consent, but a purchaser shall not be concerned to see or inquire whether such consent has been given.

24 As to a tenant for life who has parted with his interest

(1) If it is shown to the satisfaction of the court that a tenant for life, who has by reason of bankruptcy, assignment, incumbrance, or otherwise ceased in the opinion of the court to have a substantial interest in his estate or interest in the settled land or any part thereof, has unreasonably refused to exercise any of the powers conferred on him by this Act, or consents to an order under this section, the court may, on the application of any person interested in the settled land or the part thereof affected, make an order authorising the trustees of the settlement, to exercise in the name and on behalf of the tenant for life, any of the powers of a tenant for life under this Act, in relation to the settled land or the part thereof affected, either generally and in such manner and for such period as the court may think fit, or in a particular instance, and the court may by the order direct that any documents of title in the possession of the tenant for life relating to the settled land be delivered to the trustees of the settlement.

(2) While any such order is in force, the tenant for life shall not, in relation to the settled land or the part thereof affected, exercise any of the powers thereby authorised to be exercised in his name and on his behalf, but no person dealing with the tenant for life shall be affected by any such order, unless the order is for the time being registered as an order affecting land.

(3) An order may be made under this section at any time after the estate or interest of the tenant for life under the settlement has taken effect in possession, and notwithstanding that he disposed thereof when it was an estate or interest in remainder or reversion.

25 Married woman, how to be affected

(1) The foregoing provisions of this Act apply to a married woman of full age, whether or not she is entitled to her estate or interest for her separate use or as her separate property, and she, without her husband, may exercise the powers of a tenant for life under this Act.

(2) . . .

Amendment

Sub-s (2): repealed by the Married Women (Restraint upon Anticipation) Act 1949, s 1(4), Sch 2.

26 Infants, how to be affected

(1) Where an infant is beneficially entitled in possession to land for an estate in fee simple or for a term of years absolute or would if of full age be a tenant for life of or have the powers of a tenant for life over settled land, then, during the minority of the infant—

(a) if the settled land is vested in a personal representative, the personal representative, until a principal vesting instrument has been executed pursuant to the provisions of this Act; and

(b) in every other case, the trustees of the settlement;

shall have, in reference to the settled land and capital money, all the powers conferred by this Act and the settlement on a tenant for life, and on the trustees of the settlement.

(2) If the settled land is vested in a personal representative, then, if and when during the minority the infant, if of full age, would have been entitled to have the legal estate in the settled land conveyed to or otherwise vested in him pursuant to the provisions of this Act, a principal vesting instrument shall, if the trustees of the settlement so require, be executed, at the cost of the trust estate, for vesting the legal estate in themselves, and in the meantime the personal representative shall, during the minority, give effect to the directions of the trustees of the settlement, and shall not be concerned with the propriety of any conveyance directed to be made by those trustees if the conveyance appears to be a proper conveyance under the powers conferred by this Act or by the settlement, and the capital money, if any, arising under the conveyance is paid to or by the direction of the trustees of the settlement or into court, but a purchaser dealing with the personal representative and paying the capital money, if any, to him shall not be concerned to see that the money is paid to trustees of the settlement or into court, or to inquire whether the personal representative is liable to give effect to any such directions, or whether any such directions have been given.

(3) Subsection (2) of this section applies whether the infant becomes entitled before or after the commencement of this Act, and has effect during successive minorities until a person of full age becomes entitled to require the settled land to be vested in him.

(4) This section does not apply where an infant is beneficially entitled in possession to land for an estate in fee simple or for a term of years absolute jointly with a person of full age (for which case provision is made in the Law of Property Act 1925), but it applies to two or more infants entitled as aforesaid jointly, until one of them attains full age.

(5) This section does not apply where an infant would, if of full age, constitute the tenant for life or have the powers of a tenant for life together with another person of full age, but it applies to two or more infants who would, if all of them were of full age, together constitute the tenant for life or have the powers of a tenant for life, until one of them attains full age.

(6) Nothing in this section affects prejudicially any beneficial interest of an infant.

27 . . .

. . .

Amendment

Repealed by the Trusts of Land and Appointment of Trustees Act 1996, s 25(2), Sch 4.

28 . . .

. . .

Amendment

Repealed by the Mental Health Act 1959, s 149(2), Sch 8, Pt I.

29 Charitable and public trusts

(1) For the purposes of this section, all land vested or to be vested in trustees on or for charitable, ecclesiastical, or public trusts or purposes shall be deemed to be settled land, and the trustees shall, without constituting them statutory owners, have in reference to the land, all the powers which are by this Act conferred on a tenant for life and on the trustees of a settlement.

In connexion only with the exercise of those powers, and not so as to impose any obligation in respect of or to affect—

(a) the mode of creation or the administration of such trusts; or
(b) the appointment or number of trustees of such trusts;

the statute or other instrument creating the trust or under which it is administered shall be deemed the settlement, and the trustees shall be deemed the trustees of the settlement, and, save where the trust is created by a will coming into operation after the commencement of this Act, a separate instrument shall not be necessary for giving effect to the settlement.

Any conveyance of land held on charitable, ecclesiastical or public trusts shall state that the land is held on such trusts, and, where a purchaser has notice that the land is held on charitable, ecclesiastical, or public trusts, he shall be bound to see that any consents or orders requisite for authorising the transaction have been obtained.

(2) The said powers shall be exercisable subject to such consents or orders, if any, being obtained as would, if this Act had not been passed, have been requisite if the transaction were being effected under an express power conferred by the instrument creating the trust, and where the land is vested in . . . persons having no powers of management, the said powers shall be exercisable by the managing trustees or committee of management, and the . . . persons aforesaid shall not be liable for giving effect to directions given by the managing trustees or committee of management:

Provided that where—

(a) a disposition or dealing is to be effected for a nominal price or rent, or for less than the best price or rent that can be reasonably obtained or gratuitously; or

(b) any interest in land is to be acquired;

the like consent or order (if any) shall be required in reference to the disposition, dealing or acquisition, as would have been requisite if the intended transaction were a sale.

(3) Nothing in this section affects the jurisdiction of the court, [Charity Commission], Board of Education, or other competent authority, in regard to the administration of charitable, ecclesiastical, or public trusts.

(4) . . .

(5) Where any trustees or the majority of any set of trustees have power to transfer or create any legal estate, that estate shall be transferred or created by them in the names and on behalf of the persons . . . in whom the legal estate is vested.

(6) This section applies (save as otherwise provided) whether the trust was created before or after the commencement of this Act, but does not apply to land to which the Universities and College Estates Act 1925, applies.

Amendment

Repealed, except in relation to the deed of settlement set out in the Schedule to the Chequers Estate Act 1917 or the trusts instrument set out in the Schedule to the Chevening Estate Act 1959, by the Trusts of Land and Appointment of Trustees Act 1996, s 25(2), Sch 4.

Sub-s (2): first words omitted repealed by the Charities Act 1960, s 48(2), Sch 7, Pt I.

Sub-s (2): final words omitted repealed by the Charities Act 1960, s 48(2), Sch 7, Pt I.

Sub-s (3): words "Charity Commission" in square brackets substituted by the Charities Act 2006, s 75(1), Sch 8, para 19.

Sub-s (5): words omitted repealed by the Charities Act 1960, s 48(2), Sch 7, Pt I.

TRUSTEES OF SETTLEMENT

30 Who are trustees for purposes of Act

(1) Subject to the provisions of this Act, the following persons are trustees of a settlement for the purposes of this Act, and are in this Act referred to as the "trustees of the settlement" or "trustees of a settlement", namely—

(i) the persons, if any, who are for the time being under the settlement trustees with power of sale of the settled land (subject or not to the consent of any person), or with power of consent to or approval of the exercise of such a power of sale, or if there are no such persons; then

(ii) the persons, if any, for the time being, who are by the settlement declared to be trustees thereof for the purposes of the Settled Land Acts 1882 to 1890, or any of them, or this Act, or if there are no such persons; then

(iii) the persons, if any, who are for the time being under the settlement trustees with [a power or duty to sell] any other land comprised in the settlement and subject to the same limitations as the land to be sold or otherwise dealt with, or with power of consent to or approval of the exercise of such a power of sale, or, if there are no such persons; then

(iv) the persons, if any, who are for the time being under the settlement trustees with [a future power or duty to sell] the settled land, or with power of consent to or approval of the exercise of such a future power of sale, and whether the power [or duty] takes effect in all events or not, or, if there are no such persons; then

(v) the persons, if any, appointed by deed to be trustees of the settlement by all the persons who at the date of the deed were together able, by virtue of their beneficial interests or by the exercise of an equitable power, to dispose of the settled land in equity for the whole estate the subject of the settlement.

(2) Paragraphs (i) (iii) and (iv) of the last preceding subsection take effect in like manner as if the powers therein referred to had not by this Act been made exercisable by the tenant for life or statutory owner.

(3) Where a settlement is created by will, or a settlement has arisen by the effect of an intestacy, and apart from this subsection there would be no trustees for the purposes of this Act of such settlement, then the personal representatives of the deceased shall, until other trustees are appointed, be by virtue of this Act the trustees of the settlement, but where there is a sole personal representative, not being a trust corporation, it shall be obligatory on him to appoint an additional trustee to act with him for the purposes of this Act, and the provisions of the Trustee Act 1925, relating to the appointment of new trustees and the vesting of trust property shall apply accordingly.

Amendment

Sub-s (1): words in square brackets substituted by the Trusts of Land and Appointment of Trustees Act 1996, s 25(1), Sch 3, para 2(9); for savings in relation to entailed interests created before the commencement of that Act, and savings consequential upon the abolition of the doctrine of conversion, see s 25(4), (5) thereof.

31 As to trustees of compound settlements

(1) Persons who are for the time being trustees for the purposes of this Act of an instrument which is a settlement, or is deemed to be a subsisting settlement for the purposes of this Act, shall be the trustees for the purposes of this Act of any settlement constituted by that instrument and any instruments subsequent in date or operation.

[Where there are trustees for the purposes of this Act of the instrument under which there is a tenant for life or statutory owner but there are no trustees for those purposes of a prior instrument, being one of the instruments by which a compound settlement is constituted, those trustees shall, unless and until trustees are appointed of the prior instrument or of the compound settlement, be the trustees for the purposes of this Act of the compound settlement.]

(2) This section applies to instruments coming into operation before as well as after the commencement of this Act, but shall have effect without prejudice to any appointment made by the court before such commencement of trustees of a settlement constituted by more than one instrument, and to the power of the court in any case after such commencement to make any such appointment, and where any such appointment has been made before such commencement or is made thereafter this section shall not apply or shall cease to apply to the settlement consisting of the instruments to which the appointment relates.

Amendment

Sub-s (1): words in square brackets inserted by the Law of Property (Amendment) Act 1926, s 7, Schedule.

32 As to trustees of referential settlements

(1) Where a settlement takes or has taken effect by reference to another settlement, the trustees for the time being of the settlement to which reference is made shall be the trustees of the settlement by reference, but this section does not apply if the settlement by reference contains an appointment of trustees thereof for the purposes of the Settled Land Acts 1882 to 1890, or any of them, or this Act.

(2) This section applies to instruments coming into operation before as well as after the commencement of this Act, but shall have effect without prejudice to any appointment made by the court before such commencement of trustees of a settlement by reference, or of the compound settlement consisting of a settlement and any other settlement or settlements made by reference thereto, and to the power of the court in any case after such commencement to make any such appointment, and where any such appointment has been made before such commencement or is made thereafter this section shall not apply or shall cease to apply.

(3) In this section "a settlement by reference to another settlement" means a settlement of property upon the limitations and subject to the powers and provisions of an existing settlement, with or without variation.

33 Continuance of trustees in office, and as to certain compound settlements

(1) Where any persons have been appointed or constituted trustees of a settlement, whether by an order of the court or otherwise, or have by reason of [a power or duty to sell], or by reason

of a power of consent to, or approval of, the exercise of a power of sale, or by virtue of this Act, or otherwise at any time become trustees of a settlement for the purposes of the Settled Land Acts 1882 to 1890, or this Act, then those persons or their successors in office shall remain and be trustees of the settlement as long as that settlement is subsisting or deemed to be subsisting for the purposes of this Act.

In this subsection "successors in office" means the persons who, by appointment or otherwise, have become trustees for the purposes aforesaid.

(2) Where settled land is or has been expressed to be disposed of under a compound settlement of which trustees were appointed by the court, and the capital money (if any) arising on the disposition is or was paid to the persons who by virtue of the order or any subsequent appointment appear to be or to have been the trustees of that settlement, and where the person by or on whose behalf the disposition is or was made is or was the tenant for life or statutory owner of the land disposed of under an instrument mentioned in the order as constituting part of such compound settlement (in this subsection called "the principal instrument") then the title of the person to whom the disposition is made shall not be impeachable on the ground—

- (a) that the instruments mentioned in the order did not constitute a compound settlement; or
- (b) that those instruments were not all the instruments at the date of the order or of the disposition constituting the compound settlement of the land disposed of; or
- (c) that any of the instruments mentioned in the order did not form part of the settlement of the land disposed of, or had ceased to form part of the settlement at the date of the disposition;

but nothing in this subsection shall prejudice the rights of any person in respect of any estate, interest or charge under any instrument existing at the date of the order and not mentioned therein which would not have been overreached if the disposition had been made by or on behalf of the tenant for life or statutory owner under the principal instrument as such, and there had been trustees of that instrument for the purposes of the Settled Land Acts 1882 to 1890, or this Act, and the capital money, if any, arising on the disposition had been paid to the trustees.

(3) The foregoing provisions of this section operate to confirm all dispositions made before the commencement of this Act, but not so as to render invalid or prejudice any order of the court, or any title or right acquired before the commencement of this Act, and operates without prejudice to any appointment already made by the court of trustees of a settlement, and to the power of the court in any case hereafter to make any such appointment.

Amendment

Sub-s (1): words in square brackets substituted by the Trusts of Land and Appointment of Trustees Act 1996, s 25(1), Sch 3, para 2(10); for savings in relation to entailed interests created before the commencement of that Act, and savings consequential upon the abolition of the doctrine of conversion, see s 25(4), (5) thereof.

34 Appointment of trustees by court

(1) If at any time there are no trustees of a settlement, or where in any other case it is expedient, for the purposes of this Act, that new trustees of a settlement be appointed, the court may, if it thinks fit, on the application of the tenant for life, statutory owner, or of any other person having, under the settlement, an estate or interest in the settled land, in possession, remainder or otherwise, or, in the case of an infant, of his testamentary or other guardian or next friend, appoint fit persons to be trustees of the settlement.

(2) The persons so appointed, and the survivors and survivor of them, while continuing to be trustees or trustee, and, until the appointment of new trustees, the personal representatives or representative for the time being of the last surviving or continuing trustee, shall become and be the trustees or trustee of the settlement.

35 Procedure on appointment of new trustees

(1) Whenever a new trustee for the purposes of this Act is appointed of a trust instrument or a trustee thereof for the purposes aforesaid is discharged from the trust without a new trustee being appointed, a deed shall be executed supplemental to the last or only principal vesting instrument containing a declaration that the persons therein named, being the persons who after such appointment or discharge, as the case may be, are the trustees of the trust instrument

for the purposes aforesaid, are the trustees of the settlement for those purposes; and a memorandum shall be endorsed on or annexed to the last or only principal vesting instrument in accordance with the Trustee Act 1925.

(2) Every such deed as aforesaid shall, if the trustee was appointed or discharged by the court be executed by such person as the court may direct, and, in any other case, shall be executed by—

(i) the person, if any, named in the principal vesting instrument as the person for the time being entitled to appoint new trustees of the settlement, or if no person is so named, or the person is dead or unable or unwilling to act, the persons who if the principal vesting instrument had been the only instrument constituting the settlement would have had power to appoint new trustees thereof;
(ii) the persons named in the deed of declaration as the trustees of the settlement; and
(iii) any trustee who is discharged as aforesaid or retires.

(3) A statement contained in any such deed of declaration as is mentioned in this section to the effect that the person named in the principal vesting instrument as the person for the time being entitled to appoint new trustees of the settlement is unable or unwilling to act, or that a trustee has remained outside the United Kingdom for more than twelve months, or refuses or is unfit to act, or is incapable of acting, shall in favour of a purchaser of a legal estate be conclusive evidence of the matter stated.

PROVISIONS AS TO UNDIVIDED SHARES

36 Undivided shares to take effect behind a [trust of land]

(1) If and when, after the commencement of this Act, settled land is held in trust for persons entitled in possession under a trust instrument in undivided shares, the trustees of the settlement (if the settled land is not already vested in them) may require the estate owner in whom the settled land is vested (but in the case of a personal representative subject to his rights and powers for purposes of administration), at the cost of the trust estate, to convey the land to them, or assent to the land vesting in them as joint tenants, and in the meantime the land shall be held on the same trusts as would have been applicable thereto if it had been so conveyed to or vested in the trustees.

(2) If and when the settled land so held in trust in undivided shares is or becomes vested in the trustees of the settlement, the land shall be held by them (subject to any incumbrances affecting the settled land which are secured by a legal mortgage, but freed from any incumbrances affecting the undivided shares or not secured as aforesaid, and from any interests, powers and charges subsisting under the trust instrument which have priority to the trust for the persons entitled to the undivided shares) [in trust for the persons interested in the land].

(3) If the estate owner refuses or neglects for one month after demand in writing to convey the settled land so held in trust in undivided shares in manner aforesaid, or if by reason of his being outside the United Kingdom or being unable to be found, or by reason of the dissolution of a corporation, or for any other reason, the court is satisfied that the conveyance cannot otherwise be made, or cannot be made without undue delay or expense, the court may, on the application of the trustees of the settlement, make an order vesting the settled land in them [in trust for the persons interested in the land].

(4) An undivided share in land shall not be capable of being created except under a trust instrument or under the Law of Property Act 1925, and shall then only take effect behind a [trust of land].

(5) Nothing in this section affects the priority inter se of any incumbrances whether affecting the entirety of the land or an undivided share.

[(6) In subsections (2) and (3) of this section references to the persons interested in the land include persons interested as trustees or personal representatives (as well as persons beneficially interested).]

(7) The provisions of this section bind the Crown.

Amendment

Section heading: words in square brackets substituted by the Trusts of Land and Appointment of Trustees Act 1996, s 25(1), Sch 3, para 2(11)(d); for savings in relation to entailed interests created before the commencement of that Act, and savings consequential upon the abolition of the doctrine of conversion, see s 25(4), (5) thereof.

Sub-ss (2)-(4): words in square brackets substituted by the Trusts of Land and Appointment of Trustees Act 1996, s 25(1), Sch 3, para 2(11)(a), (b); for savings in relation to entailed interests created before the commencement of that Act, and savings consequential upon the abolition of the doctrine of conversion, see s 25(4), (5) thereof.

Sub-s (6): substituted by the Trusts of Land and Appointment of Trustees Act 1996, s 25(1), Sch 3, para 2(11)(c); for savings in relation to entailed interests created before the commencement of that Act, and savings consequential upon the abolition of the doctrine of conversion, see s 25(4), (5) thereof.

TRANSITIONAL PROVISIONS

37 Transitional provisions with respect to existing settlements, etc

The transitional provisions set out in the Second Schedule to this Act shall have effect as regards settlements existing at the commencement of this Act.

PART II
POWERS OF A TENANT FOR LIFE

SALE AND EXCHANGE

38 Powers of sale and exchange.

A tenant for life—

(i) May sell the settled land, or any part thereof, or any easement, right or privilege of any kind over or in relation to the land; and

(ii) . . .

(iii) May make an exchange of the settled land, or any part thereof, or of any easement, right, or privilege of any kind, whether or not newly created, over or in relation to the settled land, or any part thereof, for other land, or for any easement, right or privilege of any kind, whether or not newly created, over or in relation to other land, including an exchange in consideration of money paid for equality of exchange.

Amendment

Words omitted repealed by the Statute Law (Repeals) Act 1969, s 1, Schedule, Part III.

39 Regulations respecting sales

(1) Save as hereinafter provided every sale shall be made for the best consideration in money that can reasonably be obtained.

(2) A sale may be made in consideration wholly or partially of a perpetual rent, or a terminable rent consisting of principal and interest combined, payable yearly or half yearly to be secured upon the land sold, or the land to which the easement, right or privilege sold is to be annexed in enjoyment or an adequate part thereof.

In the case of a terminable rent, the conveyance shall distinguish the part attributable to principal and that attributable to interest, and the part attributable to principal shall be capital money arising under this Act:

Provided that, unless the part of the terminable rent attributable to interest varies according to the amount of the principal repaid, the trustees of the settlement shall, during the subsistence of the rent, [accumulate the profits from the capital money by investing them and any resulting profits under the general power of investment in section 3 of the Trustee Act 2000 and shall add the accumulations to capital].

(3) The rent to be reserved on any such sale shall be the best rent that can reasonably be obtained, regard being had to any money paid as part of the consideration, or laid out, or to be laid out, for the benefit of the settled land, and generally to the circumstances of the case, but a peppercorn rent, or a nominal or other rent less than the rent ultimately payable, may be made payable during any period not exceeding five years from the date of the conveyance.

(4) Where a sale is made in consideration of a rent, the following provisions shall have effect—

(i) The conveyance shall contain a covenant by the purchaser for payment of the rent, and [the statutory powers and remedies for the recovery of the rent shall apply];

(ii) A duplicate of the conveyance shall be executed by the purchaser and delivered to the tenant for life or statutory owner, of which execution and delivery the execution of the conveyance by the tenant for life or statutory owner shall be sufficient evidence;

(iii) A statement, contained in the conveyance or in an indorsement thereon, signed by the tenant for life of statutory owner, respecting any matter of fact or of calculation under this Act in relation to the sale, shall, in favour of the purchaser and of those claiming under him, be sufficient evidence of the matter stated.

(5) The consideration on a sale to any company incorporated by special Act of Parliament or by provisional order confirmed by Parliament or by any other order, scheme or certificate having the force of an Act of Parliament, may, with the consent of the tenant for life, consist, wholly or in part, of fully-paid securities of any description of the company, and such securities shall be vested in the trustees of the settlement and shall be subject to the provisions of this Act relating to securities representing capital money arising under this Act, and may be retained and held by the trustees in like manner as if they had been authorised by this Act for the investment of capital money.

(6) A sale may be made in one lot or in several lots, and either by auction or by private contract, and may be made subject to any stipulations respecting title, or evidence of title, or other things.

(7) On a sale the tenant for life may fix reserve biddings and may buy in at an auction.

Amendment

Sub-s (2): words from “accumulate the profits” to “accumulations to capital” in square brackets substituted by the Trustee Act 2000, s 40(1), Sch 2, Pt II, para 8.

Sub-s (4): in para (i) words “the statutory powers and remedies for the recovery of the rent shall apply” in square brackets substituted by the Law of Property (Amendment) Act 1926, s 7, Schedule.

40 Regulations respecting exchanges

(1) Save as in this Part of this Act provided, every exchange shall be made for the best consideration in land or in land and money that can reasonably be obtained.

(2) An exchange may be made subject to any stipulations respecting title, or evidence of title, or other things.

(3) Settled land in England or Wales shall not be given in exchange for land out of England or Wales.

LEASING POWERS

41 Power to lease for ordinary or building or mining or forestry purposes

A tenant for life may lease the settled land, or any part thereof, or any easement, right, or privilege of any kind over or in relation to the land, for any purpose whatever, whether involving waste or not, for any term not exceeding—

(i) In case of a building lease, nine hundred and ninety-nine years;

(ii) In case of a mining lease, one hundred years;

(iii) In case of a forestry lease, nine hundred and ninety-nine years;

(iv) In case of any other lease, fifty years.

42 Regulations respecting leases generally

(1) Save as hereinafter provided, every lease—

(i) shall be by deed, and be made to take effect in possession not later than twelve months after its date, or in reversion after an existing lease having not more than seven years to run at the date of the new lease;

(ii) shall reserve the best rent that can reasonably be obtained, regard being had to any fine taken, and to any money laid out or to be laid out for the benefit of the settled land, and generally to the circumstances of the case;

(iii) shall contain a covenant by the lessee for payment of the rent, and a condition of re-entry on the rent not being paid within a time therein specified not exceeding thirty days.

(2) A counterpart of every lease shall be executed by the lessee and delivered to the tenant for life or statutory owner, of which execution and delivery the execution of the lease by the tenant for life or statutory owner shall be sufficient evidence.

(3) A statement, contained in a lease or in an indorsement thereon, signed by the tenant for life or statutory owner, respecting any matter of fact or of calculation under this Act in relation to the lease, shall, in favour of the lessee and of those claiming under him, be sufficient evidence of the matter stated.

(4) A fine received on the grant of a lease under any power conferred by this Act shall be deemed to be capital money arising under this Act.

(5) A lease at the best rent that can be reasonably obtained without fine, and whereby the lessee is not exempted from punishment for waste, may be made—

(i) Where the term does not exceed twenty-one years—

(a) without any notice of an intention to make the lease having been given under this Act; and

(b) notwithstanding that there are no trustees of the settlement; and

(ii) Where the term does not extend beyond three years from the date of the writing, by any writing under hand only containing an agreement instead of a covenant by the lessee for payment of rent.

43 Leasing powers for special objects

The leasing power of a tenant for life extends to the making of—

(i) a lease for giving effect (in such manner and so far as the law permits) to a covenant of renewal, performance whereof could be enforced against the owner for the time being of the settled land; and

(ii) a lease for confirming, as far as may be, a previous lease being void or voidable, but so that every lease, as and when confirmed, shall be such a lease as might at the date of the original lease have been lawfully granted under this Act or otherwise, as the case may require.

PROVISIONS AS TO BUILDING, MINING AND FORESTRY LEASES

44 Regulations respecting building leases

(1) Every building lease shall be made partly in consideration of the lessee, or some person by whose direction the lease is granted, or some other person, having erected or agreeing to erect buildings, new or additional, or having improved or repaired or agreeing to improve or repair buildings, or having executed or agreeing to execute on the land leased, an improvement authorised by this Act for or in connexion with building purposes.

(2) A peppercorn rent or a nominal or other rent less than the rent ultimately payable, may be made payable for the first five years or any less part of the term.

(3) Where the land is contracted to be leased in lots, the entire amount of rent to be ultimately payable may be apportioned among the lots in any manner:

Provided that—

(i) the annual rent reserved by any lease shall not be less than [50p]; and

(ii) the total amount of the rents reserved on all leases for the time being granted shall not be less than the total amount of the rents which, in order that the leases may be in conformity with this Act, ought to be reserved in respect of the whole land for the time being leased; and

(iii) the rent reserved by any lease shall not exceed one-fifth part of the full annual value of the land comprised in that lease with the buildings thereon when completed.

Amendment

Sub-s (3): sum in square brackets substituted by virtue of the Decimal Currency Act 1969, s 10(1).

45 Regulations respecting mining leases

(1) In a mining lease—

(i) the rent may be made to be ascertainable by or to vary according to the acreage worked, or by or according to the quantities of any mineral or substance gotten, made merchantable, converted, carried away, or disposed of, in or from the settled land, or any other land, or by or according to any facilities given in that behalf; and

(ii) the rent may also be made to vary according to the price of the minerals or substances gotten, or any of them, and such price may be the saleable value, or the price or value appearing in any trade or market or other price list or return from time to time, or may be the marketable value as ascertained in any manner prescribed by the lease (including a reference to arbitration), or may be an average of any such prices of values taken during a specified period; and

(iii) a fixed or minimum rent may be made payable, with or without power for the lessees, in case the rent, according to acreage or quantity or otherwise, in any specified period does not produce an amount equal to the fixed or minimum rent, to make up the deficiency in any subsequent specified period, free of rent other than the fixed or minimum rent.

(2) A lease may be made partly in consideration of the lessee having executed, or agreeing to execute, on the land leased an improvement authorised by this Act, for or in connexion with mining purposes.

46 Variation of building or mining lease according to circumstances of district

(1) Where it is shown to the court with respect to the district in which any settled land is situate, either—

(i) that it is the custom for land therein to be leased for building or mining purposes for a longer term or on other conditions than the term or conditions specified in that behalf in this Act; or

(ii) that it is difficult to make leases for building or mining purposes of land therein, except for a longer term or on other conditions than the term and conditions specified in that behalf in this Act;

the court may, if it thinks fit, authorise generally the tenant for life or statutory owner to make from time to time leases of or affecting the settled land in that district, or parts thereof for any term or on any conditions as in the order of the court expressed, or may, if it thinks fit, authorise the tenant for life or statutory owner to make any such lease in any particular case.

(2) Thereupon the tenant for life or statutory owner, and, subject to any direction in the order of the court to the contrary, each of his successors in title being a tenant for life or statutory owner, may make in any case, or in the particular case, a lease of the settled land, or part thereof, in conformity with the order.

47 Capitalisation of part of mining rent

Under a mining lease, whether the mines or minerals leased are already opened or in work or not, unless a contrary intention is expressed in the settlement there shall be from time to time set aside, as capital money arising under this Act, part of the rent as follows, namely—where the tenant for life or statutory owner is impeachable for waste in respect of minerals, three fourth parts of the rent, and otherwise one fourth part thereof, and in every such case the residue of the rent shall go as rents and profits.

48 Regulations respecting forestry leases

(1) In the case of a forestry lease—

(i) a peppercorn rent or a nominal or other rent less than the rent ultimately payable, may be made payable for the first ten years or any less part of the term;

(ii) the rent may be made to be ascertainable by, or to vary according to the value of the timber on the land comprised in the lease, or the produce thereof, which may during any year be cut, converted carried away, or otherwise disposed of;

(iii) a fixed or minimum rent may be made payable, with or without power for the lessee, in case the rent according to value in any specified period does not produce an amount equal to the fixed or minimum rent, to make up the deficiency in any subsequent specified period, free of rent other than the fixed or minimum rent; and

(iv) any other provisions may be made for the sharing of the proceeds or profits of the user of the land between the reversioner and the Forestry Commissioners.

(2) In this expression "timber" includes all forest products.

MISCELLANEOUS POWERS

49 Power on dispositions to impose restrictions and make reservations and stipulations

(1) On a sale or other disposition or dealing under the powers of this Act—

(a) any easement, right, or privilege of any kind may be reserved or granted over or in relation to the settled land or any part thereof or other land, including the land disposed of, and, in the case of an exchange, the land taken in exchange; and

(b) any restriction with respect to building on or other user of land, or with respect to mines and minerals, or with respect to or for the purpose of the more beneficial working thereof, or with respect to any other thing, may be imposed and made binding, as far as the law permits, by covenant, condition or otherwise, on the tenant for life or statutory owner and the settled land or any part thereof, or on the other party and any land disposed of to him; and

(c) the whole or any part of any capital or annual sum (and in the case of an annual sum whether temporary or perpetual) charged on or payable out of the land disposed of, or any part thereof, and other land subject to the settlement, may as between the tenant for life or statutory owner and his successors in title, and the other party and persons deriving title under or in succession to him (but without prejudice to the rights of the person entitled to such capital or annual sum) be charged exclusively on the land disposed of, or any part thereof, or such other land as aforesaid, or any part thereof, in exoneration of the rest of the land on or out of which such capital or annual sum is charged or payable.

(2) A sale of land may be made subject to a stipulation that all or any of the timber and other trees, pollards, tellers, underwood, saplings and plantations on the land sold (in this section referred to as "timber") or any articles attached to the land (in this section referred to as "fixtures") shall be taken by the purchaser at a valuation and the amount of the valuation shall form part of the price of the land, and shall be capital money accordingly.

(3) Where on a sale the consideration attributable to any timber or fixtures is by mistake paid to a tenant for life or other person not entitled to receive it, then, if such person or the purchaser or the persons deriving title under either of them subsequently pay the aforesaid consideration, with such interest, if any, thereon as the court may direct to the trustees of the settlement or other persons entitled thereto or into court, the court may, on the application of the purchaser or the persons deriving title under him, declare that the disposition is to take effect as if the whole of the consideration had at the date thereof been duly paid to the trustees of the settlement or other persons entitled to receive the same.

The person, not entitled to receive the same, to whom the consideration is paid, and his estate and effects shall remain liable to make good any loss attributable to the mistake.

50 Separate dealing with surface and minerals with or without wayleaves, etc

A sale, exchange, lease or other authorised disposition, may be made either of land, with or without an exception or reservation of all or any of the mines and minerals therein, or of any mines and minerals, and in any such case with or without a grant or reservation of powers of working, wayleaves or rights of way, rights of water and drainage, and other powers, easements, rights, and privileges for or incident to or connected with mining purposes, in relation to the settled land, or any part thereof, or any other land.

51 Power to grant options

(1) A tenant for life may at any time, either with or without consideration, grant by writing an option to purchase or take a lease of the settled land, or any part thereof, or any easement, right, or privilege over or in relation to the same at a price or rent fixed at the time of the granting of the option.

(2) Every such option shall be made exercisable within an agreed number of years not exceeding ten.

(3) The price or rent shall be the best which, having regard to all the circumstances, can reasonably be obtained and either—

(a) may be a specified sum of money or rent, or at a specified rate according to the superficial area of the land with respect to which the option is exercised: or the frontage thereof or otherwise; or

(b) in the case of an option to purchase contained in a lease or agreement for a lease, may be a stated number of years' purchase of the highest rent reserved by the lease or agreement; or

(c) if the option is exercisable as regards part of the land comprised in the lease or agreement, may be a proportionate part of such highest rent;

and any aggregate price or rent may be made to be apportionable in any manner, or according to any system, or by reference to arbitration.

(4) An option to take a mining lease may be coupled with the grant of a licence to search for and prove any mines or minerals under the settled land, or any part thereof, pending the exercise of the option.

(5) The consideration for the grant of the option shall be capital money arising under this Act.

52 Surrenders and regrants

(1) A tenant for life may accept, with or without consideration, a surrender of any lease of settled land, whether made under this Act or not, or a regrant of any land granted in fee simple, whether under this Act or not, in respect of the whole land leased or granted, or any part thereof, with or without an exception of all or any of the mines and minerals therein, or in respect of mines and minerals, or any of them, and with or without an exception of any easement, right or privilege of any kind over or in relation to the land surrendered or regranted.

(2) On a surrender of a lease, or a regrant of land granted in fee simple, in respect of part only of the land or mines and minerals leased or granted, the rent or rentcharge may be apportioned.

(3) On a surrender or regrant, the tenant for life may in relation to the land or mines and minerals surrendered or regranted, or of any part thereof, make a new or other lease, or grant in fee simple, or new or other leases, or grants in fee simple, in lots.

(4) A new or other lease, or grant in fee simple, may comprise additional land or mines and minerals, and may reserve any apportioned or other rent or rentcharge.

(5) On a surrender or regrant, and the making of a new or other lease, whether for the same or for any extended or other term, or of a new or other grant in fee simple, and whether or not subject to the same or to any other covenants, provisions, or conditions, the value of the lessee's or grantee's interests in the lease surrendered, or the land regranted, may be taken into account in the determination of the amount of the rent or rentcharge to be reserved, and of any fine or consideration in money to be taken, and of the nature of the covenants, provisions, and conditions to be inserted in the new or other lease, or grant in fee simple.

(6) Every new or other lease, or grant in fee simple, shall be in conformity with this Act.

(7) All money, not being rent or rentcharge, received on the exercise by the tenant for life of the powers conferred by this section, shall, unless the court, on an application made within six months after the receipt thereof or within such further time as the court may in special circumstances allow, otherwise directs, be capital money arising under this Act.

(8) A regrant shall be made to the tenant for life or statutory owner, and shall be deemed a subsidiary vesting deed, and the statements and particulars required in the case of subsidiary vesting deeds shall be inserted therein.

(9) In this section "land granted in fee simple" means land so granted with or subject to a reservation thereout of a perpetual or terminable rentcharge which is or forms part of the settled land, and "grant in fee simple" has a corresponding meaning.

53 Acceptance of leases

(1) A tenant for life may accept a lease of any land, or of any mines and minerals or of any easement, right, or privilege, convenient to be held or worked with or annexed in enjoyment to

the settled land, or any part thereof, for such period, and upon such terms and conditions, as the tenant for life thinks fit:

Provided that no fine shall be paid out of capital money in respect of such lease.

(2) The lease shall be granted to the tenant for life or statutory owner, and shall be deemed a subsidiary vesting deed, and the statements and particulars required in the case of subsidiary vesting deeds shall either be inserted therein or endorsed thereon.

(3) The lease may contain an option to purchase the reversion expectant on the term thereby granted.

54 Power to grant water rights to statutory bodies

(1) For the development, improvement, or general benefit of the settled land, or any part thereof, a tenant for life may make a grant in fee simple or absolutely, or a lease for any term of years absolute, for a nominal price or rent, or for less than the best price or rent that can reasonably be obtained, or gratuitously, to any statutory authority, of any water or streams or springs of water in, upon, or under the settled land, and of any rights of taking, using, enjoying and conveying water, and of laying, constructing, maintaining, and repairing mains, pipes, reservoirs, dams, weirs and other works of any kind proper for the supply and distribution of water, and of any part of the settled land required as a site for any of the aforesaid works, and of any easement, right or privilege over or in relation to the settled land or any part thereof in connexion with any of the aforesaid works.

(2) This section does not authorise the creation of any greater rights than could have been created by a person absolutely entitled for his own benefit to the settled land affected.

(3) In this section "statutory authority" means an authority or company for the time being empowered by any Act of Parliament, public general, or local or private, or by any order or certificate having the force of an Act of Parliament, to provide with a supply of water any town, parish or place in which the settled land or any part thereof is situated.

(4) All money, not being rent, received on the exercise of any power conferred by this section shall be capital money arising under this Act.

55 Power to grant land for public and charitable purposes

(1) For the development, improvement, or general benefit of the settled land, or any part thereof, a tenant for life may make a grant in fee simple, or absolutely, or a lease for any term of years absolute, for a nominal price or rent, or for less than the best price or rent that can reasonably be obtained, or gratuitously, of any part of the settled land, with or without any easement, right or privilege over or in relation to the settled land or any part thereof, for all or any one or more of the following purposes, namely—

(i) For the site, or the extension of any existing site, of a place of religious worship, residence for a minister of religion, school house, town hall, market house, public library, public baths, museum, hospital, infirmary, or other public building, literary or scientific institution, drill hall, working-men's club, parish room, reading room or village institute, with or without in any case any yard, garden, or other ground to be held with any such building; or

(ii) For the construction, enlargement, or improvement of any railway, canal, road (public or private), dock, sea-wall, embankment, drain, watercourse, or reservoir; or

(iii) For any other public or charitable purpose in connexion with the settled land, or any part thereof, or tending to the benefit of the persons residing, or for whom dwellings may be erected, on the settled land, or any part thereof.

Not more than one acre shall in any particular case be conveyed for any purpose mentioned in paragraphs (i) and (iii) of this subsection, nor more than five acres for any purpose mentioned in paragraph (ii) of this subsection, unless the full consideration be paid or reserved in respect of the excess.

(2) All money, not being rent, received on the exercise of any power conferred by this section shall be capital money arising under this Act.

56 Dedication for streets, open spaces, etc

(1) On or after or in connexion with a sale or grant for building purposes, or a building lease, or the development as a building estate of the settled land, or any part thereof, or at any other reasonable time, the tenant for life, for the general benefit of the residents on the settled land, or on any part thereof—

(i) may cause or require any parts of the settled land to be appropriated and laid out for streets, roads, paths, squares, gardens, or other open spaces, for the use, gratuitously or on payment, of the public or of individuals, with sewers, drains, water courses, fences, paving, or other works necessary or proper in connexion therewith; and

(ii) may provide that the parts so appropriated shall be conveyed to or vested in the trustees of the settlement, or other trustees, or any company or public body, on trusts or subject to provisions for securing the continued appropriation thereof to the purposes aforesaid, and the continued repair or maintenance of streets and other places and works aforesaid, with or without provision for appointment of new trustees when required; and

(iii) may execute any general or other deed necessary or proper for giving effect to the provisions of this section (which deed may be inrolled in the Central Office of the *Supreme Court* [Senior Courts]), and thereby declare the mode, terms, and conditions of the appropriation, and the manner in which and the persons by whom the benefit thereof is to be enjoyed, and the nature and extent of the privileges and conveniences granted.

(2) In regard to the dedication of land for the public purposes aforesaid, a tenant for life shall be in the same position as if he were an absolute owner.

(3) A tenant for life shall have power—

(a) to enter into any agreement for the recompense to be made for any part of the settled land which is required for the widening of a highway under [the Highways Act 1980], or otherwise;

(b) to consent to the diversion of any highway over the settled land under [the Highways Act 1980], or otherwise; and

(c) . . .

and any agreement or consent so made or given shall be valid and effectual, for all purposes, as if made or given by an absolute owner of the settled land.

(4) All money, not being rent, received on the exercise of any power conferred by this section shall be capital money arising under this Act.

Amendment

Sub-s (1): in para (iii) words "Supreme Court" in italics repealed and subsequent words in square brackets substituted, from a date to be appointed, by the Constitutional Reform Act 2005, s 59(5), Sch 11, Pt 2, para 4(1), (3).

Sub-s (3): words in square brackets in paras (a), (b) substituted by the Highways Act 1980, s 343(2), Sch 24; para (c) repealed by the Highways Act 1959, s 312(2), Sch 25.

57 Provision of land for small dwellings, small holdings and dwellings for working classes

(1) Where land is sold, or given in exchange or leased—

(a) for the purpose of the erection on such land of small dwellings; or

(b) to the council of a county or county borough for the purposes of small holdings;

the sale, exchange, or lease may, notwithstanding anything contained in this Act, be made for such consideration in money, or land, or in land and money, or may reserve such rent, as having regard to the said purposes and to all the circumstances of the case, is the best that can reasonably be obtained, notwithstanding that a better consideration or rent might have been obtained if the land were sold, exchanged, or leased, for another purpose.

(2) Notwithstanding anything contained in, and in addition to the other powers conferred by this Act, a tenant for life may at any time—

(a) for the purpose of the erection of dwellings for the working classes, or the provision of gardens to be held therewith; or

(b) for the purpose of the Small Holdings and Allotments Acts 1908 to 1919;

make a grant in fee simple or absolutely, or a lease for any term of years absolute of any part of the settled land, with or without any easement, right or privilege of any kind over or in relation to the settled land or any part thereof, for a nominal price or rent, or for less than the best price or rent that can reasonably be obtained or gratuitously:

Provided that, except under an order of the court, not more than two acres in the case of land situate in an urban district, or ten acres in the case of land situate in a rural district, in any one parish shall be granted or leased under the powers conferred by this subsection, unless the full consideration be paid or reserved in respect of the excess.

(3) All money, not being rent, received on the exercise of any power conferred by this section shall be capital money arising under this Act.

58 Power to compromise claims and release restrictions, etc

(1) A tenant for life may, with the consent in writing of the trustees of the settlement, either with or without giving or taking any consideration in money or otherwise, compromise, compound, abandon, submit to arbitration, or otherwise settle any claim, dispute, or question whatsoever relating to the settled land, or any part thereof, including in particular claims, disputes or questions as to boundaries, the ownership of mines and minerals, rights and powers of working mines and minerals, local laws and customs relative to the working of mines and minerals and other matters . . . easements, and restrictive covenants, and for any of those purposes may enter into, give, execute, and do such agreements, assurances, releases, and other things as the tenant for life may, with such consent as aforesaid, think proper.

(2) A tenant for life may, with the consent in writing of the trustees of the settlement, at any time, by deed or writing, either with or without consideration in money or otherwise, release, waive, or modify, or agree to release, waive, or modify any covenant, agreement, or restriction imposed on any other land for the benefit of the settled land, or any part thereof, or release, or agree to release, any other land from any easement, right or privilege, including a right of pre-emption, affecting the same for the benefit of the settled land, or any part thereof.

(3) A tenant for life may contract that a transaction effected before or after the commencement of this Act, which (whether subject or not to any variation authorised by this subsection) is affected by section seventy-eight of the Railway Clauses Consolidation Act 1845, or by section twenty-two of the Waterworks Clauses Act 1847 (relating to support by minerals) shall take effect as if some other distance than forty yards or the prescribed distance had been mentioned in such sections or had been otherwise prescribed.

In any case where section seventy-eight aforesaid has effect as amended and re-enacted by Part II of the Mines (Working Facilities and Support) Act 1923, a tenant for life may make any agreement authorised by section eighty-five A of the Railway Clauses Consolidation Act 1845, as enacted in the said Part II.

Amendment

Sub-s (1): words omitted repealed by the Statute Law (Repeals) Act 1969, s 1, Schedule, Part III.

59 Power to vary leases and grants and to give licences and consents

(1) A tenant for life may, at any time, by deed, either with or without consideration in money or otherwise, vary, release, waive or modify, either absolutely or otherwise, the terms of any lease whenever made of the settled land or any part thereof, or any covenants or conditions contained in any grant in fee simple whenever made of land with or subject to a reservation thereout of a rent which is or forms part of the settled land, and in either case in respect of the whole or any part of the land comprised in any such lease or grant, but so that every such lease or grant shall, after such variation, release, waiver or modification as aforesaid, be such a lease or grant as might then have been lawfully made under this Act if the lease had been surrendered, or the land comprised in the grant had never been so comprised, or had been regranted.

(2) Where land is or has been disposed of subject to any covenant requiring the licence, consent, or approval of the covenantee or his successors in title as to—

- (a) the user of the land in any manner; or
- (b) the erection construction or alteration of or addition to buildings or works of any description on the land; or

(c) the plans or elevations of any proposed buildings or other works on the land; or
(d) any other act, matter, or thing relating to the land, or any buildings or works thereon; or
(e) any assignment, under-letting or parting with the possession of all or any part of the property comprised in any lease affecting the settled land;

and the covenant enures for the benefit of settled land (including, where the disposition is a lease, the reversion expectant on the determination thereof), the licence, consent or approval may be given by the tenant for life of the settled land affected.

60 Power to apportion rents

(1) A tenant for life may, at any time, by deed, either with or without consideration in money or otherwise, agree for the apportionment of any rent reserved or created by any such lease or grant as mentioned in the last preceding section, or any rent being or forming part of the settled land, so that the apportioned parts of such rent shall thenceforth be payable exclusively out of or in respect of such respective portions of the land subject thereto as may be thought proper, and also agree that any covenants, agreements, powers, or remedies for securing such rent and any other covenants or agreements by the lessee or grantee and any conditions shall also be apportioned and made applicable exclusively to the respective portions of the land out of or in respect of which the apportioned parts of such rent shall thenceforth be payable.

(2) Where the settled land, or any part thereof, is held or derived under a lease, or under a grant reserving rent, or subject to covenants, agreements or conditions, whether such lease or grant comprises other land or not, the tenant for life may at any time by deed, with or without giving or taking any consideration in money or otherwise, procure the variation, release, waiver, or modification, either absolutely or otherwise, of the terms, covenants, agreements, or conditions contained in such lease or grant, in respect of the whole or any part of the settled land comprised therein, including the apportionment of any rent, covenants, agreements, conditions, and provisions reserved, or created by, or contained in, such lease or grant.

(3) This section applies to leases or grants made either before or after the commencement of this Act.

61 Provisions as to consideration

(1) All money, not being rent, payable by the tenant for life in respect of any transaction to which any of the three last preceding sections relates shall be paid out of capital money arising under this Act, and all money, not being rent, received on the exercise by the tenant for life of the powers conferred by any of those sections, shall, unless the court, on an application made within six months after the receipt thereof or within such further time as the court may in special circumstances allow, otherwise directs, be capital money arising under this Act.

(2) For the purpose of the three last preceding sections "consideration in money or otherwise" means—
(a) a capital sum of money or a rent;
(b) land being freehold or leasehold for any term of years whereof not less than sixty years shall be unexpired;
(c) any easement, right or privilege over or in relation to the settled land, or any part thereof, or any other land;
(d) the benefit of any restrictive covenant or condition; and
(e) the release of the settled land, or any part thereof, or any other land, from any easement, right or privilege, including a right of pre-emption, or from the burden of any restrictive covenant or condition affecting the same.

62 Special provisions as to manorial incidents, etc

(1)–(3) . . .

(4) In reference to the conversion of a perpetually renewable lease or underlease into a long term, a tenant for life may enter into such agreements and do such acts and things as the lessor or lessee or under lessee, as the case may require, is, by any enactment authorised to enter into or do.

Amendment

Sub-ss (1)–(3): repealed by the Statute Law (Repeals) Act 1969, s 1, Schedule, Part III.

63 Power to complete predecessor's contracts

A tenant for life may make any disposition which is necessary or proper for giving effect to a contract entered into by a predecessor in title, and which if made by that predecessor would have been valid as against his successors in title.

64 General power for the tenant for life to effect any transaction under an order of the court

(1) Any transaction affecting or concerning the settled land, or any part thereof, or any other land (not being a transaction otherwise authorised by this Act, or by the settlement) which in the opinion of the court would be for the benefit of the settled land, or any part thereof, or the persons interested under the settlement, may, under an order of the court, be effected by a tenant for life, if it is one which could have been validly effected by an absolute owner.

(2) In this section "transaction" includes any sale, . . . exchange, assurance, grant, lease, surrender, reconveyance, release, reservation, or other disposition, and any purchase or other acquisition, and any covenant, contract, or option, and any application of capital money . . . and any compromise or other dealing, or arrangement . . . ; and "effected" has the meaning appropriate to the particular transaction; and the references to land include references to restrictions and burdens affecting land.

Amendment

Sub-s (2): first words omitted repealed by the Statute Law (Repeals) Act 1969, s 1, Schedule, Part III; other words omitted repealed by the Settled Land and Trustee Acts (Court's General Powers) Act 1943, s 2.

PROVISIONS AS TO SPECIAL CLASSES OF PROPERTY

65 Power to dispose of mansion

(1) The powers of disposing of settled land conferred by this Act on a tenant for life may be exercised as respects the principal mansion house, if any, on any settled land, and the pleasure grounds and park and lands, if any, usually occupied therewith:

Provided that those powers shall not be exercised without the consent of the trustees of the settlement or an order of the court—

- (a) if the settlement is a settlement made or coming into operation before the commencement of this Act and the settlement does not expressly provide to the contrary; or
- (b) if the settlement is a settlement made or coming into operation after the commencement of this Act and the settlement expressly provides that these powers or any of them shall not be exercised without such consent or order.

(2) Where a house is usually occupied as a farmhouse, or where the site of any house and the pleasure grounds and park and lands, if any, usually occupied therewith do not together exceed twenty-five acres in extent, the house is not to be deemed a principal mansion house within the meaning of this section, and may accordingly be disposed of in like manner as any other part of the settled land.

66 Cutting and sale of timber, and capitalisation of part of proceeds

(1) Where a tenant for life is impeachable for waste in respect of timber, and there is on the settled land timber ripe and fit for cutting, the tenant for life, on obtaining the consent of the trustees of the settlement or an order of the court, may cut and sell that timber, or any part thereof.

(2) Three fourth parts of the net proceeds of the sale shall be set aside as and be capital money arising under this Act, and the other fourth part shall go as rents and profits.

67 Sale and purchase of heirlooms under order of court

(1) Where personal chattels are settled so as to devolve with settled land, or to devolve therewith as nearly as may be in accordance with the law or practice in force at the date of the

settlement, or are settled together with land, or upon trusts declared by reference to the trusts affecting land, a tenant for life of the land may sell the chattels or any of them.

(2) The money arising by the sale shall be capital money arising under this Act, and shall be paid, invested, or applied and otherwise dealt with in like manner in all respects as by this Act directed with respect to other capital money arising under this Act, or may be invested in the purchase of other chattels of the same or any other nature, which, when purchased, shall be settled and held on the same trusts, and shall devolve in the same manner as the chattels sold.

(3) A sale or purchase of chattels under this section shall not be made without an order of the court.

(4) Any reference in any enactment to personal chattels settled as heirlooms shall extend to any chattels to which this section applies.

DEALINGS AS BETWEEN TENANTS FOR LIFE AND THE ESTATE

68 Provision enabling dealings with tenant for life

(1) In the manner mentioned and subject to the provisions contained in this section—

(a) a sale, grant, lease, mortgage, charge or other disposition of settled land, or of any easement, right, or privilege over the same may be made to the tenant for life; or

(b) capital money may be advanced on mortgage to him; or

(c) a purchase may be made from him of land to be made subject to the limitations of the settlement; or

(d) an exchange may be made with him of settled land for other land; and

(e) any such disposition, advance, purchase, or exchange as aforesaid may be made to, from, or with any persons of whom the tenant for life is one.

(2) In every such case the trustees of the settlement shall, in addition to their powers as trustees, have all the powers of a tenant for life in reference to negotiating and completing the transaction, and shall have power to enforce any covenants by the tenant for life, or, where the tenant for life is himself one of the trustees, then the other or others of them shall have such power, and the said powers of a tenant for life may be exercised by the trustees of the settlement in the name and on behalf of the tenant for life.

(3) This section applies, notwithstanding that the tenant for life is one of the trustees of the settlement, or that an order has been made authorising the trustees to act on his behalf, or that he is [suffering from mental disorder] but does not apply to dealings with any body of persons which includes a trustee of the settlement, not being the tenant for life, unless the transaction is either previously or subsequently approved by the court.

Amendment

Sub-s (3): words in square brackets substituted by the Mental Health Act 1959, s 149, Sch 7, Part I.

INCUMBRANCES

69 Shifting of incumbrances

Where there is an incumbrance affecting any part of the settled land (whether capable of being overreached on the exercise by the tenant for life of his powers under this Act or not), the tenant for life, with the consent of the incumbrancer, may charge that incumbrance on any other part of the settled land, or on all or any part of the capital money or securities representing capital money subject or to become subject to the settlement, whether already charged therewith or not, in exoneration of the first mentioned part, and, by a legal mortgage, or otherwise, make provision accordingly.

70 Power to vary provisions of an incumbrance and to charge by way of additional security

(1) Where an incumbrance affects any part of the settled land, the tenant for life may, with the consent of the incumbrancer, vary the rate of interest charged and any of the other provisions of the instrument, if any, creating the incumbrance, and with the like consent charge that incumbrance on any part of the settled land, whether already charged therewith or not, or on all or any part of the capital money or securities representing capital money subject or to

become subject to the settlement, by way of additional security, or of consolidation of securities, and by a legal mortgage or otherwise, make provision accordingly.

(2) "Incumbrance" in this section includes any annual sum payable during a life or lives or during a term of years absolute or determinable, but in any such case an additional security shall be effected so as only to create a charge or security similar to the original charge or security.

RAISING OF MONEY

71 Power to raise money by mortgage

(1) Where money is required for any of the following purposes namely—

(i) Discharging an incumbrance on the settled land or part thereof;

(ii) Paying for any improvement authorised by this Act or by the settlement;

(iii) Equality of exchange;

(iv), (v) . . . ;

(vi) Redeeming a compensation rentcharge in respect of the extinguishment of manorial incidents and affecting the settled land;

(vii) Commuting any additional rent made payable on the conversion of a perpetually renewable leasehold interest into a long term;

(viii) Satisfying any claims for compensation on the conversion of a perpetually renewable leasehold interest into a long term by any officer, solicitor, or other agent of the lessor in respect of fees or remuneration which would have been payable by the lessee or under-lessee on any renewal;

(ix) Payment of the costs of any transaction authorised by this section or either of the two last preceding sections;

the tenant for life may raise the money so required, on the security of the settled land, or of any part thereof, by a legal mortgage, and the money so raised shall be capital money for that purpose, and may be paid or applied accordingly.

(2) "Incumbrance" in this section does not include any annual sum payable only during a life or lives or during a term of years absolute or determinable.

(3) The restrictions imposed by this Part of this Act on the leasing powers of a tenant for life do not apply in relation to a mortgage term created under this Act.

Amendment

Sub-s (1): words omitted repealed by the Statute Law (Repeals) Act 1969, s 1, Schedule, Part III.

Modification

References to solicitors etc modified to include references to bodies recognised under the Administration of Justice Act 1985, s 9, by the Solicitors' Incorporated Practices Order 1991, SI 1991/2684, arts 4, 5, Sch 1.

CONVEYANCE

72 Completion of transactions by conveyance

(1) On a sale, exchange, lease, mortgage, charge, or other disposition, the tenant for life may, as regards land sold, given in exchange, leased, mortgaged, charged, or otherwise disposed of, or intended so to be, or as regards easements or other rights or privileges sold, given in exchange, leased, mortgaged, or otherwise disposed of, or intended so to be, effect the transaction by deed to the extent of the estate or interest vested or declared to be vested in him by the last or only vesting instrument affecting the settled land or any less estate or interest, in the manner requisite for giving effect to the sale, exchange, lease, mortgage, charge, or other disposition, but so that a mortgage shall be effected by the creation of a term of years absolute in the settled land or by charge by way of legal mortgage, and not otherwise.

(2) Such a deed, to the extent and in the manner to and in which it is expressed or intended to operate and can operate under this Act, is effectual to pass the land conveyed, or the easements, rights, privileges or other interests created, discharged from all the limitations, powers, and provisions of the settlement, and from all estates, interests, and charges subsisting or to arise thereunder, but subject to and with the exception of—

(i) all legal estates and charges by way of legal mortgage having priority to the settlement; and

(ii) all legal estates and charges by way of legal mortgage which have been conveyed or created for securing money actually raised at the date of the deed; and

(iii) all leases and grants at fee-farm rents or otherwise, and all grants of easements, rights of common, or other rights or privileges which—

(a) were before the date of the deed granted or made for value in money or money's worth, or agreed so to be, by the tenant for life or statutory owner, or by any of his predecessors in title, or any trustees for them, under the settlement, or under any statutory power, or are at that date otherwise binding on the successors in title of the tenant for life or statutory owner; and

(b) are at the date of the deed protected by registration under the Land Charges Act 1925, if capable of registration thereunder.

(3) Notwithstanding registration under the Land Charges Act 1925, of—

(a) an annuity within the meaning of Part II of that Act;

(b) a limited owner's charge or a general equitable charge within the meaning of that Act;

a disposition under this Act operates to overreach such annuity or charge which shall, according to its priority, take effect as if limited by the settlement.

(4) Where a lease is by this Act authorised to be made by writing under hand only, such writing shall have the same operation under this section as if it had been a deed.

PART III
INVESTMENT OR OTHER APPLICATION OF CAPITAL MONEY

73 Modes of investment or application

(1) Capital money arising under this Act, subject to payment of claims properly payable thereout and to the application thereof for any special authorised object for which the capital money was raised, shall, when received, be invested or otherwise applied wholly in one, or partly in one and partly in another or others, of the following modes (namely)—

[(i) In investment in securities either under the general power of investment in section 3 of the Trustee Act 2000 or under a power to invest conferred on the trustees of the settlement by the settlement;]

i(ii) In discharge, purchase, or redemption of incumbrances affecting the whole estate the subject of the settlement, or of . . . , rentcharge in lieu of tithe, Crown rent, chief rent, or quit rent, charged on or payable out of the settled land, or of any charge in respect of an improvement created on a holding under the [Agricultural Holdings Act 1986], or any similar previous enactment;

(iii) In payment for any improvement authorised by this Act;

(iv) In payment as for an improvement authorised by this Act of any money expended and costs incurred by a landlord under or in pursuance of the [Agricultural Holdings Act 1986], or any similar previous enactment, or under custom or agreement or otherwise, in or about the execution of any improvement comprised in [Schedule 7] to the said Agricultural Holdings Act;

(v) In payment for equality of exchange of settled land;

(vi), (vii) . . . ;

(viii) In redemption of any compensation rentcharge created in respect of the extinguishment of manorial incidents, and affecting the settled land;

(ix) In commuting any additional rent made payable on the conversion of a perpetually renewable leasehold interest into a long term, and in satisfying any claim for compensation on such conversion by any officer, solicitor, or other agent of the lessor in respect of fees or remuneration which would have been payable by the lessee or under-lessee on any renewal;

(x) In purchase of the freehold reversion in fee of any part of the settled land, being leasehold land held for years;

(xi) In purchase of land in fee simple, or of leasehold land held for sixty years or more unexpired at the time of purchase, subject or not to any exception or reservation of or in respect of mines or minerals therein, or of or in respect of rights or powers relative to the working of mines or minerals therein, or in other land;

(xii) In purchase either in fee simple, or for a term of sixty years or more, of mines and minerals convenient to be held or worked with the settled land, or of any easement, right, or privilege convenient to be held with the settled land for mining or other purposes;

(xiii) In redemption of an improvement rentcharge, that is to say, a rentcharge (temporary or permanent) created, whether before or after the commencement of this Act, in pursuance of any Act of Parliament, with the object of paying off any money advanced for defraying the expenses of an improvement of any kind authorised by Part I of the Third Schedule to this Act;

(xiv) In the purchase, with the leave of the court, of any leasehold interest where the immediate reversion is settled land, so as to merge the leasehold interest (unless the court otherwise directs) in the reversion, and notwithstanding that the leasehold interest may have less than sixty years to run;

(xv) In payment of the costs and expenses of all plans, surveys, and schemes, including schemes under the Town Planning Act 1925, or any similar previous enactment, made with a view to, or in connexion with the improvement or development of the settled land, or any part thereof, or the exercise of any statutory powers, and of all negotiations entered into by the tenant for life with a view to the exercise of any of the said powers, notwithstanding that such negotiations may prove abortive, and in payment of the costs and expenses of opposing any such proposed scheme as aforesaid affecting the settled land, whether or not the scheme is made;

(xvi) . . .

(xvii) In payment to a local or other authority of such sum as may be agreed in consideration of such authority taking over and becoming liable to repair a private road on the settled land or a road for the maintenance whereof a tenant for life is liable ratione tenurae;

(xviii) In financing any person who may have agreed to take a lease or grant for building purposes of the settled land, or any part thereof, by making advances to him in the usual manner on the security of an equitable mortgage of his building agreement;

(xix) In payment to any person becoming absolutely entitled or empowered to give an absolute discharge;

(xx) In payment of costs, charges, and expenses of or incidental to the exercise of any of the powers, or the execution of any of the provisions of this Act including the costs and expenses incidental to any of the matters referred to in this section;

(xxi) In any other mode authorised by the settlement with respect to money produced by the sale of the settled land.

(2) Notwithstanding anything in this section capital money arising under this Act from settled land in England or Wales shall not be applied in the purchase of land out of England and Wales, unless the settlement expressly authorises the same.

Amendment

Sub-s (1): para (i) substituted by the Trustee Act 2000, s 40(1), Sch 2, Pt II, para 9.
Sub-s (1): in para (ii) words omitted repealed by the Finance Act 1963, s 73(8)(b), Sch 11, Pt VI.
Sub-s (1): in paras (ii), (iv) words "Agricultural Holdings Act 1986" in square brackets, in each place they occur, substituted by the Agricultural Holdings Act 1986, s 100, Sch 14, para 11(a).
Sub-s (1): in para (iv) words "Schedule 7" in square brackets substituted by the Agricultural Holdings Act 1986, s 100, Sch 14, para 11(b).
Sub-s (1): paras (vi), (vii) repealed by the Statute Law Repeals Act 1969, s 1.
Sub-s (1): para (xvi) repealed by the Statute Law (Repeals) Act 1998.

Modification

References to solicitors etc modified to include references to bodies recognised under the Administration of Justice Act 1985, s 9, by the Solicitors' Incorporated Practices Order 1991, SI 1991/2684, arts 4, 5, Sch 1.

74 Power to acquire land subject to certain incumbrances

(1) Land may be acquired on a purchase or exchange to be made subject to a settlement, notwithstanding that the land is subject to any Crown rent, quit rent, chief rent, or other incident of tenure, or to any easement, right or privilege, or to any restrictive covenant, or to any liability to maintain or repair walls, fences, sea-walls, river banks, dykes, roads, streets,

sewers, or drains, or to any improvement rentcharge which is capable under this Act of being redeemed out of capital money.

(2) The acquisition on a purchase or exchange before the commencement of this Act of any land subject to any such burden as aforesaid is hereby confirmed.

75 Regulations respecting investment, devolution, and income of securities, etc

(1) Capital money arising under this Act shall, in order to its being invested or applied as aforesaid, be paid either to the trustees of the settlement or into court at the option of the tenant for life, and shall be invested or applied by the trustees, or under the direction of the court, as the case may be, accordingly.

[(2) Subject to Part IV of the Trustee Act 2000, to section 75A of this Act and to the following provisions of this section—

- (a) the investment or other application by the trustees shall be made according to the discretion of the trustees, but subject to any consent required or direction given by the settlement with respect to the investment or other application by the trustees of trust money of the settlement, and]
- ([b) any investment shall be in the names or under the control of the trustees.]

(3) The investment or other application under the direction of the court shall be made on the application of the tenant for life, or of the trustees.

[(4) The trustees, in exercising their power to invest or apply capital money, shall—

- (a) so far as practicable, consult the tenant for life; and
- (b) so far as consistent with the general interest of the settlement, give effect to his wishes.

(4A) Any investment or other application of capital money under the direction of the court shall not during the subsistence of the beneficial interest of the tenant for life be altered without his consent.

(4B) The trustees may not under section 11 of the Trustee Act 2000 authorise a person to exercise their functions with respect to the investment or application of capital money on terms that prevent them from complying with subsection (4) of this section.

(4C) A person who is authorised under section 11 of the Trustee Act 2000 to exercise any of their functions with respect to the investment or application of capital money is not subject to subsection (4) of this section.]

(5) Capital money arising under this Act while remaining uninvested or unapplied, and securities on which an investment of any such capital money is made shall for all purposes of disposition, transmission and devolution be treated as land, and shall be held for and go to the same persons successively, in the same manner and for and on the same estates, interests, and trusts, as the land wherefrom the money arises would, if not disposed of, have been held and have gone under the settlement.

(6) The income of those securities shall be paid or applied as the income of that land, if not disposed of, would have been payable or applicable under the settlement.

(7) Those securities may be converted into money, which shall be capital money arising under this Act.

(8) All or any part of any capital money paid into court may, if the court thinks fit, be at any time paid out to the trustees of the settlement.

Amendment

Sub-s (2): substituted by the Trustee Act 2000, s 40(1), Sch 2, Pt II, para 10(1); for transitional provisions in relation to directions of the tenant for life given, but not acted upon by the trustees, see para 10(3) thereof.
Sub-ss (4)-(4C): substituted, for sub-s (4) as originally enacted, by the Trustee Act 2000, s 40(1), Sch 2, Pt II, para 10(2); for transitional provisions in relation to directions of the tenant for life given, but not acted upon by the trustees, see para 10(3) thereof.

[75A Power to accept charge as security for part payment for land sold]

[(1) Where—

- (a) land subject to the settlement is sold by the tenant for life or statutory owner, for an estate in fee simple or a term having at least five hundred years to run, and
- (b) the proceeds of sale are liable to be invested,

the tenant for life or statutory owner may, with the consent of the trustees of the settlement, contract that the payment of any part, not exceeding two-thirds, of the purchase money shall be secured by a charge by way of legal mortgage of the land sold, with or without the security of any other property.

(2) If any buildings are comprised in the property secured by the charge, the charge must contain a covenant by the mortgagor to keep them insured for their full value against loss or damage due to any event.

(3) A person exercising the power under subsection (1) of this section, or giving consent for the purposes of that subsection—

- (a) is not required to comply with section 5 of the Trustee Act 2000 before giving his consent, and
- (b) is not liable for any loss incurred merely because the security is insufficient at the date of the charge.

(4) The power under subsection (1) of this section is exercisable subject to the consent of any person whose consent to a change of investment is required by the instrument, if any, creating the trust.

(5) Where the sale referred to in subsection (1) of this section is made under the order of the court, the power under that subsection applies only if and as far as the court may by order direct.]

Amendment

Inserted by the Trustee Act 2000, s 40(1), Sch 2, Pt II, para 11.

76 Application of money in court under Lands Clauses and other Acts

Where, under an Act, or an order or scheme confirmed by or having the force of an Act of Parliament, incorporating or applying, wholly or in part, the Lands Clauses Acts, or under any Act, public general or local or private, money is at the commencement of this Act in court, or is afterwards paid into court, and is liable to be laid out in the purchase of land to be made subject to a settlement, then, in addition to any mode of dealing therewith authorised by the Act under which the money is in court, that money may be invested or applied as capital money arising under this Act, on the like terms, if any, respecting costs and other things, as nearly as circumstances admit, and notwithstanding anything in this Act according to the same procedure, as if the modes of investment or application authorised by this Act were authorised by the Act under which the money is in court.

77 Application of money in hands of trustees under powers of settlement

Where—

- (a) under any instrument coming into operation either before or after the commencement of this Act money is in the hands of trustees, and is liable to be laid out in the purchase of land to be made subject to the trusts declared by that instrument; or
- (b) under any instrument coming into operation after the commencement of this Act money or securities or the proceeds of sale of any property is or are held by trustees on trusts creating entailed interests therein;

then, in addition to such powers of dealing therewith as the trustees have independently of this Act, they may, at the option of the tenant for life, invest or apply the money securities or proceeds as if they were capital money arising under this Act.

78 Provision as to personal estate settled by reference to capital money, or on trusts corresponding with the limitations of land

(1) Where money or securities or the proceeds of sale of any property is or are by any instrument coming into operation either before or after the commencement of this Act directed to be held on trusts declared by reference to capital money arising under this Act from land settled by that instrument or any other instrument, the money securities or proceeds shall be held on the like trusts as if the same had been or represented money which had actually arisen under this Act from the settled land.

[This subsection operates without prejudice to the rights of any person claiming under a disposition for valuable consideration of any such money securities or proceeds, made before the commencement of this Act].

(2) Where money or securities or the proceeds of sale of any property is or are by any instrument coming into operation after the commencement of this Act directed to be held on the same trusts as, or on trusts corresponding as nearly as may be with the limitations of land settled by that instrument or any other instrument, the money, securities or proceeds shall be held on the like trusts as if the same had been or represented capital money arising under this Act from the settled land.

(3) Such money, securities, or proceeds of sale shall be paid or transferred to or retained by the trustees of the settlement of the settled land, or paid or transferred into court, and invested or applied accordingly.

(4) Where the settled land includes freehold land, the money, securities, or proceeds of sale aforesaid shall be held on the like trusts as if the same had been or represented capital money arising from the freehold land.

(5) This section has effect notwithstanding any direction in the instrument creating the trust that the trust property is not to vest absolutely in any tenant in tail or in tail male or in tail female under the limitations of the settled land who dies under a specified age, or before the happening of a specified event, but, save as aforesaid, has effect with any variations and subject to any contrary intention expressed in the instrument creating the trust.

Amendment

Sub-s (1): words in square brackets inserted by the Law of Property (Amendment) Act 1926, Schedule.

79 Application of money paid for lease or reversion

Where capital money arising under this Act is purchase-money paid in respect of—

- (a) a lease for years; or
- (b) any other estate or interest in land less than the fee simple; or
- (c) a reversion dependent on any such lease, estate, or interest;

the trustees of the settlement or the court, as the case may be, and in the case of the court on the application of any party interested in that money, may, notwithstanding anything in this Act, require and cause the same to be laid out, invested, accumulated, and paid in such manner as, in the judgment of the trustees or of the court, as the case may be, will give to the parties interested in that money the like benefit therefrom as they might lawfully have had from the lease, estate, interest, or reversion in respect whereof the money was paid, or as near thereto as may be.

80 As to money received by way of damages for breach of covenant

(1) Money, not being rent, received by way of damages or compensation for breach of any covenant by a lessee or grantee contained in any lease or grant of settled land shall, unless in any case the court on the application of the tenant for life or the trustees of the settlement otherwise directs, be deemed to be capital money arising under this Act, and shall be paid to or retained by the trustees of the settlement, or paid into court, and invested or applied, accordingly.

(2) In addition to the other modes in which capital money may be applied under this Act or the settlement, money so received as aforesaid or any part thereof may, if the circumstances permit, be applied at any time within twelve months after such receipt, or such extended period as the court may allow, in or towards payment of the costs of making good in whole or in part the breach of covenant in respect of which it was so received, or the consequences thereof, and the trustees of the settlement, if they think fit, may require any money so received or any part thereof to be so applied.

(3) In the application of any such money in or towards payment of the cost of making good any such breach or the consequences of any such breach as aforesaid, the work required to be done for the purpose shall be deemed to be an improvement authorised by Part I of the Third Schedule to this Act.

(4) This section does not apply to money received by way of damages or compensation for the breach of a covenant to repay to the lessor or grantor money laid out or expended by him, or

to any case in which if the money received were applied in making good the breach of covenant or the consequences thereof such application would not enure for the benefit of the settled land, or any buildings thereon.

(5) This section does not apply to money received by way of damages or compensation before the commencement of this Act, but it applies whether the lease or grant was made before or after the commencement of this Act, and whether under the powers conferred by the Settled Land Acts 1882 to 1890, or this Act or not.

(6) The provisions of this section apply only if and as far as a contrary intention is not expressed in the settlement, and have effect subject to the terms of the settlement, and to any provisions therein contained, but a contrary intention shall not be deemed to be expressed merely by words negativing impeachment for waste.

81 As to capital arising otherwise than under the Act

Any money which after the commencement of this Act arises from settled land otherwise than under this Act, as well as any money or securities in the names or under the control of the tenant for life or the trustees of the settlement, being or representing money which had arisen before the commencement of this Act from the settled land otherwise than under the Settled Land Acts 1882 to 1890, and which ought, as between the persons interested in the settled land, to be or to have been treated as capital, shall (without prejudice to any other statutory provisions affecting the same) be deemed to be or to represent capital money arising under this Act, and shall be paid or transferred to or retained by the trustees of the settlement, or paid or transferred into court, and invested or applied, accordingly.

82 Land acquired may be made a substituted security for released charges

(1) Land acquired by purchase or in exchange or otherwise under the powers of this Act, may be made a substituted security for any charge from which the settled land or any part thereof has theretofore been released on the occasion and in order to the completion of a sale, exchange or other disposition:

Provided that, where a charge does not affect the whole of the settled land, the land acquired shall not be subjected thereto, unless the land is acquired either by purchase with money arising from sale of land which was before the sale subject to the charge, or by an exchange of land which was before the exchange subject to the charge.

(2) On land being so acquired, any person who, by the direction of the tenant for life, so conveys the land as to subject it to any legal estate or charge by way of legal mortgage, is not concerned to inquire whether or not it is proper that the land should be subjected to such legal estate or charge.

PART IV
IMPROVEMENTS

IMPROVEMENTS WITH CAPITAL MONEY

83 Description of improvements authorised by Act

Improvements authorised by this Act are the making or execution on, or in connexion with, and for the benefit of settled land, of any of the works mentioned in the Third Schedule to this Act, or of any works for any of the purposes mentioned in that Schedule, and any operation incident to or necessary or proper in the execution of any of those works, or necessary or proper for carrying into effect any of those purposes, or for securing the full benefit of any of those works or purposes.

84 Mode of application of capital money

(1) Capital money arising under this Act may be applied in or towards payment for any improvement authorised by this Act or by the settlement, without any scheme for the execution of the improvement being first submitted for approval to, or approved by, the trustees of the settlement or the court.

(2) Where the capital money to be expended is in the hands of the trustees of the settlement, they may apply that money in or towards payment for the whole or any part of any work or operation comprised in the improvement, on—

(i) a certificate to be furnished by a competent engineer or able practical surveyor employed independently of the tenant for life, certifying that the work or operation comprised in the improvement or some specific part thereof, has been properly executed, and what amount is properly payable in respect thereof, which certificate shall be conclusive in favour of the trustees as an authority and discharge for any payment made by them in pursuance thereof; or

(ii) an order of the court directing or authorising the trustees so to apply a specified portion of the capital money:

Provided that—

(a) In the case of improvements not authorised by Part I of the Third Schedule to this Act or by the settlement, the trustees may, if they think fit, and shall if so directed by the court, before they make any such application of capital money require that that money, or any part thereof, shall be repaid to them out of the income of the settled land by not more than fifty half-yearly instalments, the first of such instalments to be paid or to be deemed to have become payable at the expiration of six months from the date when the work or operation, in payment for which the money is to be applied, was completed;

(b) No capital money shall be applied by the trustees in payment for improvements not authorised by Parts I and II of the Third Schedule to this Act, or by the settlement, except subject to provision for the repayment thereof being made in manner mentioned in the preceding paragraph of this proviso.

(3) Where the capital money to be expended is in court, the court may, if it thinks fit, on a report or certificate of the [Secretary of State], or of a competent engineer or able practical surveyor approved by the court, or on such other evidence as the court may think sufficient, make such order and give such directions as it thinks fit for the application of the money, or any part thereof, in or towards payment for the whole or any part of any work or operation comprised in the improvement.

(4) Where the court authorises capital money to be applied in payment for any improvement or intended improvement not authorised by Part I of the Third Schedule to this Act or by the settlement, the court, as a condition of making the order, may in any case require that the capital money or any part thereof, and shall as respects an improvement mentioned in Part III of that Schedule (unless the improvement is authorised by the settlement), require that the whole of the capital money shall be repaid to the trustees of the settlement out of the income of the settled land by a fixed number of periodical instalments to be paid at the times appointed by the court, and may require that any incumbrancer of the estate or interest of the tenant for life shall be served with notice of the proceedings.

(5) All money received by the trustees of the settlement in respect of any instalments under this section shall be held by them as capital money arising from freehold land under the settlement, unless the court otherwise directs.

Amendment

Sub-s (3): words "Secretary of State" in square brackets substituted by SI 2002/794, art 5(1), Sch 1, para 2.

85 Creation of rentcharges to discharge instalments

(1) When the tenant for life is required by the trustees to repay by instalments the capital money expended, or any part thereof, the tenant for life is by this section authorised to create out of the settled land, or any part thereof, a yearly rentcharge in favour of the trustees of the settlement sufficient in amount to discharge the said half-yearly instalments.

(2) Where an order is made requiring repayment by instalments, the settled land shall stand charged with the payment to the trustees of the settlement of a yearly rentcharge sufficient in amount to discharge the periodical instalments, and the rentcharge shall accrue from day to day, and be payable at the times appointed for payment of the periodical instalments, and shall have effect as if limited by the settlement prior to the estate of the tenant for life, and the trustees of the settlement shall have all statutory and other powers for recovery thereof.

(3) A rentcharge created by or under this section shall not be redeemed out of capital money, but may be overreached in like manner as if the same were limited by the settlement, and shall cease if and when the land affected by the improvement ceases to be settled or is sold or exchanged, but if part of the land so affected remains subject to the settlement the rentcharge shall remain in force in regard to the settled land.

SUNDRY PROVISIONS AS TO IMPROVEMENTS

86 Concurrence in improvements

The tenant for life may join or concur with any other person interested in executing any improvement authorised by this Act, or in contributing to the cost thereof.

87 Court may order payment for improvements executed

The court may, in any case where it appears proper, make an order directing or authorising capital money to be applied in or towards payment for any improvement authorised by the Settled Land Acts 1882 to 1890, or this Act, notwithstanding that a scheme was not, before the execution of the improvement, submitted for approval, as required by the Settled Land Act 1882, to the trustees of the settlement or to the court, and notwithstanding that no capital money is immediately available for the purpose.

88 Obligation on tenant for life and successors to maintain, insure, etc

(1) The tenant for life, and each of his successors in title having under the trust instrument a limited estate or interest only in the settled land, shall, during such period, if any, as the [Secretary of State] by certificate in any case prescribes, maintain and repair, at his own expense, every improvement executed under the foregoing provisions of this Act or the enactments replaced thereby, and where a building or work in its nature insurable against damage by fire is comprised in the improvement, shall at his own expense insure and keep insured the improvement in such amount, if any, as the [Secretary of State] by certificate in any case prescribes.

(2) The tenant for life, or any of his successors as aforesaid, shall not cut down or knowingly permit to be cut down, except in proper thinning, any trees planted as an improvement under the foregoing provisions of this Act, or under the enactments replaced by those provisions.

(3) The tenant for life, and each of his successors as aforesaid, shall from time to time, if required by the [Secretary of State] on or without the application of any person having under the trust instrument any estate or interest in the settled land in possession, remainder, or otherwise, report to the [Secretary of State] the state of every improvement executed under this Act, and the fact and particulars of fire insurance, if any.

(4) The [Secretary of State] may vary any certificate made by him under this section in such manner or to such extent as circumstances appear to him to require, but not so as to increase the liabilities of the tenant for life, or any of his successors as aforesaid.

(5) If the tenant for life, or any of his successors as aforesaid, fails in any respect to comply with the requisitions of this section, or does any act in contravention thereof, any person having, under the trust instrument, any estate or interest in the settled land in possession, remainder, or reversion, shall have a right of action, in respect of that default or act, against the tenant for life; and the estate of the tenant for life, after his death, shall be liable to make good to the persons entitled under the trust instrument any damages occasioned by that default or act.

(6) Where in connexion with any improvement an improvement rentcharge, as hereinbefore defined, has been created, and that rentcharge has been redeemed out of capital money, this section shall apply to the improvement as if it had been an improvement executed under this Act.

Amendment

Sub-s (1): words "Secretary of State" in square brackets in both places they occur substituted by SI 2002/794, art 5(1), Sch 1, para 3(1), (2).

Sub-s (3): words "Secretary of State" in square brackets in both places they occur substituted by SI 2002/794, art 5(1), Sch 1, para 3(1), (3).

Sub-s (4): words "Secretary of State" in square brackets substituted by SI 2002/794, art 5(1), Sch 1, para 3(1), (4).

89 Protection as regards waste in execution and repair of improvements

The tenant for life, and each of his successors in title having, under the trust instrument, a limited estate or interest only in the settled land and all persons employed by or under contract with the tenant for life or any such successor, may from time to time enter on the settled land, and, without impeachment of waste by any remainderman or reversioner, thereon execute any improvement authorised by this Act, or inspect, maintain, and repair the same, and for the purposes thereof do, make, and use on the settled land, all acts, works, and conveniences proper for the execution, maintenance, repair, and use thereof, and get and work freestone, limestone, clay, sand, and other substances, and make tramways and otherways, burn and make bricks, tiles, and other things, and cut down and use timber and other trees not planted or left standing for shelter or ornament.

PART V
MISCELLANEOUS PROVISIONS

90 Power for tenant for life to enter into contracts

(1) A tenant for life—

(i) may contract to make any sale, exchange, mortgage, charge or other disposition authorised by this Act; and

(ii) may vary or rescind, with or without consideration, the contract in the like cases and manner in which, if he were absolute owner of the settled land, he might lawfully vary or rescind the same, but so that the contract as varied be in conformity with this Act; and

(iii) may contract to make any lease, and in making the lease may vary the terms, with or without consideration, but so that the lease be in conformity with this Act; and

(iv) may accept a surrender of a contract for a lease or a grant in fee simple at a rent, in like manner and on the like terms in and on which he might accept a surrender of a lease or a regrant, and thereupon may make a new or other contract for or relative to a lease or leases, or a grant or grants in fee simple at a rent, in like manner and on the like terms in and on which he might make a new or other lease or grant, or new or other leases or grants, where a lease or a grant in fee simple at a rent had been executed; and

(v) may enter into a contract for or relating to the execution of any improvement authorised by this Act, and may vary or rescind any such contract; and

(vi) may, in any other case, enter into a contract to do any act for carrying into effect any of the purposes of this Act, and may vary or rescind any such contract.

(2) Every contract, including a contract arising by reason of the exercise of an option, shall be binding on and shall enure for the benefit of the settled land, and shall be enforceable against and by every successor in title for the time being of the tenant for life, or statutory owner, and may be carried into effect by any such successor, but so that it may be varied or rescinded by any such successor, in the like case and manner, if any, as if it had been made by himself.

(3) The court may, on the application of the tenant for life, or statutory owner, or of any such successor as aforesaid, or of any person interested in any contract, give directions respecting the enforcing, carrying into effect, varying, or rescinding thereof.

(4) A preliminary contract under this Act for or relating to a lease, and a contract conferring an option, shall not form part of the title or evidence of the title of any person to the lease, or to the benefit thereof, or to the land the subject of the option.

(5) All money, not being rent, received on the exercise by the tenant for life or statutory owner of the powers conferred by subsection (1) of this section, shall, unless the court on an application made within six months after the receipt of the money, or within such further time as the court may in special circumstances allow, otherwise directs, be capital money arising under this Act.

91 Provisions as to different estates settled upon the same limitations

(1) Where estates are settled by different settlements upon the same limitations, whether by reference or otherwise, the following provisions shall have effect:—

(i) The estates or any two or more of them, as the case may require, may be treated as one aggregate estate, in which case the aggregate estate shall be the settled land for all the purposes of this Act;

(ii) Where the trustees for the purposes of this Act of the two or several settlements are the same persons they shall be the trustees of the settlement of the aggregate estate for all the purposes of this Act, and all or any part of the capital money arising from one of the estates may be applied by the direction of the tenant for life or statutory owner as if the same had arisen from any other of the estates;

(iii) Where the trustees for the purposes of this Act of the settlements or of any two or more of them are not the same persons—

(a) any notice required to be given by this Act to the trustees of the settlement and to the solicitor of such trustees shall be given to the trustees of every settlement which comprises any part of the land to which such notice relates and to the solicitor of such trustees;

(b) any capital money arising on any sale, exchange, lease, mortgage, charge, or other disposition of land comprised in more than one settlement, shall be apportioned between the trustees of the different settlements in such manner as the tenant for life or statutory owner may think fit;

(c) all or any part of the capital money arising from the land comprised in one of the settlements may be paid by the trustees of that settlement, by such direction as aforesaid, to the trustees of any of the other settlements, to be applied by such last-mentioned trustees as if the same had arisen from land comprised in that other settlement:

(iv) For the purposes of this subsection, money liable to be laid out in the purchase of land to be settled upon the same limitations as other land may be applied and dealt with in like manner in all respects as if land had been purchased and settled, and the money were capital money arising therefrom.

(2) Estates shall be deemed to be settled upon the same limitations, notwithstanding that any of them may be subject to incumbrances, charges, or powers of charging to which the other or others of them may not be subject:

Provided that, in any such case as last aforesaid, the powers of this section relating to the payment or application of capital money shall not, unless the settlement under which the capital money is held otherwise provides, be exercisable without an order of the court.

(3) This section has effect without prejudice to any appointment made by the court before the commencement of this Act of trustees of the settlement of an aggregate estate, and to the power of the court in any case after such commencement to make any such appointment, and where any such appointment has been made before such commencement, or is made thereafter, this section has effect as if the trustees so appointed and their successors in office were the trustees for the purposes of this Act of each of the settlements constituting the settlement of the aggregate estate, and there were no other trustees thereof for the purposes of this Act.

(4) In this section "estate" means the land, capital money, and securities representing capital money for the time being subject to a particular settlement.

Modification

References to solicitors etc modified to include references to bodies recognised under the Administration of Justice Act 1985, s 9, by the Solicitors' Incorporated Practices Order 1991, SI 1991/2684, arts 4, 5, Sch 1.

92 Proceedings for protection or recovery of land settled or claimed as settled

The court may, if it thinks fit, approve of any action, defence, petition to Parliament, parliamentary opposition, or other proceeding taken or proposed to be taken for the protection of settled land, or of any action or proceeding taken or proposed to be taken for the recovery of land being or alleged to be subject to a settlement, and may direct that any costs, charges, or expenses incurred or to be incurred in relation thereto, or any part thereof, be paid out of property subject to the settlement.

93 Reference of questions to court

If a question arises or a doubt is entertained—

(a) respecting the exercise or intended exercise of any of the powers conferred by this Act, or any enactment replaced by this Act, or the settlement, or any matter relating thereto; or

(b) as to the person in whose favour a vesting deed or assent ought to be executed, or as to the contents thereof; or

(c) otherwise in relation to property subject to a settlement;

the tenant for life or statutory owner, or the trustees of the settlement, or any other person interested under the settlement, may apply to the court for its decision or directions thereon, or for the sanction of the court to any conditional contract, and the court may make such order or give such directions respecting the matter as the court thinks fit.

PART VI
GENERAL PROVISIONS AS TO TRUSTEES

94 Number of trustees to act

(1) Notwithstanding anything in this Act, capital money arising under this Act shall not be paid to fewer than two persons as trustees of a settlement, unless the trustee is a trust corporation.

(2) Subject as aforesaid the provisions of this Act referring to the trustees of a settlement apply to the surviving or continuing trustees or trustee of the settlement for the time being.

95 Trustees' receipts

The receipt or direction in writing of or by the trustees of the settlement, or where a sole trustee is a trust corporation, of or by that trustee, or of or by the personal representatives of the last surviving or continuing trustee, for or relating to any money or securities, paid or transferred to or by the direction of the trustees, trustee, or representatives, as the case may be, effectually discharges the payer or transferor therefrom, and from being bound to see to the application or being answerable for any loss or misapplication thereof, and, in case of a mortgagee or other person advancing money, from being concerned to see that any money advanced by him is wanted for any purpose of this Act, or that no more than is wanted is raised.

96 . . .

. . .

Amendment
Repealed by the Trustee Act 2000, s 40(1), (3), Sch 2, Pt II, para 12, Sch 4, Pt II.

97 Protection of trustees generally

The trustees of a settlement, or any of them—

(a) are not liable for giving any consent, or for not making, bringing, taking, or doing any such application, action, proceeding, or thing, as they might make, bring, take, or do; and

(b) in case of a purchase of land with capital money arising under this Act, or of an exchange, lease, or other disposition, are not liable for adopting any contract made by the tenant for life or statutory owner, or bound to inquire as to the propriety of the purchase, exchange, lease, or other disposition, or answerable as regards any price, consideration, or fine; and

(c) are not liable to see to or answerable for the investigation of the title, or answerable for a conveyance of land, if the conveyance purports to convey the land in the proper mode; and

(d) are not liable in respect of purchase-money paid by them by the direction of the tenant for life or statutory owner to any person joining in the conveyance as a conveying party, or as giving a receipt for the purchase-money, or in any other character, or in respect of any other money paid by them by the direction of the tenant for life or statutory owner on the purchase, exchange, lease, or other disposition.

98 Protection of trustees in particular cases

(1) . . .

(2) . . .

(3) The trustees of the settlements shall not be liable in any way on account of any vesting instrument or other documents of title relating to the settled land, other than securities for capital money, being placed in the possession of the tenant for life or statutory owner:

Provided that where, if the settlement were not disclosed, it would appear that the tenant for life had a general power of appointment over, or was absolutely and beneficially entitled to the settled land, the trustees of the settlement shall, before they deliver the documents to him, require that notice of the last or only principal vesting instrument be written on one of the documents under which the tenant for life acquired his title, and may, if the documents are not in their possession, require such notice to be written as aforesaid, but, in the latter case, they shall not be liable in any way for not requiring the notice to be written.

(4) This section applies to dealings and matters effected before as well as after the commencement of this Act.

Amendment
Sub-ss (1), (2): repealed by the Trustee Act 2000, s 40(1), (3), Sch 2, Pt II, para 13, Sch 4, Pt II.

99 Indemnities to personal representatives and others

Personal representatives, trustees, or other persons who have in good faith, pursuant to this Act, executed a vesting deed, assent, or other conveyance of the settled land, or a deed of discharge of trustees, shall be absolutely discharged from all liability in respect of the equitable interests and powers taking effect under the settlement, and shall be entitled to be kept indemnified at the cost of the trust estate from all liabilities affecting the settled land, but the person to whom the settled land is conveyed (not being a purchaser taking free therefrom) shall hold the settled land upon the trusts, if any, affecting the same.

100 . . .

. . .

Amendment
Repealed by the Trustee Act 2000, s 40(1), (3), Sch 2, Pt II, para 14, Sch 4, Pt II.

101 Notice to trustees

(1) Save as otherwise expressly provided by this Act, a tenant for life or statutory owner, when intending to make a sale, exchange, lease, mortgage, or charge or to grant an option—

(a) shall give notice of his intention in that behalf to each of the trustees of the settlement, by posting registered letters, containing the notice, addressed to the trustees severally, each at his usual or last known place of abode in the United Kingdom; and

(b) shall give a like notice to the solicitor for the trustees, if any such solicitor is known to the tenant for life or statutory owner, by posting a registered letter, containing the notice, addressed to the solicitor at his place of business in the United Kingdom;

every letter under this section being posted not less than one month before the making or granting by the tenant for life or statutory owner of the sale, exchange, lease, mortgage, charge, or option, or of a contract for the same:

Provided that a notice under this section shall not be valid unless at the date thereof the trustee is a trust corporation, or the number of trustees is not less than two.

(2) The notice required by this section of intention to make a sale, exchange, or lease, or to grant an option, may be notice of a general intention in that behalf.

(3) The tenant for life or statutory owner is, upon request by a trustee of the settlement, to furnish to him such particulars and information as may reasonably be required by him from time to time with reference to sales, exchanges, or leases effected, or in progress, or immediately intended.

(4) Any trustee, by writing under his hand, may waive notice either in any particular case, or generally, and may accept less than one month's notice.

(5) A person dealing in good faith with the tenant for life is not concerned to inquire respecting the giving of any such notice as is required by this section.

Modification

References to solicitors etc modified to include references to bodies recognised under the Administration of Justice Act 1985, s 9, by the Solicitors' Incorporated Practices Order 1991, SI 1991/2684, arts 4, 5, Sch 1.

102 Management of land during minority or pending contingency

(1) If and as long as any person who is entitled to a beneficial interest in possession affecting land is an infant, the trustees appointed for this purpose by the settlement, or if there are none so appointed, then the trustees of the settlement, unless the settlement or the order of the court whereby they or their predecessors in office were appointed to be such trustees expressly provides to the contrary, or if there are none, then any persons appointed as trustees for this purpose by the court on the application of a guardian or next friend of the infant, may enter into and continue in possession of the land on behalf of the infant, and in every such case the subsequent provisions of this section shall apply.

(2) The trustees shall manage or superintend the management of the land, with full power—

- (a) to fell timber or cut underwood from time to time in the usual course for sale, or for repairs or otherwise; and
- (b) to erect, pull down, rebuild, and repair houses, and other buildings and erections; and
- (c) to continue the working of mines, minerals, and quarries which have usually been worked; and
- (d) to drain or otherwise improve the land or any part thereof; and
- [(e) to insure against risks of loss or damage due to any event under section 19 of the Trustee Act 1925;]
- (f) to make allowances to and arrangements with tenants and others; and
- (g) to determine tenancies, and to accept surrenders of leases and tenancies; and
- (h) generally to deal with the land in a proper and due course of management;

but so that, where the infant is impeachable for waste, the trustees shall not commit waste, and shall cut timber on the same terms only, and subject to the same restrictions, on and subject to which the infant could, if of full age, cut the same.

(3) The trustees may from time to time, out of the income of the land, including the produce of the sale of timber and underwood, pay the expenses incurred in the management, or in the exercise of any power conferred by this section, or otherwise in relation to the land, and all outgoings not payable by any tenant or other person, and shall keep down any annual sum, and the interest of any principal sum, charged on the land.

(4) This section has effect subject to an express appointment by the settlement, or the court, of trustees for the purposes of this section or of any enactment replaced by this section.

(5) Where any person is contingently entitled to land, this section shall, subject to any prior interests or charges affecting that land, apply until his interest vests, or, if his interest vests during his minority, until he attains [the age of eighteen years].

This subsection applies only where a person becomes contingently entitled under an instrument coming into operation after the commencement of this Act.

(6) This section applies only if and as far as a contrary intention is not expressed in the instrument, if any, under which the interest of the infant or person contingently entitled as aforesaid arises, and has effect subject to the terms of that instrument and to the provisions therein contained.

Amendment

Sub-s (2): para (e) substituted by the Trustee Act 2000, s 40(1), Sch 2, Pt II, para 15.
Sub-s (5): words in square brackets substituted by the Family Law Reform Act 1969, s 1(3), Sch 1.

PART VII
RESTRICTIONS, SAVINGS AND PROTECTION OF PURCHASERS

103 Legal estate in settled land not to vest in trustee in bankruptcy of estate owner

[For the purposes of determining, where the estate owner of any settled land is bankrupt, whether the legal estate in the settled land is comprised in, or is capable of being claimed for, the bankrupt's estate, the legal estate in the settled land shall be deemed not to vest in the] estate owner unless and until the estate owner becomes absolutely and beneficially entitled to the settled land free from all limitations, powers, and charges taking effect under the settlement.

Amendment

Words in square brackets substituted by the Insolvency Act 1985, s 235, Sch 8, para 3.

104 Powers not assignable, and contract not to exercise powers void

(1) The powers under this Act of a tenant for life are not capable of assignment or release, and do not pass to a person as being, by operation of law or otherwise, an assignee of a tenant for life, and remain exercisable by the tenant for life after and notwithstanding any assignment, by operation of law or otherwise, of his estate or interest under the settlement.

This subsection applies notwithstanding that the estate or interest of the tenant for life under the settlement was not in possession when the assignment was made or took effect by operation of law.

(2) A contract by a tenant for life not to exercise his powers under this Act or any of them shall be void.

(3) Where an assignment for value of the estate or interest of the tenant for life was made before the commencement of this Act, this section shall operate without prejudice to the rights of the assignee, and in that case the assignee's rights shall not be affected without his consent, except that—

- (a) unless the assignee is actually in possession of the settled land or the part thereof affected, his consent shall not be requisite for the making of leases thereof by the tenant for life or statutory owner, provided the leases are made at the best rent that can reasonably be obtained, without fine, and in other respects are in conformity with this Act; and
- (b) the consent of the assignee shall not be required to an investment of capital money for the time being affected by the assignment in securities . . . .

(4) Where such an assignment for value is made or comes into operation after the commencement of this Act, the consent of the assignee shall not be requisite for the exercise by the tenant for life of any of the powers conferred by this Act:

Provided that—

- (a) the assignee shall be entitled to the same or the like estate or interest in or charge on the land, money, or securities for the time being representing the land, money, or securities comprised in the assignment, as he had by virtue of the assignment in the last-mentioned land, money, or securities; and
- (b) if the assignment so provides, or if it takes effect by operation of the law of bankruptcy, and after notice thereof to the trustees of the settlement, [the consent of the assignee shall be required to an investment of capital money for the time being affected by the assignment in investments other than securities, and to any application of such capital money]; and
- (c) notice of the intended transaction shall, unless the assignment otherwise provides, be given to the assignee, but a purchaser shall not be concerned to see or inquire whether such notice has been given.

(5) Where such an assignment for value was made before the commencement of this Act, then on the exercise by the tenant for life after such commencement of any of the powers conferred by this Act—

- (a) a purchaser shall not be concerned to see or inquire whether the consent of the assignee has been obtained; and
- (b) the provisions of paragraph (a) of the last subsection shall apply for the benefit of the assignee.

(6) A trustee or personal representative who is an assignee for value shall have power to consent to the exercise by the tenant for life of his powers under this Act, or to any such investment or application of capital money as aforesaid, and to bind by such consent all persons interested in the trust estate, or the estate of the testator or intestate.

(7) If by the original assignment, or by any subsequent disposition, the estate or interest assigned or created by the original assignment, or any part thereof, or any derivative interest is

settled on persons in succession, whether subject to any prior charge or not, and there is no trustee or personal representative in whom the entirety of the estate or interest so settled is vested, then the person for the time being entitled in possession under the limitations of that settlement, whether as trustee or beneficiary, or who would, if of full age, be so entitled, and notwithstanding any charge or incumbrance subsisting or to arise under such settlement, shall have power to consent to the exercise by the tenant for life of his powers under this Act, or to any such investment or application of capital money as aforesaid, and to bind by such consent all persons interested or to become interested under such settlement.

(8) Where an assignee for value, or any person who has power to consent as aforesaid under this section, is an infant, the consent may be given on his behalf by his parents or parent or testamentary or other guardian in the order named.

(9) The court shall have power to authorise any person interested under any assignment to consent to the exercise by the tenant for life of his powers under this Act, or to any such investment or application of capital money as aforesaid on behalf of himself and all other persons interested, or who may become interested under such assignment.

(10) An assignment by operation of the law of bankruptcy, where the assignment comes into operation after the commencement of this Act, shall be deemed to be an assignment for value for the purposes of this section.

(11) An instrument whereby a tenant for life, in consideration of marriage or as part or by way of any family arrangement, not being a security for payment of money advanced, makes an assignment of or creates a charge upon his estate or interest under the settlement is to be deemed one of the instruments creating the settlement, and not an assignment for value for the purposes of this section:

Provided that this subsection shall not have effect with respect to any disposition made before the eighteenth day of August, eighteen hundred and ninety, if inconsistent with the nature or terms of the disposition.

(12) This section extends to assignments made or coming into operation before or after the commencement of this Act, and in this section "assignment" includes assignment by way of mortgage, and any partial or qualified assignment, and any charge or incumbrance, "assignee" has a corresponding meaning, and "assignee for value" includes persons deriving title under the original assignee.

Amendment

Sub-s (3): in para (b) words omitted repealed by the Trustee Act 2000, s 40(1), (3), Sch 2, Pt II, para 16(1)(a), Sch 4, Pt II.

Sub-s (4): in para (b) words from "the consent of" to "such capital money" in square brackets substituted by the Trustee Act 2000, s 40(1), Sch 2, Pt II, para 16(1)(b).

105 Effect of surrender of life estate to the next remainderman

(1) Where the estate or interest of a tenant for life under the settlement has been or is absolutely assured with intent to extinguish the same, either before or after the commencement of this Act, to the person next entitled in remainder or reversion under the settlement, then, . . . the statutory powers of the tenant for life under this Act shall, in reference to the property affected by the assurance, and notwithstanding the provisions of the last preceding section, cease to be exercisable by him, and the statutory powers shall thenceforth become exercisable as if he were dead, but without prejudice to any incumbrance affecting the estate or interest assured, and to the rights to which any incumbrancer would have been entitled if those powers had remained exercisable by the tenant for life.

This subsection applies whether or not any term of years or charge intervenes, or the estate of the remainderman or reversioner is liable to be defeated, and whether or not the estate or interest of the tenant for life under the settlement was in possession at the date of the assurance.

This subsection does not prejudice anything done by the tenant for life before the commencement of this Act, in exercise of any power operating under the Settled Land Acts 1882 to 1890, or, unless the assurance provides to the contrary, operate to accelerate any such intervening terms of years or charge as aforesaid.

(2) In this section "assurance" means any surrender, conveyance, assignment or appointment under a power (whether vested in any person solely, or jointly in two or more persons) which

operates in equity to extinguish the estate or interest of the tenant for life, and "assured" has a corresponding meaning.

Amendment
Words omitted repealed by the Law of Property (Amendment) Act 1926, s 7, Schedule.

106 Prohibition or limitation against exercise of powers void, and provision against forfeiture

(1) If in a settlement, will, assurance, or other instrument executed or made before or after, or partly before and partly after, the commencement of this Act a provision is inserted—

(a) purporting or attempting, by way of direction, declaration, or otherwise, to forbid a tenant for life or statutory owner to exercise any power under this Act, or his right to require the settled land to be vested in him; or

(b) attempting, or tending, or intended, by a limitation, gift, or disposition over of settled land, or by a limitation, gift, or disposition of other real or any personal property, or by the imposition of any condition, or by forfeiture, or in any other manner whatever, to prohibit or prevent him from exercising, or to induce him to abstain from exercising, or to put him into a position inconsistent with his exercising any power under this Act, or his right to require the settled land to be vested in him;

that provision, as far as it purports, or attempts, or tends, or is intended to have, or would or might have, the operation aforesaid, shall be deemed to be void.

(2) For the purposes of this section an estate or interest limited to continue so long only as a person abstains from exercising any such power or right as aforesaid shall be and take effect as an estate or interest to continue for the period for which it would continue if that person were to abstain from exercising the power or right, discharged from liability to determination or cesser by or on his exercising the same.

(3) Notwithstanding anything in a settlement, the exercise by the tenant for life or statutory owner of any power under this Act shall not occasion a forfeiture.

107 Tenant for life trustee for all parties interested

(1) A tenant for life or statutory owner shall, in exercising any power under this Act, have regard to the interests of all parties entitled under the settlement, and shall, in relation to the exercise thereof by him, be deemed to be in the position and to have the duties and liabilities of a trustee for those parties.

[(1A) The following provisions apply to the tenant for life as they apply to the trustees of the settlement—

(a) sections 11, 13 to 15 and 21 to 23 of the Trustee Act 2000 (power to employ agents subject to certain restrictions),

(b) section 32 of that Act (remuneration and expenses of agents etc),

(c) section 19 of the Trustee Act 1925 (power to insure), and

(d) in so far as they relate to the provisions mentioned in paragraphs (a) and (c), Part I of, and Schedule 1 to, the Trustee Act 2000 (the duty of care).]

(2) The provision by a tenant for life or statutory owner, at his own expense, of dwellings available for the working classes on any settled land shall not be deemed to be an injury to any interest in reversion or remainder in that land, but such provision shall not be made by a tenant for life or statutory owner without the previous approval in writing of the trustees of the settlement.

Amendment
Sub-s (1A): inserted by the Trustee Act 2000, s 40(1), Sch 2, Pt II, para 17.

108 Saving for and exercise of other powers

(1) Nothing in this Act shall take away, abridge, or prejudicially affect any power for the time being subsisting under a settlement, or by statute or otherwise, exercisable by a tenant for life, or (save as hereinafter provided) by trustees with his consent, or on his request, or by his direction, or otherwise, and the powers given by this Act are cumulative.

(2) In case of conflict between the provisions of a settlement and the provisions of this Act, relative to any matter in respect whereof the tenant for life or statutory owner exercises or

contracts or intends to exercise any power under this Act, the provisions of this Act shall prevail; and, notwithstanding anything in the settlement, any power (not being merely a power of revocation or appointment) relating to the settled land thereby conferred on the trustees of the settlement or other persons exercisable for any purpose, whether or not provided for in this Act, shall, after the commencement of this Act, be exercisable by the tenant for life or statutory owner as if it were an additional power conferred on the tenant for life within the next following section of this Act and not otherwise.

(3) If a question arises or a doubt is entertained respecting any matter within this section, the tenant for life or statutory owner, or the trustees of the settlement, or any other person interested, under the settlement may apply to the court for its decision thereon, and the court may make such order respecting the matter as the court thinks fit.

109 Saving for additional or larger powers under settlement

(1) Nothing in this Act precludes a settlor from conferring on the tenant for life, or (save as provided by the last preceding section) on the trustees of the settlement, any powers additional to or larger than those conferred by this Act.

(2) Any additional or larger powers so conferred shall, as far as may be, notwithstanding anything in this Act, operate and be exercisable in the like manner, and with all the like incidents, effects, and consequences, as if they were conferred by this Act, and, if relating to the settled land, as if they were conferred by this Act on a tenant for life.

110 Protection of purchasers, etc

(1) On a sale, exchange, lease, mortgage, charge, or other disposition, a purchaser dealing in good faith with a tenant for life or statutory owner shall, as against all parties entitled under the settlement, be conclusively taken to have given the best price, consideration, or rent, as the case may require, that could reasonably be obtained by the tenant for life or statutory owner, and to have complied with all the requisitions of this Act.

(2) A purchaser of a legal estate in settled land shall not, except as hereby expressly provided, be bound or entitled to call for the production of the trust instrument or any information concerning that instrument or any ad valorem stamp duty thereon, and whether or not he has notice of its contents he shall, save as hereinafter provided, be bound and entitled if the last or only principal vesting instrument contains the statements and particulars required by this Act to assume that—

- (a) the person in whom the land is by the said instrument vested or declared to be vested is the tenant for life or statutory owner and has all the powers of a tenant for life under this Act, including such additional or larger powers, if any, as are therein mentioned;
- (b) the persons by the said instrument stated to be the trustees of the settlement, or their successors appearing to be duly appointed, are the properly constituted trustees of the settlement;
- (c) the statements and particulars required by this Act and contained (expressly or by reference) in the said instrument were correct at the date thereof;
- (d) the statements contained in any deed executed in accordance with this Act declaring who are the trustees of the settlement for the purposes of this Act are correct;
- (e) the statements contained in any deed of discharge, executed in accordance with this Act, are correct:

Provided that, as regards the first vesting instrument executed for the purpose of giving effect to—

- (a) a settlement subsisting at the commencement of this Act; or
- (b) an instrument which by virtue of this Act is deemed to be a settlement; or
- (c) a settlement which by virtue of this Act is deemed to have been made by any person after the commencement of this Act; or
- (d) an instrument inter vivos intended to create a settlement of a legal estate in land which is executed after the commencement of this Act and does not comply with the requirements of this Act with respect to the method of effecting such a settlement;

a purchaser shall be concerned to see—

- (i) that the land disposed of to him is comprised in such settlement or instrument;

(ii) that the person in whom the settled land is by such vesting instrument vested, or declared to be vested, is the person in whom it ought to be vested as tenant for life or statutory owner;

(iii) that the persons thereby stated to be the trustees of the settlement are the properly constituted trustees of the settlement.

(3) A purchaser of a legal estate in settled land from a personal representative shall be entitled to act on the following assumptions—

(i) If the capital money, if any, payable in respect of the transaction is paid to the personal representative, that such representative is acting under his statutory or other powers and requires the money for purposes of administration;

(ii) If such capital money is, by the direction of the personal representative, paid to persons who are stated to be the trustees of a settlement, that such persons are the duly constituted trustees of the settlement for the purposes of this Act, and that the personal representative is acting under his statutory powers during a minority;

(iii) In any other case, that the personal representative is acting under his statutory or other powers.

(4) Where no capital money arises under a transaction, a disposition by a tenant for life or statutory owner shall, in favour of a purchaser of a legal estate, have effect under this Act notwithstanding that at the date of the transaction there are no trustees of the settlement.

(5) If a conveyance of or an assent relating to land formerly subject to a vesting instrument does not state who are the trustees of the settlement for the purposes of this Act, a purchaser of a legal estate shall be bound and entitled to act on the assumption that the person in whom the land was thereby vested was entitled to the land free from all limitations, powers, and charges taking effect under that settlement, absolutely and beneficially, or, if so expressed in the conveyance or assent, as personal representative, or [trustee of land] or otherwise, and that every statement of fact in such conveyance or assent is correct.

Amendment

Sub-s (5): words in square brackets substituted by the Trusts of Land and Appointment of Trustees Act 1996, s 25(1), Sch 3, para 2(12); for savings in relation to entailed interests created before the commencement of that Act, and savings consequential upon the abolition of the doctrine of conversion, see s 25(4), (5) thereof.

111 Purchaser of beneficial interest of tenant for life to have remedies of a legal owner

Where—

(a) at the commencement of this Act the legal beneficial interest of a tenant for life under a settlement is vested in a purchaser; or

(b) after the commencement of this Act a tenant for life conveys or deals with his beneficial interest in possession in favour of a purchaser, and the interest so conveyed or created would, but for the restrictions imposed by statute on the creation of legal estates, have been a legal interest;

the purchaser shall (without prejudice to the powers conferred by this Act on the tenant for life) have and may exercise all the same rights and remedies as he would have had or have been entitled to exercise if the interest had remained or been a legal interest and the reversion, if any, on any leases or tenancies derived out of the settled land had been vested in him:

Provided that, where the conveyance or dealing is effected after the commencement of this Act, the purchaser shall not be entitled to the possession of the documents of title relating to the settled land, but shall have the same rights with respect thereto as if the tenant for life had given to him a statutory acknowledgment of his right to production and delivery of copies thereof, and a statutory undertaking for the safe custody thereof.

The tenant for life shall not deliver any such documents to a purchaser of his beneficial interest, who is not also a purchaser of the whole of the settled land to which such documents relate.

112 Exercise of powers; limitation of provisions, etc

(1) Where a power of sale, exchange, leasing, mortgaging, charging, or other power is exercised by a tenant for life, or statutory owner or by the trustees of a settlement, he and they may respectively execute, make, and do all deeds, instruments, and things necessary or proper in that behalf.

(2) Where any provision in this Act refers to sale, purchase, exchange, mortgaging, charging, leasing, or other disposition or dealing, or to any power, consent, payment, receipt, deed, assurance, contract, expenses, act, or transaction, it shall (unless the contrary appears) be construed as extending only to sales, purchases, exchanges, mortgages, charges, leases, dispositions, dealings, powers, consents, payments, receipts, deeds, assurances, contracts, expenses, acts, and transactions under this Act.

PART VIII
COURT, MINISTRY OF AGRICULTURE AND FISHERIES, PROCEDURE

113 Jurisdiction and procedure

(1) All matters within the jurisdiction of the court under this Act shall, subject to the enactments for the time being in force with respect to the procedure of the *Supreme Court of Judicature* [Senior Courts], be assigned to the Chancery Division of the High Court.

(2) . . .

[(3) The powers of the court may, as regards land not exceeding in capital value the county court limit, or in net annual value for rating the county court limit, and, as regards capital money arising under this Act, and securities in which the same is invested, not exceeding in amount or value the county court limit, and as regards personal chattels settled or to be settled, as in this Act mentioned, not exceeding the county court limit, be exercised by any county court. Section 147(2) and (3) of the County Courts Act 1984 (construction of references to net annual value for rating) shall apply for the purposes of this subsection as it applies for the purposes of that Act.]

[(3A) In the preceding subsection "the county court limit" means the county court limit for the time being specified by an Order in Council under [section 145 of the County Courts Act 1984] as the county court limit for the purposes of that subsection.]

(4) Payment of money into court effectually exonerates therefrom the person making the payment.

(5) Every application to the court under this Act shall, subject to any rules of court to the contrary, be by summons at Chambers.

(6) On an application by the trustees of a settlement notice shall be served in the first instance on the tenant for life.

(7) On any application notice shall be served on such persons, if any, as the court thinks fit.

(8) The court shall have full power and discretion to make such order as it thinks fit respecting the costs, charges, or expenses of all or any of the parties to any application, and may, if it thinks fit, order that all or any of those costs, charges, or expenses be paid out of property subject to the settlement.

(9) The provisions of the Trustee Act 1925, relating to vesting orders and orders appointing a person to convey shall apply to all vesting orders authorised to be made by this Act.

Amendment

Sub-s (1): words "Supreme Court of Judicature" in italics repealed and subsequent words in square brackets substituted, from a date to be appointed, by the Constitutional Reform Act 2005, s 59(5), Sch 11, Pt 2, para 4(1), (3).
Sub-s (2): repealed by the Courts Act 1971, s 56(4), Sch 11, Part II.
Sub-s (3): substituted by the County Courts Act 1984, s 148(1), Sch 2, para 20.
Sub-s (3A): inserted by the Administration of Justice Act 1982, s 37, Sch 3, Part II, para 4; amended by the County Courts Act 1984, s 148(1), Sch 2, para 20.

114 Payment of costs out of settled property

Where the court directs that any costs, charges, or expenses be paid out of property subject to a settlement, the same shall, subject and according to the directions of the court, be raised and paid—

(a) out of capital money arising under this Act, or other money liable to be laid out in the purchase of land to be made subject to the settlement; or

(b) out of securities representing such money, or out of income of any such money or securities; or
(c) out of any accumulations of income of land, money, or securities; or
(d) by means of a sale of part of the settled land in respect whereof the costs, charges or expenses are incurred, or of other settled land comprised in the same settlement and subject to the same limitations; or
(e) by means of a legal mortgage of the settled land or any part thereof to be made by such person as the court directs;

or partly in one of those modes and partly in another or others, or in any such other mode as the court thinks fit.

115 Powers of the [Secretary of State]

(1) The [Secretary of State] shall, by virtue of this Act, have for the purposes of any Act, public general or local or private, making provision for the execution of improvements on settled land, all such powers and authorities as he has for the purposes of the Improvement of Land Act 1864.

(2) The provisions of the last-mentioned Act relating to proceedings and inquiries, and to authentication of instruments, and to declarations, statements, notices, applications, forms, security for expenses, inspections and examinations, shall extend and apply, as far as the nature and circumstances of the case admit, to acts and proceedings done or taken by or in relation to the [Secretary of State] under any Act making provision as last aforesaid.

(3) The provisions of any Act relating . . . to security for costs to be taken in respect of the business transacted under the Acts administered by the [Secretary of State] as successor of the Land Commissioners for England shall extend and apply to the business transacted by or under the direction of the [Secretary of State] under any Act, public general or local or private, by which any power or duty is conferred or imposed on him as such successor.

Amendment

Section heading: words "Secretary of State" in square brackets substituted by virtue of SI 2002/794, art 5(1), Sch 1, para 4.
Sub-s (1): words "Secretary of State" in square brackets substituted by SI 2002/794, art 5(1), Sch 1, para 4(1), (2).
Sub-s (2): words "Secretary of State" in square brackets substituted by SI 2002/794, art 5(1), Sch 1, para 4(1), (3).
Sub-s (3): words omitted repealed by the Agriculture (Miscellaneous Provisions) Act 1963, s 28, Schedule, Pt II.
Sub-s (3): words "Secretary of State" in square brackets in both places they occur substituted by SI 2002/794, art 5(1), Sch 1, para 4(1), (4).

116 Filing of certificates, etc at the Ministry of Agriculture

(1) Every certificate and report approved and made by the [Secretary of State] under this Act shall be filed in the office of [the [Secretary of State]].

(2) An office copy of any certificate or report so filed shall be delivered out of such office to any person requiring the same, on payment of the proper fee, and shall be sufficient evidence of the certificate or report whereof it purports to be a copy.

Amendment

Sub-s (1): words "Secretary of State" in square brackets in both places they occur substituted by SI 2002/794, art 5(1), Sch 1, para 5.
Sub-s (1): words in square brackets beginning with the word "the" substituted by the Transfer of Functions (Ministry of Food) Order 1955, SI 1955/554, art 3.

Miscellaneous

Following the substitution of the words "Secretary of State" as noted above, the reference to the Ministry of Agriculture in the section heading should be construed accordingly.

PART IX
SUPPLEMENTARY PROVISIONS

117 Definitions

(1) In this Act, unless the context otherwise requires, the following expressions have the meanings hereby assigned to them respectively, that is to say—

(i) "Building purposes" include the erecting and the improving of, and the adding to, and the repairing of buildings; and a "building lease" is a lease for any building purposes or purposes connected therewith;

(ii) "Capital money arising under this Act" means capital money arising under the powers and provisions of this Act or the Acts replaced by this Act, and receivable for the trusts and purposes of the settlement and includes securities representing capital money;

(iii) "Death duty" means estate duty . . . and every other duty leviable or payable on death;

(iv) "Determinable fee" means a fee determinable whether by limitation or condition;

(v) "Disposition" and "conveyance" include a mortgage, charge by way of legal mortgage, lease, assent, vesting declaration, vesting instrument, disclaimer, release and every other assurance of property or of an interest therein by any instrument, except a will, and "dispose of" and "convey" have corresponding meanings;

(vi) "Dower" includes "freebench";

(vii) "Hereditaments" mean real property which on an intestacy might before the commencement of this Act have devolved on an heir;

(viii) "Instrument" does not include a statute unless the statute creates a settlement;

(ix) "Land" includes land of any tenure, and mines and minerals whether or not held apart from the surface, buildings or parts of buildings (whether the division is horizontal, vertical or made in any other way) and other corporeal hereditaments; also a manor, an advowson, and a rent and other incorporeal hereditaments, and an easement, right, privilege, or benefit in, over, or derived from land, and any estate or interest in land[, but does not (except in the phrase "trust of land") include] an undivided share in land;

(x) "Lease" includes an agreement for a lease, and "forestry lease" means a lease to the Forestry Commissioners for any purpose for which they are authorised to acquire land by the Forestry Act 1919;

(xi) "Legal mortgage" means a mortgage by demise or sub-demise or a charge by way of legal mortgage, and "legal mortgagee" has a corresponding meaning; "legal estate" means an estate interest or charge in or over land (subsisting or created at law) which is by statute authorised to subsist or to be created at law; and "equitable interests" mean all other interests and charges in or over land or in the proceeds of sale thereof; an equitable interest "capable of subsisting at law" means such an equitable interest as could validly subsist at law, if clothed with the legal estate; and "estate owner" means the owner of a legal estate;

(xii) "Limitation" includes a trust, and "trust" includes an implied or constructive trust;

(xiii) . . .

(xiv) "Manor" includes lordship, and reputed manor or lordship; and "manorial incident" has the same meaning as in the Law of Property Act 1922;

(xv) "Mines and minerals" mean mines and minerals whether already opened or in work or not, and include all minerals and substances in, on, or under the land, obtainable by underground or by surface working; and "mining purposes" include the sinking and searching for, winning, working, getting, making merchantable, smelting or otherwise converting or working for the purposes of any manufacture, carrying away, and disposing of mines and minerals, in or under the settled land, or any other land, and the erection of buildings, and the execution of engineering and other works suitable for those purposes; and a "mining lease" is a lease for any mining purposes or purposes connected therewith, and includes a grant or licence for any mining purposes;

(xvi) . . .

(xvii) "Notice" includes constructive notice;

(xviii) "Personal representative" means the executor, original or by representation, or administrator, for the time being of a deceased person, and where there are special personal representatives for the purposes of settled land means those personal representatives;

(xix) "Possession" includes receipt of rents and profits, or the right to receive the same, if any; and "income" includes rents and profits;

(xx) "Property" includes any thing in action, and any interest in real or personal property;

(xxi) "Purchaser" means a purchaser in good faith for value, and includes a lessee, mortgagee or other person who in good faith acquires an interest in settled land for value; and in reference to a legal estate includes a chargee by way of legal mortgage;

(xxii) "Rent" includes yearly or other rent, and toll, duty, royalty, or other reservation, by the acre, or the ton, or otherwise; and in relation to rent, "payment" includes delivery; and "fine" includes premium or fore-gift, and any payment, consideration, or benefit in the nature of a fine, premium, or fore-gift;

(xxiii) "Securities" include stocks, funds, and shares;

(xxiv) "Settled land" includes land which is deemed to be settled land; "settlement" includes an instrument or instruments which under this Act or the Acts which it replaces is or are deemed to be or which together constitute a settlement, and a settlement which is deemed to have been made by any person or to be subsisting for the purposes of this Act; "a settlement subsisting at the commencement of this Act" includes a settlement created by virtue of this Act immediately on the commencement thereof; and "trustees of the settlement" mean the trustees thereof for the purposes of this Act howsoever appointed or constituted;

(xxv) "Small dwellings" mean dwelling-houses of a rateable value not exceeding one hundred pounds per annum;

(xxvi) "Statutory owner" means the trustees of the settlement or other persons who, during a minority, or at any other time when there is no tenant for life, have the powers of a tenant for life under this Act, but does not include the trustees of the settlement, where by virtue of an order of the court or otherwise the trustees have power to convey the settled land in the name of the tenant for life;

(xxvii) "Steward" includes deputy steward, or other proper officer, of a manor;

(xxviii) "Tenant for life" includes a person (not being a statutory owner) who has the powers of a tenant for life under this Act, and also (where the context requires) one of two or more persons who together constitute the tenant for life, or have the powers of a tenant for life; and "tenant in tail" includes a person entitled to an entailed interest in any property; and "entailed interest" has the same meaning as in the Law of Property Act 1925;

(xxix) A "term of years absolute" means a term of years, taking effect either in possession or in reversion, with or without impeachment for waste, whether at a rent or not and whether subject or not to another legal estate, and whether certain or liable to determination by notice, re-entry, operation of law, or by a provision for cesser on redemption, or in any other event (other than the dropping of a life, or the determination of a determinable life interest), but does not include any term of years determinable with life or lives or with the cesser of a determinable life interest, nor, if created after the commencement of this Act, a term of years which is not expressed to take effect in possession within twenty-one years after the creation thereof where required by statute to take effect within that period; and in this definition the expression "term of years" includes a term for less than a year, or for a year or years and a fraction of a year or from year to year;

(xxx) "Trust corporation" means the Public Trustee or a corporation either appointed by the court in any particular case to be a trustee or entitled by rules made under subsection (3) of section four of the Public Trustee Act 1906, to act as custodian trustee, and "trust for sale" [has the same meaning] as in the Law of Property Act 1925;

(xxxi) In relation to settled land "vesting deed" or "vesting order" means the instrument whereby settled land is conveyed to or vested or declared to be vested in a tenant for life or statutory owner; "vesting assent" means the instrument whereby a personal representative, after the death of a tenant for life or statutory owner, or the survivor of two or more tenants for life or statutory owners, vests settled land in a person entitled as tenant for life or statutory owner; "vesting instrument" means a vesting deed, a vesting assent or, where the land affected remains settled land, a vesting order; "principal vesting instrument" includes any vesting instrument other than a subsidiary vesting deed; and "trust instrument" means the instrument whereby the trusts of the settled land are declared, and includes any two or more such instruments and a settlement or instrument which is deemed to be a trust instrument;

(xxxii) "United Kingdom" means Great Britain and Northern Ireland;

(xxxiii) "Will" includes codicil.

[(1A) Any reference in this Act to money, securities or proceeds of sale being paid or transferred into court shall be construed as referring to the money, securities or proceeds being paid or transferred into the *Supreme Court* [Senior Courts] or any other court that has jurisdiction, and any reference in this Act to the court, in a context referring to the investment or application of money, securities or proceeds of sale paid or transferred into court, shall be construed, in the case of money, securities or proceeds paid or transferred into the *Supreme Court* [Senior Courts], as referring to the High Court, and, in the case of money, securities or proceeds paid or transferred into another court, as referring to that other court.]

(2) Where an equitable interest in or power over property arises by statute or operation of law, references to the "creation" of an interest or power include any interest or power so arising.

(3) References to registration under the Land Charges Act 1925, apply to any registration made under any statute which is by the Land Charges Act 1925, to have effect as if the registration had been made under that Act.

Amendment

Sub-s (1): in para (iii) words omitted repealed by the Finance Act 1949, s 52, Sch 11, Pt IV.
Sub-s (1): in paras (ix), (xxx) words ", but does not (except in the phrase "trust of land") include" in square brackets substituted by the Trusts of Land and Appointment of Trustees Act 1996, s 25(1), Sch 3, para 2(13); for savings in relation to entailed interests created before the commencement of that Act, and savings consequential upon the abolition of the doctrine of conversion, see s 25(4), (5) thereof.
Sub-s (1): para (xiii) repealed by the Mental Health Act 1959, s 149(2), Sch 8, Pt I.
Sub-s (1): para (xvi) repealed by SI 2002/794, art 5(2), Sch 2.
Sub-s (1A): inserted by the Administration of Justice Act 1965, s 17(1), Sch 1.
Sub-s (1A): words "Supreme Court" in italics in both places they occur repealed and subsequent words in square brackets substituted, from a date to be appointed, by the Constitutional Reform Act 2005, s 59(5), Sch 11, Pt 2, para 4(1), (3).

Modification

Definition "Trust corporation" modified, in relation to Charities, by the Charities Act 1993, s 35.

118 . . .

. . .

Amendment

Repealed by the Statute Law (Repeals) Act 2004.

119 Repeals, savings, and construction

(1) . . . without prejudice to the provisions of section thirty-eight of the Interpretation Act 1889—

(a) Nothing in this repeal shall affect the validity or legality of any dealing in land or other transaction completed before the commencement of this Act, or any title or right acquired or appointment made before the commencement of this Act, but, subject as aforesaid, this Act shall, except where otherwise expressly provided, apply to and in respect of settlements and other instruments whether made or coming into operation before or after the commencement of this Act;

(b) Nothing in this repeal shall affect any rules, orders, or other instruments made under any enactment so repealed, but all such rules, orders and instruments shall continue in force as if made under the corresponding enactment in this Act;

(c) References in any document to any enactment repealed by this Act shall be construed as references to this Act or the corresponding enactment in this Act.

(2) References in any statute to the Settled Estates Act 1877, and to any enactment which it replaced shall be construed as references to this Act.

(3) . . .

Amendment
Sub-s (1): words omitted repealed by the Statute Law Revision Act 1950.
Sub-s (3): repealed by the Land Registration Act 2002, ss 133, 135, Sch 11, para 1, Sch 13.

120 Short title, commencement and extent

(1) This Act may be cited as the Settled Land Act 1925.

(2) . . .

(3) This Act extends to England and Wales only.

Amendment
Sub-s (2): repealed by the Statute Law Revision Act 1950.

SCHEDULE 1

. . .

Amendment
Repealed by the Statute Law (Repeals) Act 2004.

SCHEDULE 2
TRANSITIONAL PROVISIONS AFFECTING EXISTING SETTLEMENTS

Section 37

PROVISIONS FOR VESTING LEGAL ESTATE IN TENANT FOR LIFE OR STATUTORY OWNER

1 (1) A settlement subsisting at the commencement of this Act is for the purposes of this Act, a trust instrument.

(2) As soon as practicable after the commencement of this Act, the trustees for the purposes of this Act of every settlement of land subsisting at the commencement of this Act (whether or not the settled land is already vested in them), may and on the request of the tenant for life or statutory owner, shall at the cost of the trust estate, execute a principal vesting deed (containing the proper statements and particulars) declaring that the legal estate in the settled land shall vest or is vested in the person or persons therein named (being the tenant for life or statutory owner, and including themselves if they are the statutory owners), and such deed shall (unless the legal estate is already so vested) operate to convey or vest the legal estate in the settled land to or in the person or persons aforesaid and, if more than one, as joint tenants.

(3) If there are no trustees of the settlement then (in default of a person able and willing to appoint such trustees), an application shall be made to the court by the tenant for life or statutory owner, or by any other person interested, for the appointment of such trustees.

(4) If default is made in the execution of any such principal vesting deed, the provisions of this Act relating to vesting orders of settled land shall apply in like manner as if the trustees of the settlement were persons in whom the settled land is wrongly vested.

(5) This paragraph does not apply where, at the commencement of this Act, settled land is held at law or in equity in undivided shares vested in possession.

(6) In the case of settlements subsisting at the commencement of this Act, all the estates, interests and powers thereby limited which are not by statute otherwise converted into equitable interests or powers, shall, as from the date of the principal vesting deed or the vesting order, take effect only in equity.

[This sub-paragraph shall not apply to any legal estate or interest vested in a mortgagee or other purchaser for money or money's worth.]

(7) This paragraph does not apply where settled land is vested in personal representatives at the commencement of this Act, or where settled land becomes vested in personal representatives before a principal vesting deed has been executed pursuant to this paragraph.

(8) No ad valorem stamp duty shall be payable in respect of a vesting deed or order made for giving effect to an existing settlement.

PROVISIONS WHERE SETTLED LAND IS AT COMMENCEMENT OF ACT VESTED IN PERSONAL REPRESENTATIVES

2 (1) Where settled land remains at the commencement of this Act vested in the personal representatives of a person who dies before such commencement, or becomes vested in personal representatives before a principal vesting deed has been executed pursuant to the last preceding paragraph, the personal representatives shall hold the settled land on trust, if and when required so to do, to convey the same to the person who, under the trust instrument, or by virtue of this Act, is the tenant for life or statutory owner and, if more than one, as joint tenants.

(2) A conveyance under this paragraph shall be made at the cost of the trust estate and may be made by an assent in writing signed by the personal representatives which shall operate as a conveyance. No stamp duty is payable in respect of a vesting assent.

(3) The obligation to convey settled land imposed on the personal representatives by this paragraph is subject and without prejudice—

(a) to their rights and powers for purposes of administration, and

(b) to their being satisfied that provision has been or will be made for the payment of any unpaid death duties in respect of the land or any interest therein for which they are accountable, and any interest and costs in respect of such duties, or that they are otherwise effectually indemnified against such duties, interest and costs.

(4) A conveyance under this paragraph shall—

(a) if by deed, be a principal vesting deed, and

(b) if by an assent, be a vesting assent, which shall contain the like statements and particulars as are required by this Act in the case of a principal vesting deed.

(5) Nothing contained in this paragraph affects the rights of personal representatives to transfer or create such legal estates to take effect in priority to a conveyance under this paragraph as may be required for giving effect to the obligations imposed on them by statute.

(6) A conveyance by personal representatives under this paragraph, if made by deed, may contain a reservation to themselves of a term of years absolute in the land conveyed upon trusts for indemnifying them against any unpaid death duties in respect of the land conveyed or any interest therein, and any interest and costs in respect of such duties.

(7) Nothing contained in this paragraph affects any right which a person entitled to an equitable charge for securing money actually raised, and affecting the whole estate the subject of the settlement, may have to require effect to be given thereto by a legal mortgage, before the execution of a conveyance under this section.

PROVISIONS AS TO INFANTS

3 (1) Where, at the commencement of this Act, an infant is beneficially entitled to land in possession for an estate in fee simple or for a term of years absolute, or would, if of full age, be a tenant for life or have the powers of a tenant for life, the settled land shall, by virtue of this Act, vest in the trustees (if any) of the settlement upon such trusts as may be requisite for giving effect to the rights of the infant and other persons (if any) interested:

Provided that, if there are no such trustees, then—

(i) Pending their appointment, the settled land shall, by virtue of this Act, vest in the Public Trustee upon the trusts aforesaid:

(ii) The Public Trustee shall not be entitled to act in the trust, or charge any fee, or be liable in any manner unless and until requested in writing to act on behalf of the infant by his parents or parent or testamentary or other guardian in the order named:

(iii) After the Public Trustee has been so requested to act, and has accepted the trust, he shall become the trustee of the settlement, and no trustee shall (except by an order of the court) be appointed in his place without his consent:

(iv) If there is no other person able and willing to appoint trustees the parents or parent or testamentary or other guardian of the infant, if respectively able and willing to act, shall (in the order named) have power by deed to appoint trustees of the settlement in place of the Public Trustee in like manner as if the Public Trustee had refused to act in the trust, and to vest the settled land in them on the trusts aforesaid, and the provisions of the Trustee Act 1925, relating to the appointment of new trustees, and the vesting of trust property shall apply as if the persons aforesaid (in the order named) had been nominated by the settlement for the purpose of appointing new trustees thereof; and in default of any such appointment the infant by his next friend, may, at any time during the minority, apply to the court for the appointment of trustees of the settlement, and the court may make such order as it thinks fit, and if thereby trustees of the settlement are appointed, the settled land shall, by virtue of this Act, vest in the trustees as joint tenants upon the trusts aforesaid:

Provided that in favour of a purchaser a statement in the deed of appointment that the father or mother or both are dead or are unable or unwilling to make the appointment shall be conclusive evidence of the fact stated.

(v) If land to which an infant is beneficially entitled in possession for an estate in fee simple or for a term of years absolute vests in the Public Trustee, but the Public Trustee does not become the trustee of the settlement, and trustees of the settlement are not appointed in his place, then, if and when the infant attains the age of twenty-one years, the land shall vest in him.

(2) The provisions of this paragraph shall extend to the legal estate in the settled land, except where such legal estate is, at or immediately after the commencement of this Act, vested in personal representatives, in which case this paragraph shall have effect without prejudice to the provisions of paragraph two of this Schedule.

(3) Where, at the commencement of this Act, any persons appointed under section sixty of the Settled Land Act 1882, have power to act generally or for any specific purpose on behalf of an infant, then those persons shall, by virtue of this Act, become and be the trustees of the settlement.

(4) Notwithstanding that the settled land is by virtue of this paragraph vested in the trustees of the settlement, they shall, at the cost of the trust estate, in accordance with this Act, execute a principal vesting deed declaring that the settled land is vested in them.

(5) This paragraph does not apply where an infant is beneficially entitled in possession to land for an estate in fee simple or for a term of years absolute jointly with a person of full age (for which case provision is made in the Law of Property Act 1925), but it applies to two or more infants entitled as aforesaid jointly.

(6) This paragraph does not apply where an infant would, if of full age, constitute the tenant for life or have the powers of a tenant for life together with another person of full age, but it applies to two or more infants who would, if all of them were of full age, together constitute the tenant for life or have the powers of a tenant for life.

Amendment

Para 1(6): words in square brackets inserted by the Law of Property (Amendment) Act 1926, s 7, Schedule.

SCHEDULE 3

Section 83

PART I
IMPROVEMENTS, THE COSTS OF WHICH ARE NOT LIABLE TO BE REPLACED BY INSTALMENTS

(i) Drainage, including the straightening, widening, or deepening of drains, streams, and watercourses:
(ii) Bridges:
(iii) Irrigation; warping:
(iv) Drains, pipes, and machinery for supply and distribution of sewage as manure:
(v) Embanking or weiring from a river or lake, or from the sea, or a tidal water:
(vi) Groynes; sea walls; defences against water:
(vii) Inclosing; straightening of fences; re-division of fields:
(viii) Reclamation; dry warping:
(ix) Farm roads; private roads; roads or streets in villages or towns:
(x) Clearing; trenching; planting:

(xi) Cottages for labourers, farm-servants, and artisans, employed on the settled land or not:
(xii) Farmhouses, offices, and outbuildings, and other buildings for farm purposes:
(xiii) Saw-mills, scutch-mills, and other mills, water-wheels, engine-houses, and kilns, which will increase the value of the settled land for agricultural purposes or as woodland or otherwise:
(xiv) Reservoirs, tanks, conduits, watercourses, pipes, wells, ponds, shafts, dams, weirs, sluices, and other works and machinery for supply and distribution of water for agricultural, manufacturing, or other purposes, or for domestic or other consumption:
(xv) Tramways; railways; canals; docks:
(xvi) Jetties, piers, and landing places on rivers, lakes, the sea, or tidal waters, for facilitating transport of persons and of agricultural stock and produce, and of manure and other things required for agricultural purposes, and of minerals, and of things required for mining purposes:
(xvii) Markets and market-places:
(xviii) Streets, roads, paths, squares, gardens, or other open spaces for the use, gratuitously or on payment, of the public or of individuals, or for dedication to the public, the same being necessary or proper in connexion with the conversion of land into building land:
(xix) Sewers, drains, watercourses, pipe-making, fencing, paving, brick-making, tile-making, and other works necessary or proper in connexion with any of the objects aforesaid:
(xx) Trial pits for mines, and other preliminary works necessary or proper in connexion with development of mines:
(xxi) Reconstruction, enlargement, or improvement of any of those works:
(xxii) The provision of small dwellings, either by means of building new buildings or by means of the reconstruction, enlargement, or improvement of existing buildings, if that provision of small dwellings is, in the opinion of the court, not injurious to the settled land or is agreed to by the tenant for life and the trustees of the settlement:
(xxiii) Additions to or alterations in buildings reasonably necessary or proper to enable the same to be let:
(xxiv) Erection of buildings in substitution for buildings within an urban sanitary district taken by a local or other public authority, or for buildings taken under compulsory powers, but so that no more money be expended than the amount received for the buildings taken and the site thereof:
(xxv) The rebuilding of the principal mansion house on the settled land:

Provided that the sum to be applied under this head shall not exceed one-half of the annual rental of the settled land.

PART II
IMPROVEMENTS, THE COSTS OF WHICH THE TRUSTEES OF THE SETTLEMENT OR THE COURT MAY REQUIRE TO BE REPLACED BY INSTALMENTS

(i) Residential houses for land or mineral agents, managers, clerks, bailiffs, woodmen, gamekeepers and other persons employed on the settled land, or in connexion with the management or development thereof:
(ii) Any offices, workshops and other buildings of a permanent nature required in connexion with the management or development of the settled land or any part thereof:
(iii) The erection and building of dwelling houses, shops, buildings for religious, educational, literary, scientific, or public purposes, market places, market houses, places of amusement and entertainment, gasworks, electric light or power works, or any other works necessary or proper in connexion with the development of the settled land, or any part thereof as a building estate:
(iv) Restoration or reconstruction of buildings damaged or destroyed by dry rot:

(v) Structural additions to or alterations in buildings reasonably required, whether the buildings are intended to be let or not, or are already let:

(vi) Boring for water and other preliminary works in connexion therewith.

PART III
IMPROVEMENTS, THE COSTS OF WHICH THE TRUSTEES OF THE SETTLEMENT AND THE COURT MUST REQUIRE TO BE REPLACED BY INSTALMENTS

(i) Heating, hydraulic or electric power apparatus for buildings, and engines, pumps, lifts, rams, boilers, flues, and other works required or used in connexion therewith:

(ii) Engine houses, engines, gasometers, dynamos, accumulators, cables, pipes, wiring, switchboards, plant and other works required for the installation of electric, gas, or other artificial light, in connexion with any principal mansion house, or other house or buildings; but not electric lamps, gas fittings, or decorative fittings required in any such house or building:

(iii) Steam rollers, traction engines, motor lorries and moveable machinery for farming or other purposes.

SCHEDULE 4

. . .

Amendment
Repealed by the Statute Law (Repeals) Act 2004.

APPENDIX III

INTESTATE SUCCESSION (INTEREST AND CAPITALISATION) ORDER 1977

SI 1977/1491

1 Citation and Interpretation

(1) This Order may be cited as the Intestate Succession (Interest and Capitalisation) Order 1977 and shall come into operation on 15th September 1977.

(2) The Interpretation Act 1889 shall apply to the interpretation of this Order as it applies to the interpretation of an Act of Parliament.

2 Interest of Statutory Legacy

For the purposes of section 46(1)(i) of the Administration of Estates Act 1925, as it applies both in respect of persons dying before 1953 and in respect of persons dying after 1952, the specified rate of interest shall be [6] per cent, per annum.

Amendment

Number "6" in square brackets substituted by SI 1983/1374, art 2.

3 Capitalisation of Life Interests

(1) Where after the coming into operation of this Order an election is exercised in accordance with subsection (6) or (7) of section 47A of the Administration of Estates Act 1925, the capital value of the life interest of the surviving spouse [or civil partner] shall be reckoned in accordance with the following provisions of this article.

(2) There shall be ascertained, by reference to the index compiled by the Financial Times, The Institute of Actuaries and the Faculty of Actuaries, the average gross redemption yield on medium coupon fifteen-year Government Stocks at the date on which the election was exercised or, if the index was not compiled on that date, by reference to the index on the last date before that date on which it was compiled; and the column which corresponds to that yield in whichever of the Tables set out in the Schedule hereto is applicable to the sex of the surviving spouse [or civil partner] shall be the appropriate column for the purposes of paragraph (3) of this article.

(3) The capital value for the purposes of paragraph (1) of this article is the product of the part of the residuary estate (whether or not yielding income) in respect of which the election was exercised and the multiplier shown in the appropriate column opposite the age which the surviving spouse [or civil partner] had attained at the date on which the election was exercised.

Amendment

Words "or civil partner" in square brackets in each place they occur inserted by SI 2005/2114, art 2(6), Sch 6, para 1(1), (2).

SCHEDULE

Table 1

Multiplier to be applied to the part of the residuary estate in respect of which the election is exercised to obtain the capital value of the life interest of a surviving husband [or a surviving male civil partner], when the average gross redemption yield on medium coupon fifteen-year Government Stocks is at the rate shown.

Age Last Birthday of Husband or Civil Partner	Less than 8.50%	8.50% or Between 8.50% and 9.50%	9.50% or Between 9.50% and 10.50%	10.50% or Between 10.50% and 11.50%	11.50% or Between 11.50% and 12.50%	12.50% or Between 12.50% and 13.50%	13.50% or Between 13.50% and 14.50%	14.50% or Between 14.50% and 15.50%	15.50% or More
16	0.882	0.897	0.908	0.917	0.923	0.927	0.931	0.934	0.936
17	0.879	0.895	0.906	0.915	0.921	0.926	0.930	0.933	0.935
18	0.876	0.892	0.904	0.913	0.920	0.925	0.929	0.932	0.934
19	0.873	0.890	0.902	0.911	0.918	0.923	0.928	0.931	0.933
20	0.870	0.887	0.900	0.909	0.917	0.922	0.926	0.930	0.933
21	0.866	0.884	0.897	0.907	0.915	0.921	0.925	0.929	0.932
22	0.863	0.881	0.895	0.905	0.913	0.919	0.924	0.928	0.931
23	0.859	0.878	0.892	0.903	0.911	0.918	0.923	0.927	0.930
24	0.855	0.875	0.890	0.901	0.909	0.916	0.921	0.925	0.929
25	0.852	0.872	0.887	0.898	0.907	0.914	0.920	0.924	0.928
26	0.847	0.868	0.884	0.896	0.905	0.912	0.918	0.923	0.926
27	0.843	0.864	0.880	0.893	0.903	0.910	0.916	0.921	0.925
28	0.838	0.860	0.877	0.890	0.900	0.908	0.914	0.919	0.923
29	0.834	0.856	0.873	0.887	0.897	0.905	0.912	0.917	0.922
30	0.828	0.851	0.869	0.883	0.894	0.903	0.910	0.915	0.920
31	0.823	0.847	0.865	0.879	0.891	0.900	0.907	0.913	0.918
32	0.818	0.842	0.861	0.876	0.887	0.897	0.904	0.911	0.916
33	0.812	0.837	0.856	0.871	0.884	0.893	0.901	0.908	0.913
34	0.806	0.831	0.851	0.867	0.880	0.890	0.898	0.905	0.911
35	0.799	0.825	0.846	0.862	0.875	0.886	0.895	0.902	0.908
36	0.792	0.819	0.840	0.857	0.871	0.882	0.891	0.899	0.905
37	0.785	0.813	0.834	0.852	0.866	0.878	0.887	0.895	0.902
38	0.778	0.806	0.828	0.846	0.861	0.873	0.883	0.891	0.898
39	0.771	0.799	0.822	0.840	0.856	0.868	0.879	0.887	0.894
40	0.763	0.792	0.815	0.834	0.850	0.863	0.874	0.883	0.890
41	0.755	0.784	0.808	0.828	0.844	0.857	0.869	0.878	0.886
42	0.746	0.776	0.801	0.821	0.838	0.852	0.863	0.873	0.881
43	0.737	0.768	0.793	0.814	0.831	0.845	0.857	0.868	0.876
44	0.728	0.759	0.785	0.806	0.824	0.839	0.851	0.862	0.871
45	0.719	0.750	0.776	0.798	0.816	0.832	0.845	0.856	0.866

Age Last Birthday of Husband or Civil Partner	Less than 8.50%	8.50% or Between 8.50% and 9.50%	9.50% or Between 9.50% and 10.50%	10.50% or Between 10.50% and 11.50%	11.50% or Between 11.50% and 12.50%	12.50% or Between 12.50% and 13.50%	13.50% or Between 13.50% and 14.50%	14.50% or Between 14.50% and 15.50%	15.50% or More
46	0.709	0.741	0.768	0.790	0.809	0.825	0.838	0.850	0.860
47	0.699	0.731	0.758	0.781	0.801	0.817	0.831	0.843	0.853
48	0.688	0.721	0.749	0.772	0.792	0.809	0.823	0.836	0.847
49	0.678	0.711	0.739	0.763	0.783	0.800	0.815	0.828	0.839
50	0.666	0.700	0.729	0.753	0.774	0.791	0.807	0.820	0.832
51	0.655	0.689	0.718	0.743	0.764	0.782	0.798	0.812	0.824
52	0.643	0.678	0.707	0.732	0.754	0.772	0.789	0.803	0.815
53	0.631	0.666	0.695	0.721	0.743	0.762	0.779	0.794	0.807
54	0.619	0.654	0.684	0.710	0.732	0.752	0.769	0.784	0.797
55	0.606	0.641	0.671	0.698	0.721	0.741	0.758	0.774	0.787
56	0.594	0.628	0.659	0.685	0.709	0.729	0.747	0.763	0.777
57	0.580	0.615	0.646	0.673	0.696	0.717	0.735	0.752	0.766
58	0.567	0.602	0.633	0.660	0.683	0.705	0.723	0.740	0.755
59	0.553	0.588	0.619	0.646	0.670	0.692	0.711	0.728	0.743
60	0.539	0.574	0.605	0.632	0.657	0.678	0.698	0.715	0.731
61	0.525	0.560	0.590	0.618	0.642	0.664	0.684	0.702	0.718
62	0.510	0.545	0.576	0.603	0.628	0.650	0.670	0.688	0.704
63	0.496	0.530	0.561	0.588	0.613	0.636	0.656	0.674	0.691
64	0.481	0.515	0.546	0.573	0.598	0.621	0.641	0.659	0.676
65	0.466	0.500	0.530	0.558	0.583	0.605	0.626	0.644	0.661
66	0.451	0.485	0.515	0.542	0.567	0.590	0.610	0.629	0.646
67	0.436	0.469	0.499	0.526	0.551	0.574	0.594	0.613	0.631
68	0.421	0.454	0.483	0.510	0.535	0.557	0.578	0.597	0.615
69	0.407	0.438	0.467	0.494	0.518	0.541	0.562	0.581	0.598
70	0.392	0.423	0.452	0.478	0.502	0.524	0.545	0.564	0.582
71	0.377	0.407	0.436	0.462	0.485	0.508	0.528	0.547	0.565
72	0.362	0.392	0.420	0.445	0.469	0.491	0.511	0.530	0.548
73	0.348	0.377	0.404	0.429	0.452	0.474	0.494	0.513	0.531
74	0.333	0.362	0.388	0.413	0.436	0.457	0.477	0.496	0.513
75	0.319	0.347	0.373	0.397	0.419	0.441	0.460	0.479	0.496

Age Last Birthday of Husband or Civil Partner	Less than 8.50%	8.50% or Between 8.50% and 9.50%	9.50% or Between 9.50% and 10.50%	10.50% or Between 10.50% and 11.50%	11.50% or Between 11.50% and 12.50%	12.50% or Between 12.50% and 13.50%	13.50% or Between 13.50% and 14.50%	14.50% or Between 14.50% and 15.50%	15.50% or More
76	0.305	0.332	0.357	0.381	0.403	0.424	0.443	0.461	0.479
77	0.292	0.318	0.342	0.365	0.387	0.407	0.426	0.444	0.461
78	0.278	0.304	0.328	0.350	0.371	0.391	0.410	0.427	0.444
79	0.265	0.290	0.313	0.335	0.355	0.375	0.393	0.410	0.427
80	0.253	0.277	0.299	0.320	0.340	0.359	0.377	0.394	0.410
81	0.241	0.264	0.285	0.306	0.325	0.343	0.361	0.377	0.393
82	0.229	0.251	0.272	0.292	0.310	0.328	0.345	0.361	0.377
83	0.218	0.239	0.259	0.278	0.296	0.313	0.330	0.346	0.361
84	0.207	0.227	0.246	0.265	0.282	0.299	0.315	0.331	0.345
85	0.196	0.216	0.234	0.252	0.269	0.285	0.301	0.316	0.330
86	0.186	0.205	0.223	0.240	0.256	0.272	0.287	0.302	0.315
87	0.177	0.195	0.212	0.228	0.244	0.259	0.274	0.288	0.301
88	0.168	0.185	0.201	0.217	0.232	0.247	0.261	0.275	0.288
89	0.159	0.176	0.191	0.207	0.221	0.235	0.249	0.262	0.275
90	0.151	0.167	0.182	0.197	0.211	0.224	0.237	0.250	0.262
91	0.144	0.159	0.173	0.187	0.201	0.214	0.227	0.239	0.251
92	0.137	0.151	0.165	0.179	0.192	0.205	0.217	0.229	0.240
93	0.130	0.144	0.158	0.171	0.183	0.196	0.208	0.219	0.230
94	0.124	0.138	0.151	0.163	0.175	0.187	0.199	0.210	0.221
95	0.119	0.132	0.144	0.156	0.168	0.179	0.190	0.201	0.212
96	0.113	0.126	0.138	0.149	0.161	0.172	0.182	0.193	0.203
97	0.108	0.120	0.132	0.143	0.154	0.164	0.175	0.185	0.195
98	0.103	0.115	0.126	0.137	0.147	0.157	0.167	0.177	0.187
99	0.098	0.109	0.119	0.130	0.140	0.150	0.159	0.169	0.178
100 and over	0.093	0.103	0.112	0.123	0.133	0.143	0.151	0.161	0.169

Amendment

Words "or a surviving male civil partner" in square brackets inserted by SI 2005/2114, art 2(6), Sch 6, para 1(1), (3)(a).

Table: amended by SI 2005/2114, art 2(6), Sch 6, para 1(1), (3)(b).

Table 2

Multiplier to be applied to the part of the residuary estate in respect of which the election is exercised to obtain the capital value of the life interest of a surviving wife [or a surviving female civil partner], when the average gross redemption yield on medium coupon fifteen-year Government Stocks is at the rate shown.

Age Last Birthday of Wife or Civil Partner	Less than 8.50%	8.50% or Between 8.50% and 9.50%	9.50% or Between 9.50% and 10.50%	10.50% or Between 10.50% and 11.50%	11.50% or Between 11.50% and 12.50%	12.50% or Between 12.50% and 13.50%	13.50% or Between 13.50% and 14.50%	14.50% or Between 14.50% and 15.50%	15.50% or More
16	0.892	0.905	0.915	0.922	0.927	0.930	0.933	0.936	0.937
17	0.889	0.903	0.913	0.920	0.925	0.929	0.933	0.935	0.937
18	0.887	0.901	0.911	0.919	0.924	0.929	0.932	0.934	0.936
19	0.884	0.899	0.910	0.917	0.923	0.928	0.931	0.934	0.936
20	0.882	0.897	0.908	0.916	0.922	0.927	0.930	0.933	0.935
21	0.879	0.895	0.906	0.915	0.921	0.926	0.929	0.932	0.934
22	0.877	0.893	0.904	0.913	0.920	0.925	0.928	0.931	0.934
23	0.874	0.890	0.902	0.911	0.918	0.923	0.927	0.931	0.933
24	0.871	0.888	0.900	0.910	0.917	0.922	0.926	0.930	0.932
25	0.868	0.885	0.898	0.908	0.915	0.921	0.925	0.929	0.932
26	0.864	0.882	0.896	0.906	0.914	0.920	0.924	0.928	0.931
27	0.861	0.879	0.893	0.904	0.912	0.918	0.923	0.927	0.930
28	0.857	0.876	0.891	0.901	0.910	0.916	0.921	0.925	0.929
29	0.853	0.873	0.888	0.899	0.908	0.915	0.920	0.924	0.928
30	0.849	0.869	0.885	0.896	0.906	0.913	0.918	0.923	0.926
31	0.845	0.866	0.882	0.894	0.903	0.911	0.916	0.921	0.925
32	0.840	0.862	0.878	0.891	0.901	0.908	0.914	0.919	0.923
33	0.836	0.858	0.875	0.888	0.898	0.906	0.912	0.918	0.922
34	0.831	0.853	0.871	0.884	0.895	0.903	0.910	0.916	0.920
35	0.826	0.849	0.867	0.881	0.892	0.901	0.908	0.913	0.918
36	0.820	0.844	0.863	0.877	0.889	0.898	0.905	0.911	0.916
37	0.815	0.839	0.858	0.873	0.885	0.895	0.902	0.909	0.914
38	0.809	0.834	0.853	0.869	0.881	0.891	0.899	0.906	0.911
39	0.803	0.828	0.848	0.864	0.877	0.888	0.896	0.903	0.909
40	0.796	0.822	0.843	0.860	0.873	0.884	0.893	0.900	0.906
41	0.790	0.816	0.838	0.855	0.869	0.880	0.889	0.897	0.903
42	0.783	0.810	0.832	0.850	0.864	0.876	0.885	0.893	0.900
43	0.775	0.803	0.826	0.844	0.859	0.871	0.881	0.889	0.896
44	0.768	0.796	0.820	0.838	0.854	0.866	0.877	0.885	0.893
45	0.760	0.789	0.813	0.832	0.848	0.861	0.872	0.881	0.889

Age Last Birthday of Wife or Civil Partner	Less than 8.50%	8.50% or Between 8.50% and 9.50%	9.50% or Between 9.50% and 10.50%	10.50% or Between 10.50% and 11.50%	11.50% or Between 11.50% and 12.50%	12.50% or Between 12.50% and 13.50%	13.50% or Between 13.50% and 14.50%	14.50% or Between 14.50% and 15.50%	15.50% or More
46	0.752	0.782	0.806	0.826	0.842	0.856	0.867	0.876	0.885
47	0.744	0.774	0.799	0.819	0.836	0.850	0.862	0.872	0.880
48	0.735	0.766	0.791	0.812	0.829	0.844	0.856	0.866	0.875
49	0.726	0.757	0.783	0.804	0.822	0.837	0.850	0.861	0.870
50	0.716	0.748	0.775	0.797	0.815	0.831	0.844	0.855	0.865
51	0.707	0.739	0.766	0.788	0.807	0.823	0.837	0.849	0.859
52	0.697	0.729	0.757	0.780	0.799	0.816	0.830	0.842	0.853
53	0.686	0.719	0.747	0.771	0.791	0.808	0.822	0.835	0.846
54	0.676	0.709	0.737	0.761	0.782	0.799	0.814	0.827	0.839
55	0.664	0.698	0.727	0.751	0.772	0.790	0.806	0.820	0.831
56	0.653	0.687	0.716	0.741	0.763	0.781	0.797	0.811	0.823
57	0.641	0.676	0.705	0.730	0.752	0.771	0.788	0.802	0.815
58	0.629	0.664	0.693	0.719	0.741	0.761	0.778	0.793	0.806
59	0.616	0.651	0.681	0.707	0.730	0.750	0.767	0.783	0.796
60	0.603	0.638	0.669	0.695	0.718	0.739	0.757	0.772	0.786
61	0.590	0.625	0.656	0.683	0.706	0.727	0.745	0.761	0.776
62	0.577	0.612	0.643	0.670	0.693	0.715	0.733	0.750	0.764
63	0.563	0.598	0.629	0.656	0.680	0.702	0.721	0.738	0.753
64	0.549	0.584	0.615	0.642	0.667	0.688	0.708	0.725	0.740
65	0.534	0.569	0.600	0.628	0.653	0.674	0.694	0.712	0.728
66	0.520	0.555	0.586	0.613	0.638	0.660	0.680	0.698	0.714
67	0.505	0.540	0.570	0.598	0.623	0.645	0.666	0.684	0.700
68	0.490	0.524	0.555	0.583	0.608	0.630	0.651	0.669	0.686
69	0.475	0.509	0.539	0.567	0.592	0.615	0.635	0.654	0.671
70	0.459	0.493	0.523	0.551	0.576	0.599	0.619	0.638	0.655
71	0.444	0.477	0.507	0.535	0.560	0.582	0.603	0.622	0.640
72	0.428	0.461	0.491	0.518	0.543	0.566	0.586	0.606	0.623
73	0.413	0.445	0.475	0.501	0.526	0.549	0.570	0.589	0.606
74	0.398	0.429	0.458	0.485	0.509	0.532	0.552	0.572	0.589
75	0.382	0.413	0.442	0.468	0.492	0.514	0.535	0.554	0.572

Age Last Birthday of Wife or Civil Partner	Less than 8.50%	8.50% or Between 8.50% and 9.50%	9.50% or Between 9.50% and 10.50%	10.50% or Between 10.50% and 11.50%	11.50% or Between 11.50% and 12.50%	12.50% or Between 12.50% and 13.50%	13.50% or Between 13.50% and 14.50%	14.50% or Between 14.50% and 15.50%	15.50% or More
76	0.367	0.397	0.425	0.451	0.475	0.497	0.517	0.536	0.554
77	0.352	0.381	0.408	0.434	0.457	0.479	0.499	0.518	0.536
78	0.337	0.365	0.392	0.417	0.440	0.461	0.482	0.500	0.518
79	0.322	0.350	0.376	0.400	0.423	0.444	0.464	0.482	0.500
80	0.307	0.334	0.360	0.383	0.406	0.426	0.446	0.464	0.482
81	0.293	0.319	0.344	0.367	0.389	0.409	0.428	0.446	0.463
82	0.279	0.304	0.328	0.351	0.372	0.392	0.410	0.428	0.445
83	0.265	0.290	0.313	0.335	0.355	0.375	0.393	0.410	0.427
84	0.252	0.276	0.298	0.319	0.339	0.358	0.376	0.393	0.409
85	0.239	0.262	0.284	0.304	0.323	0.342	0.359	0.376	0.392
86	0.227	0.249	0.269	0.289	0.308	0.326	0.343	0.359	0.374
87	0.215	0.236	0.256	0.275	0.293	0.310	0.327	0.342	0.357
88	0.204	0.224	0.243	0.261	0.279	0.295	0.311	0.327	0.341
89	0.193	0.212	0.230	0.248	0.265	0.281	0.296	0.311	0.325
90	0.182	0.201	0.218	0.235	0.251	0.267	0.282	0.296	0.310
91	0.173	0.190	0.207	0.223	0.239	0.254	0.268	0.282	0.296
92	0.164	0.180	0.197	0.212	0.227	0.242	0.256	0.269	0.282
93	0.155	0.171	0.187	0.202	0.216	0.230	0.243	0.256	0.269
94	0.147	0.162	0.177	0.192	0.205	0.219	0.232	0.244	0.256
95	0.139	0.154	0.168	0.182	0.195	0.208	0.221	0.233	0.244
96	0.132	0.146	0.159	0.173	0.185	0.198	0.210	0.222	0.233
97	0.125	0.138	0.151	0.164	0.176	0.188	0.199	0.211	0.222
98	0.118	0.130	0.143	0.155	0.167	0.178	0.189	0.200	0.210
99	0.110	0.122	0.134	0.146	0.157	0.168	0.178	0.189	0.199
100 and over	0.102	0.114	0.125	0.137	0.147	0.158	0.167	0.178	0.188

Amendment

Words "or a surviving female civil partner" in square brackets inserted by SI 2005/2114, art 2(6), Sch 6, para 1(1), (4)(a).

Table: amended by SI 2005/2114, art 2(6), Sch 6, para 1(1), (4)(b).

Appendix IV

JUDICIAL TRUSTEE RULES1983

SI 1983/370

1 Citation and commencement

These Rules may be cited as the Judicial Trustee Rules 1983 and shall come into operation on 1st April 1983.

2 Interpretation

(1) In these Rules, unless the context otherwise requires—

"the Act" means the Judicial Trustees Act 1896;

"the Court" has the same meaning as in the Rules of the Supreme Court;

"Corporate Trustee" means the Official Solicitor, the Public Trustee or a corporation either appointed by the Court in any particular case to be a trustee or entitled by rules made under section 4(3) of the Public Trustee Act 1906 to act as custodian trustee;

"judicial trustee" means a sole judicial trustee or two or more judicial trustees appointed to act together;

"master" means a master of the Supreme Court other than a master of the Supreme Court (Taxing Office) and includes a [district judge] of a district registry of the High Court;

"official of the Court" means the holder of any paid office in or connected with the Supreme Court and includes the Official Solicitor to the Supreme Court;

"Official Solicitor" means the Official Solicitor to the Supreme Court;

"qualified accountant" means a person who is a member or a firm all the partners in which are members of the Institute of Chartered Accountants in England and Wales or of the Association of Certified and Corporate Accountants;

"Rules of the Supreme Court" has the same meaning as in section 151(4) of the *Supreme Court Act 1981* [Senior Courts Act 1981].

(2) Subject to the provisions of these Rules and of any enactment, the Rules of the Supreme Court shall apply with the necessary modification to proceedings under the Act and these Rules.

Amendment

Para (1): in definition "master" words "district judge" in square brackets substituted by the Courts and Legal Services Act 1990, s 74(1)(b), (3).

Para (1): in definition "Rules of the Supreme Court" words "Supreme Court Act 1981" in italics revoked and subsequent words in square brackets substituted, from a date to be appointed, by the Constitutional Reform Act 2005, s 59(5), Sch 11, Pt 1, para 1(2).

APPOINTMENT OF JUDICIAL TRUSTEE

3 Making of application

(1) An application to the Court for the appointment of a judicial trustee must be made by originating summons or, if it is made in a pending cause or matter, by summons or motion in the cause or matter.

(2) An application for an injunction ancillary or incidental to an order appointing a judicial trustee may be joined with the application for such order.

(3) The Court hearing an application under paragraph (2) may grant an injunction restraining any trustee or person entitled to any interest in the property of which a judicial trustee is sought from assigning, charging or otherwise dealing with that property until after the hearing of a summons for the appointment of the judicial trustee and may require such summons returnable on such date as the Court may direct, to be issued.

(4) The evidence in support of such an application must include an affidavit by the applicant containing the following particulars so far as the applicant can gain information with regard to them—

(a) a short description of the trust and instrument by which it is, or is to be, created;
(b) short particulars of the trust property, with an approximate estimate of its income, and capital value;
(c) short particulars of the incumbrances (if any) affecting the trust property;
(d) particulars as to the persons who are in possession of the documents relating to the trust;
(e) the names and addresses of the beneficiaries and short particulars of their respective interests; and
(f) the name, address and description of the proposal judicial trustee (if any) together with any proposal the applicant may make for his remuneration.

(5) Where the applicant cannot gain the information required on any point he must mention his inability in the affidavit.

4 Service of summons and notice

(1) Subject to any direction of the Court—
(a) the summons shall be served on every existing trustee who is not an applicant and on such of the beneficiaries as the applicant thinks fit; but
(b) a summons issued by or on behalf of a person creating or intending to create a trust need not be served on any person.

(2) The Court may give such directions as it thinks fit for the service of the summons or the dispensing with service of the summons on any person.

(3) Where an applicant has no nomination for a judicial trustee he may, if he thinks fit, give not less than four days notice of the hearing of the application to any official of the Court who may be appointed judicial trustee.

(4) Where an official of the Court receives notice under paragraph (3) of this rule he shall not be a party to the proceedings but shall be entitled to attend the hearing.

5 Service of order

A copy of the order appointing a judicial trustee shall be served by the party having conduct of the proceedings on the judicial trustee, such beneficiaries, former trustees and other persons as the Court may direct.

6 Security

(1) This rule shall apply where the judicial trustee is not an official of the Court.

(2) Subject to paragraph (3) below, an order appointing a judicial trustee may include such directions as the Court thinks fit for the giving of security by the person appointed.

(3) The Court shall not, except for special reasons, require security to be given when the application is made by a person creating or intending to create a trust.

(4) Where, by virtue of paragraph (2), a person is required to give security in accordance with this rule he must give security approved by the Court duly to account for what he receives as judicial trustee and to deal with it as the Court directs.

(5) Unless the Court otherwise directs, the security shall be by guarantee.

(6) Any guarantee or undertaking ordered to be filed as security shall be filed in Chancery Chambers or, if the cause or matter is proceeding in a district registry, that registry.

7 Custody of trust funds, property and documents

The Court may give such directions as it thinks fit as to the manner in which and the conditions subject to which—
(a) the trust fund is to be held;
(b) any title deeds, certificates or other documents which are evidence of the title to the trust property are to be held or disposed of;
(c) trust property may be vested in the judicial trustee; and
(d) any payments received or made on behalf of the trust are to be dealt with and accounts thereof are to be kept.

8 Applications for directions

(1) A judicial trustee or any person interested in the trust may at any time request the Court to give directions as to the trust or its administration, including a direction that there shall cease to be a judicial trustee, and such request shall state in writing the matters with regard to which directions are required.

(2) The Court may require the trustee or any other person to attend at chambers (if it appears that such attendance is necessary or convenient) or may direct a summons to be issued in the proceedings, or direct an issue or issues to be tried.

ACCOUNTS AND EXAMINATION

9 Preparation of accounts

Unless the Court otherwise orders a judicial trustee shall make up his accounts (in such form as the Court shall require) in each year to the anniversary of his appointment and shall deliver them in accordance with rules 12 or 13, as the case may be, within one calendar month after such anniversary.

10 A judicial trustee shall endorse on his accounts a certificate of the approximate capital value of the trust property at the commencement of the year of account.

11 Remuneration and disbursements

(1) A person appointed judicial trustee shall be allowed on the examination of his accounts—

- (a) by way of remuneration, if any, such reasonable amount in respect of work reasonably performed as may be authorised by the Court and the Court may direct that such remuneration shall be fixed by reference to such scales or rates of professional charges as it thinks fit provided that remuneration authorised under this rule shall not, in any year of account, exceed 15 per cent of the capital value of the trust property.
- (b) such disbursements as have actually and properly been expended in his trusteeship.

(2) For the purpose of sub-paragraph (1)(a) of this rule—

- (a) the capital value shall be ascertained from the certificate under rule 10 in respect of the year of account, or, if the Court sees fit in the case of a final account, from the certificate in respect of the preceding year.
- (b) The Court may, if it thinks fit, indicate to a judicial trustee upon his appointment the scale or rate of professional charges that it considers would be appropriate in relation to the appointment.

12 Filing, examination and inspection of accounts

(1) This rule shall apply where the judicial trustee is not a corporate trustee.

(2) Unless the Court otherwise directs a judicial trustee must submit his accounts to the Court.

(3) The accounts shall be examined by the Court unless it considers that the accounts are likely to involve questions of difficulty and refers them to a qualified accountant for report, in which case the Court may order payment to him out of the trust of such reasonable amount in respect of his report as it thinks fit.

(4) Following examination by or on behalf of he Court, the result of such examination must be certified by a master and an order may thereupon be made as to the incidence of any costs or expenses incurred.

(5) The judicial trustee shall send a copy of the accounts, or if the Court thinks fit, a summary of the accounts, of the trust to such beneficiaries or other persons as the Court may direct.

(6) If an application is made by any person to inspect the filed accounts, the Court may, if it thinks fit, having regard to the nature of the relation of the applicant to the trust, allow them to be inspected on giving reasonable notice.

(7) Any person who is served with a copy of the accounts, or a summary of the accounts under paragraph (5), or, after inspection of the accounts under paragraph (6), remains dissatisfied with them, may apply to the Court for directions.

13 (1) This rule shall apply where the judicial trustee is a corporate trustee.

(2) A judicial trustee shall submit for examination such account to such persons as the Court may direct.

(3) Any person to whom a judicial trustee is required to submit accounts may, on giving reasonable notice to the judicial trustee, inspect, either personally or by an agent, the books and other papers relating to such accounts.

(4) Any person to whom the judicial trustee is required to submit accounts, or any beneficiary, who is dissatisfied with them may give notice specifying the item or items as to which objection is taken and requiring the judicial trustee within not less than 14 days to lodge his accounts with the Court and a copy of such notice shall be lodged in Chancery Chambers or, if the cause or matter is proceeding in a district registry, that registry.

(5) Following an examination by or on behalf of the Court of an item or items in an accounts to which objection is taken the result of such examination must be certified by a master and an order may thereupon be made as to the incidence of any costs or expenses incurred.

14 Default by judicial trustee

(1) Where a judicial trustee fails to submit his account in the prescribed manner or do any other thing which he is required to submit, provide or do, he and any or all of the beneficiaries and such other persons as the Court may direct may be required to attend in chambers to show cause for the failure and the Court may, either in chambers or after adjourning into Court, give such directions as it thinks proper, including if necessary, directions for the discharge of the judicial trustee and the appointment of another and the payment of costs.

(2) Without prejudice to paragraph (1) of this Rule, where the judicial trustee has failed to comply with the Act or with these Rules or with any direction of the Court made in accordance with these Rules or has otherwise misconducted himself in relation to the trust the Court may disallow any remuneration claimed in any subsequent account.

(3) If the Court is satisfied that the judicial trustee has failed to pay any sum into the trust account within a reasonable period of time it may charge him with interest at the rate currently payable in respect of judgment debts on that sum while in his possession.

SPECIAL PROVISIONS RELATING TO OFFICIALS OF THE COURT

15 An official of the Court shall not be appointed or act as judicial trustee—

- (a) for any persons in their capacity as members or debenture holders of, or being in any other relation to, any corporation or unincorporated body, or any club, or
- (b) of a trust which involves the carrying on of any trade or business unless the Court, with or without special conditions to ensure the proper supervision of the trade or business, specifically directs.

16 (1) The appointment of an official of the Court as a judicial trustee shall be an appointment of the holder of that office for the time being, and no further order or appointment shall be necessary by reason only of the person appointed dying or ceasing to hold office.

(2) Any property vested in an official of the Court as a judicial trustee shall, on his dying or ceasing to hold office, vest in the person appointed to succeed him without any conveyance, assignment or transfer.

17 District Registries

(1) Notwithstanding any provisions contained in the Rules of the Supreme Court, an originating summons may be issued out of a district registry for the purpose of an application to appoint a judicial trustee.

(2) Where a judicial trustee is appointed on a summons or motion or in a cause or matter proceeding in a district registry all proceedings with respect to the trust and the administration thereof under the Act or these Rules shall, subject to paragraph (3) of this rule, be taken in the district registry.

(3) The Court may transfer any trust of which there is a judicial trustee from a district registry to Chancery Chambers or from Chancery Chambers to a district registry, or from one district registry to another, according as it appears convenient for the administration of the trust.

18 Fees

Where in any matter proceeding under these Rules a fee would be payable under the Order for the time being in force relating to Supreme Court Fees, that fee shall be paid.

19 Revocations

(1) . . .

(2) The provisions of the rules in force immediately before the commencement of the Judicial Trustee Rules 1972 shall continue to apply to proceedings taken before that date in a county court.

Amendment

Para (1): revokes SI 1972/1096.

Appendix V

NON-CONTENTIOUS PROBATE RULES 1987

SI 1987/2024

1 Citation and commencement

These Rules may be cited as the Non-Contentious Probate Rules 1987 and shall come into force on 1st January 1988.

2 Interpretation

(1) In these Rules, unless the context otherwise requires—

"the Act" means the *Supreme Court Act 1981* [Senior Courts Act 1981];

"authorised officer" means any officer of a registry who is for the time being authorised by the President to administer any oath or to take any affidavit required for any purpose connected with his duties;

"the Crown" includes the Crown in right of the Duchy of Lancaster and the Duke of Cornwall for the time being;

["district judge" means a district judge of the Principal Registry;]

"grant" means a grant of probate or administration and includes, where the context so admits, the resealing of such a grant under the Colonial Probates Acts 1892 and 1927;

"gross value" in relation to any estate means the value of the estate without deduction for debts, incumbrances, funeral expenses or inheritance tax (or other capital tax payable out of the estate);

["judge" means a judge of the High Court;]

"oath" means the oath required by rule 8 to be sworn by every applicant for a grant;

"personal applicant" means a person other than a trust corporation who seeks to obtain a grant without employing a solicitor [or probate practitioner], and "personal application" has a corresponding meaning;

["probate practitioner" means a person to whom section 23(1) of the Solicitors Act 1974 does not apply by virtue of section 23(2) of that Act [or section 55 of the Courts and Legal Services Act 1990;]]

["registrar" means the district probate registrar of the district probate registry—

(i) to which an application for a grant is made or is proposed to be made,

(ii) in rules 26,40,41 and 61(2), from which the grant issued, and

(iii) in rules 46,47 and 48, from which the citation has issued or is proposed to be issued;]

"registry" means the Principal Registry or a district probate registry;

["the senior district judge" means the Senior District Judge of the Family Division or, in his absence, the senior of the district judges in attendance at the Principal Registry;]

. . .

. . .

"the Treasury Solicitor" means the solicitor for the affairs of Her Majesty's Treasury and includes the solicitor for the affairs of the Duchy of Lancaster and the solicitor of the Duchy of Cornwall;

"trust corporation" means a corporation within the meaning of section 128 of the Act as extended by section 3 of the Law of Property (Amendment) Act 1926.

(2) A form referred to by number means the form so numbered in the First Schedule; and such forms shall be used wherever applicable, with such variation as a [district judge or] registrar may in any particular case direct or approve.

Amendment

Para (1): in definition "the Act" words "Supreme Court Act 1981" in italics revoked and subsequent words in square brackets substituted, from a date to be appointed, by the Constitutional Reform Act 2005, s 59(5), Sch 11, Pt 1, para 1(2).

Para (1): definition "district judge" inserted by SI 1991/1876, r 6(a).

Para (1): definition "judge" inserted by SI 1991/1876, r 6(b).
Para (1): in definition "personal applicant" words "or probate practitioner" in square brackets inserted by SI 1998/1903, r 3(a).
Para (1): definition "probate practitioner" inserted by SI 1998/1903, r 3(b).
Para (1): in definition "probate practitioner" words "or section 55 of the Courts and Legal Services Act 1990;" in square brackets inserted by SI 2004/2985, r 2.
Para (1): definition "registrar" substituted by SI 1991/1876, r 6(c).
Para (1): definition "the senior district judge" substituted, for definition "the Senior Registrar" as originally enacted, by SI 1991/1876, r 6(d).
Para (1): definition "statutory guardian" omitted revoked by SI 1991/1876, r 2.
Para (1): definition "testamentary guardian" omitted revoked by SI 1991/1876, r 2.
Para (2): words in square brackets substituted by SI 1991/1876, r 7(1).

Modification
References to solicitors etc modified to include references to bodies recognised under the Administration of Justice Act 1985, s 9, by the Solicitors' Incorporated Practices Order 1991, SI 1991/2684, arts 4, 5, Sch 1.

[3 Application of other rules]

[(1) Subject to the provisions of these rules and to any enactment, the Rules of the Supreme Court 1965 as they were in force immediately before 26th April 1999 shall apply, with any necessary modifications to non-contentious probate matters, and any reference in these rules to those rules shall be construed accordingly.

(2) Nothing in Order 3 of the Rules of the Supreme Court shall prevent time from running in the Long Vacation.]

Amendment
Substituted by SI 1999/1015, r 2.

4 Applications for grants through solicitors [or probate practitioners]

(1) A person applying for a grant through a solicitor [or probate practitioner] may apply at any registry or sub-registry.

(2) Every solicitor [or probate practitioner] through whom an application for a grant is made shall give the address of his place of business within England and Wales.

Amendment
Provision heading: words "or probate practitioners" in square brackets inserted by SI 1998/1903, r 4(a).
Para (1): words "or probate practitioner" in square brackets inserted by SI 1998/1903, r 4(b).
Para (2): words "or probate practitioner" in square brackets inserted by SI 1998/1903, r 4(b).

Modification
References to solicitors etc modified to include references to bodies recognised under the Administration of Justice Act 1985, s 9, by the Solicitors' Incorporated Practices Order 1991, SI 1991/2684, arts 4, 5, Sch 1.

5 Personal applications

(1) A personal applicant may apply for a grant at any registry or sub-registry.

(2) Save as provided for by rule 39 a personal applicant may not apply through an agent, whether paid or unpaid, and may not be attended by any person acting or appearing to act as his adviser.

(3) No personal application shall be proceeded with if—

- (a) it becomes necessary to bring the matter before the court by action or summons[, unless a judge, district judge or registrar so permits];
- (b) an application has already been made by a solicitor [or probate practitioner] on behalf of the applicant and has not been withdrawn; or
- (c) the [district judge or] registrar so directs.

(4) After a will has been deposited in a registry by a personal applicant, it may not be delivered to the applicant or to any other person unless in special circumstances the [district judge or] registrar so directs.

(5) A personal applicant shall produce a certificate of the death of the deceased or such other evidence of the death as the [district judge or] registrar may approve.

(6) A personal applicant shall supply all information necessary to enable the papers leading to the grant to be prepared in the registry.

(7) Unless the [district judge or] registrar otherwise directs, every oath or affidavit required on a personal application shall be sworn or executed by all the deponents before an authorised officer.

(8) No legal advice shall be given to a personal applicant by an officer of a registry and every such officer shall be responsible only for embodying in proper form the applicant's instructions for the grant.

Amendment

Para (3): in sub-para (a) words ", unless a judge, district judge or registrar so permits" in square brackets inserted by SI 1998/1903, r 5.
Para (3): in sub-para (b) words "or probate practitioner" in square brackets inserted by SI 1998/1903, r 6.
Para (3): in sub-para (c) words "district judge or" in square brackets inserted by SI 1991/1876, r 7(1).
Para (4): words "district judge or" in square brackets inserted by SI 1991/1876, r 7(1).
Para (5): words "district judge or" in square brackets inserted by SI 1991/1876, r 7(1).
Para (7): words "district judge or" in square brackets inserted by SI 1991/1876, r 7(1).

Modification

References to solicitors etc modified to include references to bodies recognised under the Administration of Justice Act 1985, s 9, by the Solicitors' Incorporated Practices Order 1991, SI 1991/2684, arts 4, 5, Sch 1.

6 Duty of [district judge or] registrar on receiving application for grant

(1) A [district judge or] registrar shall not allow any grant to issue until all inquiries which he may see fit to make have been answered to his satisfaction.

(2) Except with the leave of a [district judge or] registrar, no grant of probate or of administration with the will annexed shall issue within seven days of the death of the deceased and no grant of administration shall issue within fourteen days thereof.

Amendment

Provision heading: words in square brackets inserted by SI 1991/1876, r 7(1).
Paras (1), (2): words in square brackets inserted by SI 1991/1876, r 7(1).

7 Grants by district probate registrars

(1) No grant shall be made by a . . . registrar—

(a) in any case in which there is contention, until the contention is disposed of; or

(b) in any case in which it appears to him that a grant ought not to be made without the directions of a judge or a [district judge].

(2) In any case in which paragraph (1)(b) applies, the . . . registrar shall send a statement of the matter in question to the Principal Registry for directions.

(3) A [district judge] may either confirm that the matter be referred to a judge and give directions accordingly or may direct the . . . registrar to proceed with the matter in accordance with such instructions as are deemed necessary, which may include a direction to take no further action in relation to the matter.

Amendment

Paras (1), (3): words omitted revoked, and words in square brackets substituted, by SI 1991/1876, r 7(2), (3).
Para (2): words omitted revoked by SI 1991/1876, r 7(2).

8 Oath in support of grant

(1) Every application for a grant other than one to which rule 39 applies shall be supported by an oath by the applicant in the form applicable to the circumstances of the case, and by such other papers as the [district judge or] registrar may require.

(2) Unless otherwise directed by a [district judge or] registrar, the oath shall state where the deceased died domiciled.

(3) Where the deceased died on or after 1st January 1926, the oath shall state whether or not, to the best of the applicant's knowledge, information and belief, there was land vested in the deceased which was settled previously to his death and not by his will and which remained settled land notwithstanding his death.

(4) On an application for a grant of administration the oath shall state in what manner all persons having a prior right to a grant have been cleared off and whether any minority or life interest arises under the will or intestacy.

Amendment
Paras (1), (2): words in square brackets inserted by SI 1991/1876, r 7(1).

9 Grant in additional name

Where it is sought to describe the deceased in a grant by some name in addition to his true name, the applicant shall depose to the true name of the deceased and shall specify some part of the estate which was held in the other name, or give any other reason for the inclusion of the other name in the grant.

10 Marking of wills

(1) Subject to paragraph (2) below, every will in respect of which an application for a grant is made—

(a) shall be marked by the signatures of the applicant and the person before whom the oath is sworn; and

(b) shall be exhibited to any affidavit which may be required under these Rules as to the validity, terms, condition or date of execution of the will.

(2) The [district judge or] registrar may allow a facsimile copy of a will to be marked or exhibited in lieu of the original document.

Amendment
Para (2): words in square brackets inserted by SI 1991/1876, r 7(1).

11 Engrossments for purposes of record

(1) Where the [district judge or] registrar considers that in any particular case a facsimile copy of the original will would not be satisfactory for purposes of record, he may require an engrossment suitable for facsimile reproduction to be lodged.

(2) Where a will—

(a) contains alterations which are not to be admitted to proof; or

(b) has been ordered to be rectified by virtue of section 20(1) of the Administration of Justice Act 1982,

there shall be lodged an engrossment of the will in the form in which it is to be proved.

(3) Any engrossment lodged under this rule shall reproduce the punctuation, spacing and division into paragraphs of the will and shall follow continuously from page to page on both sides of the paper.

Amendment
Para (1): words in square brackets inserted by SI 1991/1876, r 7(1).

12 Evidence as to due execution of will

(1) Subject to paragraphs (2) and (3) below, where a will contains no attestation clause or the attestation clause is insufficient, or where it appears to the [district judge or] registrar that there is doubt about the due execution of the will, he shall before admitting it to proof require an affidavit as to due execution from one or more of the attesting witnesses or, if no attesting witness is conveniently available, from any other person who was present when the will was executed; and if the [district judge or] registrar, after considering the evidence, is satisfied the will was not duly executed, he shall refuse probate and mark the will accordingly.

(2) If no affidavit can be obtained in accordance with paragraph (1) above, the [district judge or] registrar may accept evidence on affidavit from any person he may think fit to show that the signature on the will is in the handwriting of the deceased, or of any other matter which may raise a presumption in favour of due execution of the will, and may if he thinks fit require that notice of the application be given to any person who may be prejudiced by the will.

(3) A [district judge or] registrar may accept a will for proof without evidence as aforesaid if he is satisfied that the distribution of the estate is not thereby affected.

Amendment
Para (3): words in square brackets inserted by SI 1991/1876, r 7(1).

13 Execution of will of blind or illiterate testator

Before admitting to proof a will which appears to have been signed by a blind or illiterate testator or by another person by direction of the testator, or which for any other reason raises doubt as to the testator having had knowledge of the contents of the will at the time of its execution, the [district judge or] registrar shall satisfy himself that the testator had such knowledge.

Amendment
Words in square brackets inserted by SI 1991/1876, r 7(1).

14 Evidence as to terms, condition and date of execution of will

(1) Subject to paragraph (2) below, where there appears in a will any obliteration, interlineation, or other alteration which is not authenticated in the manner prescribed by section 21 of the Wills Act 1837, or by the re-execution of the will or by the execution of a codicil, the [district judge or] registrar shall require evidence to show whether the alteration was present at the time the will was executed and shall give directions as to the form in which the will is to be proved.

(2) The provisions of paragraph (1) above shall not apply to any alteration which appears to the [district judge or] registrar to be of no practical importance.

(3) If a will contains any reference to another document in such terms as to suggest that it ought to be incorporated in the will, the [district judge or] registrar shall require the document to be produced and may call for such evidence in regard to the incorporation of the document as he may think fit.

(4) Where there is a doubt as to the date on which a will was executed, the [district judge or] registrar may require such evidence as he thinks necessary to establish the date.

Amendment
Paras (1), (4): words in square brackets inserted by SI 1991/1876, r 7(1).

15 Attempted revocation of will

Any appearance of attempted revocation of a will by burning, tearing, or otherwise destroying and every other circumstance leading to a presumption of revocation by the testator, shall be accounted for to the [district judge's or] registrar's satisfaction.

Amendment
Words in square brackets inserted by SI 1991/1876, r 7(5).

16 Affidavit as to due execution, terms etc, of will

A [district judge or] registrar may require an affidavit from any person he may think fit for the purpose of satisfying himself as to any of the matters referred to in rules 13, 14 and 15, and in any such affidavit sworn by an attesting witness or other person present at the time of the execution of a will the deponent shall depose to the manner in which the will was executed.

Amendment
Words in square brackets inserted by SI 1991/1876, r 7(1).

17 Wills proved otherwise than under section 9 of the Wills Act 1837

(1) Rules 12 to 15 shall apply only to a will that is to be established by reference to section 9 of the Wills Act 1837 (signing and attestation of wills).

(2) A will that is to be established otherwise than as described in paragraph (1) of this rule may be so established upon the [district judge or] registrar being satisfied as to its terms and validity, and includes (without prejudice to the generality of the foregoing)—

- (a) any will to which rule 18 applies; and
- (b) any will which, by virtue of the Wills Act 1963, is to be treated as properly executed if executed according to the internal law of the territory or state referred to in section 1 of that Act.

Amendment
Para (2): words in square brackets inserted by SI 1991/1876, r 7(1).

18 Wills of persons on military service and seamen

Where the deceased died domiciled in England and Wales and it appears to the [district judge or] registrar that there is prima facie evidence that a will is one to which section 11 of the Wills Act 1837 applies, the will may be admitted to proof if the registrar is satisfied that it was signed by the testator or, if unsigned, that it is in the testator's handwriting.

Amendment
Words in square brackets inserted by SI 1991/1876, r 7(1).

19 Evidence of foreign law

Where evidence as to the law of any country or territory outside England and Wales is required on any application for a grant, the [district judge or] registrar may accept—

(a) an affidavit from any person whom, having regard to the particulars of his knowledge or experience given in the affidavit, he regards as suitably qualified to give expert evidence of the law in question; or
(b) a certificate by, or an act before, a notary practising in the country or territory concerned.

Amendment
Words in square brackets inserted by SI 1991/1876, r 7(1).

20 Order of priority for grant where deceased left a will

Where the deceased died on or after 1 January 1926 the person or persons entitled to a grant in respect of a will shall be determined in accordance with the following order of priority, namely—

(a) the executor (but subject to rule 36(4)(d) below);
(b) any residuary legatee or devisee holding in trust for any other person;
(c) any other residuary legatee or devisee (including one for life) or where the residue is not wholly disposed of by the will, any person entitled to share in the undisposed of residue (including the Treasury Solicitor when claiming bona vacantia on behalf of the Crown), provided that—
  (i) unless a [district judge or] registrar otherwise directs, a residuary legatee or devisee whose legacy or devise is vested in interest shall be preferred to one entitled on the happening of a contingency, and
  (ii) where the residue is not in terms wholly disposed of, the [district judge or] registrar may, if he is satisfied that the testator has nevertheless disposed of the whole or substantially the whole of the known estate, allow a grant to be made to any legatee or devisee entitled to, or to share in, the estate so disposed of, without regard to the persons entitled to share in any residue not disposed of by the will;
(d) the personal representative of any residuary legatee or devisee (but not one for life, or one holding in trust for any other person), or of any person entitled to share in any residue not disposed of by the will;
(e) any other legatee or devisee (including one for life or one holding in trust for any other person) or any creditor of the deceased, provided that, unless a [district judge or] registrar otherwise directs, a legatee or devisee whose legacy or devise is vested in interest shall be preferred to one entitled on the happening of a contingency;
(f) the personal representative of any other legatee or devisee (but not one for life or one holding in trust for any other person) or of any creditor of the deceased.

Amendment
Paras (c), (e): words in square brackets inserted by SI 1991/1876, r 7(1).

21 Grants to attesting witnesses, etc

Where a gift to any person fails by reason of section 15 of the Wills Act 1837, such person shall not have any right to a grant as a beneficiary named in the will, without prejudice to his right to a grant in any other capacity.

22 Order of priority for grant in case of intestacy

(1) Where the deceased died on or after 1 January 1926, wholly intestate, the person or persons having a beneficial interest in the estate shall be entitled to a grant of administration in the following classes in order of priority, namely—

(a) the surviving [spouse or civil partner];
(b) the children of the deceased and the issue of any deceased child who died before the deceased;
(c) the father and mother of the deceased;
(d) brothers and sisters of the whole blood and the issue of any deceased brother or sister of the whole blood who died before the deceased;
(e) brothers and sisters of the half blood and the issue of any deceased brother or sister of the half blood who died before the deceased;
(f) grandparents;
(g) uncles and aunts of the whole blood and the issue of any deceased uncle or aunt of the whole blood who died before the deceased;
(h) uncles and aunts of the half blood and the issue of any deceased uncle or aunt of the half blood who died before the deceased.

(2) In default of any person having a beneficial interest in the estate, the Treasury Solicitor shall be entitled to a grant if he claims bona vacantia on behalf of the Crown.

(3) If all persons entitled to a grant under the foregoing provisions of this rule have been cleared off, a grant may be made to a creditor of the deceased or to any person who, notwithstanding that he has no immediate beneficial interest in the estate, may have a beneficial interest in the event of an accretion thereto.

(4) Subject to paragraph (5) of rule 27, the personal representative of a person in any of the classes mentioned in paragraph (1) of this rule or the personal representative of a creditor of the deceased shall have the same right to a grant as the person whom he represents provided that the persons mentioned in sub-paragraphs (b) to (h) of paragraph (1) above shall be preferred to the personal representative of a spouse [or a civil partner] who has died without taking a beneficial interest in the whole estate of the deceased as ascertained at the time of the application for the grant.

Amendment

Para (1): in sub-para (a) words "spouse or civil partner" in square brackets substituted by SI 2005/2114, art 2(6), Sch 6, para 2(1), (2).

Para (4): words "or a civil partner" in square brackets inserted by SI 2005/2114, art 2(6), Sch 6, para 2(1), (3).

23 Order of priority for grant in pre-1926 cases

Where the deceased died before 1st January 1926, the person or persons entitled to a grant shall, subject to the provisions of any enactment, be determined in accordance with the principles and rules under which the court would have acted at the date of death.

24 Right of assignee to a grant

(1) Where all the persons entitled to the estate of the deceased (whether under a will or on intestacy) have assigned their whole interest in the estate to one or more persons, the assignee or assignees shall replace, in the order of priority for a grant of administration, the assignor or, if there are two or more assignors, the assignor with the highest priority.

(2) Where there are two or more assignees, administration may be granted with the consent of the others to any one or more (not exceeding four) of them.

(3) In any case where administration is applied for by an assignee the original instrument of assignment shall be produced and a copy of the same lodged in the registry.

25 Joinder of administrator

(1) A person entitled in priority to a grant of administration may, without leave, apply for a grant with a person entitled in a lower degree, provided that there is no other person entitled in a higher degree to the person to be joined, unless every other such person has renounced.

(2) Subject to paragraph (3) below, an application for leave to join with a person entitled in priority to a grant of administration a person having no right or no immediate right thereto shall be made to a [district judge or] registrar, and shall be supported by an affidavit by the person entitled in priority, the consent of the person proposed to be joined as administrator and such other evidence as the [district judge or] registrar may direct.

(3) Unless a [district judge or] registrar otherwise directs, there may without any such application be joined with a person entitled in priority to administration—

(a) any person who is nominated under paragraph (3) of rule 32 or paragraph (3) of rule 35;

(b) a trust corporation.

Amendment

Paras (2), (3): words in square brackets inserted by SI 1991/1876, r 7(1).

26 Additional personal representatives

(1) An application under section 114(4) of the Act to add a personal representative shall be made to a [district judge or] registrar and shall be supported by an affidavit by the applicant, the consent of the person proposed to be added as personal representative and such other evidence as the [district judge or] registrar may require.

(2) On any such application the [district judge or] registrar may direct that a note shall be made on the original grant of the addition of a further personal representative, or he may impound or revoke the grant or make such other order as the circumstances of the case may require.

Amendment

Words in square brackets inserted by SI 1991/1876, r 7(1).

27 Grants where two or more persons entitled in same degree

[(1) Subject to paragraphs (1A), (2) and (3) below, where, on an application for probate, power to apply for a like grant is to be reserved to such other of the executors as have not renounced probate, notice of the application shall be given to the executor or executors to whom power is to be reserved; and, unless the district judge or registrar otherwise directs, the oath shall state that such notice has been given.

(1A) Where power is to be reserved to executors who are . . . partners in a firm, . . . notice need not be given to them under paragraph (1) above if probate is applied for by another partner in that firm.]

(2) Where power is to be reserved to partners of a firm, notice for the purposes of paragraph (1) above may be given to the partners by sending it to the firm at its principal or last known place of business.

(3) A [district judge or] registrar may dispense with the giving of notice under paragraph (1) above if he is satisfied that the giving of such a notice is impracticable or would result in unreasonable delay or expense.

(4) A grant of administration may be made to any person entitled thereto without notice to other persons entitled in the same degree.

(5) Unless a [district judge or] registrar otherwise directs, administration shall be granted to a person of full age entitled thereto in preference to a guardian of a minor, and to a living person entitled thereto in preference to the personal representative of a deceased person.

(6) A dispute between persons entitled to a grant in the same degree shall be brought by summons before a [district judge or] registrar.

[(7) The issue of a summons under this rule in a registry shall be noted forthwith in the index of pending grant applications.]

(8) If the issue of a summons under this rule is known to the [district judge or] registrar, he shall not allow any grant to be sealed until such summons is finally disposed of.

Amendment

Paras (1), (1A): substituted for original para (1) by SI 1991/1876, r 8(1).
Para (1A): words omitted revoked by SI 1998/1903, r 7(1).
Paras (3), (5), (6), (8): words in square brackets inserted by SI 1991/1876, r 7(1).
Para (7): substituted by SI 1998/1903, r 7(2).

28 Exceptions to rules as to priority

(1) Any person to whom a grant may or is required to be made under any enactment shall not be prevented from obtaining such a grant notwithstanding the operation of rules 20, 22, 25 or 27.

(2) Where the deceased died domiciled outside England and Wales rules 20, 22, 25 or 27 shall not apply except in a case to which paragraph (3) of rule 30 applies.

[29 Grants in respect of settled land]

[(1) In this rule "settled land" means land vested in the deceased which was settled prior to his death and not by his will, and which remained settled land notwithstanding his death.

(2) The person or persons entitled to a grant of administration limited to settled land shall be determined in accordance with the following order of priority—

(i) the special executors in regard to settled land constituted by section 22 of the Administration of Estates Act 1925;

(ii) the trustees of the settlement at the time of the application for the grant; and

(iii) the personal representatives of the deceased.

(3) Where there is settled land and a grant is made in respect of the free estate only, the grant shall expressly exclude the settled land.]

Amendment

Substituted by SI 1991/1876, r 9.

30 Grants where deceased died domiciled outside England and Wales

(1) Subject to paragraph (3) below, where the deceased died domiciled outside England and Wales, [a district judge or registrar may order that a grant, limited in such way as the district judge or registrar may direct,] do issue to any of the following persons—

(a) to the person entrusted with the administration of the estate by the court having jurisdiction at the place where the deceased died domiciled; or

(b) where there is no person so entrusted, to the person beneficially entitled to the estate by the law of the place where the deceased died domiciled or, if there is more than one person so entitled, to such of them as the [district judge or] registrar may direct; or

(c) if in the opinion of the [district judge or] registrar the circumstances so require, to such person as the [district judge or] registrar may direct.

(2) A grant made under paragraph (1)(a) or (b) above may be issued jointly with such person as the [district judge or] registrar may direct if the grant is required to be made to not less than two administrators.

(3) Without any order made under paragraph (1) above—

(a) probate of any will which is admissible to proof may be granted—

(i) if the will is in the English or Welsh language, to the executor named therein; or

(ii) if the will describes the duties of a named person in terms sufficient to constitute him executor according to the tenor of the will, to that person; or

(b) where the whole or substantially the whole of the estate in England and Wales consists of immovable property, a grant in respect of the whole estate may be made in accordance with the law which would have been applicable if the deceased had died domiciled in England and Wales.

Amendment

Para (1): first words in square brackets substituted and other words in square brackets inserted by SI 1991/1876, rr 7(1), 10.

Para (2): words in square brackets inserted by SI 1991/1876, r 7(1).

31 Grants to attorneys

(1) Subject to paragraphs (2) and (3) below, the lawfully constituted attorney of a person entitled to a grant may apply for administration for the use and benefit of the donor, and such grant shall be limited until further representation be granted, or in such other way as the [district judge or] registrar may direct.

(2) Where the donor referred to in paragraph (1) above is an executor, notice of the application shall be given to any other executor unless such notice is dispensed with by the [district judge or] registrar.

[(3) Where the donor referred to in paragraph (1) above lacks capacity within the meaning of the Mental Capacity Act 2005 (c 9) and the attorney is acting under an enduring power of attorney or lasting power of attorney, the application shall be made in accordance with rule 35.]

Amendment

Paras (1), (2): words in square brackets inserted by SI 1991/1876, r 7(1).
Para (3): substituted by SI 2007/1898, art 6, Sch 1, para 13(1), (2).

32 Grants on behalf of minors

(1) Where a person to whom a grant would otherwise be made is a minor, administration for his use and benefit, limited until he attains the age of eighteen years, shall, unless otherwise directed, and subject to paragraph (2) of this rule, be granted to

[(a) a parent of the minor who has, or is deemed to have, parental responsibility for him in accordance with—
  (i) section 2(1), 2(2) or 4 of the Children Act 1989,
  (ii) paragraph 4 or 6 of Schedule 14 to that Act, or
  (iii) an adoption order within the meaning of section 12(1) of the Adoption Act 1976 [or section 46(1) of the Adoption and Children Act 2002], or

[(aa) a person who has, or is deemed to have, parental responsibility for the minor by virtue of section 12(2) of the Children Act 1989(a) where the court has made a residence order under section 8 of that Act in respect of the minor in favour of that person; or]

[(ab) a step-parent of the minor who has parental responsibility for him in accordance with section 4A of the Children Act 1989; or]

(b) a guardian of the minor who is appointed, or deemed to have been appointed, in accordance with section 5 of the Children Act 1989 or in accordance with paragraph 12, 13 or 14 of Schedule 14 to that Act]; [or]

[(ba) a special guardian of the minor who is appointed in accordance with section 14A of the Children Act 1989; or

(bb) an adoption agency which has parental responsibility for the minor by virtue of section 25(2) of the Adoption and Children Act 2002; or]

[(c) a local authority which has, or is deemed to have, parental responsibility for the minor by virtue of section 33(3) of the Children Act 1989 where the court has made a care order under section 31(1)(a) of that Act in respect of the minor and that local authority is designated in that order;]

provided that where the minor is sole executor and has no interest in the residuary estate of the deceased, administration for the use and benefit of the minor limited as aforesaid, shall, unless a [district judge or] registrar otherwise directs, be granted to the person entitled to the residuary estate.

[(2) A district judge or registrar may by order appoint a person to obtain administration for the use and benefit of the minor, limited as aforesaid, in default of, or jointly with, or to the exclusion of, any person mentioned in paragraph (1) of this rule; and the person intended shall file an affidavit in support of his application to be appointed.]

(3) Where there is only one person competent and willing to take a grant under the foregoing provisions of this rule, such person may, unless a [district judge or] registrar otherwise directs, nominate any fit and proper person to act jointly with him in taking the grant.

Amendment

Para (1): sub-paras (a), (b) substituted by SI 1991/1876, r 3.
Para (1): in sub-para (a)(iii) words "or section 46(1) of the Adoption and Children Act 2002" in square brackets inserted by SI 2005/3504, art 4(a).
Para (1): sub-para (aa) inserted by SI 1998/1903, r 8(1).
Para (1): sub-para (ab) inserted by SI 2005/3504, art 4(b).
Para (1): in sub-para (b) word "or" in square brackets inserted by SI 1998/1903, r 8(2).
Para (1): sub-paras (ba), (bb) inserted by SI 2005/3504, art 4(c).
Para (1): sub-para (c) inserted by SI 1998/1903, r 8(3).
Para (1): words "district judge or" in square brackets inserted by SI 1991/1876, r 7(1).
Para (2): substituted by SI 1991/1876, r 4.
Para (3): words in square brackets inserted by SI 1991/1876, r 7(1).

33 Grants where a minor is a co-executor

(1) Where a minor is appointed executor jointly with one or more other executors, probate may be granted to the executor or executors not under disability with power reserved to the minor executor, and the minor executor shall be entitled to apply for probate on attaining the age of eighteen years.

(2) Administration for the use and benefit of a minor executor until he attains the age of eighteen years may be granted under rule 32 if, and only if, the executors who are not under disability renounce or, on being cited to accept or refuse a grant, fail to make an effective application therefor.

34 Renunciation of the right of a minor to a grant

(1) The right of a minor executor to probate on attaining the age of eighteen years may not be renounced by any person on his behalf.

(2) The right of a minor to administration may be renounced only by a person [appointed] under paragraph (2) of rule 32, and authorised by the [district judge or] registrar to renounce on behalf of the minor.

Amendment

Para (2): first word in square brackets substituted and second words in square brackets inserted by SI 1991/1876, rr 5, 7(1).

35 Grants in case of [lack of mental capacity]

(1) Unless a [district judge or] registrar otherwise directs, no grant shall be made under this rule unless all persons entitled in the same degree as the [person who lacks capacity within the meaning of the Mental Capacity Act 2005] referred to in paragraph (2) below have been cleared off.

(2) Where a [district judge or] registrar is satisfied that a person entitled to a grant [lacks capacity within the meaning of the Mental Capacity Act 2005 to manage] his affairs, administration for his use and benefit, limited until further representation be granted or in such other way as the [district judge or] registrar may direct, may be granted in the following order of priority—

(a) to the person authorised by the Court of Protection to apply for a grant;

(b) where there is no person so authorised, to the lawful attorney of the [person who lacks capacity within the meaning of the Mental Capacity Act 2005] acting under a registered enduring power of attorney [or lasting power of attorney];

(c) where there is no such attorney entitled to act, or if the attorney shall renounce administration for the use and benefit of the [person who lacks capacity within the meaning of the Mental Capacity Act 2005], to the person entitled to the residuary estate of the deceased.

(3) Where a grant is required to be made to not less than two administrators, and there is only one person competent and willing to take a grant under the foregoing provisions of this rule, administration may, unless a [district judge or] registrar otherwise directs, be granted to such person jointly with any other person nominated by him.

(4) Notwithstanding the foregoing provisions of this rule, administration for the use and benefit of the [person who lacks capacity within the meaning of the Mental Capacity Act 2005] may be granted to such [other person] as the [district judge or] registrar may by order direct.

(5) [Unless the applicant is the person authorised in paragraph (2)(a) above,] Notice of an intended application under this rule shall be given to the Court of Protection.

Amendment

Heading: words "person who lacks capacity within the meaning of the Mental Capacity Act 2005" substituted by SI 2007/1898, art 6, Sch 1, para 13(1), (3).
Para (1): words "district judge or" inserted by SI 1991/1876, r 7(1).
Para (2): words substituted by SI 2007/1898, art 6, Sch 1, para 13(1), (3).
Para (2): words "district judge or" in both places they occur inserted by SI 1991/1876, r 7(1).
Para (2): words "lacks capacity within the meaning of the Mental Capacity Act 2005 to manage" substituted by SI 2007/1898, art 6, Sch 1, para 13(1), (5)(a).
Para (2): words "person who lacks capacity within the meaning of the Mental Capacity Act 2005" in both places they occur substituted by SI 2007/1898, art 6, Sch 1, para 13(1), (5)(b).
Para (2): words "or lasting power of attorney" inserted by SI 2007/1898, art 6, Sch 1, para 13(1), (5)(c).

Para (3): words "district judge or" inserted by SI 1991/1876, r 7(1).
Para (4): words "person who lacks capacity within the meaning of the Mental Capacity Act 2005" substituted by SI 2007/1898, art 6, Sch 1, para 13(1), (6).
Para (4): words "other person" substituted by SI 1998/1903, r 9(1).
Para (4): words "district judge or" inserted by SI 1991/1876, r 7(1).
Para (5): words from "Unless" to "paragraph (2)(a) above," inserted by SI 1998/1903, r 9(2).

36 Grants to trust corporations and other corporate bodies

(1) An application for a grant to a trust corporation shall be made through one of its officers, and such officer shall depose in the oath that the corporation is a trust corporation as defined by these Rules and that it has power to accept a grant.

(2) (a) Where the trust corporation is the holder of an official position, any officer whose name is included on a list filed with the [senior district judge] of persons authorised to make affidavits and sign documents on behalf of the office holder may act as the officer through whom the holder of that official position applies for the grant.

(b) In all other cases a certified copy of the resolution of the trust corporation authorising the officer to make the application shall be lodged, or it shall be deposed in the oath that such certified copy has been filed with the [senior district judge], that the officer is therein identified by the position he holds, and that such resolution is still in force.

(3) A trust corporation may apply for administration otherwise than as a beneficiary or the attorney of some person, and on any such application there shall be lodged the consents of all persons entitled to a grant and of all persons interested in the residuary estate of the deceased save that the [district judge or] registrar may dispense with any such consents as aforesaid on such terms, if any, as he may think fit.

(4) (a) Subject to sub-paragraph (d) below, where a corporate body would, if an individual, be entitled to a grant but is not a trust corporation as defined by these Rules, administration for its use and benefit, limited until further representation be granted, may be made to its nominee or to its lawfully constituted attorney.

(b) A copy of the resolution appointing the nominee or the power of attorney (whichever is appropriate) shall be lodged, and such resolution or power of attorney shall be sealed by the corporate body, or be otherwise authenticated to the [district judge's or] registrar's satisfaction.

(c) The nominee or attorney shall depose in the oath that the corporate body is not a trust corporation as defined by these Rules.

(d) The provisions of paragraph (4)(a) above shall not apply where a corporate body is appointed executor jointly with an individual unless the right of the individual has been cleared off.

Amendment

Para (2): words in square brackets substituted by SI 1991/1876, r 7(4).
Paras (3), (4): words in square brackets inserted by SI 1991/1876, r 7(1), (5).

37 Renunciation of probate and administration

(1) Renunciation of probate by an executor shall not operate as renunciation of any right which he may have to a grant of administration in some other capacity unless he expressly renounces such right.

(2) Unless a [district judge or] registrar otherwise directs, no person who has renounced administration in one capacity may obtain a grant thereof in some other capacity.

[(2A) Renunciation of probate or administration by members of a partnership—

(a) may be effected, or

(b) subject to paragraph (3) below, may be retracted by any two of them with the authority of the others and any such renunciation or retraction shall recite such authority.]

(3) A renunciation of probate or administration may be retracted at any time with the leave of a [district judge or] registrar; provided that only in exceptional circumstances may leave be

given to an executor to retract a renunciation of probate after a grant has been made to some other person entitled in a lower degree.

(4) A direction or order giving leave under this rule may be made either by the registrar of a district probate registry where the renunciation is filed or by a [district judge].

Amendment

Paras (2), (3): words in square brackets inserted by SI 1991/1876, r 7(1).
Para (2A): inserted by SI 1998/1903, r 10.
Para (4): words in square brackets substituted by SI 1991/1876, r 7(3).

38 Notice to Crown of intended application for grant

In any case in which it appears that the Crown is or may be beneficially interested in the estate of a deceased person, notice of intended application for a grant shall be given by the applicant to the Treasury Solicitor, and the [district judge or] registrar may direct that no grant shall issue within 28 days after the notice has been given.

Amendment

Words in square brackets inserted by SI 1991/1876, r 7(1).

39 Resealing under Colonial Probates Acts 1892 and 1927

(1) An application under the Colonial Probates Acts 1892 and 1927 for the resealing of probate or administration granted by the court of a country to which those Acts apply may be made by the person to whom the grant was made or by any person authorised in writing to apply on his behalf.

(2) On any such application an Inland Revenue affidavit or account shall be lodged.

(3) Except by leave of a [district judge or] registrar, no grant shall be resealed unless it was made to such a person as is mentioned in sub-paragraph (a) or (b) of paragraph (1) of rule 30 or to a person to whom a grant could be made under sub-paragraph (a) of paragraph (3) of that rule.

(4) No limited or temporary grant shall be resealed except by leave of a [district judge or] registrar.

(5) Every grant lodged for resealing shall include a copy of any will to which the grant relates or shall be accompanied by a copy thereof certified as correct by or under the authority of the court by which the grant was made, and where the copy of the grant required to be deposited under subsection (1) of section 2 of the Colonial Probates Act 1892 does not include a copy of the will, a copy thereof shall be deposited in the registry before the grant is resealed.

(6) The [district judge or] registrar shall send notice of the resealing to the court which made the grant.

(7) Where notice is received in the Principal Registry of the resealing of a grant issued in England and Wales, notice of any amendment or revocation of the grant shall be sent to the court by which it was resealed.

Amendment

Paras (3), (4), (6): words in square brackets inserted by SI 1991/1876, r 7(1).

40 Application for leave to sue on guarantee

An application for leave under section 120(3) of the Act or under section 11(5) of the Administration of Estates Act 1971 to sue a surety on a guarantee given for the purposes of either of those sections shall, unless the [district judge or] registrar otherwise directs under rule 61, be made by summons to a [district judge or] registrar and notice of the application shall be served on the administrator, the surety and any co-surety.

Amendment

Words in square brackets inserted by SI 1991/1876, r 7(1).

41 Amendment and revocation of grant

(1) Subject to paragraph (2) below, if a [district judge or] registrar is satisfied that a grant should be amended or revoked he may make an order accordingly.

(2) Except on the application or with the consent of the person to whom the grant was made, the power conferred in paragraph (1) above shall be exercised only in exceptional circumstances.

Amendment

Para (1): words in square brackets inserted by SI 1991/1876, r 7(1).

42 Certificate of delivery of Inland Revenue affidavit

Where the deceased died before 13th March 1975 the certificate of delivery of an Inland Revenue affidavit required by section 30 of the Customs and Inland Revenue Act 1881 to be borne by every grant shall be in Form 1.

43 Standing searches

[(1) Any person who wishes to be notified of the issue of a grant may enter a standing search for the grant by lodging at, or sending by post to any registry or sub-registry, a notice in Form 2.]

(2) A person who has entered a standing search will be sent an office copy of any grant which corresponds with the particulars given on the completed Form 2 and which—

(a) issued not more than twelve months before the entry of the standing search; or

(b) issues within a period of six months after the entry of the standing search.

(3) (a) Where an applicant wishes to extend the said period of six months, he or his solicitor [or probate practitioner] may lodge at, or send by post to, [the registry or sub-registry at which the standing search was entered] written application for extension.

(b) An application for extension as aforesaid must be lodged, or received by post, within the last month of the said period of six months, and the standing search shall thereupon be effective for an additional period of six months from the date on which it was due to expire.

(c) A standing search which has been extended as above may be further extended by the filing of a further application for extension subject to the same conditions as set out in sub-paragraph (b) above.

Amendment

Para (1): substituted by SI 1991/1876, r 11(1).
Para (3): in sub-para (a) words "or probate practitioner" in square brackets inserted by SI 1998/1903, r 6.
Para (3): in sub-para (a) words from "the registry" to "search was entered" in square brackets substituted by SI 1991/1876, r 11(2).

Modification

References to solicitors etc modified to include references to bodies recognised under the Administration of Justice Act 1985, s 9, by the Solicitors' Incorporated Practices Order 1991, SI 1991/2684, arts 4, 5, Sch 1.

44 Caveats

(1) Any person who wishes to show cause against the sealing of a grant may enter a caveat in any registry or sub-registry, and the [district judge or] registrar shall not allow any grant to be sealed (other than a grant ad colligenda bona or a grant under section 117 of the Act) if he has knowledge of an effective caveat; provided that no caveat shall prevent the sealing of a grant on the day on which the caveat is entered.

(2) Any person wishing to enter a caveat (in these Rules called "the caveator"), or a solicitor [or probate practitioner] on his behalf, may effect entry of a caveat—

(a) by completing Form 3 in the appropriate book at any registry or sub-registry; or

(b) by sending by post at his own risk a notice in Form 3 to any registry or sub-registry and the proper officer shall provide an acknowledgement of the entry of the caveat.

(3) (a) Except as otherwise provided by this rule or by rules 45 or 46, a caveat shall be effective for a period of six months from the date of entry thereof, and where a caveator wishes to extend the said period of six months, he or his solicitor [or probate practitioner] may lodge at, or send by post to, the registry or sub-registry at which the caveat was entered a written application for extension.

(b) An application for extension as aforesaid must be lodged, or received by post, within the last month of the said period of six months, and the caveat shall thereupon (save as otherwise provided by this rule) be effective for an additional period of six months from the date on which it was due to expire.

(c) A caveat which has been extended as above may be further extended by the filing of a further application for extension subject to the same conditions as set out in sub-paragraph (b) above.

[(4) An index of caveats entered in any registry or sub-registry shall be maintained and upon receipt of an application for a grant, the registry or sub-registry at which the application is made shall cause a search of the index to be made and the appropriate district judge or registrar shall be notified of the entry of a caveat against the sealing of a grant for which the application has been made.]

(5) Any person claiming to have an interest in the estate may cause to be issued from the [nominated registry] a warning in Form 4 against the caveat, and the person warning shall state his interest in the estate of the deceased and shall require the caveator to give particulars of any contrary interest in the estate; and the warning or a copy thereof shall be served on the caveator forthwith.

(6) A caveator who has no interest contrary to that of the person warning, but who wishes to show cause against the sealing of a grant to that person, may within eight days of service of the warning upon him (inclusive of the day of such service), or at any time thereafter if no affidavit has been filed under paragraph (12) below, issue and serve a summons for directions.

(7) On the hearing of any summons for directions under paragraph (6) above the [district judge or] registrar may give a direction for the caveat to cease to have effect.

(8) Any caveat in force when a summons for directions is issued shall remain in force until the summons has been disposed of unless a direction has been given under paragraph (7) above [or until it is withdrawn under paragraph (11) below].

(9) The issue of a summons under this rule shall be notified forthwith to the [nominated registry].

(10) A caveator having an interest contrary to that of the person warning may within eight days of service of the warning upon him (inclusive of the day of such service) or at any time thereafter if no affidavit has been filed under paragraph (12) below, enter an appearance in the [nominated registry] by filing Form 5 . . . ; and he shall serve forthwith on the person warning a copy of Form 5 sealed with the seal of the court.

(11) A caveator who has not entered an appearance to a warning may at any time withdraw his caveat by giving notice at the registry or sub-registry at which it was entered, and the caveat shall thereupon cease to have effect; and, where the caveat has been so withdrawn, the caveator shall forthwith give notice of withdrawal to the person warning.

(12) If no appearance has been entered by the caveator or no summons has been issued by him under paragraph (6) of this rule, the person warning may at any time after eight days of service of the warning upon the caveator (inclusive of the day of such service) file an affidavit in the [nominated registry] as to such service and the caveat shall thereupon cease to have effect provided that there is no pending summons under paragraph (6) of this rule.

(13) Unless a [district judge or, where application to discontinue a caveat is made by consent, a registrar] by order made on summons otherwise directs, any caveat in respect of which an appearance to a warning has been entered shall remain in force until the commencement of a probate action.

(14) Except with the leave of a [district judge], no further caveat may be entered by or on behalf of any caveator whose caveat is either in force or has ceased to have effect under paragraphs (7) or (12) of this rule or under rule 45(4) or rule 46(3).

[(15) In this rule, "nominated registry" means the registry nominated for the purpose of this rule by the senior district judge or in the absence of any such nomination the Leeds District Probate Registry.]

Amendment

Para (1): words "district judge or" in square brackets inserted by SI 1991/1876, r 7(1).
Para (2): words "or probate practitioner" in square brackets inserted by SI 1998/1903, r 6.

Para (3): in sub-para (a) words "or probate practitioner" in square brackets inserted by SI 1998/1903, r 6.
Para (4): substituted by SI 1998/1903, r 11(1).
Para (5): words "nominated registry" in square brackets substituted by SI 1998/1903, r 11(2).
Para (7): words "district judge or" in square brackets inserted by SI 1991/1876, r 7(1).
Para (8): words in square brackets inserted by SI 1991/1876, r 12(1).
Para (9): words "nominated registry" in square brackets substituted by SI 1998/1903, r 11(2).
Para (10): words "nominated registry" in square brackets substituted by SI 1998/1903, r 11(2).
Para (10): words omitted revoked by SI 1991/1876, r 12(2).
Para (12): words "nominated registry" in square brackets substituted by SI 1998/1903, r 11(2).
Para (13): words in square brackets substituted by SI 1991/1876, rr 7(3), 12(3).
Para (14): words in square brackets substituted by SI 1991/1876, r 7(3).
Para (15): inserted by SI 1998/1903, r 11(3).

Modification

References to solicitors etc modified to include references to bodies recognised under the Administration of Justice Act 1985, s 9, by the Solicitors' Incorporated Practices Order 1991, SI 1991/2684, arts 4, 5, Sch 1.

45 Probate actions

(1) Upon being advised by the court concerned of the commencement of a probate action the [senior district judge] shall give notice of the action to every caveator other than the plaintiff in the action in respect of each caveat that is in force.

(2) In respect of any caveat entered subsequent to the commencement of a probate action the [senior district judge] shall give notice to that caveator of the existence of the action.

(3) Unless a [district judge] by order made on summons otherwise directs, the commencement of a probate action shall operate to prevent the sealing of a grant (other than a grant under section 117 of the Act) until application for a grant is made by the person shown to be entitled thereto by the decision of the court in such action.

(4) Upon such application for a grant, any caveat entered by the plaintiff in the action, and any caveat in respect of which notice of the action has been given, shall cease to have effect.

Amendment

Paras (1), (2): words in square brackets substituted by SI 1991/1876, r 7(4).
Para (3): words in square brackets substituted by SI 1991/1876, r 7(3).

46 Citations

(1) Any citation may issue from the Principal Registry or a district probate registry and shall be settled by a [district judge or] registrar before being issued.

(2) Every averment in a citation, and such other information as the registrar may require, shall be verified by an affidavit sworn by the person issuing the citation (in these Rules called the "citor"), provided that the [district judge or] registrar may in special circumstances accept an affidavit sworn by the citor's solicitor [or probate practitioner].

(3) The citor shall enter a caveat before issuing a citation and, unless a [district judge] by order made on summons otherwise directs, any caveat in force at the commencement of the citation proceedings shall, unless withdrawn pursuant to paragraph (11) of rule 44, remain in force until application for a grant is made by the person shown to be entitled thereto by the decision of the court in such proceedings, and upon such application any caveat entered by a party who had notice of the proceedings shall cease to have effect.

(4) Every citation shall be served personally on the person cited unless the [district judge or] registrar, on cause shown by affidavit, directs some other mode of service, which may include notice by advertisement.

(5) Every will referred to in a citation shall be lodged in a registry before the citation is issued, except where the will is not in the citor's possession and the [district judge or] registrar is satisfied that it is impracticable to require it to be lodged.

(6) A person who has been cited to appear may, within eight days of service of the citation upon him (inclusive of the day of such service), or at any time thereafter if no application has been made by the citor under paragraph (5) of rule 47 or paragraph (2) of rule 48, enter an appearance in the registry from which the citation issued by filing Form 5 and shall forthwith thereafter serve on the citor a copy of Form 5 sealed with the seal of the registry.

Amendment

Para (1): words "district judge or" in square brackets inserted by SI 1991/1876, r 7(1).
Para (2): words "district judge or" in square brackets inserted by SI 1991/1876, r 7(1).
Para (2): words "or probate practitioner" in square brackets inserted by SI 1998/1903, r 6.
Para (3): words in square brackets substituted by SI 1991/1876, r 7(3).
Para (4): words "district judge or" in square brackets inserted by SI 1991/1876, r 7(1).
Para (5): words "district judge or" in square brackets inserted by SI 1991/1876, r 7(1).

47 Citation to accept or refuse or to take a grant

(1) A citation to accept or refuse a grant may be issued at the instance of any person who would himself be entitled to a grant in the event of the person cited renouncing his right thereto.

(2) Where power to make a grant to an executor has been reserved, a citation calling on him to accept or refuse a grant may be issued at the instance of the executors who have proved the will or the survivor of them or of the executors of the last survivor of deceased executors who have proved.

(3) A citation calling on an executor who has intermeddled in the estate of the deceased to show cause why he should not be ordered to take a grant may be issued at the instance of any person interested in the estate at any time after the expiration of six months from the death of the deceased, provided that no citation to take a grant shall issue while proceedings as to the validity of the will are pending.

(4) A person cited who is willing to accept or take a grant may, after entering an appearance, apply ex parte by affidavit to a [district judge or] registrar for an order for a grant to himself.

(5) If the time limited for appearance has expired and the person cited has not entered an appearance, the citor may—

(a) in the case of a citation under paragraph (1) of this rule, apply to a [district judge or] registrar for an order for a grant to himself;

(b) in the case of a citation under paragraph (2) of this rule, apply to a [district judge or] registrar for an order that a note be made on the grant that the executor in respect of whom power was reserved has been duly cited and has not appeared and that all his rights in respect of the executorship have wholly ceased; or

(c) in the case of a citation under paragraph (3) of this rule, apply to a [district judge or] registrar by summons (which shall be served on the person cited) for an order requiring such person to take a grant within a specified time or for a grant to himself or to some other person specified in the summons.

(6) An application under the last foregoing paragraph shall be supported by an affidavit showing that the citation was duly served.

(7) If the person cited has entered an appearance but has not applied for a grant under paragraph (4) of this rule, or has failed to prosecute his application with reasonable diligence, the citor may—

(a) in the case of a citation under paragraph (1) of this rule, apply by summons to a [district judge or] registrar for an order for a grant to himself;

(b) in the case of a citation under paragraph (2) of this rule, apply by summons to a [district judge or] registrar for an order striking out the appearance and for the endorsement on the grant of such a note as is mentioned in sub-paragraph (b) of paragraph (5) of this rule; or

(c) in the case of a citation under paragraph (3) of this rule, apply by summons to a [district judge or] registrar for an order requiring the person cited to take a grant within a specified time or for a grant to himself or to some other person specified in the summons;

and the summons shall be served on the person cited.

Amendment

Paras (4), (5), (7): words in square brackets inserted by SI 1991/1876, r 7(1).

48 Citation to propound a will

(1) A citation to propound a will shall be directed to the executors named in the will and to all persons interested thereunder, and may be issued at the instance of any citor having an interest contrary to that of the executors or such other persons.

(2) If the time limited for appearance has expired, the citor may—

(a) in the case where no person has entered an appearance, apply to a [district judge or] registrar for an order for a grant as if the will were invalid and such application shall be supported by an affidavit showing that the citation was duly served; or

(b) in the case where no person who has entered an appearance proceeds with reasonable diligence to propound the will, apply to a [district judge or] registrar by summons, which shall be served on every person cited who has entered an appearance, for such an order as is mentioned in paragraph (a) above.

Amendment
Para (2): words in square brackets inserted by SI 1991/1876, r 7(1).

49 Address for service

All caveats, citations, warnings and appearances shall contain an address for service in England and Wales.

50 Application for order to attend for examination or for subpoena to bring in a will

(1) An application under section 122 of the Act for an order requiring a person to attend for examination may, unless a probate action has been commenced, be made to a [district judge or] registrar by summons which shall be served on every such person as aforesaid.

(2) An application under section 123 of the Act for the issue by a [district judge or] registrar of a subpoena to bring in a will shall be supported by an affidavit setting out the grounds of the application, and if any person served with the subpoena denies that the will is in his possession or control he may file an affidavit to that effect in the registry from which the subpoena issued.

Amendment
Words in square brackets inserted by SI 1991/1876, r 7(1).

51 Grants to part of an estate under section 113 of the Act

An application for an order for a grant under section 113 of the Act to part of an estate may be made to a [district judge or] registrar, and shall be supported by an affidavit setting out the grounds of the application, and

(a) stating whether the estate of the deceased is known to be insolvent; and

(b) showing how any person entitled to a grant in respect of the whole estate in priority to the applicant has been cleared off.

Amendment
Words in square brackets inserted by SI 1991/1876, r 7(1).

52 Grants of administration under discretionary powers of court, and grants ad colligenda bona

An application for an order for—

(a) a grant of administration under section 116 of the Act; or

(b) a grant of administration ad colligenda bona,

may be made to a [district judge or] registrar and shall be supported by an affidavit setting out the grounds of the application.

Amendment
Words in square brackets inserted by SI 1991/1876, r 7(1).

53 Applications for leave to swear to death

An application for leave to swear to the death of a person in whose estate a grant is sought may be made to a [district judge or] registrar, and shall be supported by an affidavit setting out the grounds of the application and containing particulars of any policies of insurance effected on the life of the presumed deceased together with such further evidence as the [district judge or] registrar may require.

Amendment
Words in square brackets inserted by SI 1991/1876, r 7(1).

54 Grants in respect of nuncupative wills and copies of wills

(1) Subject to paragraph (2) below, an application for an order admitting to proof a nuncupative will, or a will contained in a copy or reconstruction thereof where the original is not available, shall be made to a [district judge or] registrar.

(2) In any case where a will is not available owing to its being retained in the custody of a foreign court or official, a duly authenticated copy of the will may be admitted to proof without the order referred to in paragraph (1) above.

(3) An application under paragraph (1) above shall be supported by an affidavit setting out the grounds of the application, and by such evidence on affidavit as the applicant can adduce as to—

- (a) the will's existence after the death of the testator or, where there is no such evidence, the facts on which the applicant relies to rebut the presumption that the will has been revoked by destruction;
- (b) in respect of a nuncupative will, the contents of that will; and
- (c) in respect of a reconstruction of a will, the accuracy of that reconstruction.

(4) The [district judge or] registrar may require additional evidence in the circumstances of a particular case as to due execution of the will or as to the accuracy of the copy will, and may direct that notice be given to persons who would be prejudiced by the application.

Amendment
Paras (1), (4): words in square brackets inserted by SI 1991/1876, r 7(1).

55 Application for rectification of a will

(1) An application for an order that a will be rectified by virtue of section 20(1) of the Administration of Justice Act 1982 may be made to a [district judge or] registrar, unless a probate action has been commenced.

(2) The application shall be supported by an affidavit, setting out the grounds of the application, together with such evidence as can be adduced as to the testator's intentions and as to whichever of the following matters as are in issue—

- (a) in what respects the testator's intentions were not understood; or
- (b) the nature of any alleged clerical error.

(3) Unless otherwise directed, notice of the application shall be given to every person having an interest under the will whose interest might be prejudiced[, or such other person who might be prejudiced,] by the rectification applied for and any comments in writing by any such person shall be exhibited to the affidavit in support of the application.

(4) If the [district judge or] registrar is satisfied that, subject to any direction to the contrary, notice has been given to every person mentioned in paragraph (3) above, and that the application is unopposed, he may order that the will be rectified accordingly.

Amendment
Paras (1), (4): words in square brackets inserted by SI 1991/1876, r 7(1).
Para (3): words ", or such other person who might be prejudiced," in square brackets inserted by SI 1998/1903, r 12.

56 Notice of election by surviving spouse [or civil partner] to redeem life interest

(1) Where a surviving spouse [or civil partner] who is the sole or sole surviving personal representative of the deceased is entitled to a life interest in part of the residuary estate and elects under section 47A of the Administration of Estates Act 1925 to have the life interest redeemed, he may give written notice of the election to the [senior district judge] in pursuance of subsection (7) of that section by filing a notice in Form 6 in the Principal Registry or in the district probate registry from which the grant issued.

(2) Where the grant issued from a district probate registry, the notice shall be filed in duplicate.

(3) A notice filed under this rule shall be noted on the grant and the record and shall be open to inspection.

Amendment
Provision heading: words "or civil partner" in square brackets inserted by SI 2005/2114, art 2(6), Sch 6, para 2(1), (4).

Para (1): words "or civil partner" in square brackets inserted by SI 2005/2114, art 2(6), Sch 6, para 2(1), (4).
Para (1): words "senior district judge" in square brackets substituted by SI 1991/1876, r 7(4).

[57 Index of grant applications]

[(1) The senior district judge shall maintain an index of every pending application for a grant made in any registry or sub-registry.

(2) Every registry or sub-registry in which an application is made shall cause the index to be searched and shall record the result of the search.]

Amendment
Substituted by SI 1998/1903, r 13.

58 Inspection of copies of original wills and other documents

An original will or other document referred to in section 124 of the Act shall not be open to inspection if, in the opinion of a [district judge or] registrar, such inspection would be undesirable or otherwise inappropriate.

Amendment
Words in square brackets inserted by SI 1991/1876, r 7(1).

59 Issue of copies of original wills and other documents

Where copies are required of original wills or other documents deposited under section 124 of the Act, such copies may be facsimile copies sealed with the seal of the court and issued either as office copies or certified under the hand of a [district judge or] registrar to be true copies.

Amendment
Words in square brackets inserted by SI 1991/1876, r 7(1).

[60 Costs]

[(1) Order 62 of the Rules of the Supreme Court 1965 shall not apply to costs in non-contentious probate matters, and Parts 43, 44 (except rules 44.9 to 44.12), 47 and 48 of the Civil Procedure Rules 1998 ("the 1998 Rules") shall apply to costs in those matters, with the modifications contained in paragraphs (3) to (7) of this rule.

(2) Where detailed assessment of a bill of costs is ordered, it shall be referred—

- (a) where the order was made by a district judge, to a district judge, a costs judge or an authorised court officer within rule 43.2(1)(d)(iii) or (iv) of the 1998 Rules;
- (b) where the order was made by a registrar, to that registrar or, where this is not possible, in accordance with sub-paragraph (a) above.

(3) Every reference in Parts 43, 44, 47 and 48 of the 1998 Rules to a district judge shall be construed as referring only to a district judge of the Principal Registry.

(4) The definition of "costs officer" in rule 43.2(1)(c) of the 1998 Rules shall have effect as if it included a paragraph reading—

"(iv) a district probate registrar."

(5) The definition of "authorised court officer" in rule 43.2(1)(d) of the 1998 Rules shall have effect as if paragraphs (i) and (ii) were omitted.

(6) Rule 44.3(2) of the 1998 Rules (costs follow the event) shall not apply.

(7) Rule 47.4(2) of the 1998 Rules shall apply as if after the words "Supreme Court Costs Office" there were inserted ", the Principal Registry of the Family Division or such district probate registry as the court may specify".

(8) Except in the case of an appeal against a decision of an authorised court officer (to which rules 47.20 to 47.23 of the 1998 Rules apply), an appeal against a decision in assessment proceedings relating to costs in non-contentious probate matters shall be dealt with in accordance with the following paragraphs of this rule.

(9) An appeal within paragraph (8) above against a decision made by a district judge, a costs judge (as defined by rule 43.2(1)(b) of the 1998 Rules) or a registrar, shall lie to a judge of the High Court.

(10) Part 52 of the 1998 Rules applies to every appeal within paragraph (8) above, and any reference in Part 52 to a judge or a district judge shall be taken to include a district judge of the Principal Registry of the Family Division.

(11) The 1998 Rules shall apply to an appeal to which Part 52 or rules 47.20 to 47.23 of those Rules apply in accordance with paragraph (8) above in the same way as they apply to any other appeal within Part 52 or rules 47.20 to 47.23 of those Rules as the case may be; accordingly the Rules of the Supreme Court 1965 and the County Court Rules 1981 shall not apply to any such appeal.]

Amendment
Substituted by SI 1991/1876, r 13.
Substituted by SI 2003/185, rr 4, 5.

61 Power to require applications to be made by summons

(1) [Subject to rule 7(2),] a [district judge or] registrar may require any application to be made by summons to a [district judge or] registrar in chambers or a judge in chambers or open court.

(2) An application for an inventory and account shall be made by summons to a [district judge or] registrar.

(3) A summons for hearing by a [district judge or] registrar shall be issued out of the registry in which it is to be heard.

(4) A summons to be heard by a judge shall be issued out of the Principal Registry.

Amendment
Paras (1)–(3): words in square brackets inserted by SI 1991/1876, rr 7(1), 14.

62 Transfer of applications

A registrar to whom any application is made under these Rules may order the transfer of the application to another [district judge or] registrar having jurisdiction.

Amendment
Words in square brackets inserted by SI 1991/1876, r 7(1).

[62A Exercise of a registrar's jurisdiction by another registrar]

[A registrar may hear and dispose of an application under these Rules on behalf of any other registrar by whom the application would otherwise have been heard, if that other registrar so requests or an application in that behalf is made by a party making an application under these Rules; and where the circumstances require it, the registrar shall, without the need for any such request or application, hear and dispose of the application.]

Amendment
Inserted by SI 1998/1903, r 14.

63 Power to make orders for costs

On any application dealt with by him on summons, the . . . registrar shall have full power to determine by whom and to what extent the costs are to be paid.

Amendment
Words omitted revoked by SI 1991/1876, r 7(2).

64 Exercise of powers of judge during Long Vacation

All powers exercisable under these Rules by a judge in chambers may be exercised during the Long Vacation by a [district judge].

Amendment
Words in square brackets substituted by SI 1991/1876, r 7(3).

65 Appeals from [district judges or] registrars

(1) An appeal against a decision or requirement of a [district judge or] registrar shall be made by summons to a judge.

(2) If, in the case of an appeal under the last foregoing paragraph, any person besides the appellant appeared or was represented before the [district judge or] registrar from whose decision

or requirement the appeal is brought, the summons shall be issued within seven days thereof for hearing on the first available day and shall be served on every such person as aforesaid.

[(3) This rule does not apply to an appeal against a decision in proceedings for the assessment of costs.]

Amendment

Para (1): words "district judge or" in square brackets inserted by SI 1991/1876, r 7(1), (6).
Para (2): words "district judge or" in square brackets inserted by SI 1991/1876, r 7(1), (6).
Para (3): inserted by SI 2003/185, r 6.

66 Service of summons

(1) A judge or [district judge] or, where the application is to be made to a district probate registrar, that registrar, may direct that a summons for the service of which no other provision is made by these Rules shall be served on such person or persons as the [judge, district judge or registrar] [may direct].

(2) Where by these Rules or by any direction given under the last foregoing paragraph a summons is required to be served on any person, it shall be served not less than two clear days before the day appointed for the hearing, unless a judge or [district judge or] registrar at or before the hearing dispenses with service on such terms, if any, as he may think fit.

Amendment

Para (1): words "district judge" in square brackets substituted by SI 1991/1876, r 7(3).
Para (1): words "judge, district judge or registrar" in square brackets substituted by SI 1998/1903, r 15.
Para (1): words "may direct" in square brackets substituted by SI 1991/1876, r 7(7).
Para (2): words "district judge or" in square brackets inserted by SI 1991/1876, r 7(1).

67 Notices, etc

Unless a [district judge or] registrar otherwise directs or these Rules otherwise provide, any notice or other document required to be given to or served on any person may be given or served in the manner prescribed by Order 65 Rule 5 of the Rules of the Supreme Court 1965.

Amendment

Words in square brackets inserted by SI 1991/1876, r 7(1).

68 Application to pending proceedings

Subject in any particular case to any direction given by a judge or [district judge or] registrar, these Rules shall apply to any proceedings which are pending on the date on which they come into force as well as to any proceedings commenced on or after that date.

Amendment

Words in square brackets inserted by SI 1991/1876, r 7(1).

69 Revocation of previous rules

(1) Subject to paragraph (2) below, the rules set out in the Second Schedule are hereby revoked.

(2) The rules set out in the Second Schedule shall continue to apply to such extent as may be necessary for giving effect to a direction under rule 68.

SCHEDULE 1
FORMS

Rule 2(2)

FORM 1
CERTIFICATE OF DELIVERY OF INLAND REVENUE AFFIDAVIT

Rule 42

And it is hereby certified that an Inland Revenue affidavit has been delivered wherein it is shown that the gross value of the said estate in the United Kingdom (exclusive of what the said deceased may have been possessed of or entitled to as a trustee and not beneficially) amounts to £ . . . . and that the net value of the estate amounts to £ . . . .

And it is further certified that it appears by a receipt signed by an Inland Revenue officer on the said affidavit that £ .... on account of estate duty and interest on such day has been paid.

FORM 2
STANDING SEARCH

Rule 43(1)

In the High Court of Justice Family Division

[The Principal (or .... District Probate) Registry]

I/We apply for the entry of a standing search so that there shall be sent to me/us an office copy of every grant of representation in England and Wales in the estate of—

Full name of deceased: ....

Full address: ....

Alternative or alias names: ....

Exact date of death: ....

which either has issued not more than 12 months before the entry of this application or issues within 6 months thereafter.

Signed ....

Name in block letters ....

Full address ....

Reference No. (if any) ....

Amendment
Words in square brackets substituted by SI 1991/1876, r 11(3).

FORM 3
CAVEAT

Rule 44(2)

In the High Court of Justice Family Division

The Principal (*or* .... District Probate) Registry.

Let not grant be sealed in the estate of (*full name and address*) deceased, who died on the .... day of 19 .... without notice to (*name of party by whom or on whose behalf the caveat is entered*).

Dated this .... day of .... 19 ....

(*Signed*) .... (*to be signed by the caveator's solicitor* [*or probate practitioner*] *or by the caveator if acting in person*)

whose address for service is: ....

Solicitor[/probate practitioner] for the said .... (*If the caveator is acting in person, substitute "In person*".)

Amendment
Words "or probate practitioner" in square brackets inserted by SI 1998/1903, r 16(a).
Words "/probate practitioner" in square brackets inserted by SI 1998/1903, r 16(b).

FORM 4
WARNING TO CAVEATOR

Rule 44(5)

In the High Court of Justice Family Division

[(The nominated registry as defined by rule 44(15))]

To .... of .... a party who has entered a caveat in the estate of .... deceased.

You have eight days (starting with the day on which this warning was served on you):

(i) to enter an appearance either in person or by your solicitor [or probate practitioner], at the [(name and address of the nominated registry)] setting out what interest you have in the estate of the above-named . . . . of . . . . deceased contrary to that of the party at whose instance this warning is issued; or

(ii) if you have no contrary interest but wish to show cause against the sealing of a grant to such party, to issue and serve a summons for [directions by a district judge of the Principal Registry or a registrar of] a district probate registry.

If you fail to do either of these, the court may proceed to issue a grant of probate or administration in the said estate notwithstanding your caveat.

Dated this . . . . day of . . . . 19 . . . .

Issued at the instance of . . . .

(*Here set out the name and interest (including the date of the will, if any, under which the interest arises) of the party warning, the name of his solicitor* [*or probate practitioner*] *and the address for service. If the party warning is acting in person, this must be stated.*). . . . . Registrar

Amendment

Words "(The nominated registry as defined by rule 44(15))" in square brackets substituted by SI 1998/1903, r 17(b).
Words "or probate practitioner" in square brackets in both places they occur inserted by SI 1998/1903, r 17(a).
Words "(name and address of the nominated registry)" in square brackets substituted by SI 1998/1903, r 17(c).
Words from "directions by" to "a registrar of" in square brackets substituted by SI 1991/1876, r 7(8).

FORM 5
APPEARANCE TO WARNING OR CITATION

Rules 44(10), 46(6)

In the High Court of Justice Family Division

The Principal (*or* . . . . District Probate) Registry Caveat No . . . . dated the . . . . day of . . . . 19 . . . . (Citation dated the . . . . day of . . . . 19 . . . .)

Full name and address of deceased: . . . .

Full name and address of person warning (*or* citor): . . . .

(*Here set out the interest of the person warning, or citor, as shown in warning or citation.*)

Full name and address of caveator (or person cited).

(*Here set out the interest of the caveator or person cited, stating the date of the will (if any) under which such interest arises.*)

Enter an appearance for the above-named caveator (*or* person cited) in this matter.

Dated this . . . . day of . . . . 19 . . . .

(*Signed*) . . . .

whose address for service is: . . . .

. . . . Solicitor[/probate practitioner] (*or* In person).

Amendment

Words "/probate practitioner" in square brackets inserted by SI 1998/1903, r 18.

FORM 6
NOTICE OF ELECTION TO REDEEM LIFE INTEREST

Rule 56

In the High Court of Justice Family Division

The Principal (*or* .... District Probate) Registry

In the estate of .... deceased.

Whereas .... of .... died on the .... day of .... 19 .... wholly/ partially intestate leaving his/her/lawful wife/husband[/civil partner] and .... lawful issue of the said deceased;

And whereas Probate/Letters of Administration of the estate of the said .... were granted to me, the said .... (and to .... of ....) at the Probate Registry on the............ ....day of .... 19 ....;

And whereas (the said .... has ceased to be a personal representative because ....) and I am (now) the sole personal representative;

Now I, the said .... hereby given notice in accordance with section 47A of the Administration of Estates Act 1925 that I elect to redeem the life interest to which I am entitled in the estate of the late .... by retaining £ .... its capital value, and £ .... the costs of the transaction.

Dated this .... day of .... 19 ....

(Signed) ....

To the [senior district judge] of the Family Division.

Amendment

Words "/civil partner" in square brackets inserted by SI 2005/2114, art 2(6), Sch 6, para 2(1), (5).
Words "senior district judge" in square brackets substituted by SI 1991/1876, r 7(4).

SCHEDULE 2
REVOCATIONS

Rule 69

Rules revoked	*References*
The Non-Contentious Probate Rules 1954	SI 1954/796
The Non-Contentious Probate (Amendment) Rules 1961	SI 1961/72
The Non-Contentious Probate (Amendment) Rules 1962	SI 1962/2653
The Non-Contentious Probate (Amendment) Rules 1967	SI 1967/748
The Non-Contentious Probate (Amendment) Rules 1968	SI 1968/1675
The Non-Contentious Probate (Amendment) Rules 1969	SI 1969/1689
The Non-Contentious Probate (Amendment) Rules 1971	SI 1971/1977
The Non-Contentious Probate (Amendment) Rules 1974	SI 1974/597
The Non-Contentious Probate (Amendment) Rules 1976	SI 1976/1362
The Non-Contentious Probate (Amendment) Rules 1982	SI 1982/446
The Non-Contentious Probate (Amendment) Rules 1983	SI 1983/623
The Non-Contentious Probate (Amendment) Rules 1985	SI 1985/1232

APPENDIX VI

CIVIL PARTNERSHIP ACT 2004

2004 Chapter 33

PART 2
CIVIL PARTNERSHIP: ENGLAND AND WALES

Chapter 3
Property and Financial Arrangements

71 Wills, administration of estates and family provision

Schedule 4 amends enactments relating to wills, administration of estates and family provision so that they apply in relation to civil partnerships as they apply in relation to marriage.

PART 4
CIVIL PARTNERSHIP: NORTHERN IRELAND

Chapter 3
Property and Financial Arrangements

195 Wills, administration of estates and family provision

Schedule 14 amends enactments relating to wills, administration of estates and family provision so that they apply in relation to civil partnerships as they apply in relation to marriage.

SCHEDULE 4
WILLS, ADMINISTRATION OF ESTATES AND FAMILY PROVISION

Section 71

PART 1
WILLS

1 Amend the Wills Act 1837 (c 26) as follows.

2 After section 18A insert—

"18B Will to be revoked by civil partnership

(1) Subject to subsections (2) to (6), a will is revoked by the formation of a civil partnership between the testator and another person.

(2) A disposition in a will in exercise of a power of appointment takes effect despite the formation of a subsequent civil partnership between the testator and another person unless the property so appointed would in default of appointment pass to the testator's personal representatives.

(3) If it appears from a will—

- (a) that at the time it was made the testator was expecting to form a civil partnership with a particular person, and
- (b) that he intended that the will should not be revoked by the formation of the civil partnership,

the will is not revoked by its formation.

(4) Subsections (5) and (6) apply if it appears from a will—

- (a) that at the time it was made the testator was expecting to form a civil partnership with a particular person, and

(b) that he intended that a disposition in the will should not be revoked by the formation of the civil partnership.

(5) The disposition takes effect despite the formation of the civil partnership.

(6) Any other disposition in the will also takes effect, unless it appears from the will that the testator intended the disposition to be revoked by the formation of the civil partnership.

18C Effect of dissolution or annulment of civil partnership on wills

(1) This section applies if, after a testator has made a will—

(a) a court of civil jurisdiction in England and Wales dissolves his civil partnership or makes a nullity order in respect of it, or

(b) his civil partnership is dissolved or annulled and the dissolution or annulment is entitled to recognition in England and Wales by virtue of Chapter 3 of Part 5 of the Civil Partnership Act 2004.

(2) Except in so far as a contrary intention appears by the will—

(a) provisions of the will appointing executors or trustees or conferring a power of appointment, if they appoint or confer the power on the former civil partner, take effect as if the former civil partner had died on the date on which the civil partnership is dissolved or annulled, and

(b) any property which, or an interest in which, is devised or bequeathed to the former civil partner shall pass as if the former civil partner had died on that date.

(3) Subsection (2)(b) does not affect any right of the former civil partner to apply for financial provision under the Inheritance (Provision for Family and Dependants) Act 1975."

3 The following provisions—

(a) section 15 of the Wills Act 1837 (c 26) (avoidance of gifts to attesting witnesses and their spouses), and

(b) section 1 of the Wills Act 1968 (c 28) (restriction of operation of section 15),

apply in relation to the attestation of a will by a person to whose civil partner there is given or made any such disposition as is described in section 15 of the 1837 Act as they apply in relation to a person to whose spouse there is given or made any such disposition.

4 In section 16 of the 1837 Act, after "wife or husband" insert "or civil partner".

5 Except where a contrary intention is shown, it is presumed that if a testator—

(a) devises or bequeaths property to his civil partner in terms which in themselves would give an absolute interest to the civil partner, but

(b) by the same instrument purports to give his issue an interest in the same property,

the gift to the civil partner is absolute despite the purported gift to the issue.

PART 2
ADMINISTRATION OF ESTATES AND FAMILY PROVISION

PUBLIC TRUSTEE ACT 1906 (C 55)

6 In section 6(1), after "widower, widow" (in both places) insert ", surviving civil partner".

ADMINISTRATION OF ESTATES ACT 1925 (C 23)

7 In section 46 (succession to real and personal estate on intestacy), for "husband or wife" (in each place) substitute "spouse or civil partner".

8 (1) Amend section 47(1) (meaning of "the statutory trusts") as follows.

(2) In paragraph (i), after "or marry under that age" (in the first place) insert "or form a civil partnership under that age".

(3) In that paragraph, after "or marry" (in the second place) insert ", or form a civil partnership,".

(4) In paragraph (ii), after "marries" insert ", or forms a civil partnership,".

9 In section 47A, in subsection (1) and in the proviso to subsection (5), for "husband or wife" substitute "spouse or civil partner".

10 In section 48(2), for "husband or wife" (in each place) substitute "spouse or civil partner".

11 In section 51(3) (devolution of certain estates vested in infant who dies without having married and without issue), after "without having been married" insert "or having formed a civil partnership,".

12 In section 55(1)(xviii) (which defines "valuable consideration" as including marriage), after "includes marriage," insert "and formation of a civil partnership,".

INTESTATES' ESTATES ACT 1952 (C 64)

13 (1) Amend section 5 and Schedule 2 (rights of surviving spouse as respects the matrimonial home) as follows.

(2) For "husband or wife" (in each place) substitute "spouse or civil partner".

(3) In section 5, after "matrimonial" insert "or civil partnership".

(4) In the heading of each—

(a) after "spouse" insert "or civil partner", and

(b) after "matrimonial" insert "or civil partnership".

FAMILY PROVISION ACT 1966 (C 35)

14 In section 1(1) (fixed net sum payable to surviving spouse of person dying intestate), for "husband or wife" substitute "spouse or civil partner".

INHERITANCE (PROVISION FOR FAMILY AND DEPENDANTS) ACT 1975 (C 63)

15 (1) Amend section 1 (application for financial provision from deceased person's estate) as follows.

(2) For subsection (1)(a) and (b) (application may be made by spouse or by former spouse who has not remarried) substitute—

"(a) the spouse or civil partner of the deceased;

(b) a former spouse or former civil partner of the deceased, but not one who has formed a subsequent marriage or civil partnership;".

(3) In subsection (1)(ba) (application may be made by person living as husband or wife of the deceased), after "subsection (1A)" insert "or (1B)".

(4) In subsection (1)(d) (application may be made by child of the family), after "marriage" (in each place) insert "or civil partnership".

(5) After subsection (1A) insert—

"(1B) This subsection applies to a person if for the whole of the period of two years ending immediately before the date when the deceased died the person was living—

(a) in the same household as the deceased, and

(b) as the civil partner of the deceased."

(6) In subsection (2) (meaning of "reasonable financial provision"), after paragraph (a) insert—

"(aa) in the case of an application made by virtue of subsection (1)(a) above by the civil partner of the deceased (except where, at the date of death, a separation order under Chapter 2 of Part 2 of the Civil Partnership Act 2004 was in force in relation to the civil partnership and the separation was continuing), means such financial provision as it would be reasonable in all the circumstances of the case for a civil partner to receive, whether or not that provision is required for his or her maintenance;".

16 In section 2(1) (orders which may be made on an application), after paragraph (f) insert—

"(g) an order varying any settlement made—

(i) during the subsistence of a civil partnership formed by the deceased, or

(ii) in anticipation of the formation of a civil partnership by the deceased,

on the civil partners (including such a settlement made by will), the variation being for the benefit of the surviving civil partner, or any child of both the civil partners, or any person who was treated by the deceased as a child of the family in relation to that civil partnership."

17 (1) Amend section 3(2) (application by spouse or former spouse: matters to which court is to have regard) as follows.

(2) For the words from the beginning to "1(1)(b) of this Act" substitute—

"This subsection applies, without prejudice to the generality of paragraph (g) of subsection (1) above, where an application for an order under section 2 of this Act is made by virtue of section 1(1)(a) or (b) of this Act."

(3) The words from "the court shall, in addition" to the end of paragraph (b) shall become a second sentence of the subsection and, in paragraph (a) of the sentence so formed, after "duration of the marriage" insert "or civil partnership".

(4) The words from "in the case of an application by the wife or husband" to the end shall become a third sentence of the subsection.

(5) At the end insert the following sentence—

"In the case of an application by the civil partner of the deceased, the court shall also, unless at the date of the death a separation order under Chapter 2 of Part 2 of the Civil Partnership Act 2004 was in force and the separation was continuing, have regard to the provision which the applicant might reasonably have expected to receive if on the day on which the deceased died the civil partnership, instead of being terminated by death, had been terminated by a dissolution order."

18 In section 3(2A) (application by person living as husband or wife of deceased: matters to which court is to have regard), in paragraph (a), after "wife" insert "or civil partner".

19 In section 6(3) and (10) (variation etc of orders which cease on occurrence of specified event other than remarriage of former spouse), for " (other than the remarriage of a former wife or former husband)" substitute "(other than the formation of a subsequent marriage or civil partnership by a former spouse or former civil partner)".

20 After section 14 insert—

"14A Provision as to cases where no financial relief was granted in proceedings for the dissolution etc of a civil partnership

(1) Subsection (2) below applies where—

(a) a dissolution order, nullity order, separation order or presumption of death order has been made under Chapter 2 of Part 2 of the Civil Partnership Act 2004 in relation to a civil partnership,

(b) one of the civil partners dies within twelve months from the date on which the order is made, and

(c) either—

(i) an application for a financial provision order under Part 1 of Schedule 5 to that Act or a property adjustment order under Part 2 of that Schedule has not been made by the other civil partner, or

(ii) such an application has been made but the proceedings on the application have not been determined at the time of the death of the deceased.

(2) If an application for an order under section 2 of this Act is made by the surviving civil partner, the court shall, notwithstanding anything in section 1 or section 3 of this Act, have power, if it thinks it just to do so, to treat the surviving civil partner as if the order mentioned in subsection (1)(a) above had not been made.

(3) This section shall not apply in relation to a separation order unless at the date of the death of the deceased the separation order was in force and the separation was continuing."

21 After section 15 insert—

"15ZA Restriction imposed in proceedings for the dissolution etc of a civil partnership on application under this Act

(1) On making a dissolution order, nullity order, separation order or presumption of death order under Chapter 2 of Part 2 of the Civil Partnership Act 2004, or at any time after making

such an order, the court, if it considers it just to do so, may, on the application of either of the civil partners, order that the other civil partner shall not on the death of the applicant be entitled to apply for an order under section 2 of this Act.

(2) In subsection (1) above "the court" means the High Court or, where a county court has jurisdiction by virtue of Part 5 of the Matrimonial and Family Proceedings Act 1984, a county court.

(3) In the case of a dissolution order, nullity order or presumption of death order ("the main order") an order may be made under subsection (1) above before (as well as after) the main order is made final, but if made before the main order is made final it shall not take effect unless the main order is made final.

(4) Where an order under subsection (1) above made in connection with a dissolution order, nullity order or presumption of death order has come into force with respect to a civil partner, then, on the death of the other civil partner, the court shall not entertain any application for an order under section 2 of this Act made by the surviving civil partner.

(5) Where an order under subsection (1) above made in connection with a separation order has come into force with respect to a civil partner, then, if the other civil partner dies while the separation order is in force and the separation is continuing, the court shall not entertain any application for an order under section 2 of this Act made by the surviving civil partner."

22 After section 15A insert—

"15B Restriction imposed in proceedings under Schedule 7 to the Civil Partnership Act 2004 on application under this Act

(1) On making an order under paragraph 9 of Schedule 7 to the Civil Partnership Act 2004 (orders for financial provision, property adjustment and pension-sharing following overseas dissolution etc of civil partnership) the court, if it considers it just to do so, may, on the application of either of the civil partners, order that the other civil partner shall not on the death of the applicant be entitled to apply for an order under section 2 of this Act.

(2) In subsection (1) above "the court" means the High Court or, where a county court has jurisdiction by virtue of Part 5 of the Matrimonial and Family Proceedings Act 1984, a county court.

(3) Where an order under subsection (1) above has been made with respect to one of the civil partners in a case where a civil partnership has been dissolved or annulled, then, on the death of the other civil partner, the court shall not entertain an application under section 2 of this Act made by the surviving civil partner.

(4) Where an order under subsection (1) above has been made with respect to one of the civil partners in a case where civil partners have been legally separated, then, if the other civil partner dies while the legal separation is in force, the court shall not entertain an application under section 2 of this Act made by the surviving civil partner."

23 In section 16(1) (power to vary secured periodical payments orders)—

(a) after "the Matrimonial Causes Act 1973" insert "or Schedule 5 to the Civil Partnership Act 2004", and
(b) after "that Act" insert "of 1973 or Part 11 of that Schedule".

24 In section 17(4) (meaning of "maintenance agreement")—

(a) for "entered into a marriage" substitute "formed a marriage or civil partnership",
(b) after "of the parties to that marriage" insert "or of the civil partners", and
(c) after "marriage" (in the third and fourth places) insert "or civil partnership".

25 After section 18 insert—

"18A Availability of court's powers under this Act in applications under paragraphs 60 and 73 of Schedule 5 to the Civil Partnership Act 2004

(1) Where—

(a) a person against whom a secured periodical payments order was made under Schedule 5 to the Civil Partnership Act 2004 has died and an application is made under paragraph 60 of that Schedule for the variation or discharge of that order or for the revival of the operation of any suspended provision of the order, or

(b) a party to a maintenance agreement within the meaning of Part 13 of that Schedule has died, the agreement being one which provides for the continuation of payments under the agreement after the death of one of the parties, and an application is made under paragraph 73 of that Schedule for the alteration of the agreement under paragraph 69 of that Schedule,

the court shall have power to direct that the application made under paragraph 60 or 73 of that Schedule shall be deemed to have been accompanied by an application for an order under section 2 of this Act.

(2) Where the court gives a direction under subsection (1) above it shall have power, in the proceedings on the application under paragraph 60 or 73 of that Schedule, to make any order which the court would have had power to make under the provisions of this Act if the application under that paragraph had been made jointly with an application for an order under section 2 of this Act; and the court shall have power to give such consequential directions as may be necessary for enabling the court to exercise any of the powers available to the court under this Act in the case of an application for an order under section 2.

(3) Where an order made under section 15ZA(1) of this Act is in force with respect to a civil partner, the court shall not give a direction under subsection (1) above with respect to any application made under paragraph 60 or 73 of that Schedule by that civil partner on the death of the other civil partner."

26 (1) Amend section 19 (effect, duration and form of orders) as follows.

(2) In subsection (2)(a), for "former husband or former wife" substitute "former spouse or former civil partner".

(3) In subsection (2), after paragraph (b) insert

"or

(c) an applicant who was the civil partner of the deceased in a case where, at the date of death, a separation order under Chapter 2 of Part 2 of the Civil Partnership Act 2004 was in force in relation to their civil partnership and the separation was continuing,".

(4) In that subsection, in the words after paragraph (b), for "on the remarriage of the applicant" onwards substitute "on the formation by the applicant of a subsequent marriage or civil partnership, except in relation to any arrears due under the order on the date of the formation of the subsequent marriage or civil partnership."

(5) In subsection (3), after "section 15(1)" insert "or 15ZA(1)".

27 (1) Amend section 25 (interpretation) as follows.

(2) In subsection (1), in the definition of "former wife" and "former husband", for ""former wife" or "former husband"" substitute ""former spouse"".

(3) In that subsection, before that definition insert—

""former civil partner" means a person whose civil partnership with the deceased was during the lifetime of the deceased either—

(a) dissolved or annulled by an order made under the law of any part of the British Islands, or

(b) dissolved or annulled in any country or territory outside the British Islands by a dissolution or annulment which is entitled to be recognised as valid by the law of England and Wales;".

(4) In subsection (4)—

(a) before "wife" insert "spouse," and

(b) in paragraph (b), for "entered into a later marriage" substitute "formed a subsequent marriage or civil partnership".

(5) For subsection (5) substitute—

"(4A) For the purposes of this Act any reference to a civil partner shall be treated as including a reference to a person who in good faith formed a void civil partnership with the deceased unless either—

(a) the civil partnership between the deceased and that person was dissolved or annulled during the lifetime of the deceased and the dissolution or annulment is recognised by the law of England and Wales, or

(b) that person has during the lifetime of the deceased formed a subsequent civil partnership or marriage.

(5) Any reference in this Act to the formation of, or to a person who has formed, a subsequent marriage or civil partnership includes (as the case may be) a reference to the formation of, or to a person who has formed, a marriage or civil partnership which is by law void or voidable.

(5A) The formation of a marriage or civil partnership shall be treated for the purposes of this Act as the formation of a subsequent marriage or civil partnership, in relation to either of the spouses or civil partners, notwithstanding that the previous marriage or civil partnership of that spouse or civil partner was void or voidable."

(6) After subsection (6) insert—

"(6A) Any reference in this Act to an order made under, or under any provision of, the Civil Partnership Act 2004 shall be construed as including a reference to anything which is deemed to be an order made (as the case may be) under that Act or provision."

SCHEDULE 14
WILLS, ADMINISTRATION OF ESTATES AND FAMILY PROVISION: NORTHERN IRELAND

Section 195

PART 1
WILLS

1 Amend the Wills and Administration Proceedings (Northern Ireland) Order 1994 (SI 1994/1899 (NI 13)) as follows.

2 In Article 4(1) (will made by person under 18 invalid unless he is or has been married), for "married" substitute "a spouse or civil partner".

3 In Article 8(1) and (3) (avoidance of gifts to attesting witnesses and their spouses), after "spouse" (in each place) insert "or civil partner".

4 In Article 9 (witnessing by creditor), after "spouse" insert "or civil partner".

5 After Article 13 insert—

"Effect of civil partnership

13A (1) Subject to paragraphs (2) to (6), a will is revoked by the formation of a civil partnership between the testator and another person.

(2) A disposition in a will in exercise of a power of appointment takes effect despite the formation of a subsequent civil partnership between the testator and another person unless the property so appointed would in default of appointment pass to the testator's personal representatives.

(3) If it appears from a will—

(a) that at the time it was made the testator was expecting to form a civil partnership with a particular person, and

(b) that he intended that the will should not be revoked by the formation of the civil partnership,

the will is not revoked by its formation.

(4) Paragraphs (5) and (6) apply if it appears from a will—

(a) that at the time it was made the testator was expecting to form a civil partnership with a particular person, and

(b) that he intended that a gift in the will should not be revoked by the formation of the civil partnership.

(5) The gift takes effect despite the formation of the civil partnership.

(6) Any other gift in the will also takes effect, unless it appears from the will that the testator intended the gift to be revoked by the formation of the civil partnership.

Effect of dissolution or annulment of civil partnership

13B (1) This Article applies if, after a testator has made a will—

(a) a court of civil jurisdiction in Northern Ireland dissolves his civil partnership or makes a nullity order in respect of it, or

(b) his civil partnership is dissolved or annulled and the dissolution or annulment is entitled to recognition in Northern Ireland under Chapter 3 of Part 5 of the Civil Partnership Act 2004.

(2) Subject to any contrary intention appearing from the will—

(a) provisions of the will appointing executors or trustees or conferring a power of appointment, if they appoint or confer the power on the former civil partner, take effect as if the former civil partner had died on the date on which the civil partnership is dissolved or annulled, and

(b) except as provided in paragraph (3), any property comprising or included in a gift to the former civil partner passes as if the former civil partner had died on that date.

(3) Where property comprising or included in a gift to the former civil partner is a share of residue, the will takes effect as if the gift of the residue were to the other person or persons entitled to it (and, if more than one, in such shares as to preserve the ratio of their former shares), to the exclusion of the former civil partner.

(4) Paragraph (2)(b) does not affect any right of the former civil partner to apply for financial provision under the Inheritance (Provision for Family and Dependants) (Northern Ireland) Order 1979 (SI 1979/ 924 (NI 8))."

6 In Article 14 (revocation), in paragraph (1)(a), after "Article 12 (marriage)" insert "or Article 13A (civil partnership)".

7 (1) Amend Article 23 (presumption as to effect of gift to spouses) as follows.

(2) After "spouse" (in each place) insert "or civil partner".

(3) In the heading to Article 23, after "spouses" insert "or civil partners".

8 In Article 27(3) (construction and effect of references to failure of issue), after "married" insert "or formed a civil partnership".

PART 2
ADMINISTRATION OF ESTATES AND FAMILY PROVISION

ADMINISTRATION OF ESTATES ACT (NORTHERN IRELAND) 1955 (C 24 (NI))

9 (1) Amend section 6A (spouse dying within 28 days of intestate) as follows.

(2) After "spouse" (in each place) insert "or civil partner".

(3) In the sidenote to section 6A, after "Spouse" insert "or civil partner".

10 (1) Amend section 7 (rights of surviving spouse) as follows.

(2) After "spouse" (in each place) insert "or civil partner".

(3) In subsection (7), after "husband" insert ", or of section 180 of the Civil Partnership Act 2004".

(4) In the sidenote to section 7, after "spouse" insert "or civil partner".

11 In section 8 (rights of issue), after "spouse" insert "or civil partner".

12 In section 9 (rights of parents), after "spouse" insert "or civil partner".

13 In section 10 (rights of brothers and sisters and their issue), after "spouse" (in both places) insert "or civil partner".

14 In section 11 (rights of next-of-kin), in subsection (1) after "neither spouse" insert "nor civil partner".

15 In section 38 (power to appoint trustees of infant's property), in subsection (5) after "marries" insert ", or forms a civil partnership,".

INHERITANCE (PROVISION FOR FAMILY AND DEPENDANTS) (NORTHERN IRELAND) ORDER 1979 (SI 1979/ 924 (NI 8))

16 (1) Amend Article 2 (interpretation) as follows.

(2) In paragraph (2), after the definition of "child" insert—

""civil partnership proceedings county court" has the same meaning as in the Civil Partnership Act 2004;".

(3) In that paragraph, in the definition of "former wife" and "former husband", for ""former wife" or "former husband" "substitute ""former spouse"".

(4) In that paragraph, before that definition insert—

""former civil partner" means a person whose civil partnership with the deceased was during the lifetime of the deceased either—

(a) dissolved or annulled by an order made under the law of any part of the United Kingdom or the Channel Islands or the Isle of Man, or

(b) dissolved or annulled in any country or territory outside the United Kingdom, the Channel Islands and the Isle of Man by a dissolution or annulment which is entitled to be recognised as valid by the law of Northern Ireland;".

(5) In that paragraph, in the definition of "reasonable financial provision", after paragraph (a) insert—

"(aa) in the case of an application made by virtue of Article 3(1)(a) by the civil partner of the deceased (except where, at the date of death, a separation order under Chapter 2 of Part 4 of the Civil Partnership Act 2004 was in force in relation to the civil partnership and the separation was continuing), means such financial provision as it would be reasonable in all the circumstances of the case for a civil partner to receive, whether or not that provision is required for his or her maintenance;".

(6) In paragraph (5)—

(a) before "wife" insert "spouse,", and

(b) in sub-paragraph (b), for "entered into a later marriage" substitute "formed a subsequent marriage or civil partnership".

(7) For paragraph (6) substitute—

"(5A) For the purposes of this Order any reference to a civil partner shall be treated as including a reference to a person who in good faith formed a void civil partnership with the deceased unless either—

(a) the civil partnership between the deceased and that person was dissolved or annulled during the lifetime of the deceased and the dissolution or annulment is recognised by the law of Northern Ireland, or

(b) that person has during the lifetime of the deceased formed a subsequent civil partnership or marriage.

(6) Any reference in this Order to the formation of, or to a person who has formed, a subsequent marriage or civil partnership includes (as the case may be) a reference to the formation of, or to a person who has formed, a marriage or civil partnership which is by law void or voidable.

(6A) The formation of a marriage or civil partnership shall be treated for the purposes of this Order as the formation of a subsequent marriage or civil partnership, in relation to either of the spouses or civil partners, notwithstanding that the previous marriage or civil partnership of that spouse or civil partner was void or voidable."

17 (1) Amend Article 3 (application for financial provision from deceased person's estate) as follows.

(2) For paragraph (1)(a) and (b) (application may be made by spouse or by former spouse who has not remarried) substitute—

"(a) the spouse or civil partner of the deceased;

(b) a former spouse or former civil partner of the deceased, but not one who has formed a subsequent marriage or civil partnership;".

(3) In paragraph (1)(ba) (application may be made by person living as husband or wife of the deceased), after "paragraph (1A)" insert "or (1B)".

(4) In paragraph (1)(d) (application may be made by child of the family), after "marriage" (in each place) insert "or civil partnership".

(5) After paragraph (1A) insert—

"(1B) This paragraph applies to a person if for the whole of the period of two years ending immediately before the date when the deceased died the person was living—

(a) in the same household as the deceased, and
(b) as the civil partner of the deceased."

18 In Article 4(1) (orders which may be made on an application), after sub-paragraph (f) insert—

"(g) an order varying any settlement made—

(i) during the subsistence of a civil partnership formed by the deceased, or
(ii) in anticipation of the formation of a civil partnership by the deceased,

on the civil partners (including such a settlement made by will), the variation being for the benefit of the surviving civil partner, or any child of both the civil partners, or any person who was treated by the deceased as a child of the family in relation to that civil partnership."

19 (1) Amend Article 5(2) (application by spouse or former spouse: matters to which court is to have regard) as follows.

(2) For the words from the beginning to "or (b)" substitute—

"This paragraph applies, without prejudice to the generality of sub-paragraph (g) of paragraph (1), where an application for an order under Article 4 is made by virtue of Article 3(1)(a) or (b)."

(3) The words from "the court shall, in addition" to the end of sub-paragraph (b) shall become a second sentence of the paragraph and, in sub-paragraph (a) of the sentence so formed, after "duration of the marriage" insert "or civil partnership".

(4) The words from "in the case of an application by the wife or husband" to the end shall become a third sentence of the paragraph, omitting the immediately preceding "and".

(5) At the end insert the following sentence—

"In the case of an application by the civil partner of the deceased, the court shall also, unless at the date of the death a separation order under Chapter 2 of Part 4 of the Civil Partnership Act 2004 was in force and the separation was continuing, have regard to the provision which the applicant might reasonably have expected to receive if on the day on which the deceased died the civil partnership, instead of being terminated by death, had been terminated by a dissolution order."

20 In Article 5(2A) (application by person living as husband or wife of deceased: matters to which court is to have regard), in sub-paragraph (a), after "wife" insert "or civil partner".

21 (1) In Article 8(3) and (10) (variation etc of orders which cease on occurrence of specified event other than remarriage of former spouse), for " (other than the remarriage of a former wife or former husband)" substitute " (other than the formation of a subsequent marriage or civil partnership by a former spouse or former civil partner)".

(2) In Article 8(9), for "or (f)" substitute "(f) or (g)".

22 After Article 16 insert—

"Provision as to cases where no financial relief was granted in proceedings for the dissolution etc of a civil partnership

16A (1) Paragraph (2) applies where—

(a) a dissolution order, nullity order, separation order or presumption of death order has been made under Chapter 2 of Part 4 of the Civil Partnership Act 2004 in relation to a civil partnership,
(b) one of the civil partners dies within twelve months from the date on which the order is made, and
(c) either—

(i) an application for a financial provision order under Part 1 of Schedule 15 to that Act or a property adjustment order under Part 2 of that Schedule has not been made by the other civil partner, or

(ii) such an application has been made but the proceedings on the application have not been determined at the time of the death of the deceased.

(2) If an application for an order under Article 4 is made by the surviving civil partner, the court shall, notwithstanding anything in Article 3 or 5, have power, if it thinks it just to do so, to treat the surviving civil partner as if the order mentioned in paragraph (1)(a) had not been made.

(3) This Article shall not apply in relation to a separation order unless at the date of the death of the deceased the separation order was in force and the separation was continuing."

23 After Article 17 insert—

"Restriction imposed in proceedings for the dissolution etc of a civil partnership on application under this Order

17ZA (1) On making a dissolution order, nullity order, separation order or presumption of death order under Chapter 2 of Part 4 of the Civil Partnership Act 2004, or at any time after making such an order, the High Court or a civil partnership proceedings county court, if it considers it just to do so, may, on the application of either of the civil partners, order that the other civil partner shall not on the death of the applicant be entitled to apply for an order under Article 4.

(2) In the case of a dissolution order, nullity order or presumption of death order ("the main order") an order may be made under paragraph (1) before (as well as after) the main order is made final, but if made before the main order is made final it shall not take effect unless the main order is made final.

(3) Where an order under paragraph (1) made in connection with a dissolution order, nullity order or presumption of death order has come into force with respect to a civil partner, then, on the death of the other civil partner, the court shall not entertain any application for an order under Article 4 made by the surviving civil partner.

(4) Where an order under paragraph (1) made in connection with a separation order has come into force with respect to a civil partner, then, if the other civil partner dies while the separation order is in force and the separation is continuing, the court shall not entertain any application for an order under Article 4 made by the surviving civil partner."

24 After Article 17A insert—

"Restriction imposed in proceedings under Schedule 17 to the Civil Partnership Act 2004 on application under this Order

17B (1) On making an order under paragraph 9 of Schedule 17 to the Civil Partnership Act 2004 (orders for financial provision, property adjustment and pension-sharing following overseas dissolution etc of civil partnership) the High Court, if it considers it just to do so, may, on the application of either of the civil partners, order that the other civil partner shall not on the death of the applicant be entitled to apply for an order under Article 4.

(2) Where an order under paragraph (1) has been made with respect to one of the civil partners in a case where a civil partnership has been dissolved or annulled, then, on the death of the other civil partner, the court shall not entertain an application under Article 4 made by the surviving civil partner.

(3) Where an order under paragraph (1) has been made with respect to one of the civil partners in a case where civil partners have been legally separated, then, if the other civil partner dies while the legal separation is in force, the court shall not entertain an application under Article 4 made by the surviving civil partner."

25 In Article 18(1) (power to vary secured periodical payments orders)—

(a) after "Matrimonial Causes (Northern Ireland) Order 1978" insert "or Schedule 15 to the Civil Partnership Act 2004", and

(b) after "that Order" insert "or Part 10 of that Schedule".

26 In Article 19(4) (meaning of "maintenance agreement")—

(a) for "entered into a marriage" substitute "formed a marriage or civil partnership",
(b) after "of the parties to that marriage" insert "or of the civil partners", and
(c) after "marriage" (in the third and fourth places) insert "or civil partnership".

27 After Article 20 insert—

"Availability of court's powers under this Order in applications under paragraphs 53 and 66 of Schedule 15 to the Civil Partnership Act 2004

20A (1) Where—

(a) a person against whom a secured periodical payments order was made under Schedule 15 to the Civil Partnership Act 2004 has died and an application is made under paragraph 53 of that Schedule for the variation or discharge of that order or for the revival of the operation of any suspended provision of the order, or
(b) a party to a maintenance agreement within the meaning of Part 12 of that Schedule has died, the agreement being one which provides for the continuation of payments under the agreement after the death of one of the parties, and an application is made under paragraph 66 of that Schedule for the alteration of the agreement under paragraph 62 of that Schedule,

the court to which the application is made under paragraph 53 or 66 shall have power to direct that the application shall be deemed to have been accompanied by an application for an order under Article 4.

(2) Where the court to which an application is made under paragraph 53 or 66 gives a direction under paragraph (1), that court shall have power—

(a) to make any order which the court would have had power to make under the provisions of this Order if the application under paragraph 53 or 66 had been made jointly with an application for an order under Article 4; and
(b) to give such consequential directions as may be necessary for enabling it to exercise any of the powers available to it under this Order in the case of an application for an order under Article 4.

(3) Where an order made under Article 17ZA(1) is in force with respect to a civil partner, a direction shall not be given under paragraph (1) with respect to any application made under paragraph 53 or 66 by that civil partner on the death of the other civil partner."

28 (1) Amend Article 21 (effect, duration and form of orders) as follows.

(2) In paragraph (2)(a), for "former husband or former wife" substitute "former spouse or former civil partner".

(3) In paragraph (2), after sub-paragraph (b) insert

"or

(c) an applicant who was the civil partner of the deceased in a case where, at the date of death, a separation order under Chapter 2 of Part 4 of the Civil Partnership Act 2004 was in force in relation to their civil partnership and the separation was continuing,".

(4) In that paragraph, in the words after sub-paragraph (b), for "on the remarriage of the applicant" onwards substitute "on the formation by the applicant of a subsequent marriage or civil partnership, except in relation to any arrears due under the order on the date of the formation of the subsequent marriage or civil partnership."

APPENDIX VII

CIVIL PROCEDURE RULES 1998

SI 1998/3132

PART 8
ALTERNATIVE PROCEDURE FOR CLAIMS

Rule 8.1 Types of claim in which Part 8 procedure may be followed

(1) The Part 8 procedure is the procedure set out in this Part.

(2) A claimant may use the Part 8 procedure where—
  (a) he seeks the court's decision on a question which is unlikely to involve a substantial dispute of fact; or
  (b) paragraph (6) applies.

(3) The court may at any stage order the claim to continue as if the claimant had not used the Part 8 procedure and, if it does so, the court may give any directions it considers appropriate.

(4) Paragraph (2) does not apply if a practice direction provides that the Part 8 procedure may not be used in relation to the type of claim in question.

(5) Where the claimant uses the Part 8 procedure he may not obtain default judgment under Part 12.

(6) A rule or practice direction may, in relation to a specified type of proceedings—
  (a) require or permit the use of the Part 8 procedure; and
  (b) disapply or modify any of the rules set out in this Part as they apply to those proceedings.

(Rule 8.9 provides for other modifications to the general rules where the Part 8 procedure is being used).

Rule 8.2 Contents of the claim form

Where the claimant uses the Part 8 procedure the claim form must state—
  (a) that this Part applies;
  (b) (i) the question which the claimant wants the court to decide; or
      (ii) the remedy which the claimant is seeking and the legal basis for the claim to that remedy;
  (c) if the claim is being made under an enactment, what that enactment is;
  (d) if the claimant is claiming in a representative capacity, what that capacity is; and
  (e) if the defendant is sued in a representative capacity, what that capacity is.

(Part 22 provides for the claim form to be verified by a statement of truth).

(Rule 7.5 provides for service of the claim form).

[(The costs practice direction sets out the information about a funding arrangement to be provided with the claim form where the claimant intends to seek to recover an additional liability).

("Funding arrangement" and "additional liability" are defined in rule 43.2).]

Amendment
Third and fourth cross-references inserted by SI 2000/1317, r 5.

[Rule 8.2A Issue of claim form without naming defendants

[(1) A practice direction may set out the circumstances in which a claim form may be issued under this Part without naming a defendant.

(2) The practice direction may set out those cases in which an application for permission must be made by application notice before the claim form is issued.]

(3) The application notice for permission—
   (a) need not be served on any other person; and
   (b) must be accompanied by a copy of the claim form that the applicant proposes to issue.

(4) Where the court gives permission it will give directions about the future management of the claim.]

Amendment

Inserted by SI 2000/221, r 5.
Paras (1), (2): substituted by SI 2001/256, r 5.

Rule 8.3 Acknowledgment of service

(1) The defendant must—
   (a) file an acknowledgment of service in the relevant practice form not more than 14 days after service of the claim form; and
   (b) serve the acknowledgment of service on the claimant and any other party.

(2) The acknowledgment of service must state—
   (a) whether the defendant contests the claim; and
   (b) if the defendant seeks a different remedy from that set out in the claim form, what that remedy is.

(3) The following rules of Part 10 (acknowledgment of service) apply—
   (a) rule 10.3(2) (exceptions to the period for filing an acknowledgment of service); and
   (b) rule 10.5 (contents of acknowledgment of service).

(4) . . .

[(The costs practice direction sets out the information about a funding arrangement to be provided with the acknowledgment of service where the defendant intends to seek to recover an additional liability).

("Funding arrangement" and "additional liability" are defined in rule 43.2).]

Amendment

Para (4): revoked by SI 2001/4015, r 11.
First and second cross-references inserted by SI 2000/1317, r 6.

Rule 8.4 Consequence of not filing an acknowledgment of service

(1) This rule applies where—
   (a) the defendant has failed to file an acknowledgment of service; and
   (b) the time period for doing so has expired.

(2) The defendant may attend the hearing of the claim but may not take part in the hearing unless the court gives permission.

Rule 8.5 Filing and serving written evidence

(1) The claimant must file any written evidence on which he intends to rely when he files his claim form.

(2) The claimant's evidence must be served on the defendant with the claim form.

(3) A defendant who wishes to rely on written evidence must file it when he files his acknowledgment of service.

(4) If he does so, he must also, at the same time, serve a copy of his evidence on the other parties.

(5) The claimant may, within 14 days of service of the defendant's evidence on him, file further written evidence in reply.

(6) If he does so, he must also, within the same time limit, serve a copy of his evidence on the other parties.

(7) The claimant may rely on the matters set out in his claim form as evidence under this rule if the claim form is verified by a statement of truth.

Rule 8.6 Evidence—general

(1) No written evidence may be relied on at the hearing of the claim unless—

(a) it has been served in accordance with rule 8.5; or

(b) the court gives permission.

(2) The court may require or permit a party to give oral evidence at the hearing.

(3) The court may give directions requiring the attendance for cross-examination(GL) of a witness who has given written evidence.

(Rule 32.1 contains a general power for the court to control evidence).

Rule 8.7 Part 20 claims

Where the Part 8 procedure is used, Part 20 (counterclaims and other additional claims) applies except that a party may not make a Part 20 claim (as defined by rule 20.2) without the court's permission.

Rule 8.8 Procedure where defendant objects to use of the Part 8 procedure

(1) Where the defendant contends that the Part 8 procedure should not be used because—

(a) there is a substantial dispute of fact; and

(b) the use of the Part 8 procedure is not required or permitted by a rule or practice direction, he must state his reasons when he files his acknowledgment of service.

(Rule 8.5 requires a defendant who wishes to rely on written evidence to file it when he files his acknowledgment of service).

(2) When the court receives the acknowledgment of service and any written evidence it will give directions as to the future management of the case.

(Rule 8.1(3) allows the court to make an order that the claim continue as if the claimant had not used the Part 8 procedure).

Rule 8.9 Modifications to the general rules

Where the Part 8 procedure is followed—

(a) provision is made in this Part for the matters which must be stated in the claim form and the defendant is not required to file a defence and therefore—

(i) Part 16 (statements of case) does not apply;

(ii) Part 15 (defence and reply) does not apply;

(iii) any time limit in these Rules which prevents the parties from taking a step before a defence is filed does not apply; and

(iv) the requirement under rule 7.8 to serve on the defendant a form for defending the claim does not apply;

(b) the claimant may not obtain judgment by request on an admission and therefore—

(i) rules 14.4 to 14.7 do not apply; and

(ii) the requirement under rule 7.8 to serve on the defendant a form for admitting the claim does not apply; and

(c) the claim shall be treated as allocated to the multi-track and therefore Part 26 does not apply.

[PART 57
[PROBATE AND INHERITANCE]]

Amendment

Part inserted by SI 2001/1388, r 14, Schedule.
Part heading: substituted by SI 2002/2058, r 23(a).

[Rule 57.1 Scope of this Part and definitions]

[(1) This Part contains rules about—

(a) probate claims;

(b) claims for the rectification of wills; . . .

(c) claims and applications to—

(i) substitute another person for a personal representative; or

(ii) remove a personal representative[; and

(d) claims under the Inheritance (Provision for Family and Dependants) Act 1975].

(2) In this Part:
- (a) "probate claim" means a claim for—
  - (i) the grant of probate of the will, or letters of administration of the estate, of a deceased person;
  - (ii) the revocation of such a grant; or
  - (iii) a decree pronouncing for or against the validity of an alleged will;

not being a claim which is non-contentious (or common form) probate business;
(Section 128 of the *Supreme Court Act 1981* [Senior Courts Act 1981] defines non-contentious (or common form) probate business.)

- (b) "relevant office" means—
  - (i) in the case of High Court proceedings in a Chancery district registry, that registry;
  - (ii) in the case of any other High Court proceedings, Chancery Chambers at the Royal Courts of Justice, Strand, London, WC2A 2LL; and
  - (iii) in the case of county court proceedings, the office of the county court in question;
- (c) "testamentary document" means a will, a draft of a will, written instructions for a will made by or at the request of, or under the instructions of, the testator, and any document purporting to be evidence of the contents, or to be a copy, of a will which is alleged to have been lost or destroyed;
- (d) "will" includes a codicil.]

Amendment

Inserted by SI 2001/1388, r 14, Schedule.
Para (1): in sub-para (b) word omitted revoked by SI 2002/2058, r 23(c)(i).
Para (1): sub-para (d) and word "and" immediately preceding it inserted by SI 2002/2058, r 23(c)(ii).
Para (2): words "Supreme Court Act 1981" in italics revoked and subsequent words in square brackets substituted by the Constitutional Reform Act 2005, s 59(5), Sch 11, Pt 1, para 1(2).

[SECTION I—PROBATE CLAIMS]

Amendment

Inserted by SI 2001/1388, r 14, Schedule.

[Rule 57.2 General]

[(1) This Section contains rules about probate claims.

(2) Probate claims in the High Court are assigned to the Chancery Division.

[(3) Probate claims in the county court must only be brought in—
- (a) a county court where there is also a Chancery district registry; or
- (b) the Central London County Court.]

(4) All probate claims are allocated to the multi-track.]

Amendment

Inserted by SI 2001/1388, r 14, Schedule.
Para (3): substituted by SI 2003/2113, r 15.

[Rule 57.3 How to start a probate claim]

[A probate claim must be commenced—
- (a) in the relevant office; and
- (b) using the procedure in Part 7.]

Amendment

Inserted by SI 2001/1388, r 14, Schedule.

[Rule 57.4 Acknowledgement of service and defence]

[(1) A defendant who is served with a claim form must file an acknowledgement of service.

(2) Subject to paragraph (3), the period for filing an acknowledgement of service is—
- (a) if the defendant is served with a claim form which states that particulars of claim are to follow, 28 days after service of the particulars of claim; and
- (b) in any other case, 28 days after service of the claim form.

(3) If the claim form is served out of the jurisdiction under rule 6.19, the period for filing an acknowledgement of service is 14 days longer than the relevant period specified in rule 6.22 or the practice direction supplementing Section 3 of Part 6.

(4) Rule 15(4) (which provides the period for filing a defence) applies as if the words "under Part 10" were omitted from rule 15.4(1)(b).]

Amendment

Inserted by SI 2001/1388, r 14, Schedule.

[Rule 57.5 Lodging of testamentary documents and filing of evidence about testamentary documents]

[(1) Any testamentary document of the deceased person in the possession or control of any party must be lodged with the court.

(2) Unless the court directs otherwise, the testamentary documents must be lodged in the relevant office—

(a) by the claimant when the claim form is issued; and

(b) by a defendant when he acknowledges service.

(3) The claimant and every defendant who acknowledges service of the claim form must in written evidence—

(a) describe any testamentary document of the deceased of which he has any knowledge or, if he does not know of any such testamentary document, state that fact, and

(b) if any testamentary document of which he has knowledge is not in his possession or under his control, give the name and address of the person in whose possession or under whose control it is or, if he does not know the name or address of that person, state that fact.

(A specimen form for the written evidence about testamentary documents is annexed to the practice direction.)

(4) Unless the court directs otherwise, the written evidence required by paragraph (3) must be filed in the relevant office—

(a) by the claimant, when the claim form is issued; and

(b) by a defendant when he acknowledges service.

(5) Except with the permission of the court, a party shall not be allowed to inspect the testamentary documents or written evidence lodged or filed by any other party until he himself has lodged his testamentary documents and filed his evidence.

(6) The provisions of paragraphs (2) and (4) may be modified by a practice direction under this Part.]

Amendment

Inserted by SI 2001/1388, r 14, Schedule.

[Rule 57.6 Revocation of existing grant]

[(1) In a probate claim which seeks the revocation of a grant of probate or letters of administration every person who is entitled, or claims to be entitled, to administer the estate under that grant must be made a party to the claim.

(2) If the claimant is the person to whom the grant was made, he must lodge the probate or letters of administration in the relevant office when the claim form is issued.

(3) If a defendant has the probate or letters of administration under his control, he must lodge it in the relevant office when he acknowledges service.

(4) Paragraphs (2) and (3) do not apply where the grant has already been lodged at the court, which in this paragraph includes the Principal Registry of the Family Division or a district probate registry.]

Amendment

Inserted by SI 2001/1388, r 14, Schedule.

[Rule 57.7 Contents of statements of case]

[(1) The claim form must contain a statement of the nature of the interest of the claimant and of each defendant in the estate.

(2) If a party disputes another party's interest in the estate he must state this in his statement of case and set out his reasons.

(3) Any party who contends that at the time when a will was executed the testator did not know of and approve its contents must give particulars of the facts and matters relied on.

(4) Any party who wishes to contend that—

(a) a will was not duly executed;

(b) at the time of the execution of a will the testator [lacked testamentary capacity]; or

(c) the execution of a will was obtained by undue influence or fraud,

must set out the contention specifically and give particulars of the facts and matters relied on.

(5) (a) A defendant may give notice in his defence that he does not raise any positive case, but insists on the will being proved in solemn form and, for that purpose, will cross-examine the witnesses who attested the will.

(b) If a defendant gives such a notice, the court will not make an order for costs against him unless it considers that there was no reasonable ground for opposing the will.]

Amendment

Inserted by SI 2001/1388, r 14, Schedule.

Para (4): in sub-para (b) words "was not of sound mind, memory and understanding" in italics revoked and subsequent words in square brackets substituted by SI 2007/3543, r 8.

[Rule 57.8 Counterclaim]

[(1) A defendant who contends that he has any claim or is entitled to any remedy relating to the grant of probate of the will, or letters of administration of the estate, of the deceased person must serve a counterclaim making that contention.

(2) If the claimant fails to serve particulars of claim within the time allowed, the defendant may, with the permission of the court, serve a counterclaim and the probate claim shall then proceed as if the counterclaim were the particulars of claim.]

Amendment

Inserted by SI 2001/1388, r 14, Schedule.

[Rule 57.9 Probate counterclaim in other proceedings]

[(1) In this rule "probate counterclaim" means a counterclaim in any claim other than a probate claim by which the defendant claims any such remedy as is mentioned in rule 57.1(2)(a).

(2) Subject to the following paragraphs of this rule, this Part shall apply with the necessary modifications to a probate counterclaim as it applies to a probate claim.

(3) A probate counterclaim must contain a statement of the nature of the interest of each of the parties in the estate of the deceased to which the probate counterclaim relates.

(4) Unless an application notice is issued within 7 days after the service of a probate counterclaim for an order under rule 3.1(2)(e) or 3.4 for the probate counterclaim to be dealt with in separate proceedings or to be struck out, and the application is granted, the court shall order the transfer of the proceedings to either—

(a) the Chancery Division (if it is not already assigned to that Division) and to either the Royal Courts of Justice or a Chancery district registry (if it is not already proceeding in one of those places); or

(b) if the county court has jurisdiction, to a county court where there is also a Chancery district registry [or the Central London County Court].

(5) If an order is made that a probate counterclaim be dealt with in separate proceedings, the order shall order the transfer of the probate counterclaim as required under paragraph (4).]

Amendment

Inserted by SI 2001/1388, r 14, Schedule.

Para (4): in sub-para (b) words "or the Central London County Court" in square brackets inserted by SI 2003/3361, r 14.

[Rule 57.10 Failure to acknowledge service or to file a defence]

[(1) A default judgment cannot be obtained in a probate claim and rule 10.2 and Part 12 do not apply.

(2) If any of several defendants fails to acknowledge service the claimant may—

(a) after the time for acknowledging service has expired; and

(b) upon filing written evidence of service of the claim form and (if no particulars of claim were contained in or served with the claim form) the particulars of claim on that defendant;

proceed with the probate claim as if that defendant had acknowledged service.

(3) If no defendant acknowledges service or files a defence then, unless on the application of the claimant the court orders the claim to be discontinued, the claimant may, after the time for acknowledging service or for filing a defence (as the case may be) has expired, apply to the court for an order that the claim is to proceed to trial.

(4) When making an application under paragraph (3) the claimant must file written evidence of service of the claim form and (if no particulars of claim were contained in or served with the claim form) the particulars of claim on each of the defendants.

(5) Where the court makes an order under paragraph (3), it may direct that the claim be tried on written evidence.]

Amendment
Inserted by SI 2001/1388, r 14, Schedule.

[Rule 57.11 Discontinuance and dismissal]

[(1) Part 38 does not apply to probate claims.

(2) At any stage of a probate claim the court, on the application of the claimant or of any defendant who has acknowledged service, may order that—

(a) the claim be discontinued or dismissed on such terms as to costs or otherwise as it thinks just; and

(b) a grant of probate of the will, or letters of administration of the estate, of the deceased person be made to the person entitled to the grant.]

Amendment
Inserted by SI 2001/1388, r 14, Schedule.

[SECTION II—RECTIFICATION OF WILLS]

Amendment
Inserted by SI 2001/1388, r 14, Schedule.

[Rule 57.12]

[(1) This Section contains rules about claims for the rectification of a will.

(Section 20 of the Administration of Justice Act 1982 provides for rectification of a will. Additional provisions are contained in rule 55 of the Non-Contentious Probate Rules 1987.)

(2) Every personal representative of the estate shall be joined as a party.

(3) The practice direction makes provision for lodging the grant of probate or letters of administration with the will annexed in a claim under this Section.]

Amendment
Inserted by SI 2001/1388, r 14, Schedule.

[SECTION III—SUBSTITUTION AND REMOVAL OF PERSONAL REPRESENTATIVES]

Amendment
Inserted by SI 2001/1388, r 14, Schedule.

[Rule 57.13]

[(1) This Section contains rules about claims and applications for substitution or removal of a personal representative.

(2) Claims under this Section must be brought in the High Court and are assigned to the Chancery Division.

(Section 50 of the Administration of Justice Act 1985 gives the High Court power to appoint a substitute for, or to remove, a personal representative.)

(3) Every personal representative of the estate shall be joined as a party.

(4) The practice direction makes provision for lodging the grant of probate or letters of administration in a claim under this Section.

(5) If substitution or removal of a personal representative is sought by application in existing proceedings, this rule shall apply with references to claims being read as if they referred to applications.]

Amendment

Inserted by SI 2001/1388, r 14, Schedule.

[SECTION IV—CLAIMS UNDER THE INHERITANCE (PROVISION FOR FAMILY AND DEPENDANTS) ACT 1975]

Amendment

Inserted by SI 2002/2058, r 23(d), Sch 4, Pt II.

[57.14 Scope of this Section]

[This Section contains rules about claims under the Inheritance (Provision for Family and Dependants) Act 1975 ("the Act").]

Amendment

Inserted by SI 2002/2058, r 23(d), Sch 4, Pt II.

[57.15 Proceedings in the High Court]

[(1) Proceedings in the High Court under the Act shall be issued in either—

(a) the Chancery Division; or

(b) the Family Division.

(2) The Civil Procedure Rules apply to proceedings under the Act which are brought in the Family Division, except that the provisions of the Family Proceedings Rules 1991 relating to the drawing up and service of orders apply instead of the provisions in Part 40 and its practice direction.]

Amendment

Inserted by SI 2002/2058, r 23(d), Sch 4, Pt II.

[57.16 Procedure for claims under section 1 of the Act]

[(1) A claim under section 1 of the Act must be made by issuing a claim form in accordance with Part 8.

(2) Rule 8.3 (acknowledgment of service) and rule 8.5 (filing and serving written evidence) apply as modified by paragraphs (3) to (5) of this rule.

(3) The written evidence filed and served by the claimant with the claim form must have exhibited to it an official copy of—

(a) the grant of probate or letters of administration in respect of the deceased's estate; and

(b) every testamentary document in respect of which probate or letters of administration were granted.

(4) [Subject to paragraph (4A), the time] within which a defendant must file and serve—

(a) an acknowledgment of service; and

(b) any written evidence,

is not more than 21 days after service of the claim form on him.

[(4A) If the claim form is served out of the jurisdiction under rule 6.19, the period for filing an acknowledgment of service and any written evidence is 7 days longer than the relevant period specified in rule 6.22 or the practice direction supplementing Section III of Part 6.]

(5) A defendant who is a personal representative of the deceased must file and serve written evidence, which must include the information required by the practice direction.]

Amendment
Inserted by SI 2002/2058, r 23(d), Sch 4, Pt II.
Para (4): words "Subject to paragraph (4A), the time" in square brackets substituted by SI 2004/1306, r 17(a).
Para (4A): inserted by SI 2004/1306, r 17(b).

[PART 64
ESTATES, TRUSTS AND CHARITIES]

Amendment
Inserted by SI 2002/2058, r 26(a), Sch 5.

[Rule 64.1 General]

[(1) This Part contains rules—
- (a) in Section I, about claims relating to—
  - (i) the administration of estates of deceased persons, and
  - (ii) trusts; and
- (b) in Section II, about charity proceedings.

(2) In this Part and its practice directions, where appropriate, references to trustees include executors and administrators.

(3) All proceedings in the High Court to which this Part applies must be brought in the Chancery Division.]

Amendment
Inserted by SI 2002/2058, r 26(a), Sch 5.

[SECTION I—CLAIMS RELATING TO THE ADMINSITRATION OF ESTATES AND TRUSTS]

Amendment
Inserted by SI 2002/2058, r 26(a), Sch 5.

[Rule 64.2 Scope of this Section]

[This Section of this Part applies to claims—
- (a) for the court to determine any question arising in—
  - (i) the administration of the estate of a deceased person; or
  - (ii) the execution of a trust;
- (b) for an order for the administration of the estate of a deceased person, or the execution of a trust, to be carried out under the direction of the court ("an administration order");
- (c) under the Variation of Trusts Act 1958; or
- (d) under section 48 of the Administration of Justice Act 1985.]

Amendment
Inserted by SI 2002/2058, r 26(a), Sch 5.

[Rule 64.3 Claim form]

[A claim to which this Section applies must be made by issuing a Part 8 claim form.]

Amendment
Inserted by SI 2002/2058, r 26(a), Sch 5.

[Rule 64.4 Parties]

[(1) In a claim to which this Section applies, other than an application under section 48 of the Administration of Justice Act 1985—
- (a) all the trustees must be parties;
- (b) if the claim is made by trustees, any of them who does not consent to being a claimant must be made a defendant; and

(c) the claimant may make parties to the claim any persons with an interest in or claim against the estate, or an interest under the trust, who it is appropriate to make parties having regard to the nature of the order sought.

(2) In addition, in a claim under the Variation of Trusts Act 1958, unless the court directs otherwise any person who—

(a) created the trust; or

(b) provided property for the purposes of the trust,

must, if still alive, be made a party to the claim.

(The court may, under rule 19.2, order additional persons to be made parties to a claim.)]

Amendment

Inserted by SI 2002/2058, r 26(a), Sch 5.

[SECTION II—CHARITY PROCEEDINGS]

Amendment

Inserted by SI 2002/2058, r 26(a), Sch 5.

[Rule 64.5 Scope of this Section and interpretation]

[(1) This Section applies to charity proceedings.

(2) In this Section—

(a) "the Act" means the Charities Act 1993;

(b) "charity proceedings" has the same meaning as in section 33(8) of the Act; and

(c) "the Commissioners" means the Charity Commissioners for England and Wales.]

Amendment

Inserted by SI 2002/2058, r 26(a), Sch 5.

[Rule 64.6 Application for permission to take charity proceedings]

[(1) An application to the High Court under section 33(5) of the Act for permission to start charity proceedings must be made within 21 days after the refusal by the Commissioners of an order authorising proceedings.

(2) The application must be made by issuing a Part 8 claim form, which must contain the information specified in the practice direction.

(3) The Commissioners must be made defendants to the claim, but the claim form need not be served on them or on any other person.

(4) The judge considering the application may direct the Commissioners to file a written statement of their reasons for their decision.

(5) The court will serve on the applicant a copy of any statement filed under paragraph (4).

(6) The judge may either—

(a) give permission without a hearing; or

(b) fix a hearing.]

Amendment

Inserted by SI 2002/2058, r 26(a), Sch 5.

Appendix VIII

MENTAL CAPACITY ACT 2005 (TRANSITIONAL AND CONSEQUENTIAL PROVISIONS) ORDER 2007

SI 2007/1898

1 Citation and commencement

This Order may be cited as the Mental Capacity Act 2005 (Transitional and Consequential Provisions) Order 2007, and comes into force on 1 October 2007.

2 Interpretation

In this Order—

(a) "the Act" means the Mental Capacity Act 2005; and
(b) "Court of Protection" refers—
   (i) the first time the expression appears in article 4, to the office of the Supreme Court called the Court of Protection mentioned in section 45(6) of the Act, and
   (ii) where the expression appears in articles 3, 4(a) and (b), to the superior court of record established by section 45(1) of the Act.

3 Proceedings begun in the High Court before 1 October 2007

(1) This article applies to any proceedings about P's personal welfare begun in the High Court before 1 October 2007 in respect of which the Court of Protection would, but for this article, have jurisdiction on and after that date under section 16 of the Act.

(2) The proceedings may continue to be dealt with, until they are finally decided, in accordance with the arrangements existing immediately before 1 October 2007.

(3) For the purposes of paragraph (2), an application is finally decided when it is determined and there is no possibility of the determination being reversed or varied on an appeal.

(4) In dealing with proceedings under this article, the High Court retains all the powers and jurisdiction in relation to any matter that is the subject of the proceedings that it had immediately before the commencement of the Act.

(5) In this article—

(a) "P" means any person (other than a protected party) who lacks, or so far as consistent with the context is alleged to lack, capacity to make a decision or decisions in relation to any matter that is the subject of an application to the court and references to a person who lacks capacity are to be construed in accordance with the Act;
(b) "personal welfare" is to be construed in accordance with section 17 of the Act; and
(c) "protected party" means a party, or an intended party (other than P or a child), who lacks capacity to conduct the proceedings.

4 Senior Judge of the Court of Protection

The person who, immediately before the commencement of Part 2 of the Act, holds the office of Master of the Court of Protection, shall be treated as—

(a) being a circuit judge nominated under section 46(1) of the Act to exercise the jurisdiction of the Court of Protection; and
(b) having been appointed the Senior Judge of the Court of Protection under section 46(4) of the Act.

5 Advance decisions to refuse life-sustaining treatment

(1) An advance decision refusing life-sustaining treatment shall be treated as valid and applicable to a treatment and does not have to satisfy the requirements mentioned in paragraph (3) if the conditions in paragraph (2) are met.

(2) The conditions that must be met are that—

(a) a person providing health care for a person ("P") reasonably believes that—

(i) P has made the advance decision refusing life-sustaining treatment before 1 October 2007, and

(ii) P has lacked the capacity to comply with the provisions mentioned in paragraph (3) since 1 October 2007;

(b) the advance decision is in writing;

(c) P has not—

(i) withdrawn the decision at a time when he had capacity to do so, or

(ii) done anything else clearly inconsistent with the advance decision remaining his fixed decision;

(d) P does not have the capacity to give or refuse consent to the treatment in question at the material time;

(e) the treatment in question is the treatment specified in the advance decision;

(f) any circumstances specified in the advance decision are present; and

(g) there are no reasonable grounds for believing that circumstances exist which P did not anticipate at the time of the advance decision and which would have affected his decision had he anticipated them.

(3) The requirements that do not have to be satisfied are as follows—

(a) the requirement for the decision to be verified by a statement by P to the effect that the advance decision is to apply to that treatment even if life is at risk (section 25(5)(a) of the Act); and

(b) the requirement for a signed and witnessed advance decision (section 25(6)(b) to (d) of the Act).

(4) In this article, "advance decision" has the meaning given in section 24(1) of the Act.

6 Minor and consequential amendments

Schedule 1 contains minor and consequential amendments.

SCHEDULE 1
MINOR AND CONSEQUENTIAL AMENDMENTS

Article 6

TRUSTEE SAVINGS BANK LIFE ANNUITY REGULATIONS 1930

1 In regulation 16(2) of the Trustee Savings Bank Life Annuity Regulations 1930—

(a) for the words "a person who is incapable, by reason of mental disorder within the meaning of the Mental Health Act 1959, of managing and administering his property and affairs" substitute "a person who lacks mental capacity within the meaning of the Mental Capacity Act 2005 (c 9) to administer and manage his property and affairs"; and

(b) for the word "receiver" substitute "deputy".

SAVINGS CONTRACT REGULATIONS 1969

2 (1) The Savings Contract Regulations 1969 are amended in accordance with this paragraph.

(2) In regulation 2(1) (interpretation), omit the entries for "mentally disordered person" and "receiver" and, in the appropriate alphabetical position, insert—

(a) ""deputy" in the application of these Regulations to England and Wales, means, in relation to any decision made for a person who lacks capacity, a deputy appointed by the Court of Protection for that person with power to make decisions in relation to the matters in question;"; and

(b) ""person who lacks capacity" means a person who lacks capacity within the meaning of the Mental Capacity Act 2005 (c 9);".

(3) In regulation 7 (payment in case of mentally disordered persons)—

(a) in the title, for "mentally disordered persons" substitute "persons who lack capacity"; and

(b) in paragraphs (1) and (2) in each place—
  (i) for "mentally disordered person" substitute "person who lacks capacity", and
  (ii) for "receiver" substitute "deputy".

(4) In regulation 12 (persons under disability)—
  (a) for "mentally disordered person" substitute "person who lacks capacity"; and
  (b) for "receiver" substitute "deputy".

(5) In regulation 27 (application to Scotland)—
  (a) in paragraph (a), for "mentally disordered person" substitute "person who lacks capacity"; and
  (b) in paragraph (b), for "receiver in relation to a mentally disordered person" substitute "deputy in relation to a person who lacks capacity".

(6) In regulation 28(2) (application to Northern Ireland)—
  (a) in sub-paragraph (a), for "mentally disordered person" substitute "person who lacks capacity"; and
  (b) in sub-paragraph (b), for "receiver in relation to a mentally disordered person" substitute "deputy in relation to a person who lacks capacity".

(7) In regulation 29(2)(a) (application to the Isle of Man), for "receiver in relation to a mentally disordered person" substitute "deputy in relation to a person who lacks capacity".

(8) In regulation 30 (application to the Channel Islands)—
  (a) in paragraphs (2)(a) and (3)(a), for "mentally disordered person" substitute "person who lacks capacity"; and
  (b) in paragraphs (2)(b) and (3)(b), for "receiver in relation to a mentally disordered person" substitute "deputy in relation to a person who lacks capacity".

PENSIONS INCREASE (JUDICIAL PENSIONS) REGULATIONS 1972

3 In paragraph 9 of the Schedule to the Pensions Increase (Judicial Pensions) Regulations 1972, omit the reference to a Master of the Court of Protection except in the case of a person holding that office immediately before the commencement of this paragraph or who had previously retired from that office or died.

NATIONAL SAVINGS BANK REGULATIONS 1972

4 (1) The National Savings Bank Regulations 1972 are amended in accordance with this paragraph.

(2) In regulation 2(1) (interpretation), omit the entries for "mentally disordered person" and "receiver" and, in the appropriate alphabetical position, insert—
  (a) ""deputy" in the application of these Regulations to England and Wales, means, in relation to any decision made for a person who lacks capacity, a deputy appointed by the Court of Protection for that person with power to make decisions in relation to the matters in question;"; and
  (b) ""person who lacks capacity" means a person who lacks capacity within the meaning of the Mental Capacity Act 2005 (c 9);".

(3) In regulation 7 (mentally disordered persons)—
  (a) in the title, for "Mentally disordered persons" substitute "Persons who lack capacity";
  (b) in paragraph (1), for "mentally disordered person, by his receiver" substitute "person who lacks capacity, by his deputy";
  (c) in paragraphs (2), (3) and (4) in each place—
    (i) for "mentally disordered person" substitute "person who lacks capacity", and
    (ii) for "receiver" substitute "deputy";

(4) In regulation 8(4)(c) (joint accounts)—
  (a) for "mentally disordered person" substitute "person who lacks capacity"; and
  (b) for "receiver" substitute "deputy".

(5) In regulation 9(4) (trust accounts)—
  (a) for both references to "mentally disordered person" substitute "person who lacks capacity"; and
  (b) for "receiver" substitute "deputy".

(6) In regulation 37(1)(b) (payment under nomination)—

(a) for "mentally disordered person" substitute "person who lacks capacity"; and

(b) for "receiver" substitute "deputy".

(7) In regulation 45 (persons under disability)—

(a) for "mentally disordered person" substitute "person who lacks capacity"; and

(b) for "receiver" substitute "deputy".

(8) In regulation 57(2)(a) (application to the Isle of Man), for "receiver in relation to a mentally disordered person" substitute "deputy in relation to a person who lacks capacity".

(9) In regulation 58 (application to the Channel Islands)—

(a) in paragraphs (2)(a) and (3)(a), for "mentally disordered person" substitute "person who lacks capacity"; and

(b) in paragraphs (2)(b) and (3)(b), for "receiver in relation to a mentally disordered person" substitute "deputy in relation to a person who lacks capacity".

PREMIUM SAVINGS BOND REGULATIONS 1972

5 (1) The Premium Savings Bond Regulations 1972 are amended in accordance with this paragraph.

(2) In regulation 2(1) (interpretation), omit the entries for "mentally disordered person" and "receiver" and, in the appropriate alphabetical position, insert—

(a) ""deputy" in the application of these Regulations to England and Wales, means, in relation to any decision made for a person who lacks capacity, a deputy appointed by the Court of Protection for that person with power to make decisions in relation to the matters in question;"; and

(b) ""person who lacks capacity" means a person who lacks capacity within the meaning of the Mental Capacity Act 2005 (c 9);".

(3) In regulation 4 (persons entitled to purchase and hold bonds)—

(a) in paragraph (3)(b), for "mentally disordered person, by his receiver" substitute "a person who lacks capacity, by his deputy"; and

(b) in paragraph (5)(b), for "mentally disordered person" substitute "person who lacks capacity".

(4) In regulation 10 (payment in case of mentally disordered persons)—

(a) in the title, for "Mentally disordered persons" substitute "Persons who lack capacity";

(b) in paragraph (1)—

(i) for "mentally disordered person" substitute "person who lacks capacity", and

(ii) for "receiver" substitute "deputy"; and

(c) in paragraph (2), for "mentally disordered person for whose estate no receiver" substitute "person who lacks capacity for whom no deputy has been appointed in relation to his property and affairs".

(5) In regulation 16 (persons under disability)—

(a) for "mentally disordered person" substitute "person who lacks capacity"; and

(b) for "receiver" substitute "deputy".

(6) In regulation 31 (application to Scotland)—

(a) in paragraph (a), for "mentally disordered person" substitute "person who lacks capacity"; and

(b) in paragraph (b), for "receiver in relation to a mentally disordered person" substitute "deputy in relation to a person who lacks capacity".

(7) In regulation 32(2) (application to Northern Ireland)—

(a) in paragraph (a), for "mentally disordered person" substitute "person who lacks capacity"; and

(b) in paragraph (b), for "receiver in relation to a mentally disordered person" substitute "deputy in relation to a person who lacks capacity".

(8) In regulation 33(2)(a) (application to the Isle of Man), for "receiver in relation to a mentally disordered person" substitute "deputy in relation to a person who lacks capacity".

(9) In regulation 34 (application to the Channel Islands)—
- (a) in paragraphs (2)(a) and (3)(a), for "mentally disordered person" substitute "person who lacks capacity"; and
- (b) in paragraphs (2)(b) and (3)(b), for "receiver in relation to a mentally disordered person" substitute "deputy in relation to a person who lacks capacity".

NATIONAL SAVINGS STOCK REGISTER REGULATIONS 1976

6 (1) The National Savings Stock Register Regulations 1976 are amended in accordance with this paragraph.

(2) In regulation 2(1) (interpretation), omit the entries for "mentally disordered person" and "receiver" and, in the appropriate alphabetical position, insert—
- (a) " "deputy" in the application of these Regulations to England and Wales, means, in relation to any decision made for a person who lacks capacity, a deputy appointed by the Court of Protection for that person with power to make decisions in relation to the matters in question;"; and
- (b) " "person who lacks capacity" means a person who lacks capacity within the meaning of the Mental Capacity Act 2005 (c 9);".

(3) In regulation 31 (persons under disability)—
- (a) in paragraphs (1) and (2) in each place—
  - (i) for "mentally disordered person" substitute "person who lacks capacity"; and
  - (ii) for "receiver" substitute "deputy"; and
- (b) in paragraphs (3) and (4), for "mentally disordered person" substitute "person who lacks capacity".

(4) In regulation 59 (application to Scotland)—
- (a) in paragraph (a), for "mentally disordered person" substitute "person who lacks capacity"; and
- (b) in paragraph (b), for "receiver in relation to a mentally disordered person" substitute "deputy in relation to a person who lacks capacity".

(5) In regulation 60(2) (application to Northern Ireland)—
- (a) in paragraph (a), for "mentally disordered person" substitute "person who lacks capacity"; and
- (b) in paragraph (b), for "receiver in relation to a mentally disordered person" substitute "deputy in relation to a person who lacks capacity".

(6) In regulation 61(2)(a) (application to the Isle of Man), for "receiver in relation to a mentally disordered person" substitute "deputy in relation to a person who lacks capacity".

(7) In regulation 62 (application to the Channel Islands)—
- (a) in paragraphs (2)(a) and (3)(a), for "mentally disordered person" substitute "person who lacks capacity"; and
- (b) in paragraphs (2)(b) and (3)(b), for "receiver in relation to a mentally disordered person" substitute "deputy in relation to a person who lacks capacity".

MOTOR VEHICLES (TESTS) REGULATIONS 1981

7 In regulation 9(1)(c) (cessations: general) of the Motor Vehicles (Tests) Regulations 1981, for the words from "patient" to "Mental Health Act 1983" substitute "person who lacks capacity (within the meaning of the Mental Capacity Act 2005 (c 9)) to carry on the activities covered by the authorisation".

THE MENTAL HEALTH REVIEW TRIBUNAL RULES 1983

8 For rule 7(c) (notice to other persons interested) of the Mental Health Review Tribunal Rules 1983, substitute—

"(c) where there is an extant order of either—
- (i) the office of the Supreme Court called the Court of Protection mentioned in section 45(6) of the Mental Capacity Act 2005 (c 9), or
- (ii) the superior court of record established by section 45(1) of the Mental Capacity Act 2005,

to the court referred to in sub-paragraph (ii) of this rule;"

SAVINGS CERTIFICATES (YEARLY PLAN) REGULATIONS 1984

9 (1) The Savings Certificates (Yearly Plan) Regulations 1984 are amended in accordance with this paragraph.

(2) In regulation 2 (interpretation), omit the entries for "mentally disordered person" and "receiver" and, in the appropriate alphabetical position, insert—

(a) ""deputy" in the application of these Regulations to England and Wales, means, in relation to any decision made for a person who lacks capacity, a deputy appointed by the Court of Protection for that person with power to make decisions in relation to the matters in question;"; and

(b) ""person who lacks capacity" means a person who lacks capacity within the meaning of the Mental Capacity Act 2005 (c 9);".

(3) In regulation 4(2)(b) (persons entitled to enter into agreements and to hold certificates), for "mentally disordered person, by his receiver" substitute "person who lacks capacity, by his deputy".

(4) In regulation 5(2) (maximum payments), for "mentally disordered person" substitute "person who lacks capacity".

(5) In regulation 8 (repayment in case of persons under 7 years of age and mentally disordered persons)—

(a) in the title, for "mentally disordered persons" substitute "persons who lack capacity";

(b) in paragraph (2), for "mentally disordered person, by his receiver" substitute "person who lacks capacity, by his deputy"; and

(c) in paragraph (3), for "mentally disordered person for whose estate no receiver" substitute "person who lacks capacity for whom no deputy".

(6) In regulation 9(1)(a) (repayment in case of joint trustees)—

(a) for "mentally disordered person" substitute "person who lacks capacity"; and

(b) for "receiver" substitute "deputy".

(7) In regulation 10(1)(a) (repayment in case of certificate held by person jointly)—

(a) for "mentally disordered person" substitute "person who lacks capacity"; and

(b) for "receiver" substitute "deputy".

(8) In regulation 18 (persons under disability)—

(a) for "mentally disordered person" substitute "person who lacks capacity"; and

(b) for "receiver" substitute "deputy".

(9) In regulation 33 (application to Scotland)—

(a) in paragraph (a), for "mentally disordered person" substitute "person who lacks capacity"; and

(b) in paragraph (b), for "receiver in relation to a mentally disordered person" substitute "deputy in relation to a person who lacks capacity".

(10) In regulation 34(2) (application to Northern Ireland)—

(a) in paragraph (a), for "mentally disordered person" substitute "person who lacks capacity"; and

(b) in paragraph (b), for "receiver in relation to a mentally disordered person" substitute "deputy in relation to a person who lacks capacity".

(11) In regulation 35(2)(a) (application to the Isle of Man), for "receiver in relation to a mentally disordered person" substitute "deputy in relation to a person who lacks capacity".

(12) In regulation 36 (application to the Channel Islands)—

(a) in paragraphs (2)(a) and (3)(a), for "mentally disordered person" substitute "person who lacks capacity"; and

(b) in paragraphs (2)(b) and (3)(b), for "receiver in relation to a mentally disordered person" substitute "deputy in relation to a person who lacks capacity".

ROAD VEHICLES (CONSTRUCTION AND USE) REGULATIONS 1986

10 In paragraph 5(1)(c) of Part 1 of Schedule 3B (authorised sealers) to the Road Vehicles (Construction and Use) Regulations 1986, for the words from "patient" to "Mental Health Act 1983", substitute "person who lacks capacity (within the meaning of the Mental Capacity Act 2005 (c 9)) to carry on the activities covered by the authorisation".

OPERATION OF PUBLIC SERVICE VEHICLES (PARTNERSHIP) REGULATIONS 1986

11 On the entry as to section 57(2) of the Public Passenger Vehicles Act 1981, in column 2 of Part 1 of the Schedule to the Operation of Public Service Vehicles (Partnership) Regulations 1986, for the words from "patient" to "Mental Health Act 1983", substitute "person who lacks capacity (within the meaning of the Mental Capacity Act 2005 (c 9)) to carry on the activities covered by the licence".

INSOLVENCY RULES 1986

12 (1) The Insolvency Rules 1986 are amended in accordance with this paragraph.

(2) In rule 4.214 (witness unfit for examination)—
- (a) in paragraph (1)—
  - (i) omit the words "mental disorder or", and
  - (ii) before "is suffering" insert "is a person who lacks capacity within the meaning of the Mental Capacity Act 2005 (c 9) or", and
- (b) in paragraph (3)(a), for the words "patient within the meaning of the Mental Health Act 1983" substitute "person who lacks capacity within the meaning of the Mental Capacity Act 2005".

(3) In rule 6.174 (bankrupt unfit for examination)—
- (a) in paragraph (1)—
  - (i) omit the words "mental disorder or", and
  - (ii) before "is suffering" insert "is a person who lacks capacity within the meaning of the Mental Capacity Act 2005 or", and
- (b) in paragraph (3)(a), for the words "patient within the meaning of the Mental Health Act 1983", substitute "person who lacks capacity within the meaning of the Mental Capacity Act 2005".

(4) In the heading to Part 7 of Chapter 7, for "Persons Incapable of Managing their Affairs", substitute "Persons who Lack Capacity to Manage their Affairs".

(5) In rule 7.43 (introductory)—
- (a) in paragraph (1), for "is incapable of managing and administering his property and affairs", substitute "lacks capacity within the meaning of the Mental Capacity Act 2005 to manage and administer his property and affairs"; and
- (b) in paragraph (1)(a), for "mental disorder within the meaning of the Mental Health Act 1983", substitute "lacking capacity within the meaning of the Mental Capacity Act 2005".

(6) In paragraph 4.64 of Part 4 of Schedule 4, Forms Index (companies winding up)—
- (a) after the words "person who", insert "lacks capacity to manage and administer his property and affairs or"; and
- (b) for the words "mental disorder or", substitute "a".

(7) In paragraph 6.57 of Part 6 of Schedule 4, Forms Index (bankruptcy)—
- (a) after the words "bankrupt who", insert "lacks capacity to manage and administer his property and affairs or"; and
- (b) for the words "mental disorder or", substitute "a".

(8) For form 4.64 in Schedule 4 (forms), substitute the form in Schedule 2 (Part 1).

(9) For form 6.57 in Schedule 4 (forms), substitute the form in Schedule 2 (Part 2).

NON-CONTENTIOUS PROBATE RULES 1987

13 (1) Rule 31 (grant to attorneys) and 35 (grants in case of mental incapacity) of the Non-contentious Probate Rules 1987 are amended in accordance with this paragraph.

(2) For rule 31(3) substitute—

> "(3) Where the donor referred to in paragraph (1) above lacks capacity within the meaning of the Mental Capacity Act 2005 (c 9) and the attorney is acting under an enduring power of attorney or lasting power of attorney, the application shall be made in accordance with rule 35."

(3) For rule 35, in the title, for the words "mental incapacity" substitute "lack of mental capacity".

(4) In rule 35(1), for the words "incapable person" substitute "person who lacks capacity within the meaning of the Mental Capacity Act 2005".

(5) In rule 35(2)—

(a) for the words "is by reason of mental incapacity incapable of managing", substitute "lacks capacity within the meaning of the Mental Capacity Act 2005 to manage";

(b) for each reference to an incapable person substitute a reference to a person who lacks capacity within the meaning of the Mental Capacity Act 2005; and

(c) at the end of sub-paragraph (b), insert "or lasting power of attorney".

(6) In rule 35(4), for the words "incapable person", substitute "person who lacks capacity within the meaning of the Mental Capacity Act 2005".

JUDICIAL PENSION (PRESERVATION OF BENEFITS) ORDER 1988

14 In Schedule 2 to the Judicial Pension (Preservation of Benefits) Order 1988, omit the reference to a Master of the Court of Protection except in the case of a person holding that office immediately before the commencement of this paragraph or who had previously retired from that office or died.

JUDICIAL PENSIONS (REQUISITE BENEFITS) ORDER 1988

15 In Schedule 2 (office) to the Judicial Pensions (Requisite Benefits) Order 1988, omit the reference to a Master of the Court of Protection except in the case of a person holding that office immediately before the commencement of this paragraph or who had previously retired from that office or died.

CHURCH OF ENGLAND PENSIONS REGULATIONS 1988

16 (1) Regulation 30 (payment of pensions in respect of persons suffering from mental disorder) of the Church of England Pensions Regulations 1988 is amended in accordance with this paragraph.

(2) In paragraph (1)—

(a) for the words "is incapable by reason of mental disorder within the meaning of the Mental Health Act, 1983, of managing and administering", substitute "lacks capacity (within the meaning of the Mental Capacity Act 2005 (c 9)) to manage and administer"; and

(b) in sub-paragraph (a), for the words "suffering from mental disorder", substitute "a person lacking capacity (within the meaning of the Mental Capacity Act 2005) to manage and administer his property and affairs".

(3) In paragraph (2)—

(a) for the words "authority having jurisdiction under Part VII of the Mental Health Act, 1983", substitute "Court of Protection"; and

(b) for each reference to "that authority" substitute a reference to "the Court of Protection".

(4) In paragraph (3)—

(a) for the words "the authority having jurisdiction under Part VII of the Mental Health Act, 1983 give", substitute "the Court of Protection gives"; and

(b) for the words "that authority", substitute "the Court of Protection".

SAVINGS CERTIFICATES REGULATIONS 1991

17 (1) The Savings Certificates Regulations 1991 are amended in accordance with this paragraph.

(2) In regulation 2(1) (interpretation), omit the entries for "mentally disordered person" and "receiver" and, in the appropriate alphabetical position, insert—

(a) ""deputy" in the application of these Regulations to England and Wales, means, in relation to any decision made for a person who lacks capacity, a deputy appointed by the Court of Protection for that person with power to make decisions in relation to the matters in question;"; and

(b) ""person who lacks capacity" means a person who lacks capacity within the meaning of the Mental Capacity Act 2005 (c 9);".

(3) In regulation 4(2)(c) (persons entitled to purchase and hold certificates), for "mentally disordered person, by his receiver" substitute "person who lacks capacity, by his deputy".

(4) In regulation 9 (repayment in case of persons under 7 years of age and mentally disordered persons)—

(a) in the title, for "mentally disordered persons" substitute "persons who lack capacity";
(b) in paragraph (2), for "mentally disordered person shall be made by his receiver" substitute "person who lacks capacity shall be made by his deputy"; and
(c) in paragraph (4), for the words from "mentally disordered person for" to "of the mentally disordered person" substitute "person who lacks capacity in respect of whom no deputy has been appointed, the Director of Savings may, if he thinks fit, pay the whole or any part of the amount repayable in respect of the certificate to any person who satisfies him that he will apply the payment for the maintenance or otherwise for the benefit of the person who lacks capacity".

(5) In regulation 10(1)(a) (repayment in case of certificate held by persons jointly)—

(a) for "mentally disordered person" substitute "person who lacks capacity"; and
(b) for "receiver" substitute "person who lacks capacity".

(6) In regulation 18 (persons under disability)—

(a) for "mentally disordered person" substitute "person who lacks capacity"; and
(b) for "receiver" substitute "deputy".

(7) In regulation 33 (application to Scotland)—

(a) in paragraph (a), for "mentally disordered person" substitute "person who lacks capacity"; and
(b) in paragraph (b), for "receiver in relation to a mentally disordered person" substitute "deputy in relation to a person who lacks capacity".

(8) In regulation 34 (application to Northern Ireland)—

(a) in paragraph (b), for "mentally disordered person" substitute "person who lacks capacity"; and
(b) in paragraph (c), for "receiver in relation to a mentally disordered person" substitute "deputy in relation to a person who lacks capacity".

(9) In regulation 35(2) (application to the Isle of Man)—

(a) in paragraph (a), for "mentally disordered person" substitute "person who lacks capacity"; and
(b) in paragraph (b), for "receiver in relation to any act or thing done in respect of a mentally disordered person shall be construed as a reference to a receiver" substitute "deputy in relation to any decision made for a person who lacks capacity shall be construed as a reference to a deputy".

(10) In regulation 36 (application to the Channel Islands)—

(a) in paragraphs (2)(a) and (3)(a), for "mentally disordered person" substitute "person who lacks capacity"; and
(b) in paragraphs (2)(b) and (3)(b), for "receiver in relation to a mentally disordered person" substitute "deputy in relation to a person who lacks capacity".

(11) In paragraph 2 of Part 1 of Schedule 1 (persons entitled to hold index-linked certificates to be purchased before 7th September 1981), for "receiver on behalf of and in the name of a mentally disordered person" substitute "deputy on behalf of and in the name of a person who lacks capacity".

SAVINGS CERTIFICATES (CHILDREN'S BONUS BONDS) REGULATIONS 1991

18 (1) The Savings Certificates (Children's Bonus Bonds) Regulations 1991 are amended in accordance with this paragraph.

(2) In regulation 2(1) (interpretation), omit the entries for "mentally disordered person" and "receiver" and, in the appropriate alphabetical position, insert—

(a) ""deputy" in the application of these Regulations to England and Wales, means, in relation to any decision made for a person who lacks capacity, a deputy appointed by the Court of Protection for that person with power to make decisions in relation to the matters in question;"; and
(b) ""person who lacks capacity" means a person who lacks capacity within the meaning of the Mental Capacity Act 2005 (c 9);".

(3) In regulation 8(2) (repayment in case of persons under 16 years of age), for "mentally disordered person" substitute "person who lacks capacity".

(4) In regulation 9 (repayment in case of mentally disordered persons)—
(a) in the title, for "mentally disordered persons" substitute "persons who lack capacity";
(b) in paragraph (1), for "mentally disordered person shall be made by his receiver" substitute "person who lacks capacity shall be made by his deputy"; and
(c) in paragraph (2), for "mentally disordered person for whose estate no receiver" substitute "person who lacks capacity for whom no deputy".

(5) In regulation 15 (persons under disability)—
(a) for "mentally disordered person" substitute "person who lacks capacity"; and
(b) for "receiver" substitute "deputy".

(6) In regulation 29 (application to Scotland)—
(a) in paragraph (a), for "mentally disordered person" substitute "person who lacks capacity"; and
(b) in paragraph (b), for "receiver in relation to a mentally disordered person" substitute "deputy in relation to a person who lacks capacity".

(7) In regulation 30 (application to Northern Ireland)—
(a) in paragraph (a), for "mentally disordered person" substitute "person who lacks capacity"; and
(b) in paragraph (b), for "receiver in relation to a mentally disordered person" substitute "deputy in relation to a person who lacks capacity".

(8) In regulation 31(2) (application to the Isle of Man)—
(a) in paragraph (a), for "mentally disordered person" substitute "person who lacks capacity"; and
(b) in paragraph (b), for "receiver in relation to any act or thing done in respect of a mentally disordered person shall be construed as a reference to a receiver" substitute "deputy in relation to any decision made for a person who lacks capacity shall be construed as a reference to a deputy".

(9) In regulation 32 (application to the Channel Islands)—
(a) in paragraphs (2)(a) and (3)(a), for "mentally disordered person" substitute "person who lacks capacity"; and
(b) in paragraphs (2)(b) and (3)(b), for "receiver in relation to a mentally disordered person" substitute "deputy in relation to a person who lacks capacity".

JUDICIAL PENSIONS (TRANSFER BETWEEN JUDICIAL PENSION SCHEMES) REGULATIONS 1995

19 In Schedule 2 (existing judicial scheme judicial offices included in each arrangement) to the Judicial Pensions (Transfer Between Judicial Pension Schemes) Regulations 1995, under the cross-heading "District Judiciary Scheme", omit the reference to a Master of the Court of Protection except in the case of a person holding that office immediately before the commencement of this paragraph or who had previously retired from that office or died.

JUDICIAL PENSIONS (ADDITIONAL VOLUNTARY CONTRIBUTIONS) REGULATIONS 1995

20 In Schedule 4 (existing judicial scheme judicial offices included in each arrangement) to the Judicial Pensions (Additional Voluntary Contributions) Regulations 1995, under the cross-heading "District Judiciary Scheme", omit the reference to a Master of the Court of Protection except in the case of a person holding that office immediately before the commencement of this paragraph or who had previously retired from that office or died.

GOODS VEHICLES (LICENSING OF OPERATORS) REGULATIONS 1995

21 (1) Regulations 29 (partnerships) and 31 (continuance of licence on death, bankruptcy etc) of the Goods Vehicles (Licensing of Operators) Regulations 1995 are amended in accordance with this paragraph.

(2) In regulation 29(11)(b), for the words from "patient" to "Mental Health Act 1983", substitute "person who lacks capacity (within the meaning of the Mental Capacity Act 2005 (c 9)) to carry on the activities covered by the licence".

(3) In regulation 31—

- (a) in paragraph (2), for the words from "patient" to "Mental Health Act 1983", substitute "person who lacks capacity (within the meaning of the Mental Capacity Act 2005) to carry on the activities covered by the licence"; and
- (b) in paragraph (3), for the words from "patient" to "Mental Health Act 1983", substitute "person who lacks capacity (within the meaning of the Mental Capacity Act 2005) to carry on the activities covered by the licence".

LANDFILL TAX REGULATIONS 1996

22 For regulation 33(1C)(a) (bodies eligible for approval) of the Landfill Tax Regulations 1996, substitute—

"(a) in England and Wales, the person lacks capacity within the meaning of the Mental Capacity Act 2005 (c 9) to administer and manage his property and affairs;".

FAMILY LAW ACT 1996 (ALLOCATION OF PROCEEDINGS) ORDER 1997

23 In article 8(2)(b) (transfer from family proceedings court to county court) of the Family Law Act 1996 (Allocation of Proceedings) Order 1997, for the words "a person who, by reason of mental disorder within the meaning of the Mental Health Act 1983, is incapable of managing and administering his property and affairs" substitute "a person lacking capacity within the meaning of the Mental Capacity Act 2005 (c 9) to conduct the proceedings".

GENERAL CHIROPRACTIC COUNCIL (CONSTITUTION AND PROCEDURE) RULES ORDER 1999

24 In rule 2 (grounds of removal) of the General Chiropractic Council (Constitution and Procedure) Rules Order of Council 1999, in paragraph (1)(d) for "or is otherwise incapable, by reason of mental disorder, of properly managing his property or affairs", substitute "or lacks capacity within the meaning of the Mental Capacity Act 2005 (c 9), to properly manage his property or affairs".

HEALTH SERVICE MEDICINES (PRICE CONTROL APPEALS) REGULATIONS 2000

25 In regulation 7 (appointment of tribunal) of the Health Service Medicines (Price Control Appeals) Regulations 2000, in paragraph (3)(b), for "incapacity" substitute "lack of capacity (within the meaning of the Mental Capacity Act 2005 (c 9))".

IONISING RADIATION (MEDICAL EXPOSURE) REGULATIONS 2000

26 In regulation 7 (optimisation) of the Ionising Radiation (Medical Exposure) Regulations 2000—

- (a) in paragraph (5)(b), after "capacity" insert "(within the meaning of the Mental Capacity Act 2005 (c 9) in the case of a child aged sixteen or seventeen)"; and
- (b) in paragraph (5)(c), after "capacity" insert "(within the meaning of the Mental Capacity Act 2005)".

CARERS (SERVICES) AND DIRECT PAYMENTS (AMENDMENT) (ENGLAND) REGULATIONS 2001

27 For regulation 2(2) (services of an intimate nature and prescribed circumstances) of the Carers (Services) and Direct Payments (Amendment) (England) Regulations 2001, substitute—

"(2) Where a service (A) is being delivered to the person cared for, a service of an intimate nature may be provided if—

(a) during the delivery of service A, the person cared for asks the person delivering that service to provide a service of an intimate nature;

(b) the person lacks capacity (within the meaning of the Mental Capacity Act 2005 (c 9)) to consent to the provision of a service of an intimate nature and it is provided in accordance with the principles of that Act; or

(c) except where sub-paragraph (b) applies, the person cared for is in a situation in which he is likely to suffer serious personal harm unless a service of an intimate nature is provided to him and the person providing service A reasonably believes that it is necessary to provide a service of an intimate nature because the likelihood of serious personal harm to the person cared for is imminent.".

CARE HOMES REGULATIONS 2001

28 (1) The Care Homes Regulations 2001 are amended in accordance with this paragraph.

(2) In regulation 2 (interpretation), in paragraph (1), in the appropriate alphabetical position, insert—

(a) ""the 2005 Act" means the Mental Capacity Act 2005 (c 9);" and

(b) ""lacks capacity" means lacks capacity within the meaning of the 2005 Act;".

(3) In regulation 13 (further requirements as to health and welfare), for paragraph (7) substitute—

"(7) The registered person shall ensure that no service user is subject to physical restraint unless—

(a) restraint of the kind employed is the only practicable means of securing the welfare of that or any other service user and there are exceptional circumstances; or

(b) in the case of a person who lacks capacity in relation to the matter in question, the act meets the conditions of section 6 of the 2005 Act.".

PRIVATE AND VOLUNTARY HEALTH CARE (ENGLAND) REGULATIONS 2001

29 (1) The Private and Voluntary Health Care (England) Regulations 2001 are amended in accordance with this paragraph.

(2) In regulation 2 (interpretation)—

(a) in paragraph (1), at the beginning insert—

""the 2005 Act" means the Mental Capacity Act 2005 (c 9);"; and

(b) at the end, add—

"(4) For the purpose of any decision required to be made under these Regulations as to a person's capacity, lack of capacity shall be interpreted in accordance with the 2005 Act and any reference to a person who lacks capacity shall be construed accordingly.".

(3) In regulation 9 (policies and procedures), in paragraph (3)—

(a) in sub-paragraph (a), for "competence" substitute "capacity";

(b) in sub-paragraph (b), for "competent patient" substitute "patient who has capacity"; and

(c) for sub-paragraph (c), substitute—

"(c) in the case of patient who lacks capacity the requirements of the 2005 Act are complied with before any treatment proposed for him is administered; and".

(4) In regulation 16 (care and welfare of patients), in paragraphs (1) and (3), after "so far as practicable," insert "(and, where the person lacks capacity, in accordance with the principles of the 2005 Act)".

(5) In regulation 35 (resuscitation), in paragraph (2)—

(a) in sub-paragraph (a), for "are competent" substitute "have the capacity"; and

(b) after sub-paragraph (a), insert—

"(aa) take proper account of valid and applicable advance decisions made by patients under the 2005 Act;".

(6) In regulation 37 (surgical procedures)—

(a) in paragraph (2), after "a patient" insert "who has the capacity to do so";
(b) in paragraph (3), for "is not competent" substitute "lacks the capacity"; and
(c) after paragraph (3), insert—

"(4) In the case of a patient who lacks capacity to consent to surgery, the registered person shall take proper account of any valid and applicable advance decisions made by the patient under the 2005 Act.".

DOMICILIARY CARE AGENCIES REGULATIONS 2002

30 (1) The Domiciliary Care Agencies Regulations 2002 are amended in accordance with this paragraph.

(2) In regulation 2 (interpretation), in paragraph (1), in the appropriate alphabetical position, insert—

" "the 2005 Act" means the Mental Capacity Act 2005 (c 9);
"lacks capacity" means lacks capacity within the meaning of the 2005 Act;".

(3) In regulation 14 (arrangements for the provision of personal care), for paragraph (10) substitute—

"(10) The registered person shall ensure that no service user is subject to physical restraint unless—

(a) restraint of the kind employed is the only practicable means of securing the welfare of that or any other service user and there are exceptional circumstances; or
(b) in the case of a person who lacks capacity in relation to the matter in question, the act meets the conditions of section 6 of the 2005 Act.".

LAND REGISTRATION RULES 2003

31 (1) Rule 61 (documents executed by attorney) of, and Schedule 3 (forms referred to in rule 206) to, the Land Registration Rules 2003 are amended in accordance with this paragraph.

(2) In rule 61—

(a) for paragraph (1)(c) substitute—

"(c) a document which under section 4 of the Evidence and Powers of Attorney Act 1940, paragraph 16 of Part 2 of Schedule 1, or paragraph 15(3) of Part 5 of Schedule 4 to the Mental Capacity Act 2005 (c 9) is sufficient evidence of the contents of the power, or"; and

(b) for paragraph (2) substitute—

"(2) If an order or direction under section 22 or 23 of, or paragraph 16 of Part 5 of Schedule 4 to, the Mental Capacity Act 2005 has been made with respect to a power or the donor of the power or the attorney appointed under it, the order or direction must be produced to the registrar.".

(3) In Schedule 3—

(a) in Form 1 (certificate as to execution of power of attorney (rule 61))—
(i) for the first bullet point substitute—

"the power of attorney ("the power") is in existence [and is made and, where required, has been registered under (*state statutory provisions under which the power is made and, where required, has been registered, if applicable*)],", and

(ii) in the fourth bullet point, for the words "or section 7(3) of the Enduring Powers of Attorney Act 1985", substitute—

", paragraph 16 of Part 2 of Schedule 1, or paragraph 15(3) of Part 5 of Schedule 4 to the Mental Capacity Act 2005"; and

(b) in Form 2 (statutory declaration/certificate as to non-revocation for powers more than 12 months old at the date of the disposition for which they are used (rule 62)—
(i) in the third bullet point, for the words "valid enduring power", substitute "valid lasting or enduring power of attorney",

(ii) after the third bullet point, insert—

"Where the power is in the form prescribed for a lasting power of attorney—
—that a lasting power of attorney was not created, or
—of circumstances which, if the lasting power of attorney had been created, would have terminated the attorney's authority to act as an attorney, or", and

(iii) in the heading immediately before the fourth bullet point, after the words "enduring power", insert "of attorney".

NATIONAL HEALTH SERVICE (TRAVEL EXPENSES AND REMISSION OF CHARGES) REGULATIONS 2003

32 In regulation 7 (claims to entitlement) of the National Health Service (Travel Expenses and Remission of Charges) Regulations 2003, for paragraph (3), substitute—

"(3) A claim may be made on behalf of another person where that person—
(a) is unable by reason of physical incapacity; or
(b) lacks capacity within the meaning of the Mental Capacity Act 2005 (c 9),

to make the claim himself.".

CHILD TRUST FUNDS REGULATIONS 2004

33 In regulation 33A(2) (the official solicitor or accountant of court to be the person who has the authority to manage an account) of the Child Trust Funds Regulations 2004, in Condition 4—

(a) in sub-paragraph (a), for the word "receiver" substitute "deputy";
(b) for sub-paragraph (b), substitute "(b) determined that such a person lacks capacity within the meaning of the Mental Capacity Act 2005 (c 9) to manage the child's property and affairs"; and
(c) in the modifications of condition 4 for Scotland—
(i) in sub-paragraph (b), for the word "receiver" substitute "deputy"; and
(ii) in sub-paragraph (c), for the word "patient" substitute "person lacking capacity".

NATIONAL HEALTH SERVICE (COMPLAINTS) REGULATIONS 2004

34 In regulation 8 (person who may make complaints) of the National Health Service (Complaints) Regulations 2004—

(a) in paragraph (2)(c), omit "or mental" and "or";
(b) after paragraph(2)(c), insert—
"(cc) is unable because he lacks capacity within the meaning of the Mental Capacity Act 2005 (c 9) to make the complaint himself; or";
(c) in paragraph (3), after "who is" insert "physically"; and
(d) after paragraph (3) insert—

"(3A) In the case of a patient or person affected who lacks capacity within the meaning of the Mental Capacity Act 2005 the representative must be either a person appointed or authorised to act on his behalf under the 2005 Act or another person who, in the opinion of the complaints manager, had or has a sufficient interest in his welfare and is a suitable person to act as representative".

COMMONHOLD REGULATIONS 2004

35 (1) In the table of contents in Schedule 2 (articles of association) to the Commonhold Regulations 2004, under the heading "Votes of Members", for the words "Entitlement to vote—Mental Capacity" substitute "Entitlement to vote—lack of mental capacity".

(2) In the title to article 29 of Schedule 2 (articles of association) to the Commonhold Regulations 2004, for the words "mental incapacity" substitute "lack of mental capacity".

(3) In article 29 of Schedule 2 (articles of association) to the Commonhold Regulations 2004, for each reference to "receiver" substitute a reference to "deputy".

ADULT PLACEMENT SCHEMES (ENGLAND) REGULATIONS 2004

36 (1) The Adult Placement Schemes (England) Regulations 2004 are amended in accordance with this paragraph.

(2) In regulation 2 (interpretation), in the appropriate alphabetical position, insert—

(a) ““the 2005 Act” means the Mental Capacity Act 2005 (c 9);”; and

(b) ““lacks capacity” means lacks capacity within the meaning of the 2005 Act;”.

(3) In regulation 17 (carer agreements), for paragraph (2)(e) substitute—

“(e) specifies that a service user is not to be subject to physical restraint unless—

(i) restraint of the kind employed is the only practicable means of securing the welfare of that, or another, service user; or

(ii) in the case of a person who lacks capacity in relation to the matter in question, the act meets the conditions of section 6 of the 2005 Act;”

(4) In regulation 19 (adult placement carer handbook), for paragraph (3)(c) substitute—

“(c) specifies that a service user is not to be subject to physical restraint unless—

(i) restraint of the kind employed is the only practicable means of securing the welfare of that, or another, service user, or

(ii) in the case of a person who lacks capacity in relation to the matter in question, the act meets the conditions of section 6 of the 2005 Act;”.

DAMAGES (VARIATION OF PERIODICAL PAYMENTS) ORDER 2005

37 For article 3(d) (defendant’s financial resources) of the Damages (Variation of Periodical Payments) Order 2005, substitute—

“(d) the order is made by consent and the claimant is neither a child, nor a person who lacks capacity within the meaning of the Mental Capacity Act 2005 (c 9) to administer and manage his property and affairs nor a patient within the meaning of Part VII of the Mental Health (Northern Ireland) Order 1986,”.

DISABILITY DISCRIMINATION (SERVICE PROVIDERS AND PUBLIC AUTHORITIES CARRYING OUT FUNCTIONS) REGULATIONS 2005

38 In regulation 3(b) (circumstances in which mental incapacity justification does not apply) of the Disability Discrimination (Service Providers and Public Authorities Carrying Out Functions) Regulations 2005, for the words “functions conferred by or under Part 7 of the Mental Health Act 1983”, substitute “being a deputy appointed by the Court of Protection”.

DISABILITY DISCRIMINATION (PRIVATE CLUBS ETC) REGULATIONS 2005

39 (1) In regulation 3(b) (circumstances in which mental incapacity justification does not apply) of the Disability Discrimination (Private Clubs etc) Regulations 2005, for the words “functions conferred by or under Part 7 of the Mental Health Act 1983”, substitute “being a deputy appointed by the Court of Protection”.

(2) In regulation 13(3)(b) (duty of associations to make adjustments: justification) of these regulations, for the words “functions conferred by or under Part 7 of the Mental Health Act 1983”, substitute “being a deputy appointed by the Court of Protection”.

DISABILITY DISCRIMINATION (PREMISES) REGULATIONS 2006

40 In regulation 2(b) (circumstances in which mental incapacity justification does not apply) of the Disability Discrimination (Premises) Regulations 2006 , for the words “functions conferred by or under Part 7 of the Mental Health Act 1983”, substitute “being a deputy appointed by the Court of Protection”.

SCHEDULE 2
AMENDMENTS TO FORMS IN SCHEDULE 4 (FORMS) OF THE INSOLVENCY RULES 1986: FORM 4.64 AND FORM 6.57

…

MENTAL CAPACITY ACT 2005 (TRANSFER OF PROCEEDINGS) ORDER 2007

SI 2007/1899

1 Citation and commencement

(1) This Order may be cited as the Mental Capacity Act 2005 (Transfer of Proceedings) Order 2007.

(2) This Order shall come into force on 1st October 2007.

(3) In this Order "the Children Act" means the Children Act 1989.

2 Transfers from the Court of Protection to a court having jurisdiction under the Children Act

(1) This article applies to any proceedings in the Court of Protection which relate to a person under 18.

(2) The Court of Protection may direct the transfer of the whole or part of the proceedings to a court having jurisdiction under the Children Act where it considers that in all the circumstances, it is just and convenient to transfer the proceedings.

(3) In making a determination, the Court of Protection must have regard to—
- (a) whether the proceedings should be heard together with other proceedings that are pending in a court having jurisdiction under the Children Act;
- (b) whether any order that may be made by a court having jurisdiction under that Act is likely to be a more appropriate way of dealing with the proceedings;
- (c) the need to meet any requirements that would apply if the proceedings had been started in a court having jurisdiction under the Children Act; and
- (d) any other matter that the court considers relevant.

(4) The Court of Protection—
- (a) may exercise the power to make an order under paragraph (2) on an application or on its own initiative; and
- (b) where it orders a transfer, must give reasons for its decision.

(5) Any proceedings transferred under this article—
- (a) are to be treated for all purposes as if they were proceedings under the Children Act which had been started in a court having jurisdiction under that Act; and
- (b) are to be dealt with after the transfer in accordance with directions given by a court having jurisdiction under that Act.

3 Transfers from a court having jurisdiction under the Children Act to the Court of Protection

(1) This article applies to any proceedings in a court having jurisdiction under the Children Act which relate to a person under 18.

(2) A court having jurisdiction under the Children Act may direct the transfer of the whole or part of the proceedings to the Court of Protection where it considers that in all circumstances, it is just and convenient to transfer the proceedings.

(3) In making a determination, the court having jurisdiction under the Children Act must have regard to—
- (a) whether the proceedings should be heard together with other proceedings that are pending in the Court of Protection;
- (b) whether any order that may be made by the Court of Protection is likely to be a more appropriate way of dealing with the proceedings;
- (c) the extent to which any order made as respects a person who lacks capacity is likely to continue to have effect when that person reaches 18; and
- (d) any other matter that the court considers relevant.

(4) A court having jurisdiction under the Children Act—
- (a) may exercise the power to make an order under paragraph (2) on an application or on its own initiative; and
- (b) where it orders a transfer, must give reasons for its decision.

(5) Any proceedings transferred under this article—
- (a) are to be treated for all purposes as if they were proceedings under the Mental Capacity Act 2005 which had been started in the Court of Protection; and
- (b) are to be dealt with after the transfer in accordance with directions given by the Court of Protection.

4 Avoidance of double liability for fees

Any fee paid for the purpose of starting any proceedings that are transferred under article 2 or 3 is to be treated as if it were the fee that would have been payable if the proceedings had started in the court to which the transfer is made.

LASTING POWERS OF ATTORNEY, ENDURING POWERS OF ATTORNEY AND PUBLIC GUARDIAN REGULATIONS 2007

SI 2007/1253

PART 1
PRELIMINARY

1 Citation and commencement

(1) These Regulations may be cited as the Lasting Powers of Attorney, Enduring Powers of Attorney and Public Guardian Regulations 2007.

(2) These Regulations shall come into force on 1 October 2007.

2 Interpretation

(1) In these Regulations—

"the Act" means the Mental Capacity Act 2005;

"court" means the Court of Protection;

"LPA certificate", in relation to an instrument made with a view to creating a lasting power of attorney, means the certificate which is required to be included in the instrument by virtue of paragraph 2(1)(e) of Schedule 1 to the Act;

"named person", in relation to an instrument made with a view to creating a lasting power of attorney, means a person who is named in the instrument as being a person to be notified of any application for the registration of the instrument;

"prescribed information", in relation to any instrument intended to create a lasting power of attorney, means the information contained in the form used for the instrument which appears under the heading "prescribed information".

3 Minimal differences from forms prescribed in these Regulations

(1) In these Regulations, any reference to a form—
- (a) in the case of a form set out in Schedules 1 to 7 to these Regulations, is to be regarded as including a Welsh version of that form; and
- (b) in the case of a form set out in Schedules 2 to 7 to these Regulations, is to be regarded as also including—
  - (i) a form to the same effect but which differs in an immaterial respect in form or mode of expression;
  - (ii) a form to the same effect but with such variations as the circumstances may require or the court or the Public Guardian may approve; or
  - (iii) a Welsh version of a form within (i) or (ii).

4 Computation of time

(1) This regulation shows how to calculate any period of time which is specified in these Regulations.

(2) A period of time expressed as a number of days must be computed as clear days.

(3) Where the specified period is 7 days or less, and would include a day which is not a business day, that day does not count.

(4) When the specified period for doing any act at the office of the Public Guardian ends on a day on which the office is closed, that act will be done in time if done on the next day on which the office is open.

(5) In this regulation—

"business day" means a day other than—

(a) a Saturday, Sunday, Christmas Day or Good Friday; or

(b) a bank holiday under the Banking and Financial Dealings Act 1971, in England and Wales; and

"clear days" means that in computing the number of days—

(a) the day on which the period begins, and

(b) if the end of the period is defined by reference to an event, the day on which that event occurs,

are not included.

PART 2
LASTING POWERS OF ATTORNEY

INSTRUMENTS INTENDED TO CREATE A LASTING POWER OF ATTORNEY

5 Forms for lasting powers of attorney

The forms set out in Parts 1 and 2 of Schedule 1 to these Regulations are the forms which, in the circumstances to which they apply, are to be used for instruments intended to create a lasting power of attorney.

6 Maximum number of named persons

The maximum number of named persons that the donor of a lasting power of attorney may specify in the instrument intended to create the power is 5.

7 Requirement for two LPA certificates where instrument has no named persons

Where an instrument intended to create a lasting power of attorney includes a statement by the donor that there are no persons whom he wishes to be notified of any application for the registration of the instrument—

(a) the instrument must include two LPA certificates; and

(b) each certificate must be completed and signed by a different person.

8 Persons who may provide an LPA certificate

(1) Subject to paragraph (3), the following persons may give an LPA certificate—

(a) a person chosen by the donor as being someone who has known him personally for the period of at least two years which ends immediately before the date on which that person signs the LPA certificate;

(b) a person chosen by the donor who, on account of his professional skills and expertise, reasonably considers that he is competent to make the judgments necessary to certify the matters set out in paragraph (2)(1)(e) of Schedule 1 to the Act.

(2) The following are examples of persons within paragraph (1)(b)—

(a) a registered health care professional;

(b) a barrister, solicitor or advocate called or admitted in any part of the United Kingdom;

(c) a registered social worker; or

(d) an independent mental capacity advocate.

(3) A person is disqualified from giving an LPA certificate in respect of any instrument intended to create a lasting power of attorney if that person is—

(a) a family member of the donor;

(b) a donee of that power;

(c) a donee of—

(i) any other lasting power of attorney, or

(ii) an enduring power of attorney,

which has been executed by the donor (whether or not it has been revoked);

(d) a family member of a donee within sub-paragraph (b);
(e) a director or employee of a trust corporation acting as a donee within sub-paragraph (b);
(f) a business partner or employee of—
  (i) the donor, or
  (ii) a donee within sub-paragraph (b);
(g) an owner, director, manager or employee of any care home in which the donor is living when the instrument is executed; or
(h) a family member of a person within sub-paragraph (g).

(4) In this regulation—
"care home" has the meaning given in section 3 of the Care Standards Act 2000;
"registered health care professional" means a person who is a member of a profession regulated by a body mentioned in section 25(3) of the National Health Service Reform and Health Care Professions Act 2002; and
"registered social worker" means a person registered as a social worker in a register maintained by—
(a) the General Social Care Council;
(b) the Care Council for Wales;
(c) the Scottish Social Services Council; or
(d) the Northern Ireland Social Care Council.

9 Execution of instrument

(1) An instrument intended to create a lasting power of attorney must be executed in accordance with this regulation.

(2) The donor must read (or have read to him) all the prescribed information.

(3) As soon as reasonably practicable after the steps required by paragraph (2) have been taken, the donor must—
(a) complete the provisions of Part A of the instrument that apply to him (or direct another person to do so); and
(b) subject to paragraph (7), sign Part A of the instrument in the presence of a witness.

(4) As soon as reasonably practicable after the steps required by paragraph (3) have been taken—
(a) the person giving an LPA certificate, or
(b) if regulation 7 applies (two LPA certificates required), each of the persons giving a certificate,

must complete the LPA certificate at Part B of the instrument and sign it.

(5) As soon as reasonably practicable after the steps required by paragraph (4) have been taken—
(a) the donee, or
(b) if more than one, each of the donees,

must read (or have read to him) all the prescribed information.

(6) As soon as reasonably practicable after the steps required by paragraph (5) have been taken, the donee or, if more than one, each of them—
(a) must complete the provisions of Part C of the instrument that apply to him (or direct another person to do so); and
(b) subject to paragraph (7), must sign Part C of the instrument in the presence of a witness.

(7) If the instrument is to be signed by any person at the direction of the donor, or at the direction of any donee, the signature must be done in the presence of two witnesses.

(8) For the purposes of this regulation—
(a) the donor may not witness any signature required for the power;
(b) a donee may not witness any signature required for the power apart from that of another donee.

(9) A person witnessing a signature must—
(a) sign the instrument; and
(b) give his full name and address.

(10) Any reference in this regulation to a person signing an instrument (however expressed) includes his signing it by means of a mark made on the instrument at the appropriate place.

REGISTERING THE INSTRUMENT

10 Notice to be given by a person about to apply for registration of lasting power of attorney

Schedule 2 to these Regulations sets out the form of notice ("LPA 001") which must be given by a donor or donee who is about to make an application for the registration of an instrument intended to create a lasting power of attorney.

11 Application for registration

(1) Schedule 3 to these Regulations sets out the form ("LPA 002") which must be used for making an application to the Public Guardian for the registration of an instrument intended to create a lasting power of attorney.

(2) Where the instrument to be registered which is sent with the application is neither—

(a) the original instrument intended to create the power, nor

(b) a certified copy of it,

the Public Guardian must not register the instrument unless the court directs him to do so.

(3) In paragraph (2) "a certified copy" means a photographic or other facsimile copy which is certified as an accurate copy by—

(a) the donor; or

(b) a solicitor or notary.

12 Period to elapse before registration in cases not involving objection or defect

The period at the end of which the Public Guardian must register an instrument in accordance with paragraph 5 of Schedule 1 to the Act is the period of 6 weeks beginning with—

(a) the date on which the Public Guardian gave the notice or notices under paragraph 7 or 8 of Schedule 1 to the Act of receipt of an application for registration; or

(b) if notices were given on more than one date, the latest of those dates.

13 Notice of receipt of application for registration

(1) Part 1 of Schedule 4 to these Regulations sets out the form of notice ("LPA 003A") which the Public Guardian must give to the donee (or donees) when the Public Guardian receives an application for the registration of a lasting power of attorney.

(2) Part 2 of Schedule 4 sets out the form of notice ("LPA 003B") which the Public Guardian must give to the donor when the Public Guardian receives such an application.

(3) Where it appears to the Public Guardian that there is good reason to do so, the Public Guardian must also provide (or arrange for the provision of) an explanation to the donor of—

(a) the notice referred to in paragraph (2) and what the effect of it is; and

(b) why it is being brought to his attention.

(4) Any information provided under paragraph (3) must be provided—

(a) to the donor personally; and

(b) in a way that is appropriate to the donor's circumstances (for example using simple language, visual aids or other appropriate means).

14 Objection to registration: notice to Public Guardian [to be given by the donee of the power or a named person]

(1) This regulation deals with any objection to the registration of an instrument as a lasting power of attorney which is to be made to the Public Guardian [by the donee of the power or a named person].

(2) Where [the donee of the power or a named person]—

(a) is entitled to receive notice under paragraph 6, 7 or 8 of Schedule 1 to the Act of an application for the registration of the instrument, and

(b) wishes to object to registration on a ground set out in paragraph 13(1) of Schedule 1 to the Act, he must do so before the end of the period of 5 weeks beginning with the date on which the notice is given.

(3) A notice of objection must be given in writing, setting out—

- (a) the name and address of the objector;
- (b) . . . the name and address of the donor of the power;
- (c) if known, the name and address of the donee (or donees); and
- (d) the ground for making the objection.

(4) The Public Guardian must notify the objector as to whether he is satisfied that the ground of the objection is established.

(5) At any time after receiving the notice of objection and before giving the notice required by paragraph (4), the Public Guardian may require the objector to provide such further information, or produce such documents, as the Public Guardian reasonably considers necessary to enable him to determine whether the ground for making the objection is established.

(6) Where—

- (a) the Public Guardian is satisfied that the ground of the objection is established, but
- (b) by virtue of section 13(7) of the Act, the instrument is not revoked,

the notice under paragraph (4) must contain a statement to that effect.

(7) Nothing in this regulation prevents an objector from making a further objection under paragraph 13 of Schedule 1 to the Act where—

- (a) the notice under paragraph (4) indicates that the Public Guardian is not satisfied that the particular ground of objection to which that notice relates is established; and
- (b) the period specified in paragraph (2) has not expired.

Amendment

Provision heading: words "to be given by the donee of the power or a named person" in square brackets inserted by SI 2007/2161, regs 2, 3(1).
Para (1): words "by the donee of the power or a named person" in square brackets inserted by SI 2007/2161, regs 2, 3(2).
Para (2): words "the donee of the power or a named person" in square brackets substituted by SI 2007/2161, regs 2, 3(3).
Para (3): in sub-para (b) words omitted revoked by SI 2007/2161, regs 2, 3(4).

[14A Objection to registration: notice to Public Guardian to be given by the donor]

[(1) This regulation deals with any objection to the registration of an instrument as a lasting power of attorney which is to be made to the Public Guardian by the donor of the power.

(2) Where the donor of the power—

- (a) is entitled to receive notice under paragraph 8 of Schedule 1 to the Act of an application for the registration of the instrument, and
- (b) wishes to object to the registration,

he must do so before the end of the period of 5 weeks beginning with the date on which the notice is given.

(3) The donor of the power must give notice of his objection in writing to the Public Guardian, setting out—

- (a) the name and address of the donor of the power;
- (b) if known, the name and address of the donee (or donees); and
- (c) the ground for making the objection.]

Amendment

Inserted by SI 2007/2161, regs 2, 4.

15 Objection to registration: application to the court

(1) This regulation deals with any objection to the registration of an instrument as a lasting power of attorney which is to be made to the court.

(2) The grounds for making an application to the court are—

- (a) that one or more of the requirements for the creation of a lasting power of attorney have not been met;
- (b) that the power has been revoked, or has otherwise come to an end, on a ground other than the grounds set out in paragraph 13(1) of Schedule 1 to the Act;

(c) any of the grounds set out in paragraph (a) or (b) of section 22(3) of the Act.

(3) Where any person—

(a) is entitled to receive notice under paragraph 6, 7 or 8 of Schedule 1 to the Act of an application for the registration of the instrument, and

(b) wishes to object to registration on one or more of the grounds set out in paragraph (2),

he must make an application to the court before the end of the period of 5 weeks beginning with the date on which the notice is given.

(4) The notice of an application to the court, which a person making an objection to the court is required to give to the Public Guardian under paragraph 13(3)(b)(ii) of Schedule 1 to the Act, must be in writing.

16 Notifying applicants of non-registration of lasting power of attorney

Where the Public Guardian is prevented from registering an instrument as a lasting power of attorney by virtue of—

(a) paragraph 11(1) of Schedule 1 to the Act (instrument not made in accordance with Schedule),

(b) paragraph 12(2) of that Schedule (deputy already appointed),

(c) paragraph 13(2) of that Schedule (objection by donee or named person on grounds of bankruptcy, disclaimer, death etc),

(d) paragraph 14(2) of that Schedule (objection by donor), or

(e) regulation 11(2) of these Regulations (application for registration not accompanied by original instrument or certified copy),

he must notify the person (or persons) who applied for registration of that fact.

17 Notice to be given on registration of lasting power of attorney

(1) Where the Public Guardian registers an instrument as a lasting power of attorney, he must—

(a) retain a copy of the instrument; and

(b) return to the person (or persons) who applied for registration the original instrument, or the certified copy of it, which accompanied the application for registration.

(2) Schedule 5 to these Regulations sets out the form of notice ("LPA 004") which the Public Guardian must give to the donor and donee (or donees) when the Public Guardian registers an instrument.

(3) Where it appears to the Public Guardian that there is good reason to do so, the Public Guardian must also provide (or arrange for the provision of) an explanation to the donor of—

(a) the notice referred to in paragraph (2) and what the effect of it is; and

(b) why it is being brought to his attention.

(4) Any information provided under paragraph (3) must be provided—

(a) to the donor personally; and

(b) in a way that is appropriate to the donor's circumstances (for example using simple language, visual aids or other appropriate means).

(5) "Certified copy" is to be construed in accordance with regulation 11(3).

POST-REGISTRATION

18 Changes to instrument registered as lasting power of attorney

(1) This regulation applies in any case where any of paragraphs 21 to 24 of Schedule 1 to the Act requires the Public Guardian to attach a note to an instrument registered as a lasting power of attorney.

(2) The Public Guardian must give a notice to the donor and the donee (or, if more than one, each of them) requiring him to deliver to the Public Guardian—

(a) the original of instrument which was sent to the Public Guardian for registration;

(b) any office copy of that registered instrument; and

(c) any certified copy of that registered instrument.

(3) On receipt of the document, the Public Guardian must—
(a) attach the required note; and
(b) return the document to the person from whom it was obtained.

19 Loss or destruction of instrument registered as lasting power of attorney

(1) This regulation applies where—
(a) a person is required by or under the Act to deliver up to the Public Guardian any of the following documents—
(i) an instrument registered as a lasting power of attorney;
(ii) an office copy of that registered instrument;
(iii) a certified copy of that registered instrument; and
(b) the document has been lost or destroyed.

(2) The person required to deliver up the document must provide to the Public Guardian in writing—
(a) if known, the date of the loss or destruction and the circumstances in which it occurred;
(b) otherwise, a statement of when he last had the document in his possession.

20 Disclaimer of appointment by a donee of lasting power of attorney

(1) Schedule 6 to these Regulations sets out the form ("LPA 005") which a donee of an instrument registered as a lasting power of attorney must use to disclaim his appointment as donee.

(2) The donee must send—
(a) the completed form to the donor; and
(b) a copy of it to—
(i) the Public Guardian; and
(ii) any other donee who, for the time being, is appointed under the power.

21 Revocation by donor of lasting power of attorney

(1) A donor who revokes a lasting power to attorney must—
(a) notify the Public Guardian that he has done so; and
(b) notify the donee (or, if more than one, each of them) of the revocation.

(2) Where the Public Guardian receives a notice under paragraph (1)(a), he must cancel the registration of the instrument creating the power if he is satisfied that the donor has taken such steps as are necessary in law to revoke it.

(3) The Public Guardian may require the donor to provide such further information, or produce such documents, as the Public Guardian reasonably considers necessary to enable him to determine whether the steps necessary for revocation have been taken.

(4) Where the Public Guardian cancels the registration of the instrument he must notify—
(a) the donor; and
(b) the donee or, if more than one, each of them.

22 Revocation of a lasting power of attorney on death of donor

(1) The Public Guardian must cancel the registration of an instrument as a lasting power of attorney if he is satisfied that the power has been revoked as a result of the donor's death.

(2) Where the Public Guardian cancels the registration of an instrument he must notify the donee or, if more than one, each of them.

PART 3
ENDURING POWERS OF ATTORNEY

23 Notice of intention to apply for registration of enduring power of attorney

(1) Schedule 7 to these Regulations sets out the form of notice ("EP1PG") which an attorney (or attorneys) under an enduring power of attorney must give of his intention to make an application for the registration of the instrument creating the power.

(2) In the case of the notice to be given to the donor, the attorney must also provide (or arrange for the provision of) an explanation to the donor of—

(a) the notice and what the effect of it is; and
(b) why it is being brought to his attention.

(3) The information provided under paragraph (2) must be provided—
(a) to the donor personally; and
(b) in a way that is appropriate to the donor's circumstances (for example using simple language, visual aids or other appropriate means).

24 Application for registration

(1) Schedule 8 to these Regulations sets out the form ("EP2PG") which must be used for making an application to the Public Guardian for the registration of an instrument creating an enduring power of attorney.

(2) Where the instrument to be registered which is sent with the application is neither—
(a) the original instrument creating the power, nor
(b) a certified copy of it,

the Public Guardian must not register the instrument unless the court directs him to do so.

(3) "Certified copy", in relation to an enduring power of attorney, means a copy certified in accordance with section 3 of the Powers of Attorney Act 1971.

25 Notice of objection to registration

(1) This regulation deals with any objection to the registration of an instrument creating an enduring power of attorney which is to be made to the Public Guardian under paragraph 13(4) of Schedule 4 to the Act.

(2) A notice of objection must be given in writing, setting out—
(a) the name and address of the objector;
(b) if different, the name and address of the donor of the power;
(c) if known, the name and address of the attorney (or attorneys); and
(d) the ground for making the objection.

26 Notifying applicants of non-registration of enduring power of attorney

Where the Public Guardian is prevented from registering an instrument creating an enduring power of attorney by virtue of—
(a) paragraph 13(2) of Schedule 4 to the Act (deputy already appointed),
(b) paragraph 13(5) of that Schedule (receipt by Public Guardian of valid notice of objection from person entitled to notice of application to register),
(c) paragraph 13(7) of that Schedule (Public Guardian required to undertake appropriate enquiries in certain circumstances), or
(d) regulation 24(2) of these Regulations (application for registration not accompanied by original instrument or certified copy),

he must notify the person (or persons) who applied for registration of that fact.

27 Registration of instrument creating an enduring power of attorney

(1) Where the Public Guardian registers an instrument creating an enduring power of attorney, he must—
(a) retain a copy of the instrument; and
(b) return to the person (or persons) who applied for registration the original instrument, or the certified copy of it, which accompanied the application.

(2) "Certified copy" has the same meaning as in regulation 24(3).

28 Objection or revocation not applying to all joint and several attorneys

In a case within paragraph 20(6) or (7) of Schedule 4 to the Act, the form of the entry to be made in the register in respect of an instrument creating the enduring power of attorney is a stamp bearing the following words (inserting the information indicated, as appropriate)—

"THE REGISTRATION OF THIS ENDURING POWER OF ATTORNEY IS QUALIFIED AND EXTENDS TO THE APPOINTMENT OF .... (insert name of attorney(s) not affected by ground(s) of objection or revocation) ONLY AS THE ATTORNEY(S) OF .... (insert name of donor)".

29 Loss or destruction of instrument registered as enduring power of attorney

(1) This regulation applies where—

(a) a person is required by or under the Act to deliver up to the Public Guardian any of the following documents—

(i) an instrument registered as an enduring power of attorney;

(ii) an office copy of that registered instrument; or

(iii) a certified copy of that registered instrument; and

(b) the document has been lost or destroyed.

(2) The person who is required to deliver up the document must provide to the Public Guardian in writing—

(a) if known, the date of the loss or destruction and the circumstances in which it occurred;

(b) otherwise, a statement of when he last had the document in his possession.

PART 4
FUNCTIONS OF THE PUBLIC GUARDIAN

THE REGISTERS

30 Establishing and maintaining the registers

(1) In this Part "the registers" means—

(a) the register of lasting powers of attorney,

(b) the register of enduring powers of attorney, and

(c) the register of court orders appointing deputies,

which the Public Guardian must establish and maintain.

(2) On each register the Public Guardian may include—

(a) such descriptions of information about a registered instrument or a registered order as the Public Guardian considers appropriate; and

(b) entries which relate to an instrument or order for which registration has been cancelled.

31 Disclosure of information on a register: search by the Public Guardian

(1) Any person may, by an application made under paragraph (2), request the Public Guardian to carry out a search of one or more of the registers.

(2) An application must—

(a) state—

(i) the register or registers to be searched;

(ii) the name of the person to whom the application relates; and

(iii) such other details about that person as the Public Guardian may require for the purpose of carrying out the search; and

(b) be accompanied by any fee provided for under section 58(4)(b) of the Act.

(3) The Public Guardian may require the applicant to provide such further information, or produce such documents, as the Public Guardian reasonably considers necessary to enable him to carry out the search.

(4) As soon as reasonably practicable after receiving the application—

(a) the Public Guardian must notify the applicant of the result of the search; and

(b) in the event that it reveals one or more entries on the register, the Public Guardian must disclose to the applicant all the information appearing on the register in respect of each entry.

32 Disclosure of additional information held by the Public Guardian

(1) This regulation applies in any case where, as a result of a search made under regulation 31, a person has obtained information relating to a registered instrument or a registered order which confers authority to make decisions about matters concerning a person ("P").

(2) On receipt of an application made in accordance with paragraph (4), the Public Guardian may, if he considers that there is good reason to do so, disclose to the applicant such additional information as he considers appropriate.

(3) "Additional information" means any information relating to P—
- (a) which the Public Guardian has obtained in exercising the functions conferred on him under the Act; but
- (b) which does not appear on the register.

(4) An application must state—
- (a) the name of P;
- (b) the reasons for making the application; and
- (c) what steps, if any, the applicant has taken to obtain the information from P.

(5) The Public Guardian may require the applicant to provide such further information, or produce such documents, as the Public Guardian reasonably considers necessary to enable him to determine the application.

(6) In determining whether to disclose any additional information to P, the Public Guardian must, in particular, have regard to—
- (a) the connection between P and the applicant;
- (b) the reasons for requesting the information (in particular, why the information cannot or should not be obtained directly from P);
- (c) the benefit to P, or any detriment he may suffer, if a disclosure is made; and
- (d) any detriment that another person may suffer if a disclosure is made.

SECURITY FOR DISCHARGE OF FUNCTIONS

33 Persons required to give security for the discharge of their functions

(1) This regulation applies in any case where the court orders a person ("S") to give to the Public Guardian security for the discharge of his functions.

(2) The security must be given by S—
- (a) by means of a bond which is entered into in accordance with regulation 34; or
- (b) in such other manner as the court may direct.

(3) For the purposes of paragraph (2)(a), S complies with the requirement to give the security only if—
- (a) the endorsement required by regulation 34(2) has been provided; and
- (b) the person who provided it has notified the Public Guardian of that fact.

(4) For the purposes of paragraph (2)(b), S complies with the requirement to give the security—
- (a) in any case where the court directs that any other endorsement must be provided, only if—
  - (i) that endorsement has been provided; and
  - (ii) the person who provided it has notified the Public Guardian of that fact;
- (b) in any case where the court directs that any other requirements must be met in relation to the giving of the security, only if the Public Guardian is satisfied that those other requirements have been met.

34 Security given under regulation 33(2)(a): requirement for endorsement

(1) This regulation has effect for the purposes of regulation 33(2)(a).

(2) A bond is entered into in accordance with this regulation only if it is endorsed by—
- (a) an authorised insurance company; or
- (b) an authorised deposit-taker.

(3) A person may enter into the bond under—
- (a) arrangements made by the Public Guardian; or
- (b) other arrangements which are made by the person entering into the bond or on his behalf.

(4) The Public Guardian may make arrangements with any person specified in paragraph (2) with a view to facilitating the provision by them of bonds which persons required to give security to the Public Guardian may enter into.

(5) In this regulation—

"authorised insurance company" means—

(a) a person who has permission under Part 4 of the Financial Services and Markets Act 2000 to effect or carry out contracts of insurance;

(b) an EEA firm of the kind mentioned in paragraph 5(d) of Schedule 3 to that Act, which has permission under paragraph 15 of that Schedule to effect or carry out contracts of insurance;

(c) a person who carries on insurance market activity (within the meaning given in section 316(3) of that Act); and

"authorised deposit-taker" means—

(a) a person who has permission under Part 4 of the Financial Services and Markets Act 2000 to accept deposits;

(b) an EEA firm of the kind mentioned in paragraph 5(d) of Schedule 3 to that Act, which has permission under paragraph 15 of that Schedule to accept deposits.

(6) The definitions of "authorised insurance company" and "authorised deposit-taker" must be read with—

(a) section 22 of the Financial Services and Markets Act 2000;

(b) any relevant order under that section; and

(c) Schedule 2 to that Act.

35 Security given under regulation 33(2)(a): maintenance or replacement

(1) This regulation applies to any security given under regulation 33(2)(a).

(2) At such times or at such intervals as the Public Guardian may direct by notice in writing, any person ("S") who has given the security must satisfy the Public Guardian that any premiums payable in respect of it have been paid.

(3) Where S proposes to replace a security already given by him, the new security is not to be regarded as having been given until the Public Guardian is satisfied that—

(a) the requirements set out in sub-paragraphs (a) and (b) of regulation 33(3) have been met in relation to it; and

(b) no payment is due from S in connection with the discharge of his functions.

36 Enforcement following court order of any endorsed security

(1) This regulation applies to any security given to the Public Guardian in respect of which an endorsement has been provided.

(2) Where the court orders the enforcement of the security, the Public Guardian must—

(a) notify any person who endorsed the security of the contents of the order; and

(b) notify the court when payment has been made of the amount secured.

37 Discharge of any endorsed security

(1) This regulation applies to any security given by a person ("S") to the Public Guardian in respect of which an endorsement has been provided.

(2) The security may be discharged if the court makes an order discharging it.

(3) In any other case, the security may not be discharged until the end of the period of 7 years commencing with whichever of the following dates first occurs—

(a) if the person on whose behalf S was appointed to act dies, the date of his death;

(b) if S dies, the date of his death;

(c) if the court makes an order which discharges S but which does not also discharge the security under paragraph (2), the date of the order;

(d) the date when S otherwise ceases to be under a duty to discharge the functions in respect of which he was ordered to give security.

(4) For the purposes of paragraph (3), if a person takes any step with a view to discharging the security before the end of the period specified in that paragraph, the security is to be treated for all purposes as if it were still in place.

DEPUTIES

38 Application for additional time to submit a report

(1) This regulation applies where the court requires a deputy to submit a report to the Public Guardian and specifies a time or interval for it to be submitted.

(2) A deputy may apply to the Public Guardian requesting more time for submitting a particular report.

(3) An application must—

(a) state the reason for requesting more time; and

(b) contain or be accompanied by such information as the Public Guardian may reasonably require to determine the application.

(4) In response to an application, the Public Guardian may, if he considers it appropriate to do so, undertake that he will not take steps to secure performance of the deputy's duty to submit the report at the relevant time on the condition that the report is submitted on or before such later date as he may specify.

39 Content of reports

(1) Any report which the court requires a deputy to submit to the Public Guardian must include such material as the court may direct.

(2) The report must also contain or be accompanied by—

(a) specified information or information of a specified description; or

(b) specified documents or documents of a specified description.

(3) But paragraph (2)—

(a) extends only to information or documents which are reasonably required in connection with the exercise by the Public Guardian of functions conferred on him under the Act; and

(b) is subject to paragraph (1) and to any other directions given by the court.

(4) Where powers as respects a person's property and affairs are conferred on a deputy under section 16 of the Act, the information specified by the Public Guardian under paragraph (2) may include accounts which—

(a) deal with specified matters; and

(b) are provided in a specified form.

(5) The Public Guardian may require—

(a) any information provided to be verified in such manner, or

(b) any document produced to be authenticated in such manner,

as he may reasonably require.

(6) "Specified" means specified in a notice in writing given to the deputy by the Public Guardian.

40 Power to require final report on termination of appointment

(1) This regulation applies where—

(a) the person on whose behalf a deputy was appointed to act has died;

(b) the deputy has died;

(c) the court has made an order discharging the deputy; or

(d) the deputy otherwise ceases to be under a duty to discharge the functions to which his appointment relates.

(2) The Public Guardian may require the deputy (or, in the case of the deputy's death, his personal representatives) to submit a final report on the discharge of his functions.

(3) A final report must be submitted—

(a) before the end of such reasonable period as may be specified; and

(b) at such place as may be specified.

(4) The Public Guardian must consider the final report, together with any other information that he may have relating to the discharge by the deputy of his functions.

(5) Where the Public Guardian is dissatisfied with any aspect of the final report he may apply to the court for an appropriate remedy (including enforcement of security given by the deputy).

(6) "Specified" means specified in a notice in writing given to the deputy or his personal representatives by the Public Guardian.

41 Power to require information from deputies

(1) This regulation applies in any case where—

(a) the Public Guardian has received representations (including complaints) about—
(i) the way in which a deputy is exercising his powers; or
(ii) any failure to exercise them; or
(b) it appears to the Public Guardian that there are other circumstances which—
(i) give rise to concerns about, or dissatisfaction with, the conduct of the deputy (including any failure to act); or
(ii) otherwise constitute good reason to seek information about the deputy's discharge of his functions.

(2) The Public Guardian may require the deputy—
(a) to provide specified information or information of a specified description; or
(b) to produce specified documents or documents of a specified description.

(3) The information or documents must be provided or produced—
(a) before the end of such reasonable period as may be specified; and
(b) at such place as may be specified.

(4) The Public Guardian may require—
(a) any information provided to be verified in such manner, or
(b) any document produced to be authenticated in such manner,

as he may reasonably require.

(5) "Specified" means specified in a notice in writing given to the deputy by the Public Guardian.

42 Right of deputy to require review of decisions made by the Public Guardian

(1) A deputy may require the Public Guardian to reconsider any decision he has made in relation to the deputy.

(2) The right under paragraph (1) is exercisable by giving notice of exercise of the right to the Public Guardian before the end of the period of 14 days beginning with the date on which notice of the decision is given to the deputy.

(3) The notice of exercise of the right must—
(a) state the grounds on which reconsideration is required; and
(b) contain or be accompanied by any relevant information or documents.

(4) At any time after receiving the notice and before reconsidering the decision to which it relates, the Public Guardian may require the deputy to provide him with such further information, or to produce such documents, as he reasonably considers necessary to enable him to reconsider the matter.

(5) The Public Guardian must give to the deputy—
(a) written notice of his decision on reconsideration, and
(b) if he upholds the previous decision, a statement of his reasons.

MISCELLANEOUS FUNCTIONS

43 Applications to the Court of Protection

The Public Guardian has the function of making applications to the court in connection with his functions under the Act in such circumstances as he considers it necessary or appropriate to do so.

44 Visits by the Public Guardian or by Court of Protection Visitors at his direction

(1) This regulation applies where the Public Guardian visits, or directs a Court of Protection Visitor to visit, any person under any provision of the Act or these Regulations.

(2) The Public Guardian must notify (or make arrangements to notify) the person to be visited of—
(a) the date or dates on which it is proposed that the visit will take place;

(b) to the extent that it is practicable to do so, any specific matters likely to be covered in the course of the visit; and

(c) any proposal to inform any other person that the visit is to take place.

(3) Where the visit is to be carried out by a Court of Protection Visitor—

(a) the Public Guardian may—

(i) give such directions to the Visitor, and

(ii) provide him with such information concerning the person to be visited,

as the Public Guardian considers necessary for the purposes of enabling the visit to take place and the Visitor to prepare any report the Public Guardian may require; and

(b) the Visitor must seek to carry out the visit and take all reasonable steps to obtain such other information as he considers necessary for the purpose of preparing a report.

(4) A Court of Protection Visitor must submit any report requested by the Public Guardian in accordance with any timetable specified by the Public Guardian.

(5) If he considers it appropriate to do so, the Public Guardian may, in relation to any person interviewed in the course of preparing a report—

(a) disclose the report to him; and

(b) invite him to comment on it.

45 Functions in relation to persons carrying out specific transactions

(1) This regulation applies where, in accordance with an order made under section 16(2)(a) of the Act, a person ("T") has been authorised to carry out any transaction for a person who lacks capacity.

(2) The Public Guardian has the functions of—

(a) receiving any reports from T which the court may require;

(b) dealing with representations (including complaints) about—

(i) the way in which the transaction has been or is being carried out; or

(ii) any failure to carry it out.

(3) Regulations 38 to 41 have effect in relation to T as they have effect in relation a deputy.

46 Power to require information from donees of lasting power of attorney

(1) This regulation applies where it appears to the Public Guardian that there are circumstances suggesting that the donee of a lasting power of attorney may—

(a) have behaved, or may be behaving, in a way that contravenes his authority or is not in the best interests of the donor of the power,

(b) be proposing to behave in a way that would contravene that authority or would not be in the donor's best interests, or

(c) have failed to comply with the requirements of an order made, or directions given, by the court.

(2) The Public Guardian may require the donee—

(a) to provide specified information or information of a specified description; or

(b) to produce specified documents or documents of a specified description.

(3) The information or documents must be provided or produced—

(a) before the end of such reasonable period as may be specified; and

(b) at such place as may be specified.

(4) The Public Guardian may require—

(a) any information provided to be verified in such manner, or

(b) any document produced to be authenticated in such manner,

as he may reasonably require.

(5) "Specified" means specified in a notice in writing given to the donee by the Public Guardian.

47 Power to require information from attorneys under enduring power of attorney

(1) This regulation applies where it appears to the Public Guardian that there are circumstances suggesting that, having regard to all the circumstances (and in particular the

attorney's relationship to or connection with the donor) the attorney under a registered enduring power of attorney may be unsuitable to be the donor's attorney.

(2) The Public Guardian may require the attorney—
- (a) to provide specified information or information of a specified description; or
- (b) to produce specified documents or documents of a specified description.

(3) The information or documents must be provided or produced—
- (a) before the end of such reasonable period as may be specified; and
- (b) at such place as may be specified.

(4) The Public Guardian may require—
- (a) any information provided to be verified in such manner, or
- (b) any document produced to be authenticated in such manner,

as he may reasonably require.

(5) "Specified" means specified in a notice in writing given to the attorney by the Public Guardian.

48 Other functions in relation to enduring powers of attorney

The Public Guardian has the following functions—
- (a) directing a Court of Protection Visitor—
  - (i) to visit an attorney under a registered enduring power of attorney, or
  - (ii) to visit the donor of a registered enduring power of attorney,

  and to make a report to the Public Guardian on such matters as he may direct;
- (b) dealing with representations (including complaints) about the way in which an attorney under a registered enduring power of attorney is exercising his powers.

SCHEDULE 1
FORM FOR INSTRUMENT INTENDED TO CREATE A LASTING POWER OF ATTORNEY

Regulation 5

PART 1
FORM FOR INSTRUMENT INTENDED TO CREATE A PROPERTY AND AFFAIRS LASTING POWER OF ATTORNEY

...

PART 2
FORM FOR INSTRUMENT INTENDED TO CREATE A PERSONAL WELFARE LASTING POWER OF ATTORNEY

...

SCHEDULE 2
NOTICE OF INTENTION TO APPLY FOR REGISTRATION OF A LASTING POWER OF ATTORNEY: LPA 001

Regulation 10

...

SCHEDULE 3
APPLICATION TO REGISTER A LASTING POWER OF ATTORNEY: LPA 002

Regulation 11

...

SCHEDULE 4
NOTICE OF RECEIPT OF AN APPLICATION TO REGISTER A LASTING POWER OF ATTORNEY: LPA 003A AND LPA 003B

Regulation 13

PART 1
NOTICE TO AN ATTORNEY OF RECEIPT OF AN APPLICATION TO REGISTER A LASTING POWER OF ATTORNEY

. . .

PART 2
NOTICE TO DONOR OF RECEIPT OF AN APPLICATION TO REGISTER A LASTING POWER OF ATTORNEY

. . .

SCHEDULE 5
NOTICE OF REGISTRATION OF A LASTING POWER OF ATTORNEY: LPA 004

Regulation 17

. . .

SCHEDULE 6
DISCLAIMER BY DONEE OF A LASTING POWER OF ATTORNEY: LPA 005

Regulation 20

. . .

SCHEDULE 7
NOTICE OF INTENTION TO APPLY FOR REGISTRATION OF AN ENDURING POWER OF ATTORNEY

Regulation 23

. . .

Amendment
Amended by SI 2007/2051, reg 12.

SCHEDULE 8
APPLICATION TO REGISTER AN ENDURING POWER OF ATTORNEY

Regulation 24

. . .

PUBLIC GUARDIAN (FEES, ETC) REGULATIONS 2007

SI 2007/2051

1 Citation and commencement

These Regulations may be cited as the Public Guardian (Fees, etc) Regulations 2007 and shall come into force on 1 October 2007.

2 Interpretation

In these Regulations—

"the Act" means the Mental Capacity Act 2005;

"court" means the Court of Protection;

"P" means the person in respect of whom a deputy has been appointed under section 16 of the Act; and

"Public Guardian" means the officer appointed in accordance with section 57 of the Act;

"the registers" means—

(a) the register of lasting powers of attorney,

(b) the register of enduring powers of attorney, and

(c) the register of court orders appointing deputies,

established and maintained by the Public Guardian under section 58(1)(a) and (b) of and paragraph 14 of Schedule 4 to the Act.

3 Schedule of fees

The fees set out in the Schedule to these Regulations shall apply in accordance with the following provisions of these Regulations.

4 Enduring power of attorney registration fee

(1) A fee for the registration of an enduring power of attorney shall be payable by the person seeking to register the enduring power of attorney under regulation 24 of the Lasting Powers of Attorney, Enduring Powers of Attorney and Public Guardian Regulations 2007 (application for registration).

(2) The fee prescribed by paragraph (1) shall be payable upon the application to register the enduring power of attorney.

5 Lasting power of attorney registration fee

(1) A fee for the registration of a lasting power of attorney shall be payable by the person seeking to register the lasting power of attorney under regulation 11 of the Lasting Powers of Attorney, Enduring Powers of Attorney and Public Guardian Regulations 2007 (application for registration).

(2) The fee prescribed by paragraph (1) shall be payable upon the application to register the lasting power of attorney.

6 Application to search the registers fee

(1) A fee for an application to search the registers made under regulation 31 of the Lasting Powers of Attorney, Enduring Powers of Attorney and Public Guardian Regulations 2007 (disclosure of information on a register: search by the Public Guardian) shall be payable by the person making the application.

(2) The fee prescribed by paragraph (1) shall be payable upon the application to search the registers.

(3) The fee prescribed by paragraph (1) shall not be payable where the person making the application is a—

(a) registered health care professional; or

(b) a representative of a public authority.

(4) In paragraph (3) "registered health care professional" means a person who is a member of a profession regulated by a body mentioned in section 25(3) of the National Health Service Reform and Health Care Professions Act 2002.

7 Appointment of deputy fee

(1) This regulation applies where—

(a) the court has appointed a deputy under section 16 of the Act (powers to make decisions and appoint deputies: general); or

(b) an existing receiver is treated as if he were a deputy appointed by the court under paragraph 1(2)(a) of Schedule 5 to the Act.

(2) Where paragraph (1) applies a fee shall be payable by P.

(3) The fee prescribed by paragraph (2) shall be payable by P within 30 days of the date of the invoice for the fee.

8 Appointment of deputy: supervision fees

(1) This regulation applies where—

(a) the court has appointed a deputy under section 16 of the Act (powers to make decisions and appoint deputies: general); or

(b) an existing receiver is treated as if he were a deputy appointed by the court under paragraph 1(2)(a) of Schedule 5 to the Act.

(2) Where paragraph (1) applies the Public Guardian shall determine the level of supervision required under section 58(1)(c) of the Act.

(3) The levels of supervision are—

(a) type I (highest);

(b) type II (lower); and

(c) type III (minimal).

(4) Where the level of supervision determined by the Public Guardian in accordance with paragraph (2) is type I (highest) or type II (lower) an annual supervision fee shall be payable by P until the appointment of the deputy is terminated.

(5) Subject to paragraphs (6) and (7), the appropriate supervision fee prescribed by paragraph (2) shall be due on 31 March each year and shall be payable by P within 30 days of the date of the invoice for the fee.

(6) Where the period for which the fee prescribed by paragraph (4) is payable is less than one year, the amount of the fee payable shall be such proportion of the full fee as that period bears to one year.

(7) Where the deputy's appointment terminates, the appropriate fee prescribed by paragraph (4) shall be due on the date of termination and shall be payable within 30 days of the date of the invoice for the fee.

(8) In the event of termination of the appointment due to P's death, the appropriate fee prescribed by paragraph (2) shall be payable by P's estate.

9 Exemptions

(1) Subject to paragraph (2) no fee shall be payable under these regulations when, at the time when the fee would otherwise become payable, the relevant person is in receipt of any qualifying benefit.

(2) Paragraph (1) does not apply to a person who has an award of damages in excess of £16,000 which has been disregarded for the purposes of determining eligibility for that benefit.

(3) For the purposes of regulation 4 the relevant person is the donor of the enduring power of attorney.

(4) For the purposes of regulation 5 the relevant person is the donor of the lasting power of attorney.

(5) For the purposes of regulation 6 the relevant person is the person making the application.

(6) For the purposes of regulations 7 and 8 the relevant person is P.

(7) The following are qualifying benefits for the purposes of paragraph (1)—

(a) income support under the Social Security Contributions and Benefits Act 1992;

(b) working tax credit, provided that—

(i) child tax credit is being paid to the relevant person, or to a couple (as defined in section 3(5)(A) of the Tax Credits Act 2002) which includes the relevant person; or

(ii) there is a disability element or severe disability element (or both) to the . . . tax credit received by the relevant person;

(c) income-based job-seeker's allowance under the Jobseekers Act 1995;

(d) guarantee credit under the State Pensions Credit Act 2002;

(e) council tax benefit under the Social Security Contributions and Benefits Act 1992; and

(f) housing benefit under the Social Security Contributions and Benefits Act 1992.

Amendment

Para (7): in sub-para (b)(ii) word omitted revoked by SI 2007/2616, reg 2.

10 Reductions and remissions in exceptional circumstances

Where it appears to the Public Guardian that the payment of any fee prescribed by these Regulations would, owing to the exceptional circumstances of the particular case, involve undue hardship, he may reduce or remit the fee in that case.

11 Transitional provision

(1) In respect of the administration fee that would have been payable under rule 78 of the Court of Protection Rules 2001 on 31 March 2008, the appropriate proportion of that fee shall be due on 30 September 2007 and shall be payable within 30 days of the date of the invoice for the fee.

(2) Where the period for which the fee prescribed by paragraph (1) is payable is less than six months, the amount of the fee payable shall be such proportion of that fee as that period bears to six months.

12 Amendment to Schedule 7 of the Lasting Powers of Attorney, Enduring Powers of Attorney and Public Guardian Regulations 2007

(1) Schedule 7 of the Lasting Powers of Attorney, Enduring Powers of Attorney and Public Guardian Regulations 2007 is amended as follows.

(2) For paragraph 1 of Form EP1PG substitute "You have the right to object to the proposed registration on one or more of the grounds set out below. You must notify the Office of the Public Guardian of your objection within five weeks from the day this notice was given to you. You may make an application to the Court of Protection under rule 68 of the Court of Protection Rules 2007 for a decision on the matter. No fee is payable for such an application. If you do not make such an application, the Public Guardian will ask for the court's directions about registration."

SCHEDULE
FEES TO BE TAKEN

Regulation 3

Column 1	*Column 2*
Enduring power of attorney registration (regulation 4)	£120.00
Lasting power of attorney registration (regulation 5)	£150.00
Application to search the registers (regulation 6)	£25.00
Appointment of deputy (regulation 7)	£125.00
Type I (highest) supervision (regulation 8)	£800.00 per annum
Type II (lower) supervision (regulation 8)	£175.00 per annum
Type III (minimal) supervision (regulation 8)	No fee

INDEX

[*references are to paragraph number*]